PERSPECTIVES ON THE AMERICAN CATHOLIC CHURCH,
1789-1989

Perspectives on the American Catholic Church

1789-1989

Edited by Stephen J. Vicchio, Ph.D.
and Virgina Geiger, S.S.N.D., Ph.D.
College of Notre Dame of Maryland

Christian Classics, Inc.
Post Office Box 30, Westminster, Maryland 21157
1989

First published, 1989

© 1989 by Stephen J. Vicchio $ 19.96

ISBN 0 87061 171 2

Library of Congress Card Number: 89-62319

Printed in U.S.A.

In gratitude to

ARCHBISHOP WILLIAM DONALD BORDERS

yet another example of the grace bestowed on the

ARCHDIOCESE OF BALTIMORE

Foreword

by John Tracy Ellis
Catholic University

That highly perceptive observer and critic of the contemporary scene, Monsignor George G. Higgins, recently commented on the growing maturity of Americans in general and of American Catholics in particular. *Inter alia,* he stated:

> The very fact that we no longer think, as the Puritans did, that we have a divine commission in the world or that our nation has a God given manifest destiny is a sign of hope, I believe, a sign not of decadence, but a growing maturity....
>
> Self-doubt and self-criticism, of course, can be destructive if indulged in cynically or uncritically. Yet I think we are better off as a nation because Americans, and American Catholics in particular, are more willing to question, to criticize, to challenge and, if necessary, to oppose government policies.[1]

I would thoroughly agree, and I welcome this changed attitude in all aspects of American Catholic life, and especially in my own discipline of church history. In a word, it is heartening to see the increasing number of examples of this maturing process, a process displayed in the fifteen essays of this volume.

As we enter the 200th anniversary of the organized American Catholic community, our fellow Americans of other and no religious affiliation, to say nothing of Catholics themselves, are warranted in anticipating that the restrictive, defensive and exclusive attitudes that marked the Catholic community of an earlier time would have been set aside, and the intervening time given to a changed mentality that reflects the presence in 1989 of a religious family numbering roughly 53,500,000 members whose economic and social status are such as to offer a striking contrast to that of their great grandparents. The essays contained in this book demonstrate that intellectual maturity in that they do not hesitate to be critical in tone when that is thought necessary, as well as giving evidence of a professional approach that will, I think, satisfy the specialists in each aspect of American Catholic affairs, whether that be the schools, liturgy, social reform or the position of American Catholic women.

These essays, it seems to me, portray the same spirit of openness and intellectual honesty that characterize the six-volume *Makers of the American Catholic Community,* competently edited by Christopher J. Kauffman, a work that reflects high credit on all concerned: the respective authors, the sponsoring National Conference of Catholic Bishops and the financial supporters such as the Knights of Columbus. On a smaller scale, *Perspectives on the American*

---

[1] George G. Higgins, "Today's America—A Growing Maturity," *Catholic New York,* March 9, 1989, p. 10.

Catholic Church has done the same for the topics surveyed for the two centuries between 1789 and 1989.

It is a universally recognized fact that American Catholics have come of age, so to speak, in many aspects of our national life, for example, in politics, labor, the professions and the business community. We have yet to realize our full potential in cultural and intellectual achievements, commensurate with our numbers, our financial resources and our commitment in terms of educational institutions on the post-secondary level. While that may be true, I believe it to be equally true that a volume such as the present one edited by Sister Virgina Geiger and Dr. Stephen Vicchio points the way toward a richer contribution in that regard. Each of these fifteen essays might well be expanded to book length and thus extend in a detailed way our knowledge in the particular areas on which the individual essays focus.

One of the characteristics of maturity is a lack of fear, a feeling of security vis-à-vis those around us, a readiness to encounter criticism with a serenity that properly balances and measures the significant from the trivial. In general it may be said that the essays here meet that standard, and that is to say much about their sophistication and their mature approach. Thinking in terms of the Catholic community when John Carroll received his appointment as the first American Bishop in 1789, the change has been not only striking but little short of miraculous. True, the Church in the United States is still passing through a severe crisis, the final outcome of which remains clouded in mystery. Yet the tone and content of these essays are reassuring for the time ahead. In that regard, Judge John T. Noonan, Jr., has been brave enough to predict certain developments within the American Catholic community, a series of predictions which, it is to be hoped, may in the main find fulfillment as the human family reaches beyond the third millennium. Among the learned Judge's points, there is one which applies to what I have tried to say here. He declared:

> The Catholic Church will give greater weight to the necessity of truthtelling in all human relations, personal and professional, ecclesiastical and governmental. Especially will the Church prize the truth in the history of its own life, in the exegesis of Scripture, and in the preaching of the word.[1]

In the gradual working out of that desired goal these essays will serve a useful purpose in pointing the way by their honest appraisal of the past and their up-to-date knowledge of the present. What more could reasonably be asked of the editors and authors in their commemoration of the American Catholic community's 200th birthday?

John Tracy Ellis
Professorial Lecturer in Church History
The Catholic University of America

---

[1]John R. Noonan, Jr., "Visions of the Church in America," *Church* (Spring, 1989), p. 52.

Contents

PART I   HISTORICAL PERSPECTIVES

PART II   PROBLEMS AND ISSUES

Introduction

To think it is to thank it, to remember it with gratitude.
William Barrett[1]

In his excellent introduction to the life and times of John Carroll, Father Peter Guilday uses the metaphor of a river to talk about the many sources of American Independence.[2] "Like the great rivers of the country," he says

> American Independence had many sources; and while each of these sources can be traced to its origin, it is difficult to fix upon the spot where each one joins itself to the great river that swept the country into freedom in 1776. The religious source is the most turbulent and crooked of all these tributary streams and upon its flow the frail bark of the Catholic Church in the country, while directed by its leaders towards the meeting of the waters, was not uncertain of the wreckage in the mighty rivers below.[3]

If anyone fully understood the possibility of the Catholic ship running aground or breaking up at sea it was Archbishop Carroll. In 1829, his cousin Charles Carroll reflected that he had signed the Declaration of Independence for the purpose of bringing about full religious liberty for Catholics in the new nation, but by 1829 these were the remembrances of a man in his 90th year. The truth of the matter was that John Carroll and other great religious leaders of the emerging Catholic Church of America had as much reason to disbelieve as to believe that they would ever have full religious toleration in the United States.

If the revolutionary years to the close of the eighteenth century were difficult, the waters became no calmer in the nineteenth century. The rise of the Know-Nothings in the middle of the century, followed by the Civil War, and severe internal tensions within the Church brought American Catholicism into the twentieth century, a ship somewhat battered but with sails still trimmed.

This book is intended to act as a kind of abbreviated ship's log. November of 1989 marks the 200th anniversary of the establishment of the Catholic Church in America. The ship is in dry dock while we repair some wear and tear. It is perhaps prudent to take a close look at where she has been, in order that we might chart a truer course for the future.

You will find entries in the log from lay and religious, black and white, women and men, all who have added their expertise to the interpreting of a long and eventful voyage.

[1]William Barrett, *Irrational Man* (New York: Doubleday, 1962), p. 235. In this section of the book, Barrett reflects on a passage in Martin Heidegger's *Discourse on Thinking*.
[2]Peter Guilday, *The Life and Times of John Carroll: Archbishop of Baltimore* (Westminster: Newman Press, 1954).
[3]Ibid., p. 85.

Sister Virgina Geiger begins the book with "The Miracle of Grace," an overview with commentary on the establishment of the 188 dioceses and 33 archdioceses established in this country since the first in Baltimore in 1789.

Sister Dolores Liptak's insightful article on Catholic immigration patterns documents the growth of our immigrant Church. She points out the early immigrants' desire to be fully integrated into American life. With the enormous increase in southern and eastern European Catholics in the 1880's, however, ideological and ethnic differences changed the face of American Catholicism.

Stephen Vicchio's entry in the log deals with the causes and manifestations of anti-Catholic sentiment in America from the early Colonies to the election of John Kennedy as the first Catholic president in America. He points out that anti-Catholic attitudes remained a constant threat, first with sentiments borrowed from the Reformation and the English revolutions, but later with a variety of nativist movements that stretched well into the twentieth century.

Father Cyprian Davis' "God's Image in Black," judiciously outlines the Black Catholic community in slavery and freedom. He uses two important focal points: 1889, the centenary of the American Catholic hierarchy and the date of the first Black Catholic Lay Congress in the United States, a time Father Davis marks as the beginning of self-awareness among Black Catholics. What the results were for the black Catholic community is the story he unfolds.

Margaret Susan Thompson's article on women in the American Catholic Church is an original piece of historical scholarship on an often neglected area of religious history. Dr. Thompson skillfully outlines what she sees as "separate spheres" traditionally occupied by American Catholic women. As she points out, some of these were in the world: the home, single-sex schools and voluntary associations, while others, particularly women's religious congregations, provided more public leadership as teachers, social workers, role models and symbols.

"Catholic Religious Thought in the United States," Patrick Carey's contribution to this anniversary volume, is a thoughtful essay about the changing conceptions of the Catholic intellectual tradition in the United States. Professor Carey convincingly argues that one can only understand Catholic interpretations of Christianity in a given age if one first understands not only what is distinctive about that age, but also the continuity which exists from age to age.

Father Joel Rippinger's "History of American Catholic Monasticism," reveals original insights as it carefully traces the growth of American Catholic monasticism, from its European roots to its peculiarly American manifestations.

In "John Carroll and the Shape of the American Catholic Liturgy," Father Gurrieri takes an incisive look at the history and structure of Catholic worship and liturgical practices in the beginning of the American Church. Carroll's rational and pious approach was evident in the "Diocesan Synod in 1791, his pastoral letter of 1792, his views on the use of English in the liturgy and his practical approach to cultural adaptation and domestic liturgy."

Father Harold Buetow provides an excellent short history of the development of Catholic schools in America, as well as some keen observations on the present state of American Catholic education.

Philip Gleason's article on the history of Catholic higher education in some ways acts as a companion piece to Father Buetow's article. The focus of Professor Gleason's remarks are the elements of continuity and change. He points out two great periods of change, one of structure, the other of ideological modernization, and adds an insightful section on the causes and resolutions of these crises.

In "American Catholic Sexual Ethics," Leslie Griffin provides an excellent discussion of the emergence and development of American Catholic sexual ethics. It begins with an analysis of the early European influences on American Catholic sexual ethics evident in moral manuals, and traces the history through major changes brought about by the Second Vatican Council. She pays particular attention to the role played by ecumenism and authority in contemporary discussions of Catholic sexual ethics.

David Kelly's scholarly work on Catholic health care ethics serves as a good companion piece to Professor Griffin's article. Dr. Kelly traces the development of health care ethics from its roots in European Pastoral Medicine and Moral Theology to the contemporary state of American Catholic Medical Ethics.

Father Robert Leavitt's article explores the changing roles of the laity that have evolved since the early years of the American Church with few priests, an evolution providing new challenges not only to how the hierarchy sees the laity, but also to how the laity sees itself.

Sonya Quitslund, in her essay "The Contribution of the Laity and Religious in the Development of American Catholic Spirituality," provides a thoughtful analysis of the history of spirituality in an American Catholic context. She points out that American Puritanism and republicanism created an environment for Catholics that demanded a religious response for which there were no models. The article demonstrates that it was only in the later nineteenth century that a set of historical circumstances and a spiritual crisis brought about what might be properly called American Catholic spirituality.

In "American Catholics and Social Reform," Mel Piehl adds a third important essay on Catholic morality. He describes social reform and social change as one dimension of the Church's larger engagement with American society and culture. In his thoughtful essay, he interprets the relationship of American Catholicism to larger social movements of the last two centuries as essentially a reciprocal one, with three major forces influencing the dynamics of this interaction.

All of these essays act as clear and judicious annotations on various aspects of the ship's log that is our collective history. The foreword has been provided by Monsignor John Tracy Ellis, a man who for several decades has been the standard for scholarship on American Catholic history. More times than any other scholar in the second half of this century, he has given insightful interpretation when the documents that reveal our past were less than clear. We owe a great debt of gratitude to Monsignor Ellis for his life and work.

Gratitude must also be expressed to Sister Kathleen Feeley, the President of the College of Notre Dame of Maryland, and to Sister Delia Dowling, our Dean. Their constant encouragement and support moved this work from an idea to a book. We must also thank Mary Jordan and Frances Nilsson for their excellent help in preparing the manuscript, and Diane Markert for the attractive photograph on the cover. The College of Notre Dame's Council for Faculty Research and Development and The Raskob Foundation provided funds and stipends to help in the completion of this project. For the cartography we owe a special word of thanks to James Doherty. Elizabeth McHale provided valuable editing and proofreading expertise. Lastly, we must thank John McHale, the publisher, for recognizing the importance of this project, and making its publication possible.

Stephen J. Vicchio, Ph.D.
Sister Virgina Geiger, S.S.N.D., Ph.D.
College of Notre Dame of Maryland
Spring 1989

CHAPTER ONE

A Miracle of Grace: The Growth of the Dioceses and Archdioceses in the United States

Virgina Geiger, S.S.N.D.
College of Notre Dame of Maryland

To study the history of the dioceses and archdioceses in the United States is to undergo a spiritual journey that deepens our understanding of Christ's promise to be with us always and opens up new ways of thinking about the message of Vatican Council II that the Church is "all people of God." A miracle of grace has enabled laity and religious to work together for the presence and growth of the American Catholic Church.

Early in our history, four areas witnessed Christ's presence among us: 1) the role of lay people prior to the arrival of missionaries; 2) the population growth within the Catholic Church; 3) the contribution of European religious orders and diocesan priests in the establishment of the dioceses in the United States; and 4) the financial help given to the American immigrant Church.

The history of Catholicism in the United States is replete with examples of God's working in the life of His people. The faith of Indians in New England was often kept alive without benefit of clergy during the seventeenth and early eighteenth centuries until their plea to send someone "to keep us from what is bad, correct our lives, absolve our sins,"[1] was answered with the sending of missionaries. Lay men and women took the initiative in preserving and spreading the faith where there were no bishops or priests, and no churches or schools. The work of the clergy was to gather together into congregations the scattered that were already there and to build churches, meeting halls and, wherever possible, schools,[2] the formation of dioceses following as a natural result.

One need but reflect on the growth of the Catholic population in the United States to realize the miracle of grace mysteriously working throughout the history of the country. On March 17, 1785 in a letter from the Propaganda Archives it was estimated that the Catholic population in the United States was 44,500 with 24 priests in the various states of the Union. There were at this time no seminary-trained priests in this country apart from the few Jesuits who were secular priests, but many French Sulpicians who were fleeing the persecution of the French Revolution were willing to come to the United States and accept administrative positions to serve in the dioceses. Young, well-educated men trained by masters of the spiritual life in France, they contributed a remarkable service to the formation of our dioceses. "Thirty-five Sulpicians served the Church in the United States . . . Ten Sulpicians became Archbishops and Bishops . . . and many served as official and unofficial advisors to several bishops at

---

[1] John Tracy Ellis, *Catholics in Colonial America* (Helicon Press, 1963), p. 142.
[2] Thomas T. McAvoy, *A History of the Catholic Church in the United States* (University of Notre Dame, 1970), p. 51. Cf. David O'Brien, *Faith and Friendship* (Catholic Diocese of Syracuse, 1987), p. 39.

the provincial councils of Baltimore."[1] Additional priests were solicited for the American Church by bishops travelling individually to Europe.

The lack of money for the immigrant Church was a constant problem, despite the great generosity of God's people, and often the American bishops were required to go to Europe for funds to support their young dioceses. In addition to contributions made to individual bishops, three organizations were noteworthy in their response to the appeals of the American Bishops. The Society for the Propagation of the Faith in Paris, organized for the purpose of maintaining Catholic missions throughout the world, donated $7,000,000 between 1822 and 1921.[2] The Leopoldine Society in Vienna supplied over $700,00 for the dioceses and for religious communities of Austrian-Hungarian membership in the United States.[3] The Ludwig-Missionsverein Society in Munich gave $900,000 for the dioceses of the German bishops and German religious orders in North America.[4] Grateful for this support, the Church in the United States began to repay the Society for the Propagation of the Faith and by 1922 almost $11,000,000, slightly more than had been received, had been raised for this cause.

Besides the European contributors, many more established dioceses in the East helped the newer dioceses. In the twentieth century the Catholic Extension Society, a national organization in the United States, raised money for the missionary needs of the seminaries and clergymen in the southern and western states, and in Alaska, Hawaii, Puerto Rico and the Philippines. Over 7,000 small churches were erected with funds from this organization.[5] Scant attention has been directed to the vast and complex contributions these three groups made to both American Catholicism and to our national heritage.

Today the total Catholic population for the United States is 53,496,862, or 22% of the population. Of this number there are 530,616 Eastern Rite Catholics. Statistical information for these figures is taken from *The Official Catholic Directory, 1988.*

In many areas in the United States today religious women and laity acting in the capacity of parish ministers continue to represent the Church where no priests are available. Truly the contribution of the priests, religious men and brothers, women religious and innumerable laity within the Church is a phenomenon so grace-filled that the real story merits further development to do justice to the topic.

[1]Christopher Kauffman, *Tradition and Transformation in Catholic Culture* (Macmillan & Co., 1988), p. 69-70.
[2]Monsignor Edward Hickey, *The Society for the Propagation of the Faith: Its Foundation, Organization and Success (1822-1921)* (Washington, DC, 1922), p. 153.
[3]B.J. Blied, "Leopoldinen Stiftung," *New Catholic Encyclopedia,* Vol. 8, p. 664.
[4]B.J. Blied, "Ludwig Missionsverein," *New Catholic Encyclopedia,* Vol. 8, p. 1064. Cf. Theodore Roemer, *Ten Decades of Alms* (Herder Book Co., 1942), passim.
[5]J.L. May, "Catholic Extension Society," *New Catholic Encyclopedia,* Vol. 3, p. 266.

In the following pages I present a study of the development of the archdioceses and dioceses of the American Catholic Church. For purposes of clarity, certain definitions may be helpful.

Prefecture Apostolic is the first stage in the ecclesiastical organization of a missionary land under the direct authority of the Pope and administered by a Prefect Apostolic (he is *not* a bishop). *Vicariate Apostolic* is the next stage in the ecclesiastical organization of a missionary land under the direct authority of the Pope and administered by a Vicar Apostolic (he *is* a bishop). *Province* is the territory over which an archbishop exercises metropolitan jurisdiction, namely in his own diocese and at least one suffragan diocese. *Eparchy* is a diocese of the Eastern Rite churches.

I would like to take this opportunity to express my gratitude to each person in the dioceses and archdioceses throughout the United States and in the Territories who so graciously offered assistance to me in this project.

PROVINCE OF BALTIMORE

The Archdiocese of Baltimore has the unique distinction of being the Premiere See in the United States. On November 6, 1789 John Carroll was named the first bishop of the United States by Pope Pius VI in the brief *Ex Hac Apostolicae*. Recognition of the honor bestowed on Baltimore was given on July 25, 1858, when Pope Pius IX conferred the "Prerogative of Place" on the Archdiocese of Baltimore, an honor that has never been revoked:

> By the explicit words of the decree of the Holy See the archbishop of Baltimore takes precedence over all archbishops of the United States (not Cardinals) in Councils, gatherings and meetings of whatever kind of the Hierarchy...regardless of the seniority of the other archbishops in promotion or ordination. Decree signed by Cardinal Barnabo, August 15, 1858.[1]

The ecclesiastical jurisdiction of the bishop of Baltimore in 1789 was identical to the jurisdiction given Carroll when he became prefect apostolic in 1784. It was coterminous with the new Republic. It extended from the Atlantic Ocean to the Mississippi River, and from Canada to Florida (then owned by Spain), an area with only 35 priests and approximately 50,000 Catholics.[2] Because of the encroachment of the bishop of Quebec in the Northwest Territory, the Sacred Congregation affirmed that the entire territory of the United States was under the jurisdiction of Bishop Carroll in 1791.[3] In 1803, his jurisdiction had been increased by the purchase of Louisiana, and extended from the Atlantic Ocean on

---

[1]P.J. Kenedy & Sons, *The Official Catholic Directory*, 1988, p. 49. In the Seventh Provincial Council in 1849 the Prelates had asked that this honor be conferred on the Archbishop of Baltimore for the First Plenary Council of the American Church in 1850, but it was delayed until 1858. Peter Guilday, *A History of the Councils of Baltimore,* p. 157.
[2]Peter Guilday, *The Life and Times of John Carroll,* (The Newman Press, 1954), p. 386-387. "A generous number of Catholics in the United States would be. . . 50,000."
[3]*Ibid.,* p. 387.

the east to the Rocky Mountains on the west, and from Quebec on the north to New Orleans on the south. In 1808, when Bishop Carroll was named the first archbishop of the United States, his province extended to almost two-thirds of the United States.

The impossibility of settling difficulties in so vast an area caused Archbishop Carroll to ask the Holy See for a division of the province. In 1808, four suffragan sees were erected: Bardstown, Philadelphia, New York and Boston, but there still remained under the archbishop's jurisdiction the extensive Louisiana Territory, Maryland, Virginia, North and South Carolina, Georgia, the Territory of Mississippi and the future Territory of Alabama.[1] Baltimore was the only archdiocese until 1846, when Oregon City (now Portland in Oregon) became the second province, and in 1847, when St. Louis became the third province in the United States.

Throughout the next century a miracle of grace was evident. The Church kept pace with the growing nation. Dioceses and archdioceses were formed from the "territorial contraction" of the Baltimore Province. While this province today measures only 4,801 miles, it has been the Mother Church of most of the provinces in the United States. Only five archdioceses and sections of two other archdioceses have not been a part of the original Baltimore Province.

The important role the Archdiocese of Baltimore played in the growth of the American Catholic Church can hardly be exaggerated. It was Archbishop John Carroll, the founder of the American hierarchy, who insisted on an unprecedented independence for the American Catholic Church, yet still maintaining obedience to the Holy Father. Carroll's understanding of the role of the Church in the foundation of the New Republic was invaluable to the progress of the Catholic Church.

The seven Provincial Councils of Baltimore held between 1829 and 1849 laid the foundation for the establishment of an ecclesiastical discipline for the clergy and for the sacramental life of the Church. Even more important were the three Plenary Councils called by the archbishops of Baltimore: the first established the parochial school system in 1852, a unique achievement of the American Catholic Church; in 1866 the second dealt with the increase of population within the Church especially the newly freed slaves; in 1884 the third "surpassed all Councils" which compiled the Baltimore Catechism and made a general law to establish parish schools with each church.[2]

Today the Province of Baltimore includes the Archdiocese of Baltimore (except five counties in the Archdiocese of Washington, DC) and four suffragan sees: Wilmington, Delaware; Richmond and Arlington, Virginia; and Wheeling-Charleston, West Virginia.

Delaware was part of the Diocese of Baltimore from 1789 until 1808 when it was added to the Philadelphia Diocese. In October 1866 the bishops of the Second Plenary Council of Baltimore petitioned the Holy See to erect a new diocese in Wilmington, covering the area of the state of Delaware, nine counties in Maryland and two counties in Virginia, an area known as the Delmarva

---

[1] Rose Gibbons Lovett, *Catholic Church in the Deep South*, (privately printed, 1980), p. 4.
[2] T.L. Jenkins, *Christian Schools* (Baltimore, 1889), p. 134. Quoted in P. Guilday, *History of the Councils*, p. 238.

Peninsula. In March of 1868 Pope Pius IX granted their request. June 17, 1974 Pope Paul VI returned the Virginia territory to the Diocese of Richmond, because with the "construction of the Chesapeake Bay Tunnel access to the mainland of Virginia was now much easier."[1] Today the Diocese of Wilmington includes the state of Delaware and the nine counties on the eastern shore of Maryland.

In the papal bull of July 11, 1820 Pope Pius VII established the Diocese of Richmond, encompassing the entire state of Virginia and the area now known as West Virginia. The diocese underwent further territorial changes in the next 150 years.

July 19, 1850: The Diocese of Wheeling (Virginia) was cut from the Diocese of Richmond to include the trans-Allegheny area, one of the few populations centers west of the mountains.

August 15, 1858: The city of Alexandria was transferred to the Diocese of Richmond because the federal government had receded Alexandria (part of the District of Columbia) to Virginia in 1846.

March 3, 1968: The Eastern Shore counties of Northampton and Accomac in Virginia were given to the Diocese of Wilmington. June 17, 1974: Pope Paul VI transferred these two Virginia counties back to the Diocese of Richmond.

August 13, 1974: Pope Paul VI established Arlington as a second diocese in Virginia because of its proximity to Washington and its 25% Catholic population.[2]

In 1863, thirteen years after the Diocese of Wheeling was formed, the state of West Virginia was admitted to the Union (comprised of what had been western counties in Virginia that refused to secede during the war between the states). On August 13, 1974 the boundaries of the Diocese of Wheeling were adjusted to encompass the state of West Virginia. To give greater prominence to the city of Charleston, the capital of West Virginia and also to place a co-cathedral and some administrative services in the southern part of the state, the Diocese of Wheeling-Charleston was formed October 4, 1974.[3]

The Province of Baltimore has one archdiocese and four suffragan sees with a total Catholic population of 1,027,413 or 17% of the total population of Maryland, 17% of Delaware, 6% of Virginia and 6% of West Virginia.

PROVINCE OF ANCHORAGE

Alaska, a Russian possession since 1741, proved to be a liability to the czars of Russia. In 1867 the United States purchased this "Seward's Folly," an investment which proved to be the most valuable of all American acquisitions.

Ecclesiastically, the vicar apostolic of British Columbia in Victoria had jurisdiction over Alaska, but few missionaries went to this faraway area. The first

[1]Edward B. Curley, *The Catholic Directory, A Brief History of the Diocese of Wilmington, 1874*, pp. 17, 25.
[2]Correspondence with Reverend Msgr. William T. Reinicke, Chancellor, Diocese of Richmond, June 12, 1988.
[3]Correspondence with Reverend Robert C. Nash, Chancellor, Diocese of Wheeling-Charleston, February 2 and 25, 1988.

Catholic priest went to Alaska in 1862, which was still Russian American. Not until 1870 did another priest enter the territory.[1] In 1874, Alaska was assigned to the bishop of Vancouver Island and, although the archbishop made five journeys to Alaska, the last one ended in his tragic murder. The scarcity of priests, the vastness of the area, the limited population and the rigors of the climate made the conversion of the Indians a painful and hazardous endeavor. From 1877, when missionaries began gradually to come to Alaska, until 1960, when travel was more accessible, Alaska proved to be "one of the most difficult mission areas of the world."[2]

Pope Leo XIII, recognizing the importance of the Alaskan mission territory, raised it to a prefecture apostolic on July 17, 1884. In September 1895 the territory of Alaska was separated from Vancouver Island making the Alaskan mission autonomous. In 1917 Pope Benedict XV designated Alaska as a vicariate apostolic. On June 23, 1951 Juneau was made a diocese, and on the same day the Diocese of Seattle was raised to a metropolitan see, with Juneau as its suffragan. The vicariate apostolic of Alaska was then transferred to Northern Alaska. On August 8, 1962 the vicariate of Northern Alaska became the diocese of Fairbanks.[3]

Alaska remained part of the Province of Seattle from 1917 until February 9, 1966, when the Province of Anchorage was created from the dioceses of Fairbanks and Juneau. This province became coterminous with the state of Alaska.

Today the Province of Anchorage has two suffragan sees and a Catholic population of 45,940 or 11% of the total population of the state of Alaska.

PROVINCE OF ATLANTA

The states of North and South Carolina and Georgia are included in the Archdiocese of Atlanta. Catholics have always been few in number and even today constitute only 3% of the total population of that area. Many reasons account for this.

Legislation against Catholics was rampant in this Protestant area. In Charleston, Bishop England recalled:

> The Catholics were settled as a colony by English emigrants; the penal laws against Catholics were then in full force, and the hatred to their religion was violent in England...nor was there a corrective—the colony received all its literature from the mother country.[4]

The laws of 1689 prohibiting Catholics from exercising their religion was repealed only in 1791.

[1]Gerard G. Steckler, S.J., "The Diocese of Juneau, Alaska," *Historical Records and Studies,* 47 (1959), p. 236.
[2]Wilfred P Schoenberg, "Diocese of Anchorage," *New Catholic Encyclopedia,* Vol. I, p. 244.
[3]Correspondence with Father Steven C. Moore, Vicar General, Archdiocese of Anchorage, February 6, 1988.
[4]*The Catholic Church in the United States,* undertaken to celebrate the Golden Jubilee of His Holiness, Pope Pius X, the Province of Baltimore and the Province of New York, Vol. III (The Catholic Editing Co., 1914), p. 123.

North Carolina's constitution stated that "any man who shall deny the existence of God or the truth of the Protestant religion...shall not hold office." No
early constitution of any state, except Massachusetts, equalled that of North
Carolina's prejudice against Catholics.[1] Georgia, the most backward state in the
colonies, forbade "slavery, rum and Catholics." The prohibition against slavery
and rum was immediately rescinded because of self-interest but it took twenty
years for the laws against Catholics to be changed.[2]

Another reason for the anti-Catholic feeling was evident: the question of
slavery in the state presented a problem if Catholics were allowed to enter. The
slaves exercised menial tasks on the plantations; the Irish if they entered would
take the same jobs and in addition would be encouraging the practice of the
Catholic religion. The owners would tolerate neither.[3]

Difficulties in South Carolina with the trustees of the Church and among
the priests made the Archbishop of Baltimore realize that the three southern
states were too far distant to be governed by Baltimore. He urged the Holy See
to establish a diocese in Charleston, South Carolina. On June 18, 1820 this
was granted and it included North and South Carolina and Georgia. Because the
bishop of Havana could no longer take care of East Florida, the bishop of
Charleston was asked to include this area in the new diocese.

An increasing population in Georgia resulted in the creation of a new diocese in Savannah including in its territory Georgia and East Florida. On January
5, 1937 it was designated as Savannah-Atlanta and renamed Savannah on
November 8, 1956. On the same date Atlanta was made a new diocese.

The Civil War devastated these new southern states, but since so many
Catholics had been loyal to the Confederate cause less antagonism was shown to
them. The Holy See believed that the erection of a diocese in North Carolina,
the least Catholic of all states in the union, might prove advantageous to the
Church. Pope Pius IX separated North Carolina from the diocese of Charleston
on March 3, 1868 and created the vicariate apostolic of North Carolina with only
700 Catholics and three priests in the state. By 1924 the number of Catholics
had grown to 6,000 and on December 12, 1924 Pope Pius XI raised North Carolina to a diocese with its see in Raleigh.[4]

Atlanta's growing importance earned for it the title of "the Capital of the
New South" because it was becoming a magnet for post-war growth: roads, railroads and an airport made it the hub of the south and a gateway to the west.[5] On
February 21, 1962 Atlanta was made a metropolitan see extending its area
through Georgia, the Carolinas and East Florida (this was given to Miami when
it became a province on May 8, 1969).

The last diocese to be erected in the Province of Atlanta was Charlotte,
North Carolina, an area lacking a harbor but recently developing as the largest
furniture market in the country, and an important hosiery, textile and manufac-

[1]*Ibid.*, p. 260
[2]*Ibid.*, p. 194.
[3]Henry De Courcey and John Gilmary Shea, *History of the Catholic Church in the
United States, 1879* (P.J. Kenedy & Sons), p. 529.
[4]Rev. Gerald L. Lewis, *History of the Diocese of Raleigh* (1984), p. 1.
[5]Thea Jarvin, "Diocese's Growth, Faith-Torch Passed," *The Georgia Bulletin,* May
2, 1988, p. 1.

turing center.[1] Because the area had doubled in size within the last decade, Pope Paul VI designated Charlotte as a new diocese on November 31, 1971.

All three states have been blessed with many outstanding leaders, among them: Bishop John England of Charleston, "the light of the American Hierarchy," whose "learning, eloquence, vigor of mind, and administrative ability, has rarely been equalled,"[2] and Bishop James Gibbons who became Vicar Apostolic of North Carolina, Bishop of Richmond, Archbishop and later Cardinal of Baltimore (the latter for 35 years). His book, the classic *Faith of Our Fathers*, had won Cardinal Gibbons an international reputation. And in our own day, on May 2, 1988, Josephite Eugene Marino, Auxiliary Bishop of Washington, DC was elevated to the archbishopric in Atlanta, the first and only black archbishop in the United States.

The Province of Atlanta has an archdiocese and four suffragan sees with a Catholic population of 216,368 or 3% of the total population of Georgia; 140,288 is the total Catholic population or 2% of the total population of the state of North Carolina; and 75,382 is the total Catholic population or 2% of the total population of the state of South Carolina.

PROVINCE OF BOSTON

The Diocese of Boston, created from the Archdiocese of Baltimore in 1808, comprised the New England states of Massachusetts, Maine, Connecticut, Rhode Island, New Hampshire and Vermont.[3] The early history of the Boston Diocese is markedly different from that of other Catholic dioceses because of the extremely small number of Catholics in New England until the mid-nineteenth century. Whereas Catholicism was an important factor in the French settlements of the Ohio and Mississippi valleys, as was also true in the Spanish areas of California, the Southwest and for a time Florida, it was not true of the New England colonies. Here Catholics were a decided minority. According to a report of Bishop John Carroll in 1785, there were approximately 25,000 Catholics in the United States but only 600 in New England[4] including the Indians, the French and the Irish.

The virtual absence of Catholicism in New England was primarily the result of the strong anti-Catholic sentiment of the Puritans as evidenced by severe anti-Catholic legislation. In 1647 the Massachusetts Bay Colony passed laws forbidding all Jesuits, seminary priests or ecclesiastical persons to enter or live within its borders. In 1681 a new charter allowed liberty of conscience and worship to all but papists, and in 1700 legislation stated that no priest could legally be a priest in Massachusetts Territory, including Maine, under penalty of perpet-

[1]Sister Miriam Miller, *A History of the Early Years of the Roman Catholic Diocese of Charlotte* (Laney Smith, Inc., 1984), p. 6-7.
[2]De Courcey and Shea, *op. cit.,* p. 527.
[3]Peter Guilday, *Life and Times of John Carroll* (The Newman Press, 1954), p. 621. Quote from "A letter from Bishop Jean-Louis Lefebre de Cheverus."
[4]Patrick Conley and Matthew J. Smith, *Catholicism in Rhode Island. The Formative Era* (Diocese of Providence, 1976), p. 4.

ual imprisonment.[1] So successful was anti-Catholic legislation in New England that John Adams remarked that "papist and rascally Jacobites were as rare in his hometown as a comet or an earthquake."[2]

By the time of the American Revolution (1776), Catholics accounted for 1% of the total population but in New England there were no openly professed Catholics, except a few Indians of the Penobscot tribe, and there was no priest to serve them. The Penobscots kept the faith alive by gathering to pray, and continued to beg for a priest to minister to them. When a delegation of Penobscots petitioned the Governor of Massachusetts for assistance in obtaining a priest, their spokesman voiced the urgency of their need: "We want a Father to baptise our children, & administer the Sacraments to us...to keep us from what is bad, and correct our lives...."[3] Finally, they appealed to the Bishop of Quebec. "It is thirty-one years since we have had prayer in our village, because we have had no priest....Our heart is sad...All our young folk have been baptised only by our own hands...Nor have we anyone to teach us."[4]

Independence in 1783 brought relief from most laws disabling Catholics from practicing religious freedom and from holding office. In Massachusetts the religious qualification for holding office was abandoned and religious freedom was allowed, but New Hampshire passed anti-Catholic legislation granting only to Protestants the right to hold office (for the next 90 years) and the right to teach in public schools (until 1986).[5]

When the Diocese of Boston was created in 1808, there were only three churches and three priests, including the bishop, in the entire New England area. The Catholic population was 720 persons. This number grew to 3,000 in 1829 and to 7,000 in 1830, but the rate of increase was insignificant in comparison with that in other areas where the Irish immigrants were in large numbers. So weak and insignificant did the Diocese of Boston appear that in 1825 the Bishop of Louisiana suggested that it seemed advisable to unite the Sees of Boston and New York.[6]

Although the first three priests who came to administer the parishes were undesirable, the flowering of the Church did begin at the turn of the century when genuine spiritual leadership began to emerge. The real growth of the Church in New England can be traced to the remarkable administration of Bishop

[1]Reverend Msgr. Wilfrid H. Paradis, *Catholicism in New Hampshire: An Historical Summary* (a pub. of the Diocese of Manchester Centennial Committee), p. 2.

[2]John Adams, *Works* (Boston, 1856), Vol. 9, p. 355. Quoted in James Hennesey, S.J., *American Catholics* (Oxford University Press, 1981), p. 77.

[3]John Tracy Ellis, *op. cit.*, pp. 142, 145. Msgr. Ellis also remarks that "the redmen and their families were the most loyal and peaceful Catholic communities" within New England.

[4]Hennesey, *op. cit.*, p. 80.

[5]Paradis, *op. cit.*, p. 5.

[6]Robert H. Lord, John E. Sexton, Edward T. Harrington, *History of the Archdiocese of Boston* (Sheed & Ward, 1944), Vol. ll, p. 30. Reprinted in Robert W. Hayman, *Catholicism in Rhode Island 1780-1886* (Diocese of Providence, 1982), p. 17.

Benedict Joseph Fenwick (1823-1846) in the Diocese of Boston. He transformed the diocese from one of the weakest to the strongest in the United States.[1]

Because of the need for closer contact with bishops in this vast area, the Diocese of Hartford, which included Connecticut and Rhode Island, was created in 1843. In 1850 when New York became an archdiocese, Boston and Hartford became suffragan sees. But the distance from Boston to Maine was so vast that the bishops of the Fifth Provincial Council petitioned the Holy See for two new dioceses in New England. Consequently two sees were erected within the Boston Diocese on July 29, 1853: the Diocese of Burlington in Vermont and the Diocese of Portland for Maine and New Hampshire.

The first black priest in the United States, Reverend James Augustine Healy, was elevated to the Bishopric of Portland. The son of a plantation owner and a slave girl, he was born in Georgia where the law required that a child born of a slave mother became a slave. Bishop Healy was, therefore, legally born a slave. Another unique event in New England was the large number of conversions that took place, unparalleled in any other area of the country.[2]

It is a known fact that New England received very few immigrants other than the Irish until the late nineteenth century. One-fifth of all Irish immigrants resided in the six states of New England. This was due to the great Irish famine and cheaper fare on faster and larger commercial ships taking the oceanic routes. Jobs were also available for the building of canals, railroads and highways. Gradually the new roads linking New England and Canada brought into the Northeast a large influx of Canadians especially after the Civil War. In the late nineteenth century immigrants from southern and eastern Europe swelled the population to such an extent that "Catholics outnumbered any other religious denomination in Massachusetts, and fifty years later, they were twice as numerous as all other denominations combined."[3] Opposition to this growth created the strong anti-Catholic movements that harassed the Boston Diocese for nearly a century.

As the population continued to grow, especially in central and western Massachusetts, the bishops requested a new diocese with Springfield as the see city. This occurred on June 14, 1870. The phenomenal progress of the Church in New England (the Catholic population now numbered 863,000) resulted in the erection of Boston as a metropolitan see on May 2, 1875, including in its territory all of New England. Because of the lessening of anti-Catholicism in New Hampshire and the renewed influx of Catholics into this area, the Diocese of Manchester was erected on April 14, 1884. On March 12, 1904 the Diocese of Falls River was carved from the southeastern part of the Province of Boston. Finally, the Diocese of Worcester was established on January 14, 1950.

Territorially, the Archdiocese of Boston remained the same until 1953 when Hartford became an archdiocese and the Boston Province then encompassed the states of Massachusetts, Maine, New Hampshire and Vermont.

The Province of Boston has one archdiocese and six suffragan sees within four states. It has a total Catholic population of 2,842,040 or 50% of the total

---

[1] T.F. Casey, "Benedict Joseph Fenwick," *New Catholic Encyclopedia*, Vol. 6, p. 885.

[2] Paradis, *op. cit.*, pp. 8-9, 13.

[3] Lord, Sexton, Harrington, *op. cit.*, p. x.

population of the state of Massachusetts; 279,000 or 25% of the total population of Maine; 295,930 or 29% of the total population of New Hampshire and 147,816 or 27% of the total population of Vermont.

PROVINCE OF CHICAGO

The Province of Chicago has the second largest Catholic population in the United States. As early as the seventeenth century French missionaries came to the area, then administered by a vicar apostolic from Canada. On April 11, 1675 the Catholic Church was officially established in the Territory of Illinois when Father Jacques Marquette, S.J., named the first mission, Immaculate Conception.[1]

Illinois Territory, originally part of Virginia, then part of the Northwest Territory, was administered by the bishop of Quebec until 1789 when the ecclesiastical jurisdiction was transferred to Bishop John Carroll of Baltimore. In 1808 when the Diocese of Bardstown was created, Illinois Territory was under its jurisdiction. In 1826 when the Diocese of St. Louis was created the bishops of St. Louis and Bardstown agreed to divide the administration of the state. Bardstown administered the southern and eastern sections and St. Louis the northern and western sections.[2] In 1834 the administration of the eastern one-third of Illinois passed to the newly created Diocese of Vincennes in Indiana and resided with the bishop of that diocese until Chicago was created a diocese in 1843.

When St. Louis was elevated to a metropolitan see in 1847 Illinois came under its ecclesiastical jurisdiction. In the 1840's and 1850's the population of Illinois grew rapidly. From 1840 construction of the canal built up those cities that were close to water and land routes. Immigrants were in such demand as laborers for the construction of roads and railroads that many times the railroad companies had to recruit in New York City for immigrants to work in Illinois.[3] The majority of these immigrants were Irish and German. As the roads and railroads neared completion, farmers were able to send their wares to market, people could be easily relocated and manufacturing plants were begun. The rapid growth of population within a short period of time necessitated the building of many new churches, organization of new parishes and the establishment of various missions.[4]

Dioceses had to be formed to meet the needs of the Catholic population. The Diocese of Quincey was created on July 29, 1853 in southern Illinois, but this bishopric was left vacant for four years because no one was found to accept it and in 1857 the see was transferred to Alton. In 1923 it was again transferred to Springfield, Illinois. On May 22, 1877 the Diocese of Peoria was created due to the rapid expansion of industry, the building of schools and hospitals and the tremendous activity that resulted from the increase of population.

[1]Robert R. Miller, *That All May Be One, A History of the Rockford Diocese* (The Diocese of Rockford, 1976), p. 42.
[2]Correspondence with John J. Treanor, Archivist, Archdiocese of Chicago, June 10, 1988.
[3]Alice O'Rourke, O.P., *The Good Work Begun* (The Lakeside Press, 1970), p. 15.
[4]*Ibid.*, p. 25.

12   *Perspectives on the American Catholic Church*

As early as the Second Plenary Council of Baltimore (1866), Archbishop Kenrick of St. Louis had requested that Chicago be elevated to an archbishopric. Thirteen years later it was again requested (1879), stating that this city was larger in population than St. Louis and it was "already the center of the mid-continental rail networks." Chicago was also more populated and had more churches than five other metropolitan sees.[1] Finally, on September 10, 1880, the Archdiocese of Chicago was established in the northern part of Illinois.

Between 1880 and 1910 seventeen million people came to the United States, mainly from southern and eastern Europe. Many settled in the Chicago area necessitating the establishment of national parishes where each one's language could be preserved, often causing the boundary lines of the dioceses to be reshaped.

After this period of flux three dioceses ultimately were established: on January 7, 1887 the Diocese of Belleville in southern Illinois; on September 23, 1908 Rockford, a centrally located region known for its rich agricultural land and large manufacturing center; and on March 24, 1949 the Diocese of Joliet, carved out of Peoria and the Chicago Diocese.

Chicago has welcomed people from all over the globe and is, as a noted historian states, "the ideal laboratory in which to study [immigrants'] impact on city and church alike."[2]

Currently, the Province of Chicago has an archdiocese and five suffragan sees with a total Catholic population of 3,535,524 or 31% of the total population of the state of Illinois.

PROVINCE OF CINCINNATI

The Diocese of Cincinnati is one of the oldest dioceses in the United States. However, until 1791, the ecclesiastical jurisdiction over this area was complex, because Ohio had been the cause of contention between England and France in the eighteenth century. The French claimed Louisiana and all waters drained by the Mississippi and its tributaries, which included northern Ohio. France needed this territory for easy access from Canada to Louisiana; England disputed France's claim as a military stronghold near her territory.[3]

By the Quebec Act of 1774, which guaranteed religious freedom in Canada and extended it to the Ohio River, ecclesiastical jurisdiction should have passed to the bishop of Quebec. But after the Treaty of Peace in 1783 England still maintained forts in Michigan and Ohio, relinquishing them only after Jay's Treaty of 1794.

The question of ecclesiastical jurisdiction soon followed: Did the bishop of Quebec or the vicar apostolic of the London District or Bishop Carroll, the only bishop in the United States, have ecclesiastical jurisdiction over Ohio? Even the *Propaganda de Fide* recognized the problem, and sent a missionary to see if

[1]William Barnaby Faherty, S.J., *Dream by the River* (River City Publishers), p. 102.
[2]James Hennesey, S.J., *American Catholics* (Oxford University Press, 1981), p. 174.
[3]W.A. Jurgens, H.E.D., *A History of the Diocese of Cleveland*, (Catholic Publishing Co., Youngstown, Ohio, 1980), Vol. 1, p. 47.

Bishop Carroll's jurisdiction would be recognized in Ohio.[1] Fortunately, it was. Ohio remained without priests, however, from 1751 to 1795, when the first one arrived. In the meantime, the few Catholics in Ohio were dependent upon priests who came to them from Kentucky.[2]

When Bishop Carroll's vast diocese was divided in 1808, Bardstown, Kentucky, one of the divisions, included Ohio. In order to increase population and have a bishop closer to the people, Pope Pius VII, on June 19, 1821, established the Diocese of Cincinnati, a "bustling riverport city" which included the entire state of Ohio and until 1833 all of the Northwest Territory.

Irish immigration into Ohio coincided with the demand for laborers to build canals. These workers earned "30 cents a day, food, whiskey, and a shanty." Later in the western part of the state, German immigrants received $26 plus board per month. Malaria killed so many that the canal system was called the "Irish graveyard," and it was estimated that there was "a dead Irishman for every mile of canal."[3]

The constant increase of Irish and German immigrants due to the Irish famine and German persecution in Europe led Pope Pius IX to create the Diocese of Cleveland on April 23, 1847, carving it out of the northern part of the Diocese of Cincinnati. At that time this diocese of 10,000 had no schools, hospitals or orphanages, and the first bishop (1847-1870) worked to increase the numbers of these institutions. With the opening of the canals in 1832 and the building of the Commodore Vanderbilt Railroad linking it with New York in 1848-1849, Cleveland's growth as an industrial center was assured. On July 15, 1850 Cincinnati was established as an archdiocese.

Immigration from the Civil War until 1910 brought immigrants of varied ethnic backgrounds, mainly from eastern and southern Europe. Since national parishes were part of each diocese, there was always a problem of finding priests who could speak the languages of the immigrants.

Organization again followed population. The Diocese of Columbus was carved from the south central part of Ohio on March 3, 1868. On April 20, 1910 the western portion of the Cleveland Diocese was established as the new Diocese of Toledo, with three additional counties added on June 1, 1922. On May 15, 1943 the Diocese of Youngstown was carved from Cleveland. The youngest diocese, Steubenville, taken from the eastern part of the Columbus Diocese, was formed on November 11, 1944.

Thousands of Byzantines, following their own rite, settled in Cleveland. Today, they are centered in Parma, Ohio, and their cathedral parish is that of the Byzantine Eparchy (diocese) of Parma.

Today the Province of Cincinnati has an archdiocese and five suffragan sees with a total Catholic population of 2,219,167 or 21% of the total population of the state of Ohio.

---

[1]*Ibid.*, p. 58.
[2]*Ibid.*, p. 47.
[3]Albert Hamilton, *The Catholic Journey through Ohio,* (Catholic Conference of Ohio, 1796), p. 11.

PROVINCE OF DENVER

Over a half a century before the Pilgrims landed at Plymouth Rock in 1620, the Spanish had colonized the New World. The Denver Diocese was "a child of the much older church of Mexico" in the Diocese of Durango in 1562. Eleven churches were planted in New Mexico before 1620 and it was from these churches that missionaries ventured into Colorado.[1]

In 1706 Colorado was claimed for King Philip V of Spain. Constant expeditions against the French in Colorado finally ended in 1763 in victory for the Spanish. Spain received all land west of the Mississippi, but secretly gave it back to France in 1800. The Colorado land south of the Arkansas River was not included in the transaction when it was sold to the United States and it remained in Spanish hands, "the reason why the residence south of the Arkansas River continued to enjoy a special dispensation from Friday abstinence."[2] When the United States purchased it, the same privilege held.

The land ceded by Mexico to the United States in 1848 by the Treaty of Guadalupe-Hildago included the area of Colorado. On July 19, 1850 Pope Pius IX placed Colorado in the newly erected vicariate apostolic of Indian Territory. The bishop's residence for ecclesiastical jurisdiction was in Kansas but, geographically, Colorado was closer to the Diocese of Santa Fe to which it was transferred in 1861.[3]

The gold rush of 1858 brought numerous eastern money-seekers into Denver, Pueblo and Colorado Springs, so much so that the population of Colorado rose to 50,000. Catholics, however, numbered only 30 or 40 people. Because of the growth of the population, the bishops of the Second Plenary Council of 1866 requested that a new vicariate apostolic be formed for Colorado and Utah.[4] In 1866, the discovery of silver triggered the rise of towns and parishes, while at the same time, the arrival of the railroad tripled the population of Colorado. In 1868 the vicariate apostolic was established. In 1870, since one-third of the 47 parishes in the Colorado Territory was Catholic, it was decided to ease the work of the diocesan priests in Denver by transferring Utah to the Archdiocese of San Francisco.

One year after Colorado became a state, the Diocese of Denver was established (August 16, 1887). Throughout the next several decades, the Church in Colorado had grown to such proportions that the Holy See divided the Denver Diocese in 1941 and created the Diocese of Pueblo from the southern counties of Denver. In that same year, Pope Pius XII raised Denver to a metropolitan see and made Cheyenne a suffragan of the Denver Archdiocese.

---

[1]Thomas Noel, "Hispanic Roots of Colorado Catholicism," *The Denver Catholic Register,* Vol. LXIII, No. 30, August 5, 1987, p. 3.
[2]Mary Papa, "History of the Diocese," Appendix A, *Colorado Dateline,* 1968. This so-called Spanish privilege had been granted to Spain and her territories by Papal proclamation but was revoked in 1945.
[3]*Ibid.*
[4]Peter Guilday, *A History of the Councils,* p. 222.

Cheyenne is an interesting diocese since it has been under a number of ec-clesiastical jurisdictions: French, Spanish and Mexican bishops all governed this area, though many did it with a *"de jure* jurisdiction rather than *de facto,"* since only a few white settlers occupied this land and in the beginning only one priest cared for the conversion of the Indians.[1]

In 1827 Wyoming was under the jurisdiction of St. Louis; in 1851 it was a part of the vicariate apostolic of the Indian Territory; by 1857 it was included in the vicariate apostolic of Nebraska; on October 2, 1885, when Omaha was made a diocese, it included the Territory of Wyoming; and on August 9, 1887 Cheyenne and Lincoln became suffragans of Omaha. In 1893 Cheyenne became a suffragan of the Province of Dubuque. Lastly, in 1941, when Denver was made a metropolitan see, Cheyenne and Pueblo were created suffragans of the Province of Denver. On January 30, 1894 Colorado Springs, created from the nine counties of the Denver Archdiocese and one from Pueblo, became the last diocese to be formed in the Province of Denver.

Today the Province of Denver has one archdiocese and three suffragan sees with a total Catholic population of 545,356 or 13% of the total population in the states of Colorado and Wyoming.

PROVINCE OF DETROIT

Over 350 years ago the history of the Catholic Church in Michigan began with the arrival of missionaries in the area surrounding the Straits of Mackinac. Jesuits like Isaac Jogues and Jacques Marquette, and the Sulpician Francois Dol-lier were among the intrepid missionaries who met the tremendous challenges of bringing Christianity to the Native Americans.[2] The entire area of Michigan and most of Wisconsin until the end of the eighteenth century had only one church, St. Anne's, "the Mother Parish of the Northwest."[3]

In 1763 England took possession of all land east of the Mississippi, but by the Treaty of Paris in 1783, England ceded all this land to the new American government. The missions were under the bishop of Quebec until November 6, 1789 when authority over all Catholics in the United States was exercised by Bishop John Carroll of Baltimore. When the division of the Baltimore Diocese occurred in 1808, Detroit and the Michigan Territory were assigned to Bard-stown, Kentucky. When the Diocese of Cincinnati was created in 1821, Michigan became part of this diocese. On March 4, 1827 Pope Leo XII issued a bull for the erection of a diocese in Detroit but it was never implemented. On March 8, 1833 another bull established the Diocese of Detroit.

The Detroit Diocese included Michigan, Wisconsin, Iowa, Minnesota and portions of North and South Dakota east of the Mississippi River.[4] The original

[1]Most Rev. Patrick A. McGovern, *History of the Diocese of Cheyenne* (Diocese of Cheyenne, 1941), p. 4.
[2]Msgr. Francis X. Canfield, *A Condensed History of the Catholic Church in the Archdiocese of Detroit* (Archdiocese of Detroit, 1983), p. 2.
[3]Willard M.J. Baird, *A Heritage of Faith* (privately published, 1983), pp. 2, 3. Quoted from John W. McGee, *The Catholic Church in the Grand River Valley, 1833-1950* (Diocese of Grand Rapids, Michigan, 1950), p. 8.
[4]Canfield, *New Catholic Encyclopedia,* Vol. IV, p. 817.

extent of territory was considerably reduced when the Diocese of Dubuque (1837) and the Diocese of Milwaukee (1843) were created. On July 19, 1850, when Cincinnati was raised to a metropolitan see, Detroit became one of its suffragans.

On July 29, 1853 the Upper Peninsula of Michigan was made into a vicariate apostolic of Sault Ste. Marie and raised to diocesan status on January 9, 1857 within the Archdiocese of Cincinnati. Sault Ste. Marie was transferred to Marquette, October 23, 1865, and later to the Milwaukee Province when an archdiocese was named on February 12, 1875.[1]

In the nineteenth century upper and lower Michigan saw a surging of population and a growth of membership within the Catholic Church. The completion of the Erie Canal, the building of railroads which became "the main conduit of people and freight during the second half of the nineteenth century," the logging industry and the fertile land contributed to this growth linking the eastern seaboard with Detroit. Various ethnic groups from southern and eastern Europe came to work in the factories and on the roads[2] and the population figures indicate the growth resulting from these movements. In 1838 there were between 20,000 and 24,000 Catholics, most of whom were French; by 1882 the population of the Diocese of Detroit had grown to 100,000 Catholics.[3]

The influx of people into this area necessitated new dioceses. On May 19, 1882 the Diocese of Grand Rapids was established in the northwestern sector of Michigan. Prospects for employment in Detroit's new automobile industry helped the Catholic population to reach 386,000 by 1918.[4] The Archdiocese of Detroit was created on August 3, 1937 and in the same year the Diocese of Lansing in the southern sector was established (May 22, 1937) followed by the erection of the Diocese of Saginaw in the east central area in 1938.

It was during the bishopric of the first archbishop of Detroit that the great automotive unions came into existence. This archdiocese played a great part in establishing organizations to implement the social teachings of the Church such as the Associations of Catholic Trade Unionists and the Archdiocesan Labor Institutes.

In 1971 two more dioceses created in the Province of Detroit necessitated a change in boundaries: the Diocese of Gaylord on July 20th in the northern part of Michigan and the Diocese of Kalamazoo on July 21st in the southwestern sector of the state.

The Province of Detroit is renowned for its outstanding record of spiritual and material help to Detroit's various ethnic groups. A universal archdiocese, Detroit has extended its charity to many different nationalities. There are 100 different ethnic groups receiving help; there are quasi-parishes for other immigrants such as Vietnamese, Koreans, Kerala Indians and Syriac Rite Catholics as

[1]Correspondence with Rev. John J. Shiverski, Chancellor, Diocese of Marquette, February 17, 1988.
[2]Canfield, *A Condensed History*, p. 6.
[3]*Ibid.*, pp. 8, 13.
[4]*Ibid.*, p. 14.

well as those from the Far East. There are also Eucharistic celebrations in the various languages to retain their cultures.[1]

Today the Province of Detroit has an archdiocese and six suffragan sees with a total Catholic population of 2,281,181 or 25% of the total population of the state of Michigan.

PROVINCE OF DUBUQUE

The American Midwest (the Mississippi Valley and the Great Lakes region) first came under the ecclesiastical jurisdiction of the Province of Rouen, France, when the Vicariate Apostolic of Quebec was established during the years 1653 and 1674. Later, from 1674 to 1763, it was placed under the bishop of Quebec, but this vast territory was impossible to administer spiritually from Canada; hence no bishop visited there. Many letters are extant, however, which indicate interest in correcting abuses among fur traders who were scandalizing the Indians.[2]

The suppression of the Jesuits in 1763 in the Mississippi Valley ended their missionary work among the Indians until 1830. In the meantime ecclesiastical jurisdiction passed to the Spanish (from 1763 to 1803) and later to the archbishop of Baltimore.

In 1804 when Congress divided the Louisiana Territory into the Territory of Orleans (Lower Louisiana) and the District of Louisiana (Upper Louisiana), the last name was changed to the Territory of Missouri, because Orleans used the name Louisiana for its state.[3]

The Diocese of St. Louis was created in 1826, extending from Missouri to Canada and from the Mississippi to the Rocky Mountains. Because of its size, the Third Provincial Council of Baltimore in 1837 asked in language that was purposely vague that a diocese be established at Dubuque, Iowa: "Since it was a land of strangers and mystery," it was to have jurisdiction in the state of Wisconsin,[4] i.e., all the territory lying between the Missouri and Mississippi rivers. On April 22, 1837 Dubuque became a diocese one year before the Territory of Iowa was established (1838). This Territory included what is presently Minnesota, eastern parts of North and South Dakota and, until the dioceses of Chicago and Minnesota were formed in 1843, the bishops of Dubuque exercised jurisdiction over these areas.[5]

The phenomenal population growth in Iowa was seen in many areas within the United States. in 1838 there were 500 Catholics in Iowa served by one priest and one bishop, who also administered the dioceses of St. Louis and Milwaukee.[6] The Catholic population was 7,050 in 1840, but by 1880 it had reached 120,000. The land, opened to white settlers by the Indian treaties of

---

[1]Correspondence with Roman P. Godzak, Archivist, January 3, 1989. Letter of Edmund Cardinal Szoka, in *Michigan Catholic Newspaper*.
[2]Sister Madeleine Marie Schmidt, C.H.M., *Seasons of Growth, History of the Diocese of Davenport, 1881-1981* (The Diocese of Davenport, 1981), p. 12.
[3]*Ibid.*, p. 18.
[4]Peter Guilday, *A History of the Councils*, p. 34.
[5]Schmidt, *op. cit.*, p. 34.
[6]S.D. Luby, *New Catholic Encyclopedia*, Vol. IV, p. 1081.

1833-1851, was alluring and its easy access by steamboat to the Mississippi and the Ohio rivers brought hungry American pioneers to follow the paths to the fertile soil of the Midwest.

With the increase of the number of Catholics in Iowa, the bishop of Dubuque requested a division of the diocese. In 1850 the Diocese of St. Paul was created, removing from the Diocese of Dubuque all land in Minnesota, and North and South Dakota, making the boundary of Dubuque coterminous with that of Iowa.

Other territorial changes followed: In 1881 Davenport was cut from the southern part of Dubuque which, in 1883, was raised to a metropolitan see with suffragans in Davenport, Iowa; Cheyenne, Wyoming; and Lincoln and Omaha, Nebraska. In Iowa two other dioceses were created in the twentieth century: Sioux City was cut from the western part of Dubuque in 1902 and, after repeated pleas from the priests and the people of Des Moines to establish a diocese in the capital of the state, because of its large Catholic population and because of its importance to the Church, in 1911 Des Moines was made a diocese.

Other changes reduced the size of the Archdiocese of Dubuque: Denver was made a metropolitan see in 1941 with Cheyenne as one of its suffragans. In 1945 Omaha, Nebraska, became a metropolitan see with Lincoln as its suffragan. The Province of Dubuque was then coterminous with the state of Iowa.

The Province of Dubuque has three suffragan sees and a Catholic population of 510,388 or 18% of the total population of the state of Iowa.

PROVINCE OF HARTFORD

Before 1830 Catholicism in Connecticut and Rhode Island presented a very different picture from that found in other parts of New England. In both states there were no laws prohibiting the presence of priests nor was there any burning of buildings by anti-Catholic rioters. But this does not say that Catholics were accepted for the Puritans held them in low esteem.[1] Catholic worship was proscribed and a fine was imposed for harboring a Catholic. The law of 1784 in Connecticut did allow freedom of worship for all except Catholics and Jews. Rhode Island had a "notorious reputation" for tolerating different religious opinions.[2] But there were only 600 Catholics in all of New England with perhaps none in Connecticut and Rhode Island.

The *Connecticut Gazette* of January 5, 1764 carried this pathetic advertisement: "Just Imported from Dublin...A Parcel of Irish servants, both men and women, and to be sold cheap."[3] But no opportunity was given anyone to practice his or her religion as there were no priests, no churches and no bishop in this area until 1823 when the first resident pastor arrived.[4] In 1808, although the

[1]Rev. John S. Kennedy, "Catholicism in Connecticut," *The Hartford Courant*, October 25, 1953, p. 3.
[2]Robert W. Hayman, *Catholicism in Rhode Island, and the Diocese of Providence*, (Diocese of Providence, 1982), p. 4.
[3]Kennedy, *op. cit.*
[4]M.J. Scholsky, "Archdiocese of Hartford," *New Catholic Encyclopedia*, Vol VI, p. 933.

Archdiocese of Baltimore

Bishop Carro
Administrator Apo
1804-1815

Archbishop John Carroll's jurisdiction co

Cartographer James L. Doherty

its four Suffragan Sees 1808

the vast territory within the dotted lines.

bishop of Boston had jurisdiction over all New England, the distance made it impossible to exercise it to any extent.

The growth of the Catholic population and material prosperity was so low in the New England states that the bishop of New Orleans "suggested to Rome in 1824 and again in 1825 that the Sees of Boston and New York be united."[1] However, the unprecedented influx of immigrants into this territory from 1820 to 1860, coupled with the great "Transportation Revolution" that offered numerous job opportunities on roads, turnpikes and railroads, soon proved to be the folly of that idea.

While the earliest immigrants of New England were educated and financially able to exist in the New World, the Irish who followed in the years from 1820 to 1860 were mainly impoverished Catholics, often illiterate, fleeing from the ravages of famine, "the worst disaster that had befallen a nation in Western History."

By 1840 there were almost 68,000 Catholics in Boston but the distance to Connecticut and Rhode Island to care for the 10,000 there proved such an obstacle that the bishop of Boston requested that his diocese be divided. Even though Providence was a larger city, was free from debt and had a large Catholic population, the bishops at the Fifth Provincial Council in 1843 deemed Hartford the best place for a diocese because of its centrally located position. The bishop, however, chose for his residence not Hartford but Providence, retaining the name Hartford for the diocese.[2] This remained until 1872.

The Diocese of Hartford was so poor that the plea to the Propagation of the Faith and the Leopoldine Society in Vienna did not go unheeded and a generous contribution was made to the diocese, despite the fact that there was but one Austrian-born seminarian in the state. Because of the shortage of priests the bishops sought help from the seminaries at Maynooth and All Hallows, Dublin.[3] To encourage more vocations to the priesthood a seminary was established in Hartford.

With the increase of immigration from the 1870's to 1910, particularly of French Canadian Catholics and people from southern and eastern Europe, the Hartford Diocese reached a Catholic population of 200,000. A division of the diocese was again requested but Vatican Council I was in session and the request was tabled until January 31, 1872 when Pope Pius IX formally established a new diocese in Providence which included all of Rhode Island and southeastern Massachusetts.[4]

The Diocese of Hartford was raised to a metropolitan see in 1953. At the same time two new dioceses were established in Connecticut: Bridgeport, a prosperous Catholic area from southwest Hartford; and Norwich, a less prosperous area but with a deeply religious population. Time saw the wisdom of this division.

There is a very large number of foreign-born in the Archdiocese of Hartford. From 1880 to 1914, Connecticut and particularly Rhode Island had larger num-

[1]Patrick T. Conley and Matthew J. Smith, *Catholicism in Rhode Island, The Formation* (Diocese of Providence, 1976).
[2]Hayman, *op. cit.*, p. 59.
[3]Conley and Smith, *op. cit.*, p. 72.
[4]Kennedy, *op. cit.*, October 27, 1953.

bers than any other state in the Union. This necessitated additional priests, particularly those who could speak the languages of southern and eastern Europe. The Archdiocese of Hartford has been successful in its mission. This territory which in 1828 was served by only one priest had, in 1988, over 2,000 diocesan and religious clergy. The story of the religious sisters, brothers and laity throughout the diocese has yet to be told.

The province of Hartford currently includes an archdiocese and three suffragan sees with a total population of 1,362,970 Catholics or 42% of the total population of the state of Connecticut and 625,170 Catholics or 63% of the total population of the state of Rhode Island.

PROVINCE OF INDIANAPOLIS

One of the earliest dioceses to be erected in the United States (the 13th) was Vincennes (later called Indianapolis), colonized by French missionaries from Canada. The bishop of Quebec exercised ecclesiastical jurisdiction over it until it was assigned to Bishop John Carroll of Baltimore in 1789 and later to the bishop of Bardstown, Kentucky, in 1808.

Vincennes was one of the "most cosmopolitan cities in the United States," because of the victorious battles fought by the Patriots. Her history is fascinating reading:

> she was founded under France, developed under England, became the parent of the American Union in the Northwest Territory and the mother of five sister states, [among them] Indiana, Ohio, Wisconsin and Michigan.[1]

Vincennes was also the "cradle of world power" since the military victories extended our western frontier to the Mississippi.

By the early nineteenth century, the French inhabitants were outnumbered by the Irish and German immigrants (1820-1880) of Maryland and Kentucky. The Irish engaged first in building canals, then farming and factory work, and later railroads. The Germans were adept as farmers and construction builders.[2] Naturally, organization of dioceses followed population growth.

As early as 1825, the bishops realized that a multiplication of bishoprics "was the only agency to direct the spiritual care of the scattered population."[3] The problem remained untouched, however, until May 6, 1834, when Pope Gregory XVI established the Diocese of Vincennes coterminous with the state of Indiana and including the eastern part of Illinois. This was relinquished in 1843, when Chicago became a diocese.[4] Population increases were noticeable. The number of parishes grew from 23 in 1834 to 140 in 1877 with a total of 80,000 Catholics. To meet this demand, Pope Pius IX, on January 8, 1857, erected Fort Wayne (redesignated as Fort Wayne-South Bend on July 22, 1960) in the

---

[1]Sister M. Salesia Godecker, O.S.B., *Simon Bruté de Remur, First Bishop of Vincennes* (St. Meinrad, 1931), p. 161.
[2]James J. Divita, "Archdiocese of Indianapolis" (booklet, 1979), p. 2.
[3]Godecker, *op. cit.*, p. 198.
[4]Guilday, *A History of the Councils*, p. 106.

northern half of the state and the remaining southern half of the state became the Diocese of Vincennes.

The second bishop of Vincennes was permitted a choice of residences: at Vincennes, Madison, Lafayette or Indianapolis. Vincennes was, however, to remain the see city. This permission, except for the city of Lafayette, was renewed for the next two bishops. It was also realized that, although Vincennes was growing in population, most of the inhabitants were Protestants and that Indianapolis, the state capital, included most of the Catholics. The Holy See, therefore, moved the bishop's residence to Indianapolis, although the title of the see remained at Vincennes. By the Apostolic Brief dated March 23, 1898, the title of the diocese was changed to "Diocese of Indianapolis," and the episcopal see located in Indianapolis.[1]

On December 21, 1944 Pope Pius XII created the Archdiocese of Indianapolis. At the same time, two other dioceses were erected, the Dioceses of Evansville and Lafayette. The last diocese to be erected was Gary, established on February 25, 1957.

The state of Indiana has a small number of Catholics, perhaps due to the fact that for a century and a half (1820-1950) many anti-Catholic movements, particularly in the southern part of the state, engendered prejudice and intolerance.

Today the Province of Indianapolis has an archdiocese and four suffragan sees with a total Catholic population of 695,551 or 13% of the total population of the state of Indiana.

KANSAS AND NEBRASKA

BACKGROUND

It was in 1682 that De La Salle, the first white man to reach the mouth of the Mississippi, planted his cross and proclaimed the river and all lands watered by it for the King of France, Louis XIV. This vast territory, named Louisiana in his honor, was under the ecclesiastical jurisdiction of the bishop of Quebec.

In 1763, at the end of the Seven Years War, Spain took possession of this land with the bishop of Santiago de Cuba exercising jurisdiction. When the Holy See divided this diocese to form San Cristobal as Havana's second diocese in 1787, Louisiana and Florida belonged ecclesiastically to the bishop of Havana.

In 1803 the United States purchased Louisiana from France, to whom Spain secretly had given it. Hence, the future Kansas and Nebraska territory came under another ecclesiastical jurisdiction, the Baltimore Archdiocese. The archbishop of Baltimore was asked to care for this Diocese of Louisiana because of the confused jurisdiction after the resignation of the bishop of Havana (who remained until 1806). When the archbishop died in 1815, the jurisdiction passed to the bishop of New Orleans and later, in 1826, to the bishop of St. Louis.[2]

In 1849 the bishops of the Seventh Provincial Council in Baltimore requested that an apostolic vicariate be established in this "Indian Territory." In

---

[1] Archdiocese of Indianapolis, *Directory, 1987-88,* pp. 4-5.
[2] Sister Loretta Gosen, *History of the Catholic Church in the Diocese of Lincoln, Nebraska, 1887-1987* (The Catholic Bishop of Lincoln, 1986), p. 1.

1850 the Holy See decreed that the territory was to extend "from the Kansas River at its mouth north to the British possessions and from the Missouri River west to the Rocky Mountains," 650 miles from north to south and 600 from east to west.[1] This included the present states of Nebraska, Kansas, North and South Dakota, Wyoming, and parts of Montana, Idaho and Colorado. At the time Kansas had neither priests nor churches.

In 1854 the Kansas-Nebraska Act permitted settlers to enter these territories. The vast influx of people who immediately responded necessitated another division of the original vicariate. In 1857 the territories of Kansas and Nebraska became two vicariates. Between 1868 and 1883, four new vicariates were made from the Nebraska Territory. Kansas remained one vicariate.[2]

PROVINCE OF KANSAS CITY, KANSAS

From 1860 to 1877 Kansas suffered from severe drought, a crop failure caused by a plague of grasshoppers destroying the land and its products and the unemployment that followed the "panic of 1873." Prosperity, however, came to the state with the construction of three major railroads, bringing an increased number of immigrants from Germany and other parts of Europe seeking employment. A request for a diocese in Leavenworth came as early as 1874, and by May 22, 1877 it became a reality. On August 2, 1887 Pope Leo XIII, responding to the request of the bishop of St. Louis, established two new dioceses in Kansas, that of Wichita and Concordia on the west side of Leavenworth.

New boundaries were formed to enlarge the Diocese of Wichita and on July 10, 1897, it was extended to the southern part of Kansas. On December 23, 1944 the Diocese of Concordia was transferred to that of Salina, the largest city in the diocese, because it was situated on two transcontinental railroads and "its population is twice as great as any other city."[3] On May 10, 1947 the Diocese of Leavenworth was transferred to Kansas City in Kansas and five years later, August 9, 1952, it became an archdiocese. The distance of 400 miles across the Diocese of Wichita seemed too great to offer spiritual help, so another diocese was established on the western side at Dodge City on May 19, 1951.

All dioceses in Kansas were suffragan sees of St. Louis until 1952, when Kansas City in Kansas became an archdiocese coterminous with the state of Kansas.

The Province of Kansas City in Kansas has an archdiocese and three suffragan sees with a total Catholic population of 373,770 or 16% of the total population of Kansas.

---

[1]Father John M. Moeder, J.C.D., *History of the Diocese of Wichita* (privately printed, 1963), p. 12. Also Guilday, *A History of the Councils,* p. 15.
[2]Gosen, *op. cit.,* p. 472.
[3]Mary Frances Lahey, *Harvest of Faith, History of the Diocese of Saline—100 Years* (Dallas: Taylor Publishing Company, 1987), p. 34.

PROVINCE OF OMAHA

Nebraska suffered the same hardships of poverty and unemployment as the surrounding areas. Here, the inability of the steamboats and covered wagons to compete with the growth of railroads and other means of transportation, the available and generous land offers, and the increase of rainfall turned the land of destruction to one of prosperity in the 1870's.[1] On October 3, 1885 the vicariate of Nebraska, which included the state of Nebraska and the territory of Wyoming, was raised to the status of a diocese, with Omaha as the see city. Within two years the diocese was divided into three dioceses with two new dioceses: Lincoln, Nebraska and Cheyenne, Wyoming.

Because of the increase of population due to this new prosperity, the diocese became so distant from the western end of the state that a new diocese was established in Kearney on March 8, 1912. In 1916 the diocese was expanded to include four new counties, and a year later Pope Benedict XV transferred this see to Grand Island, April 11, 1917, because it was a center of good transportation and could offer easy access to the other dioceses.[2]

The difficulty that confronted most dioceses in other parts of the country—the cultural differences in ethnic groups—also faced Omaha, especially in Lincoln. National parishes for each language group helped to ease the tension often caused by isolation in predominantly Protestant areas. Ethnic groups demanded that the priests speak their language; the need for the knowledge of finance, building experience and teaching ability often called for more than physical stamina in these areas.[3] The growth in the number of Catholics at a time when the state seemed to be decreasing in population, indicated again that a miracle of grace was taking place in this vast land.

The three dioceses remained under the ecclesiastical jurisdiction of the St. Louis Province from 1826 until 1893. When Dubuque, Iowa became an archdiocese in 1893, it exercised jurisdiction over Nebraska and Wyoming. On August 7, 1945 Omaha was elevated to a province and its jurisdiction was coterminous with Nebraska. Wyoming became part of the Province of Denver in 1941.

Today the Province of Omaha has an archdiocese and two suffragan sees with a total Catholic population of 329,925 or 21% of the total population of the state of Nebraska.

[1]Gosen, *op. cit.*, pp. 2-3.
[2]*The Nebraska Register*, September 14, 1962, p. 6.
[3]Gosen, *op. cit.*, pp. 3-4.

CALIFORNIA

BACKGROUND

Although California was claimed by Spanish explorers as early as 1542, Spanish missionaries were late in coming to this region, but the fear of the Russians in Alaska made the Spanish aware of the need for colonization and mission sites in the area now known as Upper California.[1] One of the well-known Franciscan missionaries was Father Junipero Serra, who was instrumental in founding the first mission in San Diego (1769). From this time until 1845, there were 146 Franciscans who labored for the spread of the faith. They taught the art of Christian as well as civilized living and taught agricultural skills to the native farmers, the results of which are regarded as phenomenal, even today.

The ecclesiastical jurisdiction over Upper and Lower California was administered by the Diocese of Sonora in the Province of Durango, Mexico. Mexico became independent from Spain in 1821, and California was made a part of Mexico in 1825. Political and financial difficulties in Spain had repercussions in Mexico: Secularization of the mission lands followed in 1830, ending the evangelization by the Franciscan missions. The vast grazing lands of the missions were "parcelled out as land grants to retired soldiers."[2]

The Mexican government did, however, negotiate with Pope Gregory XVI to erect a Diocese of Upper and Lower California on April 27, 1840, creating a "gigantic diocese" which extended from the Oregon line (42nd° north latitude) to the southern part of Baja (Lower) California.[3]

1846 marked the year that changed the United States politically and the Church's ecclesiastical jurisdiction territorially. The Mexican War ended with victory for the United States. Mexico ceded California (now Baja, California) to our country and New Mexico to the Rio Grande boundary. The Diocese of Upper California was now officially Monterey (1849). Lower California was placed under the jurisdiction of the archbishop of Mexico, where it has remained.

PROVINCE OF SAN FRANCISCO

The influx of people into California due to the gold rush, the opening of new trade routes and the transfer of sovereignty in California necessitated a delineation of boundaries. On July 17, 1853, Rome removed the Baja California area from the Diocese of Monterey, and on July 29 Pope Pius IX created the metropolitan see at San Francisco, with the larger suffragan see at Monterey, an area that remained intact for the "next seven decades."[4] On July 8, 1859 the diocese was moved to Los Angeles and renamed Monterey-Los Angeles.

In 1860, the Vicariate Apostolic of Marysville was established as a diocese in the Province of San Francisco; it became the Diocese of Grass Valley in 1868, and then part of the new Diocese of Sacramento in 1886. In 1962 three

---

[1]John Tracy Ellis, *op. cit.,* p. 108.
[2]*Official Directory* of the Oakland Diocese, 1987, p. 74.
[3]"Archdiocese of Los Angeles," *The Holy Father in California's Southland,* p. 55.
[4]*Ibid.,* p. 55.

more dioceses were created for this Province: Stockton (January 13) and Oakland and Santa Rosa (February 21). The last diocese to be erected was San Jose on January 27, 1981.

The archdiocese also included the states of Utah, Nevada and Hawaii, the Equatorial Islands of Christmas, Palmyra and Fanning. "As the Territory of Utah had been withdrawn from Denver and placed temporarily under the direction of the Archbishop of San Francisco, constant communication existed between the parishes of Utah and southern and eastern Nevada."[1] When Utah became a vicariate apostolic on January 25, 1887, Utah and southern Nevada were withdrawn from the Province of San Francisco. On January 27, 1891 this vicariate apostolic became the Diocese of Salt Lake, renamed Salt Lake City Diocese on March 31, 1951. At the same time, the Holy See detached the territory within northern Nevada that was held partially by Sacramento and Salt Lake and returned it to the Nevada Territory, thereby creating the Diocese of Reno and bringing ecclesiastical unity for the first time to the state of Nevada. Reno was redesignated the Diocese of Reno-Las Vegas by Pope Paul VI on October 13, 1976.

A good example of how a diocese embraces different ecclesiastical jurisdictions within its lifetime is seen in the Diocese of Reno, created on March 27, 1931. "The people have been 'subjects' in turn of the Archdiocese of San Francisco, the Vicariate of Marysville, the Diocese of Grass Valley, the Diocese of Sacramento, the Vicariate of Utah and the Diocese of Salt Lake."[2]

The prefecture apostolic of the Hawaiian Islands (then known as the Sandwich Islands) was established in 1826; these islands were erected into a vicariate apostolic in 1844, and then created the Diocese of Honolulu on September 10, 1941. The former Diocese of Agana (Guam), which originally belonged to San Francisco, was elevated to a metropolitan see on May 20, 1984.

Now the Province of San Francisco embraces Northern California, Utah, Nevada and Hawaii and includes an archdiocese and eight suffragan sees. It has a total Catholic population of 1,720,058 in California or 19% of the total population; 69,944 in Utah or 4% of the total population; 147,000 in Nevada or 15% of the total population; and 191,520 or 18% in Honolulu.

PROVINCE OF LOS ANGELES

The Province of Los Angeles was formed in the twentieth century. It was originally part of the San Francisco Province as the Diocese of Monterey-Los Angeles. Despite the many proposals to dismember the territory, it remained intact for seven decades until Pope Pius XI in 1922 created the Diocese of Monterey-Fresno from the northern part of the diocese and left the southern part as the Diocese of Los Angeles-San Diego.

On July 11, 1936 the Province of Los Angeles was created from the Province of San Francisco, detaching Monterey-Fresno and Los Angeles-San Diego from its territory. At the same time, the separation involved the creation of San Diego as a new diocese, the continuance of Monterey-Fresno as an established diocese and the addition of Tucson, Arizona. In 1969 Monterey and

[1]Most Rev. Thomas K. Gorman, *Seventy-Five Years of Catholic Life in Nevada* (The Journal Press, Reno, Nevada, 1935), p. 12.
[2]*Ibid.*, p. 14.

Fresno became separate dioceses and Tucson was given to the Santa Fe Archdiocese. When Los Angeles was raised to a metropolitan see, California became the only state in the union which had two separate archdioceses. Los Angeles has the unique distinction of being the largest Catholic-populated archdiocese in the nation.

The above territory adjustments remained until June 18, 1976 when the Diocese of Orange was created, an area which has experienced a spectacular growth in population from a rich agricultural region into a progressively industrial region.[1] The last diocese to be formed in Los Angeles was that of the Diocese of San Bernadino on November 6, 1978, carved from the Diocese of San Diego.

The Province of Los Angeles has one archdiocese and five suffragan sees with a total Catholic population of 2,416,948 or 20% of the total population.

PROVINCE OF LOUISVILLE

With the exception of the Florida-Louisiana Diocese under Spanish jurisdiction, Baltimore was the only diocese in the United States until 1808. When the Archdiocese of Baltimore was divided into four dioceses, Bardstown, Kentucky, became one of the suffragan sees. This area was called "The American Holy Land" because of its large number of Catholics, religious leaders and professional lawyers. It was also the first inland diocese in America.[2]

Strange as it may seem Catholicism was more prominent in Kentucky than it was anywhere else in this vast territory. Other parts of this area such as Cleveland, Detroit or Chicago were little known and unimportant at this time. By 1805 Catholics in Bardstown numbered six to eight thousand, and immigration into this area was constantly increasing. It was not only a good choice but the best one to preserve the faith.[3]

Immigrants profited religiously and economically by moving into this region. They had the spiritual guidance of some of the best minds in the country because the educated French priests of the Sulpician Society came to Kentucky to escape the anti-clerical laws of the French Revolution and its aftermath, the Reign of Terror. In fact, a Sulpician became the first bishop in the Bardstown Diocese and many Sulpicians became leaders in other areas.

The territory of the Bardstown Diocese was vast. It included not only the three existent states of Kentucky, Tennessee and Ohio, but also the areas of the present states of Indiana, Illinois, Michigan, Wisconsin and part of Minnesota.

During the episcopate of Bishop Flaget a number of dioceses were formed from that of Bardstown: Cincinnati (1821), Detroit (1833), Vincennes (now Indianapolis, 1834), and Nashville (1837). It was Bishop Flaget who petitioned the Holy See to remove the episcopal see from Bardstown to Louisville, which, because of the coming of the steamboat of the Ohio River, became an important

---

[1]"Our Extended Family," *The Holy Father in California's Southland,* p. 16.
[2]Clyde F. Crews, *An American Holy Land, A History of the Archdiocese of Louisville,* (Michael Glazier, Inc., 1987), pp. 76-77.
[3]Rev. William A. Jurgens, H.E.D., *A History of the Diocese of Cleveland, The Prehistory of the Diocese to its Establishment in 1847* (The Catholic Diocese of Cleveland, 1980), Vol. I, p. 74.

shipping and warehouse center and the producer of food products. The ecclesiastical center in Louisville was "more urban and less ethnically diverse."[1]

The bishops of the Fourth Provincial Council responded favorably to Bishop Flaget's request and a petition was sent to the Holy See. On February 13, 1841 the seat of the diocese was transferred to Louisville. In 1837 the entire state of Tennessee was created as the Diocese of Nashville and the state of Kentucky as the Diocese of Louisville. Nashville was under the Province of St. Louis after the latter became an archdiocese in 1847 and Louisville was under the Province of Cincinnati when it became a province in 1850. In 1883 Nashville (all of Tennessee) was transferred from St. Louis to become part of the Province of Cincinnati. When Louisville itself became a metropolitan see in 1937, it included the entire states of Kentucky and Tennessee. Nashville then became a part of this province.[2]

Covington, a territory which comprised the eastern third of Kentucky and which remains rural even today was made a diocese in 1853 under the Archdiocese of Cincinnati. It became part of the Province of Louisville in 1937. Because of the moving population two more dioceses were created in this province: Owensboro, Kentucky (February 23, 1938) and Memphis, Tennessee (January 6, 1971).

In 1988 two new dioceses were created from the Province of Louisville. On March 2, 1988, because of the growth of population and new highway construction, Lexington was made a diocese. On September 8, 1988, the Diocese of Knoxville was created in response to demographic increase and, although most of the population was not Catholic, the bishops realized that the proximity to the few Catholics there might foster evangelization in this area.

The Province of Louisville has an archdiocese and six suffragan sees with a total population of 376,688 or 10% of the total population of Kentucky and 127,220 or 3% of the total population of the state of Tennessee.

PROVINCE OF MIAMI

In 1565 St. Augustine in Florida was the site of the first Spanish settlement in America, over 420 years ago and long before colonists settled in Jamestown or the Pilgrims in Massachusetts.[3] From the sixteenth to the middle of the nineteenth century, Spain had the largest holdings in the New World. During this period, while her story of bringing Catholicism to the North American land was filled with success, there was often tragedy as well. In the twentieth century, when no longer a possession of Spain or England, Florida experienced a remarkable growth of Catholicism, especially in the east coast in Miami.

As early as 1521 to 1526, Florida was founded by explorers eager to aid the Indian missions. Success marked their endeavors until 1702-1704, when the English completely destroyed the mission territory of St. Augustine. In 1763,

[1]Crews, *op. cit.,* p. 109.
[2]Correspondence with Rev. Stephen A. Klasek, Chancellor, Diocese of Nashville, August 23, 1988 and William Barnaby Faherty, S.J., Archivist, Jesuit Mission Province Archives, September 7, 1988.
[3]Michael V. Gannon, *The Cross in the Sand* (University of Florida Press, 1965), pp. xii-xiii.

Florida passed into English hands, and for the next 20 years Catholicism was almost obliterated. If ever the statement, "the blood of the martyrs is the seed of the Church," is questioned, the growth of Catholicism in Florida proves its truth. In 1763 only eight priests and one brother remained to care for the demoralized state population. One year later, these missionaries were withdrawn and 190 years of Franciscan missionary work was destroyed.[1]

The exodus of the Catholic families to Cuba to escape annihilation brought additional hardships to the Church, because the English seized all its possessions, declaring it property of the Spanish crown and not of the Church. While a second spring did seem to be on the horizon in 1777, especially after Spain took possession of Florida again in 1783, it was short-lived. Even though the United States purchased this land from Spain in 1819, the Church gained little benefit.

From 1783 until the Civil War period, the Indian missions were wiped out, and from 1821 until 1858 the history of the Church was one of dismal failure. In pre-Civil War days, there were only three priests and 3,000 Catholics. But by 1870, after remarkable growth, Florida had 12 priests and 10,000 Catholics.[2]

In 1763 England had territorially divided Florida into two areas: East Florida including the land to the Chattahoochee River and West Florida, including the land along the Gulf of Mexico. Ecclesiastically, the jurisdiction for this area was administered by the bishop of Santiago de Cuba (1565-1787) and by St. Cristobal de Havana (1789-1793). In 1793 an episcopal see was erected in Louisiana called "The Diocese of Louisiana and the Floridas" which severed the ecclesiastical authorities from Cuba. But, because of continual factions of government within the Church, Florida was again under the Diocese of Havana (1801-1819). However, the bishop of Baltimore was requested in 1807 to "temporarily" take care of Louisiana and Florida. In 1825, when a bishop of Louisiana and the Floridas was elevated for the Diocese of New Orleans, Florida was again under the Diocese of Louisiana (1819-1825).

It was obvious that some control had to be exercised in Florida, since the distance from New Orleans made it impossible for the bishop to visit the Florida territory. In 1825 the Holy See created the Vicariate Apostolic of Florida and Alabama, becoming part of the Diocese of Mobile when the latter was made a diocese in 1829. But the destruction of orange groves due to the weather and the Seminole wars, plus other problems which faced the city of St. Augustine, caused many to write to the bishop in Havana to rescue them, not knowing that the Havana Diocese was also in ruins.[3]

Finally East Florida was transferred from Mobile to the new Diocese of Savannah in 1850-1870. Following the Civil War, the Church of St. Augustine began to enjoy some prosperity and the Holy See erected a diocese in St.

---

[1]J.P. Hurley, *New Catholic Encyclopedia,* Vol XII, p. 862.

[2]Gannon, *op. cot.,* pp. xiii-xiv.

[3]*Ibid.,* p. 150. There is an excellent but pitiful letter written in Gannon's book that made clear the situation that faced the Church and its people: "Since this poverty-stricken town was ceded to the United States, we have experienced nothing but ill fortune and disgraces. The severe freeze of the winter has just destroyed entirely our abundant orange groves...we find ourselves under arms day and night protecting our lives and homes against Indian savages..."

Augustine in 1870, the first and only diocese in Florida in the nineteenth century. This included all of East Florida. West Florida still remained within the Mobile Diocese.

All additional dioceses in Florida were established in the twentieth century. In 1958 the first diocese to be formed from the St. Augustine Diocese was that of Miami on the southern East Coast. Up to 1962 East Florida, now including the St. Augustine and Miami dioceses, was part of the Province of Baltimore. With the creation of the Province of Atlanta in 1962, this eastern part of Florida was included in the Province of Atlanta and remained there until 1968.

In 1968, because of the immigration of many Cubans after the Castro Revolution, and the arrival of older citizens desirous of the milder climate and a more affordable cost of living, the vast increase in Catholic population required a large church expansion. At the request of the bishops, Miami became a metropolitan see on June 13, 1968. Within the next week, two more dioceses were created: the Diocese of St. Petersburg comprising the west central coast, and the Diocese of Orlando comprising the east central section of Florida.

In 1975 the Diocese of St. Augustine relinquished her westernmost counties to form the Diocese of Pensacola-Tallahassee. The latest division occurred in October of 1984, with the creation of two additional dioceses: the Diocese of Palm Beach on the lower east coast and the Diocese of Venice in southwest Florida.

Thus the Province of Miami, which began as the site of the first Catholic city after enduring for centuries cruel persecution and virtual destruction, had witnessed a miracle of grace in the extraordinary population growth of the Church in Florida with a large number of parishes and dioceses to serve the people. Today the Province of Miami has one archdiocese and six suffragan sees with a total Catholic population of 1,494,360 or 13% of the total population of the state.

ARCHDIOCESE FOR THE MILITARY SERVICES

There has been an unbroken tradition in the United States of appointing military chaplains to serve the armed forces. From 1775 to the present, Catholic priests have been among those who have given spiritual help in time of war and, since the twentieth century, have served in peace as well as war. After World War II, 1,026 priests were serving in either the Army or the Navy.

Because of the large number of priests working as chaplains throughout the world, the Holy See appointed a bishop for the military in each country. On November 24, 1917 Benedict XV appointed Bishop Patrick Hayes, Auxiliary of New York, as "Ordinary of all Catholics who fight in the army and the navy during the present war." The military diocese was divided into five vicariates, and was known as the military vicariate and its offices as the military ordinariate. In World II 2,453 priests, or 9% of the nation's clergy, served as noncommissioned chaplains and 2,000 as civilian army chaplains.

In 1946 the Holy See extended the vicariate's jurisdiction to civilians serving in the United States government overseas, the Veterans Administration and, in 1947, to the newly established Air Force. In 1950 the Catholic chaplains of all countries in the Korean War were placed under the American military vicar.

The need for a military chaplaincy on a permanent basis resulted in the creation of a military vicariate and the ordinariate in 1957 under the archbishop of New York, operating as a separate office with its own staff and tribunal. In 1983 it was determined that the vicariate have its own status to function as any other diocese. The Archbishop of New York was named the ordinary of this separate archdiocese. Today this archdiocese is called the "Archdiocese for the Military Services, USA," and is located in the nation's capital.[1]

The archdiocese for the Military Services has been "especially established to serve the unique religious needs of the American military personnel and their families at home and abroad." Ordained priests serve in over 700 facilities, bases and shops.[2] The military ordinariates have "a distinct form of ecclesiastical jurisdiction with their own constitution and statutes and place in Canon Law."[3] In the United States there are 2,290,349 members of the Archdiocese for the Military Services.

PROVINCE OF MILWAUKEE

Spanish missionaries for the conversion of the Indians entered the South and Southwest of the New World at the same time French missionaries and explorers came to the North and Northwest. This was the pattern for the territory of Wisconsin where many familiar names come to mind: Fathers Rene Menard, Claude Allouez and particularly, Jacques Marquette were among the many French Jesuits who served the people of this region.[4] Despite the remarkable missionary work accomplished from 1661, this area was abandoned in 1728 and "with an exception of a missionary or two, no priest entered Wisconsin for about a century."[5] Wars, liquor and the suppression of the Jesuits all contributed to its failure. From 1840 to 1870 another difficult time occurred because of the nativist attacks and violent threats to the Church. Truly a miracle of grace transformed the suffering of the members of the Church into the blessing of growth in members and fervor that followed.

The Diocese of Quebec was established on October 1, 1674 by Pope Clement X and had a jurisdictional tie to Wisconsin for the next century. When France ceded the territory east of the Mississippi to England in 1763, the same ecclesiastical jurisdiction continued. This ended in 1784 when John Carroll, "The Superior of the Faithful," exercised jurisdiction over all the territory east of the Mississippi.

When Bardstown, Kentucky, one of the four suffragan sees of the Archdiocese of Baltimore, became a diocese in 1808, Wisconsin (a part of Michigan in the Northwest Territory) was included. Wisconsin was also included when the

---

[1]*A Brief History of the Catholic Chaplaincy and the Archdiocese for the Military Services, U.S.A.*
[2]Flyer for the Archdiocese for the Military Services, U.S.A.
[3]Correspondence with Rev. Richard Saudia, Chancellor, Archdiocese for the Military Services, January 26, 1988.
[4]Rev. Leo Rummel, *History of the Catholic Church in Wisconsin* (Knights of Columbus, 1976), p. 30.
[5]P.L. Johnson, "Archdiocese of Milwaukee," *New Catholic Encyclopedia,* Vol. IX, pp. 862-863.

Cincinnati Diocese was carved from Bardstown in 1821 and the Detroit Diocese from Cincinnati in 1833. Evidently the bishop of Detroit gave little spiritual attention to the Wisconsin area so the bishop of Dubuque, Iowa, exercised administrative functions over this part for several years. Because of its growing importance Milwaukee was recommended as a site for a new diocese by the bishops of the Fifth Provincial Council in 1843. This was accomplished on November 23, 1843, five years before Wisconsin was admitted to the Union.[1] The new diocese included all of Wisconsin, parts of Minnesota and all of upper Michigan.

The great influx of the Catholic population into Wisconsin kept pace with the growth of the total population. In 1842 there were 7,000 white Catholics; by 1844 there were 19,000. Two-thirds of these were Irish and one-third was German. From the first year of Bishop Henni's term (1843), great attention was given to the "cultural linguistic needs" of the German people, evident in the phenomenal growth of the German population. In 1850 15,000 were Catholics; in 1860 the total reached 180,000 and two-thirds of these were of German origin.

There was great need for priests to serve this large number of Catholics. The number of priests grew from 17 in 1844 to 64 in 1853; by 1860 there were 160 priests, but this was still not sufficient. What occurred in this diocese occurred in so many others: priests were solicited from Europe and the response was encouraging. Bishop Henni's German determination took him to Switzerland, Bavaria, Ireland and The Netherlands and in each place he found recruits for Wisconsin. He opened a seminary in 1856 and received financial help from the three Catholic societies in Europe who were assisting so many dioceses in America. Between 1856 and 1858, 83 churches were established in Wisconsin; by 1896 there were 396.[2]

The growth of population was also due to the incentives that Wisconsin offered the immigrant. The liberal land policy and easy transportation by rail, stagecoach and steamboat as well as the agricultural and lumbering industries attracted vast numbers to this western state.

Because of the rapid growth in population the bishops of the Second Plenary Council in October 1866 requested that two new dioceses be formed.[3] On March 3, 1868 the Diocese of Green Bay was carved from the northeast part of Milwaukee and La Crosse from the northwest part. The large number of Catholics in Wisconsin urged the bishops in the Second Plenary Council in 1866 to recommend that Milwaukee be elevated to an archbishopric. This was not done, however, until February 12, 1875, predating the Archdiocese of Chicago by five years. The Province of Milwaukee included the states of Wisconsin, Minnesota, North and South Dakota and the Upper Peninsula of Michigan.

More territorial changes occurred on May 3, 1905 when the Diocese of Superior was created from the northwest part of Wisconsin and on February 22, 1945 when the last diocese, Madison, was erected on February 22, 1945 from the western part of Milwaukee. With the creation of the Province of St. Paul (later called St. Paul and Minneapolis) in 1888 and the Province of Detroit in 1917 the

[1]Gerald Edward Fisher, *Dusk is my Dawn* (privately printed), pp. 9-10.
[2]Rummel, *op. cit.,* p. 127; Fisher, *op. cit.,* p. 17.
[3]Guilday, *A History of the Councils,* p. 222.

extent of the Province of Milwaukee was reduced and became coterminous with the state of Wisconsin.

Today the Province of Milwaukee has four suffragan sees with a total Catholic population of 1,531,706 or 31% of the population of the state.

PROVINCE OF MOBILE

This Province of Mobile includes the states of Alabama and Mississippi. As early as 1519, Spanish explorers and missionaries came to Mobile Bay, then moved to East Florida at St. Augustine in 1565 and Pensacola in 1696. The French arrived in Mobile in 1702. In 1763 the English obtained this land by conquest; in 1783 the Spanish took possession of Florida and finally the Americans acquired it through the Treaty of Peace in 1783.[1] Pinckney's Treaty of 1795 fixed the disputed southern boundary of Mississippi and Alabama and proclaimed the land a United States possession.

This shift in jurisdiction was duplicated politically in the shift in ecclesiastical jurisdiction. Louisiana (which included Mobile) belonged to France before 1763, hence the ecclesiastical jurisdiction came from the bishop of Quebec.[2] Florida (which included the Gulf Coast) was under the jurisdiction of Santiago de Cuba. In 1763, when Spain acquired Louisiana, jurisdiction came from Santiago de Cuba but the bishop of Quebec continued to exercise authority over the area. In 1763 Florida was ceded to England; the promise that the inhabitants could continue their Catholic religion was not trusted and most fled to Cuba and Mexico, leaving eight laymen in all of Florida.[3] In 1783 Florida was returned to Spain with Spanish ecclesiastical jurisdiction. By 1819, when the United States purchased Florida, it was an area destitute of spiritual growth.

Mississippi and Alabama were in the area called "Georgia's western lands" which Georgia finally ceded to the United States. In 1789 the Mississippi Territory was created from western Georgia and admitted as a state in 1817. The eastern part of the Mississippi Territory, between Mississippi and Georgia, was more populous and richer than the western. It was, therefore, believed that the Territory had to be divided or the eastern part would "overwhelm the backwoods."[4] This was accomplished and from this new part Alabama became a territory in 1817 and a state in 1819.

The archbishop of Baltimore had jurisdiction over all territory within the United States but the impossibility of one person's caring for the spiritual welfare of the Catholics was soon evident. Finally, an administrator apostolic was appointed for Louisiana and the Floridas which included the future states of Mississippi and Alabama. Again there was confusion because the bishop of Havana, no longer holding jurisdiction in the United States, resumed charge of Florida. To solve this problem the Holy See established a vicariate apostolic for Alabama and Mississippi in 1822 but it had to be revoked because of the impracticality of the decision. Finally, in August of 1825, Mississippi was created a vicariate

[1]Oscar Lipscomb, "History of the Diocese of Mobile," *The Catholic Week*, November 14, 1980, p. 13.
[2]De Courcey and Shea, *op. cit.*, p. 623.
[3]Gannon, *op. cit.*, pp. 83-84.
[4]John Ray Skates, *Mississippi* (W.W. Norton, 1979), p. 75-76.

apostolic under "the Bishop of Louisiana and the states of Alabama and Florida were erected into a like jurisdiction with a titular Bishop as Vicar Apostolic."[1]

On May 15, 1829 Mobile was made a diocese with the extent of its territory including Alabama and the Territory of Florida. On July 28, 1837 Natchez was chosen by Pope Gregory XVI as a diocese at a time when there was "neither Church nor a priest in permanent residency," although there was a group of organized Catholics. Natchez was an economical center of the state with the largest population in Mississippi and easily accessible by steamboat. It was renamed Natchez-Jackson in 1957 and on March 8, 1977 it became the Diocese of Jackson. At the same time a new diocese, Biloxi, was formed in the southern part of Mississippi, the area with the largest number of Catholics.[2]

On July 20, 1980 Pope John Paul II raised Mobile to a metropolitan see with three suffragan sees: Jackson, Birmingham and Biloxi.

The Province of Mobile has an archdiocese and three suffragan sees with a total Catholic population of 126,774 or 4% of the total population of the state of Alabama, and 99,197 or 4% of the total population of the state of Mississippi.

PROVINCE OF NEWARK

When New York and Philadelphia were established as dioceses in 1808, the ecclesiastical jurisdiction of the area of New Jersey was divided between both dioceses: New York included the eastern part of New Jersey, and Philadelphia the western.

By the year 1800 the number of Catholics in New Jersey reached almost 1,000. Fifty years later because of immigration the number had reached 825,000, predominantly Irish and German with the ratio of three Irish to one German.[3] Employment was easily available because of the growth of industry that accompanied the building of the railroads and canals. Since the Catholic population was so large, Pope Pius IX created the Diocese of Newark on July 29, 1853 at the request of the bishops of the First Plenary Council of Baltimore. Newark was now coterminous with the state of New Jersey and a suffragan of the Province of New York. This remained the only diocese in the state until 1881.

The depression of 1870 affected all workers: on the railroads, on the farms and in the factories. Poverty was so widespread that often the churches were robbed of their sacred vessels.[4] Despite the financial distress, the growth of the Diocese of Newark from 1873 to 1880 was remarkable.

In the last part of the nineteenth century, tension arose among the Irish who adopted American ways and the Germans who wished to keep their customs and language. From 1870-1900, a new wave of immigration added to the conflict. These immigrants, many of whom were Roman Catholic, were mostly from the southern and eastern European countries, groups that were different from the ear-

[1]Lipscomb, *op. cit.*, p. 13.
[2]Special Edition of *Mississippi Today* (newspaper) Sesquicentennial Edition on "The Church in Mississippi, 1827-1987," p. 6.
[3]New Jersey Historical Records Commission, *The Bishops of Newark, 1853-1978*, p. 4.
[4]*Ibid.*, p. 28.

lier settlers. They were willing to work in industries that Newark offered and they were close to the port of New York. The most numerous were the Italians who were unskilled and who became victims of social rejection by the residents.[1] The Poles, Slavs and Lithuanians presented a problem because they wished to retain their language and have their own churches. This difficulty was emerging in other areas of the country as well. In 1881, in addition to the English-speaking parishes, there were seven German-speaking parishes; by 1900 there were 35 foreign language parishes.[2] In 1978 the diocese faced the problem as to what to do with these churches since the need was no longer present. It was solved in one of two ways: either they were closed or they merged with another parish church. It must be remembered, however, that these parishes did maintain the unity of the Church at the time they were erected.

This influx of population caused Pope Leo XIII in 1881 to separate the fourteen southern counties of the state and create the Diocese of Trenton. The northern counties remained with the Diocese of Newark. On December 8, 1937 Pope Pius XI separated New Jersey from the Ecclesiastical Province of New York and then raised the Newark Diocese to a metropolitan see. On the following day, December 9, the Diocese of Paterson was carved from the Newark Diocese and the Diocese of Camden was separated from the Diocese of Trenton. The last diocese was formed in 1981 when the Diocese of Metuchen was separated from the Trenton Diocese.[3]

In 1963 Pope Paul VI divided the Byzantine Diocese of Pittsburgh and established a diocese for Catholics of the Ruthenian Byzantine Rite located in Passaic. This diocese is distinct from the above Latin Rite dioceses.

Currently the Province of Newark consists of an archdiocese and four suffragan sees with a total Catholic population of 3,072,758 or 40% of the total population of the state of New Jersey.

PROVINCE OF NEW ORLEANS

New Orleans, the second oldest diocese in the United States, has its roots in Christianity as far back as 1632, when La Salle took this land in the name of the King of France. The restriction imposed upon the Church through French (1731-1762) and Spanish (1762-1801) domination impeded the growth of Christianity in the United States. The unfortunate result of this tight, secular control over spiritual affairs far outweighed the efforts of the missionary priests and religious, men and women, to bring Christianity to the people.[4]

When the Diocese of Louisiana and the two Floridas (East and West) were established on March 25, 1793 as the Diocese of New Orleans, "the vast territory of the original diocese, except for the area under the jurisdiction of the Diocese of Baltimore, stretched from the Rocky Mountains to the Atlantic and from Canada to the Gulf of Mexico."[5] This territory was under the jurisdiction of the bishop

[1] *Ibid.,* p. 59.
[2] *Ibid.,* p. 65.
[3] Correspondence with Rev. Raymond J. Kupke, Archivist of the Archdiocese of Newark, February 13, 1988.
[4] Msgr. Henry C. Bezou, *Clarion Herald,* September 10, 1987, p. 9.
[5] "Archdiocese of New Orleans," *New Catholic Encyclopedia,* Vol. X, p. 383.

of Havana until 1801, but uncertainty about the government in New Orleans, now a French possession, and the inability to know who within the Church to appoint as a successor, left the diocese without a resident bishop for a number of years (1801-1815). The Cathedral Canons governed locally and the care of the diocese was given to Archbishop Carroll of Baltimore.[1]

In 1815 the Holy See asked the Archbishop of Baltimore to appoint an administrator to care for Upper and Lower Louisiana. A bishop was consecrated, but continuing difficulties in administering the churches led to the bishop's resignation in 1826. The year previous, the eastern section of the Diocese of New Orleans had been formed into the new apostolic vicariate of Alabama and the Floridas; in 1829 this became the Diocese of Mobile.

In 1826, when St. Louis became a diocese, its bishop continued to administer both the St. Louis Diocese and the New Orleans Diocese until the appointment of the third bishop of New Orleans in 1830, whose jurisdiction extended over the states of Louisiana and Mississippi. In 1837 Mississippi was separated from the Diocese of New Orleans when the Diocese of Natchez (later Jackson) was created.

On July 19, 1850 New Orleans was elevated to a metropolitan see as the second province in the United States, with four suffragan sees: Galveston (all of Texas), Little Rock (including Indian Territory), Natchez and Mobile (including the western section of Florida).[2] The Province retained these boundaries until 1926.

From 1926 the Diocese of New Orleans was gradually reduced in size. In 1926 the Texas Diocese and Oklahoma City (changed to Oklahoma City-Tulsa in 1930) became part of the Diocese of San Antonio. In 1973 the Diocese of Little Rock was transferred to the newly created Province of Oklahoma City. In 1980 the Diocese of Mobile and Jackson became part of the new Province of Mobile, leaving the Province of New Orleans coterminous with the state of Louisiana.

The Province of New Orleans consists of six dioceses: In 1853 the oldest permanent settlement in the Louisiana Purchase, Natchitoches, was made a diocese; in 1910 this see city was transferred to Alexandria; in 1977 its title was changed to Alexandria-Shreveport and on June 24, 1986 it was divided into two dioceses: Alexandria, and Shreveport in the northwestern corner.

In 1918 the Diocese of Lafayette was created; in 1961, Baton Rouge; in 1977, Houma-Thibodaux; in 1980, the Diocese of Lake Charles; and in 1986, Shreveport.

The question as to whether this diocese was called Louisiana or New Orleans before it was made an archdiocese in not too easy to answer. Certainly the diocese in 1793 was termed Louisiana and Floridas. It was the same term used in letters of the Church in 1801-1803. In 1815 when William Du Bourg was appointed bishop his appointment was described as New Orleans *or* Louisiana and in another place just as New Orleans. In 1825 the Holy See erected the Vicariate of Alabama and the Floridas which ended the discussion of Louisiana and the Floridas, but it was not certain that the title of the diocese in Louisiana was ac-

[1]Bezou, *Clarion Herald,* p. 10.
[2]Correspondence with Rev. Msgr. Earl C. Woods, Chancellor of the Archdiocese of New Orleans, February 8, 1988.

tually New Orleans or Louisiana. It was settled when St. Louis and New Orleans were made the new dioceses.[1]

Today the Province of New Orleans has an archdiocese and six suffragan sees with a Catholic population of 1,404,411 or 32% of the total population of the state of Louisiana.

PROVINCE OF NEW YORK

It is very difficult to picture the state of New York without Catholic priests yet this was the situation in 1784. Catholics were forbidden to enter the state because the New York statute of 1700 condemned priests to death or imprisonment if found, and the penal laws of England excluded Catholics from the rights of citizenship. In the eighteenth century there was scarcely a trace of Catholicity among the whites or Indians,[2] but after the Treaty of Paris in 1783, by which the state legislature guaranteed religious freedom, there were 1,000 Catholics in New York. There was, regrettably, not a single priest in the state at the time.[3]

It is important to remember that in places where there were no priests, "many communities of lay people took the initiative in forming Catholic organizations...that marked the formation of American parishes" so that when priests came to the cities in 1835 there were already "houses of prayer" established. This period of history in the Church was followed by one of strong pastors who brought to the Church a vision that enabled the educational and spiritual growth necessary for the survival of the dioceses.[4]

The phenomenal growth of the Church was due to the rapid rise in immigration. Between 1820 and 1860, because of the Irish famine and the German revolutions, Irish and German immigration increased. Approximately 100,000 Germans entered the port of New York between 1840 and 1860 and 40% were Catholics. The Irish that came to New York numbered 221,213 in 1851. Fortunately these immigrants came when employment on the canals, roads and railroads was readily available. From 1890 to 1910 there was a noticeable change in the nationalities of the immigrant. Now the southern and eastern European peoples came in greater numbers and most of them were Catholics.[5]

Blessings and hardships marked the immigrants' paths to the United States. They increased the Catholic population and contributed a rich cultural heritage that led to spiritual progress. But problems arose with these new immigrants. The Germans demanded national parishes with German priests to preserve their language and culture. They wished to be German and Catholic without compromising either and wished their churches to be built on ethnic as well as on

[1]Correspondence with Very Rev. J. Edgar Bruns, Archdiocesan Historian, Archdiocese of New Orleans, December 18, 1988.
[2]J.A. Reynolds, "Archdiocese of New York," *The New Catholic Encyclopedia,* Vol. X, p. 399.
[3]Sister Mary Christine Taylor, *A History of Catholicism in the North Country* (Farnsworth Sons, Inc., 1972), p. 7. There were but 24 priests in the entire United States in 1789, and they were all in Maryland and Pennsylvania.
[4]Rev. Msgr. Florence D. Cohalan (United States Catholic Historical Society, 1983), p. 61.
[5]David O'Brien, *Faith and Friendship, Catholicism in the Diocese of Syracuse, 1886-1986* (Catholic Diocese of Syracuse, 1987), pp. 39, 53.

doctrinal beliefs. Another difficulty was trusteeism, the control of property and elections of prelates by lay groups. In many cases good resulted from this system but it also caused much tension, anxiety and disaster for ecclesiastical authority.

The vast territory within the Diocese of New York necessitated a division of jurisdiction. At the Sixth Provincial Council of Baltimore (1846) the bishops requested that two more dioceses be given to New York. On April 23, 1849 Albany and Buffalo were created from the north and west of New York City. In May 1849 the bishops of the Seventh Provincial Council of Baltimore requested that New York be made a metropolitan see. This was granted on July 19, 1850. The Province of New York then included the state of New York and the Boston Diocese which included New England (removed from New York when Boston became an archdiocese in 1875).

Other dioceses were created. On July 29, 1853 Brooklyn, including the whole of Long Island, was separated from New York. On March 3, 1868 Rochester was carved out of Buffalo; on February 16, 1872 Ogdensburg was created and on November 26, 1886 Syracuse was severed from the northern and western part of Albany. Lastly, on April 6, 1957 the Diocese of Brooklyn was divided so that Long Island became the Diocese of Rockville Center and the Diocese of Brooklyn comprised the two boroughs of Brooklyn and Queens, also known as Kings and Queens counties.

The Province of New York is coterminous with the boundaries of the state of New York with one exception. For practical purposes, Fisher's Island, which belongs to Suffolk County, Long Island, has been included under the jurisdiction of the Norwich (Connecticut) Diocese. From 1885 to 1932 the Bahama Islands were under the jurisdiction of the New York Archdiocese, but on September 5, 1960 they became the Diocese of Nassau and a suffragan of the Province of Kingston, Jamaica.[1]

Today the Province of New York has an archdiocese and seven suffragan sees with a total Catholic population of 6,771,854 or 38% of the total population of the state of New York.

[1]Correspondence with Rev. Robert F. McNamara, Former Archivist, Diocese of Rochester, February 3, 1988.

PROVINCE OF OKLAHOMA CITY

Although Oklahoma, "the land of the red people," was only established as an archdiocese in 1973, the territory itself was inhabited by Plains Indians over 400 years ago and was visited by Catholic missionaries as early as 1540. In the sixteenth and seventeenth centuries, religious and secular Spanish priests accompanied the Spanish explorers and fur traders, and in the eighteenth century, French explorers arrived with missionaries to convert the Indians. By the nineteenth century Catholic missionary endeavor was on a permanent basis in Oklahoma.

When the Louisiana Territory was purchased in 1803, the explorers stated that the land was suitable only for Indians and not for white settlers.[1] Removal of the Indians to an area designated as unorganized territory began in 1817, was continued by the Indian Removal Act of 1830, and was accomplished by the creation of the Indian Territory in 1833, the present site of Oklahoma. The "Trail of Tears," the usurping of their land by the railroads, and land runs of 1889-1899 resulted in the white settlers becoming the final owners of the land.

In 1889 Congress created the Territory of Oklahoma out of the Indian lands and the Panhandle, called "No Man's Land." These twin territories, Oklahoma on the west and the Indian Territory on the east, were finally admitted as the state of Oklahoma in 1905.

Ecclesiastically, this area called "Unorganized Land" was under the jurisdiction of Baltimore until 1803, and then under the Diocese of St. Louis in 1826, perhaps until 1893. Missionaries visited this territory from Kansas and Arkansas since there were no priests. The papal bull establishing the Diocese of Little Rock in 1843 does not indicate that its jurisdiction extended into the Indian Territory. In fact, it explicitly mentioned that its jurisdiction is coterminous with the state of Arkansas. There is documentation that the Bishop of Little Rock authorized a Benedictine to visit the Indian Territory for the spiritual welfare of the Indians.[2]

On July 9, 1876 Pope Pius IX established a prefect apostolic for the Indian Territory. Maps of the United States for 1880 and 1888 show that the Indian Territory was in the Province of St. Louis, but a map of 1893 indicates the newly erected vicariate apostolic of Oklahoma City in 1881 as part of the New Orleans Province.[3] A recent study proves that Oklahoma continued to be part of this Province until 1927.[4]

A significant event for the Catholic Church occurred with the "last run of 1899." One million people poured into the Indian Territory in one day, April

[1]Howard R. Kalmar, *The American West* (Thomas Crowell, 1934), p. 866.
[2]Papal Bull of Pope Gregory XVI, November 28, 1843. Correspondence with Sister Catherine Markey, M.H.S., Archivist for the Diocese of Little Rock, March 7, 1988.
[3]Thomas Nolan, *Historical Geography of the Catholic Church in the United States, 1789-1931*. Stated in correspondence with Rev. James D. White, Historian, Diocese of Tulsa, to Rev. Paul Thomas, Archivist, Archdiocese of Baltimore, August 24, 1988.
[4]James P. Gaffey, *Francis Clement Kelley and the American Catholic Dream* (The Heritage Foundation, Inc., Bensenville, Illinois), Vol. II, p. 276.

22nd, and this hastened the Holy See to raise the Twin Territories in 1891 to the status of a vicariate apostolic with the right of a resident bishop.[1]

Two years before the admission of Oklahoma as a state, the Twin Territories became the Diocese of Oklahoma (1905). Oklahoma City became the state capital in 1923. Because of the provincialism of Tulsa and the need to strengthen the ties of the bishop to eastern Oklahoma, the official title was changed to the Diocese of Oklahoma City and Tulsa on November 14, 1930. It was officially proclaimed in February 1931.[2]

On August 3, 1926 the Holy See established the Metropolitan See of San Antonio with five suffragan sees, one of which was Oklahoma. It remained in this province until February 6, 1973, when the Archdiocese of Oklahoma City was established with suffragan sees of Tulsa and Little Rock, Arkansas.[3]

The dioceses in Oklahoma have played a significant role for the Church in the work of Catholic priests in the military encampments. Beginning as early as 1819, 1834, 1869 and as recently as 1975, Benedictine priests assumed responsibility for the management of the camps. Between 1941 and 1945, because of a favorable climate, numerous training camps and air fields were created here. But it was the concern of Pope Pius XII and the archdiocese for German prisoners of war that diocesan influence was most remarkable. Thirty priests were included among these prisoners, and many German-speaking priests of the dioceses ministered to their spiritual and temporal needs. The camps closed in 1945.[4]

Today the Province of Oklahoma City has two suffragan sees with a Catholic population of 143,226 Catholics or 5% of the total population of Oklahoma and 69,416 Catholics or 3% of the total population of Arkansas.

PROVINCE OF PHILADELPHIA

The story of the English colonies in the East is vastly different from that of the French and Spanish west of the Mississippi. The French and Spanish settlements were mainly Catholic undertakings; the English were motivated by the desire for lands and material wealth, superiority of the seas and the determination to crush Catholicism.[5] The Spanish and French came in the late sixteenth century; the English in the seventeenth. Also, in the English colonies there was "an absence of any regulated form of ecclesiastical government either in America or in England." The vicar apostolic of the London District for the American Catholics was appointed to administer but he had "remote and vague jurisdiction."[6] The Spanish were well-organized. In 1784 the London juris-diction passed to Bishop Vicar Apostolic John Carroll who would have the sole responsibility over all of America.

---

[1]Privately printed article, Diocese of Oklahoma.
[2]Gaffey, *op. cit.,* pp. 188-189.
[3]Correspondence with Dr. Patrick Foley, Editor, *Journal of Texas Catholic History and Culture,* September 3, 1988.
[4]James D. White, *The Souls of the Just* (The Sarto Press, 1983), pp. 523-529.
[5]John Tracy Ellis, *op. cit.,* p. 316.
[6]*Ibid.*

Although their number was small, Catholic immigrants were greatly feared by the majority. The heightened sense of national identity to maintain their own language and culture resulted in the establishment of numerous national parishes. The small number of Catholic immigrants settled mainly in Maryland, Pennsylvania or New York, experiencing a dismal period for almost a century and a half.

Philadelphia, the largest city in the colonies and the home of the first government, was one of the four suffragan sees in the Province of Baltimore in 1808. The diocese comprised the states of Delaware and Pennsylvania and the western part of New Jersey. It enjoyed a great deal of freedom and toleration due to William Penn and his "Frame of Government." While the laws of the government of Pennsylvania (1705) stated that no Catholic could hold office, William Penn did almost nothing to enforce it. It was only in Pennsylvania that religious freedom was safeguarded.

While Philadelphia seems to promise great spiritual leadership for the Church, "in the course of time it suffered more than the Church in other parts of the country from enemies within and to a terrible extent from enemies without."[1] This disturbed condition continued for over a half century because of the abuses of the trustee system, unruly priests and distrust of the French, Irish and English clergy. To make matters worse, Philadelphia had no bishop for six years.

Irish famine, the wars in Europe, and English oppression resulted in a tremendous rise in immigration to the United States between 1820 and 1860. Over two million entered the country, the Irish heading the national lists, followed by the Germans, the French and the English. Philadelphia was exceptionally attractive to immigrants because of work in the building of canals and roads or in factories or farms, and the many opportunities in the iron mines. The immigrants offered their "productive years" to this country and in return it was possible to succeed.[2]

On August 11, 1843 Pope Gregory XVI created the Diocese of Pittsburgh transferring the western half of the state of Pennsylvania into the new diocese. Over the years new dioceses were erected. In 1853 the Diocese of Erie was created out of the northwestern part of Pittsburgh, and Newark was removed from the Philadelphia Diocese to become a diocese of the Province of New York. Two years later (March 3, 1866) Delaware became the new Diocese of Wilmington in the Province of Baltimore. On March 3, 1868 Harrisburg and Scranton were created from the western and northern Philadelphia Diocese. On March 15, 1875 Pope Pius IX elevated Philadelphia to the rank of an archdiocese. On May 27, 1901 Altoona became a diocese and was redesignated as Altoona-Johnstown on October 9, 1957 because of size and growth of population. The Diocese of Greensburg was formed from the western and southern counties of Pittsburgh (1951) and Allentown from the northwestern part of Philadelphia (1961).

---

[1]Guilday, *The Life and Times of John Carroll,* p. 644.
[2]James F. Connolly, Ed., *History of the Archdiocese of Philadelphia* (The Archdiocese of Philadelphia, 1976), pp. 127-128. The population rose considerably during the next 30 years: in 1820-1830 it was 143,000; 1831-1840, 492,000; 1841-1851, 1,551,000.

Today the Province of Philadelphia consists of an archdiocese and seven suffragan sees with a total Catholic population of 3,579,707 or 30% of the total population of the state.

OREGON AND WASHINGTON

BACKGROUND

When we speak of the Catholic Church in the Pacific Northwest, we are referring today to an area of half a million square miles bordering the Pacific Ocean and including four states (Oregon, Washington, Montana and Idaho) and two metropolitan sees of Portland in Oregon (with four dioceses) and Seattle (with two dioceses). This area has been called "the most unchurched area in the United States" because of its small number of Catholics.[1]

Until the beginning of the nineteenth century, all attempts at missionary work in this northwest area were short-lived. Explorers and fur traders, especially the Canadian Hudson Bay Company and the Pacific Fur Company of the American, John Jacob Astor, contended for the Oregon Territory and strengthened their claim in the name of England and the United States. Since no government existed here, and Spain had withdrawn in 1818 from land north of California, England and the United States had a joint agreement to the Oregon Country, "all territory between the Rockies and the Pacific from California to Alaska." But with two governments, there was no government at all.[2] In 1846 a settlement was made in which the United States acquired the land that became the state of Oregon (1859), and the states of Washington (1889), Montana (1889) and Idaho (1890).

These early fur traders and explorers were accompanied by Canadian Catholics and Catholic Iroquois Indians, who pleaded for missionaries to care for them. Repeated requests finally brought the first missionaries in 1838, 63 years after the Declaration of Independence. Until then, there was no priest or church in the entire northwest. The ecclesiastical jurisdiction was actually exercised by the Bishop of Quebec, for as late as 1822 the Bishop of Manitoba had jurisdiction over Northwest America.[3]

When the United States acquired Louisiana in 1803, part of the Oregon Territory was considered within its western limits. From 1818, both the bishops of upper and lower Louisiana claimed jurisdiction, and St. Louis from 1826, "despite the fact that in 1834 Pope Gregory XVI, in defining diocesan limits in the United States, assigned Oregon to no diocese."[4] Thus confusion persisted.

[1]Wilfred P. Schoenberg, *A History of the Catholic Church in the Pacific Northwest, 1743-1983* (The Pastoral Press, 1987), p. 1.
[2]*Ibid.*, pp. 13-14.
[3]*Ibid.*, p. 17.
[4]Cornelia M. Flaherty, *Go with Haste into the Mountains* (Catholic Diocese of Helena, 1984), p. 29.

PROVINCE OF PORTLAND IN OREGON

It was deemed necessary that a resident bishop be appointed for this distant land, since much time was required to get a message to Canada and travel in this land was extremely difficult. The Fifth Provincial Council of Baltimore in 1843 recommended that the Holy See erect a vicariate apostolic west of the Rocky Mountains,[1] and at the end of the same year, the Oregon Vicariate was established.

When the bishop elect arrived in Rome for his orders, he presented a *Memoriale* in glowing terms in which he proposed—not a plan for the establishment of a vicariate apostolic—but a plan for the establishment of an archdiocese with seven suffragan sees. Pope Gregory XVI, instead of confirming the vicariate, actually created an archdiocese of Oregon City in a brief dated July 24, 1846, and the two dioceses of Walla Walla and Vancouver Islands. Additionally, there were to be five districts that were to become districts in the future "at a time when there were no city, no state, no roads, no postal service and but 16 priests and 6,000 Catholics!"[2]   The erection of the second province in the country was one of the most amazing decisions in the history of the American Catholic Church. What was even more amazing was the size of the province which included all of Alaska (a metropolitan see in Anchorage in 1966), British Columbia (which became part of Canada), Montana, Idaho, Washington (a metropolitan see in Seattle in 1951), Oregon and a part of Wyoming (Cheyenne was made a suffragan see of the metropolitan see of Denver in 1941).

The Diocese of Walla Walla was short-lived. On May 31, 1850 Pope Pius IX transferred it to Oregon City because of political reasons and Indian unrest, and established the Diocese of Nesqually.

Although funds were sent from Europe and parts of the United States, the Church in this area suffered miserably from 1850-1856.[3] The discovery of gold in California brought about a mass exodus from Oregon to California. Incessant wars and government interference ruined many missions.[4] The episcopal residence was moved to Portland in 1862, although it kept the name of Oregon City. At this time, Oregon was still the only state in the Pacific Northwest and remained such for the next 30 years.

The size of the Archdiocese was reduced considerably during the next several decades. Idaho was greatly affected by the gold rush era which brought such an increase of population that the Holy See established the Vicariate of Idaho on March 3, 1868, a territory including western Montana, Idaho and Wyoming. Twenty-four years later, on August 25, 1893, Boise became a diocese coterminous with the state of Idaho. It has remained the only diocese in Idaho.

Montana has suffered from a dual jurisdiction with a strange political situation following the Louisiana Purchase in 1803. Western Montana (west of the

[1]Guilday, *History of the Councils of Baltimore,* p. 136.
[2]Schoenberg, *op. cit.,* p. 95.
[3]*Ibid.,* p. 137.
[4]F.M. Campbell, "Portland," *New Catholic Encyclopedia,* Vol. XI, p. 603.

Continental Divide) belonged to Oregon, jointly held by England and the United States, and the eastern part within the Louisiana Purchase was United States territory. When the Territory of Idaho was created in 1863 Montana was united politically but ecclesiastically it was not and would not be for twenty years. On March 3, 1883, after repeated requests from the bishops and people, Pope Leo XIII established a vicariate apostolic, terminating the dual jurisdiction. On March 9th it was made a part of the Province of Oregon City. On April 18, 1884 Helena was created a diocese "because it was the capital city, the center of the territory, the richest city and had the largest Catholic Church."[1]

On May 18, 1904 Pope Pius X created an eastern Montana diocese with Great Falls as its episcopal see. In June 1980, when Great Falls observed its seventy-fifth anniversary as a diocese, its name was changed to Great Falls-Billings as a concession to the people in Billings, who wished to be a separate diocese. Although a diocese for the city of Eugene was also considered, it never materialized.

The last diocese to be erected in the Province of Oregon City was Baker City, June 29, 1903, occupying two-thirds of the eastern part of Oregon. The title was changed to Baker on March 7, 1952. Lastly, the name Province of Oregon City was changed to Province of Portland-in-Oregon, September 26, 1928.

In the history of the American Church, Oregon is the one place where diocesan priests were present before the coming of missionaries, such as the Jesuits and the Oblates of Mary Immaculate. Beginning in 1838, this country endured many hardships and set-backs before it saw an age of expansion. This land, still young in terms of Catholic growth, has served the church in many educational and missionary activities.

Today the Province of Portland in Oregon covers three states, has an archdiocese and four suffragan sees with a total Catholic population of 483,226 in the three states, or 17% in Montana, 7% in Idaho and 10% in Oregon of the total population.

PROVINCE OF SEATTLE

Until 1850 the history of the Province of Seattle in the Pacific Northwest is linked with the history of the Province of Oregon City. Catholicism was brought to the present city of Vancouver on November 24, 1838 by two diocesan priests who were sent by the Bishop of Quebec to care for the spiritual needs of 26 Catholic fur traders and explorers. In 1846, when the Province of Oregon City was created, two other dioceses, Walla Walla and Vancouver Island, resulted in the transfer of the Diocese to Nesqually and the eventual suppression of the former diocese in 1853. Nesqually included the eastern sections of Washington and Oregon, the state of Idaho, western Montana and the northwestern corner of Wyoming.[2] The Cathedral remained at Vancouver until 1907.

In 1868, the creation of the Vicariate Apostolic of Idaho greatly reduced the area of the diocese and limited Nesqually to the present state of Washington. When the seat of government was transferred to Seattle in 1903 and this city be-

---

[1] Flaherty, *op. cit.,* pp. 29-33.
[2] J. McCorkle, "Seattle," *New Catholic Encyclopedia*, Vol. XIII, p. 15.

came the center for activities for a growing Catholic population, it was too difficult to administer the diocese from Vancouver. The Holy See, therefore, transferred the diocese to Seattle on September 11, 1907.

The rapidly growing Catholic population in eastern Washington necessitated the creation of the Diocese of Spokane, "the Catholic city," a populous, enterprising and prosperous area, on December 17, 1913.[1] With the phenomenal rise of new industrial, agricultural and military projects, especially electronics and airplane production during and after World War II, the Diocese of Seattle was further divided on June 23, 1951 when the Diocese of Yakima was erected. Simultaneously, the Diocese of Seattle was raised to a metropolitan see, including the states of Washington and Alaska.

The West Coast, especially the state of Washington, has experienced unprecedented growth. In over one decade (1940-1950), the population doubled in size. Fifteen years after the Province of Seattle was elevated to the see city, the ecclesiastical Province of Anchorage, Alaska was established (February 9, 1966), separating itself from the Province of Seattle.

The Province of Seattle became coterminous with that of the state of Washington with two suffragan sees and a total Catholic population of 434,606 or 10% of the total population of Washington.

PROVINCE OF ST. LOUIS

St. Louis, the "Catholic City"[2] is a unique diocese in the history of the Catholic Church: "Catholics began St. Louis,"[3] a city that is a composite of many nationalities, religions, industries and topography; it is a land of contrasts and contradictions, especially the contrast with the predominantly Protestant eastern seaboard states of the eighteenth century. Catholicism remains to this day the dominant religion of the state, one-sixth of which is Catholic.

St. Louis, named in 1764 for the patron of the reigning monarch, Louis XV, was the last foothold of France in the New World. It is to the credit of France that, unlike Spain, she dealt kindly with the Whites, the Blacks and the Indians.

The bishop of Quebec had jurisdiction over this area until 1763 when Spain, emerging as a world power, assumed authority. The bishops of Santiago de Cuba and Havana were its ecclesiastical leaders until 1803, when Spain gave this land to the French and France sold it to the United States, and ecclesiastical jurisdiction passed to the archbishop of Baltimore. It was not until 1808, when John Carroll was consecrated archbishop that the Holy See designated an administrator for the Louisiana Territory. There were only a dozen priests and 50,000 people there, but Archbishop Carroll was able to appoint a French-born Sulpician educator, William Louis Du Bourg, to administer upper and lower Louisiana. Word of his appointment came after Archbishop Carroll's death in 1815.

Because of troublesome conditions within the Church in New Orleans and difficulties within the St. Louis area, compounded by the vastness of the empire

[1]Schoenberg, *op. cit.,* p. 482
[2]John Gunther, *Inside U.S.A.* (New York, Harper & Brothers, 1947), p. 353.
[3]Faherty, *op. cit.,* "Introduction."

(885,000 square miles), Du Bourg requested that his see be separated from that of New Orleans and changed to St. Louis. The Diocese of St. Louis was created in 1826 after he resigned. The Diocese of New Orleans

> included the states of Louisiana and Mississippi; the Diocese of St. Louis included the states of Missouri, the western part of the state of Illinois, the territories of Arkansas and Iowa, and the remainder of the Louisiana Purchase to the Rocky Mountains. . . [1]

and north to Canada. In 1834, approximately half of the state of Illinois was added to the Diocese of St. Louis and remained until 1843, when Chicago became a diocese.

When St. Louis was made a diocese, the lands east of the Mississippi, except Florida and Michigan Territory (Michigan and Wisconsin) were states of the Union. West of the Mississippi there were but two states, Louisiana and Missouri, and the organized territory of Arkansas.[2] The land up to the Continental Divide was unorganized territory. This left the Diocese of St. Louis as the largest diocese in the nation, larger than all other nine dioceses combined. This diocese did not belong to the Province of Baltimore, but was directly under the Holy See.[3] The phenomenal rise in the population of St. Louis, from 6,000 in 1830 to 80,000 in 1850[4] increased the number of Catholics with a corresponding increase of diocesan priests to staff the many new parishes.

On July 20, 1847 St. Louis was elevated to a metropolitan see, the first province in mid-America. Many thought that this privilege should have gone to New York, created in 1808 or to New Orleans, a diocese in 1793. It is also possible that St. Louis was made an archdiocese because of the creation of the Archdiocese of Oregon City in 1846—a place that was far distant from the developing areas of Catholicism.[5] After the erection of the Archdiocese of St. Louis the Seventh Provincial Council of Baltimore (May 7, 1849) "formalized the organization of the Province of St. Louis by declaring the sees of Dubuque, Chicago, Milwaukee and Nashville as suffragans. The first three, Chicago, Dubuque and Milwaukee, formed a regional unity with the Diocese of Saint Louis"[6] in the states of Illinois, Missouri, Iowa, Wisconsin and the Indian territory to the north and west. Nashville made the province a "geographical monstrosity." On May 12 St. Paul was made a diocese under the jurisdiction of the St. Louis Province while the Indian Territory was made a vicariate apostolic in 1850.

On March 3, 1868 the first division of the archdiocese coterminous with the state of Missouri occurred when the Diocese of St. Joseph was erected. On September 10, 1880 it was transferred to the Diocese of Kansas City; on August 29, 1956 it was redesignated as the Diocese of Kansas City-St. Joseph. In 1956 two new dioceses were formed in the Province of St. Louis: on July 2nd the Diocese of Jefferson City in the north-central area, and on August 24th, the

[1]*Ibid.,* p. 31.
[2]*Ibid.,* p. 34.
[3]*Ibid.,* p. 37.
[4]*Ibid.,* p. 80.
[5]*Ibid.,* p. 74.
[6]*Ibid.,* p. 78. Guilday, *A History of the Councils of Baltimore,* pp. 157-158.

Diocese of Springfield-Cape Girardeau was formed from the entire southern part of the state.

Today the Province of St. Louis consists of an archdiocese and three suffragan sees, with a Catholic population of 788,048 or 16% of the total population of the state of Missouri.

PROVINCE OF ST. PAUL AND MINNEAPOLIS

The Province of St. Paul and Minneapolis comprises the states of Minnesota and North and South Dakota, in the territory once designated as the unoccupied lands of America. French explorers, fur traders and missionaries followed the rivers in this "land of ten thousand lakes," to trade with and to evangelize the Indians. Ecclesiastically, this area was governed by French bishops of Quebec from 1674 to 1762, and in 1763, when Spain acquired it, the jurisdiction passed to the Bishop of Santiago, and then to Havana in 1787. When the United States acquired the Louisiana territory in 1803, the archbishop of Baltimore continued to appoint French missionaries as administrators of New Orleans and Louisiana. When St. Louis became a diocese, Minnesota came under its jurisdiction.

Dubuque was made a diocese in 1837, with its jurisdiction including the unoccupied lands of Minnesota. Although a diocese was established in Milwaukee in 1843, both dioceses were too far removed from the Catholics in Minnesota. Consequently, when Minnesota was made a territory in 1849, the bishops of the Seventh Provincial Council in Baltimore correctly judged that this would mean an increase in Catholic population, and petitioned that St. Paul be named a diocese; it was formed in 1850 under the jurisdiction of the Province of St. Louis.[1]

The remarkable growth of the diocese was due to many factors: it was easily accessible to the Atlantic with low fare because of the new network of railroads; it became a leading center for lumber processing and flour milling, a market for wheat, dairy products and livestock, and a rich prairie land that brought immigrants from northern and southern Europe.[2]

The northern area of Minnesota had 15,000 Catholics and 2,200 Indians, but it was so distant from the 100,000 Catholics in the more densely populated areas of St. Paul that in 1875 the Holy See formed this northern region of Minnesota into a vicariate apostolic of Northern Minnesota. Four years later this jurisdiction was extended to Dakota.[3]

As the nineteenth century witnessed a rapid rise in population in mid-America, the bishops of the Province of Milwaukee (which then included Minnesota) required that the Diocese of St. Paul be raised to a province. The Metropolitan See of St. Paul, with the vicariates of Northern Minnesota and Dakota as suffragan churches, was established in 1888. The following year five new dioceses were created—three in Minnesota (St. Cloud, Duluth and Winona) and two in the Dakotas (Jamestown and Sioux Falls).

---

[1]Guilday, *A History of the Councils of Baltimore,* p. 158.
[2]Rev. Patrick H. Ahern, "Minnesota History," *Catholic Heritage* (Province of St. Paul), pp. 15-16.
[3]Rev. Martin R. O'Connell, "Archdiocese of St. Paul," *Catholic Heritage,* p. 28.

In the twentieth century four new dioceses were included in the Province of St. Paul: In the Dakotas: Lead, August 4, 1902 (later transferred to Rapid City, August 1, 1930); and Bismarck, December 31, 1909. In Minnesota: Crookston, December 31, 1909; and New Ulm, November 18, 1957.

In 1966 the name of the province was changed to the Archdiocese of St. Paul and Minneapolis, encompassing two large metropolitan areas known as the Twin Cities since they border each other, separated only by the Mississippi River. Originally, the impression was that the city of Minneapolis was not included in the Diocese of St. Paul and the change of name in 1966 to the Archdiocese of St. Paul and Minneapolis has prevented misunderstanding.

Today the Province of St. Paul and Minneapolis has an archdiocese and nine suffragan sees with 1,097,821 Catholics or 27% of its total population in Minnesota; North Dakota has 173,436 Catholics or 26%; and South Dakota has 146,906 Catholics or 21% of the total state population. The Province of St. Paul and Minneapolis has a total Catholic population of 25% of the entire three states.

PROVINCE OF SAN ANTONIO

The Province of San Antonio covers the largest territory, has the largest number of dioceses and the oldest Catholic sanctuary in the United States. The earliest inhabitants within Tejas (called Texas after 1836) were the Indians, and Spanish and Mexican peoples, maturing under the careful guidance of Franciscan missionaries, who planted the seeds of Christianity. It was this Coahuila-Tejas ancestry, the Texans of Mexican background, that left such a legacy to the Church and is still part of the religious culture of today.[1]

But the coming to power of the liberal government amid an environment of anti-clericalism soon confronted the Church in Mexico and Texas. Before long, tensions between political and religious groups arose, and the virtual collapse of ecclesiastical authority within the Church ended the mission system, beginning an era of secularization (1793-1830). Ordinarily, this should have been a period of growth for the Church with parishes and dioceses continuing on the foundation of the missions, but what happened instead was inevitable because of the anti-clerical atmosphere. Clerics and bishops fled the area by 1820, so that there were but four priests in all of Texas. Even in Mexico (1827-1831) no diocese had a bishop.[2]

Ecclesiastically, Texas was under the authority of the Bishop of Monterrey, formerly Bishop of Nuevo Leon. During this period, Mexico won freedom from

---

[1]Patrick Foley, "Beyond the Missions: The Immigrant Church and the Hispanics in Nineteenth-Century Texas," forthcoming in *Hispanicism and the Catholic Church: Great Forces in Motion* (Tucson: University of Arizona Press). I am indebted to Dr. Foley for this recent scholarly information on the history of the Church in the Southwest and particularly the history of the Church in Texas. See also Foley, "The Early Catholic Legacy of Texas from the Missions to the Civil War," a lecture presented to the Saint Thomas Institute, October 7, 1986; and "Bishop Odin and the Catholic Church in Texas, 1840-61," a paper read at the American Society of Church History, April 3, 1986.

[2]*Ibid.,* p. 5.

Spain in 1821 and in 1836 Texas became independent of Mexico. Recognizing the dire position of the Church, many lay people banded together, petitioning the bishops to send some priests to their mission lands for their spiritual and religious growth. Pope Gregory XVI, eager to help the Catholics, but aware of the anti-Catholicism still prevalent in Mexico and not certain of Mexico's reaction to the independence of Texas, was cautious. He realized, however, the plight of Texans and the importance of the Church in the Southwest. He, therefore, raised Texas to the status of prefecture apostolic on October 24, 1839, and vicariate apostolic on July 16, 1841.

Witnessing the depopulation of Texas, the new government of Mexico tried to attract people to settle there, offering them large land possibilities. The ploy did work, but with disastrous effects for Mexico and for the Church. The migration of peoples in 1840 began a period of the introduction of French and other priests into Texas and a migration of a considerable number of Anglo-Americans from the United States, who brought with them Protestant backgrounds prejudiced against the Catholic Church and unable to understand the Tejanos.

The migration to Texas in this first decade was an "almost unparalleled historical pageant, where a noticeable Catholic migration settled in a geographical region that already claimed a distinct Catholic heritage,"[1] that had been in existence for over a century and a half. While the immigrants did not destroy the Tejanos' religious beliefs (for they built their own ideas upon it), they did not bring the Mexicans to their "fullest potential."[2]

During this period of religious unrest, the Holy See transferred ecclesiastical jurisdiction from the bishop of Monterrey to the bishop of New Orleans. As the development of the Church continued and the need for a diocese was evident, Pope Pius IX, on May 4, 1847, established Galveston as the first diocese with its territory coterminous with the entire state of Texas.[3] This diocese was renamed Galveston-Houston on July 25, 1959. As in other dioceses throughout the country, Texas was helped not only financially but by religious personnel from the United States and Europe.

Difficulties in travelling over this vast region (by oxen carts, burro packs, steamboats and railroads) led the bishops of the Third Provincial Council of New Orleans in 1872 to recommend that another diocese be established. In 1874 Pope Pius IX made San Antonio a diocese and Brownsville a vicariate apostolic.[4]

A third diocese, Dallas, was established on July 15, 1890, redesignated as the Dallas-Fort Worth Diocese on October 20, 1953, and again redesignated on August 27, 1969 as the Dallas Diocese. A new Fort Worth diocese was created on August 22, 1969.

Phenomenal growth, expansion and increased population were the main factors in the establishment of ten new dioceses in Texas in the twentieth century. On March 23, 1912 the Diocese of Corpus Christi was created, followed in 1914 by the erection of that of El Paso, the diocese known as "two cultures" which had belonged to Tucson, then Dallas, before it was established as a diocese. It was given to the Province of Santa Fe and remained there until April 12, 1983,

[1]*Ibid.,* pp., 2, 22.
[2]*Ibid.,* p. 9.
[3]Guilday, *A History of the Councils of Baltimore,* p. 155.
[4]*Ibid.,* p. 222.

when it became a suffragan of San Antonio. On August 3, 1926 the Diocese of San Antonio was raised to a metropolitan see with jurisdiction over the entire state of Texas, attaching to it five suffragan sees, including the Diocese of Oklahoma. This diocese remained a suffragan until February 6, 1973, when it was withdrawn from San Antonio's ecclesiastical jurisdiction and established as the Archdiocese of Oklahoma City.

In the same year that San Antonio was raised to a metropolitan see, Amarillo was made a diocese. After that the following dioceses were estab-lished: Austin (April 14, 1948); San Angelo (October 16, 1961), Brownsville (July 10, 1965), Beaumont (September 29, 1966), Victoria (May 29, 1982), Lubbock (June 17, 1983) and Tyler (December 15, 1986).

The development of the Church in Texas has been a miracle of grace: within a period of 158 years, the Catholic population and the number of priests grew from four priests and very few Catholics (1830) to 2,039 priests and over three million Catholics (1988).

Today the Province of San Antonio has an archdiocese and thirteen suffragan sees with a Catholic population of 3,227,109 or 21% of the total population of the state of Texas.

PROVINCE OF SANTA FE

The Province of Santa Fe has a rich heritage that includes Indian, Spanish and Mexican cultures. Franciscan, Jesuit and diocesan priests ministered to their spiritual needs. One has only to recall the names of Francisco Garceo among the Franciscans, Eusebius Francisco Kino among the Jesuits, and bishops Jean Baptiste Lamy and John Baptiste Salpointe to realize the power of God's grace working in a region where the material and spiritual difficulties seemed, at times, insurmountable.

Centuries before the Spanish arrived in New Mexico, the Pueblo Indians were the only inhabitants in the southwest, but in 1539, Spain sent the Catholic missionaries and explorers to the New World. Franciscans built the first Church in 1598, near the present-day San Juan Indian Pueblo in northern Mexico.[1]

These Blue Franciscans[2] were the only priests in New Mexico from 1598 until 1853, when laws were passed to expel them: the Mexican laws of December 20, 1827 exiled all Spanish priests from Mexico and from 1826 to 1834 a law provided for the secularization of all missions in Mexico.[3] This persecution of the Franciscans was incited by the Pueblo revolt of 1680, the resentment of the medicine men and the feuds between the Spanish and Church officials. Despite the temporary failure of the missionary work of the Franciscans in New Mexico, they left a great spiritual and cultural legacy to this area that antedates California by a century and a half.[4]

---

[1]Correspondence with Marina Ochoa, Curator/Archivist of Santa Fe, February 3, 1988.

[2]Archdiocese of Santa Fe, *The Lord and New Mexico* (privately printed, 1976), pp. 4-5.

[3]Odie B. Faullk, ed., *John Baptiste Salpointe* (Diocese of Tucson), p. 5.

[4]Archdiocese of San Francisco, *op. cit.,* p. 5.

The Jesuits were to experience similar treatment. The great work of Father Eusebius Kino, "the Padre on Horseback," whose territory was south of Tucson, Arizona, was the forerunner of the Jesuits who followed him with such success in Arizona. With the suppression of the Jesuits in 1773, the eighteenth century witnessed one of the most disastrous decisions of the European monarchs which, unfortunately, was confirmed by Pope Clement XIV. Still, this seeming crisis was really the beginning of a great drama of Christianization and conversion.

Ecclesiastically, the bishops of Durango in the south of New Spain (called Mexico after 1821) were in charge of the New Mexican missions from 1730 to 1850. Because of the distance of over 1500 miles, only two bishops visited New Mexico from 1737 to 1760. In the nineteenth century, the bishop of Durango made three visitations and during this time the United States annexed California, New Mexico (including most of Arizona), and a portion of present-day Colorado through the Treaty of Guadalupa-Hidalgo in 1848, and the southern portion of Arizona and New Mexico by the Gadsden Purchase in 1853. The American bishops, realizing the need to supply priests to this vast area, moved the Seventh Provincial Council in Baltimore to petition for a vicariate apostolic for New Mexico. This was created on July 19, 1850 with a bishop, not Spanish but French: the renowned Jean Baptiste Lamy. It was not until 1970 that the first Hispanic became the first archbishop of Santa Fe.

On July 29, 1853 the Vicariate of New Mexico was elevated to the Diocese of Santa Fe and a suffragan of the Province of St. Louis. This diocese was extensive, comprising the states of Utah, Arizona, Colorado and New Mexico. On February 12, 1868 Colorado and Utah were created a vicariate apostolic; on September 25, 1868 the territory of Arizona became a vicariate. On February 12, 1871 Utah was transferred and placed under the jurisdiction of the Province of San Francisco.

On February 12, 1875 Santa Fe was elevated to a metropolitan see with the two suffragans of Colorado and Arizona. In 1897 Pope Leo XIII changed the Vicariate of Arizona to the Diocese of Tucson. Because the settlers in Arizona did not want to belong to New Mexico, the Holy See transferred Tucson to the Diocese of Los Angeles in 1936. In 1939 the northern counties of Arizona and several counties from New Mexico were formed into the new Diocese of Gallup, New Mexico, honoring the 400th anniversary of the arrival of the first white man in this area. The Diocese of Gallup has two distinctions: it is the diocese with the oldest mission and the oldest Indian tribe, the Navajos, and it is a diocese which crosses two states (Arizona and New Mexico).

In 1969, when the Diocese of Phoenix was formed from the western portion of Gallup as a suffragan of Santa Fe, it was thought by the archbishop of Santa Fe and the bishop of Tucson that no real ties with Los Angeles remained. Because Tucson shared a common heritage with Santa Fe, the Diocese of Tucson was returned to the Metropolitan See of New Mexico.[1]

In 1982 the last diocese in Santa Fe was created. Las Cruces, taken from the southern part of the Archdiocese of Santa Fe, was made a diocese on October 18. The one diocese that had been part of the Santa Fe Diocese since 1914, El Paso, was transferred to the Metropolitan See of San Antonio in 1982.

---

[1]Correspondence with Most Rev. Manuel D. Moreno, Bishop of Tucson, November 4, 1988.

Today the Province of Santa Fe has an archdiocese and four suffragan sees and comprises the states of Arizona and New Mexico with a Catholic population of 459,863 or 30% of the total population in the state of New Mexico and a Catholic population of 577,920 or 19% of the total population of the state of Arizona.

PROVINCE OF WASHINGTON

The Archdiocese of Washington is a young diocese, only fifty years old, but it has played a major role in the history of the American Church. Within the last 22 years, three cardinals have been appointed to this archdiocese: Pope Paul VI named Cardinal Patrick A. O'Boyle in 1967 and Cardinal William W. Baum in 1976. Pope John Paul II named Cardinal James A. Hickey in 1988. The location of the archdiocese in this capital city of the United States has added to its importance and it is the site for some of the most important organizations within the American Church.

Washington, DC was part of the Baltimore Archdiocese until 1939, when Pope Pius XII created a dual archdiocese with the name of Archdiocese of Baltimore and Washington.[1] The Washington Archdiocese embraced the District of Columbia. After World War II, when the population of the capital city was increased by the burgeoning surrounding suburbs and the distance from Baltimore was considered difficult for effective administration, the Archdiocese of Washington was separated from Baltimore (November 13, 1947). It became the Archiepiscopal See of Washington with no metropolitan jurisdiction over a suffragan see and directly subject to the Apostolic See.[2] The extent of its territorial jurisdiction was the area of Washington, DC and five Maryland counties.

On October 12, 1965 the Titular Bishop of the Virgin Islands of St. Thomas asked the Holy See to grant his church the right to become subject to Washington, DC and to be separated from San Juan in Puerto Rico, with the reasoning that the inhabitants of the Virgin Islands were not Spanish but English-speaking and subject to the civil law of the United States. They also requested that the archdiocese be made a metropolitan see. Because of the importance of Washington in the international world, it was raised to this dignity, effective December 25, 1965. "To it the Holy See made subject as a suffragan the *prelature nullius* of the Virgin Islands of St. Thomas in the Virgin Islands which were consequently withdrawn from the ecclesiastical province of San Juan in Puerto Rico."[3] On April 20, 1977 Pope Paul VI decreed the establishment of

---

[1] *Catholic Standard,* a weekly newspaper of the Archdiocese of Washington, July 14, 1988. Cardinal Gibbons of Baltimore was strongly opposed to the separation of Washington from Baltimore, and the rumor that this might happen caused him to go to Rome to convince the Holy Father of the danger to the Baltimore Archdiocese. He was not opposed to the idea that the name "Washington" be added to the title "Baltimore Archdiocese." This was accomplished only 25 years later, six months after Cardinal Gibbons' successor died. See *The New Catholic Encyclopedia,* Vol. XIV, p. 823.

[2] Correspondence with the Chancellor, Rev. Godfrey Mosley, Archdiocese of Washington, April 29, 1988.

[3] *Ibid.*

the Diocese of St. Thomas in the Virgin Islands as the suffragan see of the Archdiocese of Washington. To date, this is its only one.

Because of its location, the Archdiocese of Washington is the center for many national organizations and educational institutions: the residence of the Apostolic Pro-Nuncio, the Catholic University (a Pontifical University), other Catholic organizations with national offices in the Archdiocese of Washington, and many religious houses of study.

Today the Province of Washington, DC has an archdiocese and one suffragan see with a total Catholic population of 395,016 or 18% of the total population in Washington, DC; 30,000 in the Island of St. Thomas or 37% of the total population in the Virgin Islands.

ORIENTAL RITES

The last two decades of the nineteenth century saw vast numbers of Catholics from Europe and the Middle East emigrate to the United States, bringing with them their own liturgical and canonical disciplines. At first they were subject to the Ordinary of the Latin Rite but this proved a very unsatisfying arrangement. In 1913 the Sacred Congregation of the Propagation of the Faith granted each Eastern Rite group the privilege of full ordinary jurisdiction and independence from the Latin ordinaries and the right to establish vicariate exarchies (corresponding to our vicariate apostolics).

Because the growth of the ecclesiastical organization reached a point where a permanent hierarchy could be est., the Holy See in 1924 erected eparchies (dioceses) and an archeparchy (archdiocese) for the major Eastern Rites and apostolic exarchs for the new residential sees. There are, however, some members of Eastern Rites in the United States who do not have an ordinary of their own and they are under the jurisdiction of the local ordinary of the diocese.[1]

Within the Catholic Church there are eighteen canonical rites that are of equal dignity. All are validly and canonically approved by Rome, enjoying canonical jurisdiction with all its rights and obligations, completely independent of the members of the Latin Rite and/or another Rite. Each one possesses its own hierarchy, differs in liturgical and ecclesiastical discipline, and all are subject and in complete communion with the Holy Father.[2]

The Byzantine Rite constitutes the largest Eastern Rite in the United States. There are many subgroups of this same rite because these churches were independent or autonomous churches in Europe and/or the Middle East. The Ukrainians and the Ruthenians are different peoples with a common Slavic background, while the Melkites are Greek-speaking Arabs. Because each group reunited communion with Rome at different stages in history, each group did so as their own church. Because these churches were based on the language and cultures of its peoples each developed its own expression of the same liturgical rite.[3]

There are two metropolitan sees in the Byzantine Rite in the United States: The Byzantine Ruthenian Metropolitan Archdiocese of Pittsburgh with three eparchies (in Parma, Passaic and Van Nuys); and the Byzantine Ukrainian Metropolitan Archdiocese of Philadelphia with three eparchies (in St. Josephat in Parma, St. Nicholas and Stamford).

---

[1]*The Official Catholic Directory, op. cit.,* p. 1030.

[2]M.M. Wojnar, "Ukrainian (Ruthenian) Rite," *New Catholic Encyclopedia,* Vol. 14, p. 372.

[3]I am indebted to many who belong to the Eastern Rite for the information sent to me especially Rev. Daniel A. Magulick, Asst. Chancellor of the Metropolitan Archdiocese of Pittsburgh of the Ruthenian Rite and to the Chancellor of the Ukrainian Catholic Metropolitan Archdiocese, Sister Thomas Hrynewish, S.S.M.I. A very scholarly work on this topic is that by Victor J. Pospishil, J.C.D., Sc.Eccl.Orient, "Law on Persons" from the *Code of Oriental Canon Law* (St. Mary's Ukrainian Catholic Church, Ford City, PA, 1960).

There are four eparchies of St. Maron (Maronite), Eparchy of Newton (Melkite), Eparchy for the Chaldean Catholics, and Eparchy for the Romanian Byzantine Catholics. There is an exarchate for the Armenian Catholics.[1]

TERRITORIES

In the United States territorial sees of the Catholic Church, there are two metropolitan sees: the Metropolitan See of Agana in Guam and the Metro-politan See of San Juan, Puerto Rico.

Jesuit missionaries had come as early as 1668 to Guam to evangelize the natives. But it was not until 1911 that Pope Pius X erected the Vicariate Apostolic of Guam under the care of the Order of Friars Minor Capuchin. The vicariate apostolic was extended to all the Mariana Islands on July 4, 1946, and on June 14, 1948 it was extended to Wake Island. On October 14, 1965 Guam was elevated to a diocese and made a suffragan see of San Francisco. On May 20, 1984 it was elevated to a metropolitan see as the Archdiocese of Agana with a suffragan see in the Caroline-Marshalls. In 1985 another suffragan see, Chalan Kanoa (Saipan), was erected.[2]

The Diocese of Caroline-Marshalls spans three new nations: the Republic of the Marshalls, the Federated States of Micronesia and the Republic of Palau. These islands continue a relationship with the United States primarily for inter-national affairs. The Archdiocese of Agana is in the Northern Mariana Islands south of the Diocese of Saipan.[3]

The Diocese of Samao-Pago Pago was est. in November 1982, but the first bishop was not appointed until four years later. Missionaries first came to this island in 1845 and in 1850 the Vicariate Apostolic of the Navigator's Archipelago (Samoa) was est. in the island of Tutuila, with the capital at Pago Pago in the area called American Samoa.[4]

The Metropolitan See of Puerto Rico is one of the oldest dioceses in the New World. Erected as a diocese by Pope Julius II on August 8, 1511 as a suf-fragan see of Seville, Spain, in the passage of time it became part of the Ecclesiastical Province of Cuba. In 1903 Pope Leo XIII put Puerto Rico di-rectly under the Holy See. On November 21, 1924 Pope Pius XI created the Diocese of Ponce, Puerto Rico and changed the name of the "Diocese of Puerto Rico" to the "Diocese of San Juan de Puerto Rico." On April 30, 1960 the Diocese of San Juan de Puerto Rico was elevated to the Metropolitan See of Puerto Rico. On the same day Pope John XXIII erected the Diocese of Arecibo. Two additional sees were erected by Pope Paul VI: the Diocese of Caguas on November 4, 1964 and the Diocese of Mayagüez on March 1, 1976.

[1]*The Official Catholic Directory, op. cit.,* p. xxiv.
[2]Correspondence with Sister Ana Lee, O.P., Catholic Education Office, May 16, 1988.
[3]Correspondence with Bishop Martin J. Neylon, S.J., Bishop of Caroline-Marshalls, June 3, 1988.
[4]Correspondence with Bishop J. Quinn, M.M., Bishop of Samoa-Pago Pago, June 17, 1988.

Puerto Rico is politically connected to the United States but the Church in Puerto Rico is not related jurisdictionally to the Church in the United States. The archbishop of San Juan with the four other diocesan bishops form an independent episcopal conference. The Apostolic Delegate for Puerto Rico is the *Apostolic Nuncio* to the Dominican Republic, who resides in Santo Domingo, Dominican Republic.[1]

EPILOGUE

Following the directives of Vatican Council II, the role of the hierarchy, clergy, religious and laity within the Church brings new hope for the future especially within the United States. Recognizing the need for greater participation of all members in the life of the Church (for all are "the presence of Christ in the world"), bishops, priests, religious and laity together are, hopefully, meeting this challenge throughout the dioceses.

Closer working relationships of bishops with priests, religious and lay people in the creation of new dioceses and smaller dioceses, closer participation of laity and clergy in accomplishing the mission of parishes, and a greater application of the understanding of the dignity of all people, called to live in justice and peace, are real signs that the American Church is struggling towards a revitalization of the spiritual life of its members.

The greatest change has come in the role of the laity. When we reflect on the laity's place in the formation of early dioceses, we can feel encouraged that they are accepting the challenge in today's society. Today the laity is becoming aware of the true meaning of authority as a means of service rather than a position of power or domination. When all members of Christ's body realize this truth, we will come closer to Christ's example of service which is the nucleus of a Christian community and the foundation of all dioceses.

[1]Correspondence with Ms. Gilda R. Leguori, Assistant to the Vicar of Administration, June 29, 1988.

ADDENDUM

Number of Dioceses: According to the *Official Catholic Directory 1988,* there are 187 dioceses in the United States. The Diocese of Knoxville is the 188th (est. September 8, 1988). The Directory includes 12 Eastern Rite Eparchies (dioceses) as well as the Military Archdiocese. It does not include several Eastern Rite jurisdictions immediately subject to the Holy See, nor does it include any of the US territorial sees.

Black Bishops: There are 13 black bishops in the United States. One is an archbishop (Atlanta, Georgia), one is a bishop (Biloxi, Mississippi), and the other 11 are auxiliary bishops.[1]

Establishing a New Diocese: In establishing a new diocese, a bishop or archbishop is simply installed if he has previously been ordained or consecrated. Three papal orders or mandates are read: the mandate of appointment to office, the mandate of establishing the new diocese, and the mandate elevating the designated church to its status as a Cathedral.[2]

Corporation Sole: The corporation sole, an American derivative of an English common law form, is essentially the incorporation of an office in the name of the present incumbent and his successor. Almost one-third of the dioceses in the United States are so incorporated with the archbishop or bishop as the corporation sole. The purpose is to secure a method for both ownership of property and daily operations. In most of these dioceses today the parish and institution are incorporated separately to limit insurance liabilities.[3]

[1]Information submitted by the National Office for Black Catholics, February 2, 1989.
[2]Correspondence with Anthony J. Spence, Journalist, *The Tennessee Register,* March 1988 and October 20, 1988.
[3]James B. O'Hara, "The Modern Corporation Sole," *Dickinson Law Review,* Vol. 93, No. 1, Fall 1988, pp. 23-29.

PROVINCES / ARCHDIOCESES

1. Baltimore (MD) 1808
2. Oregon City (OR) 1846
   name changed to "Portland in Oregon" 1928
3. St. Louis (MO) 1847
4. Cincinnati (OH) 1850
5. New York (NY) 1850
6. New Orleans (LA) 1850
7. San Francisco (CA) 1853
8. Sante Fe (NM) 1875
9. Milwaukee (WI) 1875
10. Boston (MA) 1875
11. Philadelphia (PA) 1875
12. Chicago (IL) 1880
13. St. Paul and Minneapolis (MN) 1888
14. Dubuque (IA) 1893
15. San Antonio (TX) 1926
16. Los Angeles (CA) 1936
17. Detroit (MI) 1937
18. Louisville (KY) 1937
19. Newark (NJ) 1937
20. Denver (CO) 1941
21. Indianapolis (IN) 1944
22. Omaha (NE) 1945
23. Seattle (WA) 1951
24. Kansas City in Kansas 1952
25. Hartford (CT) 1953
26. Atlanta (GA) 1962
27. Washington (DC) 1965
28. Anchorage (AK) 1966
29. Miami (FL) 1968
30. Oklahoma City (OK) 1973
31. Mobile (AL) 1980

EASTERN RITE

32. Philadelphia (PA) 1956
    Ukrainian Byzantine
33. Pittsburgh (PA) 1969
    Ruthenian Byzantine

DIOCESES

1. Baltimore (MD)* 1789[1]
2. New Orleans (LA) 1793
3. Bardstown (KY) 1808
   trans. to Louisville* 1841
4. New York (NY)* 1808
5. Philadelphia (PA)* 1808
6. Boston (MA)* 1808
7. Richmond (VA) 1820
8. Charleston (SC) 1820
9. Cincinnati (OH) 1821
10. St. Louis (MO)* 1826
11. Mobile (AL)* 1829
    name changed to Mobile-Birmingham
    1954; redes. Mobile 1969
12. Detroit (MI)* 1833
13. Vincennes (IN) 1834
    trans. to Indianapolis* 1898
14. Nashville (TN) 1837
15. Dubuque (IA)* 1837
16. Natchez (MS) 1837
    name changed to Natchez-Jackson 1957
    name changed to Jackson 1977
17. San Diego (CA) 1840
    name changed to Monterey 1849
    name changed to Santa Barbara 1853/4
    name changed to Monterey-Los Angeles
    1859; reest. as Los Angeles-
    San Diego 1922; reest. as
    Los Angeles* 1936
18. Milwaukee (WI)* 1843
19. Pittsburgh (PA) 1843
20. Chicago (IL)* 1843
21. Little Rock (AR) 1843
22. Hartford (CT)* 1843
23. Oregon City (OR)* 1843[3]
    name changed to
    Portland in Oregon 1928
24. Albany (NY) 1847

25. Buffalo (NY) 1847
26. Cleveland (OH) 1847
27. Galveston (TX) 1847
    redes. Galveston-Houston 1959
28. Monterey (CA) 1849
    redes. Monterey-Los Angeles 1859
    redes. Monterey-Fresno 1922
    redes. Monterey 1967
29. Wheeling (WV) 1850
    redes. Wheeling-Charleston 1974
30. St. Paul and Minneapolis (MN)* 185(
31. Savannah (GA) 1850
    name changed to Savannah-Atlanta
    1837; redes. Savannah 1956
32. Nesqually (WA) 1850
    name changed to Seattle* 1907
33. Santa Fe (NM)* 1850
34. Natchitoches (LA) 1853
    trans. to Alexandria 1910
    redes. Alexandria-Shreveport 1977
    redes. Alexandria 1986
35. Newark (NJ)* 1853
36. Quincey (IL) 1853
    trans. to Alton 1857
    trans. to Springfield in Illinois 1923
37. Portland (ME) 1853
38. Erie (PA) 1853
39. Brooklyn (NY) 1853
40. Covington (KY) 1853
41. Burlington (VT) 1853
42. San Francisco (CA)* 1853[2]
43. Fort Wayne (IN) 1857
    redes. Fort Wayne-South Bend 1960
44. Marquette (WI) 1857
45. Columbus (OH) 1868
46. Green Bay (WI) 1868
47. Harrisburg (PA) 1868

[1] An asterisk indicates that the diocese has been made into an archdiocese.
[2] This is the official date for the establishment of San Francisco as an archdiocese.
It was never made a diocese.
[3] This is the official date for the establishment of a vicariate apostolic for Oregon
City. It was never made a diocese.

48. La Crosse (WI) 1868
49. Wilmington (DE) 1868
50. Rochester (NY) 1868
51. Scranton (PA) 1868
52. Springfield (MA) 1870
53. St. Augustine (FL) 1870
54. Ogdensburg (NY) 1872
55. Providence (RI) 1872
56. San Antonio (TX)* 1874
57. Peoria (IL) 1877
58. Leavenworth (KS) 1877
    trans. to Kansas City in Kansas* 1947
59. Kansas City (MO) 1880
    Diocese of St. Joseph 1868 previously est.;
    redes. Kansas City-St. Joseph 1956
60. Davenport (LA) 1881
61. Trenton (NJ) 1881
62. Grand Rapids (MI) 1882
63. Helena (MT) 1884
64. Manchester (NH) 1884
65. Omaha (NE)* 1885
66. Sacramento (CA) 1886
67. Syracuse (NY) 1886
68. Belleville (IL) 1887
69. Denver (CO) 1887
70. Concordia (KS) 1887
    trans. to Salina 1944
71. Wichita (KS) 1887
72. Lincoln (NE) 1887
73. Cheyenne (WY) 1887
74. St. Cloud (MN) 1889
75. Duluth (MN) 1889
76. Sioux Falls (SD) 1889
77. Jamestown (ND) 1889
    trans. to Fargo 1889
78. Winona (MN) 1889
79. Dallas (TX) 1890
80. Salt Lake City (UT) 1891
81. Boise (ID) 1893
82. Tucson (AZ) 1897
83. Altoona (PA) 1901
    redes. Altoona-Johnstown 1957
84. Sioux City (IA) 1902
85. Lead (SD) 1902
    trans. to Rapid City 1930
86. Baker (OR) 1903
87. Fall River (MA) 1904
88. Great Falls (MT) 1904
    name changed to Great Falls-Billings 1980
89. Oklahoma (OK)* 1905
    name changed to Oklahoma City and Tulsa 1930; Oklahoma City est. as Archdiocese 1973
90. Superior (WI) 1905
91. Rockford (IL) 1908
92. Bismarck (ND) 1909
93. Crookston (MN) 1909
94. Toledo (OH) 1910
95. Des Moines (IA) 1911
96. Kearney (NE) 1912
    trans. to Grand Island 1917
97. Corpus Christi (TX) 1912
98. Spokane (WA) 1913
99. El Paso (TX) 1914
100. Lafayette (LA) 1918
101. Raleigh (NC) 1924
102. Amarillo (TX) 1926
103. Reno (NV) 1931
    redes. Reno-Las Vegas 1976
104. San Diego (CA) 1936
105. Lansing (MI) 1937
106. Paterson (NJ) 1937
107. Camden (NJ) 1937
108. Owensboro (KY) 1938
109. Saginaw (MI) 1938
110. Washington (DC)* 1939[1]
111. Gallup (NM) 1939
112. Honolulu (HI) 1941
113. Pueblo (CO) 1941

[1]This is the date Washington, DC was established as an archdiocese with the Archdiocese of Baltimore on equal status. It was separated from Baltimore in 1947 and became a metropolitan see in 1965.

114. Youngstown (OH) 1943
115. Steubenville (OH) 1944
116. Evansville (IN) 1944
117. Lafayette (IN) 1944
118. Madison (WI) 1946
119. Austin (TX) 1948
120. Joliet (IL) 1949
121. Worcester (MA) 1950
122. Greensburg (PA) 1951
123. Dodge City (KS) 1951
124. Yakima (WA) 1951
125. Juneau (AK) 1951
126. Bridgeport (CT) 1953
127. Norwich (CT) 1953
128. Atlanta (GA)* 1956
129. Jefferson City (MO) 1956
130. Springfield-Cape Girardeau (MO) 1956
131. Gary (IN) 1956
132. Rockville Center (NY) 1957
133. New Ulm (MN) 1957
134. Miami (FL) * 1958
135. Allentown (PA) 1961
136. Baton Rouge (LA) 1961
137. San Angelo (TX) 1961
138. Stockton (CA) 1962
139. Oakland (CA) 1962
140. Santa Rosa (CA) 1962
141. Fairbanks (AK) 1962
142. Brownsville (TX) 1965
143. Beaumont (TX) 1966
144. Anchorage (AK)* 1966[2]
145. Fresno (CA) 1967

146. St. Petersburg (FL) 1968
147. Orlando (FL) 1968
148. Birmingham (AL) 1969
149. Fort Worth (TX) 1969
150. Phoenix (AZ) 1969
151. Memphis (TN) 1971
152. Gaylord (MI) 1971
153. Kalamazoo (MI) 1971
154. Charlotte (SC) 1972
155. Tulsa (OK) 1973
156. Arlington (VA) 1974
157. Pensacola-Tallahassee (FL) 197?
158. Orange (CA) 1976
159. Biloxi (MS) 1977
160. Houma-Thibodaux (LA) 1977
161. St. Thomas (Virgin Islands) 19?
162. San Bernardino (CA) 1978
163. Lake Charles (LA) 1980
164. San Jose (CA) 1981
165. Metuchen (NJ) 1981
166. Victoria (TX) 1982
167. Las Cruces (NM) 1982
168. Lubbock (TX) 1983
169. Palm Beach (FL) 1984
170. Colorado Springs (CO) 1984
171. Venice (FL) 1984
172. Military Archdiocese (DC)* 198
173. Shreveport (LA) 1986
174. Tyler (TX) 1986
175. Lexington (KY) 1988
176. Knoxville (KY) 1988

[1]This is a special Archdiocese for Military Services for USA. The headquarters are in Washington, DC because all military bases are located there but their parishes are in every diocese of the country. It serves US Catholics of the Army, Navy, Air Force, Marine Corps, Coast Guard, Veterans Administration and those in government service overseas and their dependents.
[2]This is the official date for the establishment of Anchorage as an archdiocese. It was never made a diocese.

EASTERN RITE

177. Philadelphia (PA)* 1913
178. Pittsburgh (PA)* 1924
179. Stamford (CT) 1956
180. St. Nicholas (IL) 1961
181. Passaic (NJ) 1963
182. Parma (OH) 1969
183. St. Maron, Brooklyn (NY) 1971
184. Newton (MA) 1976
185. Van Nuys (West) 1981
186. Romanian 1982
187. St. Josephat in Parma 1983
188. St. Thomas 1985

CHAPTER TWO

Catholic Immigrant Patterns, 1789-1989
Dolores Liptak
Catholic Archival and Historical Services

Even before the official establishment of the United States Catholic Church in 1789 when John Carroll (1735-1815) was appointed its first bishop, the scattered bands of the nation's Catholic population were viewed as being "foreign." Carroll himself worried about this. He described Catholic membership, which numbered approximately 23,000 in 1785, as being constantly added to by immigrants who poured "in upon us in large numbers from the various European countries."[1] From his time on, the ethnic character of the new membership of the Church continued to be an inescapable reality and concern. Although some measures were taken in every generation to avoid the characterization, the immigrant designation of the nation's Catholics only became more clear with each passing decade. Even to the present-day restriction and quota systems, immigrants and migrants continue not only to increase the Church's membership in the United States but also to cause concern among some Catholics that their Church will continue to be evaluated as immigrant. For this reason it is important to see how immigrant patterns developed and altered the composition of the Church in the United States and to evaluate in what ways, both positive and negative, these patterns have influenced American and American Catholic perceptions of U.S. Catholicism.

If one reviews the variety of changes and the nature of growth that typified the development of the Catholic Church in the United States in general, one can discern two basic immigrant patterns. Each influenced the way the nation's Catholics perceived themselves and were perceived by their fellow Americans. Lasting almost one century, when immigration came mostly from Ireland and German lands, the first pattern revealed an attitude especially on the part of Catholic leaders of openness to the new environment and willingness to trust in the possibility of integration and acceptance among Catholics and the Anglo-American Protestant establishment. A delicate balance, interrupted sporadically after the 1830's by episodes of anti-Catholic response to specific social or economic crises, allowed church leaders and members to proclaim their admiration for their adopted nation even while they encouraged the development of parallel institutions to protect their place in the new society. For the most part, a growing sense that the Church was meeting with acceptance confirmed the soundness of their stance.

By the third quarter of the nineteenth century, however, the pattern was clear. The revolution in the nation's industrial and transportation sectors altered the more harmonious social climate. As the massive and rapid influx of southern and eastern Europeans swelled the nation's population to number more than thirty million and raised the Church's membership to over four and one half

---

[1] James Hennesey, S.J., *American Catholics: A History of the Roman Catholic Church in the United States* (New York, 1983), p. 73.

million (or 13% of the total population) by 1870, new pressures occasioned increased tension between both church and society. The second century of Catholic growth was to reflect the breakdown of the openness and acceptance that had typified the earlier time, dictate a more defensive stance on the part of a church made more conscious of its immigrant base, and require a recasting of church policy with respect to immigrants.

Why immigrant Catholics were able to achieve a more harmonious pattern of accommodation and integration until the 1880's, and how they negotiated the demographic changes that altered their struggle to find an acceptable posture in the second century will be the focus of this chapter.

During the first stage of the development of the U.S. Catholic Church, when immigration caused membership to escalate dramatically every decade, Catholic leaders followed Carroll's earlier conviction that the Church in the United States needed to be perceived as an American institution; they, too, acted under the belief that this was the only way that the Church could expect freedom to expand within the anti-Catholic environment. The steady development of dioceses and Catholic institutions that occurred as a result is a testimony to the soundness of that *modus vivendi*. This strategy, furthermore, was sanctioned by Roman officials who also recognized the sensitive nature of being both Catholic and immigrant in a strongly Protestant nation. Even though guided to a great extent by immigrant bishops and clergy, they saw America as the promised land and often verbalized the same rhetoric of republicanism that their fellow Americans espoused. In particular, they seemed to see no problem with using every liberty that the nation offered and building every institution that it allowed. Becoming part of the American experiment meant, for all practical appearances, being able to build the kind of church that would not only protect their Catholic religious heritage but could ultimately serve the American nation they greatly admired.

The attitude of these nineteenth-century Catholic leaders toward American institutions and political theory created a positive and integrating point of view with respect to new membership in the Church. It cultivated the delicate accord that allowed for consistent growth in every growing sector of the nation while it allowed church officials to acknowledge and respond to the needs of newcomers by taking advantage of the opportunities afforded by the free business and legal climate that flourished in the United States. By the 1850's, even as the numbers of immigrant Catholics reached beyond the million mark, this pattern of accommodation continued without serious negative consequences, enabling leaders to continue to find creative ways to foster adaptation and understanding of the advantages of becoming acceptable to Americans. Through the appointment of clergy and the establishment of parishes where ethnic needs were at least acknowledged, church leaders were also able to convey the degree to which they viewed such means necessary, albeit temporary, solutions to finding the Church's appropriate place in American society. Well into the third quarter of the nineteenth century, church leaders seemed to succeed in proving the ability of the Church to adapt to the American environment in this way.

Despite local episodes of tension and prejudice, twin products of hard times, they managed to maintain a delicate balance between the preservation of Catholic belief and the integration of progressive cultural values.

The Anglo-Irish American Bishop, John Carroll, was the first to demonstrate this perspective. Although Carroll realized early that few of the pioneer priests and even fewer of the Catholic laity of the newly established Church fit the ethnic and cultural description that best suited his Protestant American colleagues, he deliberately took measures to portray the Church as one that could meet their fancy. Thus he chose Lulworth Castle in England as the site for his episcopal ordination, apparently intending that his choice serve to clarify its international, rather than its Roman, identification.[1] Furthermore, despite growing indications that the Catholic Church was meeting with some degree of acceptance even in the most bigoted areas of his widespread diocese, Carroll continued his efforts to adhere to standards and develop institutions that Americans would both approve of and find appealing.

The popular Greco-Roman architectural style of the cathedral that Carroll commissioned at Baltimore was merely one indication of his desire to impress Americans with the accommodating efforts of the Catholic Church. Likewise, the schools he established were meant to show his investment in American society. Georgetown Academy (later Georgetown University) in Washington, DC and St. Mary's Seminary and College in Baltimore, founded within the first years of his administration, both stood as institutional signs of his desire to take advantage of America's religious and educational opportunities. From the start, the outstanding Catholic graduates from these schools entered fully into the mainstream of American social and religious leadership. In the first seminary class at St. Mary's was Stephen Badin, the stern, circuit-riding builder of the Church of Kentucky, Ohio, Tennessee, Indiana, Illinois and Michigan; his ministry alone is said to have spread the gospel over one hundred thousand miles. From Georgetown's first class came another outstanding American and Catholic, the statesman William Gaston, who served the state of North Carolina as both senator and congressman for eleven terms and later enhanced the Supreme Court through his efforts as associate justice.[2]

Carroll found ways to promote both the contemplative and active forms of religious life for American women. He encouraged the return to America of three Maryland natives, Mother Bernardina Matthews and her two nieces, who had entered the English Carmel at Hoogstraet (then located in the Low Countries). In 1790 these three women, together with a fourth Carmelite from Antwerp and their spiritual director, the American Reverend Charles Neale, travelled to the United States and settled at Port Tobacco, Maryland, where they founded what may be considered the first religious congregation officially established in the United Sates. In need of active coworkers, Carroll also encouraged the foundation of communities of religious women who would be available for ministry. When a girl's school was opened in Baltimore in 1808 by the future American saint, Elizabeth Bayley Seton, his dream for apostolic service first became reality. The Sisters of Charity, the religious congregation that Elizabeth Seton helped to found during the same period, was to set a remarkable pattern for subsequent religious communities. Before Carroll's death in 1815, the Visi-

---

[1]*Ibid.*, pp. 87-88.

[2]Dolores Liptak, R.S.M., *Immigrants and Their Church* (New York, 1989), p. 6; Hennesey, *op. cit.*, p. 101.

tandines at Georgetown and two 1812 Kentucky groups, the Sisters of Charity of Nazareth and the Sisters of Loretto, were also educating young women, visiting the sick, or otherwise providing for the rapidly growing Catholic population in both urban and frontier settings.[1]

Sensitive about the ways Catholics were being perceived by other Americans, Carroll always tried to play down any signs of ethnic discord or competition. Concerning some unscrupulous French merchants in Baltimore during the late 1780's, for example, he wrote that their contempt for the Church was turning away both fellow Catholics and Americans. He recognized that his own unpleasant encounters with Germans in Philadelphia and Baltimore over the appointment of pastors were not merely personally humbling but were demoralizing to Catholics in general, especially to the very German Catholics that he had been trying to accommodate. Finally, when the time came to suggest bishops for the four new dioceses to be established in 1808, one of his chief concerns was that he find qualified priests of American interests and background to head these Churches. Although eventually frustrated in the second of these aims, he settled for the first requirement: finding men who were immensely able to project an image of the Church that was in conformity with American expectations.[2]

What motivated Carroll to avoid any labelling of the Church as foreign does not seem to have been dislike or distrust for those who did not share his American background. He was, in fact, immensely proud of clergymen like Ferdinand Steinmeyer, one of the most capable of several Philadelphia German-American pastors. Known in his community as Ferdinand Farmer, this missionary was well-received by Americans and much appreciated by the German-American Catholics he pastored. Carroll, himself, saw Farmer as a treasure not only because of his successful work among "our most excellent and incomparable German Brethren" but because he saw Farmer as "that great Saint."[3]

Carroll also strongly backed the remarkably creative contributions of such early missionaries as Demetrius Gallitzin, the son of a Russian prince and a Prussian countess. First choosing to identify himself as Augustine Smith, Gallitzin had received all his training for the priesthood at St. Mary's in Baltimore. By 1799 he was appointed to the Pennsylvania frontier. There he began a long-term ministry at a model commune he established in Loretto, Pennsylvania. The missionary work of both Gallitzin and Stephen Badin served to hearten and confirm Carroll's belief that European recruits were eminently fit to develop the Church in frontier circumstances.

While appreciating the contributions of these Catholic pioneers, Carroll still expressed cautious concern lest the Catholic Church in the United States be labelled as foreign because of its clergy and membership and thus fail to take its proper place alongside other American institutions. For this reason alone, segregating Catholics on the basis of their ethnicity was never Carroll's (nor was it

---

[1]Charles W. Currier, C.S.S.R., *Carmel in America: A Centennial History of the Discalced Carmelites in the United States* (Baltimore, 1890), pp. 51-56; and Historical Records, *Archives of the Carmel of Baltimore,* Baltimore, Maryland (subsequently referred to as ACB); see also Hennesey, pp. 87 and 92.

[2]Hennesey, *op. cit.,* p. 74.

[3]*Ibid.*

any of his immediate successors') preference during the first century of American growth. Nor did it appear to be the preoccupation of the vast majority of German and Irish newcomers that brought church membership to number some six million by 1880. What seemed more important was that the needs of Catholics be recognized and that the spiritual dimension of their lives be attended to by those committed and able to serve them. That responsive, responsible and resourceful missionaries were available was the original prayer for the American Church; it was the original blessing for the Church as well. That talented priests with names like Flaget, Matignon or Nerinckx first emerged to accept the invitation to serve Catholic communities during Carroll's time was appreciated from the start; that this continued into later decades, when other exemplary clergymen and women bearing such names as Neumann, Machebeuf, Baraga, Duchesne or Gerhardinger volunteered to do the same, set the American Church apart as exceedingly fortunate. Like Carroll, most of his successors knew instinctively that it was the kind of inspired and unstinting labor that these immigrant missionaries supplied that alone could overcome the major obstacles to acceptance, and strengthen the bonds of trust existing between Catholics and other members of American society.

Ironically it was advertisements published in mission journals abroad that continued to be one of the best sources of new recruits for the nation's clergy. One enticing entry announced:

> We offer you: No Salary; No Recompense; No Holidays; No Pension.
> But: Much Hard Work; A Poor Dwelling; Few Consolations; Many Disappointments; Frequent Sickness; A Violent or Lonely Death; An Unknown Grave.[1]

For many European seminarians this served as the call to adventure they needed; for others the visits of American bishops or the letters of American missionaries published in a variety of sources or disseminated by mission societies in Lyons, Vienna and Munich were the proper enticement. While native vocations lagged, the response to these invitations made all the difference for New World needs. If Carroll had once stated a preference for a native clergy, one that was accustomed to "our climate and acquainted with the tempers, manners and government of the people, to whom they are to dispense the ministry of salvation," he and his successors got, instead, a foreign-born phalanx of eager and adaptable recruits who proved as capable and dedicated as any native clergy.[2] For their part, the opportunity to work in difficult situations with the unchurched, whether Indian, Black, immigrant or American-born, was reward enough. In this way, European spiritualities and theological perspectives continued to influence American Catholics; they became enmeshed with the optimistic, pragmatic and sometimes untested values that sprang from the rich soil of the American frontier.

---

[1]Matthias M. Hoffman, *The Church Founders of the Northwest* (Milwaukee, Wisconsin, 1937), p. 23.

[2]Quoted in Jay Dolan, *The American Catholic Experience: A History from Colonial Times to the Present* (New York, 1985), p. 107.

Travelling across the broad mountains and valleys, along rivers and water-ways, down the narrow and dirty streets and alleys of rapidly growing cities from coast to coast, an immigrant Catholic clergy sought out their fellow Catholics to renew their faith, baptize their children, perform the sacraments and preside at the liturgy. So vast was the mission field to be covered in a nation constantly expanding in numbers and territory, that much of their time was spent aboard public conveyances such as trains, packetboats, steamers, on foot or in the sad-dle, riding endless rough miles to missions where they barely managed the min-imum tasks of liturgical and sacramental celebration. Furthermore, from the start, much of the pastoral work had to be left to those who could stay behind to keep the faith alive. Without the great enthusiasm, courage and faith commit-ment, but especially the financial contributions of these frontier and urban Catholics, the establishment of the Church on such a broad level could never have progressed with the remarkable steadiness and increase that typified its de-velopment.

Representative of the first century's success in directing Catholic Church growth in the United States was the "consecrated blizzard of the northwest," John Ireland (1838-1918), a French-educated Irish immigrant who became Bishop of St. Paul in 1884. Like his frontier pioneers, Ireland's aim was to build strong American Catholic communities. Even from his early days, both his energy and his eloquence were directed toward this end. As a young priest Ireland had be-come particularly interested in forming colonization projects that would bring Irish immigrants to the Midwest. As president of the Minnesota Irish Emigra-tion Society in the 1860's, for example, he worked, albeit without notable suc-cess, to encourage the migration of east coast Irish-Americans; at least four thousand families did settle in western Minnesota and Nebraska as a result of such efforts. Yet, perhaps because Ireland was so committed to the American dream, he never seemed to see himself (or to be seen) as an immigrant, certainly not as one handicapped by that status. To the contrary, his Irish background may even have made him all the more adamant about adapting his Church to the American setting and all the more able to begin a new cultural identity in the United States. So sure was Ireland of the promise of the new land and so much did he want his people to move along paths compatible with American senti-ments that he even evaluated his coworkers along the same lines. Referring on one occasion to the Dominican Samuel Mazzuchelli, another immigrant whose frontier-building projects in Wisconsin and Michigan were equally ambitious, as "a foreigner by birth" who was an "American to the tips of his fingers," Ireland unconsciously revealed the degree to which responding to the American envi-ronment and being perceived as an American were the significant test of a true American missionary.[1] His view typified a mentality shared by other like-minded Catholic leaders during the first century of church life in the United States.

The ability to see themselves as both Catholics and Americans was, in fact, often demonstrated by immigrant Catholics in the first century of the Church's development in the United States. No wonder that Irish immigrants whose facile

---

[1]Theodore Maynard, *Great Catholics in American History* (Garden City, NY, 1957), p. 179.

use of the English language allowed them to adapt more quickly to the bustling environment of the nation's cities generally appropriated the term "American," felt it their right to assume leadership positions especially in the Church, and thought it correct to compliment their fellow immigrant Catholics on the basis of their adaptability to American standards. With greater restraint, even those whose halting English revealed their German, French, Dutch or Belgian roots, often tried to do the same. Although their handicap of language and cultural difference often helped them to understand that Catholic "foreigners" would have to wait more patiently, they, too, pressed on undaunted, often mimicking American ways in their attempt to become part of the American community. Is this the reason, for example, the famed immigrant saint and acknowledged linguist, John Nepomucene Neumann, was willing to be known as "Father Newman" in his early days as a Redemptorist missionary priest in Baltimore, a fact made more significant by its repetition and use as garnered from a variety of contemporary sources, including a marble commemorative plaque still decorating one wall of St. Peter's Basilica in Rome?[1] Like Neumann or Ireland, nineteenth-century American Catholics, missionaries, founders or parishioners generally followed a similar broadminded perspective with regard to accommodating the new land. Convinced that the religion they adhered to was expansive and could only serve to create a better nation, they worked to become as much a part of American society as those for whom they labored.

The American perspective of the immigrant clergy clearly did much to win a hearing for the Catholic Church in the United States in its first hundred years of development. So great was the good impression that the French émigré priest and first Bishop of Boston, Jean Louis de Cheverus, made upon that Yankee stronghold that even within the first few years of his administration he was able to convince some of the most biased of Boston's Brahmin society to support him in the organization of his Church. One observer wrote of the "marvelous concessions" Cheverus wrought from a society more accustomed to viewing the aims of a priest, as Carroll once put it, as emanating from "the greatest monster in creation."[2] Even President John Adams, for example, felt impelled to contribute to Cheverus' fund-raising project for the building of Boston's Cathedral. In Kentucky, Benedict J. Flaget, appointed Bishop of Bardstown at the same time Cheverus was named for Boston, took on the parallel task of evangelizing the frontier with equal zeal and received, in turn, a similar respect for the solid foundation of the Church west of the Alleghenies.

Other immigrant missionaries of broad vision and ability were able to gain a hearing and interpret the faith in previously hostile settings further west and southwest. Three bishops who fit this description were John M. Okin (1801-1861) whose missionary field was Texas; Joseph Sadoc Alemany, O.P. (1814-

---

[1] Annals, ACB, on Neumann's first visit to the Carmel, he is referred to in this way, a mistake subsequently corrected; his name was pronounced that way by other religious communities with whom he worked.

[2] See details of Cheverus' ministry in Benedict Joseph Fenwick, S.J., *Memories to Serve the Future,* ed., Joseph M. McCarthy (Yonkers, NY, 1978), pp. 145-156. Regarding Carroll, who often referred to the anti-Catholicism he experienced, see James H. O'Donnell, *History of the Diocese of Hartford* (Boston, 1900), p. 116.

1888) of California, and John Baptist Lamy (1814-1888) of New Mexico. All three could be described, as Alemany later was by his biographer, as men in "sympathy with American ideas and principles."[1]   In Lamy's case, his promulgation of the 1854 proceedings of the Baltimore Second Plenary Council put him immediately at odds with the indigenous Spanish clergy who considered this action as interfering with their patronizing way of ministering to Santa Fe's Catholics. To others his aim was merely an educational one, done with the hope that he could move the new diocese more closely into the ambit of the U.S. Church.[2] In California, the Spanish-born Alemany was particularly noted for his commitment to American ways. His recruitment of the Daughters of Charity from Emmitsburg, Maryland, in 1852 and of the Sisters of Mercy who arrived from Carlow, Ireland, in 1854 indicated his desire to make the Church immediately present to his fellow Californians in the days of goldrush fever in booming San Francisco. On his behalf, both religious communities bore witness to the belief that the Church must reach out and adapt to American circumstances. Within a year after their arrival, for example, the Sisters of Mercy were making visitations to the sick poor, as well as to the county hospital and jail, and were providing health care generally. In fact their skillful response to the raging cholera epidemic of 1854 is still pointed to as an important milestone in the acceptance of the Catholic Church in California.[3]

Sometimes Catholic missionaries even proved their appreciation for and adaptability to American ways by accepting leadership roles in the political or social aspects of frontier organization. The French-born Sulpician, Gabriel Richard, who ministered in the outpost territories north and west of Ohio from 1792 until 1832, provides one example of a missionary response that was both Catholic and American. Richard's first mission was among the Indians of Illinois and Michigan. But it was not long before he was drawn to the Detroit area where he became involved in improving the education of Detroit's Catholic immigrants. This experience then led him to a leading role in championing the efforts of some of the city's most prominent citizens in crucial issues of the day, some with regard to the continued education of its entire citizenry. Because of his efforts, the state's first plan for higher education was developed; he is credited with cofounding the University of Michigan in 1817. His organizational and leadership qualities directed him to other civic projects; in each of these his ability as a polemicist served him well. Finally, after becoming a citizen in 1823, he became so associated with politics as a ministry that Michigan elected him as territorial delegate to the U.S. House of Representatives.[4]

[1]John Bernard McGloin, S.J., *California's First Archbishop: The Life of Joseph Sadoc Alemany, 1814-1888* (New York, 1966), p. 363.

[2]This thesis is developed in Frances M. Campbell, "American Catholicism in Northern New Mexico: A Kaleidoscope of Development, 1840-1850" (Ph.D. dissertation, Graduate Theological Union, University of California at Berkeley, 1985).

[3]See Sister Rose McArdle, S.M., *Mercy Undaunted: 125 Years in California* (Burlingame, 1979), *passim.*

[4]George Pare, *The Catholic Church in Detroit: 1701-1888* (Detroit, Michigan, 1951), pp. 317-318.

Farther west, the Slovenian immigrant, Frederic Baraga (1797-1868), exemplified the same ability and interest in offering his talents in affairs of state. His first work was among the Ottawa Indians of Arbre Croche mission (Michigan) yet he never saw this work as isolating him from the larger white American society. From the time of his arrival in 1830, he not only relished the challenge presented to him but he encouraged a steady stream of Slovenian missionaries to become involved as well. His mastery of Indian languages (he composed the first Chippewa grammar and dictionary) brought him into dialogue with federal officials who called upon him to assist them as intermediary and advocate of his Indian friends. It was a work Baraga would be connected with even after he became Bishop of Marquette and, later, Sault Ste. Marie. Another Slovenian, Francis Pirc, also concentrated his effort on improving the quality of Indian life; because of the inoculations he provided Indians, smallpox epidemics and cholera outbreaks were both greatly reduced. When later Slovenian missionaries modelled themselves after Baraga and Pirc, they also had to become multi-talented missionaries: preachers, teachers, Indian advocates, promoters of the Northwest territories and of the American frontier optimism.[1]

Examples similar to Baraga's abound concerning other European immigrant missionaries. Much publicity surrounded the career of the Belgian Jesuit, Pierre DeSmet, whose ability to negotiate the wilderness earned him the title "Apostle of Kansas, Oregon and the Rockies." Not only did DeSmet establish missions and successfully recruit missionary priests and sisters (it was he who brought the Sisters of Notre Dame de Namur to Oregon) but he also gained importance in secular circles as a publicist, chronicler and peace commissioner. What of the less well-known but also amazing work of French- and German-based communities of women whose members also volunteered for the missions in America? In 1840 Mother Theodore Guerin, together with five companions, led a group of the Sisters of Providence from France to answer the call of Bishop Celestin de la Hailandiere (1798-1882) to found a convent in Vincennes (Indianapolis). Although first inspired by news of an "exotic country populated by savages" she and her community went to work to the point of constant exhaustion because there was an "immense field for evangelization and education." Philippine Duchesne, American cofounder of the Religious of the Sacred Heart, devoted successful years in the urban apostolate of education at St. Louis, and still went on to do the work that had originally inspired her move to the United States in the 1820's. At 71, although unable to learn the Potawatomi language because of her advanced years, she volunteered for the mission at Sugar Creek, Kansas, where she hoped to begin a school for the Indians.[2]

---

[1] Adele K. Donchencko, "Slovene Missionaries in the Upper Midwest," in *The Other Catholics,* ed. Keith P. Dyrud, Michael Novak and Rudolph J. Vecoli (New York, 1978), pp. 1-21.

[2] On Guerin, see Mary Ewens, O.P., "The Leadership of Nuns in Immigrant Catholicism," in *Women and Religion in American, Vol I: The Nineteenth Century, A Documentary History,* ed. Rosemary Radford Ruether and Rosemary Skinner Keller (San Francisco, 1981), pp. 115-122; see also Joseph N. Tylenda, S.J., *Portraits in American Sanctity* (Chicago, 1982), pp. 146ff, and Maynard, *op. cit.,* p. 145.

Regardless of what country they immigrated from or where they labored, those clergy and religious men and women who answered the missionary call to serve the struggling nineteenth-century Church in the United States remained flexible and adaptable to the situations they discovered. Whether they worked directly with Catholics who did not speak English (German-Americans were the major recipients of this special treatment) or were allowed to venture forth to evangelize the Indians and develop frontier Catholicism, these immigrant builders of the American Church performed their tasks with great openness and resourcefulness. Despite disruptive economic crises that sometimes compromised their chances for acceptance, they guided the Catholic Church's continued expansion into new dioceses and created a variety of educational and health care institutions. During the Civil War, moreover, their reputation as loyal Americans became so enhanced by the supportive role they played that the future of the Church as an approved religious institution grew stronger than ever. At the war's end, in fact, Catholics rightly sensed the first fruits of the recognition for which their leaders had worked. In a reunified nation, they could, for the first time, savor the fruits of the many long-suffering efforts to adapt to the new surroundings.

As the second century of American Catholicism began in the reconstruction years, a more self-assured and unified Catholic community began to emerge. This was particularly obvious on the episcopal level where Irish-Americans were more numerous and most vocal. When the bishops met in plenary session at Baltimore in 1866, the congratulatory theme that reflected the posture that had brought them successfully to this moment of history was repeated by many participants. Sermon after lengthy sermon reminded Catholics of "the beauty of the Catholic Church in the United States which knows 'no nationality'...or...'no color or caste'." According to the presiding Archbishop, Martin J. Spalding of Baltimore, they were also fully aware that "...the land of Washington, affording a common nationality to the children of every clime, has become the home of men of many different nations."[1] For many, a turning point seemed inevitable in their relationship with American society. Some realized that Catholic opportunities had been enhanced; many expected that their way of accommodating people of different nationalities would find greater acceptance as well. What both Americans and church leaders failed to envision, however, was that nationality and color were to become increasingly divisive categories for Americans in general. Moreover, few understood that dissension, discord and even schism would accelerate within Catholic dioceses. In the rapidly urbanizing and industrializing post-war world, the hard-earned cohesiveness that had enhanced the Catholic image was to be once again undermined. But this time, the main cause would be the Church's constantly growing multi-ethnic, immigrant population.

Predominantly from traditionally Catholic areas of the Italian, Austro-Hungarian and Russian empires, the new and burgeoning appearance of Catholic membership in the postbellum world did more than renew Protestant xenopho-

---

[1] *Sermons Delivered During the Second Plenary Council of Baltimore, 1866 and Pastoral Letter of the Hierarchy of the United States Together with the Papal Rescript and Letters of Councils: A Complete List of Dignitaries and Officers of the Council* (Baltimore, 1866), p. 11.

bia. Especially in the decades surrounding 1900, when tens of thousands of expectant immigrants poured into the ghettoes of the nation's cities in search of jobs, Catholic leaders had to face the consequences of the dramatic changes that were occurring within their own ranks as well. The illiteracy, lack of social and occupational skills, and overall unsuitability of these newcomers especially disturbed those Irish-Americans who had, themselves, only recently risen from economic and, sometimes, social degradation. While eager to respond to their needs and include them in their midst, most church leaders found themselves at a loss to know how to handle a situation made more complex by their own newfound acceptance among Americans. As the twentieth century began and U.S. Catholics also found themselves challenged by Roman officials on the basis of so-called Americanist tendencies, any attempts to make the Church generally acceptable became more and more problematic. A second stage of the immigrant Catholic Church was in the making; it would be chiefly characterized by attempts to come to terms with the complicating factor of the multi-ethnicity of its membership.

Those bishops whose dioceses had been organized in the northeast and midwest industrial areas of the United States were the most affected by the crisis of incorporation. Sometimes they established parishes along the simple pattern set during Carroll's administration with respect to Philadelphia and New York Germans or developed models similar to the ones begun for German-speaking Catholics of St. Louis and Cincinnati. After 1884, however, when the organization of parishes for other foreign-language speaking Catholics was implicitly approved by those assembled at the Third Plenary Council, the nation's bishops began to rely upon national parishes as their favored means of providing for newcomers.[1] As a result, even by the first decade of the twentieth century, hundreds of Polish and Italian, as well as scores of Slovak, Lithuanian, Hungarian, Ruthenian and Greek-rite parishes were begun, especially in the northeastern and midwestern corridors of the nation. As these parishes proliferated, the common elements previously experienced by Catholic parishioners regardless of their different European backgrounds were weakened. If the stratification and multiplication of churches along ethnic lines had come about because ethnic differentiation seemed a necessary expedient, the decision also raised problematic considerations that would plague the Church for another century.

In the twentieth century the landscape of most of the nation's largest cities gave vivid witness to the dramatic changes of demography and to the implications of second stage immigrant Catholic life. The first-founded Catholic parishes stood within the heart of the central city; these were staffed primarily by Irish-American priests assisted by congregations of religious women and men who took charge of education and health ministries for Catholics in general. Several other Catholic Churches surrounded these parishes. Distinct styles of architecture, different languages, and colorfully diverse liturgical and devotional

---

[1] See Joseph E. Ciesluk, "National Parishes in the United States," *The Catholic University of America, Canon Law Studies,* No. 190 (Washington, DC, 1944), *passim.* Ciesluk has written the definitive monograph on the development of the national parish from the medieval European experiences to its American metamorphosis.

practices set one congregation off from the other, all contrasting sharply with the original territorial parish. The so-called "Irish" Churches retained their positions of dominance within the total picture but national parishes took on the appearance of quasi-kingdoms. Within these ethnic parishes, immigrant pastors provided every aspect of spiritual and temporal care and received in turn the undivided loyalty of their parishioners. Sometimes the separation between parishes was impermeable; an implicit agreement between pastors and bishop meant there would be no interference, providing orthodoxy of faith and practice was assured. An array of buildings and organizations, including churches, rectories, schools and social clubs, gave public testimony to the competing variety of people and services. Side by side, the different aims and needs of every Catholic group were pursued and addressed. By thus sacrificing symbolic unity, millions of newcomers were enabled to practice their Catholic faith.

If the rationale for the creation of this patchwork of ethnic parishes was simple, the results were far more complicated and complex. For one thing, contradictory messages were inevitable. Could Catholic leaders, for example, demand that the Catholic Church in the United States be perceived as a thoroughly American institution when they allowed separate parishes? Could an Irish-American leadership acknowledge the immigrants' need for special treatment and yet, at the same time work toward their adaptation to American Catholic culture in this separatist fashion? Would church leaders ever be able to move immigrant parishes into greater cultural harmony with American society if they allowed them to remain national parishes? Could bishops be sure that the clergy they recruited to staff national parishes would be acceptable to immigrants yet loyal to the diocese? If bishops and minority Catholics accepted national parishes as a way of being Catholic, could they come to a consensus about other measures of incorporating immigrants fully? Furthermore, what of those immigrants who might prefer to attend territorial parishes: would they be made to adjust to Irish-American patterns where they risked the displeasure of pastor and congregation? And finally, how were American bishops and immigrants to bridge the separate but equal worlds they were creating?

Fewer and fewer satisfactory answers seemed to be forthcoming as the development of the Church of the second century progressed. Through it all, the image of the Catholic Church as an immigrant and separatist community became more sharply etched; in this milieu, Catholics began to see themselves and one another in ethnic categories as well. So close were ethnicity and religious consciousness joined in the minds of American Catholics as the new century dawned, and so often was ethno-religious identification spelled out in the social context that it became increasingly impossible to discuss twentieth-century Catholicism without situating the particular diocese, parish, congregation, individual Catholic or special issue under study within its ethnic framework. Unlike earlier times when immigrants blended more naturally into the overall fabric of American Catholic life, the immigrant Catholic Church had finally become a clearly defined reality. In the twentieth century, the Church was to be identified, not so much for its striving to be American, but by the distinct and separate ethnic patterns that had come to characterize it.

The predominant pattern that defined American Catholicism was the one set by Irish-Americans. That their ethnic perspectives would become the most influential in the shaping of the American Catholic community was not so much based upon their predominance in numbers, even though Irish-Americans ranked almost evenly with Germans as the most numerous among nineteenth-century immigrants to the United States. Nor was their priority position a matter of years of experience in the New World, despite the fact that the Irish were among the first to arrive in large numbers. Rather it was a combination of personality traits that gave the Irish the collective edge in influencing American Catholicism. Thus, their strong religious convictions coupled with certain personality traits ensured Irish-Americans the advantage within the multi-ethnic patchwork of American Catholicism.

Irish immigrants had come to this country determined to practice a faith made especially precious because of the centuries of religious and political persecution they had endured. They looked upon the promise of the new nation as both salvific and challenging. Fluency in the English language, charming affability and a gregariousness that turned away prejudice gained them an immediate advantage; these continued as important factors in getting Irish immigrants through the initial stages of settlement. But their great faith, their practical intelligence, their penchant for dramatic oratory, as well as their organizational skills, were the key factors in making them the right people at the right time to find the right task to which to commit their energies. In the last quarter of the nineteenth century Irish-Americans were already poised to take charge of the U.S. Catholic Church.

That they had in fact been sent on "a spiritual errand into the wilderness" had been observed as early as 1884 by Rochester's Bernard J. McQuaid (1823-1909). In a speech he delivered during one session of the Third Plenary Council, McQuaid announced:

> The first immigrants coming in large numbers were from Ireland. Of all the people of Europe they were the best fitted to open the way for religion in a new country. Brave by nature, inured to poverty and hardship, just released from a struggle unto death for their faith, accustomed to the practice of religion in its simplest forms, cherishing dearly their priests whom they had learned to support directly, actively engaged in building humble chapels on the sites of ruined churches and in replacing altars, they were not appalled by the wretchedness of religious equipments and surroundings in their new homes on this side of the Atlantic.[1]

John Lancaster Spalding also saw Irish-Americans as in command of the religious mission to the American people. In his introduction to a book on that subject, he proclaimed without qualification:

> The general truth is that the Irish Catholics are the most important element in the Church of this country....Were it not for Ireland Catholicism would today be feeble and non-progressive in England, America and Australia....No other people...could have done for the Catholic faith in the United States what the Irish people have done...No other people had received the same providential

[1]*Memorials of the Third Plenary Council*, p. 12.

training for this work; of no other people had God required such proofs of love.[1]

If flattered by such praise, the Irish did not seem in need of the rhetoric of either McQuaid or Spalding. They believed in their own ability to take charge of the mission in which American Catholics were supposed to engage. Within the first generation of large-scale Irish immigration they had already demonstrated their interest in, and attraction to, the Church. In large numbers they had entered seminaries and religious communities; by 1880 even the majority of the episcopal leadership was Irish-American. Twenty years later, Irish-American bishops held all the seats of ecclesiastical power in Catholic dioceses from New York to San Francisco. By then, too, not only did Irish-Americans hold a preponderance among the clergy but the numbers of religious women had also greatly expanded largely because of Irish-American aspirants.[2] Communities from Ireland, such as the Sisters of Mercy, also experienced phenomenal growth, but even communities of French, German or Belgian origin, such as the Sisters of St. Joseph or the Sisters of Notre Dame de Namur, were early Americanized (or Hibernicized) by the increase of numbers through Irish-American vocations. These religious women became the chief organizers of schools and hospitals, the ubiquitous and cherished "co-workers" of bishops and priests who saw them, as John Ireland did, as ranking "among the Church's choicest and most valuable agencies."[3] This great reservoir of labor that Irish-American women and men provided was highly influential in shaping the direction of the Church to come.

The special gifts of Irish-American Catholics to the Church of the United States have been well-acknowledged. The institutional strength of the twentieth-century Church was largely brought about by the business acumen and organizational skills of Irish-American clergy and religious who knew how to turn the generosity of the Catholic membership to profit the Church directly. A "bricks-and-mortar" mentality, nurtured by Irish-American leadership, pervaded diocesan chanceries; it provided an example for every group within the Church to follow. Parishes and Catholic institutions multiplied. A parochial school system matured under the direction of a talented Irish-American pool of diocesan superintendents and members of boards of education. By 1900 there were 3,811 grammar schools with more than 850,000 students, and there were 63 Catholic colleges as well. Catholic benefactors like Nicholas Devereux, Edward and John Creighton or Mary Gwendolyn Caldwell made possible the inauguration of St. Bonaventure (New York), Creighton University (Omaha), and Catholic University (District of Columbia).[4] The fortunes of others helped ensure the networks of charity organizations and more specifically the establishment of the more than two hundred fifty Catholic hospitals by 1900. Almost an institution-building hysteria set in during subsequent decades, often dramatically launched by Irish-

---

[1]John Lancaster Spalding, *The Religious Mission of the Irish People* (New York, 1880), introduction.

[2]Liptak, *op. cit.,* pp. 81ff.

[3]Helen Angela Hurley, *On Good Ground: The Story of the Sisters of St. Joseph in St. Paul* (Minneapolis, 1951), p. 225.

[4]Hennesey, *op. cit.,* p. 187.

American bishops and fed by the philanthropy of other ethnic Irish Catholics. In his first ten years as Archbishop of Philadelphia, for example, Dennis Dougherty called upon the wealthy of his diocese when he opened 92 parishes, 89 parish schools, 3 diocesan high schools, 14 academies, a women's college and a preparatory seminary.[1] Other fortunes, including those of the former United States Senator James D. Phelan, or of the religious founder of the Sisters of the Blessed Sacrament, Katharine Drexel, and of the papal duchess, Genevieve Garvan Brady (Macauley), were diverted by church officials to the numerous educational and social philanthropic projects of the day.[2]

The social reform priorities and strategies for which the U.S. Catholic Church is still known also had the special touch of Irish-Americans. Their efforts were apparent from the days when the Irish political refugee and editor of the *Boston Pilot,* John Boyle O'Reilly (1844-1890), inspired one generation of Catholic readers to the Progressive and New Deal reform leadership era influenced by Monsignor John A. Ryan (1869-1945). Voices on behalf of social justice came from such grass-roots labor leaders as Elizabeth Rogers, Leonora Barry and the more controversial Terence Powderly, whose presidency of the first national labor union, the Knights of Labor, became problematic to certain American bishops. They were echoed in the 1890's by charismatic diocesan clergy like Edward McGlynn and Sylvester Malone, whose radical views also became suspect to some of the more conservative non-Irish bishops.[3]

After the turn of the century, the impetus to articulate and work toward social and labor reform derived from a still wider range of laymen and clergy and included bishops of the calibre of Cincinnati's John T. McNicholas (1877-1950), Detroit's Edward F. Mooney (1882-1958), Chicago's Bernard J. Sheil (1888-1969) and San Antonio's Robert E. Lucey (1891-1977). Because of this long line of social action-oriented Irish-American pioneers, generations of Catholics became involved in local and national labor movements as members and organizers. If they were ultimately not evaluated as radical forgers of social or labor politics, these leaders had at least promoted a respect for social reconstruction that did endure, one that strongly urged American Catholics to become involved in the social and economic crises of their times.[4]

Irish-American ethnicity also helped to create the moralistic caricature by which the U.S. Catholic Church was especially known during the second stage of the Church's immigrant history. As a result of their tendency to prefer the spoken over the sung word, for one thing, liturgical worship, as well as spiritual and devotional practices, reflected a somewhat somber ceremonial style, albeit one which always made room for oratorical display. Moreover, the Irish penchant for certain rigid Jansenistic interpretations of morality tended to control Catholics in general and even intruded into the lives of other Americans. The Legion of Decency of the 1930's and 1940's which aimed at protecting Catholics from "morally objectionable films" was but one twentieth-century manifestation

---

[1] *Ibid.*, p. 237.
[2] *Ibid.*, p. 239.
[3] Liptak, *op. cit.*, p. 88.
[4] *Ibid.*

of this mentality that had broader social ramifications. The movement was guided by Irish-Americans, such as Martin J. Quigley, a Catholic trade publisher, and Daniel A. Lord, S.J.; its impact was to affect American Catholic life into the 1960's, not only retarding the development of the movie as an art form but more especially limiting the way in which the Catholic Church was perceived by Americans.[1]

Ironically, one particular characteristic of the Irish-American mentality that was also operative during the second phase of Catholic development in the United States eventually mitigated their predominance by allowing a kind of ethnic distinctiveness previously inexperienced in the American Catholic Church. As has been pointed out, from their secure positions of ecclesiastical power, the Irish-American leadership deliberately planned for the establishment of national parishes as an acceptable way of including the newest strangers in the land. One cannot judge the motivations behind such decisions but it is possible to suggest that the rationale was "catholic" in the broadest sense of the word, and specifically influenced by the natural tendency of the Irish, as a gregarious people, to value diversity. This was clearly demonstrated in the rhetoric of contemporary Irish-American sermons and newspaper articles that consistently reported and even celebrated the growing ethnic distinctiveness within the Church.[2] Regardless of motive, however, it is clear that the business of incorporating new immigrants went on earnestly and with considerable good will at the hands of Irish-Americans during the heyday of massive immigration, despite a growing national trend toward decrying the "foreign invasion." Moreover, the practice of the accommodation of newcomers often occurred despite the ever-present possibility of discord and dissension. To be sure, some myopic church leaders exacerbated sensitive issues; on the other hand, immigrants and their spokesmen were also guilty of antagonizing or needlessly complicating their stated aims. Unfortunately, the negative results of some of these efforts to care for immigrants tended to obscure the successful efforts of Irish-Americans in this regard.

Recent investigations concerning the actions of church personnel during this period, however, have revealed a record that demonstrates that strategies for the inclusion of immigrants were specifically initiated by Irish-American bishops. These cannot simply be ignored. In the Diocese of Hartford, Connecticut, for example, serious attempts to find clergy for German and French-Canadian immigrants began with the native-born son of Irish immigrants, Francis Patrick McFarland (1819-1874); his aims were more systematically pursued by an immigrant from Ireland, Bishop Michael Tierney (1839-1908). During Tierney's administration (1894-1908), a publicized diocesan strategy was consistently engaged to assist the tens of thousands of southern and eastern European immigrants that poured into Connecticut. In the Midwest, three of Chicago's Irish-American bishops, Thomas Foley (1870-1879), Patrick Augustine Feehan (1880-1902) and James Edward Quigley (1903-1915), also manifested a determined approach toward easing the plight of new eastern and southern European

---

[1]*Ibid.*, p. 89.

[2]Example of this can be seen in Liptak "European Immigrants and the Catholic Church in Connecticut" (Ph.D. dissertation, University of Connecticut, 1978), especially pp. 206-215; pp. 386-388.

immigrants. Quigley's insistence upon the naming of the Polish-born American, Paul Rhode, to be his auxiliary bishop (representing the first appointment of a Pole to the ranks of the U.S. hierarchy) is a case in point.[1]

There was, of course, the better-known darker side to immigrant assistance and incorporation. In a number of dioceses, including Cleveland, Detroit, and Portland (Maine), German, Polish, and French-Canadian immigrants, respectively, experienced a general sense of rejection and second-class status because of either Irish-American episcopal preferences or diocesan regulations that compromised their inclusion. Where notable successes occurred and the pattern of accommodation endured, ethnic distinctiveness did take shape and multi-ethnic Catholicism became a reality. Especially in those dioceses where there was a commitment to immigrants, it became a gift to be celebrated and a colorful attribute by which the Church proudly identified itself. As a result of the admittedly limited efforts at the hands of a predominantly Irish-American hierarchy, the clear lines of the twentieth-century multi-ethnic Church were forged.[2]

Because of their advantageous situation, Irish-Americans were not only first able to influence the cultural expression of American Catholicism according to their own preferences but they also became the ones to successfully negotiate solutions to the pressing problem of immigration. If appreciation for diversity and openness to accommodate can be attributed to Irish-Americans as factors in easing the situation for immigrants and their Church, it must also be stated that, in some respects at least, their leadership alone had not made the successful inclusion of immigrants a reality. To a great extent, finding an appropriate solution to the immigrant crisis was a matter that had to become the focus of attention in every Catholic circle. Close beside Irish-Americans in terms of comparable numbers and years of settlement in the United States were the German-Americans. Gradually they too were drawn into a prominent role with regard to what some would call the "immigrant problem." A self-possessed and powerful Catholic immigrant group, German-Americans literally became the conscience of Irish-Americans. Because German-American needs for inclusion dictated an agenda that differed from the one set by the Irish-dominated hierarchy and clergy, they were to provide a challenging alternative to the Irish-American style of governance, attitude toward their adopted land, practice of faith, and especially, response to new membership.

Since colonial times, German-American Catholics had made clear that they considered it appropriate to express their faith differently than other American Catholics. Then, as in the early years of the republic, they practiced their faith in a manner that more closely reflected the liturgical and devotional life of their European forebears. During the Continental Congress meetings in revolutionary Philadelphia, the Yankee John Adams acknowledged the power of their devotional life; he commented on the spell cast by their emotion-laden ceremonies

---

[1] See Liptak, *European Immigrants and the Catholic Church in Connecticut* (Staten Island, 1987), on Tierney; and Charles Shanabruch, *Chicago's Catholics: The Evolution of an American Identity* (Notre Dame, 1981), on three Chicago bishops.

[2] Among numerous articles and monographs on the darker side is Dryud, Novak, Vecoli, eds., *The Other Catholics, passim.*

when he made his first visit to "grandmother church" in 1774.[1] Impressed with
the capacity of devotion exhibited by faithful Germans, John Carroll described
one such Pennsylvania community as "our most excellent and incomparable
German Brethren."[2] But as the population of Germans multiplied after the mid-
nineteenth century, a number of their leaders became more and more vocal about
protecting their ethnic Catholic needs in a Protestant society and even among
Catholics. Concerned that close conformity to American educational or cultural
patterns might jeopardize the faith of their fathers, for example, they pressed the
American hierarchy toward specific goals. But it was not until German-Americans numbered almost one-fourth of the U.S. Catholic population in 1870 that
they took a collective stand with regard to their place within the Church as well.
If their advancement of the Catholic school system became one of their chief
means of furthering their aims to safeguard the Catholic faith among Protestants
(95% of German parishes saw to the establishment of schools), then their pressure with regard to inclusion on every level within the ranks of the clergy were
steps they took to protect their place within the Church. In that way, they believed that their religious convictions could affect change with regard to both society and church.[3]

Perhaps because doubly concerned about influences that could deprive them
of their religious and cultural heritage, German-American Catholics tended to reinforce their Catholic, rather than their American, identity. As a result, in their
daily affairs, the parish, rather than the political meeting or the marketplace, became a preferred domain; within that setting, they found the protective environment that provided the needed freedom to express their Catholicity. The
German-American preference for a faith-community approach to life in the
United States took an even more determined direction as the nation's bishops,
priests and personnel became increasingly Hibernicized. Then, the twin fears
that either Protestant Germans or Irish-American Catholics could deprive German-Americans of the right to live by their religious tenets or express their faith
in their customary cultural style became the rationale for greater defensiveness.

Preferring to organize for economic and social reform in networks of *Vereine*
and to nurture their faith within the framework of their parish community, the
Germans became the first among ethnic Catholics to express their belief that
special status was not only good but that it was essential if Catholics were to
remain faithful in the American milieu. By the *fin de siècle*, German-Americans
had become a model to newly-arriving immigrant groups of how to adjust to a
Church whose assumption of American ways threatened to alienate them from
some aspects of faith expression with which they intended to identify.

The many positive consequences of the German-American struggle for their
proper place within the U.S. Catholic community are well-known. Their contributions to the Church range from such external manifestations as their traditional and painstakingly beautiful rendering of liturgical and paraliturgical services, to musical concerts and artistic display. Within national parishes, from

---

[1]Quoted in Hennesey, *op. cit.*, p. 62.

[2]*Ibid.*, p. 74.

[3]Liptak, *Immigrants and Their Church*, p. 96.

Baltimore to San Francisco, German-Americans consistently demonstrated their desire to share with one another the intimacy and beauty of their faith. Their serious application to the intellectual life contributed significantly to the field of Catholic education. Moreover, the sense of religious community that German-American parishes fostered through both schools and social service organizations helped to strengthen diocesan efforts to assist Catholics even as it brought psychological and spiritual renewal to those exiled by the political upheavals of the *Kulturkampf* or to the generations that followed. Especially in rural America and within the midwest "German triangle" of cities, German-American Catholics united through religious observance to their faith and their people; thus strengthened, they provided a Catholic example to the community at large. Even when twentieth-century Germans no longer stressed ethnicity as a necessary means for survival in the American setting, the model they had set endured.

In some respects, then, it can be suggested that the overall pattern in the American Catholic design had been woven by the contrasting threads of Irish- and German-American people. To the Irish warp of threads, the German had become the opposing threads; knit together, they created the broad design of the ethnic pattern of American Catholicism. Without the fabric spun by these contrasting shapers of the U.S. Catholic community the specific designs of minority Catholics could never have been as sharply focused. Because of them, the special gifts of Slavic and Italian immigrant Catholics found legitimacy within the American setting. Either singly or joined into the one design, the patterns they wove became as much a part of the U.S. Church as those first set by the Irish- or German-Americans.

How each immigrant group reflected the design already set has been the subject of much historical investigation. For our purposes, a brief review of the Polish-American experience will serve as one example of what was repeated to some degree by every ethnic Catholic minority seeking admission to the Church.

Polish-Americans were among the most numerous of latter-day immigrants expecting to be accommodated by American Catholics. Because of their rapid and overwhelming increase in numbers during the years of massive immigration and because of the characteristic firmness with which they held on to their "Polish kind of faith," they challenged the Irish-American majority in the Church to provide both special treatment and separate status. Their pattern would especially echo the experience of other new immigrants from the Austro-Hungarian and Russian empires. Early disenchanted by the way bishops and pastors provided for them, the Poles became perhaps the most severe of the church's critics with regard to their concern for fellow Catholics.

Despite fears or disappointments, however, Polish-American Catholics worked to establish themselves as members of the U.S. Catholic Church in ways that eventually had both positive and negative effects in the overall creation of the U.S. Catholic Church. Contributing generously to the creation of their own parishes, they manifested such a commitment to their faith that they often "edified" the more established Catholics by their "energy, thrift, and spirit of sacrifice."[1] If their parishes sometimes resembled fiefdoms with their pastors serving as autocratic princes, parishioners still preferred to attach themselves

---

[1]*The Catholic Transcript,* Hartford, Connecticut, July 11, 1907.

with fierce loyalty to these supportive communities. Especially in Illinois, Michigan, New York, New Jersey, Connecticut and Pennsylvania, authorized immigrant pastors ruled over parishioners with exacting discipline. A milieu of devotional and sacramental observance assured an uprooted people that they would be among God's saved. Legendary pastorates developed in factory communities from New Britain, Connecticut's Sacred Heart Parish under Monsignor Lucyan Bojnowski, to the circle of parishes in Chicago founded by the Resurrectionist, Vincent Barzynski. Mining towns in Pennsylvania cradled Polish culture in more intimate parish meetings. The presence of dynamic pastors prevailed over entire Polish communities. The famed Barzynski, for example, became the solitary genius behind the foundation of an astounding range of enterprises among Chicago's Polish community. Under him, a gigantic community system flourished. His own parish numbered some 60,000 members and administered the nation's largest Polish parochial school. Among other organizations also managed by Barzynski were the first Polish-American Catholic paper (and the first Polish daily in the United States), a national fraternal organization, an orphanage and a home for the aged.[1]

But when Polish-Americans believed their needs were slighted, the negative consequences of separatism became more apparent. Then they could act in as demanding a way as had the Germans. In fact their protests often went beyond expectations, spilling over to civil and diocesan levels. Eventually they brought their grievances to officials outside their local sphere, seemingly eager to apprise either the apostolic delegate or officials at Rome of real or imagined neglect on the part of Irish-American bishops. In a style reminiscent of the 1890's written protests of German spokesmen, Polish-Americans such as Peter Cahensly and Peter Abbelen also reacted, but they seemed even more able to go beyond words. Their "riotous behavior" divided parishes and caused humiliation or embarrassment to all parties concerned. Bitterness and frustration existed on every level but it was most keenly experienced by the Polish-American clergy who formalized their concerns in a memorial sent to Rome in 1920. In it, they argued that greater representation on the episcopal level was the chief way to change the disadvantageous plight of their people. In that way their mission "to keep alive the faith" in the new land would be made possible; only in that way was the "conservation of the Catholic religion" among Polish immigrants assured.[2]

The demand for inclusion into the mainstream of the Church's social and hierarchical framework would go largely unfulfilled, like every demand of Polish-Americans before it. Polish-Americans continued to be grossly under-utilized in chancery and episcopal positions in the nation's dioceses just as Polish laity found that they were often relegated to second-class status among fellow Catholics. In fact, the main consolation Polish-American clergy and laity had in their twentieth-century experience within the U.S. Catholic Church was that some in authority understood, appreciated and, sometimes, promoted them. Even then, their only reassurance was that the cultural and religious needs of their people would be attended to and honored within the separate world of national parishes.

[1]Liptak, *Immigrants and Their Church,* pp. 119-122.
[2]*Ibid.,* p. 127.

Unfortunately, the experience of Polish-Americans was repeated with regard to every other ethnic minority group within the Church during the second-stage of development of American Catholicism. As with the Poles, in each case, separatism became the best solution to ethnic and religious survival. And as that mutual decision was reiterated, another panel of the ethnic pattern was sewn securely into place.

Southern and eastern Europeans, especially the Italians, Slovaks, Hungarians and Lithuanians, followed the example originally influenced by the Germans and more immediately set by Polish-Americans. Each group worked in its own way to create close religious and cultural ties within a parish-community environment that reflected its cultural differences from the American norm. Despite the difficulties encountered in the shaping of the specific pattern of Catholic expression, each contributed richly to the overall design. If the massive waves of Italian immigrants, for example, seemed less interested in seeking incorporation—especially when it involved inclusion into the organizational aspects of the Church—they nevertheless clung to cultic and devotional expressions of their faith that added warmth and festival to the liturgical pattern set by Irish-Americans. Eastern Europeans differed in their approach but not in the conviction to preserve their kind of faith expression. As a result, some suffered greater hardship as they attempted to persist in old world rituals and discipline. Greek-rite eastern European Catholics were especially handicapped. Like certain Polish-Americans, some eventually chose total separation from the official Church: both the Polish National and Greek Orthodox Churches established in the early twentieth century reflected their inability to accept the limiting role enforced by American church officials. Even native Americans, like black Catholics, suffered the consequences of a segregation already imposed by society and reinforced in the new circumstances. A small minority tried to change matters; five Black Lay Congresses met in the 1890's for that purpose. But most who remained loyal took their place, like immigrant Catholics, in segregated parishes or were attracted to the greater options for expression available among Protestant denominations. The first two hundred years of creating the immigrant patterns of the United States Catholic Church were spent in this complex maze of interactions characterized sometimes by sympathetic accommodation but at other times by either angry response or carefully-nuanced reaction.[1]

The multi-textured fabric of U.S. Catholicism today represents the historically strong composition formed by this response and counter-response: Catholic people became united by faith but distinguished by the traditions unique to each. Although in need of mending time and time again, the many-patterned design created by the process has maintained its singular expression to this day; the whole has, in fact, become stronger than its parts. Yet the broken threads and worn patches of the overall design serve as a reminder that the development of the U.S. Church did not go smoothly: church leaders created and experienced difficulties in easing the way for succeeding waves of immigrants. These failures of leadership, in particular, call for a reevaluation of the very approach accepted in the past century. Especially should such a review of the incorporation

---

[1]*Ibid., passim.* On Black Experience, see *ibid.,* pp. 175-176.

of immigrants urge today's policy makers to be aware of the ways in which the previous response to immigrant concerns divided membership unfairly and helped to sustain the more negative impressions by which the Church has so often been characterized in the twentieth century.

With renewal comes the opportunity to reshape the Church's future options in this regard. As Asian, Central and South American immigrants look to the U.S. Catholic Church for both sympathy and the continuity of expression of faith on an otherwise alien soil, the Church must be ready to respond in a way that leads to a more positive integration of these diverse groups. One hopes that with the experience of two centuries of growth through immigration, the Church will continue to identify itself as living by both faith and tradition, exemplifying these values in the building of the American Catholic Church in its third century.

CHAPTER THREE

The Origins and Development of Anti-Catholicism in America

Stephen J. Vicchio
College of Notre Dame of Maryland

God is only father in the sense of being father to all. When I
hate someone or deny that God is his father—it is not he who
loses, but me; for then I have no father.
—Soren Kierkegaard

THE COLONIAL PERIOD, 1632-1800:
The Roots of American Anti-Catholicism

Anti-Catholic sentiments were already well-established in England when
seventeenth-century settlers arrived on American shores. Along with articles of
clothing, household goods and family Bibles, these colonists also transported
anti-papal sentiments to the New World.

The England they left was a nation just emerging from the Reformation, and
like all converts there was a certainty about the new and a disdain for the old.
The Puritans of New England and the Anglicans of Virginia had many fundamental religious differences, but they did share one important element in common: a fear and distrust of the Church of Rome.

Back in England the two generations who preceded these first settlers had
seen the rift between Henry VIII and Rome grow into the English Reformation.
The parents of the American settlers were still alive for a devastating series of
wars with Catholic France that brought an accompanying threat of the Restoration of Catholicism in England.

The settlers themselves had been witness to the plots and counterplots of
Elizabeth and James I, Irish Catholic uprisings, an intrigue hatched by the Duke
of Kent to take the British Isles with the help of the Spanish, and numerous efforts by Spain and France to undermine the English monarchy.

Even earlier, in the sixteenth century, anti-Catholic sentiment had been imported from the continental Reformation, and with it came a wave of anti-
Catholic literature. Martin Luther, in an introduction written in 1536 for Robert
Barnes' *History of the Popes,* gives some indication of the intention and flavor
of this literature:

> All who have the spirit of Christ know well that they can bring no higher or
> more acceptable praise offering to God than all they can say or write against
> the blood-thirsty, unclean, blasphemic whore of the devil.[1]

---

[1]M.V. Hay, *A Chain of Error in Scottish History* (New York: Harpers, 1927), pp.
3-4.

Barnes' book sold well in late sixteenth-century England and its sentiments and those of other reformation thinkers such as Zwingli and Calvin were reflected in a number of laws passed in England in the 1550's and 1560's. Chief among these was the Act of Supremacy and Uniformity enacted in 1559. In this piece of legislation, and others to follow, Catholics were forbidden to hold certain political offices, to practice law or to teach in universities. Catholic priests were banished from England under penalty of death. Less than a century later this fierce anti-Catholic sentiment accompanied the original colonists on their voyage to America.

By the end of the seventeenth century the three foci for anti-Catholic activity in Colonial America were Maryland, New York and Massachusetts, though the reasons anti-popery took hold in each were very different.

In Maryland Sir George Calvert, Lord Baltimore, was given a charter in 1632 for territory in the New World, making him a patron of all churches to be established in his grant. Because Calvert was a Catholic, and because religious toleration was guaranteed by him, Maryland saw an influx of Catholic settlers in the 1630's. This situation inspired an almost continuous battle with the neighboring Virginia colony. Indeed, William Clayborn of Virginia, backed by popular Anglican support, sailed a ship christened "The Reformation" over to Kent Island in an effort to lay claim to it, and thus save the island from Catholicism.

By 1654 England was in the midst of several decades of revolution that would finally end in 1688 with the establishment of William and Mary of Orange as the English monarchs. In the first years of the English Revolution Catholics were no longer a majority in Maryland, and Protestants spurred on by the Puritan upheavals at home passed legislation that specified "none who profess to exercise Popish religion, commonly known by the name of Roman Catholic religion, can be protected in this province."[1] Later Oliver Cromwell's government would disallow this act but instead approved a bill, subsequently passed, that excluded Catholics from holding any public office.[2]

The Massachusetts Bay Colony was also a center of anti-Catholic activity, but the justification for these sentiments was quite different. In Massachusetts there were very few Catholics and intoleration of papists was not so much a function of everyday contact with them as it was the Puritan attitude toward other faiths. Nathaniel Ward, writing in 1646, put the matter this way:

> He that is willing to tolerate any religion that is not his own, unless it be matters merely indifferent, either doubts his own, or is not sincere in it.[3]

---

[1] Ray Allen Billington, *The Protestant Crusade: 1800-1860* (New York: Rinehart & Co., 1938), p. 6.

[2] *Ibid.*

[3] Nathaniel Ward, *The Simple Cobbler of Aggawan* (Edinburgh, 1646), p. 7.

As early as 1647, the General Court of the Massachusetts Bay Colony passed an act that provided for the banishment of "any Jesuit or priest" within the Colony.[1] By 1660 another law was enacted against the celebration of Christmas, a popish holiday. In the two decades that followed, Irish immigrants were forbidden to enter the Colony, and oaths of allegiance that denounced the pope were required of all who owned land in Massachusetts.

In New York Thomas Dongan, a Catholic, had been sent out by James II to govern the colony. After the Glorious Revolution, Dongan was suspended and the Jesuits were banned from the colony. Jacob Leisler, who temporarily succeeded Dongan, immediately called an assembly that agreed to "suspend all Roman Catholics from command and places of trust."[2] Later office-holders were required to sign a declaration against the doctrine of transubstantiation.[3]

By the eighteenth century, anti-Catholic sentiment was so pervasive in the Colonies that full religious and civil rights were enjoyed by Catholics only in Rhode Island. Before 1690 the roots of intolerance toward Catholics were the Reformation and the Revolution. But after 1690, with the outbreak of wars with France and Spain, the emerging American nation felt the same Catholic threat against its national identity that the English did.

In the early eighteenth century this anti-Catholic fear can be seen in the marked stiffening of the laws against Catholics. In the south, where Florida was vulnerable to the Spanish, the new colony of Georgia was kept free of papists. Inspectors were appointed in the colony to make sure no followers of the Roman error entered the region. Oaths against transubstantiation were required of all office-holders by a 1743 act.[4] Virginia, with perhaps less justification, showed similar concerns and stiffened its existing legislation against those "practicing the popish error."[5]

The anti-papal sentiments in Maryland grew more intense in the early years of the eighteenth century as well. In 1716 the Maryland Assembly passed a law forbidding office-holders from "attending Popish assemblies" or hearing mass.[6] In 1718 all residents who did not take the necessary Protestant oaths were disenfranchised. By 1740 Catholics were barred from joining the militia for fear they would start an armed insurrection. Any priest who attempted to make converts in the colony was tried for treason and subject to the death penalty.[7]

The hatred of Catholics grew steadily in the first half of the eighteenth century, and did not disappear after the Peace Treaty of Paris. But the focus shifted from legislation in the early part of the eighteenth century to persistent propaganda, carried out largely from Protestant pulpits, by the end of the century.

[1] James Adams, *The Founding of New England* (Boston: Little Brown, 1921), pp. 149-150.
[2] *Documents Relating to the Colonial History of the State of New York* (Albany: 1856-1887), II, 71; III, 689.
[3] Sanford Cobb, *The Rise of Religious Liberty* (New York: Macmillan, 1902), p. 337.
[4] Billington, *op. cit.*, pp. 8-9.
[5] *Ibid.*
[6] *Ibid.*
[7] *Ibid.*

One of the most effective of these anti-Catholic lecturers was the Rev. Paul Dudley, who launched a series of talks at Harvard in 1750. His purpose was

> the detecting and convicting and exposing the idolatry of the Romish Church: their tyranny, usurption, damnable heresies, fatal errors, abominable super- stitions, and other crying wickedness in her high places.[1]

Numerous lectures, sermons and pamphlets from the 1740's to the 1770's had anti-popery as their central theme. This propaganda had a strong effect on those who read it. The *Gazette* of March 14, 1754 ran this message from the Maryland House of Delegates to the King:

> We, his Majesty's most dutiful and loyal subjects, the Delegates of the Freemen of Maryland, in Assembly Convened, beg leave to represent your Excellency the impending dangers we apprehend from the growth of Popery, and the valuable and extensive possessions of Popish priests and Jesuits within this province. Other Protestant states have thought it necessary to guard themselves against the Jesuits and other Popish emissaries, and we trust the same will be done here. We humbly hope, therefore, that your Excellency will put into all places of trust and profit none but tried Protestant subjects, and that you will take all possible care to have the laws duly executed for our common safety, etc.[2]

But the anti-Catholic sentiment of this period was fueled not so much by the Reformation and English revolutions as it was by fear of the French, as this item from the October 10, 1754 *Gazette* attests:

> A summary view of this Province with regard to our neighbor enemies, the French...I shall premise something on the religion of our enemies. Their na- tional religion is popery, an impious, an absurd, a persecuting, blood-shed- ding religion...The Jesuits are the bulwarks and supporters of this ungodlike religion; it is better framed to make proselytes among uncivilized and igno- rant nations, than any of our Protestant persuasions. Hence, in a great mea- sure, it is, that the Popish missionaries extend their influence upon the Con- tinent over Indians, so much more than we do; and this is one of the reasons we have to dread and guard against these, our enemies.[3]

These colonial resentments found a focus in the Quebec Act of 1774, a law designed to extend religious toleration to French settlers of the Ohio Valley. The migration of the French to that area was seen as a Roman plot to establish popery in the West.

The feelings aroused against French Catholics remained strong even through the early part of the Revolutionary War. Indeed, John Witherspoon, president of Princeton at the time, suggested in one of his sermons that it was the common hatred of popery caused by the Quebec Act that galvanized different religious fac- tions in the Colonies, allowing them to make war against the English. In fact,

[1]*Ibid.,* p. 16.
[2]*United States Catholic Historical Magazine* (January, 1887), No. 1, p. 88.
[3]*Ibid.,* (April, 1887), No. 2, pp. 205-206.

a number of pamphlets of the period suggested a secret alliance between the Pope and the English monarchy for the purposes of making the West a papal state. The presence of Catholics among British troops was seen by some as evidence of the conspiracy.[1]

The French alliance in 1778 brought an abrupt shift away from the hatred of French Catholics. French troops now fought and died alongside American revolutionaries. By the end of the war, and the period immediately following it, there was a short respite from anti-Catholic sentiment in America.

In addition to the French alliance during the war, one of the chief reasons for the lessening of tensions between Protestants and Catholics was the work of John Carroll, who became first bishop of Baltimore and the nation in 1789. Carroll was a member of an illustrious Maryland family whose members included Charles Carroll, the only Catholic to sign the Declaration of Independence, and Daniel Carroll who journeyed with four other Marylanders to represent their state at the Constitutional Convention of 1787.

With the appointment of John Carroll as bishop much of the polemic threat against Catholics was diverted, for he was a member of an old and well-established Maryland family. When he took the oath of office he convinced the Roman hierarchy to delete the words "to seek out and oppose heretics."[2] He avoided open confrontation with Protestant clergy, refusing to disturb what he called "the harmony now subsisting amongst all Christianity in this nation."[3]

Elsewhere in the new nation, the flush of victory had made some kinder to Catholicism. Travelling to Boston, John Carroll made these observations:

> It is wonderful to tell what great civilities have been done to me in this town, where a few years ago a popish priest was thought to be the greatest monster in creation. Many here, even of their principal people, have acknowledged to me that they would have crossed to the opposite side of the street rather than meet a Roman Catholic some time ago.[4]

But anti-Catholicism had already survived on American soil for 150 years. Although the Declaration of Independence announced liberty for all, the state constitutions told a different and more familiar tale.

The Constitution enacted in New Jersey in 1776 forbade Catholics from serving in state offices; in Connecticut similar laws were passed. Vermont required all voters to be professed of the Protestant faith; New Hampshire developed a series of state constitutions, each containing a number of anti-Catholic provisions. The New York State Constitution of 1777 had a provision barring from citizenship all who failed to repudiate allegiance in spiritual matters to any foreign prince or potentate. This anti-Catholic provision was inserted under

---

[1]*Ibid.,* pp. 206-207.
[2]Quoted in Thomas O'Gorman, *History of the Roman Catholic Church in the United States* (New York: Harpers, 1985), p. 277.
[3]Florence D. Cohlan, *A Popular History of the Archdiocese of New York* (Yonkers: United States Catholic Historical Society, 1983), p. 13.
[4]Billington, *op. cit.,* p. 20.

pressure from John Jay. It lasted until the federal government took charge of naturalization in 1790.[1]

1800-1850: THE RISE AND DEVELOPMENT OF NATIVISM

The post-revolutionary period, with its glow of victory and the promise of equality, brought a reduction in the expression of anti-Catholicism. But by the late 1820's a new brand of anti-popery was in its embryonic stages, and became fully grown by the 1850's. Sidney Ahlstrom described the period this way:

> Late in the 1820's, however, a new kind of anti-Catholic mood began to flow in American life, gradually changing its form and becoming increasingly political both in action and ideology. Religious and political adventurers, profit seekers, publicity hounds, fanatics, opportunists, "joiners" of all kinds, and some men who in retrospect seem almost mad played their unseemly roles. Yet, respectable church leaders did not avoid the fray, abetted by the great interdenominational voluntary associations and puritanical movements for temperance and Sabbath reform.[2]

Ahlstrom suggests that the causes of this nativist sentiment were "not altogether mysterious."

> The inner security of individuals rests upon a sense of group identity. Groups define themselves against other groups. People are also disturbed by rapid social change. When one of the transitional factors is a rapidly accelerating immigration rate which disrupts established group relationships, a strong response is likely to ensue. Xenophobia is thus latent in almost every self-conscious people, and especially near the surface in a country which has only recently achieved full national status and which is vigorously engaged on many fronts in asserting its special character and destiny.[3]

In addition to this xenophobia, Ahlstrom also points to some social factors which help to explain the rise of American nativism:

> The social factor was probably foremost: urban concentrations of working people were obvious intrusions on the traditional patterns of American life...Protestant reformers had for years been castigating the strong thirst for gin and the disorderliness of the "lower orders," but now immigration and the growth of cities added an identifiable brogue and a new religious dimension to the old problem.[4]

---

[1]Cohlan, *op. cit.,* p. 13.
[2]Sidney Ahlstrom, *A Religious History of the American People* (New Haven: Yale University Press, 1972), p. 559.
[3]*Ibid.,* p. 555.
[4]*Ibid.,* p. 556.

Later in the same chapter Ahlstrom adds these reflections:

> As the immigrants kept coming and the Roman church kept growing, grave doubts about the future of American democracy began to displace the earlier optimism. During the 1820's, when the battle began to reach new heights of intensity and depths of vulgarity, other catalysts besides immigration statistics began to have their effect. In 1827 the First Provincial Council not only made the growth of American Catholicism manifest, but also castigated the King James Version of the Bible and encouraged the founding of parochial schools.[1]

It is of no little interest that Professor Ahlstrom sees the fight over the use of the King James Bible and the founding of Catholic schools as causes of anti-Catholic sentiment in the 1820's. But another view, one at least as plausible as Ahlstrom's, is that the controversy over reading the Protestant version of the biblical text and the establishment of parochial schools in America were not causes of anti-Catholicism but rather common sense responses to it.

Whatever the causes of the rise of American nativism in the 1820's, and they were clearly economic and social as well as religious, by the 1830's a new wave of anti-Catholic propaganda had surfaced in most of the great eastern cities of this nation. The very influential *New York Observer*, founded in 1823, was particularly active in the anti-Catholic cause. It was joined in the 1830's by *The Protestant* and *The Protestant Vindicator*, established by Rev. William Craig Brownlee, a Dutch Reformed minister in New York. At the same time, similar papers were established in Boston and Philadelphia, all with the expressed purpose of establishing "what articles of faith, found in the Scriptures in *express* terms, must be believed in order to be saved."[2]

By the early 1830's most of these papers included "debates" between local ministers who represented the views of the papers and Catholic priests invited to respond to charges which included allegations that subterranean dungeons existed for the murder and burial of illegitimate babies strangled by their wayward mothers, nuns living in cloistered convents.[3]

At the same time, several English anti-Catholic tracts were imported into the United States. Anthony Gavin's *Master Key to Popery*, Scippio de Ricci's *Female Convents: Secret of Nunneries Disclosed,* as well as many other British books of the period, all depicted Catholicism as a highly immoral system in which orgies were a regular practice of its love-starved priests and nuns. The strong impression left by all this literature was that monasteries and convents were dens of iniquity in which the clergy wallowed in some combination of ignorance, insanity, luxury and debauchery.

By 1835 this salacious material found its way into American books as well. The first and perhaps the best of the genre was Rebecca Theresa Reed's *Six Months in a Convent,* published in Boston. The social antipathies, class conflicts and unbridled religious jealousies of the period can all be seen in this book, as well as the controversy that surrounded it.

---

[1]*Ibid.*, p. 559.
[2]Quoted in Billington, *op. cit.*, p. 58.
[3]*Ibid.*, pp. 58-70.

Rebecca Reed, at least by her account, had been a nun among the Ursuline sisters of Charlestown, Massachusetts. After her "escape," she claimed an assortment of lurid details as regular happenings in the convent. In her book she recounted this collection of bizarre tales along with a plan hatched by her Superior to have her carried off to Canada to check her from making the revelations.

Despite a detailed rebuttal by the Mother Superior who pointed out the convent was not even remotely similar in structure to that outlined by Reed, the book was widely praised and almost universally believed by the Protestant press. In six months, it became a bestseller.[1]

In order to fully understand the story of Rebecca Reed, however, we must know something of the 1830's Charlestown in which this fantastic tale unfolded. The Ursuline convent, and the school to which it was connected, stood in a rural community whose population was made up principally of laborers who worked as brickmakers and truckmen. The distrust of the Ursuline school, Mount Benedict, was heightened by the fact that the pupils were drawn mostly from upper class families in nearby Boston. Many of the students were daughters of Unitarians and free thinkers who had rebelled against the strict Congregationalism of the public schools. A conservative Congregationalism was also the creed of the working class Charlestonians.

The issue came to a head when a rural school, the Charlestown Female Seminary, was established in 1831, but the liberal Boston families continued to send their daughters to Mount Benedict.

The success of the Ursuline school not only angered the working class residents of Charlestown, but it also infuriated the Orthodox ministers of Boston. Lyman Beecher, whose fiery sermons had earned his Park Street Church the nickname "Brimstone Corner,"[2] began a series of anti-Catholic sermons in the later 1830's, in which he tried to show that popery was dangerous not only for the established churches but for the national government as well. The Boston press linked these and other sermons of prominent Congregationalist ministers with Mount Benedict, by pointing out that the Ursulines' students were being converted to this dangerous popery.[3]

Finally, on the night of August 11, 1834, the antipathy for the Ursuline sisters moved from words to deeds. The convent, school and neighboring farm house were burned to the ground. The sisters escaped with the terrified children through a rear door. A group of local men were later tried for arson and acquitted on insufficient evidence.[4]

Two years later there appeared what Billington has called "the greatest of the nativist propaganda works,"[5] Maria Monk's *Awful Disclosures of the Hotel Dieu Nunnery of Montreal*. It was published (and now appears to a large extent

[1]*Ibid.*, pp. 90-92.
[2]Thomas Nichols, *Forty Years of American Life* (London: Macmillan, 1864), Vol. II, p. 89.
[3]*An Account of the Conflagration of the Ursuline Convent* (Boston: 1834), a collection of newspaper clippings on the incident.
[4]Billington, *op. cit.*, p. 76.
[5]*Ibid.*, p. 99.

to have been written) by a group of New York anti-Catholic ministers, headed by Rev. J.J. Slocum and Rev. Arthur Tappan.

Monk's book, full of the usual strangled babies and underground tunnels from the rectory to the convent, was followed in 1837 by her *Further Disclosures.* A short time later, there appeared an even more transparently fraudulent book, *The Escape of Sainte Frances Patrick, Another Nun from the Hotel Dieu Nunnery of Montreal.*

Maria Monk and Sainte Frances Patrick were brought together (apparently for the first time) at a public meeting where they tearfully embraced each other, and talked at length about their mutually horrifying experiences in the convent. Later, W.I. Stone, the editor of the *New York Advertiser,* made an examination of the Montreal convent with Maria Monk's book in hand. He came away completely convinced that the entire book had been made up. Over a decade later Maria Monk died in prison, having been arrested for picking the pockets of a "companion" at a house of prostitution. But her book had sold more than half a million copies. Professor Billington points out that a generation after its publication *Awful Disclosures* had become the "Uncle Tom's Cabin of Know-Nothingism."[1]

The American Catholic hierarchy's response to these anti-Catholic sentiments came in the form of a *Pastoral Letter,* issued on April 22, 1837. It calls to task members of the Massachusetts legislature for not seeing that justice was done in the Charlestown case. It also criticizes those members of the Protestant clergy who wrote or spread anti-Catholic propaganda. The bishops suggested that anti-Catholicism meant anti-Christianity, repeatedly mentioning the gospels as a model for Christian behavior. The Pastoral ends with this observation about the problem of divided allegiance:

> We owe no religious allegiance to any state in this Union, not to its general government. No one of them claims any supremacy or dominion over us in our spiritual or ecclesiastical concerns: nor does it claim any such right or power over any of our fellow citizens, of whatsoever religion they may be: and if such a claim was made, neither would our fellow citizens, nor would we submit thereto. They and we, by our constitutional principles, are free to give this ecclesiastical supremacy to whom we please, or to refuse it to everyone, if we so think proper: But, they and we owe civil and political allegiance to several States in which we reside, and also, to our general government. When, therefore, using our undoubted right, we acknowledge the spiritual and ecclesiastical supremacy of the chief bishop of our universal church, the Pope or bishop of Rome, we do not thereby forfeit our claim to the civil and political protection of the commonwealth; for, we do not detract from the allegiance to which the temporal governments are plainly entitled, any civil or political supremacy, or power over us in any foreign potentate or power, though that potentate might be the chief pastor of our church.[2]

---

[1]*Ibid.,* p. 108.
[2]Quoted in Peter K. Guilday, *The National Pastorals of the American Hierarchy* (Washington: National Catholic Welfare Council), pp. 118-119.

This document is clearly one of the most remarkable of its kind, but it did little to change the minds and hearts of anti-Catholics. Indeed, an incident at a Carmelite monastery in Baltimore is exemplary of the continued anti-popery sentiments. In August of 1839 Sister Isabella Neale, a 35-year old nun with a history of mental problems, "escaped" through a basement window of the monastery on Aisquith Street. As C.W. Currier describes the situation:

> The novel sight of a religious in her monastic habit, running through the street, at once attracted the attention of the residents in the neighborhood, and the cry of "escaped nun" soon spread through the city.[1]

A few paragraphs later, Currier adds the following commentary:

> This unfortunate event was fuel thrown on the fire; for the state of time was such that it needed only a slight breeze to fan into flames the sparks of religious fanaticism that was kept alive by the harangues of zealous bigots. A certain Presbyterian minister named Breckenridge, whose church was on Aisquith St., near the convent, had by his preaching excited the populace against convents and monastic institutions. The "No Popery" cry was raised, and the crowd became violent.[2]

A short time after Breckenridge's exhortations began, the mayor, S.C. Leakin, a much cooler head, arrived on the scene and ordered that Sister Isabella be taken to Washington Medical College in Baltimore for examination. But the crowd was not entirely quelled. Some wanted to burn down the monastery and liberate the rest of the nuns who, they contended, were being held against their will. Later, on the invitation of the convent's chaplain, Mayor Leakin toured the monastery and concluded the sisters were all willing participants in the life of the convent. Around-the-clock police protection was ordered for the monastery. A few days later, Leakin received the report from the Washington Medical College:

> ...we visited her several times, and from the general tenor of her conversation, we are clearly of opinion that she is not of sane mind; there is a general feebleness of intellect, and we are unanimous in the belief that she is a monomaniac.[3]

The report, signed by five physicians who examined Sister Isabella, concluded this way:

> We also feel it an act of justice to state that she made no complaint of her treatment while in the convent, other than having been compelled to take food and medicine.[4]

[1]Charles W. Currier, *Carmel in America* (Baltimore: John Murray, 1890), p. 213.
[2]*Ibid.*, pp. 213-214.
[3]*Ibid.*, p. 219.
[4]*Ibid.*, pp. 219-220.

In October, 1839, two months after the report, Rev. Robert Breckenridge published a tract condemning Mayor Leakin for his handling of the matter, calling into question the report of the physicians, and generally repeating the same accusations he had voiced immediately after the "escape." In the middle of the 35-page "Review of the Case of Olivia Neal, the Carmelite," Breckenridge suggests that the nun may have been insane, but that she became insane because of the horrible conditions inside the monastery.[1]

Concurrent with these fantastic tales of convent life, and the growing number of anti-Catholic tracts, was the entrance of national figures into what by 1835 had become a wide-ranging nativist anti-Catholic movement.[2]

The Rev. Lyman Beecher, whose sermons at least indirectly were related to the Ursuline convent disaster, began raising funds for Cincinnati's Lane Seminary, to which he had been appointed president in 1835. In his *Plea for the West,* Beecher spends the first several pages exhorting good Protestants to support theological education. But this is followed by 141 pages outlining a conspiracy he detected between the Pope and the king of Austria to turn the Ohio Valley into a papal fiefdom.[3]

Beecher had taken his cue from Samuel F.B. Morse, the inventor of the telegraph, who was the first of these nationally known figures to make an inextricable link between nativism and anti-Catholicism.

Morse began to voice his anti-Catholic sentiments in a series of anonymous letters to the editor of the *New York Observer.* These were later collected in 1834 for a volume entitled *Foreign Conspiracy Against Liberties of the United States.* Morse's nativism mixed with xenophobia is given full play in the book's pages:

> What shall be done? Shall Protestants organize themselves into a political union after the manner of papists, and the various classes of industry and even of foreigners in the country? Shall they form an Anti-Popery Union, and take their places among this strange medley of conflicting interests? And why should they not?[4]

Morse followed this book with a second series of letters, this time signed, for the *New York Journal of Commerce.* These letters were reprinted in 1835 under the ominous title *Imminent Dangers to the Free Institutions of the United States through Foreign Immigration.* A year later, Morse ran unsuccessfully as a nativist candidate in the New York City mayoral election.

---

[1]Robert Breckenridge, *Tracts to Vindicate Religion and Liberty* (Baltimore: Matchett & Neilson, 1839), pp. 16-17.

[2]Cf. Joseph Mannart, "The 1839 Baltimore Nunnery Riot: An Episode in Jacksonian Nativism and Social Violence," *Maryland Historical Society Magazine,* Vol. XI, No. 1 (Spring 1980), p. 22. Mannart suggests that Henry J. Brent, a Roman Catholic, figured prominently in the founding of the Native American Association, a group formed in 1837 to advocate anti-foreign nativism. Also listed with its ranks were "the names of many highly respectable members of the Catholic Church."

[3]Lyman Beecher, *A Plea for the West* (Cincinnati, 1835).

[4]Quoted in Ahlstrom, *op. cit.,* p. 562.

The 1840's brought renewed violence and a new development in the unfolding tale of anti-Catholicism in America. In May, 1844 violence broke out in a series of clashes between nativists and Catholic immigrants to New York. The spark that ignited the rioters was the efforts by New York Bishop John Hughes to secure a share of the state's educational funds for the new Catholic schools. At the same time, Francis Kenrick, Bishop of Philadelphia, addressed a letter to the city board of comptrollers insisting that the Protestant King James version of the Bible not be read in public schools. He asked that Catholic children be excused from religious instruction and that they be allowed to use their own version of the Bible during class readings. News of the Bishop's requests galvanized Philadelphia's anti-Catholic contingent and through the late spring and early summer attacks were made on Catholic Churches and houses in Irish neighborhoods. The Irish sometimes responded in kind and violence spread throughout the city. Other cities were not immune to similar incidents, sometimes violent, sometimes not, but always virulently anti-Catholic.

1850-1900: FROM THE KNOW-NOTHINGS TO RADICAL REPUBLICANISM

The new development in the 1840's was the rise of a politically organized version of anti-popery, the Know-Nothings, whose dramatic political rise and fall have been the subject of a great number of American religious historians' scholarly efforts.

Toward the end of the first half of the nineteenth century anti-Catholic sentiment had deepened and widened to include middle and upper class Americans. The total number of immigrants entering the United States in the 1820's was 130,000. In the 1840's it was well over a million.[1] As Ahlstrom points out:

> Between 1850 and 1860...almost a third of the nation's population growth—from 23,191,000 to 31,433,000—was accounted for by immigration. Pauperism, labor class rowdyism, and crime statistics showed that the country was facing a new kind of social problem, although immigration was merely the most easily exploited factor.[2]

Many of the middle class nativist concerns were voiced by the Know-Nothings, a group begun in 1849 by Charles B. Allen of New York. He started the group as a secret society called the Order of the Star Spangled Banner, but it was later reorganized and renamed the Know-Nothings in 1852. Membership was limited to American-born Protestants without Catholic wives or parents. The Know-Nothings swore to oppose the election of foreigners and Roman Catholics, and to renounce all other political affiliations including membership in existing political parties. Second order members were pledged to remove Roman Catholics from public office whenever possible.[3]

---

[1]*Ibid.*, p. 565.
[2]*Ibid.*
[3]Billington, *op. cit.*, p. 386.

By 1852 the Know-Nothings had made great inroads in New York City politics. By 1854 the movement was a national party sending 75 men to Congress. Maryland, despite its Catholic history and still relatively high Catholic population, succumbed to Know-Nothing fever. In 1854 the Know-Nothings elected their candidate mayor of Baltimore. A year later they had gained control of the State Legislature. They had done so strongly in state elections in Massachusetts, Delaware, New Hampshire and Connecticut that the Know-Nothings fully expected to send their candidate to the White House in 1856. But a split in the Know-Nothing ranks divided them on the issue of slavery and they were defeated soundly in the election. The Know-Nothing party was dead as a force in national politics. Maryland was the lone state won by Millard Fillmore, the Know-Nothing presidential candidate of 1856.

The extraordinary rise and abrupt fall of the Know-Nothings are difficult phenomena to explain, but chief among the reasons for their appearance was surely the widespread anti-Catholic sentiment and accompanying nativism brought on by the immigration patterns and attending social problems of the 1830's and 1840's. The election of 1856 was an important time for Catholics in America, showing for the first time that no matter how deeply held Protestant and nativist prejudices were in this country, Americans in general were not willing to deny both their moral heritage and their national ideals.

The end of the Know-Nothings was followed by the 1860's and a period of tremendous social strife. The slavery issue, civil war, and the reconstruction of a nation took center stage in this decade. But just as anti-Catholic nativism was a part of antebellum America, so would it be in the 1870's.

In 1868, after the defeat of the South, Charles Eliot Norton spoke for many Republicans of his day when he suggested the Protestant faith might now

> become the complete expression, and afford the most effective organization of the moral order which underlies the political system.[1]

Implied in this same speech was the notion that Roman Catholicism—ethnic and alien in its origins—posed a threat to the Republic, one just as pernicious as the slave-holding Democrats had been.

One of the best examples of this late nineteenth-century anti-Catholicism can be seen in the drawings of Thomas Nast, a New York cartoonist for *Harper's Weekly* and other publications.

The roots of Nast's anti-Catholicism, and that of his fellow Radical Republicans, are many and varied. Certainly his German Protestant upbringing and a youth spent in a national climate of antipathy toward Rome are two important factors. But the papal policies of Pius IX must also be pointed to as raising substantial anti-Catholic ire.

In December, 1864 Pius IX issued his "Syllabus of Errors," a compendium of the "principal errors of our time." These included, among other things, socialism, communism, rationalism, naturalism, positivism, separation of church and state, and freedom of the press. In the document the Pope bluntly proclaims:

---

[1]Morton Keller, *The Art and Politics of Thomas Nast* (New York: Oxford Press, 1968), p. 159.

It is an error to believe that the Roman pontiff can and ought to reconcile himself to, and agree with, progress, liberalism, and contemporary civilization.[1]

A few years later, at the First Vatican Council of 1870 the same pope issued a declaration proclaiming the infallibility of the papacy with respect to matters of faith and morals. *Harper's Weekly*, one of the most literate voices of Republicanism responded:

In the breaking of chains, in the increase of knowledge, in the higher welfare of the greater number of human beings, in the removal of abuses, in the extinction of superstition, in the emancipation of civilization from the mortmain of ecclesiasticism, the Pope sees only the ravages of Satan.[2]

Nast fully concurred with these sentiments but he also expressed in his cartoons many of the older prejudices: an antipathy toward Irish-Americans, a fear that the Pope had designs on America, and a conviction that Catholic schools were ruining the public school systems in the great cities of America.

The anti-Catholicism of Nast was most aroused by this last issue, the relationship of the Church to public education.

The New York State Legislature in 1868 made public funds available to Catholic schools and charitable organizations. From 1870 to 1915 renewed Catholic complaints arose in New York, Ohio, Illinois, Nebraska, Louisiana and 12 other states in which readings from the King James Bible were compulsory.

To Republicans of Nast's ilk these cases, and the granting of educational funds to Catholic schools, struck at the heart of the well-being of the Republic. His cartoons are eloquent exposition of a vigorous anti-Catholicism and an accompanying anti-Irish nativism at the end of the nineteenth century.[3]

At the same time Nast's cartoons appeared, James G. Blain, a congressman from Maine, introduced a proposed amendment to the U.S. Constitution. The amendment, which was largely aimed at Catholic schools, sought to prevent states from directly or indirectly granting public monies to schools with religious affiliations.

The case of the Notre Dame sisters' Milwaukee school, St. Mary's Institute, is illustrative of the widespread distrust of Catholic schools in the midwest in the 1870's. *The Christian Statesman*, an anti-Catholic paper, published an article entitled "The Milwaukee Nunnery" on May 21, 1873, in which various forms of extortion, carousing and idolatry were reported to be a regular part of the sisters' busy day. Students of the Institute responded with a series of articles refuting the charges. These were followed by statements signed by former students, Catholic and non-Catholic, testifying to the sisters' virtues.

Eventually, the authors of the original article, Messrs. Hauser and Storey, were sued by irate Catholics of the Milwaukee community. The newspapermen

---

[1]*Ibid.*, p. 160.
[2]Quoted in *ibid.*, p. 159.
[3]*Ibid.*, pp. 159-162.

received two years of postponements until they were forced to publish a full re-traction. The statement read in part:

> We have always been ready to meet our Catholic friends in arguments and when shown to be in error are willing to acknowledge it. With these views and feelings, we accepted the kindly offices of a leading Catholic gentleman in favoring us with a personal interview with the Lady Superior of the Convent, and on her declaring that she and the Sisters associated with her, and the pupils connected with the Convent, were willing to testify under oath that the statements in that paper and also in the issue of August 14th, were untrue, we most readily retract them and deeply regret their publication. Hauser and Storey.[1]

The school issue was hotly debated throughout the 1870's and 1880's. Blaine's proposal was defeated in 1875, but has been reintroduced 20 times since. Its effects have been felt principally in subsequent amendments or revisions of numerous state constitutions. Indeed, between 1877 and 1913 more than 30 states passed legislation forbidding financial aid to parochial schools.

In the post-Civil War South, two other intellectual movements contributed to anti-Catholic feelings. Many Protestant clergy who denounced the work of Charles Darwin in the last three decades of the nineteenth century also indicted the Catholic Church for being soft on Darwinism. This arose, not from positive statements on evolution by the Church or its individual members, but from a failure of Catholics to join in the assault on natural selection.

The other late nineteenth-century southern religious movement that became particularly inimical to Catholicism was premillennialism. Though there was a wide variety of apocalyptic movements throughout the South in this period, there was a common belief that we are dwelling in the last days of the world. Christ would come again soon and suddenly to destroy the wicked and reward the righteous. Proof of these things to come was found in the Old Testament Book of Daniel and the Apocalypse of John. "The three-horned beast" of *Revelation* was taken to be a symbol of the papacy and its reference to the "whore of Babylon," as Luther had pointed out 350 years before, was the Catholic Church.[2]

Around the same time, J. Frank Norris, the pastor of First Baptist Church of Fort Worth, Texas began to ferret out Catholic plots to capture the city government of Fort Worth. Were they to succeed, Norris wrote a friend, "They would behead every Protestant preacher and disembowel every Protestant mother in the city." In his weekly newspaper, *The Fundamentalists,* he served up another round of lurid tales like "Jesuit Murderers in the British Empire," "Traffic in Nuns," and "Priests and Women."[3]

---

[1] Sister Margaret Mary O'Connell, *The Educational Contributions of the School Sisters of Notre Dame in America for the Century of 1847-1947* (Ph.D. dissertation, Johns Hopkins University, Baltimore, 1950), p. 43.

[2] James J. Thompson, *The Church, the South and the Future* (Westminster: Christian Classics, 1988), pp. 43ff.

[3] *Ibid.*

1900-1960: ANTI-CATHOLICISM IN THE 20TH CENTURY

Immigration patterns in the first decades of the twentieth century changed dramatically from those of the post-Civil War years. The predominant ethnic groups were now eastern and southern European, particularly Italian. The result was predictable: a new wave of American nativism. Its participants were many and varied but one of the greatest ironies about the nativist movements of the 1920's is that many of the most vociferous oracles of the destruction of an America for Americans were the Irish whose fathers and grandfathers had been victims of the same kind of oppression now reserved for Italian Catholics.

A second source of nativist sentiments in the first decades of the twentieth century—one that combined nativism not only with anti-Catholicism, but also with antipathy toward Jews and Blacks—was the Ku Klux Klan. The Klan had begun in 1915 in Georgia, but soon spread to the southwest and midwest, becoming particularly influential in Texas, Oklahoma and Indiana. In Birmingham, Alabama in 1921, Edwin R. Stephenson, a Protestant preacher, shot and killed James Coyle, a Catholic priest. Stephenson was angered that Coyle had performed a marriage ceremony between the preacher's daughter and a Catholic, Pedro Grossman, a man repeatedly described in the court record as "dark and curly haired." Hugo Black, later to be named to the Supreme Court but at the time a member of the Klan, conducted Stephenson's defense. The foreman of the jury was a Klan member, as was the sheriff who testified in the preacher's defense. Stephenson was acquitted.[1]

By the mid 1920's, the Klan's message had spread to the northwest. Hiram Wesley Evans, the Imperial Wizard of the Klan, published these remarks in the *North American Review* in the spring of 1926:

> Nordic Americans for the last generation have found themselves increasingly uncomfortable and finally deeply distressed. There appeared first confusion in thought and opinion, a groping hesitancy about national affairs and private life alike, in sharp contrast to the clear, straightforward purposes of the earlier years. There was futility in religion too, which was in many ways even more distressing....Finally came the moral breakdown that has been going on for two decades. One by one all our traditional moral standards went by the boards, or were so disregarded that they ceased to be bidding. The sacredness of our Sabbath, of our homes, of chastity, and finally even of our right to teach our own children in our own schools fundamental facts and truths were torn away from us. Those who maintained the old standards did so only in the face of constant ridicule.[2]

[1]*Ibid.*
[2]*Ibid.*

Evans mentions only obliquely the causes of the Nordic American's distress: a turning away from traditional morality, the removal of the Bible from public schools and the weakening of those schools through the rise of Catholic education. The Klan found an attentive audience not only in the South, but also in pockets of the midwest where many of the southern European Catholics had settled. The greatest successes of the Ku Klux Klan were found in the great northwest, particularly in Oregon and Washington.

In the period before and immediately after World War I, the northwest had seen some of the same propaganda and sensational literature about escaped nuns and secret tunnels from rectories to convents that the east had read as early as the 1820's. Stories with titles like "Former Sister of Charity on Anti-Catholic Platform" and "Escaped Nun Tells All" appeared regularly in the Portland newspapers.[1]

In June, 1920 the Masons' Grand Lodge of Oregon adopted a resolution requiring compulsory public school education for its members' children.[2] A few years earlier a secret society, the Oregon Federation of Patriotic Societies, was formed with one of its purposes being the establishment of compulsory public school education for all the state's children. When the Grand Wizard in Atlanta sent W.J. Simmons to Oregon to work on a compulsory public school bill, the nativist anti-Catholic pump had already been primed.

After several months of masterful lobbying the Anti-Parochial School Bill, as it was called, was submitted to the electorates of 14 Oregon cities and towns on July 6, 1922. The principal terms of the bill were the following:

> Be it enacted by the people of the state of Oregon: Section I. That Section 5259, Oregon Laws be, and the same is hereby amended, so as to read as follows: Section 5259, children between the ages of eight and sixteen years. Any parent, guardian or other person in the state of Oregon, having control or charge or custody of a child under the age of sixteen and of the age of eight years or older at the commencement of a term of public school of the district in which the child resides, who shall fail or neglect or refuse to send such a child to a public school shall be held during the current year in said district, guilty of a misdemeanor and each day's failure to send such a child to a public school shall constitute a separate offense.[3]

Catholic opposition to the bill was quickly formed and led by a lawyer from Seattle, D.S. Wooten. He had been hired by Archbishop Christie who earlier had established the Catholic Civil Rights Association of Oregon. The election took place on November 7, 1922, and with growing anti-Catholic sentiment and little time to organize resistance to the bill, the measure was passed.[4]

---

[1]Hiram Wesley Evans, "The Klan's Fight for Americanism," *North American Review*, Vol. 213 (March-May, 1926), pp. 33-34.
[2]Wilfred P. Schoenberg, *A History of the Catholic Church in the Pacific Northwest, 1743-1983* (Portland: Pastoral Press, 1987), p. 522.
[3]*Ibid.*
[4]*Ibid.*, pp. 523-524.

Fresh from their victory in Oregon, the Klan's attention turned to the state of Washington where a similar bill was to be introduced. In the meantime, however, the Portland Archdiocese had more effectively marshalled its opposition to the original bill and they appealed the Oregon statute to the federal court on January 15, 1924. Three federal judges heard the case in Oregon. After two months deliberation the judges declared the bill unconstitutional.

Eventually, the sponsors of the bill made an appeal to the Supreme Court, but in the intervening time the Washington bill was defeated. If this did not take the fight out of the Klan in the northwest, then the Supreme Court's decision in June of 1925 on the Oregon bill did. The court declared the compulsory school bill of Oregon to be unconstitutional. Justice James C. McReynolds wrote the unanimous decision:

> The fundamental theory of liberty upon which all governments in this Union repose excludes any general power of the state to standardize its children by forcing them to accept instruction from public teachers only. The child is not the mere creature of the state; those who nurture him and direct his destiny have the right coupled with the high duty, to recognize and prepare him for additional obligations.[1]

After this defeat the organized anti-Catholic sentiments of the Klan, nativism and anti-Catholic antipathies promoted by the temperance movement, and a renewed campaign in the late 1920's to restrict immigration, were all forces that drew the presidential election of 1928 to a bitter focus. The Democrats nominated a Catholic, Governor Alfred E. Smith of New York. For many Americans one of the deciding factors in the election was the "religious issue" or what was sometimes called the problem of "divided allegiance."

During the campaign renewed questions about the Pope's role in world politics emerged and Smith was asked repeatedly if as a Roman Catholic he could take the oath of office and perform the functions of the presidency. Despite fierce bigotry, and a flurry of anti-Catholic nativist propaganda, Smith managed 41 percent of the vote in his defeat.

Smith's humane liberalism was a sign that a growing Catholic social consciousness was now a part of the American political landscape. But just as important, Smith's showing in the 1928 election laid the groundwork for the majorities enjoyed by Franklin Roosevelt in 1932 and 1936. And perhaps this one event, a credible showing in a presidential election, brought the beginning of the end of anti-Catholicism in the American political realm. In November, 1960, just a hundred years after the Know-Nothings ran a candidate for the same office, John F. Kennedy was elected the first Catholic president of the United States.

Yet, even as late as the election of 1960, anti-Catholic sentiment was still high. One of its chief proponents was Norman Vincent Peale, who practiced anything but positive thinking when it came to Catholics seeking national offices. In a meeting with other distinguished Protestant clergy a few months before the 1960 election Peale voiced once again the question of "divided allegiance" and said in no uncertain terms that a Catholic should never serve as

---

[1]*Ibid.,* pp. 527-530.

president. A few days later, on the editorial page of the *New York Times*, Peale was depicted seated at an organ with a hymnal open to a song entitled "No Catholic for President." An apologetic Peale has turned to the congregation; the caption reads, "I don't write the music—I only play it."[1]

The election of John Kennedy and the concomitant openness of the Second Vatican Council led by Pope John XXIII did much to eliminate what vestiges of organized anti-Catholic sentiment still existed in America in the 1960's and 1970's. But the contemporary discussion in the 1980's of what some officials in the national government call the "Mexican immigration problem" gives one cause to wonder if we are not sitting on the edge of yet another version of American nativism. And where there is nativism, as we have seen, there is often anti-Catholicism.

[1]Unsigned cartoon, *The New York Times*, September 18, 1960.

CHAPTER FOUR

God's Image in Black
The Black Community in Slavery and Freedom
Cyprian Davies
St. Meinrad Archabbey

African-American Catholics have been the forgotten people in the history of the Catholic Church in the United States. For many the religious history of American Blacks is chiefly a Protestant story. For others black Catholics warrant only a few lines in the more important history of successive immigrations of European Catholics who transplanted Catholicism to these shores. Yet if we look patiently at the earliest beginnings of Catholicism in what is now the territory of the United States, it will become clear that the lands were cleared and the churches were built, the fields were tilled and the prayers were prayed by Blacks, some of whom were slaves and others who were free. If the Church is the people, then the story of black Catholics is the story of a people of faith and love who from the beginning challenged the Church in the United States to come to terms with its catholicity.

In this bicentennial year of the American hierarchy it is important to have some idea of how the American bishops dealt with the African portion of their flock. We will look at the reality of black Catholicism prior to the Civil War, and the bishops' failure to address the issue of slavery in a manner that would have had meaning to the slaves themselves. Lastly, we will look at the lay leadership of black Catholics that, together with Roman pressure, helped finally to change the long neglect of American Catholicism.

CATHOLICS, SLAVE AND FREE

When John Carroll wrote Cardinal Antonelli, the Prefect of the Congregation of the Propaganda in 1785, four years before he became the first bishop in the United States, he described the Catholics in Maryland as numbering 15,800. Three thousand of these were "slaves of all ages, come from Africa, who are called 'Negroes' because of their color."[1] Maryland had been established as a colony for English Catholics in 1634. Slavery became common in this colony by the first part of the eighteenth century.[2]

At the time of Carroll's ordination to the episcopate in 1789, black Catholics had already made their appearance on these shores two centuries earlier, in the areas developed by the Spaniards. The Spaniards had established St. Augustine by 1565 as the center of their colonizing efforts in Florida in what was to become the oldest Catholic parish in the country. Blacks were part of this settlement: many as slaves, others as freemen. A unique aspect of this settlement was the presence of a detachment of free black soldiers from Cuba garri-

---

[1]Leonardo Antonelli (1730-1811) became prefect of the Propaganda in 1780. For Carroll's letter, see *The John Carroll Papers,* Vol. I, pp. 179-182.
[2]See Aubrey Land, *Colonial Maryland; A History* (Millwood, NY: KTO Press, 1981), pp. 165ff.

soned in the town. At the same time the Spaniards, who were constantly threatened by the English settlers to the north in the Carolinas and Georgia, actively
welcomed the arrival of black slaves from the English colonies. All who came
and who embraced the Catholic faith became free. As a result the oldest black
settlement in what is now the United States was established at the beginning of
the eighteenth century just north and east of the Spanish town of St. Augustine
and the Castillo de San Marcos. It was known as *Gracia Real de Santa Teresa de
Mose*.[1]

In 1763 Spain lost her colony in Florida as a result of the Treaty of Paris at
the end of the Seven Years War. In exchange for the port of Havana won by the
British, Spain ceded Florida to Great Britain. All the Spanish colony members,
both black and white, left for Cuba. Twenty-one years later Spain got back her
Florida colony which she would continue to govern until 1821, when Florida
became United States territory. The town of Fort Mose was not reestablished.
Blacks both slave and free resided in St. Augustine and also in Pensacola. A gar-
rison of free mulatto soldiers from Cuba was established in St. Augustine.

In much of the South separate sacramental registers were kept for whites and
Blacks. In other cases, the sacramental registers, as in Baltimore for instance,
clearly indicated whether the individual was black or a mulatto. Thanks to the
sacramental registers for St. Augustine, we have a good picture of the Blacks
who were baptized, married in the Church, or buried by the Church. What we do
not have is a clear picture of how often Blacks, both slave and free, frequented
the sacraments such as Penance and Eucharist. Still, the registers give names
and often places of origin. The black Catholic community is not, thanks to
these registers, an anonymous mass, impersonally designated as slaves.

In 1788, one year before the establishment of the diocese of Baltimore, on
August 16th, Thomas Hassett, the pastor of St. Augustine, baptized a nine-year
old "Ethiopian boy, commonly known as a *Negro*." He was the son of Prince
and Judith Husten, "fugitives from North Carolina." He was given the name
Francisco Domingo Mariano Husten to replace the name Bob.[2] On the same
day, a daughter of Prince and Judith Husten was baptized and given the name
Maria.[3] Other entries are of Blacks who came not only from Africa but from
other places in the United States, such as South Carolina, Virginia, Maryland
and even Boston.

If black Catholics were a significant portion of the Spanish population of
Florida at the time of the establishment of the Diocese of Baltimore,[4] they were

[1] See John Jay TePaske, *The Governorship of Spanish Florida 1700-1763*
(Durham: Duke University Press, 1964), pp. 140-144.
[2] St. Augustine Diocesan Archives, *The Parochial Registers of St. Augustine; Bap-
tisms Colored 1784-1793*, p. 41, no. 85. For the second Spanish period, there
are four Baptismal registers for Blacks from 1784 to 1885. In the first register
for Blacks, 1784-1793, there are 389 entries. In the Baptismal register for
whites, 1781-1792, there are 521 entries.
[3] *Ibid.*, p. 42, no. 86.
[4] In 1788 when the auxiliary Bishop of Havana, who at the time was responsible
for both Florida and Louisiana, made his episcopal visitation of Florida the census
given him listed a total of 1078 white persons in the Florida colony, 284 slaves
in St. Augustine and 367 outside the city. The number of free Blacks was not
given. See Michael J. Curley, "Church and State in the Spanish Floridas (1783-

well-represented in the region of California. At the end of the eighteenth century Spain was concerned to maintain its ownership of California. Settlers were recruited from Mexico to establish towns. In September of 1781 eleven families came to the banks of the Porciuncula River to establish a settlement known as *Nuestra Senora de Los Angeles*. The census made two months later indicated the racial characteristics of each inhabitant: These settlers, known as *Los Pobladores*, were 2 Spaniards, 8 Indians, 2 mestizos (Spanish and Indian), 2 Blacks, 8 mulattos (Spanish and Black), not counting the children.[1] Los Angeles and the rest of California did not become part of the United States until the Treaty of Guadalupe Hidalgo in 1848. It is well to note, however, that one of the largest American cities was first settled by black and Indian Spanish-speaking Catholics. This Spanish-Black population was found elsewhere in California though in time the black factor disappeared.[2]

The French colony of lower Louisiana included the sites of New Orleans and Mobile and the Gulf Coast. By the first quarter of the eighteenth century the slave trade had brought Africans into the colony. In no other part of the United States would African Catholicism become so important (with the possible exception of Maryland). In 1769 the Louisiana Territory was ceded to Spain. In 1803 it was returned to France, and in that year France sold the Territory to the United States. In that year also this French Catholic Territory came under the jurisdiction of John Carroll.

In both the Spanish and French territories, the law granted certain rights to slaves. Slaves had to be baptized, they had the right to marry, children under a certain age could not be separated from parents, and slaveowners had to permit religious instruction for the slaves. The very fact that slaves were baptized granted them a personality in law and a dignity in the eyes of the Church. In this regard the position of the slave was different than that enjoyed by slaves in the American colonies and later in pre-Civil War United States. This factor minimizes in no way the harshness and the arbitrary cruelty that was the lot of slaves in all parts of the New World.

The Catholic slaveholders in Louisiana, however, were especially reluctant to allow their Catholic slaves the enjoyment of their religion. In a letter written in 1823, Jean-Marie Odin, C.M., the future archbishop of New Orleans, wrote the seminary rector at Lyons in France:

> The greatest source of discouragement is Negro slavery. The American slave-holders permit them to marry in the church and to practice their religion; but in lower Louisiana, most of the French do not want to hear about instruction

1822)" in *The Catholic University of America Church History* (Washington, CUA Press, 1940), Vol. XXX, pp. 112-113.
[1]See *Quarterly of the Historical Society of Southern California* (1931-1932), No. 15 (later entitled the *Southern California Quarterly*). See also Harry Kelsey, "A New Look at the Founding of Old Los Angeles," *California Historical Quarterly* (1976), No. 55, pp. 326-339. For another list of the Pobladores and the race, see David Weber, ed., *Foreigners in their Native Land, Historical Roots of the Mexican Americans* (Albuquerque: University of New Mexico Press, 1981), 6th edition, pp. 34-35.
[2]See Jack D. Forbes, "Black Pioneers: The Spanish-Speaking Afro-Americans of the Southwest," *Phylon* (1966), No. 27, pp. 233-246.

for their slaves, to let them marry, and often not even to permit them to go to church.[1]

In the city of New Orleans the situation was somewhat different. The Ursuline nuns instructed young black girls and for a time the clergy gave instruction to the black youth. The future first bishop of Mobile, Michael Portier (1795-1859), who as a young seminarian from France worked as a deacon in New Orleans, described his work in a letter of 1822:

> ...One of the vicar generals...has just begun in New Orleans a course of elementary instruction for the children, who are present in large numbers. Three long catechism classes a day do not at all fatigue their attention span. Whites, Blacks, and mulattoes listen to the divine word with a recollection and a fervor that ravished the fervent catechist. When at dusk, the sound of the cannon indicates to the Black and mulatto youths the signal for curfew, they give vent in the most forceful way possible their regret at not being able to listen for a longer time...The Ursuline nuns also instruct and give formation to more than three hundred poor Negro young women.[2]

In lower Louisiana, at the beginning of its history, the colony had very few French women. One of the results was the development of a tradition of concubinage between the white males, including settlers, soldiers, merchants and adventurers and the women who were found there, both Native American and African-American. In the latter instance there emerged an extensive mulatto population, which in time was free, known as creoles of color or *les gens libres de couleur*. This population, at times very independent and sometimes wealthy, was very French in culture and Catholic in religion. In spite of this it was from this milieu that the well-to-do gentlemen of New Orleans society picked their light-skinned mistresses and concubines. And it was in this atmosphere of refined, cultivated, colorful immorality that some of the great dramas of black Catholic history were played out.

One dramatic episode took place in northern Louisiana in the French frontier settlement of Natchitoches. It is the story not so much of forbidden love and its consequences as it is the recompense afforded the courageous and the industrious. It is the story of a black female slave named Marie-Thérèze. Her African name was Coincoin. Her father, born in Africa, and her mother were both slaves in the household of the commandant of the fort in the settlement of Natchitoches in central Louisiana. When she was twenty-five, a young French merchant two years her junior from La Rochelle named Claude Thomas Pierre Metoyer made her his mistress. The year was 1767, and this domestic arrangement lasted until 1786. During this time Pierre Metoyer, without ever legally acknowledging the eight children born to him and Coincoin, purchased both her and his children and then granted them their freedom. Eventually he legally married a French woman of the colony, but he provided for Coincoin and his Afro-French children with land located not far from Natchitoches on the Cane River, a settlement later known as Isle Brevelle.

---

[1]*Les Annales de la Propaganda de la Foi* (1825), p. 74.
[2]*Ibid.*, Vol. I, 1822 (1837), p. 26.

The drama is not so much the nineteen years of life together of a young Frenchman and a young slave woman but the industry and the labor of the middle-aged black woman, newly freed from slavery, who with her sons turned the land into a thriving agricultural center. When Coincoin died in either 1816 or 1817, the family, which took the name Metoyer from the father, had developed into a prosperous settlement. Augustine Metoyer (†1856) became the patriarch of the settlement. Other free people of color married into the original Metoyer family. More land was purchased and also slaves. This settlement of Blacks, founded by a slavewoman, was also a settlement of black slaveholders. Closed in upon itself, it carried on a thriving business selling its produce of tobacco, sugarcane and indigo down river in New Orleans. French in language and culture, they were fervently Catholic in religion. The Church of St. Augustine, which was erected by Augustine Metoyer in 1829, became a parish in 1856, making it one of the oldest black Catholic Churches in the United States.[1]

The Civil War destroyed the prosperity of Isle Brevelle. It also removed some of the elitist character of the settlement. Nevertheless, the settlement remains today an important chapter in black Catholic history. Seeing themselves as more French than African, there was a certain reticence regarding racial identification. Unfailingly, however, the descendants of the original settlers have clung to their Catholic identity and their cultural roots.

Isle Brevelle, however, is not the only example in African-American history of a settlement of free people of color who maintained their own historical identity in religion and culture. Both in the region of Mobile and Mon Luis Island in Alabama and in southern Maryland were to be found African-American settlements of fairly light-skinned Blacks. The progenitors were seemingly freed slaves in origin; their faith was Roman Catholic.[2]

---

[1]See Gary Mills, *The Forgotten People, Cane River's Creoles of Color* (Baton Rouge: Louisiana State University Press, 1977), pp. 1-50. Regarding the parish church, see pp. 150ff. See also Mills, "Piety and Prejudice: A Colored Catholic Community in the Antebellum South," in *Catholics in the Old South,* Randall Miller and John Wakelyn, ed., (Macon, Georgia: Mercer University Press, 1983), pp. 171-191. A recent notice with photographs on the settlement is to be found in Patricia Smith Prather, "Coincoin: Plantation Owner Before the Nation was Born," in *American Visions,* (February 1989), No. 4., pp. 46-47.

[2]In Alabama, there are the descendants of Jean Chastang, a Spaniard, and his mulatto wife, who formed a distinct community of light-skinned Blacks near Mobile, in the region of Chastang. See Mother Mary Carroll, Order of Mercy, *A Catholic History of Alabama and the Floridas* (Freeport, NY: Books for Libraries Press, 1970. Originally published 1908), pp. 339-340.

In the area of Mon Luis Island south of Mobile a community of light-skinned African-Americans, French and Catholic, took its rise from Maximilien Colin, a freed slave who acquired property at the beginning of the nineteenth century. There is very little documentation regarding the settlements at Chastang and Mon Luis Island. For the latter the author owes a debt of gratitude to Msgr. J. Edwin Stuardi, the pastor of St. Rose of Lima Church, Mon Luis Island, for general information regarding the area and its origins. (Interview on January 13, 1988.)

A similar settlement of Catholic Blacks of mixed white, Native American and African-American ancestry is found in Charles County in southern Maryland. The names are English; the exact origin is uncertain. See William Harlan Gilbert, Jr.,

Black Catholics were found in substantial numbers in French settlements along the Mississippi River in Ste. Genevieve and St. Louis; and in the French settlements of Kaskasia and Cahokia in western Illinois.[1] Black Catholics were part of the westward trek of English Catholics from Maryland who settled in Nelson County in Kentucky at the end of the eighteenth and the beginning of the nineteenth century.

Black Catholics were also part of the economic structure of many religious communities prior to the Civil War. The Jesuits in Maryland had slaves on their extensive land holdings in southern Maryland, which supplied their material needs. When John Carroll, himself a former Jesuit, became Bishop, the Jesuits, who had been suppressed in 1773, had formed themselves into the Corporation of the Roman Catholic Clergymen. As a corporation they were one of the largest slaveholders in Maryland. Restored as a religious order in 1805, the Jesuits had almost four hundred slaves in the first quarter of the nineteenth century. In the end, by the 1830's, the slaves who had been an economic advantage earlier became a financial liability.

Father Robert Emmett Curran, S.J., in his study on the slaveholding of the Maryland Jesuits points out the differences of opinion within the ranks of the Jesuits themselves regarding the disposition of their slaves.[2] Some wished to rid themselves of the slaves to stem the financial loss. Others had a strong sense of obligation to the slaves as a responsibility of the Order despite the continued financial loss. By the 1830's the opportunity of manumission of the slaves, which many in the Jesuits desired, became virtually impossible.[3] The result was that hard-headed business interests prevailed. Thomas Mulledy, the provincial at the time, carried out the sale of 272 slaves to slave traders from the South in 1838. In some instances, it seems, families were separated. Being sold into the deep South, there was no certainty that the slaves would be able to practice their Catholic faith. One can ask today what many Jesuits and others asked then: can there ever be a justification for placing the salvation of others in jeopardy? One can only add that some of the Jesuits distressed at the sale aided some of the slaves to escape.

The mass sale by the Maryland Jesuits in 1838 created a scandal among many Catholics in the United States. In a sense it was the inevitable consequence of any compromise with the institution of slavery. The moral ambiguity of chattel slavery in the United States led inevitably into moral quicksand. This did not prevent other religious, both male and female, from engaging in slaveholding. The Jesuits in Missouri and in Louisiana owned slaves. From the beginning of the French colony in Louisiana, the Capuchins were slaveholders.

"The Wesorts of Southern Maryland: An Outcasted Group," *Journal of the Washington Academy of Sciences* (1945), No. 35, pp. 237-246.
[1] For Ste. Genevieve, see Carl Eckberg, *Colonial Ste. Genevieve, An Adventure on the Mississippi Frontier* (Gerald, Missouri: The Patrice Press, 1985). For St. Louis, see William Barnaby Faherty, S.J., *Dream by the River, Two Centuries of St. Louis Catholicism, 1766-1967* (St. Louis: 1973).
[2] R. Emmett Curran, S.J., "'Splendid Poverty': Jesuit Slaveholding in Maryland, 1805-1838," in *Catholics in the Old South*, pp. 125-146. The author is also indebted to Father Curran for the use of an unpublished article entitled, "Rome, The American Church, and Slavery."
[3] Curran, "'Splendid Poverty'...," pp. 134, 138.

The Vincentians, shortly after their arrival in this country, found it expedient to purchase slaves for their seminary in Perryville, Missouri. In 1819 the bishop of Louisiana, Louis William Du Bourg, gave the Vincentians some of his own slaves for the domestic work in the seminary. They soon became one of the largest slaveholders in the area.[1] Although the Vincentians began divesting themselves of slaves through sale as early as 1840, they continued to possess some slaves and to hire others down to the Civil War.[2]

The oldest contemplative community of nuns in this country, founded in the time of Bishop Carroll, is the Carmelite convent established at Port Tobacco in southern Maryland in 1791. These nuns had slaves[3] as did the Visitation nuns in Washington, DC. The two pioneer congregations of women in Kentucky, the Sisters of Charity of Nazareth and the Sisters of Loretto, had slaves as did also the Dominicans in the same state. In the South, the Ursulines, the Madames of the Sacred Heart, the Daughters of the Cross were all slaveholders.[4]

In a sense the slavery question was a "twilight zone" for the American bishops. Like the clergy and religious in slaveholding states, many of the southern bishops were also slaveholders. They refused to address the slavery issue as a moral question. They strove to turn it into a purely political question. They could only do this by creating for themselves an illusion that had nothing to do with American chattel slavery in the nineteenth century.

A good example of this is to be found in the actions of the American bishops when, in 1839, Pope Gregory XVI condemned the traffic in slaves in the Apostolic Letter, *In supremo apostolatus*. The Pope forbade any ecclesiastic or lay person to defend or to support the slave trade. Unfortunately, John England, bishop of Charleston, South Carolina (1820-1842) felt the necessity of proving to the American people in the South that the Pope had not condemned slavery as it existed in America. He did this in a series of letters addressed to John Forsyth (1780-1841), then Secretary of State in the cabinet of President Martin Van Buren.

Forsyth had claimed that the Pope was supporting the cause of the Abolitionists. Using the diocesan newspaper which he had founded, England published eighteen "Letters to Forsyth" in which with extensive erudition he used the Scripture, the decrees of Church synods and councils, the writings of Church fathers and doctors, the decisions of the popes to argue that the Church had never forbidden slavery and, as a consequence, accepted it as a social reality that was

[1] Stafford Poole, C.M., and Douglas Slawson, C.M., *Church and Slave in Perry County, Missouri 1818-1865*, pp. 148-189.
[2] *Ibid.*, p. 186.
[3] See "Diary of Archbishop Marechal, 1818-1825," *Records of the American Catholic Historical Society of Philadelphia* (1900), No. 11, pp. 417-454. On p. 420 the Bishop writes: "The nuns have about a 1000 acres of land with negroes, stock, a water mill...."
[4] See Sister Frances Jerome Woods, C.D.P., "Congregations of Religious Women in the Old South," *Catholics in the Old South*, pp. 99-123. See especially pp. 112-115. For the Sisters of Charity, see Anna Blanche McGill, *The Sisters of Charity of Nazareth, Kentucky* (New York: The Encyclopedia Press, 1917), pp. 104-105, 141. For the Sisters of Loretto, see Camillus Maes, *The Life of Charles Nerinckx* (Cincinnati: Robt. Clarke and Co., 1880), p. 255.

not sinful.[1] England never completed his task; in 1842, two months after announcing that "pressing duties will not permit me...to continue the letters on the compatibility of domestic slavery with practical religion," he was dead.[2] In the same announcement, in answer to the question of whether he was in favor of the continuation of slavery, he said that he was not "but I also see the impossibility of now abolishing it here. When it can and ought to be abolished, is a question for the legislature and not for me.[3]

In a similar vein, Auguste Martin, bishop of Natchitoches in Louisiana from 1853 to 1875, wrote a pastoral letter in 1861 in which he spoke of the Africans as "children of the race of Canaan" for whom "the manifest will of God" was that they be brought to this country in slavery, which was "a betterment both material and moral for a degraded class."[4] The pastoral letter found its way to Rome where it was judged very severely. Vincenzo Gatti, O.P., who later became Master of the Sacred Palace, was delegated by the Congregation of the Index to examine the doctrinal content of the letter. He found the letter objectionable on many grounds. Among other things, the bishop seemed "to attribute to God the detestable violence of men," i.e., the seizing of men and women for slavery. He seemed to approve of the slave trade even though Pope Gregory XVI had condemned it. He made a difference between whites and Blacks "as if [those who are white] did not have original sin as [did those who were black]." "Experience shows," said the theologian, "that Negroes reared among Catholics and instructed like them, [can] have the [same] capacity for virtue and culture, moral dignity and freedom."[5] Gatti considered that the letter was worthy of condemnation, but since Martin was a bishop he was to be given the opportunity to correct his errors. This decision was approved by Pius IX in 1864 and the prefect of the Congregation of the Propaganda was to inform Bishop Martin of the decision. In the light of subsequent racial strife in this country, it is unfortunate that the ending of the Civil War made the decision moot and the decision of the Holy See was not made known. Nevertheless, this decision stands as an indictment of the position of the American bishops prior to the Civil War. In no way could slavery as it existed in the United States be considered justified on moral

[1]"Letters to the Hon. John Forsyth, on the Subject of Domestic Slavery: to which are prefixed copies, in Latin and English, of the Pope's Apostolic Letter concerning the African Slave Trade, with some introductory remarks, etc.," reprinted in *The Works of the Right Rev. John England, First Bishop of Charleston* (Baltimore: 1849), Vol. III, pp. 106-191.
[2]*Ibid.*, p. 190.
[3]*Ibid.*, p. 191.
[4]University of Notre Dame Archives Microfilm. Archives of the Congregation of the Propaganda, *Scritture Riferite nei Congressi America Centrale*, Vol. 20, fols. 1207r-1213v. "Lettre Pastorale de Mgr. l'Evêque de Natchitoches à l'occasion de la Guerre du Sud pour son Indépendance," pp. 6-7. See Finbar Kenneally, O.F.M., *United States Documents in the Propaganda Fide Archives, A Calendar,* First Series, Vol. III, p. 75, no. 473.
[5]*Ibid.*, Vol. III, p. 75, no. 472; pp. 7-13. See also Maria Caravaglios, "A Roman Critique of the Pro-Slavery Views of Bishop Martin of Natchitoches, Louisiana," *Records of the American Catholic Historical Society of Philadelphia*, No. 83 (1972), pp. 67-81.

grounds, and Pope Gregory XVI in condemning the slave trade had condemned slavery itself.

THE RESPONSE OF BLACK CATHOLICS

In many ways the spiritual vitality of black Catholics themselves was a redemptive sign offered by the Church itself amid the violence and the degradation of slavery. In the Sulpician Archives in Baltimore is found a notebook entitled *Journal of the Commencement and of the proceedings of the Society of Colored People with the approbation of the Most Rev. Archp. Samuel [Eccleston]*. This journal is the little-known story of a group of over two hundred black Catholic men and women who met every Sunday evening for worship and spiritual instruction in the basement of the Cathedral hall in Baltimore from December of 1843 until September of 1845.[1] For almost two years these Catholics of African origin, some of whom may have been slaves, shared a spiritual experience. The document of this experience is probably the oldest record we have to date of a black Catholic lay community in this country. The journal seems to be the minutes of each meeting as recorded by the assistant pastor, Father John F. Hickey, a Sulpician attached to the Cathedral.

Black Churches like the African Methodist Episcopal Church and the independent black Baptist Churches enjoyed a certain independence and autonomy. Here were black Catholics with their own meetings who had the opportunity for self-determination. The name of the Holy Family was chosen and their own officials were elected. John Noel, a prominent Haitian, was chosen president, and a board was established that accepted new members into the society, which numbered some two hundred and fifty or more men and women. They were self-sustaining: dues were 6 and 1/4 cents per month, and out of this they bought needed benches and made their contribution to the cathedral fund. Two Masses were offered for each deceased member. Financial assistance was given to those in need. Later the need for a lending library was seen and books such as catechisms, lives of the saints, devotional literature and hymnals were acquired, along with a bookcase; books were lent for one cent for one month and one cent more for each additional week. Reading was important at a time when slaves were forbidden under severe penalty to learn to read and write.

The weekly meetings lasted for an hour and a half or two hours, sometimes even longer. There were prayers in common including five decades of the rosary. Father Hickey gave an instruction on a doctrinal or devotional subject. Singing was very important and normally there were four hymns sung each session, occasionally accompanied by violin. The choir and the council met during the week and there was often spontaneous prayer by at least one of the members. Then it ended. The members arrived one Sunday evening in early September 1845 and discovered that the Christian Brothers had taken over the hall. In October the decision was made to disband. There is no record as to whether the group was formed again later. The pastor of St. Peter's Church in Baltimore gave space in the basement of the Church for the lending library "for the use of Coloured people."

---

[1] Sulpician Archives in Baltimore, RG42 Box 2.

For the historian of black Catholicism, this society is not only important as a testament of faith and black Catholic spirituality but also one more indication that a black Catholic community lived and practiced its faith in the shadow of slavery.

Another important indication of the commitment to Catholicism by American Blacks is the existence of black Catholic religious women in the period prior to the Civil War. As early as 1824 an attempt had been made by Father Charles Nerinckx to establish a black sisterhood in Kentucky. In 1812 Nerinckx, a pioneer missionary from Belgium, had established a congregation of sisters who are known today as the Sisters of Loretto. He was genuinely interested in the evangelization of the slaves. As a result he conceived the project of a community of black sisters attached to the Sisters of Loretto. In 1824 his project had begun to be a reality when three young black women received the veil.[1] Forced to relinquish his position that same year, Nerinckx left Kentucky for Missouri where he died in August of 1824. Those who took over the guidance of the Sisters of Loretto saw no value in the foundation of a black sisterhood and the three sisters, it seems, were dismissed.[2]

Five years later, this time in Baltimore, a community of black religious women was established that would succeed. The community of Haitians in Baltimore attended Mass in the basement chapel of St. Mary's Seminary on Paca Street. Jacques Joubert de le Muraille (1777-1843), born in St. Jean d'Angely in the western part of France, ex-soldier, ex-colonial official for the French government in Haiti, then refugee from the Haitian Revolution, entered the Sulpicians in Baltimore following his ordination in 1810.[3] Joubert was assigned to teach catechism to the Haitian children, and discovered that they could not read. He also discovered two young Haitian women who welcomed the idea of teaching the children, particularly the girls, because they had for some time wanted to "consecrate their lives to God."[4] Impressed by this Joubert realized that he had the possible nucleus of a religious community; the original two young women soon became four.

Despite some opposition to the idea of black women becoming religious and wearing a religious habit, James Whitfield, the fourth Archbishop of Balti-

---

[1]See Camillus Maes, *The Life of Rev. Charles Nerinckx,* (Cincinnati: Robert Clarke & Co., 1880), pp. 510-511.

[2]For the difficulties of Nerinckx, see Maes, *ibid.,* pp. 512ff. See also Anna Catherine Minogue, *Annals of the Century* (New York: The America Press, 1912), pp. 95-97.

[3]Grace Sherwood, *The Oblates' One Hundred and One Years* (New York: The Macmillan Co., 1931), pp. 6-7. See also Christopher J. Kauffman, *Tradition and Transformation in Catholic Culture; The Priests of Saint Sulpice in the United States from 1791 to the Present* (New York: The Macmillan Co., 1988), pp. 113-115. For a look at the beginnings of the educational tradition of the Oblate Sisters, see Sister M. Reginald Gerdes, O.S.P., "To Educate and Evangelize: Black Catholic Schools of the Oblate Sisters of Providence (1828-1880)," *U.S. Catholic Historian,* 7 (Spring, Summer 1988), pp. 183-199.

[4]Josephite Archives, Baltimore, SAB RG 41 Box 2. Copy of the English translation of the *Original Diary of the Oblate Sisters of Providence, 1827-1842.* Both the English translation and the Diary written in French by Fr. Joubert are found in the Archives of the Oblate Sisters of Providence in Baltimore.

more, gave Joubert his support for a congregation of black women to be established in his diocese. On July 2nd, the feast of the Visitation, 1829, the four young women made vows at a Mass celebrated in their new home. A few days before, Elizabeth Lange, the young woman whose capabilities Joubert had initially recognized, had been chosen as the Superior.

Elizabeth Lange had been born in Cuba to Haitian parents who had fled Haiti in the wake of the Revolution. She arrived in the United States about 1817 probably in the South and later made her way to Baltimore and the Afro-French community of Haitians. Elizabeth Lange was not without financial resources, which she used for the welfare of the community. Later her mother was allowed to join the community.[1] The first sisters were all French-speaking. Very early on, however, African-Americans also entered. Moreover, women were able to join who had no financial resources. Some came who had only recently been freed from slavery.

From the beginning the sisters had a school for young girls. Some of the girls were boarders, and some of the boarders were orphans for whom they cared without payment. From time to time adult women found lodging with them and followed the conventual life without being sisters. A financial agreement was made in each instance.

The spiritual life of the sisters was modelled on the French spirituality of the nineteenth century. Father Tessier, the Sulpician Superior,[2] often preached the retreats and gave conferences. He introduced the custom of enrolling the sisters at the time of their reception of the habit into the Association of the Holy Slavery of the Mother of God. At that time each sister would receive a small chain: one might ask whether symbolically there was association between the African origin of the sisters and the harsh reality of slavery now sublimated into the particular form of devotion to Mary preached by St. Louis-Marie Grignion de Montfort (1673-1716).[3]

The one aspect of their spirituality that was unique to their origin as black religious was the position of St. Benedict the Moor as one of their secondary patrons. St. Benedict the Moor was a black man born in Sicily in 1526 of African slaves. Freed by his owner, he joined a group of hermits in Sicily, who lived according to the spirit of St. Francis of Assisi. When Pope Pius IV encouraged small congregations of hermits to amalgamate with the established orders in 1562, St. Benedict as superior joined the group to the Order of Friars Minor, the Brown Franciscans. He died in 1589 venerated by all, especially

---

[1] See Sherwood, *op. cit.,* pp. 28-30.

[2] Jean-Marie Tessier (1758-1840). See Kauffman, *op. cit.*

[3] St. Louis-Marie Grignion de Montfort preached a devotion to the Blessed Virgin based on the ideal of the Holy Slavery to Mary. This was set forth in his book *True Devotion to the Blessed Virgin,* but the devotion to the Holy Slavery was not original with him. It is not at all certain that the devotion preached to the Oblate Sisters of Providence was that of Grignion de Montfort since the manuscript of his book was not discovered until 1842 when it became very popular in nineteenth-century devotional life. For the biographical details of St. Louis-Marie Grignion de Montfort, see the article by Louis Perouas in the *Dictionnaire de Spiritualité,* 9:1073-1081. For information regarding the devotion of the Holy Slavery, see Stefano De Fiores, "Marie (Sainte Vierge). IV. De 1650 au début du 20e siècle. 3) l'esclavage marial." 10:461-465.

Palermo. Pope Pius VII canonized St. Benedict the Moor in 1807 partly as a statement against the slave trade.[1] Beginning in 1834, the sisters celebrated the Feast of St. Benedict the Moor on the Sunday within the Octave of the Ascension.[2]

The rule of the sisters was drawn up by Father Joubert, and it was probably he who gave them the title of Oblate Sisters of Providence. Early on, St. Francis of Rome (1384-1440) who founded the Oblates of *Tor de' Specchi* in Rome was considered one of their patrons. There was forged a spiritual relationship with this community of religious women, who lived according to the rule of St. Benedict, although they were not nuns living in strict enclosure.[3]

In 1831 the Oblate Sisters received their approval as a religious community from the Holy See, twelve years before Joubert died. Archbishop Eccleston (1801-1851) was not favorable to the sisters. The issue was race, seemingly the sentiment of many in Baltimore at that time.[4] Because of the good will of St. John Neumann (1811-1860), the future Bishop of Philadelphia and at the time Redemptorist Superior, spiritual aid was given to the sisters as the Sulpicians had ceased supplying a chaplain. In 1847 a young newly ordained Redemptorist priest, Thaddeus Anwander from Bavaria, volunteered to become their chaplain. Because of his faith and optimism, the Oblate Sisters of Providence survived and became one of the major forces for the evangelization of the black Catholic community in this country.

One of the ironies of black history in this country is the role played by African-Americans in the most unlikely times and places. Sister Therese Maxis Duchemin, one of the original founders of the Oblate Sisters, left the community in 1845 and went to Monroe, Michigan, where she and a Belgian Redemptorist priest, Louis Gillet, founded the Sisters of the Immaculate Heart of Mary. Sister Anne Constance, also an Oblate Sister, joined her in the new foundation.[5] The story of Sister Therese Duchemin is one of sorrow and suffering but what is

---

[1]See Giuseppe Morabito, "Benedetto il Moro, santo" in *Bibliotheca Sanctorum*, 2:1103-1104.

[2]Archives of the Oblate Sisters of Providence, *Journal*, English translation, p. 32, May 11, 1834. Today the feast is celebrated on April 4th.

[3]*Ibid.*, pp. 27-28, November 3, 1833. St. Frances of Rome was a widow who began a religious community of women who in the beginning did not make public vows or lead a cloistered life. They gave help to the poor and carried out other acts of mercy. St. Frances of Rome had strong ties with the Olivetan Benedictines, a reform congregation of the Order of St. Benedict. The Oblates are dependent upon the Olivetan Benedictines. See M. Monacho, "Oblates of Tor de'Specchi" in *New Catholic Encyclopedia*, Vol. 6, p. 25 and M.B. Rivaldi, "Oblate del Monastero di Tor de'Specchi" in *Dizionario degli Istituti di Perfezione*, 6:585-586.

[4]See Maria M. Lannon, *Mother Mary Elizabeth Lange, Life of Love and Service*. A brochure distributed by The Josephite Pastoral Center, Washington, DC. Sherwood is less specific about the disaffection for the Oblates; see pp. 109ff.

[5]Sister Diane Edward Shea, I.H.M., and Sister Marita Constance Supan, I.H.M., "Apostolate of the Archives—God's Mystery through History," *The Josephite Harvest*, 85 (Summer 1983), pp. 10-13. See also Sister M. Rosalita, I.H.M., *No Greater Service, The History of the Congregation of the Sisters of the Holy Family of New Orleans* (privately published in 1976), pp. 6-18. See also Roger Baudier, *The Catholic Church in Louisiana* (New Orleans, 1939), pp. 397-398.

perhaps most remarkable yet is that one of the largest communities of religious women in the United States has a black woman as its founder before the Civil War in a community where Blacks have been practically non-existent. Sister Therese Duchemin died in 1892, having spent most of her religious life as an exile in a convent in Canada away from the community she founded. She was permitted to return to the Sisters of the Immaculate Heart in West Chester, Pennsylvania, a few years before her death.

Thirteen years after the founding of the Oblate Sisters of Providence in Baltimore, another foundation of black sisters was established in New Orleans. This foundation was known as the Sisters of the Holy Family. The founder was a young, very beautiful woman of twenty-nine years, Henriette Delille (1813-1862). With her as co-founder was a young woman named Juliette Gaudin (1808-1887) who was thirty-four. Under the guidance of Père Etienne Rousselon (1800-1866), originally from Lyons in France, who at the time was vicar general in New Orleans, the two women began the community and established a home for aged women.[1]

Both women belonged to that third group of Louisiana society, the "Free People of Color," those who were of mixed African and European ancestry. Henriette Delille, despite her own social background, developed a religious vocation. She was influenced through her work with a French nun, Sister Ste-Marthe Frontier, a member of a French nursing order who eventually returned to France. She had opened a school for young girls of color and had night classes in religion for Blacks, both free and slaves. Sister Ste-Marthe had enlisted Henriette in her ministry of teaching the slaves. Another French woman, Marie-Jeanne Aliquot, who arrived in New Orleans in 1832, committed her life to the service of the black population as a result of being saved by a black man from a near drowning. She joined the teaching staff in the school opened by Sister Ste-Marthe, and later sought to start a religious community with the young women of color like Henriette and Juliette and with herself as director. The project was unfortunately prevented by the Louisiana laws against racial mixing. Finally, Henriette and Juliette launched out on their own with the help of the vicar general.

With their first ministry being a hospice for the aged poor, they were forced to meet the legal demands for a corporation. A group of free people of color formed an association of the Holy Family to provide the legal support for the community. In fact it would not be until 1852 that the members of the community were considered ready for vows. At that time they were three.

The work of the community was enlarged to include the teaching of children, some of them boarders. At night they taught catechism to adults, many of whom were slaves. By 1860 there were six religious. The community grew

---

[1]For information regarding the founders of the Holy Family Sisters and details regarding the early foundation, see Sister Audrey Marie Detiege, *Henriette Delille, Free Woman of Color* (New Orleans: Sisters of the Holy Family, 1976) and Sister Mary Francis Borgia Hart, S.S.F., *Violets in the King's Garden; A History of the Sisters of the Holy Family of New Orleans* (privately published, 1976), pp. 6-18. See also Roger Baudier, *The Catholic Church in Louisiana* (New Orleans: 1939), pp. 397-398.

slowly and faced many hardships including a precarious financial situation. In 1862 Henriette Delille died.

Like the Oblate Sisters of Providence, with whom they had no contact in the beginning, the Sisters of the Holy Family were formed in a piety that was essentially French. In a sense this was not surprising as the Free People of Color were completely French in culture. The sisters, however, only received gradual recognition as religious by the society at large. It was only in 1872 that the sisters could wear the religious habit publicly in New Orleans.

Both the Oblate Sisters and the Holy Family Sisters are significant not only because they were two black religious congregations in a region where many Blacks were either slaves or the victims of racial prejudice, but also because these were two of the oldest congregations of American sisters, independent from a European center. Moreover, they are the living proof of the existence of a vital black Catholic community prior to the Civil War. Vocations to the religious life are a palpable sign of religious fervor in a community. These intrepid women who faced untold hardships were the sisters and the daughters of a people who had paid dearly for their Catholic faith.

In the history of the Catholic Church in New York prior to the Civil War, one figure stands out before all others as an example of holiness. Tall, black-skinned, always on foot, Pierre Toussaint was a Haitian slave who had come to New York in 1787, two years before the establishment of the American Catholic hierarchy. Toussaint was born a slave on the Berard estate near St-Marc on the west coast of Haiti in 1766. He died in 1853, recognized by many as a man of extraordinary charity and holiness.[1]

Toussaint obtained his freedom in 1807. From his earnings as a hairdresser for the wealthy women of New York, he purchased the freedom of the woman who became his wife and of his sister who had also been a slave in the Berard household. Pierre Toussaint supported all types of charitable enterprises, white and black. He also lent money to the needy French refugees of the Haitian colony in New York. He cared for the sick and the penniless who came to his attention. He gave a home and training to homeless black youths. He served as confidant to many including his clients and his correspondents, who were both white and black. Mass every morning, visits to the Blessed Sacrament every evening, genial and vivacious, generous to all, a loving devoted husband to his wife and caring father to his orphaned niece who died young of tuberculosis, he managed to lead a life of simple dignity in a city where racial tensions ran high and the life of Blacks was circumscribed and cramped by poverty. Far from being the "Catholic Uncle Tom," a sobriquet some well-meaning but misguided

---

[1]Over 1100 pieces of documentation consisting of letters to Pierre Toussaint, a certain number of his own letters and other personal papers are found in the *Pierre Toussaint Papers*, Manuscript and Rare Books Section, New York Public Library. A year after his death there appeared a life of Toussaint written by a member of the Schuyler family who knew him well; see Hannah Sawyer Lee, *Memoirs of Pierre Toussaint; Born a slave in St. Domingo* (Boston, 1854), For a modern biography of Toussaint, see Ellen Tarry, *The Other Toussaint; A Post-Revolutionary Black* (Boston: St. Paul Editions, 1981).

Catholics gave him,[1] he was a man who overcame the racism of his time by
heroic charity and greatness of soul.

LOST OPPORTUNITY

In a letter to the Congregation of the Propaganda dated September 18, 1863,
Henry Binsse wrote about the position of the Catholic Church in the United
States regarding slavery. The letter seemed to suggest the possibility that the
South might win. Were it to happen, he reasoned, the bishops would no longer
be able to practice the politics of "abstention" in regard to the question of slavery. Ultimately, what the Franco-American lawyer wanted was for the bishops
to come to grips with the moral dilemma of slavery and its consequences.[2]

Three years later, when Martin J. Spalding, the Archbishop of Baltimore,
summoned the American Bishops to the Second Plenary Council of Baltimore in
1866, he had set on the agenda a plan to meet the consequences of the massive
emancipation of the slaves. He had told Cardinal McCloskey of New York that
it was most important to discuss the future evangelization of the freed Blacks.
"It is a golden opportunity for reaping a harvest of souls..."[3] For Spalding it
was time for the bishops to meet the consequences of slavery in terms of the
Church's mission to work for the salvation of all.

On the agenda was a proposal from the Congregation of the Propaganda to
set up a coordinator of ministry for Blacks on the national level. He was to be a
priest or perhaps even a bishop who would have jurisdiction over all missionary
work for the African-Americans. The idea had originally been the suggestion of
Martin J. Spalding, who as Bishop of Louisville during the Civil War had written the Congregation of the Propaganda a lengthy memorial on the Civil War
that was more or less biased to the Southern cause.[4] Now that the war was over
and he was Archbishop of Baltimore, Spalding was concerned about the future of
the freed slaves and the opportunity that was present for a new effort on the part
of the Church for the conversion of the African-American people. The Congregation of the Propaganda took up the proposal of Spalding and made it its own.
Spalding never revealed that the idea was originally his own.[5]

---

[1]See Henry Binsse, "A Catholic Uncle Tom, Pierre Toussaint," *Historical Records
and Studies,* 12 (1918), pp. 90-101.
[2]University of Notre Dame Archives. Propaganda Archives, Microfilm. "Binsse
to Propaganda. September 18, 1863." *Scritture Riferite nei Congressi America
Centrale,* fol. 410. See Kenneally, *op. cit.,* Vol. III, p. 29, no. 174. This letter
had been written in the wake of the terrible Draft riots in which so many Irish
mobs burned, attacked and injured many helpless Blacks.
[3]Edward J. Misch, *The American Bishops and the Negro from the Civil War to the
Third Plenary Council of Baltimore, (1865-1884),* (Dissertation, Gregorian University, Rome, 1968), p. 130. The letter of Spalding to McCloskey, October 9,
1865, in the New York Archdiocesan Archives.
[4]See David Spalding, "Martin John Spalding's Dissertation on the American Civil
War" in *The Catholic Historical Review,* 52 (1966-1967), pp. 66-85. Spalding
gives a translation of the entire text. Martin J. Spalding was more or less for a
gradual emancipation of the slaves; see pp. 78-79.
[5]See Misch, *op. cit.,* pp. 236ff.

The Fathers of the Second Plenary Council met in extraordinary session on October 22, 1866 to discuss this proposal. The minutes of the session were never published.[1] It was a tumultuous session, and there was a great deal of bitterness. Some of the bishops felt that the creation of an office with national jurisdiction on behalf of the Blacks would encroach on their own jurisdiction. At the same time there was resentment on the part of a few that special consideration was being shown to Blacks. The result was that nothing was done: each bishop was to deal with the question of black evangelization in his own diocese. The door of opportunity was closed.

A RENEWED BLACK CATHOLIC COMMUNITY

What the bishops were unable to do, black Catholics did. By the end of the century there was held a series of five Black Catholic Lay Congresses that brought together on a national level the leaders of the black Catholic community.

In 1889 there was published a souvenir volume dedicated to Cardinal Gibbons and the American hierarchy entitled: *Three Great Events in the History of the Catholic Church in the United States. 1. The Centenary Celebrations. 2. Proceedings of the First American Catholic Congress. 3. Dedication of the Catholic University.*[2] On page 21 there appears the photograph of the only black man in the book. It is a photograph of Daniel Rudd who was a member of the Committee on Organization for the First American Catholic Lay Congress held in Baltimore, November 11-12, 1889. The Congress was held to celebrate the centennial of the establishment of the American hierarchy. By that time Daniel Rudd had organized the first lay Catholic Congress in the United States. It was the Black Lay Catholic Congress held at St. Augustine's Church in Washington, DC, January 1-14, 1889.

Rudd was born a slave in Bardstown, Kentucky, in 1854, one of twelve children in a Catholic family. After the Civil War he followed his elder brother to Springfield, Ohio, in order to complete his secondary education. There in Springfield he began a newspaper in 1886 which subsequently became known as *The American Catholic Tribune,* the only black Catholic weekly newspaper for most of the 1890's.[3]

Rudd was an enthusiastic, devout Catholic who sincerely believed that there would be a massive influx of Blacks into the Catholic Church. He also believed that the Catholic Church would be the great instrument for uplifting the African-American people. He used the newspaper and the lecture circuit to champion the cause of Catholicism and the Church's role on behalf of American Blacks.

Rudd organized the first Black Catholic Lay Congress in January, 1889 in Washington, DC, as a means of uniting the black Catholic community. As he

---

[1]Baltimore Archdiocesan Archives, 39A-D5.

[2](Detroit: William H. Hughes, 1889).

[3]For information regarding Rudd, see David Spalding, "The Negro Catholic Congresses, 1889-1894" in *The Catholic Historical Review,* 55 (1969), pp. 337-357. See also Cyprian Davies, "The Holy See and American Black Catholics. A Forgotten Chapter in the History of the American Church" in *U.S. Catholic Historian,* 7 (Spring, Summer 1988), pp. 157-181.

wrote in his newspaper, "The Catholics of the Colored race should be the leaven, which would raise up their people not only in the eye of God but before men."[1] The delegates, all male, numbered about a hundred. The opening Mass was celebrated by Father Augustus Tolton, who was the first black priest generally recognized as such in the United States.

Tolton had been born a slave in Ralls County, Missouri, in 1854, one of three children born to Catholic parents. Tolton's father had fled slavery and joined the Union Army where he died in St. Louis at the beginning of the Civil War. Tolton's mother and her children had escaped slavery by crossing the Mississippi River and settling in Quincy, Illinois.[2] There, as a young man, Augustus Tolton became aware of a calling to the priesthood. Unfortunately no American seminary was open to receiving a black candidate. With the help of the Franciscan General, Tolton obtained entrance into the Urban College in Rome, the foreign mission seminary attached to the Congregation of the Propaganda. In 1886 he was ordained to the priesthood. He returned to the United States to the Diocese of Alton, Illinois. Unfortunatley he met opposition on the part of a neighboring priest in Quincy where Tolton was pastor of the black parish. Tolton transferred to the Archdiocese of Chicago in 1889 where he began the first black parish in that city. Tolton went to work with zeal not only on behalf of Blacks in Chicago, but also in the service of black Catholics throughout the country until his death in 1897 at the age of forty-three.

Tolton was the great inspiration of black Catholics on the national level. He was not, however, the first black priest in the United States. Three of the ten slave children of Morris Healy became priests. Michael Morris Healy was a planter and slaveholder in rural Georgia. He was not married, but he fathered ten children by his slave, Eliza Healy. Three of his sons were sent North to study by their father. The eldest son, James Augustine Healy (1830-1900) was ordained a priest in Paris for Boston. He became the second Bishop of Portland, Maine in 1875.[3] His brother, Sherwood Alexander Healy (1836-1875), was ordained in Rome also for the Boston Diocese. He was a brilliant man whose career was cut short by his death in the same year that his brother became a bishop. Another brother, Patrick Francis Healy (1834-1919), became a Jesuit and was ordained at Louvain in 1865. Patrick Healy was the builder of modern Georgetown University, where he became the first man to hold the office of president.[4] The brothers were known to be of African ancestry, although in the case of Patrick this was not widely known, but they did not readily identify with the black Catholic community. Their upbringing and training had separated

[1]*The American Catholic Tribune,* May 14, 1888. The only extant copies of the ACT are found in the archives of the Catholic Historical Society, St. Charles Borromeo Seminary, Overbrook, PA. The ACT is available on microfilm from the Board of Microtext, American Theological Library Association.
[2]See the biography of Tolton by Sister Caroline Hemesath, *From Slave to Priest; Biography of Rev. Augustine Tolton, First Afro-American Priest in the United States* (Chicago: Franciscan Herald Press, 1973).
[3]See Albert S. Foley, S.J., *Bishop Healy: Beloved Outcast* (New York: Farrar, Straus and Young, 1954).
[4]See Foley, *God's Men of Color: The Colored Catholic Priests of the United States, 1854-1954* (New York: Farrar, Straus and Young, 1955), pp. 13-31.

them from their past. As a result they were neither known nor appreciated by that community.[1]

There were four more Black Catholic Lay Congresses in the United States. The second was in Cincinnati in 1891, the next in Philadelphia in 1892; and the last two were in Chicago in 1893 and Baltimore in 1894. Among other issues these congresses took a strong position regarding such issues as racial segregation within the Church. The result of these endeavors and, in fact, the long-term influence of the Black Catholic Lay Congresses belong more properly to the second century of the Church's American history. It is in the early part of the twentieth century that Rome began to take an active part in the evangelization of black Catholics. This intervention more than anything else helped set the stage for the growth and development of the black Catholic community as it is today.

In many ways the first one hundred and ten years of black Catholics in the United States Church is the story of a people who survived as Roman Catholics in spite of "benign neglect" and at times outright opposition. They clung to a Church which in the United States often took the side of slavery and was unwilling to take many risks in their support. More numerous than many would believe, these black Catholics took leadership as laymen and laywomen with a tenacious faith too little known and too often ignored. They took a responsibility within the Church because as they said, "From the days of Christ it has been her mission to inculcate the doctrine of love and not of hate; to raise up the downtrodden, and to rebuke the proud." Finally, with pride they rejoiced "that our Church, the Church of our love, the Church of our faith, has not failed to stand by its historic record."[2] That record was one of justice regardless of race. More than any other ethnic group in the American Church, it was the faith of black Catholics that made the Church in the first century of its existence truly Catholic in the most profound meaning of the word.

[1]See Joseph Taylor Skerrett, "'Is There Anything Wrong with Being a Nigger?' Racial Identity and Three Nineteenth-Century Priests," in *Freeing the Spirit*, 5 (1977) pp. 27-37.
[2]Citation from the lengthy address of the "Colored Catholics of the United States of the Fourth Congress," Chicago, 1893. The text was published in *The Boston Pilot*, September 23, 1893, p. 6.

CHAPTER FIVE

Women and American Catholicism, 1789-1989

Margaret Susan Thompson
Syracuse University

Colonial attorney Margaret Brent was a Catholic; so was twentieth-century birth-control advocate Margaret Sanger.[1] There has been Mother Seton, now canonized, and labor organizer Mother Jones, who told us to "pray for the dead, and fight like hell for the living." Maria Madalena and Maria Costanza Bentivoglio brought the Poor Clares to this country; Clare Booth Lace served in Congress. Entertainment has produced both Helen Hayes and Madonna; political advocacy has engendered a Phyllis Schlafly and an Eleanor Smeal. In 1680 Kateri Tekakwitha became the first acknowledged North American-born martyr; exactly three centuries later, four missionaries, Maura Clarke, Jean Donovan, Ita Ford and Dorothy Kazel, experienced the same fate at the southern end of the continent. And then there have been the hundreds of thousands of those whose names have been forgotten, mostly poor, many of them immigrants: the launderers, housekeepers and cooks; factory workers, farm laborers, secretaries, sales clerks and waitresses; wives and mothers, daughters, sisters and aunts; pioneer professionals, indentured servants and slaves; prostitutes, prisoners, persons of prayer—even a few prophets.

All women. All American. All Catholic. For over two centuries, their history and experiences have been coterminous with *and* integral to those of their gender, their nation and their Church. Clearly, no single essay—even if it consisted of nothing more than a litany of names, categories and accomplishments—could hope to present more than a partial and distorted glimpse of what female American Catholics have been all about during the past two hundred years.[2] So the objective here is far more limited; indeed, my intention is only to address a single question: What has the impact of women been upon the development of American Catholicism?

I am not, in other words, interested in detailing the general achievements of women in the U.S., individually or collectively, who happen to be Catholics but

---

[1] A number of points in this paper have evolved from those in previous pieces of my work, which shall be cited when relevant; others have been generated by research in connection with a book-length study of American Sisters, *The Yoke of Grace: American Nuns and Social Change, 1808-1917,* to be published by Oxford University Press. In addition, I would like to thank the following friends for allowing me to thrash out my ideas with them: Thomas J. Costello, James Hennesey, Malcolm O'Malley, Irene Thompson and Margaret Ellen Traxler. Naturally, while I am grateful for their insights, none of these people is in any way responsible for what I have written here.

[2] A recent volume that contains a number of perspectives and insights is *American Catholic Women: A Historical Exploration,* ed. Karen Kennelly (New York: 1989); while I have benefitted from reading this book, the approach of most of its authors is quite different from mine here.

whose faith is incidental or irrelevant to what they have done. (No catalogues of "first" or "notable" Catholics: lawyers, Cabinet or military officers, doctors and doctorates, Olympic athletes and mountain climbers, Pulitzer Prize and Oscar winners, or whatever!) Similarly, I am concerned only peripherally with individuals or organizations, even those explicitly identifying themselves as Catholic, whose energies have been expended primarily in the secular domain; let others relate the sagas of particular and associated Catholic nurses and teachers, reformers and social feminists, business and union leaders, social workers, suffragists, etc. Rather, my focus will be upon women's actions and influence specifically within the sphere of Catholicism itself: upon their contributions to what it has come to mean to be Catholic in the United States.

The legacy of women has typically been ignored or taken for granted. But it is, nonetheless, profound. As we shall see, our foremothers have played roles at least equal to those of men in transmitting, defining, preserving and adapting the faith within a complex and often hostile American environment. It is unquestionably a story worth telling, even if the present essay can do little more than scratch the surface.

When American Catholicism was in its earliest stages of development—a phase that successive areas of new settlement would go through until at least the end of the nineteenth century—priests were scarce, parishes virtually nonexistent, and Catholic practice largely a matter of personal and familial responsibility.[1] Given these circumstances, laypeople, and particularly women, were crucial to the faith's survival. In a culture that increasingly regarded piety as an especially *feminine* virtue, women were expected to bear primary responsibility for catechizing their offspring, transmitting religious traditions, and maintaining individual and communal moral standards.[2] Within the Catholic community, the absence of clerics meant that parents or midwives typically baptized newborns; members of the laity witnessed each others' marriages, prayed at their neighbors' deathbeds and oversaw their funerals. And on those rare occasions when mis-

---

[1]My approach in this essay is interpretive, and is not intended to represent a chronological approach to the topic. The present reference to "earliest stages," for instance, may be taken to refer to the colonial period for Maryland, the early nineteenth century for Kentucky, New York and Pennsylvania, and the early twentieth century for places where development was still embryonic at that time. Similar statements will recur throughout; dates will be provided when necessary. Meanwhile, for background specifically pertinent to the discussion here, see James Hennesey, *American Catholics: A History of the Roman Catholic Community in the United States* (New York: 1981), esp. chapters 4-7; and Jay P. Dolan, *The American Catholic Experience: A History from Colonial Times to the Present* (Garden City, NY: 1985), esp. chapters 3-4.

[2]For general background, see Barbara Welter, "The Cult of True Womanhood, 1820-1860," *American Quarterly* 27 (1966), pp. 151-174; Colleen McDannell, *The Christian Home in Victorian America, 1840-1900* (Bloomington, IN: 1986); Ann Douglas, *The Feminization of American Culture* (New York: 1977). On roles for Catholic women, specifically, see Karen Kennelly, "Ideals of American Catholic Womanhood," and Colleen McDannell, "Catholic Domesticity, 1860," both in Kennelly, *op. cit.,* pp. 1-16, 48-80.

sionary priests passed through the vicinity, women not only provided them with accommodations, food and laundering, but offered the homes for which they cared as sites for celebration of the Mass and other sacraments. The pioneer U.S. Church, then, much like that of first-century Christians, was a preeminently domestic body and, as such, depended greatly upon those whose presumed *natural* domain was considered to be the household.

But women's influence extended beyond the sphere of their homes. Until well after the Civil War, education (and therefore provision of schools) was left largely in private hands; the same, of course, was true of other social services like medicine, care of orphans and other unfortunates, etc. Such matters tended to be viewed as natural extensions of what ought to be familial responsibilities, best undertaken by those who presumably were endowed with "maternal instinct." So it should come as no surprise that women became the principal executors of these functions. And in a nation whose populace acknowledged (however diversely and sometimes vaguely) a Judeo-Christian tradition—including its teaching on charity—it should be equally unsurprising that a substantial number of them were carried out under explicitly religious auspices.

For American Catholics in particular, who tended to be a largely impoverished, frequently foreign-born minority that was regarded with suspicion and even hatred by the Protestant majority, schools and institutions for the administration of charity became essential weapons in the battles to "preserve" the faith and to guard against "leakage" from it.[1] By 1884 the U.S. Bishops were so convinced of this that the Third Council of Baltimore mandated that every parish should have its own school and that Catholic children should be required to attend them.[2] Their edict was potent (if unwitting) testimony to the central role of women within the American Church: the overwhelming majority of these schools were staffed exclusively by members of women's religious orders.

Many standard histories of American Catholicism, Catholic education, and even religious orders tend to credit the hierarchy with having founded both parochial schools and the congregations who staffed them. But the fact is that it was primarily women who were responsible for initiating the endeavor. Between 1809 and 1829, four indigenous communities of sisters—Mother Seton's Sisters of Charity, the Sisters of Loretto, the Sisters of Charity of Nazareth, and the Oblate Sisters of Providence—evolved from informal associations of laywomen who had already been engaged in teaching the children of their neighborhoods, before they submitted to supervision from ecclesial authorities. Only after observing the usefulness of these groups did bishops and priests begin to organize additional communities or bring others from abroad.[3] The original impulses,

[1]Terminology is derivative from that in Gerald Shaughnessy, *Has the Immigrant Kept the Faith?* (New York: 1925).
[2]"The Pastoral Letter of 1884," in *The National Pastorals of the American Hierarchy (1792-1919)*, ed. Peter Guilday (Washington, DC: 1923), pp. 280-282.
[3]The only order of sisters to come from Europe between 1809 and 1829 was the Religious of the Sacred Heart (1818), who initially worked exclusively within French-speaking areas of the old Louisiana Purchase; the Bishop responsible for their arrival was already familiar with the work of Mother Seton's sisters in Maryland. Similarly, the Dominican priests who oversaw the founding of the St. Catherine Dominican Sisters in 1822 benefitted from a decade of observation of

however, came from women's own experience, and from their self-initiated responses to the needs of the people around them.

By forming themselves into religious orders, the members of the earliest
American congregations exhibited implicit acknowledgement of a fact of
Catholic life that would continue to carry weight in the United States as it had in
the Old World: whenever possible, officially-sanctioned ministers—whether ordained or not—were preferable to the laity as executors of the Church's work.[1]
Both doctrine and popular piety accorded more status to those in vows and Holy
Orders than to the ordinary rank-and-file; as presumed occupants of a "higher
state of grace," their efforts automatically assumed a legitimacy and influence
that comparable efforts by the "unconsecrated" normally could not hope to attain.
Thus, for over 150 years—from the founding of Mother Seton's community in
1809 until the Second Vatican Council of the 1960's—a disproportionate
amount of whatever influence women had within American Catholicism would
almost inevitably be exerted by sisters. And because this essay is concerned
specifically with the role of women *within* the Church, much of what follows
will be focused upon that particular segment of the female populace.[2]

The extent, range and diversity of the roles of nuns[3] changed considerably
over time, and under different circumstances. Moreover, given the limits of extant research, the virtual exclusion of all women (including sisters) from most
Catholic historiography, and the brevity of the present essay, the generalizations
that I will offer here must necessarily be tentative and at least somewhat
speculative. It is possible, however, to delineate a schema of how sisters and
other women worked within American Catholicism that is both plausible and
suggestive. If nothing else, when it is fleshed out with a few representative examples, it should indicate some of the ways in which the female contributions to
Church development in this country have been seriously underappreciated,
thereby opening the door to further inquiry.

It needs to be recognized at the outset that, at the time of Catholicism's origins in the United States, the position of nuns reflected that of all women in the
Church and in contemporary society. Like their counterparts who did not take
vows, sisters were of course ineligible for Holy Orders, and even regarded as
"occasions of sin" for the men who did. To sustain and reinforce the assumptions that placed all women in roles that were fundamentally spousal and maternal, derivative, that is, rather than primary within the patriarchal construct, nuns
were described as "brides of Christ," and their ministries seen as the manifesta-

the neighboring Lorettine and Nazareth communities. Bishop England, who
founded the Sisters of Our Lady of Mercy in Charleston in 1830, was inspired to
do so largely because of the successes he had seen elsewhere. And the catalogue
of comparable stories could be multiplied endlessly.

[1]Sisters, of course, are themselves technically members of the laity, since women
are ineligible for ordination in the Catholic Church. In this essay, use of the term
"laity" conforms to popular rather than technical usage, which distinguishes members of religious orders from the so-called "ordinary faithful."

[2]Much of what I will say here is based upon research I have done in connection
with *The Yoke of Grace, op. cit.*

[3]Again, usage here conforms to popular practice; although members of active congregations are not technically nuns, the terms "nun," "sister" and "woman religious" will be used interchangeably throughout the essay.

tions of "spiritual motherhood."[1] And just as laywomen were deemed to belong under the authority of their fathers and husbands, women religious were placed under the jurisdiction of "Ecclesiastical Superiors": clerics who, according to canon law, could overrule virtually all decisions made by sister-superiors, and who could and often did appoint those sister-superiors themselves. At least theoretically, then, sisters, like all Catholic women, should have enjoyed little independence; for at least theoretically their ecclesial position seemed to offer few opportunities for autonomous action or for discernible influence upon the shape of their church's development.

To a great extent practice did follow prescription. Nineteenth-century women who became nuns, after all, were not only products of both a culture and a Church that were intrinsically patriarchal, they were devoted enough to the latter to make perpetual commitment to its service. Everything in sisters' training and spirituality acted to reinforce the primacy of a form of obedience that equated the voice of one's superior to the voice of God, and that put all clerics (each an *Alter Christus*) above even the most exalted religious "Mother" in the hierarchy of religious authority. When this is combined with the fact that Catholic piety was exhibiting an increasingly strong Eucharistic orientation (the observance of which required ministration by one in Holy Orders), we can see why reverence for the priesthood and acquiescence in a subordinate role for women were characteristic dimensions of Victorian Catholicity, especially for those in the convent. The meek and unquestioning sister, as well as the teaching nuns who promoted docile femininity and gentility as much as erudition in their academies, are no mere products of fiction construed by subsequently disaffected alumnae; the memories of generations of Catholic women who recall "Sister's" paeans on behalf of "glorious submissiveness" are generally accurate.

Thus it would be unfair to portray the typical nineteenth-century nun as a sort of proto-feminist. Those in her charge, like Sister herself, were encouraged to accept and adjust to their "sphere," rather than challenge the appropriateness of the sphere itself. Indeed, by helping to invest images of domesticity and maternity (or, alternatively, virginity) with spiritual significance, her perorations tended to validate and reinforce the precepts that emanated regularly from the pulpit.

Still, actions often speak louder than words. However unintended it might have been, the historical record contains ample evidence that the reality of religious life for women left open the possibility of roles quite different from the "official" ones.[2] Through the very lives they led, sisters demonstrated that women were able to make unique and significant contributions to the development and maintenance of American Catholicism and American society as a

---

[1]Much of this section is derived from my "'Father Didn't Always Know Best: Sisters Versus Clerics in Nineteenth-Century American Catholicism," a paper presented at the 1987 meeting of the Social Science History Association, New Orleans.
[2]These points received greater elaboration in my "Discovering Foremothers: Sisters, Society, and the American Catholic Experience," *U.S. Catholic Historian,* 5 (1986); "To Serve the People of God: Nineteenth-Century Sisters and the Creation of an American Religious Life," Cushwa Center Working Paper (1987); and "The New Nuns of Yesteryear," *USA Today* (magazine, March 1989), pp. 84-87.

whole. Countless women they taught and otherwise worked with would be inspired to follow their example as active participants in the secular realm. Further, although their religion was founded upon sacraments that they were ineligible to administer, nuns could and did deliver a range of extra-sacramental services that were central to the survival both of the institutional Church and its faithful. By the 1830's there were already more sisters than priests in this country. And such a numerical advantage, which would grow greater over time (and still exists in the 1980's), meant that women traditionally have comprised the vast majority of professional church ministers. It was their communities that established and ran most of the schools, hospitals, home visitations, orphanages, settlement houses and asylums that came to define much of what the ordinary faithful experienced as the real presence of Catholicism in their daily lives. So it is probably fair to say that many laypeople were as likely to encounter (and depend upon) more of the various ministries of nuns than they were those of the clergy.

The eagerness with which bishops, pastors and representatives of the laity repeatedly begged for the presence of sisters and their good works, evidence of which abounds in congregational, parish and diocesan histories, provides persuasive testimony to the value which American Catholics consistently attached to the activities of religious orders. And the fact that so many of these petitions met with failure testifies equally strongly to the fact that the demand for sisters always exceeded the supply. But what has rarely been noted is that, because nuns were so eagerly sought after, they were able to retain a great deal of control over their lives, despite the very real strictures of canon law and customary patterns of ecclesial deference. Stated simply, women religious were in a seller's market; as a result, their positions frequently could prevail when disputes arose between them and the prelates who had authority over them. And because nuns very often perceived things differently from the men who served as their ecclesiastical superiors, the women's visions of what Catholicism ought to be and how it ought to be manifested very often became the defining vision in the United States.

One example (although it would come to involve several independent communities) will have to suffice here to illustrate that defining vision: that of the Sisters of Charity.[1] The first band of these in the U.S. was organized by Elizabeth Ann Bayley Seton in 1809; Seton used the Rule of the French Daughters of

---

[1]This discussion is based upon materials in the archives of the Daughters of Charity (Emmitsburg, MD), the Sisters of Charity of Nazareth (KY), and the Sisters of Charity of Mount St. Vincent (NY) and of Cincinnati. See also Anna Blanche McGill, *The Sisters of Charity of Nazareth, Kentucky* (New York: 1917); M. Columba Fox, *The Life of the Right Reverend John Baptist Mary David* (New York: 1925); James Maria Spillane, *Kentucky Spring* (St. Meinrad, IN: 1968); Mary Agnes McCann, *History of Mother Seton's Daughters* [of Cincinnati], 3 vols. (New York: 1917); Marjorie Walsh, *Sisters of Charity of New York* (New York: 1960); Ellin M. Kelly, "The Rule of St. Vincent de Paul and American Women's Religious Communities," paper presented at the Cushwa Center Conference on Perspectives on American Catholicism, Notre Dame, IN, Nov. 1982, and *Numerous Choirs: A Chronicle of Elizabeth Bayley Seton and Her Spiritual Daughters*, Vol. I (Evansville, IN: 1981).

Charity as the basis for her group's Constitution, but insisted upon modifying several of its provisions that she regarded as unsuitable to conditions in the New World. The American-born Archbishop Carroll of Baltimore concurred in this approach, but from the very beginning a number of French Sulpician and Vincentian priests tried to unite the sisters in Emmitsburg with the Parisian-based Daughters, whom they had known and admired before leaving their homeland. By 1812 one of the most persistent of those Frenchmen, Jean Baptiste David, had moved to Kentucky, where he oversaw the foundation of the Sisters of Charity of Nazareth, led by Mother Catherine Spalding, who added further amendments to the "Seton Rule" which he had brought with him. Meanwhile, within a couple of decades, women from the Emmitsburg motherhouse had established missions in cities throughout the country, including New York and Cincinnati.

Clerical pressure for union with France intensified after the deaths of Seton and Carroll; indeed, by 1850 the Maryland-based congregation was amalgamated into the French Daughters through a long series of maneuvers that the Sisters were deliberately kept in the dark about, until the merger was a *fait accompli*.[1] And just when the Maryland machinations began to gather steam, around 1840, Jean Baptiste David started his own campaign to place the Nazareth community under Emmitsburg's jurisdiction, as a precursor to its becoming part of the European order. From the outset, Spalding and her sisters actively resisted the plan, basing their position on the argument that they, and not the foreign-born David, were best able to determine the mode of life appropriate to their particular setting. After a series of verbal and written negotiations between nuns and prelates, Spalding prepared a petition that every professed member of her congregation signed; among other things, it asserted that

> it was much better for both our happiness and spiritual good that we should exist always as...a separate and distinct body....Surely religion in Kentucky can be more extensively and effectively served by us as we now exist."[2]

In the face of the pressing needs that their services were meeting in the Bardstown area, both Bishop Flaget and David (now the Coadjutor) felt it necessary to acquiesce to their resistance. For similar reasons, substantial numbers of those from the Maryland motherhouse who were stationed in New York and Cincinnati refused to submit to arguments emanating from Emmitsburg that rejection of the merger represented a "betrayal" of their vocation. And because bishops in those cities also did not want to lose the contributions that the sisters were making to the well-being of people in their dioceses, the result was creation of two more independent (and indigenous) communities of "Seton" Sisters of Charity.

---

[1]Evidence that clerics, and not the sisters themselves, orchestrated the merger is ample in the Emmitsburg archives. See, for example, Bishop Joseph Rosati to John Timon, C.M., July 8, 1840 and July 9, 1842; L.R. Deluol, 1846: Portion of document presented to Fathers of the Sixth Provincials Council of Baltimore (May 1846); "Circular" by L.R. Deluol to Sisters of the Baltimore Province, September 7, 1849; and "Father [Francis] Burlando's Notes relating to Union with France."
[2]Petition in the Nazareth Archives.

Now I do not wish to suggest that the perspectives of clerics and sisters were routinely in conflict; as I stated earlier, nineteenth-century nuns were not even implicitly the purveyors of a distinctly feminine, must less feminist, agenda. My point is more subtle than that: because they and their services were in demand, women religious were able to maintain a level of autonomy and authority over their own lives and activities that was unusual for *any* of their female contemporaries. Moreover, as persons who directly and by example were responsible for educating thousands of women (and men) who would never take vows themselves, they served as role models, inculcating those who came under their influence with the implicit message that one did not need to be ordained in order to have worth and to contribute meaningfully to the faith community. Finally, and perhaps most significantly, the success and pervasiveness of their ministries helped to foster an American understanding of Catholic Christianity in which commitment to charity and service was inseparable from devotion and participation in the sacraments.

We can see that melding of social commitment and devotion in the lives of the thousands of laypeople who contributed time, money and other forms of support to the creation and maintenance of Catholic endeavors under nuns' auspices. Housewives organized fairs and other benefits to raise funds for local schools, hospitals and orphanages, and participated in food and clothing drives to help the unfortunate. Lawyers donated their services when charters needed to be drawn up and doctors who never charged fees for visits to the convent were legion. Craftsmen contributed hours of gratuitous labor to the construction of buildings that the nuns would staff, while their wives sewed curtains and linens, and upholstered the chairs that their husbands put together. Farmers provided produce and livestock that made the difference between survival and starvation for more than one group of pioneer religious. Itinerant miners gave up portions of their ore in exchange for guarantees of care at medical facilities that they might never again live near enough to visit.

Indeed, fund drives by sisters sometimes met with such enthusiastic responses that more than a few bishops (who saw them as competitors for the same resources they themselves needed) tried various strategies to restrict or prohibit nuns from collecting in their jurisdictions. These ranged from refusing to authorize solicitations by non-diocesan congregations to demanding kickbacks of up to one-third of all the money collected.[1] But such interference could backfire: sisters might threaten to withdraw from areas where the hierarchy impeded their efforts, and more than one community went so far as to relocate completely, in order to get out from under the domination of unsupportive prelates.[2] When that

[1]The prelate who demanded a kickback was Louis Lootens, Vicar Apostolic of Idaho in the 1870's; see Mother Joseph of the Sacred Heart to Sister Praxedes, September 22 and 25, 1876 (trans. from the French, Sisters of Providence Archives, Seattle); Mother Joseph was outraged, and gave him only part of what he asked for.

[2]Two examples among many of those who moved are the Sisters of Charity of Leavenworth, Kansas (originally located in Nashville), and the Franciscan Sisters who now have their motherhouse in Clinton, Iowa, but who started out in the Diocese of Louisville.

occurred, it was often difficult for a prelate to attract replacements, and so even the threat of withdrawal might be sufficient to persuade a bishop to reconsider his policies.

Meanwhile, cooperation between women religious and the laity continued. From service on boards of directors to service alongside sisters in classrooms and hospital wards, from generous support for nun-coordinated efforts to aid nearby and faraway victims of disease and natural disasters to the countless pennies collected to "save pagan babies," from pious and mission-related periodicals that expanded parochial awareness of unfamiliar places and events to attendance at expositions and performances sponsored by the local academies—sisters and their neighbors worked together to expand the definition of what it meant to be Catholic. Such endeavors throughout the nineteenth and early twentieth centuries were effective and probably necessary precedents to the evolution of "Catholic Action" in the 1920's, 1930's and 1940's—and to the emergence of formal lay ministry in the years since Vatican II.

The range and extent of collaboration between laity and women religious may come as a surprise to those whose stereotypic impression of nineteenth-century nuns has them rigidly cloistered, severely limited in the amount of movement and activity they were permitted. In fact, the official Constitutions and Customaries of most orders did contain dire warnings about the dangers posed by "the world" and its inhabitants, and most attempted to restrict or prohibit "intercourse with seculars" beyond that absolutely required by the apostolate. Once again, however, practice departed sharply from prescription. Only a handful of the women's congregations founded in the United States—and those mainly originated under the auspices of émigré clerics—attempted to replicate the European practice of enclosure; virtually all ended up abandoning it after just a few years. Sisters who migrated from abroad also came to realize, as Mother Seton had in 1809, that rules which might have made sense in the Old World were inappropriate in the New World. German Benedictines and Dominicans, Irish Presentation Nuns, and most Ursulines were among those whose newly-autonomous American communities modified or eliminated the rule of enclosure. Meanwhile, the School Sisters of Notre Dame were among those who remained part of international congregations, but with amended regulations that applied solely to the American provinces.

Thus, another contribution that early sisters gave to the American Church was a legacy of flexibility and adaptability to new and changing circumstances. It is, in fact, a tradition older than the nation itself, traceable to the first nuns in what is now U.S. territory: the Ursulines who settled in New Orleans in 1727. In Europe, the order was strictly cloistered, and its ministry was restricted exclusively to teaching within their enclosures; in Louisiana, they immediately opened a hospital and an orphanage, and taught in many locations apart from their convent.

The Ursulines were only the first to undergo major adjustments in their ways of life, so as to meet needs very different from those of the Old World. Two of the first eight Sisters of St. Joseph to come from France to Missouri in the 1830's, for example, postponed their arrival in order to learn methods for teaching the deaf; others of their congregation opened a school for Blacks before the end of the decade. Congregations that in Europe concentrated on serving the affluent and the middle class found themselves here working primarily with impoverished and often despised immigrants. Formerly cloistered members of the German Adorers of the Blood of Christ initially supported themselves here by doing heavy farm labor in rural Illinois (several early deaths and at least one case of insanity are attributed to the rigors they underwent). Ursulines originally from a German foundation in Ohio ministered to Eskimos in Alaska; their neighbors in the territory were originally French-Canadian Sisters of Providence from Washington State and members of the Irish-founded Sisters of St. Joseph of Peace. Americans like the Sinsinawa Dominicans supported striking miners in Anaconda and Spring Valley even before Leo XIII's *Rerum Novarum,* and taught in some Minnesota public schools (as did other nuns elsewhere). And when no established order could be found to respond to particular problems, new ones were founded. The Black founders of New Orleans' Sisters of the Holy Family (1845) were inspired largely by the desire to protect freeborn young girls of mixed blood from perpetuating their mothers' pattern of becoming mistresses to white "gentlemen"; Katharine Drexel's Sisters of the Blessed Sacrament (1891) were devoted more generally to "Indians and Colored People," while Margaret Mary Healy-Murphy's Sisters of the Holy Ghost (now "Spirit") and Mary Immaculate were organized by a Texas slaveholder's widow to work with Blacks and Hispanics. Sisters of the Holy Family (California) and Mission Helpers of the Sacred Heart (Maryland) were founded to catechize those who attended public schools; Missionary Sisters of the Most Blessed Trinity (Alabama) were established to encourage collaboration with the laity; Parish Visitors of Mary Immaculate (New York) and Missionary Catechists of Our Lady of Victory (Indiana) did home visiting. And besides the numerous orders that migrated from abroad, at least a dozen were founded here specifically to work with particular nationalities: Poles, Slavs, Lithuanians, Mexicans, etc.

The catalogue could be extended almost endlessly. But one thing that most congregations (except for a few of those devoted solely to individual ethnic groups) had to deal with, especially in the early years, was that, since persons of their faith were almost everywhere a minority, much of their ministry was likely to be among persons who were not Catholic. So sometimes intentionally and sometimes by default, sisters found themselves representing the Church to a public that was either unfamiliar with or hostile to the tenets of "Popery." In a country beset by repeated waves of nativism, few non-Catholics would deliberately seek the ministrations of a priest. Yet they might well send their small children to what might be the only school around, or their older daughters to academies with reputations for instilling equal doses of gentility and erudition.

Nuns engaged in nursing were even more likely to encounter non-Catholics than were teachers. And their contributions to the scope and quality of American health care is widely recognized and carefully documented.[1] But the specifically *religious* contribution that resulted from the public's approbation of their work has gone comparatively unnoticed. Consider, for instance, how widely and disparately-sought their services were. Throughout the nineteenth century, citizens in countless towns with negligible Catholic populations initiated fund drives to bring a sisters' hospital into their midst; decidedly secular corporations of various

---

[1]For a recent overview, see *Pioneer Healers: The History of Women Religious in American Health Care,* ed. Ursula Stepsis and Dolores Liptak (New York: 1989).

sorts offered to subsidize or build facilities if nuns would staff them. Habited visiting nurses in cities all over the country were known for their willingness to offer gratuitous service to anyone in need, regardless of their faith. Meanwhile, more dramatically (and dangerously) ministries like that of the Syracuse Franciscans in the leper colony run by Father Damien, and of members from countless communities during at least twenty recurrent epidemics of diseases such as cholera, typhus, yellow fever and smallpox, won plaudits from citizens of every (or no) religious bent. The cumulative effect of all this, while impossible to document explicitly, arguably did more to undermine nativism and promote toleration of Catholicism in the United States than any other single phenomenon.

No single episode supports this contention more convincingly than the response to sisters' efforts during the Civil War. In an era when soldiers were more likely to die as a result of disease and infection than as a direct result of combat, the almost 650 "Angels of Mercy" whose services were accepted (many more volunteered) made incalculable contributions to the preservation of life. They worked tirelessly and indiscriminately among both Union and Confederate forces, and while patients' inquiries on matters of religion always received answers, even the most cynical observers testified to the absence of aggressive proselytizing. During the War, countless servicemen and their families paid tribute to these women. Plaudits were decidedly nonpartisan. Presidents Abraham Lincoln and Jefferson Davis added their voices to the chorus and, once hostilities ceased, no one advocated remuneration for the South's own Sisters of Our Lady of Mercy of Charleston more avidly than Radical Republican Ben Butler (known as "The Beast" throughout Dixie). In 1876 Ulysses Grant would invite two Dominican nursing veterans, whose service had been in the slave state of Kentucky, to participate in his dedication of a Lincoln statue in Springfield, Illinois.

However significant recognition from celebrities was, it was more crucial to the development of an American Church that thousands of non-Catholic veterans from both sides and of all creeds returned home with affection and respect for the habited women who had cared for them, as well as considerably less hostility toward the faith that so clearly inspired their ministry. As a result, the Know-Nothingism which raged rampant in the 1840's and 1850's (catalyzed by the fraudulent memoirs of Maria Monk, who ironically and falsely identified herself as a former nursing nun) did not reappear in anything like the same degree for over two decades after Appomattox. And even in 1924, at the height of the Ku Klux Klan's anti-Catholic crusade, prejudice was put aside momentarily for unveiling of the congressionally-approved monument to the "Nuns of the Battlefield."

By 1924, of course, both the country and the Church were quite different from what they had been in the preceding century. Communism had replaced Catholicism as the object of America's greatest fears, and Black migration into the same urban areas that in an earlier era had attracted Catholics gave Northern prejudice another target for its venom. Even the revived Klan, which reviled white non-Protestants and immigrants, as well as Blacks, was relatively short-lived, and did not garner the same degree of influence and support that the Know-Nothings and the APA had in the 1800's. Meanwhile, so far as religion was concerned, five interrelated and gradually evolving ecclesial developments would affect the shape of the U.S. Church, including the place and potential for influence it allowed to women during the first half of the twentieth century. These were: (1) the continual trend toward "Romanization," which concentrated more and more authority over all church affairs in the Vatican, (2) the condemnations of Modernism and "Americanism," (3) the rising emphasis upon Eucharistic devotion, (4) the "success" of American Catholicism itself, including that enjoyed by religious communities, and (5) the formal approbation (and consequent regulation) of active religious life for women.

While space precludes detailed discussion, it is possible to describe some of the cumulative effects of these phenomena, and then to suggest a few of their implications, for the American Church and especially for women. The most important and consequential was Romanization, which not only reinforced the entire hierarchical order of Catholicism, but located more power in the papacy than ever before. Everything seems to promote uniformity of teaching, practice, perspective and organization. Bolstered by the declaration of infallibility in 1870 and Rome's unprecedented insistence upon control over episcopal appointments, exemplified by condemnations of the "heresies" that Modernism and Americanism allegedly represented, and culminating in the promulgation of the 1918 Code, those in the Vatican tried to quash any real or imagined deviations from its defined doctrine and objectives.[1]

At the same time, growing emphasis on the centrality of the Eucharist to Catholic devotional life, while no doubt pastoral in both intent and much of its effect, nonetheless helped to "clericalize" the exercise of faith and to strengthen and reinforce patriarchy, since the Blessed Sacrament could only be confected by those in Holy Orders. This was in dramatic contrast to the embryonic U.S. Church, when even weekly attendance at Mass was impossible for a sizeable share of the laity, who consequently had to take most of the responsibility for their own religious practice and preservation. The new piety and its encouragement of frequent confession and communion put priests firmly at the center of what was deemed necessary to be a "good Catholic."

In America the observance of a priest-directed piety had been made possible by the Church's evident "success." This was reflected in the lifting of its "mission" status in 1908 and in its relatively plentiful supply of ordained men. By the end of World War I, Catholics comprised the nation's largest single religion and, for the first time, a majority of its bishops were native-born. Catholic parishes, institutions, orders and organizations proliferated. Never before had the Church been more visible, more active or more self-confident.

And yet, one historian described the period of burgeoning triumphalism from 1917 to Vatican II as "the Great Repression."[2] It is apt, not just in reference to the nuns she happened to be writing about, but in reference to the roles of all laypeople (particularly women) within the framework of institutional

---

[1]Gerald P. Fogarty, *The Vatican and the American Hierarchy from 1870 to 1965* (Wilmington, DE: 1985); James Hennesey, *The First Council of the Vatican: The American Experience* (New York: 1963); Thomas T. McAvoy, *The Americanist Heresy in Roman Catholicism, 1895-1900* (Notre Dame, 1963).

[2]Mary Ewens, "Removing the Veil: The Liberated American Nun in the 19th Century," Cushwa Center Working Paper #3 (Spring 1978), University of Notre Dame, p. 23.

Catholicism in the first half of the twentieth century. The situation was, to be sure, somewhat ironic. As Emile Coué might have put it, "Every day, in every way, the U.S. Church is getting better and better"—but it paid a tremendous price for its success that would only become clear in retrospect. Stated simply, the flexibility and innovative responsiveness to human circumstance that had fostered ecclesial growth and development throughout the nation's first century was replaced by an emphasis on structure, obedience and formalism that exalted the clergy and relegated all others to the status of "passive recipients of the *ecclesia docens,* consumers, not producers in the economy of the Eucharist."[1] Gone was the equilibrium between sacrament and service, the balance between Synoptic and Johannine visions of Holy Thursday, that characterized nineteenth-century American Catholic practice. And with it went the understanding of the Church that had enabled women to make such important formative contributions.

The Eucharist emphasis put severe strictures upon lay, and especially female, participation. As Leo XIII declared, in 1896: "Woman is by divine counsel and decree of Holy Church, formally excluded from what directly regards the Adorable Body of Christ"; she could not "pass the limits of the Holy of Holies," and thus had "no part in the act, by which, enveloped in a mysterious cloud of faith and love, the Man-God daily renews upon the altar the divine Holocaust of Calvary." Instead, her role was distinctly subordinate and auxiliary. The "new horizon" which Leo offered to her ("a new dignity which elevates you...consecrates you more intimately with our Lord; *associates you with* the grandeur of the Catholic priesthood") was to be achieved through "the labor of her hands, which have prepared the sacred vestment and linens and provided all that *pertains to* the divine sacrifice."[2]

Thus, the new ecclesiology was premised upon a clear hierarchy of grace and upon rigid separation between the sacred and the secular.[3] Within this construct the priest, or *Alter Christus,* occupied the highest earthly rung on the ladder to sanctity while others approached God only through his agency. Unordained persons, meanwhile, and other elements of "the world," attained spiritual legitimacy only to the degree that they could be formally attached to the Church: "Christ's Body on earth." In practical terms, this meant endorsement by and incorporation

---

[1] Joseph P. Chinnici, *Living Stones: The History and Structure of Catholic Spiritual Life in the United States* (New York: 1989), p. 150; for illuminating background, see chapter 13 in Chinnici, and Ann Taves, *The Household of Faith: Roman Catholic Devotions in Mid-Nineteenth Century America* (Notre Dame, IN: 1986), esp. chapter 5.

[2] Leo XIII quoted in Chinnici, *Living Stones, op. cit.,* p. 151 (italics added).

[3] Two important lay movements of this era, each initiated by a woman in the 1930's, suggest that creative individuals could overcome at least some of the constraints of clericalism. These were the Catholic Worker movement, founded by Dorothy Day, and Friendship House, under the leadership of Catherine de Hueck. Both focused their efforts on the very poor, and both attracted large numbers of laypeople, the majority of them female. It needs to be noted, however, that neither of these groups deviated from theological or ecclesial orthodoxy in any way; neither challenged the institutional or spiritual structures of institutional Catholicism.

into the sacramental body, whenever that was possible. Lay holiness, then, was maximized through membership in religious communities that had earned episcopal approbation by their adherence to the requirements of canon law; "lesser" mortals were blessed insofar as they received the sacraments and conducted as many of the rest of their affairs as they could under Catholic auspices. The Federation of Women's Clubs and the Catholic Daughters of American (or Elks and Knights of Columbus) might serve the same functions, but those with priest-moderators were preferred by the devout. Bishops' charitable appeals replicated the fundraising of Community Chests, but distributed their largesse only to *Catholic* recipients. Scouting for boys (and later girls) was approved within *Catholic* troops, former soldiers were encouraged to join the *Catholic* War Veterans, young people participated in sports under the aegis of CYO (rather than YMCA and YWCA) sponsorship, parallel *Catholic* occupational and professional organizations were established, and social justice was to be promoted through *Catholic* Action. The Baltimore Catechism might still proclaim that "God is everywhere," but Catholics could not be faulted if they believed that S/He was *more* present among *them*.

And where were nuns in this newly-triumphal Church? Like God, they were everywhere, but their energies were more narrowly channeled and contained than in the preceding century. Ironically, their very success and proliferation had led Rome to do what it had never done before: grant official general approbation and institutional status to uncloistered apostolic women's orders. Prior to 1900, although the numbers of such congregations continued to multiply, they had no formal standing in church law. And while this occasionally led to problems, it also enabled such communities to evolve without the constraints that fixed and uniform regulations might impose. All of that changed, however, when Leo XIII issued *Conditae a Christo* in 1900. The following year, implementing *Normae* appeared, which served as the basis for relevant sections of the code of Canon Law promulgated in 1918.

Whatever it was intended to accomplish, the effect of Roman recognition was to inhibit the flexibility enjoyed by earlier generations of American women religious. Previously tolerated or ignored activities were now prohibited; now every dimension of sisters' lives, from vow formulas to forms of prayer, from ministries to curfews, from housing to contact with outsiders, from modes of choosing superiors to modes of dress, had to conform to rules devised by men in the far-off Vatican (most of whom were not religious, and virtually all of whom were Europeans unfamiliar with circumstances in the United States).

As obedient "daughters of the Church," nuns complied with what was demanded of them. Hardly immune to the enthusiasm and confidence that imbued American Catholicism generally, their numbers and institutions continued to multiply. Remember, these women, however accomplished they might be, were hardly feminists, or radicals likely to initiate serious challenge to ecclesial pronouncements. Instead, they quietly and dutifully went on with their work, much of it with women, whom they would continue to educate and inspire. In this fashion, sisters contributed significantly to the church's success, even in its—and their—more structured and institutionalized newly triumphal guise. If anything, they touched more lives than ever before, albeit in different ways. As the modern chroniclers of countless communities have noted, developments during the first decades of the century were primarily quantitative: larger buildings, more

members, more missions, etc. To put it another way, there was plenty of expansion in *size,* but relatively little in *scope.* Thus women were as involved as
ever, but their presence was stabilizing and reinforcing, rather than catalyzing.
The U.S. Church may have been at its most triumphal between 1900 and 1950.
But the roles of women within it were at their most static position.

Still, if nuns could not expand the dimensions of their ministry, they could
and did improve its quality. While informal mentoring and on-the-job training
comprised the bulk of most sisters' professional formation during the nineteenth
century, the twentieth century saw ever rising levels of education among religious teachers, nurses, social workers and so on. Impelled by a combination of
state law mandating formal credentials, foresighted leaders and the occasional
supportive prelate,[1] sisters began to attend and eventually to found their own
nursing schools, normal institutes and colleges. While few members were able
to obtain their certification or degrees before being sent on mission, by the end
of World War II more and more congregations aspired to provide such credentials
to all those who needed them for their apostolates.

The majority of sisters' ventures into higher learning were opened to others,
thereby providing thousands of women[2] (most, but not all of them Catholic)
with accredited post-secondary education that had a significant spiritual dimension. And although the quality of Catholic women's colleges varied greatly (like
their non-Catholic counterparts, some of the early ones were little more than
glorified academies or finishing schools), the best of them offered opportunities
comparable to those at the better secular institutions. They generally did so,
moreover, with a larger female presence on the faculty. Students who were
taught mathematics and physics by habited professors were unlikely to graduate
with stereotypic notions of "feminine ineptitude" in the sciences; exposure to
sister-deans and college presidents would reveal to them that women could be capable administrators. Several studies conducted in the 1980's have shown that
women who attend single sex colleges traditionally enjoy higher levels of confidence and achievement in subsequent careers than do alumnae of coeducational
ones. What the research rarely mentions explicitly, however, is that a
disproportionate share of such women have been products of colleges run by
nuns; once again, as in the pioneer era, the role models that sisters came to provide would prove innovative and prophetic.

In retrospect, there is irony in the educational foundations that were laid in
the midst of the "Great Repression." For it was within that framework that
seeds were planted that eventually would blossom into Catholic feminism. It

---

[1]While pastors and bishops theoretically were in favor of improved training for
women religious, the need for ever more "laborers in the vineyard" frequently
overrode their ideals. Thus, materials in most congregations' archives reveal the
frustrations of sister superiors who attempted (with varying degrees of success) to
resist persistent pressures to send unprepared members on missions; a representative case is discussed in Mary Philip Ryan, "Parochial School Expansion as It
Was Known in the Adrian Dominican Congregation, 1924-33," chapter draft for an
in-progress history of the Adrian (MI) Dominicans since 1920.

[2]Prior to Vatican II, few of these institutions were coeducational.

began to happen like this:[1] (1) Since traditional church policy favored single sex institutions, especially for those beyond early childhood, communities had to develop sufficient numbers of well-trained members to staff schools for themselves and for laywomen. (2) Not surprisingly, nuns chose to pursue advanced degrees tended to be among the brightest in their orders, those most capable of benefitting from the opportunities to which they were exposed. (3) Because the first of the religious to seek higher learning were refused admission to Catholic colleges under male auspices, they attended secular ones where they were exposed to a wide range of persons and ideas.[2] (4) When the men's colleges did begin to admit women (often into segregated programs like the Sister's Institute established at CUA in 1911), they became settings for networking among nuns from different orders, who previously may have had little contact with one another. (5) That networking expanded after 1950, when Pius XII called for more aggressive efforts to improve sisters' professional qualifications.[3] Two years later, the University of Notre Dame hosted the first National Conference of Major Superiors; both the Sister Formation Movement (SFM) and the Leadership Conference of Women Religious (LCWR, initially called the Conference of Major Superiors of Women when it formally organized in 1956) would evolve from what began there. (6) In an unprecedented move, the "Sisters' Committee" that convened at Notre Dame in 1952 "politely" but firmly refused to accept a cleric as its moderator, electing instead Mother Gerald Barry of the Adrian Dominicans. [While serving as the first president of CMSW in 1959, when Roman officials told her that they would soon be sending a constitution for the organization, Barry told them, equally politely and equally firmly, that her steering committee had already written its own.] And finally, under the visionary leadership of women like Sisters Annette Walters, Mary Emil Penet and Ritamary Bradley, the SFM exposed thousands of sisters to the newest developments in theology, spirituality, psychology and sociology, as well as to the specific professional preparation they needed; the effect, as more than one observer has noted, was nothing short of revolutionary.[4]

All of this preceded Vatican II, most of it by more than a decade. So by the time *Perfectae Caritatis* and other fruits of the Council reached U.S. shores, American sisters were well prepared to respond to them. As they continued the process of "renewal" Rome mandated—which, as we have seen, really began in

[1]Much of what follows is summarized from and documented in a paper I delivered at the 1986 meeting of the American Political Science Association: "Pressures By and On a Marginal Group--Or, Are Catholic Feminists Either?"
[2]In the absence of relevant data, definitive comparisons are impossible. But it is likely that few clerics, trained (sometimes from early adolescence) strictly within seminary environments, could boast of similar exposure.
[3]Nuns themselves had made similar pleas even earlier. Sister Bertrande Meyers' 1941 doctoral dissertation, *The Education of Sisters,* and Sister Madeleva Wolff's *The Education of Sister Lucy* (1949) were widely circulated critiques and proposals for concrete action.
[4]See, for example, Mary Schnieder, "The Transformation of American Women Religious: The Sister Formation Movement as Catalyst, 1954-1964," Cushwa Center Working Paper (Spring 1986); and Marie Augusta Neal, *Catholic Sisters in Transition* (Wilmington, DE: 1984).

the 1950's—the laywomen they had been educating in their schools and colleges were being similarly inspired by the combined effects of *aggiornamento,* their teachers' formative example, and the secular feminism that began to arise after publication of Betty Friedan's *Feminine Mystique.* As nuns started to go out from the confines of their convents and institutions, they found their former students already involved in the new ventures they pursued: interracial justice and opposition to the Vietnam War, ecumenical dialogue and direct service to the disadvantaged, theological inquiry and research into both societal and religious patriarchy.

It would not take too long for these two cohorts of Catholic women to coalesce in any measurable degree. During the late 1960's and early 1970's, most sisters tended to be absorbed by the tumultuous changes occurring in their own communities, while relatively few laywomen focused their energies upon specifically ecclesial matters. But lines dividing them started, almost imperceptibly at first, to blur. For one thing, thousands of nuns left their orders and became laywomen. At the same time, some who remained began to concern themselves with issues that a short while earlier might have seemed unexpectedly secular. NETWORK, a "Catholic social justice lobby" in Washington, was founded by sisters in 1970. And the preceding year saw birth of the explicitly feminist National Coalition of American Nuns (NCAN) which soon took on such controversial causes as *Humanae Vitae,* the Equal Rights Amendment, reproductive freedom and the tenure case of lay theologian Mary Daly. NCAN was too radical to attract more than a small percentage of religious into its ranks, but by the middle of the 1970's, even larger numbers of sisters were making connections between the insights of secular feminism and the anomalies of their own position in the Church. Similarly, laywomen extended the compass of their involvement directly into the precincts of their faith.

The Women's Ordination Conference (WOC), established in 1975, was one reflection of the convergence between religious and lay Catholic feminists.[1] Only 79 years after Leo XIII had decreed that females were "formally excluded from what directly regards the Adorable Body of Christ," members of WOC and additional "fellow travelers" were openly demanding admission to Holy Orders. Initially, of course, they were regarded as radicals by the overwhelming majority of their church's communicants; less than a quarter supported their objective in early surveys. Yet ordination soon took on the charismatic significance in the ecclesial arena comparable to that of ERA in secular politics. Just three years after WOC was formed, Sister of Mercy Theresa Kane, president of the Vatican-authorized LCWR, would stand before Pope John Paul II as the television cameras rolled and plead for women's acceptance into "all church ministries." By 1985, 52% of all Catholics (and 68% of those under forty) supported women's ordination, figures only slightly below those who would approve lifting the ban on married priests. Thus it seemed unsurprising when Kane's successor at LCWR repeated her petition during John Paul's 1987 U.S. visit. What the press

[1]An even more potent symbolic event occurred in 1983, when a feminist group previously known as the "National Assembly of Women Religious" renamed itself the "National Assembly of Religious Women"—signifying that members others than nuns would be welcomed as full participants.

paid attention to that year were similar remarks by Donna Hanson: the unvowed (and hitherto largely unknown) woman who represented "the laity" to the pontiff.

Meanwhile, however, the boundaries of Catholic feminism had been extended. Critical of ecclesial structures that were "fundamentally flawed," leaders of WOC and others began to move "beyond ordination," rejecting it even in theory unless Catholicism as a whole was rid of its pervasive patriarchy (as reflected not only in an all-male priesthood but in phenomena like sexist language). Those alienated from the institution, but still identifying themselves as Catholics, started to come together in small groups to celebrate their own liturgies. By 1983, twelve hundred Catholic feminists gathered in Chicago to celebrate "Women-Church"; four years later, a similar convocation in Cincinnati attracted 3000. That same year, Mary's Pence was founded, a "Catholic women's foundation to raise funds for the needs of poor women"; in 1988 it awarded its first grants. And ever-growing numbers of books, journals, recordings and resource guides in the fields of feminist theology and spirituality, many the productions of well-trained secular scholars like Rosemary Radford Ruether and Elizabeth Schussler-Fiorenza, both reinforced and expanded awareness of what religious feminism was all about.

To be sure, not everyone supported the feminist agenda. At the opposite extreme were groups like Women for Faith, and Family and Catholics United for the Faith, who adamantly rejected any challenge to the church's traditional teachings on gender, seeing feminism as perhaps the most dangerous manifestation of what they regarded as the "modernism" that characterized post-Vatican II American Catholicism. Nuns who disapproved of what they perceived as growing feminist tendencies within LCWR left to form their own organizations: *Perfectae Caritatis* and the Institute for Religious Life. More conservative periodicals (from *Our Sunday Visitor* to *The Catholic Register, Twin Circle* and *The Wanderer*) regularly condemned and ridiculed what the feminists were saying and doing. Of course, the vast majority of female Catholics identified with neither of the poles, falling somewhere on the broad continuum in between. For them, much of the debate was esoteric and irrelevant, although surveys taken throughout the 1980's revealed that more and more of them were willing to challenge the magisterium's positions on questions like birth control, abortion, female altar servers and ordination. Nonetheless, most continued to worship in parish settings, seemingly unconcerned with (or able to ignore) both the patriarchy and the modernism that those on either side of them deplored.

As the bicentennial of organized Catholicism in the U.S. drew near, it was too soon to draw definitive conclusions about the long-term consequences to the American Church of either feminism or the backlash against it. What was clear, however, even in the backlash, was that neither the hierarchy nor the general public could ignore the voices and concerns of Catholic women. Cases like those involving three Sisters of Mercy who were forced to resign from their order after refusing to withdraw from political office, a Toledo parochial school girl who was expelled after participating in a reproductive freedom rally, excommunication of the Catholic woman who headed Planned Parenthood in Rhode Island, the pro-choice record of 1984 Democratic vice-presidential candidate Geraldine Ferraro, and the failed efforts by Rome to discipline the so-called "Vatican 24"— all received extensive play from both religious and secular media. Similarly, certain American bishops (Seattle's Raymond Hunthausen and Richmond's Walter Sullivan) and male theologians (most notably Charles Curran and Matthew Fox) found themselves under investigation, in no small measure because of controversial positions they had taken in the areas of sexuality and gender roles. Credible rumor had it that clerics who strayed from traditional church teachings on matters like birth control and an all-male celibate priesthood were automatically eliminated from consideration for the episcopacy; "doubtful" prelates of auxiliary rank, meanwhile, presumably could forget about appointments as ordinaries. But the intensity of the reaction against real or purported threats to Catholic orthodoxy is itself suggestive of the credibility that feminism had attained within the Church. After all, people do not generally become excited or disturbed by that which they perceive as unimportant.

At the very least, women could no longer be regarded as peripheral or negligible participants in the Body of Christ; issues central to their experience came to dominate center stage as American Catholicism entered its third century. Indicative of this is the 1983 decision by the National Conference of Catholic Bishops to write a pastoral on women, later changed to "women's concerns". Across the country, thousands of women testified at diocesan hearings called to acquire "input"; the pastoral's first draft, "Partners in the Mystery of Redemption" released in April 1988, incorporated dozens of voices representing "alienation" and "affirmation" into the text. While the draft hardly constitutes a feminist manifesto, it does go so far as to call sexism a "sin," and to suggest that ordination at least to the permanent deaconate deserved "further study."[1] Only a few months later, Pope John Paul II issued his own "meditation" on women's roles in Church and society (*Mulieris Dignitatem*), as well as a pastoral on the laity (*Christifideles Laici*) that contained more of his reflections. The papal documents do little beyond affirming the traditional Catholic understanding of what is "appropriate" for women--and repeating the traditional arguments against "deviant" ideas like ordination.[2] But the fact that he felt it necessary to address the subject of women at all highlights the importance that it has come to assume, even (or especially) in the Vatican.

Meanwhile, and to a greater extent than ever before, American Catholic women in the 1980's took responsibility for their own spiritual welfare. Not all of them were self-consciously feminist; indeed, female proponents of orthodoxy were among the church's most active and vocal members. But regardless of the points of view they espoused, women wanted—and expected—their presence to be acknowledged, appreciated and respected.

In short, the story of women's place within American Catholicism is complex and multifaceted: one to which an ending cannot be written. As one as-

---

[1] A more extended commentary by me on the draft pastoral ("A Subtle Sexism Flaws the Letter") appeared in the *National Catholic Reporter*, April 29, 1988.
[2] As the pontiff put it in *Christifideles Laici*, women "have exercised an oftentimes decisive role in the Church herself and accomplished tasks of considerable value on her behalf. History is marked by grand works, *quite often lowly and hidden, but not for this reason any less decisive* to the growth and holiness of the Church. It is necessary that this history continue, indeed that it be expanded and intensified..." (#49; italics added).

sesses the legacy of the past two hundred years, the only certainty is the inevitability of change; the only constant is that women have always played crucial roles in the nation's ecclesial affairs. And like the foremothers who helped to lay the foundations, future generations of women will continue to give birth to new conceptions of Church and to participate fully in the ongoing process of defining and developing what it means to be Catholic in America.

CHAPTER SIX

Catholic Religious Thought in the U.S.A.
Patrick M. Carey
Marquette University

From John Carroll (1736-1815) to the present, Catholic thinkers have tried to construct intelligible concepts to disclose the universal claims of their tradition and to discover viable ways to respond to new issues (e.g., republicanism, religious liberty, separation of church and state, Protestant cultural hegemony) created by their own American culture. The concepts they used and the methods they employed to make their tradition understandable were frequently borrowed from the prevailing intellectual movements in American and Western thought (e.g., the Enlightenment, Romanticism, Modernism, Neo-Thomism and various post-Vatican II movements). The content of their Catholic tradition and the context of their American culture, though, transformed the concepts they appropriated, and the concepts they used modified their understanding of their own tradition.

This essay demonstrates in broad strokes the changing conceptions of the Catholic tradition in the United States and shows how the conception of Christianity varied in emphasis from age to age while at the same time it remained in continuity with distinctive elements in the tradition. Tradition, as understood in this essay, refers not only to the transcendental content of Christian doctrine but also to the dynamic process of its conceptualization and transmission from age to age. The Catholic tradition—as articulated in the liturgy, prayer, pious religious practices, dogmatic statements, ecclesiastical institutions and social activities—is much larger than the limited attempts to define or to conceptualize it.

The religious thought of American Catholics has received only a modicum of historical analysis. In 1966, in the wake of the Second Vatican Council, James Hennesey, S.J., published a seminal article on the conciliar tradition in the United States, calling upon historians to examine the theological dimensions of the American Catholic experience.[1] Since then a few scholars have investigated various aspects of the American Catholic theological tradition, and I am indebted to them for their work.[2]

---

[1]James J. Hennesey, S.J., "Papacy and Episcopacy in 18th- and 19th-Century American Catholic Thought," *Records of the American Catholic Historical Society of Philadelphia* 77 (1966), pp. 175-189.
[2]Some of the more recent historical surveys of American Catholic religious thought include: "American Catholics and the Intellectual Life," *U.S. Catholic Historian* 4 (1985); Patrick W. Carey, ed., *American Catholic Religious Thought* (New York: Paulist Press, 1987); Joseph P. Chinnici, O.F.M., *Living Stones: The History and Structure of Catholic Spiritual Life in the United States* (New York: Macmillan Publishing Co., 1989); John A. Coleman, "Vision and Praxis in American Theology: Orestes Brownson, John A. Ryan, and John Courtney Murray," *Theological Studies* 37 (March 1976), pp. 3-40; Gerald P. Fogarty, S.J., *Nova et*

Most Catholics described here would have presupposed two important things about their own definition of Catholic Christianity. First, they would have accepted the dogmatic declarations of the Council of Trent (1542-1565) on revelation (perceiving Scripture and Tradition as the rule of faith and the Church as the authentic interpreter of both), original sin, justification and the sacraments. Their own self-understanding was a part of the general post-Tridentine polemical dynamic that defined Catholic positions on these issues vis-à-vis various Protestant understandings.

Second, they would have understood and accepted the fact that they lived in new political and social circumstances, very different from those of their European contemporaries. The new historical situation created problems for them in their attempts to define the meaning of their tradition. The political realities in particular separated them from the experiences and ideals of many within the European Catholic community, and those political realities had a significant bearing upon the way they thought not only about the state but also about human nature, the Church and religious life. The fact of religious pluralism and the lack of long-established Catholic institutions or educational resources, too, provided a context for the development of their religious thought that was far removed from context of the post-Tridentine European Catholicism.

ENLIGHTENMENT CATHOLICISM

Henry May's *The Enlightenment in America* makes no mention of the Catholic appropriation of the Enlightenment.[1] This should come as no surprise. Catholics were a very small minority during the eighteenth and early nineteenth centuries, and they made no intellectual contributions to Enlightenment thought. Nonetheless the Age of Reason influenced some articulate American Catholics between 1789 and 1842.

The Enlightenment was a major intellectual and cultural movement in the West from the middle of the seventeenth to the beginning of the nineteenth centuries. The term refers to a fundamental shift in consciousness, a period in which the intellectuals of the period made the subject the primary focus of atten-

Vetera: The Theology of Tradition in American Catholicism (Milwaukee: Marquette University Press, 1987); Philip Gleason, *Keeping the Faith: American Catholicism Past and Present* (Notre Dame, IN: The University of Notre Dame Press, 1987); James J. Hennesey, S.J., "American History and the Theological Enterprise," *Proceedings of the Catholic Theological Society of America* (1972), pp. 91-115; *idem*, "Roman Catholic Theology in the United States," *Louvain Studies* 6 (1976), pp. 11-22; Christopher J. Kauffman, *Tradition and Transformation in Catholic Culture: The Priests of Saint Sulpice in the United States from 1791 to the Present* (New York: Macmillan Publishing Co., 1988); J.L. Murphy, "Seventy-Five Years of Fundamental Theology in America, Part I," *American Ecclesiastical Review* 150 (1964), pp. 384-404, and "Part II," *ibid.*, 151 (1964), pp. 21-41; David O'Brien, *Public Catholicism* (New York: Macmillan Publishing Co., 1989); Margaret Mary Reher, *Catholic Intellectual Life in America: A Historical Study of Persons and Movements* (New York: Macmillan Publishing Co., 1989); G.W. Shea, "Seventy-Five Years of Special Dogmatic Theology in America," *American Ecclesiastical Review* 151 (1964), pp. 145-165.
[1](New York: Oxford University Press, 1976).

tion. Henceforth questions of method and ways of knowing came to the fore, with a primary emphasis upon the individual's autonomous reason. The scientific preoccupation with verifiable evidence and a Newtonian conception of a harmonious, law-governed universe also characterized the Enlightenment mentality. Emphasis too was placed upon the idea of historical progress and the perfectibility of human persons. Republicanism, religious liberty, separation of church and state, and voluntaryism were to some extent products of this mentality in the United States.

Some apologists from Bishop John Carroll in the late eighteenth century to Bishop John England in the early nineteenth century, like their Protestant neighbors of the "Didactic Enlightenment," were moderate in their acceptance of the values and presuppositions of the Age of Reason. They upheld the value of tradition and ecclesiastical authority, supported the doctrine of original sin, and maintained the necessity of grace for the salvation and improvement of the human race in opposition to Enlightened concepts of autonomous reason and self-perfection. But, in their inspiration, their apologetical methods, their political theory and practice, and in some of their ecclesiastical structures, they reflected the values and ideals of their age. Whether they argued with deists, Unitarians or American Protestant evangelicals, apologists asserted that the Catholic vision of Christianity was compatible with the fundamental values of reason and republicanism.

Catholic religious leaders periodically stressed the limits of reason in their sermons on Christian piety. Reason was not absolutely autonomous. It was created and limited to a knowledge of the natural world. Because of original sin, moreover, the faculty of reason had been internally weakened, although not destroyed, by unruly passions and a marred will. Natural reason, therefore, needed revelation not only to perceive truths above its own capacities, but even at times to perceive the natural laws that it was constitutionally capable of perceiving but many times prevented from doing so by the effects of sin. Carroll made such an argument to counter what he considered a prevailing spirit of Pelagianism in this "age of infidelity," when deists' arguments were making an impact in late eighteenth-century Catholic congregations. Reason was not unlimited and it was dangerous to Christian piety to consider it so.[1]

Reason, though finite, did have the capacity to perceive the truth, to understand the natural law, to weigh evidence, and to influence the will in right moral conduct. This positive view of reason's nobility comes out clearly in apologetics and political theory. Confidence in reason's powers of persuasion are clear in the evidence-apologetic of three representative tracts of the period: John Carroll's "An Address to the Roman Catholics of the United States by a Catholic Clergymen" (1784),[2] Anthony Kohlmann's *Unitarianism: Philosophically and Theo-*

---

[1] Thomas O'Brien Hanley, S.J., *The John Carroll Papers* (Notre Dame, IN: The University of Notre Dame Press, 1976), Vol. III, pp. 375-383.
[2] Hanley, *op. cit.,* Vol. I, pp. 82-144.

logically Examined (1821, 1822),[1] and John England's "Discourse Before Congress" (1826).[2]

The ultimate apologetic objective was to demonstrate the reasonableness of accepting revelation and ecclesiastical authority. The starting point of all three apologetical texts was not the objective authority of revelation or the Church, but the individual's quest to discover the historical evidence that would provide reasonable motives for the credibility of Christianity and the Catholic tradition. Apologists used the inductive method to amass from scripture and tradition, both of which were perceived as historically verifiable sources of evidence, convincing motives for a rational obedience to Catholic ecclesiastical authority. Such obedience was the result of "a full conviction of conscience" that derived from a free investigation of evidence.[3]

The appeal to historical evidence, conceived as the common reason of the Christian era, provided a standard of judgment that was universal, uncomplicated, immutable and uniform, and therefore above that of the individual reason of the current innovators, whether they be deists, Unitarians or Protestant evangelicals. The argument from proscription, as some called it, was powerful precisely because it transcended the vagaries of particular times, cultures and individuals. The individual, though, had to *use* reason to uncover the universal validity of the Catholic tradition in the common reason of the ages.

In their view of government and politics, Carroll and England embraced republicanism. Although they had serious reservations about accepting the Enlightenment's emphasis upon autonomous reason in piety, they had few such reservations when it came to political theory and practice. Unlike many of their fellow Catholics in Rome and other parts of Europe, they did not perceive or experience the Enlightenment's political consequences as evil and diabolical.[4]

American Catholics found the political side of the Enlightenment beneficial, with its call for toleration, religious liberty, separation of church and state, and ecclesiastical voluntaryism; they saw these principles and practices as consistent with right reason. One could argue that the American Catholic acceptance of this church-state relationship was motivated by expediency because of the generally beneficial historical results that these practices produced for American Catholics. There was, however, more to it than that. Many articulate American

---

[1](Washington City: Henry Guegan, 1821, 1822).
[2]Ignatius Aloysius Reynolds, ed., *The Works of the Right Rev. John England, First Bishop of Charleston* (John Murphy & Co., 1849), Vol. IV, pp. 172-190.
[3]Hanley, *op. cit.,* Vol. I, pp. 84-85.
[4]Joseph A. Komonchak, "The Enlightenment and the Construction of Roman Catholicism," *Annual of the Catholic Commission on Intellectual and Cultural Affairs* (1985), pp. 31-59. Komonchak has argued that the official Roman Catholic resistance to the Enlightenment was governed by its fear of the social and political consequences of Enlightenment ideas. From the Roman perspective in particular, the Enlightenment's political philosophy had reduced the church's influence in the political, social and cultural dimensions of European life. The church's official battle with Enlightenment intellectual issues therefore was largely the result of the political consequences those ideas produced. This was not, for the most part, the case in American Catholicism among conservatives as well as liberals from the late eighteenth century to the present.

Catholic leaders, lay as well as clerical, were intellectually convinced of the rightness of these constitutional provisions and their apologetical tracts are filled with defenses of the compatibility of Catholic doctrine and tradition with American republicanism.[1]

Carroll and England in particular were children of the Enlightenment as well as of the Catholic tradition. In the realms of apologetics and politics, they trusted human nature and the powers of rational persuasion. That this confidence was not always consistent with the deeper strains of their piety is, it seems to me, one of the intellectual aberrations of the age in which they lived. It also demonstrates very clearly that for them there were inherent limits to their acceptance of the Enlightenment, regardless of how logically inconsistent their acceptance may have been.

Enlightenment anthropology and political theory and practice had implications for the ecclesiastical organization and construction of American Catholicism. Republican enthusiasm, the formation of state and federal constitutions, the corresponding organization of ecclesiastical constitutions in various Christian denominations was part of the *élan* of the age, and American Catholics as well as other Christians were caught up in the dynamics of nationalism and the processes of institutionalization. Throughout the period, lay as well as clerical Catholics began to develop what they conceived to be a national Catholic Church—one that was united to Rome and the larger Catholic communion, but which had characteristics peculiar to American political and social conditions. In their practical ecclesiology many Catholics began to emphasize the values of participatory involvement of lay and clerical members in the formation and institutionalization of the Church, wanting to show in particular the compatibility, though not identity, of the Catholic tradition with the emerging American republican tradition.

The ecclesiological emphasis throughout the period of the American Catholic Enlightenment was on the Church's external structure. Most in the American Catholic community were preoccupied with defining the extent and limits of ecclesiastical authority, the various functions of laity and clergy, and the discipline that should guide the Church. Such preoccupations arose at a time in which the entire country was preoccupied with constitution-building.

THE ROMANTIC PERIOD

Between 1840 and 1888, American Catholic thought came under the influence of Romanticism.[2] American Catholic Romanticism not only challenged

---

[1]On American Catholic views of religious liberty during this period, see bibliography in my "American Catholics and the First Amendment, 1776-1840," *The Pennsylvania Magazine of History and Biography* (July 1989).

[2]On this, see Patrick W. Carey, "American Catholic Romanticism, 1830-1888," *The Catholic Historical Review* 74 (October 1988), pp. 590-606; John Farina, ed., *Isaac T. Hecker: The Diary, Romantic Religion in Antebellum America* (New York: Paulist Press, 1988), pp. 1, 78; William LeRoy Portier, "Providential Nation: An Historical-Theological Study of Isaac Hecker's Americanism," (unpublished Ph.D. dissertation, University of St. Michael's College, Toronto, 1980), pp. 15-101; Reher, *op. cit.*, pp. 28-60.

some of the previous age's presuppositions and values but also prepared an intellectual foundation for Americanism and modernism during the late nineteenth and early twentieth centuries.

Romanticism, like the Enlightenment, represents another shift of sensibility in modern Western culture. In religion and theology it was an attempt to create a synthesis of the pietism and rationalism or of the Jansenism and scholasticism of the eighteenth century, a harmony of heart and head. This Romantic sensibility flowed into a variety of very different theological and religious orientations—Catholic as well as Protestant, conservative as well as liberal, American as well as European. In the United States that variety was clearly evident in Transcendentalism, the Mercersburg theology, the progressive orthodoxy of Horace Bushnell, the Tractarian movement in the American Episcopal Church, and the immanence-apologetics of the Catholic converts, Orestes A. Brownson (1803-1876) and Isaac T. Hecker (1819-1888). Each of these movements emphasized a different aspect of the Romantic refrain.

Although Romanticism is difficult to define because of its manifold manifestations in late eighteenth- and early nineteenth-century Western culture, it is a useful term for describing the conversion of consciousness that was taking place during the period. In general, Romanticism was, as Sydney Ahlstrom described it, a religious revolution in the way some significant cultural lights began to perceive reality itself.[1] The Romantics were those who perceived a spiritual dimension underlying all of reality and this view affected their multiple activities and conceptions. Underlying much of the diversity within the Romantic movement was a certain cluster of interlocking ideas. The Romantic view of reality had affinities to an idealist metaphysic that emphasized an organic wholeness, a fundamental synthesis of the infinite and the finite. That view of an organic wholeness penetrated the Romantics' concepts of nature, history and community. The individual, an integral of that primeval unity, apprehended this organic totality of infinite life by feeling and/or intuition rather than by the analytic reason of the Enlightenment. In Catholicism, in particular, the doctrine of the Incarnation emerged as the heart of the entire theological enterprise.

The transformation of American Catholic thought from Enlightenment to Romantic categories was gradual and never really very widespread. The older evidence-apologetics of the age of Carroll and England continued to characterize most of American Catholic thought into the 1840's, and even well beyond that period. One can perceive, however, especially in the writings of Bishops John Hughes of New York, Martin John Spalding of Louisville, and Francis Patrick Kenrick of Philadelphia, some changes in the older apologetics.

Although they continued to demonstrate evidence for the Church's infallibility, they focused their apologetics more upon the dynamic beneficial functions of the Church in the development of culture than they did upon the Church's authority. They emphasized the Church's mission in the world as a primary demonstration of its divine character. Kenrick's *The Primacy of the Apostolic See Vindicated* (1845), for example, was a collection of biblical and historical evidences for papal primacy, but 175 of the 429 pages (of the 1867 edition) were

---

[1] "The Romantic Religious Revolution," *Church History* 46 (June 1977), pp. 149-170.

devoted to the papacy's moral, literary, social and political influences upon the development of Western civilization. This kind of functional ecclesiology was occasioned, in part, by Protestant charges, made by François Guizot and Jean Henri Merle d'Aubigné in particular, that Catholicism had been detrimental to the development of Western civilization and that Protestantism was indeed the parent of all that was good in modern civilization. Hughes, Spalding and Kenrick were not conversant with the philosophical and religious problems created by Immanuel Kant and did not appropriate the idealist or intuitionist sensitivities of the post-Kantian age, but they were concerned with the social significance of the Church in the development of civilization—Romantic themes not very evident in Carroll's and England's apologetics.

The most notable Romantic transformation in American Catholic thought, though, came from outside the American Catholic community. The 1844 conversions of Brownson and Hecker brought into American Catholicism a temperament and perspective on religious life that separated them from the dominant rationalist perspectives. Both men had participated in the intellectual revolution that was taking place among the New England Transcendentalists. Their own searches with that movement for a synthesis of mind and heart, and an organic, social and concrete wholeness led them toward Catholicism. The affinity for Catholicism in the United States as well as in Europe was another manifestation of the Romantic spirit.[1]

Brownson and Hecker were both keenly aware of the philosophical and theological issues of the post-Kantian age. Both saw the intellectual problem of the period as the correlation or reconciliation of the subject-object dialectic. Throughout their lives they tried to uncover the *a priori* conditions for the possibility of religious knowledge and of a concrete historical revelation. For them, the proper understanding of humanity's relationship to God, the possibility of supernatural revelation, the relations of the individual to the community, the church question, and the relation of religion to society and culture were in root problems that flowed from one's perception of the relationship of subject to object.[2]

Except for a brief period immediately following his conversion to Catholicism (1844-1850), Brownson's response to the post-Kantian problems unfolded in his doctrine of life by communion, which he had originally discovered in the thought of the French Saint Simonian Pierre Leroux in 1840. That doctrine asserted that life was itself the interaction of subject and object. Only in the communion of the two was religious knowledge and experience possible. For

---

[1]Examples of the Romantic affinity for Catholicism that led to personal conversions abound: Frederick von Schlegel and John Henry Newman in Europe; Clarence Walworth and James McMaster from the Oxford Movement in America; Sophia Ripley and Rose Hawthorne from American Transcendentalism. On this, see Farina, *op. cit.,* pp. 19-25, 61-66.

[2]For the development of Brownson's thought on these issues, see my forthcoming *Orestes A. Brownson: Selected Writings* (New York: Paulist Press). On Hecker, see John Farina, *An American Experience of God: The Spirituality of Isaac Hecker* (New York: Paulist Press, 1981). For a good bibliography on Hecker, see John Farina, ed., *Hecker Studies: Essays on the Thought of Isaac Hecker* (New York: Paulist Press, 1983).

him the doctrine provided objective grounds for the subjective Christian experiences. Christian life was itself the result of the joint free activity of both God and humans and was, therefore, simultaneously subjective and objective. He struggled throughout his Catholic period to come to terms with the historical, objective and sacramental dimensions of the Christian life. Such positions were reactions to a perceived diminution of these aspects of the Christian tradition in a Jacksonian America where individualism, subjectivism and freedom in religious life had been taken out of their proper dialectic relationship with communalism, objectivism and authority.

In 1850 Brownson began reading the Italian ontologist Vincenzo Gioberti, who combined in his philosophy and theology Cartesianism, Augustinian illuminationism and Traditionalism in order to avoid the pitfalls of the "psychologism" of Descartes, the empiricism of the eighteenth century, and the Kantian idealism of the nineteenth century. To overcome the subject-object dichotomy of post-Kantian idealism, Gioberti sought to establish the objective ground of both the subject and the object in Being itself. Gioberti had criticized Leroux for making the subject itself the creator of the relation between the subject and the object. Such a position ultimately led Leroux toward a pantheism, which Brownson had already acknowledged in the early 1840's, and a subjectivism which was unable to provide an objective ground for religious knowledge or revealed religion. For Gioberti, and after 1850 for Brownson, it was not the subject that provided the relation between it and the object, but the divine creative act. Thereafter Brownson accepted Gioberti's ideal formula, Being creates existence, to demonstrate that the relation between the subject and the object was in the divine creative act, making the object the creator of the relation.[1]

Brownson returned to reformulation of his doctrine of communion in *The Convert* (1857), a book intended as an intellectual apology for his conversion to Catholicism. The ultimate purpose of the apology, however, was much broader. He intended not only to show that the doctrine of communion had led him into the Catholic Church but also to demonstrate with the aid of Gioberti's formula the much firmer ontological foundations for the doctrine. That doctrine, reinforced now with Giobertian insights, could, he believed, demonstrate "the connecting link between nature and grace, the natural and the supernatural, and [it would lead the reader] to perceive that, in becoming a Catholic, a man has no occasion to divest himself of his nature, or to forego the exercise of his reason."[2]

[1]On Gioberti's philosophy, see Gerald A. McCool, *Catholic Theology in the Nineteenth Century: The Quest for a Unitary Method* (New York: The Seabury Press, 1977), pp. 113-119; and Bernard M.G. Reardon, *Religion in the Age of Romanticism: Studies in Early Nineteenth-Century Thought* (New York, 1985), pp. 146-156

[2]Henry F. Brownson, ed., *The Works of Orestes A. Brownson* (Detroit: Thorndike Nourse, 1882-1887), Vol. V, p. 2.

The synthetic method of Brownson's philosophy and theology, combining intuition and reflection, led him to view the universe and all of history as one organic "dialectical whole." The divine creative act was for him

> the real *nexus* between contraries, and hence a dialectic union means a real union of contraries made one by means of the middle term. A dialectic whole is a real living whole, an organism, and not a mere aggregation. By the creative act, the real *medius terminus* of the universe, all the parts of the universe are made one dialectic whole, in which all the parts are really connected with the whole and with one another.[1]

The ideal formula was an ontological fact, apprehended by intuition, and it became the object of reflection only through language which originated from a divine revelation that was passed on from generation to generation through tradition. By reflection and tradition, therefore, persons became aware that it was God, not merely real and necessary being, who creates creatures.

Brownson's synthetic method and his dialectical view of the universe also informed his social and political philosophy, as is evident in *The American Republic* (1866). For Brownson human beings commune with God not only through creation and the Incarnation (i.e., religion), but also through their fellow human beings (i.e., society and government), and the material world (i.e., property). Society and therefore government, which was a necessary part of society, was, in his view, one of the essential means and conditions of human existence, development, perfection and communion with God.[2]

He repeatedly blasted what he termed a growing "political atheism" in Jacksonian and post-Jacksonian American politics because he believed that some politicians had severed any fundamental link between religion and politics. Although he was convinced that the constitutional provisions for religious liberty and separation of church and state were necessary and justified, he thought that some had misinterpreted these provisions by relegating religion to the sphere of individual conscience. This was a kind of religious and political "psychologism." For him government, as indeed the whole of culture, was ultimately founded upon the divine creative act which provided the ultimate justification for all freedom and authority. To forget this was equivalent to societal suicide, leading either to anarchy on the one hand or political despotism on the other.

Brownson wrestled for the remainder of his life with his dialectical view of the universe, emphasizing in his writings on politics as well as religion at one time the individual's freedom and at another the individual's dependence upon tradition and authority in a mediating community. In his own day and many times thereafter these shifting emphases in his thought were interpreted as characteristic of his chameleon character. His forceful and at times unreserved expressions of his views certainly gave his readers grounds for such interpretations. When his writings are interpreted, however, within the context of his dialectical view of reality, they can be seen, as Brownson himself saw them, as expressions of one

[1]Brownson, *op. cit.,* Vol. VIII, p. 33, n.
[2]See *The American Republic*, in Brownson, *op. cit.,* Vol. XVIII, p. 13.

or another side of the dialectic. Communion in the divine life established the dependence and the freedom simultaneously. If he stressed authority or freedom, it was because he believed that contemporary society had neglected one or the other of them. All his shifting views, however, were not simply a part of his dialectical whole. His views did change and develop over time and he periodically acknowledged these transformations.

For most of his life, Brownson operated within the rather wide ambit of the post-Kantian Romantic movement. His primary interests were in what would today be called the philosophy of religion, although his dialectic view of reality did not allow him to separate philosophy and theology. For him every philosophical position had theological implications and indeed all knowledge, as all experience, was ultimately grounded in the divine creative act.

Isaac Hecker, friend and disciple of Brownson's as he was, brought a different temperament and different side of the Romantic impulse into American Catholicism. If Brownson was more philosophical than Hecker, Hecker was more poetic than Brownson. Hecker was directly concerned with discovering new ways of expressing the quests of the sensitive religious soul.

After his conversion to Catholicism, Hecker published three major works the titles of which indicate something of his Romantic bent: *Questions of the Soul* (1855), *Aspirations of Nature* (1857), and *The Church and the Age* (1887). The first two works are attempts to demonstrate that the subjective yearnings of the heart and reason find their realization and fulfillment in the sacramental and communitarian mediations of Christ's life in the Catholic tradition. In a fashion similar to Brownson's synthetic method, he argued that the human soul, instinct with aspirations for the higher life, had real life only by its communion with the object. Only in the organic and dialectical union of the two can the individual find true freedom, spiritual nourishment, progressive sanctification and Christian perfection.

Hecker was well aware that the primary problem of the age was the one of subjectivity. Those who would defend religion in general and Catholic Christianity in particular had to take notice of this predominant characteristic of the age. They had to show in a way that was satisfactory to reason and human feelings that Catholic Christianity was not indeed repugnant to the human passion for personal liberty and the best impulses and instincts of human nature.

The fault with much of Catholic theology, Hecker argued repeatedly, was that it was not sensitive to the dynamics of the American culture and the needs of the age. Catholic theologians and apologists had concentrated so much upon ecclesiastical authority that they were unable to respond to the real questions raised by those outside of Catholicism. Thus they were not able to reconcile the demands of freedom as well as authority in the Christian tradition. It was not enough and in fact it was absurd to argue, as some Catholic apologists were doing, that once one accepted the reasonable and historical grounds for the Catholic Church's authority one had to make an entire surrender of one's personal liberty and will. Such a method, which Brownson had previously called the "method of authority," may have been useful for those already convinced of the truth of the Catholic tradition, but they were inept to win over the minds and hearts of those outside that tradition.

For Hecker, as for Brownson, it was a gross error to declare that the essence of Christianity was authority. Authority, although necessary, was not the essence of anything, much less of Christianity. It was only secondary. The essence of Christianity was communion in the one divine life—i.e., "the elevation of rational creatures, by the power of the Holy Spirit, to a union with God above that which they enjoy by their birth."[1] The Catholic apologist had to take seriously the natural aspirations of the human soul and simultaneously the contemporary manifestations of those aspirations if he or she was to be true to the universality inherent both in the aspirations and in the revelation concretely realized in the Catholic tradition.

The age, as well as human nature, had aspirations that flowed from the instinct God had originally planted in the human soul. If Catholicism had necessary and universal answers to the questions posed by the age, then it had the responsibility to correlate those universal yearnings with the universal revelation found in the Church. This was the task of contemporary Catholicism. It was the task that Hecker established for himself, for the religious order he formed (the Paulists), and for the American Catholic Church in the later half of the nineteenth century. Catholicism had to take seriously the real constitutive principles of American society, and in particular the dynamics of freedom, scientific investigation and progress, if it would Christianize these elements and thereby elevate them to their true goal of union with God. Here was an acknowledgement that the Spirit of God was at work in the human soul, in history, as well as in the Church.

For Hecker, each age and each culture had its own characteristic genius. The movement of history, though, was toward a synthesis of the particular values of every age and culture, and the Catholic Church was to become the concrete historical agent of this union. American Catholicism, in particular, was in an historically advantageous position to carry on the providential role of reconciliation because in the United States the geniuses of various nations were coming together in a way that would eventually serve the entire world.

Such millennial optimism (which Brownson did not share) was firmly rooted in Hecker's Thomistic understanding of human nature, his Romantic perception of the potentialities inherent within that nature, his organic view of history and community, and his belief in the present activity of the Holy Spirit in the historical process. It was also particularly Catholic in its focus on the Church itself as the concrete eschatological promise of the future redemption of the world.

---

[1]Isaac T. Hecker, *The Church and the Age* (New York: Catholic Publication Society, 1887), pp. 197-198.

AMERICANISM AND MODERNISM[1]

The new generation of thinkers who began to mature in the 1880's had little time for or interest in the philosophical issues that concerned Brownson and Hecker. The previous struggle to define the role of intuition and tradition in knowing God all but disappeared. The central issue in this period was the relation of the Church to the age, a continuation of the problem as it was articulated in the former era, but not within the romantic-idealist perspective of the universe as a dialectical whole. The doctrines of creation and the Incarnation continued to inform the thinking about the relation of the Church to contemporary culture, but again without the idealist presuppositions. Even if the new generation had had the interests they would have faced some strong resistance from Rome in adopting Traditionalist and Ontologist ways of thinking because Rome had already rejected these and other non-scholastic approaches to philosophy and theology as dangerous to orthodoxy, replacing them with Neo-Thomism as the solution to contemporary problems of knowledge, faith and religious experience.

Although the Romantic temperament was absent from many of the discussions of the period, the influence of Brownson and Hecker continued on especially among some of the so-called Americanists and their friends. Bishop John Lancaster Spalding, perhaps the most capable intellectual in the American hierarchy of the period, was educated in the Traditionalist-Ontologist school at Louvain and had the highest regard for Brownson as a philosopher. Spalding, however, emphasized the practical rather than the theoretical side of his traditionalism, being preoccupied with establishing and developing a major Catholic university in the United States. Archbishop John Ireland, while studying theology in France, was a regular reader of *Brownson's Quarterly Review*. A number of his lectures, too, are studded with quotations from Brownson's and Hecker's works, particularly those dealing with the relations of Catholicism to American culture. John Keane, as priest and later as bishop, was an avid follower of Hecker and was particularly influenced by the emphasis Hecker placed on the role of the Holy Spirit in the Christian life. Denis O'Connell, too, saw

---

[1]For a general introduction to Americanism and Modernism, see especially the following: Robert D. Cross, *The Emergence of Liberal Catholicism in America* (Cambridge, MA: Harvard University Press, 1958); Thomas T. McAvoy, C.S.C., *The Great Crisis in American Catholic History: 1895-1900* (Chicago: Henry Regnery Co., 1957); Thomas E. Wangler, "The Birth of Americanism: 'Westward the Apocalyptic Candlestick'," *The Harvard Theological Review* 65 (1972), pp. 415-436; Margaret Mary Reher, "The Church and the Kingdom of God in America: The Ecclesiology of the Americanists," (unpublished Ph.D. dissertation, Fordham University, 1972); Michael B. McGarry, "Modernism in the United States: William Laurence Sullivan, 1872-1935," *Records of the American Catholic Historical Society of Philadelphia* 90 (March-December 1979), pp. 33-52; Michael J. DeVito, *The New York Review, 1905-1908* (Yonkers, NY: The United States Catholic Historical Society, 1977); Scott Appleby, "American Catholic Modernism: Dunwoodie and *The New York Review*, 1895-1910," (Series 14, no. 3, Notre Dame Cushwa Center Working Papers Series, Fall 1983).

in "A New Idea in the Life of Father Hecker" a fresh Catholic argument in favor
of the American way of life.

The late nineteenth-century cultural and political context out of which developed the Americanist programs differed considerably from the context in
which Brownson and Hecker operated. The Americanists were not struggling, as
were Brownson and Hecker, with questions originating in the context of Unitarianism and Transcendentalism. What the Americanists appropriated from the
thought of Brownson and Hecker related more to the problems raised by the *zeit-
geist* and culture of the late nineteenth century. The Americanists were preoccupied with establishing a practical rapproachment between Catholicism and some
significant values of American culture, and not with a theoretical examination of
the issues undergirding those relations.

American Catholics of the period faced new social, cultural and ecclesiastical
problems. Immigration, an old problem, brought about a new intensity because
of a rapid increase of new immigrants from southern and eastern European countries, making American Catholicism increasingly multi-ethnic and demonstrating
in most visible ways to nativists the foreign character of Catholicism. Industrialization and the rise of large urban areas, too, created new social and economic
difficulties that called for solution. Problems were also created by the post-Civil
War interests in theories of evolution, and the rise of the new sciences of critical
history, sociology and psychology. Catholics as well as Protestants became divided among themselves in their responses to the questions of the day. American Protestants had their liberal-fundamentalist divisions and Catholics had their
Americanist- (and sometimes modernist) conservative divisions.

Within the post-Civil War American Catholic community the general cultural and social transformation produced at least seven major specific issues.
American Catholics were divided into (1) those who wanted an Americanized
hierarchy and those who advocated more ethnic representation in the hierarchy,
(2) those who fought for the establishment of a national Catholic university and
those who believed such an establishment would only further Americanist plans,
(3) those who wanted Catholic schools to cooperate with the public school system and those who rejected these desires as forms of capitulation, (4) those who
wanted a Roman Apostolic delegate and those who opposed the delegation as an
unnecessary Roman intervention in American affairs, (5) those who supported
the Knights of Labor and the Church's responsibilities to address the legitimate
aspirations of the working class and those who feared such labor unions as anar-
chistic, (6) those who desired quasi-ecumenical exchanges of opinion and those
who feared such exchanges as manifestations of religious indifferentism, and
(7) those who advocated the use of the social sciences and the scientific method
in the study of the Bible and religion, and those who interpreted such usage as
contrary to orthodox Catholic scholasticism. Although liberals and
conservatives could be on the same side over one or two of the above issues,
they were generally of very different minds.

The fundamental question underlying many of the specific issues was that of
a Catholic accommodation or capitulation to values and practices in American
culture. The Americanist programs and the numerous publications and public
lectures that advanced them were attempts to reconcile what they perceived to be
best in American culture with Catholic tradition without compromising that tradition. I have argued in another place that the Americanist practical programs for

reconciling Catholic and American ideals were based upon their optimistic view of the modern world and their understanding of the dynamic character of Christianity.[1] Most Americanists had a transformationist view of the relationship of grace to nature that allowed them to perceive the possibility of the presence of the divine within nature and culture. They viewed God as immanent in the natural as well as the supernatural orders and had a providential and developmental view of history. Both of these ideas enabled them to stress the Christian's inherent responsibilities for the natural order, the necessity to accommodate Catholicism to the spirit of the age and an openness to the use of the new sciences within religion and theology.

Such ideas and attitudes were rarely presented in systematic arguments. They were, rather, recurring motifs in the Americanist popular lectures and addresses. Although the Americanists were primarily ecclesiastical pragmatists, they did create a climate of opinion in American Catholicism that was conducive to modernist attempts to come to terms with some of the religious issues created by modern scientific research and methodologies.

From the 1890's to 1908, a small number of Catholic modernist or quasi-modernist educators and theologians took up the task of demonstrating the compatibility of the new scientific methods and social sciences with religion and theology. The modernists' methods and perspectives were more analytical and critical than they were synthetic (as in the thought of Brownson and Hecker). John Zahm, C.S.C., a professor and scientist at the University of Notre Dame, argued that a theistic conception of evolution was reconcilable with the Catholic intellectual tradition. John Hogan, S.S., a theologian at New Brighton Seminary outside of Boston and later a professor at The Catholic University of America in Washington, D.C., advocated the use of historical science in theology. William Kerby and John A. Ryan, both of The Catholic University, used sociology and economics in their works and encouraged seminaries to use these new sciences in their theological and ethical discourse. Francis E. Gigot, S.S., professor of Biblical Studies at St. Joseph's Seminary in Dunwoodie, New York, called upon Catholics to use higher criticism in the study of the Scriptures. The Catholic University and Dunwoodie Seminary published, respectively, the *Catholic University Bulletin* and the *New York Review* to disseminate these incipient modernist concerns.

Protests against the Americanists' programs and the quasi-modernist theologians, analogous to the protests against Protestant liberalism, were swift and were based upon a very different conception of the values of the age. Those who opposed the Americanists and the incipient modernists (e.g., Archbishop Michael Corrigan of New York, Bishop Bernard McQuaid of Rochester, Bishop Frederick Katzer of Milwaukee, and many of the Jesuit and German clergy) had specific reasons for their opposition to particular Americanist programs, but they also shared a world view that grounded their opposition. For them, as for Pope Pius IX and the First Vatican Council which they frequently quoted, the age was one of rationalism, secularism and naturalism. Americanists, too, saw these tendencies in the age, but the tendencies themselves were not, as Archbishop Ireland frequently argued, of the essence of the age, but only aberrations.

---

[1]Patrick Carey, ed., *American Catholic Religious Thought*, pp. 32-36.

For the conservatives, however, the age pulsated with these evil tendencies and the Church, the realm of the supernatural, could not be compromised by an alignment with this age. They believed that the Americanist and quasi-modernist spirit of accommodation was essentially a disguise for cultural and theological capitulation to values that were contrary to the Catholic tradition. The Americanists were, they charged, cultural chauvinists, and the modernists were theological minimizers. By using scientific methods, social sciences and biblical criticism, the modernists tended to "limit and reduce the authority of the magisterium of the church as far as possible."[1] The conservatives had accepted the dominant post-Vatican I (1870) neo-scholastic apologetic that reasserted the authority of reason and the Church as a solution to the various fideisms, subjectivisms and autonomous rationalisms of the age. Most American Jesuit colleges in the post-Vatican I period used apologetical texts that reflected this perspective. Opposition to the Americanists and the incipient modernists was indeed part of the larger post-Vatican I official Roman Catholic mentality. Where the Americanists saw opportunity for growth and reconciliation by adaptation, the conservatives saw dangers to the preservation of a unique Catholic identity.

The divisions in the American Church soon made their way to Rome. During much of the late 1880's and early 1890's the Americanists received favorable Roman decisions on the so-called German Question, the establishment of The Catholic University of America, the school controversy, and the decision not to condemn the Knights of Labor. But Rome's condemnations of future ecumenical activities and John Zahm's book, *Evolution and Dogma* (1895), and the removal of some key Americanists from positions of leadership at the North American College in Rome and at The Catholic University indicated that by the middle of the 1890's the Roman tide had turned in favor of the conservative positions in the American Church. Because of the 1897 French translation of Walter Elliott's biography of Isaac Hecker, the Americanist program got entangled with ecclesiastical politics in France and Italy over the proper relations between Catholicism and the modern state in Europe, and Rome became increasingly more cautious about Americanist leanings.[2]

In 1899 Pope Leo XIII published *Testem benevolentiae,* censuring what he perceived to be the Pelagian tendencies inherent in the new opinions and attitudes regarding the Church's adaptation to popular modern theories and methods. Although he did not in fact denounce the Americanists or hold them personally accountable for the charges he made, he sent them a clear warning. Pope Pius X reinforced Roman opposition to the accommodating spirit of the age in *Pascendi* (1907), which condemned modernism as the "synthesis of all errors." The two encyclicals effectively and practically eliminated for some time Catholic dialogue with American culture. They also reinforced and legitimated the Neo-Thomist

---

[1]Joseph Schroder, "Theological Minimizing and Its Latest Defender," *American Ecclesiastical Review* 5 (July 1891), p. 56.
[2]Walter Elliott, *The Life of Father Hecker* (New York: Columbus, 1891); *Le Père Hecker Fondateur des "Paulistes" Américains, 1819-1888* par le Père W. Elliott, de la même Compagnie. Traduit et adapté de l'anglais avec authorization de l'auteur. Introduction par Mgr. Ireland. Préface par l'Abbé Félix Klein (Paris, 1897).

alternative to the use of modern scientific methods and modern forms of philosophy in biblical study and theology.

CATHOLIC CULTURE AND NEO-THOMISM

American Catholic liberals smarted from the sting of the two papal whips, but denied that they held the positions therein condemned. Conservatives welcomed the warnings and asserted that there were needed correctives in American Catholicism. For all practical purposes, though, the encyclicals brought to an end the overt ecclesiastical warfare that had been going on in the community since the middle of the 1880's. In the period following their promulgation, from 1920 to 1960, American Catholics experienced new social changes that encouraged another transformation in intellectual life.

Philip Gleason has aptly called this period in American Catholic thought a search for unity.[1] The dominant integrating perspective behind this search was philosophical and theological Neo-Thomism, which Gleason sees operating in part as an ideology in support of Catholic ecclesial interests.[2] Neo-Thomism offered a number of American Catholic intellectuals a synthetic vision of the universe and provided an intellectual foundation for the attempt to create a Catholic culture within the larger American society. Although there were occasional dissenting voices to this vision, it clearly dominated in Catholic intellectual circles at least until the middle of the 1950's.

The rise of Neo-Thomism to a position of hegemony in American Catholic thought was gradual. The neo-scholastic apologetic, primarily imported from Europe, had been used in some seminaries and colleges before the papal rebukes of Americanism and modernism, but there was no concerted American effort to foster neo-scholasticism before the 1920's. Brownson repeatedly challenged Neo-Thomistic scholasticism and the incipient modernists were moderately critical of it. After the papal encyclicals, however, most seminaries and many colleges began to use textbooks written exclusively from the post-Vatican I Neo-Thomistic perspective. The Jesuits in particular during the immediate aftermath of modernism raised a new breed of self-consciously anti-modernist neo-scholastics.

The Jesuits were not alone, however, in giving birth to the interests in Neo-Thomistic thought and seeing it as the correct alternative to modern forms of thought. In 1921, Virgil Michel, O.S.B., complained that there was not one journal in the entire English-speaking world devoted to neo-scholasticism, and no one outside of Catholic seminaries conversant enough with modern philosophy and neo-scholasticism to engage modern thinkers in discussion and debate.[3]

[1]"In Search of Unity: American Catholic Thought, 1920-1960," *The Catholic Historical Review* 65 (April 1979), pp. 185-205. For much of what follows in this section, I am indebted to Gleason; Arnold J. Sparr, "The Catholic Literary Revival in America, 1920-1960" (Ph.D. dissertation, University of Wisconsin, 1985); and William M. Halsey, *The Survival of American Innocence: Catholicism in an Era of Disillusionment 1920-1940* (Notre Dame, IN: The University of Notre Dame Press, 1980).
[2]Philip Gleason, "Keeping the Faith in America," *op. cit.*, p. 169.
[3]Virgil Michel, "The Mission of Catholic Thought," *American Catholic Quarterly Review* 46 (1921), p. 664.

By 1923, things were beginning to change. In that year, the 600th anniversary of the canonization of St. Thomas, the *American Ecclesiastical Review* devoted an entire issue to Thomas' thought, and advocated an American movement "back to St. Thomas."[1] In the same year the philosophy department at St. Louis University began publishing *The Modern Schoolman*, the first American publication devoted *ex professo* to neo-scholasticism. Other journals followed: in 1926, *Thought*; in 1927, *The New Scholasticism*; in 1939, *The Thomist*. Fulton Sheen, too, published his doctoral dissertation, *God and Intelligence in Modern Philosophy* (1925), reflecting the rising neo-scholastic interests among younger scholars in the 1920's.

The revival of Neo-Thomism was intended to foster a widespread vibrant intellectual life and to promote the intellectual standing of Catholics in American cultural life, to defend Catholic beliefs and practices, and to redeem the modern secularized society by integrating religion and all forms of life. The revival falls into two major periods of development. During the early phase of its revival (1920-1935), American Neo-Thomism focused its intellectual guns upon modernism, the essence of which, in Christopher Dawson's words, was the anti-dogmatic principle. Inherent in modernism was a rationalistic skepticism about the supernatural as an object of certain knowledge, an individualism and subjectivism that was fatal to all religious authority and community, and a belief that science using unaided human reason could produce unlimited progress. It was a relativistic, positivistic and completely secular movement based upon philosophical materialism. What it offered was an empty promise of human self-fulfillment and was in fact a closed system of thought that *a priori* ruled out divine intervention as the source of human redemption. It was no wonder, the Neo-Thomists argued, that modernist intellectuals in American culture were disillusioned. Neo-Thomism offered a way out of the disillusionment by placing confidence in reason's capacity to discover the intelligibility of the universe, and by the aid of revelation, to know the end for which the universe and humanity were created.

From 1935 to 1955—as American Catholic thinkers came into contact with Jacques Maritain, Etienne Gilson and a host of other French Catholic neo-scholastics—the American revival entered a new phase of its development. Although Neo-Thomists continued their assault on modernism, they began to see their Catholic faith, not just reason, as a cultural force capable of transforming Western civilization. In a variety of ways, they attempted to redeem their culture from what they perceived to be its drifting and secular tendencies.

The *élan* of American Catholic thought during the period was, in Philip Gleason's estimation, "toward an organically unified Catholic culture in which religious faith constituted the integrating principle that brought all the dimensions of life together in a comprehensive and tightly articulated synthesis."[2] Following Jacques Maritain and others, intellectuals combined both the philosophical and theological dimensions of Thomism in formulating a frankly

[1]*American Ecclesiastical Review* 69 (July 1932).
[2]Philip Gleason, "A Search for Unity," *op. cit.*, p. 187.

Christian humanism[1] which emphasized humanity's wounded nature, and its need for grace and redemption.

American Catholics were beginning to read not only the Neo-Thomism of Maritain and Etienne Gilson, but also the thought of Romano Guardini, Karl Adam, Christopher Dawson, and the novels of Leon Bloy, François Mauriac and George Bernanos. Their reading exposed them to a dimension of Catholic thought and culture to which the earlier Neo-Thomistic revival had been oblivious. Maritain's "humanism of the Incarnation" and their reflections upon the doctrine of the Mystical Body of Christ encouraged them to perceive the social and cultural implications of their Catholic faith and practice.

Attempts to integrate religion and cultural life were evident on a number of levels. College courses, especially in literature and philosophy, aimed at a synthetic vision. *Commonweal,* a journal established in 1926 and published by lay Catholics, tried to raise the consciousness of lay Catholics for the regeneration of humanity and society. The Catholic Worker Movement, established in 1930 by Peter Maurin and Dorothy Day, demonstrated the practical as well as theoretical side of the social dimensions of the Christian life. Maurin wanted Catholics to ignite the "dynamite" of the gospel and to demonstrate the Church's potential to redeem society. Maurin introduced Dorothy Day to the Christian Personalism of French philosophers like Emmanuel Mounier, and through round-table discussions at the Catholic Worker houses Maurin and Day familiarized a host of other young Catholics with the new dimensions of a social Catholicism.[2]

The revival was also reflected in the liturgical movement that was initiated in the late 1920's and early 1930's by Virgil Michel, O.S.B., of St. John's Abbey in Collegeville, Minnesota; Gerald Ellard, S.J., of St. Louis University; William Busch of St. Paul Seminary in St. Paul, Minnesota; and a host of others. The liturgical movement, too, articulated a dynamic vision of Christian life, emphasizing a doctrine of the Mystical Body of Christ and a concept of worship that attempted to integrate Christian life and work in the world. The foundation of *Orate Fratres* (1926, later *Worship*), the publication of the movement, signalled the new approach.[3]

The Catholic Worker and liturgical movements were consistent with the overall synthetic aims of the Neo-Thomistic revival, but they were also implicitly, and at times explicitly, critical of the rationalistic scholastic method in theology and the almost exclusive juridical ecclesiology with mainstream American

---

[1]Many took up this theme from Jacques Maritain's *True Humanism* (1936).
[2]On these movements, see Rodger Van Allen, *The Commonweal and American Catholicism* (Philadelphia: Fortress Press, 1974); Marc Ellis, *Peter Maurin: Prophet in the Twentieth Century* (New York: Paulist Press, 1981); William Miller, *Dorothy Day: A Biography* (San Francisco: Harper and Row, 1982); Mel Piehl, *Breaking Bread: The Catholic Worker and the Origin of Catholic Radicalism in America* (Philadelphia: Temple University Press, 1982).
[3]On Michel, see R.W. Franklin, *Virgil Michel: American Catholic* (Collegeville, MN: The Liturgical Press, 1988); Jeremy Hall, O.S.B., *The Full Stature of Christ: The Ecclesiology of Dom Virgil Michel* (Collegeville: MN: The Liturgical Press, 1976); Paul Marx, O.S.B., *Virgil Michel and the Liturgical Movement* (Collegeville, MN: The Liturgical Press, 1957).

Catholicism. The liturgical movement in particular fostered a return to the biblical and patristic sources of the Catholic tradition in doing theology. The implications of this call for a return to these sources of theology, however, would not be clear until after the Second Vatican Council. Both movements were also attempts to restore a consciousness of the Church's divine inner nature. Michel believed, for example, that the Catholic community's lost consciousness of the Mystical Body coincided historically with the loss of a "liturgical sense" and these losses combined to diminish personal and social responsibility for justice in society.

The preoccupation with integrating religion and life revealed itself in a new way in the 1940's. By then it was becoming clear to persons like John Courtney Murray, S.J., professor of theology at Woodstock College in Maryland, that Catholics could not very easily enter into the debates on social justice in American society until they removed the old suspicions that Catholicism, if not American Catholics, was doctrinally opposed to religious liberty. Catholics had to demonstrate the basis of their adherence to religious liberty. Murray's support for religious liberty, however, did not mean a divorce of religion from the issues of political life. He made it clear that for him religious liberty meant that religion should be distinct from and separated from state government on the institutional level so that religion could be more effectively integrated into the total life of society.[1]

Murray's argument for religious liberty blended the transtemporal principles of the Neo-Thomistic natural law tradition with an historical consciousness, which was not a part of that tradition, to create an understanding of the concrete human situation in which "religious pluralism is theologically the human condition." The political movements toward religious liberty were for the most part expressions of the demands of "natural law in the present moment of history."[2] Murray developed a Catholic argument for the constitutional principle and practice of religious liberty by examining the Thomistic principles of natural law in light of American political experience and the political consciousness that had evolved during the previous two centuries in the Western world. By an historical-critical examination of recent papal declarations on the state and social justice, moreover, he also tried to show that papal teachings themselves had evolved to acknowledge the dignity of the human person in modern society. The historical emergence of constitutional protections for religious liberty were in fact a legitimate development of the Catholic tradition itself.

Murray's views got him in trouble not only with American theologians like Francis J. Connell and Joseph Fenton, professors of theology at The Catholic University, but also with his Roman religious superiors and Cardinal Alfredo Ottaviani, head of the Congregation of the Holy Office in Rome. Murray's opponents argued that religious liberty was a tolerable evil in circumstances where the Catholic Church was a minority, but that in the ideal order, civil government

---

[1]On Murray, see Donald E. Pelotte, S.S.S., *John Courtney Murray: Theologian in Conflict* (New York: Paulist Press, 1975); and John Coleman, S.J., "Vision and Praxis."

[2]John Courtney Murray, S.J., *The Problem of Religious Freedom* (Westminster, MD: The Newman Press, 1965), pp. 109, 119.

had a responsibility to protect and support the Catholic Church. Murray countered that this so-called traditional argument was itself historically-conditioned and did not possess universal validity. It merely made ideal a concrete historical relationship between the church and the state. Murray's arguments, however, could not match the power of the votes against him. In 1954, therefore, he was for all practical purposes asked to remain silent on the issue. And he did so, until new winds began to blow in the Catholic Church with the announcement of the Second Vatican Council.

Another aspect of the move toward integration can be seen in the ecumenical efforts of Murray's fellow Jesuit at Woodstock, Gustave Weigel. Although it is rarely interpreted within this context, the ecumenical movement as perceived by Weigel was a part of that general dynamic in American Catholicism toward concrete unity in life, culture and Church. The disunity of Christianity was a scandal and a direct violation of the divine desires for unity. That Weigel considered the Catholic Church to be the concrete manifestation of that divine love and unity did not prevent him from seeing the necessity of a fuller concrete sign of that unity. He has been called an "uncompromising ecumenist" because for him dogma was the heart of Christian unity and the only way Christians would be able to enjoy a unity of dogma was if they all returned to Rome. Nevertheless, uncompromising though he was, he encouraged mutual dialogue and understanding between Protestants and Catholics and advocated in particular that Catholics study American Protestants from their own sources and not just from the polemical Catholic tracts. He brought many younger students into the ecumenical movement prior to the Second Vatican Council.[1]

In the midst of the 1950's, when most indexes of participation in Catholic religious life were running high and when many Catholic intellectuals were severely critical of the modernist tendencies in the secular world, the respected historian of American Catholicism, Monsignor John Tracy Ellis, published a critique of American Catholic anti-intellectualism.[2] He demonstrated some of the historical reasons for the lack of creativity and cultural contributions, but argued that these historical reasons could not excuse American Catholics from present attempts to improve. Ellis found much agreement with his criticisms, demonstrating a growing maturity within American Catholicism.[3]

American Catholic thought from 1920 to 1960 was, as Philip Gleason has argued, in pursuit of unity: an affirmation of the unicity and intelligibility of truth, a correlation of reason and revelation, a synthesis of life and thought, an integration of religion and culture, and a vision of Catholicism itself as *the* only unified religious way of life that offered a viable alternative to modern culture. Whether intellectuals sought the center of Catholic culture in the Christian ra-

---

[1]On Weigel, see Patrick W. Collins, "Gustave Weigel: Ecclesiologist and Ecumenist" (unpublished Ph.D. dissertation, Fordham University, 1972).
[2]"American Catholics and the Intellectual Life," *Thought* 30 (Autumn 1955), pp. 353-386.
[3]See, e.g., Gustave Weigel's "American Catholic Intellectualist—A Theologian's Reflection," *Review of Politics* 19 (July 1957), pp. 275-307; and Thomas F. O'Dea, *American Catholic Dilemma: An Inquiry into the Intellectual Life* (New York: Sheed & Ward, 1958).

tionalism of the thirteenth century, the liturgy or Christian Personalism, they generally agreed that there was a fundamental irreducible core that held Catholic tradition together. This did not mean that American Catholic thinkers were in fundamental agreement on any particular issue. There were significant divisions and disagreements within the Neo-Thomist school of thought. Numerous American Catholics, too, rejected the ideas, implications and attitudes associated with the liturgical and Catholic Worker movements. Educators, moreover, disagreed among themselves over what constituted the integrating core of Catholic education. The search for unity did not in fact mean uniformity, but it did reflect fundamental aspirations and created a climate of opinion and expectations that, at times, placed undue philosophical and cultural burdens upon the concept of unity itself.

Within the quest for an integral Catholicism were seeds of its own destruction. The different movements in search of unity were held together by a common goal, a common opposition to what they perceived to be the intellectual disillusionment, individualism, materialism and secularism of society, and by a common and well-organized ecclesiastical structure, all of which masked the differences that later became apparent once the goal was no longer commonly shared and modern society was viewed more positively. The Neo-Thomistic philosophy, too, was not well-integrated with or suited to the historical methods employed in biblical research and liturgical studies.

VATICAN II TO THE PRESENT

The Second Vatican Council (1962-1965) has been characterized as a religious reformation in which a paradigmatic shift in consciousness and thought occurred within the Catholic Church. It would be impossible in the few short paragraphs that follow to summarize the revolutionary impact the Council had upon American Catholic thinking from 1965 to the present. I will indicate here only one major development—i.e., what could be called the celebration, and in some cases the consecration, of diversity in the theological community.

The sixteen conciliar documents reflected not only the new biblical, historical and existential theology that had been developing in France and Germany prior to the council but also the Neo-Thomistic theology of the scholastic revival. The very combination of these different theological perspectives provided grounds for both liberal and conservative post-conciliar interpretations of the council's intentions and contained the seeds of much of the theological diversity and conflict that would characterize the post-conciliar Church.

In that post-conciliar period, as in the periods immediately following the Council of Trent and the First Vatican Council (1869-1870), the new shift in consciousness received the most attention. It was not so much the reform programs or even specific documents that brought about a change in thinking, but the theological context in which the reforms and documents were articulated. Although the documents contain some notice of the immutable in human nature, the emphasis and context was upon the historicity of humanity—an awareness of the mutable dimensions of human existence and the Christian faith. A new cognizance of reform, change, human subjectivity and freedom flowed intrinsically from the emphasis on historicity. A new respect, too, for diversity within unity had its origins in the eschatological dimensions of that historicity. A new openness to secularity and the call for a sympathetic dialogue between the Church and the modern world, moreover, created in some a receptivity to modern forms of thought that were previously considered inimical to the faith.

Conciliar talk of renewal, change and reform represented a dynamic shift of consciousness for many American Catholics who were reared in a Church that was accustomed to speaking about the Church's irreformable nature and its unchanging practices. For these, the new mentality was a frightening experience because it shattered their visions of Catholic unity and uniformity that had been developing in the most recent past. For others, the new emphasis was a liberating experience, filled with hope for the moral and institutional revitalization of Catholicism.

By the late 1960's, the intellectual community was visibly divided over the interpretation and implementation of the conciliar vision. Catholic traditionalists, the most reactionary and the least numerous group within American Catholicism, rejected the validity, not just the abuses, of the conciliar liturgical reforms. Other conservatives, like James Hitchcock, questioned the extent and uncontrolled pace of ecclesiastical reforms that the "elite" liberal bishops, clergy and theologians were imposing upon the Church. Many of the popular reforms and much of the thinking behind them, Hitchcock argued, were unwarranted by the council. In essence, the liberal program was a capitulation to modernity and secularism that deadened the sense of the supernatural.[1]

Even those who were open to new consciousness were divided among themselves in evaluating the nature and extent of the reforms. Some argued that many of the reforms were minimal and did not meet the needs of modernity. Others sought to extend the implications of Vatican II and began to revise Catholic theological concepts and methods. By 1975, the year of the "Hartford Appeal"[2] and the publication of David Tracy's *A Blessed Rage for Order*,[3] a rift was beginning to develop within liberal circles as theologians like Avery Dulles, S.J., professor of theology at The Catholic University of America, and David Tracy, professor of theology at the University of Chicago, argued about the nature and method of fundamental and systematic theology.

Dulles is a creative theological interpreter of the ecclesiology of Vatican II and represents the moderately progressive theological wing within the theological community. He is committed to a legitimate diversity in theology and defines himself as an advocate of theological adaptation to modern thought forms. For Dulles, however, adaptation has specific limits which are defined by the dis-

---

[1] See, e.g., James Hitchcock, *Catholicism and Modernity: Confrontation or Capitulation?* (New York: The Seabury Press, 1979); and George A. Kelly, *The Battle for the American Church* (New York: Doubleday and Co., Inc., 1979).

[2] "An Appeal for Theological Affirmation" (subscribed to by 24 prominent American Catholic and Protestant theologians, Avery Dulles, S.J., among them) asserted the need to recover "a sense of the transcendent" and charged that some contemporary theological themes were "false and debilitating to the church's life and work." The "Appeal" condemned thirteen current themes it so characterized. On the "Appeal," see Avery Dulles, *The Resilient Church: The Necessity and Limits of Adaptation* (Garden City, NY: Doubleday, 1977), pp. 191-195.

[3] David Tracy, *Blessed Rage for Order: The New Pluralism in Theology* (New York: Seabury Press, 1975).

tinctiveness of the Catholic tradition.[1] Although he supports an inclusive approach to theology, he does not believe, as does Tracy who is himself a committed believer, that the Catholic theologian can explain Christianity to the modern pluralistic and secular world without an explicit religious commitment. Fundamental as well as systematic theology for Dulles cannot accept even the possibility of a complete scientific objectivity, and he feared that Tracy and others were moving in that direction.

Since 1975, Tracy has argued that both systematic and fundamental theology must become a part of "public discourse." He is not, therefore, as concerned with the theology of Vatican II and its implementation as he is with carrying on a dialogue with the "present pluralism of theologies." He defines his theology as "revisionist," meaning an attempt to revise both the traditional Christian and the traditional modern self-understandings. For him revisionist theology is best understood as "philosophical reflection upon the meanings present in common human experience and the meanings present in the Christian Tradition."[2] Such a theological method provides an avenue to appropriate public discourse and tries to make meaningful the universal claims of Christianity. Dulles finds Tracy's attempts to establish public criteria for truth and meaning in theological discourse to be an unwarranted appropriation of the empirical model of the positive sciences in doing theology.[3]

Hitchcock, Dulles and Tracy represent something of the spectrum of theological orientation in the post-Vatican II period. The dialogue or battle has been and continues to be between those who are resisting the inroads of modernity, those whose primary theological concern is within the confessional tradition and its reform, and those whose "public theology" tries to demonstrate the universal claims of Christianity and human experience. In this theological pluralism, American Catholics have become partners with other ecclesiastical communities—sharing all the strengths and weaknesses of the past American experiences with pluralism.

Diversity in the theological community stemmed in part from the Council's call to dialogue with the modern world. Various schools of thought arose reflecting different theological methodologies borrowed from the social sciences, literary criticism, the study of the history of world religions, and diverse modern philosophies. In the United States, too, the diversity comes from a new openness to multifarious theological educations. No longer would promising young theologians receive their theological education exclusively in European Catholic centers of theology. During the 1960's, a number of younger theologians received their doctorates from American Protestant theological seminaries and secular universities and many were employed in new doctoral programs established at a number of American Catholic universities to respond to the need for more professionally trained theologians in the Catholic colleges. The new doctoral programs, too, reflected the varied theological backgrounds and specialities.

[1]See Dulles, *The Resilient Church, op. cit.,* p. 145.

[2]Tracy, *Blessed Rage for Order, op. cit.,* p. 34.

[3]Avery Dulles, "Authority and Criticism in Systematic Theology," *Theology Digest* 26 (Winter 1978), p. 392.

The widespread diversity within Catholic theology displaced the hegemony of Neo-Thomism in American Catholic thought. Unity of perspective and even the desire for it gave way to diversity with a suddenness that makes the memory of a unitive perspective difficult not only to recall but to value. For some in the post-Vatican II period, too, diversity has been raised to a value in itself with the same enthusiasm that blinded some of the Neo-Thomists to the weaknesses of their own almost exclusive emphasis upon unity.

American Catholic thought from John Carroll to the present has been a history of continuity and change in the various attempts to make sense of Catholic Christianity in the modern world. Whether emphasis was placed upon the reasonableness of the faith, the dialectical nature of the Christian life, the Catholic values within American ideals, the transcendental unity and integral vision of Catholicism, or the legitimate diversity of theological discourse, American Catholic religious thinkers struggled and continue to struggle to conceptualize for their own day the Catholic tradition which itself simultaneously includes and transcends each of the emphases. No one time, but only all times together, can bring forth the full meaning of Christianity as it moves in history toward the ultimate unity in Christ for which all humanity has been created. That each of these periods had its own strengths and weaknesses would be the object of a theological essay. Here I have been content to demonstrate something of the history of the various movements.

CHAPTER SEVEN

The History of American Catholic Monasticism
Joel Rippinger
Marmion Abbey

For all of its distinctive features, the historical evolution of monastic life in the United States has been, from its inception, closely connected with the development of the American Catholic Church. American monasticism's European heritage, its immigrant institutions, its capacity to assimilate and adapt to American culture—all point to distinctive traits shared by the wider American Catholic Church.

Characteristic of the monastic order throughout the centuries has been its ability to address itself to the specific needs of the Church and faith community surrounding it. This instinctive pliancy not only served well the pluralistic character of religion in North America and the multiple demands of the Catholic Church in the United States in its formative stages, but it also engendered in time the formation of a wide array of different forms of monastic life, each in turn making its own contribution to the maturing identity of American Catholicism.

The intent of this essay will be to trace some of the broad features of the history of monastic life in the United States, its contribution to the growth of the American Catholic Church over the last century and a half, its evolving variety of expression, and its spiritual itinerary in helping to shape the identity of Catholic life and thought in the United States.

THE FOUNDING ERA

The immediate context of the emergence of European monks in the United States was that of the increasing wave of German-speaking immigrants to North America in the middle of the nineteenth century. Prior to that time there had been isolated cases of individual monks who had made their way to America and even the celebrated case of a Trappist community from France attempting a foundation at the beginning of the nineteenth century, but their impact was negligible.

It was only in the 1840's that the prospect of establishing monastic foundations in the United States elicited an observable interest among European monasteries. This was the result of a confluence of factors. In Europe itself, there was a renewed interest in missionary activity to foreign lands, reflected in the rapid emergence of new missionary orders and aid societies.[1] There was also a renewal of Benedictine monasticism on the European continent where, at the beginning of the century, it had all but been eclipsed because of Napoleonic

---

[1]Africa, Asia and Australia, as well as the Americas, were the object of much of this activity. In the nineteenth century, European monastic houses established foundations on each of these continents.

Wars and revolutions.[1] In addition, there was a steady stream of petitions directed toward European religious houses during this time. These petitions emanated from an American episcopate desperate for clerical and religious personnel. Such requests were made to meet the urgent pastoral needs of a nascent American Catholic Church that was suddenly being augmented by European immigrants.

Recognizing the need for missionary assistance to be given the Catholic immigrants of North America was one thing; presenting a pastoral plan and securing both sufficient personnel and clear commitment from monastic communities was quite another. Here, too, the confluence of historical context and practical necessity played its role. The first half of the nineteenth century in Europe was witness to a revival of interest in the monastic model of the earlier Middle Ages, a time when monk-missionaries of Irish and Anglo-Saxon abbeys had Christianized the continent of Europe. The pregnant historical moment of the nineteenth century was aligned to this earlier monastic model. There emerged at the same time a select group of independent and impulsive monks who were anxious to energize this model. Imbued with the spirit of this earlier epoch, these monks wanted to serve as the vanguard of a missionary effort to North America, imitating the monastic model of their forebears. It was an effort whose expansive pastoral vision was rivaled only by the faith that their project would succeed.

Among the monastic figures representative of this missionary impulse was a young, outspoken Bavarian priest from the German Abbey of Metten, Boniface Wimmer. A man of many projects and plans, Wimmer had come to a decisive point in his personal design for Metten Abbey's missionary future in 1845. Convinced of the urgent need to establish a Benedictine monastery in North America, the thirty-six-year old monk boldly petitioned his abbot and the Congregation for the Propagation of the Faith in Rome for permission to leave Europe and found his monastery. His initial petition was summarily rejected. But with a resourcefulness and political acumen rare even in more seasoned participants in ecclesial politics, Wimmer secured the good will and financial backing of the Bavarian King (Ludwig I) and his court chaplain, charmed the papal nuncio to Bavaria into securing approval of his plan from Propaganda Fide in Rome and, after persistent pleas, badgered his abbot and community into accepting the idea of his missionary enterprise.[2]

Wimmer's missionary plan was of a piece with his own maverick style of monastic life. He recruited eighteen prospective candidates for the journey to the United States, only one of whom had ever experienced life in a Benedictine monastery. Nonetheless, the young monk of Metten was confident that his mission would succeed. He also consciously linked his proposed establishment of a Benedictine monastery in the New World with those countless monasteries established by the earlier monk missionaries of Europe, including his namesake

---

[1] Roger Aubert, "Nineteenth-Century Monastic Restoration in Western Europe," *Tjurunga* 8 (1974), pp. 5-24.

[2] Jerome Oetgen, *An American Abbot* (Latrobe, PA, 1976) is the best single resource for chronicling Wimmer's life and monastic influence.

Boniface, a millennium earlier. For Wimmer, "conditions in America are like those of Europe one thousand years ago."[1]

Nonetheless, the plan was more than a romantic pipe dream. It had a precise and pragmatic design. Wimmer was directing his missionary effort to the German-speaking Catholics of North America. He would provide priests to care for their sacramental needs, a seminary to supply them with the safeguard of future priestly and religious vocations, schools to insure a Catholic education for their children, and a monastery that would serve as a cultural and religious lifeline for an immigrant community whose ties with its rich European tradition had been severed.

Shortly after his arrival in the United States in 1846, Wimmer realized that any success in his efforts would have to be attached to his ability to adapt to the immediate and constantly changing demands facing a still fragile American Catholic Church. In this challenge, Wimmer proved himself more than equal to the task, employing his talents as monastic missionary, persuasive politician, pragmatic planner and forceful leader.

One of the first examples of the Bavarian Benedictine's adaptive ability was his decision to reject the original offer for land in the remote reaches of Cambria County, Pennsylvania, finding more compelling the invitation extended by Bishop Michael O'Connor of Pittsburgh for property near Latrobe in Westmoreland County, Pennsylvania.[2] It was at the site near Latrobe that Wimmer's vision of a monastic community was to take root in the form of the Benedictine monastery of St. Vincent.

The Diocese of Pittsburgh was also to be the backdrop of the first real standoff between a standard of European monastic life and the contrasting model of American Catholic culture. This contrast was epitomized in the persons of O'Connor and Wimmer. The Irish Bishop was accustomed to absolute episcopal control of his diocese and was a strong temperance advocate. The German superior was equally accustomed to the tradition of autonomous monastic authority and, as the son of a Bavarian tavernkeeper, saw no difficulty in allowing the construction of a brewery on his property. The clash between language and culture, and jurisdiction and tradition reflected both the German-Irish ethnic tension and the conflict between bishops and religious orders that ran throughout the nineteenth-century history of the American Catholic Church. It also underscored the determination and resoluteness of Wimmer to maintain his independence of action. For on every controversial issue that saw Wimmer and O'Connor confront one another in the first decade of St. Vincent's existence—the Bishop's power of apointment of monk-priests, acceptance of all diocesan students in the monastic seminary, the withholding of exemption from the monastic community and the removal of Wimmer as superior—Wimmer won concessions.[3]

[1] Article written by Wimmer in the *Augsburger Postzeitung,* November 8, 1845, as cited and translated in Colman Barry, *Worship and Work* (Collegeville, MN, 1980), p. 420.

[2] Oetgen, *op. cit.,* pp. 62-69.

[3] See Henry Szarnicki, "The Episcopate of Michael O'Connor, First Bishop of Pittsburgh, 1843-1860" (Ph.D. dissertation, Catholic University of America, Washington, DC, 1971), pp. 161-244; and exchange of letters and briefs between

At the same time Wimmer was consolidating his role as superior, he was widening the role of the monastic community of St. Vincent. He recruited large numbers of new members from other European monasteries to staff his new monastery. He persuaded the German immigrant aid society, the *Ludwig-Missionverein,* to bypass the Bishop of Pittsburgh and distribute funds directly to German parishes and religious communities of his diocese. Using his own lobbying contacts in Rome, Wimmer was able to have St. Vincent raised to the rank of an exempt abbey in 1855 and received the title of abbot, a position he held for thirty-three years.

In that time frame, Wimmer launched an experiment in "missionary monasticism" from St. Vincent that acquired a momentum all its own. In 1851 he drew up plans to bring Benedictine women to America, petitioning Bavarian sisters from the Benedictine community of Eichstaett to join him in Pennsylvania. Once again Wimmer's doggedness in pursuing a petition won over the initial reluctance of Eichstaett's superior and by 1852 the first contingent of sisters arrived in Pennsylvania. Despite deep set differences with Wimmer's insistence on exercising exclusive control over the work of the sisters,[1] the presence of these first Benedictine women set the pattern for the foundation of similar communities of Benedictine sisters in succeeding years.[2]

Meanwhile, the community of monks at St. Vincent experienced a surge in numbers during its early years and accelerated Wimmer's plan for expansion. Having received a number of requests to establish monastic communities in the "West," Wimmer responded by initiating new foundations in Minnesota in 1856 and Kansas in 1857. Four years later, at the start of the Civil War, the young abbot had monks in Newark and Chicago, Kentucky and Texas. This only marked the beginning of a movement that, by the time of Wimmer's death in 1887, continued westward to Colorado, made inroads into southern states from Virginia and North Carolina to Georgia and Alabama, and saw sustained growth in already established communities. In the process, Wimmer merited his title of Patriarch of American Monasticism. Even as his Bavarian brusqueness and boundless energy served him well in the ferment of the American frontier, his savvy diplomacy, missionary zeal and dedication to pastoral service were at one with the needs of the American Catholic Church in the second half of the nineteenth century. The abbot of St. Vincent did not lack opposition within his monastic foundations to the missionary strain of monasticism he propounded, nor natural obstacles to its implementation, but his single-minded determination to root Benedictine life in the New World of North America and his indefatigable efforts to make of it an evangelizing arm of the American Catholic Church con-

Wimmer and the Congregation of Propaganda Fide in Rome for the years 1851-1857, Archives of Propaganda Fide, Rome.
[1]Letter of Wimmer to Archbishop Karl Reisach of Munich, January 1, 1852, Saint Vincent Archabbey Archives.
[2]For a more extensive elaboration of the problems and the success of this pattern, see Mary Ewens, *The Role of the Nun in Nineteenth-Century America* (New York, 1978); Incarnata Girgen, *Behind the Beginnings* (St. Joseph, MN, 1981); and Judith Sutera, *True Daughters: Monastic Identity and American Benedictine Women's History* (Atchison, KA, 1987).

stitute a considerable and lasting contribution to the evolution of American Catholicism in the nineteenth century.

The missionary impulse of Boniface Wimmer had its counterpart among other European Benedictine monks as well. At the same time Wimmer was beginning his work in Pennsylvania, a young priest from the Benedictine Abbey of Einsiedeln in Switzerland, Martin Marty, was attracted to the graphic accounts of the evangelization of the North American Indians made by the famed Belgian Missionary, Pierre de Smet, during a tour of Europe.[1] Marty nurtured this missionary vision more as he read the *Annales* of the Society for the Propagation of the Faith that recounted the exploits and heroism of missionaries in North America. The opportunity for the young monk to translate his vision into action came in 1860 when his abbot asked him to embark upon a difficult task: go to the United States and try to revive the floundering monastic community that Einsiedeln had established six years earlier in Southern Indiana. Marty responded with wholehearted dedication to the task and within a decade his administrative and leadership skills helped place the monastery of St. Meinrad on a firm basis and led to his election as the community's first abbot. Not unlike the Benedictines of St. Vincent, the community at St. Meinrad dedicated itself primarily to meeting the pastoral and educational needs of the German-speaking immigrant, erecting a seminary-college and serving in parishes and missions throughout the dioceses of Vincennes and Southern Indiana.[2]

Nor was Einsiedeln the only Swiss monastery interested in making an American foundation. The parlous Swiss political situation in the middle of the nineteenth century threatened the ongoing existence of Catholic religious communities. Partly in response to the uncertain future facing his own foundation and partly in reply to the request for pastoral assistance coming from the bishops of America, the abbot of Engelberg Abbey, Anselm Villiger, sent a pair of monks in 1871 to the United States. The two Swiss Benedictines, Frowin Conrad and Adelhelm Odermatt, were formally responding to an invitation from Bishop John Hogan of the recently erected diocese of St. Joseph, Missouri, to establish a monastic community there. Informally, they were assuring Engelberg of an American political refuge in view of a possible suppression of the Swiss abbey. From this initial foundation in Nodaway County, Missouri, flowed two variant visions of Benedictine life. The first, fostered by Frowin Conrad as superior of Conception Abbey, was of a monasticism that concentrated on liturgical life within the cloister of the community and one that limited its range of pastoral commitments. The second, proposed by Conrad's Engelberg confrere Adelhelm Odermatt, opted for a more missionary and activist mode of monastic life. Odermatt moved to the West Coast in the 1880's, where his model of missionary monasticism took root in the community of Mount Angel, Oregon. Frowin Conrad continued to serve as superior of the Missouri monastery of Conception for the next half century. In their respective ventures

[1] Letter of Martin Marty, appearing in the August 7, 1876 *Wahrheitsfreund* of Cincinnati.
[2] For a comparison of the respective monastic visions of the communities of St. Vincent and St. Meinrad, see Basilius Doppelfeld, *Monchtum und Kirchlicher Heilsdienst* (Munsterschwarzach, 1974).

to implant monasticism on American soil, both men looked to Switzerland in the early years as a source for a continuing flow of recruits, including Benedictine sisters from the Swiss communities of Maria Rickenbach, Sarnen and Melchtal. The monastic vision of these two superiors was also tempered by conditions in North America. Odermatt's dream of a missionary congregation of monasteries along the West Coast was soon dispelled by the sheer struggle for physical survival of his own community of Mount Angel in its formative decade.[1] Conrad had to compromise his ideal of a largely contemplative and community-centered monasticism with the exigencies of an American Catholic Church that preferred a clerical model of sacramental service to the immigrant and a missionary outreach to Native Americans and Protestant North Americans alike.[2]

MISSION TO THE INDIGENT AND THE IMMIGRANT

An unexpectedly prominent aspect of the early American Benedictine missionary effort was the Native American Indian. The first monastery founded by Boniface Wimmer at St. John's in Collegeville had taken on the role of evangelizing the Chippewa Indian of the Northern Minnesota Vicariate, at the urging of that community's first abbot and later bishop, Rupert Seidenbusch.[3] Another abbot-bishop, Martin Marty of St. Meinrad, began an illustrious career of two decades of advocacy for the Plains Indians when he was named vicar apostolic of the Dakota Territory in 1879. Marty enlisted the assistance of a substantial contingent of monks from the monasteries of St. Meinrad and Conception, as well as Benedictine sisters, in initiating a network of schools and missions to provide for the spiritual and material needs of the Sioux Indians. He also had a determining influence in the decision of Katherine Drexel to found the Order of the Blessed Sacrament for the work of the Indian missions. Wrote Drexel of the visits made by Marty to her in Philadelphia when she was a young girl:

> The accounts of his missionary expeditions, his desire to establish schools for these people, his own sacrificing and untiring labors on their behalf, thrilled my soul with a desire to reach out to these people, and I believe that to Bishop Marty's visits I may partially ascribe the missionary vocation which God in his mercy has vouchsafed for me, and I also believe that had I not met Bishop Marty my whole future career might have been entirely different.[4]

Marty also proved to be of invaluable help to the Indian cause in the political arena. He was the only Catholic member of the Board of Regents on Indian Af-

---

[1]Lawrence McCrank, *Mount Angel Abbey* (Wilmington, DE, 1983).
[2]See Edward Malone, *Conception: A History of Conception Colony, Abbey and Schools* (Omaha, NE, 1971); and Joel Rippinger, "From the Old World to New: The Origins and Development of St. Meinrad and Conception Abbeys in the Nineteenth Century" (Rome, 1976).
[3]Barry, *op. cit.*, pp. 136-140.
[4]Letter of Drexel to Father Peter Behrman, July 22, 1922, copy in Archives of Sacred Heart Convent, Yankton, SD.

fairs, a president of the Catholic Bureau of Indian Missions and a periodic spokesman for the interests of the American Indian in personal appearances before the United States Congress.[1]

The project of educating and evangelizing the Native American was not limited to the Dakotas and Minnesota. In the Far West, Benedictine sisters established schools for the Indian tribes of the Northwest in Oregon and Washington, working in tandem with monks. In Oklahoma, in the 1870's and 1880's, French monks under Isidore Robot sponsored a school for the Pottawatomie Indian and a quarterly magazine, the *Indian Advocate*.[2]

The Benedictine involvement with the Native American was also a reflection of how many monastic communities soon moved outside the narrow compass of missionary commitment to the German-speaking immigrant. In the Protestant preserve of the American South, Benedictines made surprising inroads. The American Cassinese Congregation, composed of the Benedictine communities founded from Wimmer's original monastery, made determined strides to lay the groundwork for monastic houses throughout the southern states in the years after the Civil War. A practical reason for this was a commitment to help care for the needs of the newly freed Black citizen. But the motives for this initiative were mixed and in this regard the American Benedictines reflected the same ambivalence and paternalism toward the former slaves as their fellow Catholics. A letter of Boniface Wimmer (who made no secret of his anti-abolition and pro-Democratic political leanings) to Bishop Patrick Lynch of Charleston in the year after the Civil War's close epitomized this attitude:

> My opinion is that the Negro must, as matters are now, stand the competition with the white laborer willing or unwilling and learn to swim or perish in the stream alongside the whites, rather than in a separate colony. I have no antipathy against them; I was always against the war and abolition because I thought they are not capable of enjoying full liberty; but since they are free now, they must learn to act as free men."[3]

Nonetheless, Wimmer was willing to found Belmont Abbey in North Carolina in 1876 at the invitation of then Archbishop James Gibbons, and in 1877 to take over an industrial school for black children on Skidaway Island in Georgia. The abbot of St. Vincent also provided the stimulus for monastic foundations in Alabama and Florida before his death in 1877. In each of these Benedictine communities the combination of racial prejudice and a majority Protestant population made survival a greater priority than sensibility in serving the pastoral needs or evangelizing the local black population.

[1] See Robert Karolevitz, *Bishop Martin Marty* (Freeman, SD, 1980); and Joel Rippinger, "Martin Marty: Monk, Abbot, Missionary, Bishop - Missionary to the Indians," *American Benedictine Review* 33 (1982), pp. 376-393.
[2] The *Indian Advocate* was a journal devoted to the affairs of the Catholic missions in the Indian Territory and remains a faithful documentation of the work of the Benedictines in Oklahoma during the last two decades of the nineteenth century.
[3] Letter of Wimmer to Bishop Lynch, April 23, 1866, Charleston, South Carolina Diocesan Archives, copy in the Archives of St. Vincent Archabbey.

The other major American Benedictine Congregation of the nineteenth century, the Swiss-American, was also spreading into the South. In 1878 the community at St. Meinrad started a community in western Arkansas and in 1890 a new house was founded in Louisiana, from which the abbeys of New Subiaco and St. Joseph were to develop. Fast upon the appearance of monks from these two congregations came Benedictine sisters, with the men's communities of Arkansas, Louisiana, Florida and Alabama flanked by feminine counterparts.

The multiplication of monastic communities in the second half of the nineteenth century was at one with the heady pace of European immigration to the United States. Even though service to the German-speaking immigrant continued to hold priority of place in the ministry of most monastic houses, the new immigration from Southern and Eastern Europe opened still newer opportunities. By the turn of the century, Benedictine monks and sisters in Chicago were in charge of the Czech parish of St. Procopius and on their way to establishing an ethnic enclave of monastery, schools and publishing center for Czech immigrants. Much the same pattern took place when monks in Cleveland founded a community to care for the needs of Slovak Catholics. Later, as part of the flotsam of refugees from twentieth-century wars and revolutions, monks from Germany, Mexico, Hungary and China found sanctuary and established monastic houses in the United States.

EDUCATION

The monastic endeavor that was perhaps most influential in touching the lives of the immigrants and expediting their entry into American society was that of education. The earliest aspirations of Benedictines who came to the United States included a desire to establish a school alongside the monastic community. This school was to be not only a place of learning and a means of preserving the Catholic faith, but also a seminary that would imbibe the monastic spirit and in turn produce a core of priests and monks to serve the surrounding immigrant community.[1]

An obvious boon to the first generation of American Benedictines in establishing their educational apostolate was the affinity that had always existed between the German immigrant and the school. More than any other ethnic group in the United States, the German-Americans saw the school as the linchpin to their faith community. This fit conveniently into a more ancient tradition of monastic education that the Catholic Church had come to expect of the Order of St. Benedict over the centuries. A pioneer monk of an American Benedictine community expressed this common sentiment succinctly: "There can be no question of a monastery without a school."[2]

The eruption of educational institutions that accompanied the expansion of Benedictine communities in the United States is witness to the singular importance of the school. From storefront academies and seminaries run on a

[1]This was particularly evident in the original notion of St. Vincent and St. Meinrad. See Doppelfeld, pp. 305-306.
[2]Letter of Chrysostom Foffa to Abbot Henry Schmid of Einsiedeln, December 31, 1857, St. Meinrad Archabbey Archives.

shoestring, the American Benedictines by the twentieth century could boast of an impressive network of high schools, colleges, universities and theological seminaries that educated a growing number of American Catholics. All the while, Benedictine women staffed countless elementary and secondary schools as the first line of a formidable force of teachers in the Catholic parochial school system in the United States.

Like their religious peers, American Benedictines experienced the rigors of a frontier environment and schools that suffered from a want of comprehensive curriculum and professional faculty. But their teachers quickly matured in the proving ground of American Catholicism. Shedding some of their ethnic provincialism during the Americanist controversy at the end of the nineteenth century, Benedictine educational institutions in the first half of the twentieth century could point to first-rate faculties with graduate degrees from the best universities of Europe and the United States.

The venerable tradition of monastic scholarship attached itself to this educational evolution, even as it experienced the tension with competing claims of missionary activity and the underlying vein of anti-intellectualism in American Catholic life. The increasing size and holdings of monastic libraries in the United States gave telling testimony to the priority of research and scholarly interest. It also signaled the intention of monastic communities to serve as centers of theological research and scholarship, a marked advance from the sacramental supply image it had carried for its first few generations.

THE PROCESS OF ASSIMILATION

Given their central role in Catholic education and pastoral work with the immigrant, American Benedictines were bound to encounter the element of nativism, so much a part of the history of the American Catholic Church. In their founding period, the first Benedictines confronted the political arm of nativism, the Know-Nothing Party. The confrontation was graphically described by Boniface Wimmer:

> Our newest political sect, the Know-Nothings, would like to eat us, skin and hair, but it does not go so easily. The pressure on them is as it were on the Egyptians; they see us grow but they cannot stop us.[1]

Although the nativists did not stop the numerical surge of monastic houses, both Benedictine monks and sisters were prime targets for a literature that concentrated on criticism of continental customs of Catholic immigrants and alliance with Rome. Sisters were prevented from wearing their habits in schools in Pennsylvania, and monks in such non-Catholic sections of the country as North Carolina, Alabama and Arkansas found themselves clashing repeatedly with segments of the American Protection Association and the Ku Klux Klan as they carried on the work of education and care for Catholics and Blacks.

---

[1] Letter of Boniface Wimmer to Eugene Schwerzmann, August 8, 1854, Archives of Einsiedeln Abbey, translated copy in St. Meinrad Archabbey Archives.

German monks were also vulnerable targets for temperance advocates who railed against the "Order of Sacred Brewers." Critics contended in their broadsides that "the monk priests are largely to blame that the temperance laws of the Catholic Church in America are not observed in many sections of the country."[1]

Nonetheless, monastic communities in the United States weathered nativist attacks, the Americanist crisis, and the anti-German feeling of two World Wars, asserting themselves as assimilated Americans in much the same assertive way as their Catholic countrymen.

Benedictines in the United States also paralleled their Catholic contemporaries as builders. Many an isolated rural landscape was transformed by basilica church towers and a monastic sweep of structures that usually included a farm, mills, monastery, school and guest accommodations. The pragmatic brick and mortar buildings of early years eventually gave way to a dazzling variety of architectural and aesthetic designs, ranging from the monumentalism of Marcel Breuer's Bahaus in Collegeville, Minnesota, to an array of monasteries and libraries that carried the names of such famous architects as Aalto, Belluschi, Nakashima and Tigerman.[2]

20TH-CENTURY MONASTIC GROWTH AND INFLUENCE

The same forces that set in motion the budding pluralism of building styles also triggered a more variegated expression of monastic life in the United States in the twentieth century.

In addition to the original American Cassinese and Swiss-American Congregations of Benedictine monks, there were added three monasteries of the English Benedictine Congregation, houses of the St. Ottilien missionary congregation from Germany and Olivetan Benedictine Congregation from Italy, along with houses of the Carthusians and Camaldolese. In addition, Cistercians of the Strict Observance (Trappists) and of the Common Observance saw their monastic membership multiply rapidly midway through the century.

There was a parallel pluralism among monastic women, with the development of new communities and congregations. Some, such as the German missionary sisters of Tutzing, maintained an active role, along the lines of the American Congregations of St. Scholastica, St. Benedict and St. Gertrude. Other foundations from France and Germany chose to adopt a much more contemplative way of life, as reflected in the communities of Bethlehem, Connecticut (1947) and Boulder, Colorado (1935), as well as communities of Trappistine sisters. Still others, such as the Congregation of Perpetual Adoration, opted for a more cloistered and monastic mode of living, in contrast to their earlier activist tradition.

Just as the twentieth century witnessed a waning of the immigrant influx and the gradual breaking down of ethnic exclusiveness in American Catholicism, so the representative institutions of monasticism in the United States showed a capacity to absorb more of the elements of American culture and take a more

---

[1]George Zurcher, *Monks and Their Decline* (Buffalo, NY, 1898), p. 36.
[2]Howard Niebling, "Monastic Churches Erected by American Benedictines since World War II, Part I," *American Benedictine Review* 26 (1975), pp. 182-202.

mature and active role in tapping their monastic tradition of prayer and spirituality.

This was seen above all in the liturgical movement, whose roots extended to monastic centers in Europe and whose genesis in an American context bore a similar monastic imprint. Father Virgil Michel, a Benedictine monk of St. John's Abbey, became the central figure of the liturgical movement in the United States. Michel brought back from his graduate studies in Europe in 1924 and 1925 not only a solid grasp of the essentials of the liturgical movement there, but a conviction to transplant that movement to the Catholic Church in the United States and integrate it into what he saw as the vital social and educational mission of the Catholic community.[1] The peculiar genius of Michel's method of implanting the liturgical movement on American soil was that it focused on the education and participation of the laity and employed the best of both scholarly research and modern communications.

Moreover, Michel's prolific translations and articles in the decade of the 1930's popularized the liturgical reform for a laity that formerly had thought such topics to be the preserve of academicians and ecclesiastics. Another key to the popularity of Michel's synthetic accomplishment was his incorporation of social justice and the indigenous spiritual vision of nineteenth-century America into a previously European-based and derivative reform.[2]

All of these elements were joined in the appearance of the journal *Orate Fratres,* which first appeared in 1926 and soon became the authoritative voice of the liturgical movement in the English-speaking world. While at Collegeville, Michel also launched Liturgical Press and the Popular Liturgical Library, whose pamphlets found their way into the vestibules of many parish churches and attracted a worldwide audience. Perhaps the most impressive part of the link Michel made between American Catholic culture and the liturgical movement was his genius at drawing to his base of operations in Collegeville the diverse strands of Dorothy Day and Peter Maurin's Catholic Worker Movement, the progressive lay Catholicism of *Commonweal,* the social concerns of Catherine De Hueck's Friendship House, the liturgical leadership of Martin Hellriegel and Gerald Ellard, and the ecumenical educational vision of Mortimer Adler.

Michel's contribution to the liturgical movement had built upon the accomplishments of other American Benedictine monks as well. Father Bede Maler of St. Meinrad Archabbey and Father Augustine Walsh of St. Anselm's Priory in Washington, DC, had entertained similar ideas of reform before Michel appeared on the scene, but were unable to implement them with the singular success of the Collegeville monk.[3]

---

[1] R.W. Franklin, "Virgil Michel: An Introduction," *Worship* 62 (1988), pp. 195-196.

[2] Joseph Chinnici, in alluding to Michel's doctoral dissertation on the thought of Orestes Brownson and his ongoing interest in Isaac Hecker and nineteenth-century Americanizers, sees Michel as incorporating the transcendentalist strain of the Americanist movement to his later liturgical reform. See Chinnici's "Virgil Michel and the Tradition of Affective Prayer," *Worship* 62 (1988), pp. 225-236.

[3] Barry, *op. cit.,* p. 267.

After his untimely death in 1938, Michel's Benedictine confreres at St. John's Abbey carried on his legacy. Paschal Botz and Godfrey Diekmann widened the publishing activity of the Liturgical Press and the successor to *Orate Fratres, Worship* magazine, became the standard bearer of the liturgical movement in the United States as it passed from its frontier stages into and beyond the Second Vatican Council.

In the expanding wave of liturgical reform that followed Michel's initial efforts, the monasteries of St. Meinrad and Conception became designated centers for experimentation during the years immediately preceding the Council. The work of these communities and other monastic houses paved the way for the reforms in the vernacular and in liturgical aesthetics and architecture that followed in the wake of the Council. In 1968, St. John's Abbey responded to the request of the Bishops of the United States to become one of three research centers for pastoral liturgical development in the United States. Throughout this same post-conciliar period, communities of monastic men and women continued to offer the American Catholic Church individual examples of liturgical scholarship and collective models of community worship.

The twentieth century also witnessed a change in the forms of piety practiced by American Catholics. The role of monastic life in effecting this change was a significant one. The above-mentioned liturgical movement went a considerable distance in introducing a more communitarian dimension to the liturgy, infusing it with an American amalgam of social commitment and pragmatic adaptability. Benedictine communities also served as an ongoing source for inculcating seminarians and laity with the best elements of liturgical theology and monastic spirituality.

A NEW MONASTIC SPIRITUALITY

As the twentieth century progressed, there was also a decided change within American monasticism, one that both presaged and prompted corresponding changes in the spirituality of the American Catholic community. The largely missionary and active model of monastic life that had prevailed for the first several generations of American Benedictines began to give way to a more diversified pattern of monastic life.

The contemplative impulse that had caused such conflict in the nineteenth century and failed to take root, reemerged in new and more vibrant form in the middle of the twentieth century. New European monastic foundations of men and women in the United States after World War II made no apology about their intent to establish a cloistered community life, removed from the active pastoral involvement that had previously prevailed on the North American continent. The monastic communities of Mt. Savior Priory in New York (1950) and Weston Priory in Vermont (1952) represented the first of a new wave of smaller Benedictine communities whose accent was on prayer and detachment from the world rather than on pastoral work and education.[1] A stricter model of monastic

---

[1]Two European monks from Germany spearheaded these efforts: Damasus Winzen of Maria Laach and Leo Rudloff of Dormition Abbey.

life for women also emerged at this time with new European foundations that placed emphasis on cloistered seclusion rather than active apostolates.

The rapid spread of Trappist monasteries in the United States also had much to do with exposing more members of the American Catholic Church to the contemplative character of the monastic tradition. The spirituality of these Trappist houses, coming from the different roots of the European monasticism of Ireland and France, appeared as a far remove from the German Benedictine heretofore prevalent. However this spirituality and the austere form of monastic observance that accompanied it had little impact on the larger Catholic Church in the United States until the publication of an autobiography that is arguably the most influential single piece of literature that has come from monastic circles in the United States. *The Seven Storey Mountain* of Thomas Merton, published in 1948, was at once an evocation of a romanticized monastic ideal and the point of reference for an individual monk whose subsequent writings over the next two decades gave birth to a spirituality that was a synthesis of all that was best in the monastic tradition and still spoke in a voice that was authentically American.

Long before he became a religious folk figure of the 1960's who attracted to his home abbey of Gethsemani a collection of cultural pilgrims that stretched even the most ecumenical of minds in the Catholic Church, Merton had tapped the wellspring of what was most genuine and problematic in the American experience: contemplation in a world of action, racial discrimination and nuclear war, in a smugly suburban society that tried to sanitize both realities, the rich tradition of Eastern spirituality and non-Christian mysticism in a Catholic Church long accustomed to excluding both. Combining the seemingly contradictory roles of social critic and solitary, poet and priest, spiritual guru of Benedictine life and novice imbiber of Buddhist monasticism, Merton left a meteoric mark on monasticism of the twentieth century before his unexpected death in December of 1968. In his hermitage at Gethsemani that served as icon and progenitor of countless other monastic solitaries in the years after Vatican II, in the revitalization form of monastic life that already transformed Trappist houses in his lifetime, in the voluminous legacy of Merton's writings and the cottage industry of commentators that continue to churn out articles more than two decades after his death, one can begin to see the enormous impact and ongoing influence of the life and writings of Thomas Merton. Yet Merton's writing reflected a new era in American monasticism: spiritual renewal coincided with Vatican II.

Religious ecumenism was an alien attitude in the environment of the Catholic Church in the United States in the late nineteenth and early twentieth centuries. The prevailing Protestant ethos of American society and the defensive apologetical stance it sparked among American Catholics was part of the early experience of many monastic communities. But some of these same communities showed themselves to be agents of changing that hidebound stance, ushering in a new stage in American Catholic history.

In the 1920's the Benedictine community of St. Procopius in Lisle, Illinois, took a first step in facilitating church unity by accepting the apostolate of furthering dialogue and promoting reconciliation with Eastern Rite churches, a work that led to the founding of Holy Trinity Monastery in Butler, Pennsylvania in 1948.[1]

In 1946 the Anglican Benedictine Monastery of Nashdom, England, established a monastic foundation in Three Rivers, Michigan. The community of St. Gregory which grew from this foundation eventually became an independent abbey and took an active role in ecumenical exchange with Catholic monastic houses in the United States.[2]

The work of fostering wider ecumenical contacts, undertaken informally by the Abbey of St. John's in Collegeville and many other smaller monastic communities in the years leading up to Vatican Council II, was given a formal and institutional status with the erection of the Institute for Ecumencial and Cultural Research in Collegeville in 1967. The post-conciliar effort to encourage interdenominational scholarship and invite wider ecumenical exchange, that this Institute and other less formal projects of monastic houses in the United States facilitated, constituted a natural culmination of the earlier monastic climate that had witnessed the collaboration of Virgil Michel and Mortimer Adler, Thomas Merton and Daisetz Suzuki.

Within the boundaries of the American Catholic community, the variety of liturgical and spiritual forms spawned by a maturing American monasticism served as a rich stimulant to the broader currents of spiritual life in that community. The spectrum of spiritual activity covered by monastic houses ranged from preservation of Gregorian chant and the tradition of eremitical life to communities that identified with the Charismatic Renewal and forms of prayer that were part Benedictine tradition and part New Age experimentation.

Whereas the earlier expressions of monastic spirituality were transmitted in a centrifugal fashion, through the person of individual missionaries or teachers, the era encompassing either side of Vatican Council II was epitomized by the evolution of the monastery as centripetal force, attracting all manner of people to its spiritual center by means of its liturgy, retreat facilities and environment of solitude and space. Vast acreage that had once been prized for its ability to provide agricultural self-sufficiency for a Benedictine community, was now valued for the buffer it became from the breakneck pace of urban society and the slower rhythms and silence it offered the American Catholic layperson. This development indicated one more way in which American monasticism both affected the life of Catholics in the United States and adjusted itself to serve the changing needs of the Catholic faithful, a membership of persons who had now achieved educational levels comparable to members of mainline Protestant denominations and had become integrated into the wider social framework of American culture.

All of this coincided with the wholesale assessment made by monastic communities in the period of the late 1960's in response to the renewal of religious life mandated by the Council. The crucial time of renewal was one that tested and clarified the contributions of monasticism to the Catholic Church in the United States. The direct and collaborative way in which monastic congregations of men and women dealt with the demands of writing new consti-

---

[1]Vitus Buresch, *The Procopian Chronicle* (Lisle, IL, 1985), pp. 85-93.
[2]Brendan Harmon, "An Apostolate of Prayer: A History of St. Gregory's Abbey" (unpublished, Three Rivers, MI, 1983).

tutions and reflecting upon their role was indicative of the American attributes they had acquired. In this respect, the post-conciliar period was a coming of age in American monastic life that forced a reevaluation of the identity and purpose of the monastic charism in the Church whose situation in the world around it was of an entirely different nature than when Benedictines had first encountered it a century before.

What proved to be most distinctive about American Catholic monasticism in this post-conciliar era could serve as a hallmark for the larger role it played out in the history of the American Catholic Church: its acute sensitivity to the spiritual needs of a constantly changing community of Catholic Americans and its capacity to provide for those needs with a blend of timeless Benedictine tradition and the perspective of the lived experience of a culture they shared with American Catholics. How viable such a role will be for the future of the American Catholic community is open to question, but the perduring value of monastic life and the pressing spiritual needs of the now and future Church point to a continued place for the monastic order in the evolving life of American Catholics.

CHAPTER EIGHT

John Carroll
and the Shape of
American Catholic Liturgy

John A. Gurrieri
St. John's University, Collegeville

Forms of prayer and the practice of piety often reveal more about ecclesiology and church polity than do fundamental dogmas or structures of church government.

The European origins of the Church in the United States and its close emotional ties with Europe have never prevented American Catholics from espousing a kind of innate nationalism, and even a cultural-religious xenophobia toward their European co-religionists. Over the last two centuries of established church existence, American Catholics have sometimes looked with suspicion upon the forms of church governance and liturgical piety of the Catholic Churches of Europe. The foundational experience of American democracy and Republicanism and the sense of having overcome tyranny from abroad have sown the seeds of a sense of superiority Americans feel about their independence from Europe's fractious past and ancient rivalries, its authoritarianism, and the tensions of church and state which tragically scarred the history of every European nation. The first Catholics of the United States, being Americans, shared this fundamental American nationalism and cultural xenophobia with their fellow citizens. These elements in the American Catholic character have proved to be both a source of the American Catholic Church's strength and an irritant in its relations with European Catholicism, the Holy See not excluded.[1]

Over the past two hundred years American Catholics have viewed the world from a fresh perspective, a vision uncluttered by the debris of modern European Catholic history. That American difference is evident in the early forms of church polity and in the liturgical piety which prevailed in the period of the episcopacy of America's first Catholic bishop, John Carroll of Baltimore (1735-1815).[2] During Carroll's tenure as bishop of Baltimore, and later as archbishop, peculiarly American "experiments" in church governance (Carroll's episcopal

---

[1]See, for example, Gerald P. Fogarty, *The Vatican and the American Hierarchy from 1870-1965*, Vol. 21 in the series *Papste und Papsttum* (Stuttgart: Anton Hiersemann, 1982).

[2]For the life and times of John Carroll, see the following: Joseph Agonito, *The Building of an American Catholic Church: The Episcopacy of John Carroll* (New York/London: Garland Publishing, Inc., 1988); Annabelle Melville, *John Carroll of Baltimore: Founder of the American Catholic Hierarchy* (New York: Charles Scribner's Sons, 1955); Peter Guilday, *The Life and Times of John Carroll, Archbishop of Baltimore, 1735-1815* (New York, 1922); John Gilmary Shea, *Life and Times of the Most Reverend John Carroll, Bishop and First Archbishop of Baltimore, Embracing the History of the Catholic Church in the United States, 1763-1815* (New York, 1888).

election by the clergy, lay trusteeism, national parishes) and innovations in worship (the liturgical use of English, liturgical adaptation, domestic liturgy, etc.) not only caused both wonderment and dismay in European Catholic circles but also a consternation which would eventually change these new American Catholic ways of expressing ancient structures and liturgical expressions.

From the time of the Maryland colony's foundation in 1634 through the early years of the Republic, American Catholics sought to be Catholic in an American cultural and political context. Those first Catholic colonists were conscious that they would be "free from persecution on account of their religion."[1] Nevertheless, those Anglo-American Catholics knew just how close to the edge of persecution and harassment they were. Thus the obligation of being both Catholic and American was born in an atmosphere of tolerance which at any moment could disintegrate into bigotry. An impact on piety and liturgy was unavoidable.

The ancient adage *lex orandi, lex credendi (legem credendi lex statuat supplicandi)* is as clearly demonstrated in the history of the Catholic Church in the United States as it is in the patristic or medieval periods of European church history. The history of liturgy in Catholic America, however, must be understood against this background of *difference* between an old Europe and a new America.

From the very beginnings of the Catholic Church on American soil, forms of worship and piety have been the source of nourishment for followers of an "alien religion" and the cause of debate, even conflict, between Catholic and Protestant, and between Catholic and Catholic. Friction among Catholics was later to have a greater impact on American Catholic forms of worship. Conflict was especially sharp when successive waves of immigrants came to America and brought with them the piety and liturgical practices of cultures often as alien to fellow Catholics as to the Protestant majority. Liturgical difference is problematic enough, but when difference implies change, it prompts reaction. Such was the case during the life and times of John Carroll, for American Catholicism was in large measure shaped by the thinking and pastoral attitude of the United States' first Roman Catholic bishop.[2]

The purpose of this essay is to examine John Carroll's influence upon the shape and structure of Catholic worship and liturgical piety. As a son of the American Catholic Enlightenment, Carroll believed in a "reasonable" Catholicism formed in a liturgical piety based on an "irenic vision of Christian life." Carroll's Catholicism was, therefore, bathed in "an atmosphere of tolerance, mutual respect, and rational argument—in short, a 'system of piety and humility' that would be socially constructive."[3] To Carroll's way of thinking, "the starting point of the life of grace was always reasonable consent and personal in-

[1]Jay P. Dolan, *The American Catholic Experience: A History from Colonial Times to the Present* (Garden City, NY: Doubleday & Co., Inc., 1985), p. 73.
[2]For an overview of John Carroll's theology and ecclesiology, see Joseph P. Chinnici, *Living Stones: The History and Structure of Catholic Spiritual Life in the United States* (New York: Macmillan Publishing Co., 1988), especially Part I, "An Enlightenment Synthesis, 1776-1815" (pp. 1-34).
[3]Chinnici, *op. cit.*, p. 7.

tegrity."[1] Carroll's rational and pious approach to Catholic liturgy and worship is evident from several events in his episcopate, namely, the Diocesan Synod of 1791, his Pastoral Letter of 1792, his views on the use of English in the liturgy, and his practical approach to cultural adaptation and "domestic liturgy."

THE SYNOD OF 1791 AND
THE STATE OF AMERICAN CATHOLIC LITURGY

The Diocesan Synod of 1791 marks a watershed in the history of American liturgy.[2] The liturgical legislation of that first meeting of the clergy of the newly established Diocese of Baltimore summed up the piety and patterns of worship of the first Catholics of the new Republic of the United States of America.[3] The Synod also bears the imprint of Baltimore's first bishop, his piety and ecclesiological outlook.

The descendants of the *Catholick Colonie of Maryland* were heirs to a liturgical piety brought to American shores in the early seventeenth century. However, before going on to describe that piety and how it too shaped the legislation of the 1791 Synod, it will be important first to sort out what the Synod taught.

Perhaps the most important of its statutes, Statute 17 of the Synod, *De ordinandis divinis officiis, et festorum observatione,* gave shape to the manner in which American Catholics were to observe Sundays and feast days. The Synod held that, where possible, the *missa cantata,* begun with the *Asperges,* is to be celebrated. The priest is to proclaim the Gospel in English (or French or German) after reading it in Latin. The sermon at Mass is obligatory. The congregation sings the Litany of the Blessed Virgin. In the afternoon parishes are to celebrate Vespers and Benediction. The Synod encourages the singing of hymns in English during these liturgical celebrations. Statute 18 covers situations in which only one priest is available. In this case,

> after Mass the priest led the congregation in the recitation of the Lord's Prayer, the Hail Mary, the Apostles' Creed, and the Acts of Faith, Hope, and Charity. In *all* parishes the Prayer for the Civil Authorities, composed by Carroll himself, was to be recited immediately after the Gospel and before the sermon.[4]

---

[1]*Ibid.,* p. 13.
[2]For the acts of the Synod see *Statuta Synodi Baltimorensis anno 1791 celebratae* in *Concilia Provincialia Baltimori habita ab anno 1829 usque ad annum 1849, Editio altera* (Baltimore, 1851), pp. 17-20.
[3]By "America's first Catholics" I mean those Anglo-American Catholics who descended from the first Catholics of the Maryland Colony, those Catholics living in the United States at the time of its independence from Britain and during the first two decades of the Republican period. A broader understanding of "American Catholicism," however, will include the French of the Northwest Territories and later the Spanish-speaking Catholics of the Louisiana Territory.
[4]John A. Gurrieri, "Catholic Sunday in America: Its Shape and Early History" in *Sunday Morning: A Time for Worship,* Mark Searle, ed. (Collegeville, MN: The Liturgical Press, 1982), p. 86. See *Statuta Synodi Baltimorensis anno 1791 celebratae* in *Concilia Provincialia Baltimori habita ab anno 1829 usque ad annum*

The liturgical pattern mandated for Sundays and feast days by the Synod of 1791 summed up the colonial practice of English Catholic America. Indeed, this pattern was inspired by the liturgical tradition of English Catholicism to which Anglo-American Catholics were heir. The Synod's liturgical statutes can best be understood against the background of the devotional life of Anglo-American Catholics in the pre-revolutionary period.

ENGLISH CATHOLIC LITURGICAL PIETY

English Catholics who came to Maryland in the early seventeenth century brought with them a *liturgical* piety that was simultaneously Christocentric and devotional, and that would last until the middle of the nineteenth century. John Carroll's own piety reflected the legacy of a Catholicism shaped by, among other things, the liturgical spiritual tradition of seventeenth- and eighteenth-century England, especially exemplified in the works of John Gother (†1704) and Bishop Richard Challoner (1691-1781).[1]

The devotional writings of both Gother and Challoner were popular among colonial Anglo-American Catholics. *The Garden of the Soul: A Manual of Fervent Prayers, Pious Reflections and Solid Instructions,* first composed, edited and printed by Bishop Challoner in London around 1740, was initially meant to be a supplement to the two standard prayerbooks already in use among English Catholics, the *Primer* and the *Manual.* "That *The Garden of the Soul* was designed to supplement, rather than supersede these, is clear from the fact that long after he had published his own work, Dr. Challoner issued a new edition of the *Manual* carefully revised by himself."[2]

THE GARDEN OF THE SOUL
AND ANGLO-AMERICAN PIETY

To appreciate the importance of *The Garden of the Soul* one must also understand the role of the *Primer* and the *Manual* that Challoner sought to supplement, for it is highly probable that both works were among the treasured possessions of those first English Catholics who landed on Maryland's shores in 1634. Furthermore, both the *Primer* and the *Manual* provide an outline of the piety enshrined in the statutes of the 1791 Synod.[3]

The *Manual of Godly Prayers and Litanies,* as it was first known, was published sometime during the reign of Elizabeth I (the first extant edition dates

1849, Editio altera (Baltimore, 1851), pp. 17-20. For an adapted version of Carroll's Prayer for the Civil Authorities and a restoration of its use to Catholic piety, see *Catholic Household Blessings and Prayers,* an official prayerbook prepared and issued by the Bishops' Committee on the Liturgy of the National Conference of Catholic Bishops (Washington, DC: United States Catholic Conference, 1988), p. 196.

[1] See Chinnici, *op. cit.,* pp. 9-11. For Challoner's life and writings see E.H. Burton, *The Life and Times of Bishop Challoner, 1691-1781* (London, 1909).

[2] Burton, *op. cit.,* pp. 127-128.

[3] In 1774, Robert Bell published *A Manual of Catholic Prayers* in Philadelphia. Bell's work is the first American edition of the popular English *Manual.*

from 1595). The *Manual* contained forms of Morning Prayer and Night Prayer and a set of prayers for every day of the week, consisting of psalms, prayers, litanies and hymns. Popular devotions such as the penitential psalms, the Litany of the Holy Ghost, prayers for the Eucharist, Confession and other sacraments were also included. Finally, hymns and prayers for principal feasts of the liturgical year, the Jesus Psalter and the Golden Litany came at the end of the book.[1] The *Primer*, first published in England in 1599, "was the direct descendant of the old pre-Reformation Primers or Books of Hours of Our Lady."[2] While *The Garden of the Soul* differed in many ways from the *Primer* and the *Manual* in the emphasis placed upon liturgical piety, it was a spirituality that stressed devout participation in the sacraments and the liturgical year rather than an individualistic pietism.

All three books, especially Challoner's, became the backbone of Anglo-American Catholic spiritual life, the sources for new prayerbooks written and published in America. "It may be added that the influence of *The Garden of the Soul* on other prayerbooks has been very marked, and it may be considered the direct ancestor of such well-known and popular books as the *Golden Manual*, the *Church Manual* and the *Vade Mecum*."[3] An edition of the *Vade Mecum* was published in Philadelphia by Matthew Carey in 1789 and again in 1792.[4]

The Garden of the Soul "was widely diffused in the American Catholic settlements and became the model for later devotional works published in the newly independent United States."[5] The first American imprint was published by Joseph Cruikshank, a Quaker, in Philadelphia in 1770 or 1774.[6] *The Garden of the Soul* "became the most important devotional work in revolutionary America,"[7] containing popular devotions typical of eighteenth-century English Catholicism. The book also served as a guide for proper participation in the liturgy. Among the "Instructions" for the "devout hearing" and "assisting at" Mass were prayers which might be said silently by the congregation, English translations of the Ordinary of the Mass as well as many Mass propers in English so that the liturgy might be intelligible to the lay Catholic. *The Garden of the Soul* also contained instructions on the manner of observing Sunday at home and the liturgical texts for Sunday Vespers and Benediction.

In certain respects, *The Garden of the Soul* was not unlike Anglican devotional prayerbooks of the time. Anglican and Catholic spirituality shared a common medieval liturgical tradition by and large unaffected by the Reformation or Counter-Reformation.[8] In fact, even though separated from the mass of En-

---

[1] See Burton, *op. cit.*, Vol. I, pp. 129-130.

[2] Burton, *op. cit.*, p. 128.

[3] *Ibid.*, p. 136.

[4] See John Wright, *Early Prayer Books of America, Being a Descriptive Account of Prayer Books Published in the United States, Mexico and Canada* (St. Paul, MN, privately printed, 1896), p. 21. Later editions were published in Baltimore (1801, 1812) and New York (1840).

[5] Gurrieri, *op. cit.*, p. 83.

[6] Wright, *op. cit.*, p. 19.

[7] Chinnici, *op. cit.*, p. 10, n. 13.

[8] For example, see R. Russell, *The Devout Christian's Daily Companion and Exercise in Devotion, Containing a Posie of Prayers for Every Day in the Week, and*

glish Christians, English Catholics, most of whom were upper class, also shared with Anglicans certain forms of prayer for the welfare of England and the sovereign.[1] Nevertheless, Challoner's purpose in *The Garden of the Soul* was to "provide Catholics with a distinctive spiritual identity during a time of declining persecution [in England] and growing indifference."[2]

While Challoner's piety was principally indebted to St. Francis de Sales, his devotional writings owed much to Gother, especially the latter's *Instructions and Devotions for Hearing Mass* published posthumously in 1725. Gother's works, in turn, were similar in purpose to the *Manual of Devout Prayers* published in 1688 by Henry Hillis in England. The *Manual of Devout Prayers* "instructed Catholics

> to assist at Mass devoutly, following along with the priest in Latin, while reading devotional prayers composed to 'unveil' the meaning of the various parts of the Eucharistic liturgy, or reading the very texts of the Mass in English translation as the priest recited [or sang] them in Latin.[3]

Gother's works were irenic and non-combative in tone, relying on the personal and interior relationship of the individual with Christ.

THE SYNOD ON SUNDAY AND THE LITURGICAL YEAR

The Synod's directives pertained not only to Sundays but to feast days and holy days as well.[4] The English Catholic background is also evident in this legislation as it is for Sundays.

Alban Butler's *The Moveable Feasts, Fasts and Other Annual Observances of the Catholic Church*, published posthumously in London in 1774, was popular in America in the late eighteenth century and was reprinted several times in the United States through the first half of the nineteenth century. "Butler's historical-liturgical explanations of Sundays and feasts of the liturgical year profoundly shaped the liturgical understanding of many American Catholics in the period just after the War of Independence."[5] American devotional books, such as Robert Molyneux's *A Manual of Catholic Prayers* (Philadelphia)[6] and *The Pious Guide to Prayer and Devotion* (Georgetown, 1792), owed their appreciation of the liturgical year to Butler.

---

several Occasions: for Families and Private Persons Alone (London, 1717). This Anglican prayerbook offered spiritual guidance and appreciation for the worship of the Church.

[1] See Gurrieri, *op. cit.*, p. 82.

[2] John Coulson, "English Roman Catholics in the Eighteenth and Nineteenth Centuries" in *The Study of Spirituality*, Cheslyn Jones, Geoffrey Wainwright, Edward Yarnold, eds. (New York & Oxford: Oxford University Press, 1986), p. 425.

[3] Gurrieri, *op. cit.*, p. 82.

[4] For an historical overview of holy days in America, see John A. Gurrieri, "Holy Days in America," *Worship* 54 (September 1980), pp. 417-446; and Bishops' Committee on the Liturgy, *Holy Days in the United States: History, Theology, Celebration* (Washington, DC: United States Catholic Conference, 1984).

[5] Gurrieri, "Catholic Sunday in America," p. 84.

[6] Published in the eighteenth century; exact date of publication unknown.

THE STATE OF CATHOLIC PIETY

The 1791 Synod, which summed up the prevailing liturgical practice of Anglo-American Catholicism, was an attempt on the part of Bishop John Carroll to bolster the faith and piety of American Catholics in a pluralist Christian situation, such as in the Diocese of Baltimore where there was a shortage of priests. As early as 1785, Carroll expressed his profound concern in this regard in his first report to the Propaganda Fide:

> In Maryland a few of the leading more wealthy families still profess the Catholic faith introduced at the very foundation of the province by their ancestors. The greater part of them are planters and in Pennsylvania almost all are farmers, except the merchants and mechanics living in Philadelphia. As for piety, they are for the most part sufficiently assiduous in the exercises of religion and in frequenting the sacraments, but they lack that fervor, which frequent appeals to the sentiment of piety usually produce, as many congregations hear the word of God only once a month, and sometimes only once in two months. We are reduced to this by want of priests, by the distance of congregations from each other and by difficulty of travelling. This refers to Catholics born here, for the condition of the Catholics who in great numbers are flowing in here from different countries of Europe, is very different. For while there are few of our native Catholics who do not approach the sacraments of penance and the Holy Eucharist, at least once a year, especially in Easter time, you can scarcely find any among the newcomers who discharge this duty of religion, and there is reason to fear that the example will be very pernicious especially in commercial towns.[1]

When Carroll submitted his report to the Holy See the statistics were rather grim. For 15,800 Catholics in Maryland there were nineteen priests; for the 7,000 Catholics of Pennsylvania, there were but five. In Virginia, where the Catholic population in 1785 did not exceed 200, there were no clergy; likewise in New York there were no priests to minister to the 1500 Catholics in that state. As Carroll notes in his report, a number of the 24 priests available to him were too aged or infirm to submit to the rigors of a circuit ministry.

As in the seventeenth century, lay Catholics were spiritually very much on their own except for those few times when a priest came to lead them in liturgical and sacramental celebrations. Theirs was a domestic Catholicism nourished by the Scriptures and English prayerbooks. That they continued to be "sufficiently assiduous in the exercises of religion and the frequenting of the sacraments" was largely due, as Carroll stated, to their deep faith and their use of devotional and liturgical prayerbooks in the home and in common. There is certainly evidence for the widespread use of such books.[2] However, it should be kept in mind that the scarcity of priests and therefore of liturgical services meant

---

[1]John Carroll, "Report for the Eminent Cardinal Antonelli Concerning the State of Religion in the United States of America" in *Documents of American Catholic History,* Vol. I, John Tracy Ellis, ed. (Chicago: Henry Regnery Company, 1967), pp. 148-149.
[2]For a survey of those books, see Gurrieri, "Catholic Sunday in America."

a greater reliance on the prayerbooks and manuals available to American Catholics. "With few priests and a scarcity of pulpits, people could readily turn to their manuals of prayer and have at their fingertips a devotional guide that encouraged a type of prayer not grounded in the meditative function of priests or ritual."[1]

As for the "newcomers" from other European countries, there was little Carroll could do for them without their own clergy or other resources. His words suggest, however, that Carroll was also wary of a Catholic piety different from the Anglo-American spirituality of "native" Catholics.

Carroll embodied the principles of the "American Catholic Enlightenment." For Carroll "a good Catholic was a reasonable Catholic and one who was Catholic by rational conviction, not merely cultural association."[2] Carroll believed that American Catholics differed from their European co-religionists because of the American experience of democracy and pluralism and their firm commitment to Republicanism. He believed in much of the Enlightenment's anthropology, its political philosophy as expressed in the American experience, and the appeal to rationality.[3] Thus he also believed in the reasonableness of Catholic claims and did not hesitate to present these to the Protestant majority.

ENGLISH IN THE LITURGY

John Carroll also felt a natural reservation for European continental Catholicism, which was still embedded in a monarchical polity and expressed in a piety that did not tolerate variety. Carroll's desire for a vernacular liturgy and a native clergy, for example, was wedded to his ecclesiological reflections upon the state and role of the Catholic Church in republican America. He firmly believed in the need for independence from European forms of Catholicism that history had marked with sectarianism and an implacable hostility toward Protestants. His desire for a vernacular English liturgy for American Catholics was also quite pastoral. In a letter to his friend the Reverend Joseph Berington written in 1787, Carroll stated that

> The greater portion of our congregations must be utterly ignorant of the meaning and sense of the public offices of the Church...[T]o continue the practice of the Latin liturgy in the present state of things must be owing to chimerical fears of innovation or to indolence and inattention in the first pastors of the national Churches in not joining to solicit or indeed ordain this necessary alteration.[4]

Carroll's support for a vernacular liturgy made the use of English in worship all the more possible. In fact, English was quite commonly used in the Mass and other liturgical rites in Carroll's time.[5] The gospel was read in English at

---

[1] Dolan, *op. cit.*, p. 92.
[2] Peter W. Carey, *American Catholic Religious Thought: The Shaping of a Theological and Social Tradition* (New York/Mahwah: Paulist Press, 1987), p. 13.
[3] See Carey, *op. cit.*, p. 7.
[4] Carroll to Berington, cited in Ellis, *op. cit.*, Vol. I, p. 129.
[5] See Dolan, *op. cit.*, pp. 109-110.

Mass and many priests used English in the celebration of baptism and marriage. In 1810, when the Bishops of the United States actually passed resolutions limiting the use of the vernacular, English became an illicit liturgical language in America.

Another of his motives for actively pursuing the licit use of English in worship was Carroll's desire "to make the liturgy intelligible to Protestants," for he considered the use of Latin in the liturgy "one of the greatest obstacles, with Christians of other denominations, to a thorough union with us; or, at least, to a much more general Diffusion of our Religion, particularly in N. America."[1] In fact, Carroll believed "that some change in the discipline, which had been enforced at the time of the Reformation, should be '*insisted on*, as essential to the Service of God & Benefit of Mankind'."[2]

Neither the desire for nor the use of English in the liturgy died with the 1810 episcopal prohibition. As Joseph Chinnici notes, a priest working at St. Patrick's in Washington in 1821

> testified to the perdurance of these practices [use of the vernacular in the celebration of the sacraments]. He noted to his archbishop that 'Rev. Mr. Matthews, (the pastor) used for interments, and likewise frequently for baptisms, the English translations of the Roman Ritual instead of the Latin Original, on account of the late Right Revd. Archbishop Carroll's having formerly so stated.'[3]

English in the liturgy endured until the middle of the nineteenth century. In 1829 Francis Patrick Kenrick, who became Baltimore's sixth Archbishop, noted that English was used in the questions to parents and godparents in the Rite of Baptism. He also noted "the recitation of the marriage vows from the English ritual, the Roman rite being added afterward."[4] Bishop Joseph Rosati of St. Louis (1827-1843), who was later to publish a *Ceremonial* for parish use, questioned such practices which existed despite prohibitions such as the 1810 Bishops' decision to the contrary:

> Can the priests use the English language for the administrations of Baptism, Matrimony, Extreme Unction and in the prayers established for burial? Such use exists in some dioceses, a use which certain bishops foster by their own example.[5]

While the Synod of 1791 encouraged the use of English in the celebration of the Mass and the sacraments for reasons already noted, the presence of growing numbers of immigrants from non-English-speaking Europe and the desire to conform to the wishes of the Holy See compelled the American Bishops in 1810 to prohibit the use of the vernacular in the "essential" elements of the Mass and sacraments.

---

[1]See Chinnici, *op. cit.*, p. 16.
[2]*Ibid.*
[3]See Carey, *op. cit.*, p. 7.
[4]See Chinnici, *op. cit.*, p. 17.
[5]Cited in *ibid.*

> To achieve uniformity of practice, the bishops ordered the clergy to celebrate 'the whole Mass in the Latin language' and to use Latin in the essential prayers of the sacraments; English could be used only for the nonessential prayers connected with the administration of the sacraments.[1]

Nevertheless, priests continued to use English in the celebration of the Mass "when the priest addressed the congregation," for example, the *miseratur* and the *indulgentiam*.[2]

English in the liturgy seemed essential to Carroll in the early years of his episcopate for a variety of reasons: its pastoral utility and to make the liturgy comprehensible and reasonable to Protestants (and to Catholics as well). But Carroll also believed that a vernacular liturgy would enable the Church to be simultaneously independent and in union with Rome. In the now famous letter to Joseph Berington written on July 10, 1784, Carroll emphasized this latter point when he said:

> Can there be any thing more preposterous, than for a small district containing in extent no more than mount Libarius [Mount Lebanon] & a trifling territory at the foot of it, to say nothing of the Greeks, Armenians, Coptits [sic] &c have a liturgy in their proper idiom; & on the other hand for an immenser extent of countries, containing G.B., Ireland, all N. Am., the W. Indies &c, to be obliged to perform divine Service in an unknown tongue?[3]

In proposing the use of English in the liturgy Carroll took a position contrary to the Council of Trent's prohibitions against the vernacular.[4] Carroll was not alone in holding for the necessity of using the vernacular in the liturgy; his position was shared by the Synod of Pistoia (1786).[5] In 1794 Pius VI condemned, among other things, the Synod's proposition concerning the use of Italian in the liturgy as *"falsa, temeraria, ordinis pro mysteriorum celebratione praescripti perturbativa, plurium malorum facile productrix."*[6] Was Carroll aware of the teaching of the Synod of Pistoia and the Holy See's subsequent condemnation of its propositions?

Like his Italian counterparts Carroll believed that the Council of Trent's teaching on the use of the vernacular was valid and proper for the sixteenth cen-

---

[1]Dolan, *op. cit.*, pp. 113-114.

[2]Chinnici, *op. cit.*, p. 17.

[3]John Carroll to Joseph Berington, July 10, 1784 in *The John Carroll Papers*, Vol. I: 1755-1791, Thomas O'Brien Hanley, ed. (University of Notre Dame Press, 1976), p. 149.

[4]Council of Trent, Session XII, September 17, 1562, *De ss. Missae sacrificio*, Cap. 8. *De Missa vulgari lingua passim non celebranda, et mysteriis eius populo explicandis* and canon 9: *Si quis dixerit, Ecclesia Romanae ritum, quo submissa voce pars canonis et verba consecrationis proferuntur, damnandum est; aut lingua tantum vulgari Missam celebrari debere.... an. s.* (DS 1749,1759).

[5]For a discussion of the liturgical reforms of the Synod of Pistoia, see Enrico Cattaneo, *Problemi liturgici nel Settecento italiano* (Milan: Universita Cattolica del Sacro Cuore, 1977), pp. 99-111.

[6]ES 2666.

tury. However, he did not feel compelled to hold to that conciliar decision in the late eighteenth century. "Its retention was no longer of advantage to the religious life of Catholics in America. He said as much in 1787 to Joseph Berington,"[1] as noted earlier. Carroll's letter to Berington was widely circulated among English Catholics and became the cause for controversy in England and Ireland. Archbishop John Thomas Troy of Dublin condemned Carroll's position and informed the American that he had written a sixty-page pastoral letter against Carroll's proposal. The controversialist Arthur O'Leary, O.F.M, chaplain to the Spanish Embassy in London, also strongly disagreed with Carroll's views on the vernacular set out in the letter to Berington.[2]

Carroll was dismayed but not put off by the controversy he unwittingly instigated in the British Isles. Repeating the views he expressed in his letter to Berington, Carroll replied to O'Leary's criticism:

> In a letter to him [Berington] and before I had a thought of ever being in my present station, I expressed a wish that the pastors of the Church would see cause to grant to this extensive continent jointly with England and Ireland, etc. the same privilege as is enjoyed by many churches of infinitely less extent; that of having their liturgy in their own language; for I do indeed conceive that one of the most popular prejudices against us is that our public prayers are unintelligible to our hearers. Many of the poor people, and the negroes generally, not being able to read, have no technical help to confine their attention.[3]

In taking a stand for the liturgical use of English, Carroll expressed not only what Berington called a great "liberality of mind,"[4] but first and foremost a highly-tuned pastoral sense that English was necessary for the advancement of the Catholic Church in an America (and Britain and Ireland as well) viewed with suspicion by Protestants for foreign allegiance not only in government (the papacy) but also in prayer (Latin). Carroll's concern for poor illiterate Catholics, white and black, slave and free, and his desire to bring the Catholic faith to the poor, slave and free, was paramount in his position on the vernacular. Carroll *believed in English* as a liturgical vessel worthy of the Christian faith.

But Carroll was also a realist. As he told O'Leary in 1788, "I should find no cooperation from my clerical brethren in America, were I rash enough to attempt their introduction [liturgical reforms] upon my own authority."[5] In fact, Carroll's "advanced position on the vernacular" would be modified in the Synod of 1791. John Tracy Ellis has stated the following in this regard:

---

[1] Agonito, *op. cit.,* pp. 126-127.
[2] See John Tracy Ellis, "Archbishop Carroll and the Liturgy in the Vernacular" in *Worship* XXVI (November 1952), p. 548.
[3] John Carroll to Arthur O'Leary, Baltimore, undated, cited by Ellis from Guilday, *op. cit.,* Vol. I, p. 131.
[4] Berington to Carroll, Oscot near Birmingham, March 27, 1788, cited by Ellis from Guilday, *op. cit.,* Vol I, p. 132.
[5] Ellis, *op. cit.,* p. 549.

Whether or not he made any attempt during the synod to implement his ideas of earlier years, we have no way of knowing. In all likelihood the realization of his lack of power to decide such matters without reference to the Holy See, plus the fine balance and common sense which never seemed to fail Carroll during his long and eventful life, prompted him to pass over the question to a more propitious time.[1]

If Carroll's position was modified by 1791, it would greatly change between 1791 and 1810.

During the twenty-year period between the 1791 Synod and the 1810 meeting of the archbishop with his new suffragan bishops of the United States, such growing pastoral problems as ethnic nationalism, schism and other dangers to ecclesial unity cast a shadow on the entire pastoral enterprise of the American Church. Carroll needed help in maintaining authority and unity. In 1808 four new dioceses were erected—Boston, New York, Philadelphia and Bardstown. The bishops of the new sees, John Cheverus (Boston), Michael Egan, O.F.M. (Philadelphia), Benedict Flaget, S.S. (Bardstown), together with a coadjutor for Baltimore (Leonard Neale) met with Archbishop Carroll in Boston in November 1810. Because of differences of opinion among the five bishops and the widely divergent practices existing at that time, and perhaps because Carroll was no longer convinced of the validity or at least the possibility of his position, the Bishops enacted the following regulations to limit further the use of the vernacular in the liturgy:

It is being made known to the Archbishop and Bishops that there exists a difference of opinion and practice among some of the clergy of the United States concerning the use of the vernacular language in any part of the public service, and in the administration of the Sacraments. It is hereby enjoined on all Priests not only to celebrate the whole Mass in the Latin language, but likewise when they administer Baptism, the Holy Eucharist, Penance and Extreme Unction, to express the necessary and essential form of those Sacraments in the same tongue according to the Roman ritual; but it does not appear contrary to those Sacred forms, provided however, that no translation of those prayers shall be made use of except one authorized by the concurrent approbation of the Bishops of this ecclesiastical Province, which translation will be printed as soon as it can be prepared under their inspection. In the meantime the translation of the late venerable Bishop Challoner may be made use of.[2]

The Bishops did not realize that even the limited use of the vernacular which they permitted was likewise prohibited by Pius VI. The 1810 regulations reflected Carroll's continuing belief in the pastoral utility of the vernacular. How-

[1]*Ibid.*, p. 550.
[2]Guilday, *op. cit.*, Vol. II, p. 592, cited by Ellis, *op. cit.*, p. 552. Richard Luke Concannen was appointed Bishop of New York and consecrated in Europe without Carroll's knowledge. Concannen never arrived in America. See James Hennesey, S.J., "An Enlightenment Bishop: John Carroll of Baltimore" in *Patterns of Episcopal Leadership*, Gerald P. Fogarty, S.J., ed. (New York: Macmillan Publishing Co., 1988), p. 24.

ever, the new regulations also demonstrated the shift that was beginning to take place from the plain liturgical spirituality of the colonial and early republican periods, based on the Enlightenment view of the person, to the more devotional piety reflective of the new Catholic immigrants' more baroque tradition of over-whelming influence of the Fall and original sin. *"Garden of the Soul* Catholicism," with its simple, direct approach to God and love of the liturgy, was beginning to give way to a moralistic, more penitential (and more pessimistic) view of the Christian life.

This conservative shift, already evident in 1810, would blossom fully before 1850 and was to mark American Catholicism up to the Second Vatican Council.[1]

CARROLL — A LITURGIST?

It should be stated immediately that John Carroll was not a liturgiologist, that is, a scholar or expert in liturgical study, according to any twentieth-century definition. However, among the many values for which the American Catholic Church's first Bishop stood, the liturgy was paramount. John Carroll was imbued with the spirit of worship. For him the liturgical texts of the Church were a source of unending consolation and prayer. He drew inspiration not only from the Roman liturgy in which he was raised but also from the treasures of the *Book of Common Prayer.*[2] That personal love for the liturgy inspired him to expend himself in doing all he could as Bishop to ensure excellent forms of worship in the fledgling American Church.

Formed in the English Catholicism of the eighteenth century, Carroll hoped to leave a sound legacy for the Catholics of a new and tolerant nation, established according to reason and the principles of the Enlightenment. A gentleman of the American Catholic Enlightenment whose only and last successor would be Bishop John England (1786-1842),[3] Carroll embodied a tradition of prayer and worship that would not rise to the surface of American Catholicism until this century. As Joseph Chinnici states, "Carroll tried to inculcate in the community a genuinely liturgical spirituality."[4] The liturgy was also the source for a correct understanding and practice of devotion and piety for Carroll. For John Carroll, only the liturgy could counteract the Jansenist strains of contemporary European

---

[1]The seeds for another shift, from institution and perfect society to mystery and communion, were already sown by the liturgical movement in the late 1920's and 1930's. See Jeremy Hall, O.S.B., "The American Liturgical Movement: The Early Years," *Worship* 50 (November 1976), pp. 472-489.

[2]John Carroll's well-thumbed copy of the *Book of Common Prayer* may be found in the Rare Books Collection at The Catholic University of America in Washington, DC. From annotations in the margins, it seems clear that Carroll supplemented the Roman Divine Office by reading frequently (perhaps daily) from the Anglican Prayer Book. His respect for the language of the Prayer Book and its widespread liturgical and household use among Anglicans might help explain his convictions about the necessity of an English liturgy for Roman Catholics in the United States.

[3]See Carey, *op. cit.,* pp. 12-15, 73ff.

[4]Chinnici, *op. cit.,* p. 27.

Catholicism. In this regard, perhaps, Carroll's former Jesuit existence is also evident.

Years after his death, proponents of the vernacular defended their increasingly unpopular use of English in the liturgy by appealing to Carroll's liberal and pastoral attitude on the subject. In criticizing the use of English, opponents also pointed, negatively, to Carroll's advocacy of English. Increasingly, however, priests born and educated in Europe, and Americans formed under the tutelage of Europeans[1] learned "old world liturgical practices."[2] And, increasingly, those practices upheld the baroque piety of the new immigrants.[3]

In the end, John Carroll was the right man to be the first bishop of the Catholic Church in the United States, not only because his commitment to democracy and Republicanism enabled him to present the Church to the Protestant majority in a favorable light, but also because he laid the foundations for a future appreciation of the central role of liturgy and worship in the Christian spiritual life. While firmly holding to the rightness of an American form of Catholicism similar to the national or cultural rites of the East, Carroll never exhibited a cultural xenophobia, even if he was uncomfortable with some strains of European Catholicism. His belief in the universal importance of the liturgy and his unity with Rome prevented any appearance of nationalistic fervor of any kind.

As Chinnici states:

> John Carroll's vision of the Christian life was profoundly incarnational....His life of piety, with its liturgical orientation, strict moralism and affective prayer correlated well with his basic understanding of the person and the church. Challenged to be an example to all, John Carroll fashioned a spirituality that was Catholic, Christian, and American.[4]

Now Carroll serves as an example, a challenging example, to bishops and all Catholics for a truly American Catholicism founded on the bedrock of liturgical spirituality.

---

[1]On the education of seminarians during the episcopate of John Carroll, see Christopher J. Kauffman, *Tradition and Transformation in Catholic Culture*, pp. 69-95.

[2]See Agonito, *op. cit.*, pp. 124-125.

[3]For a survey of nineteenth-century devotions and piety, see the following: Ann Taves, *The Household of Faith: Roman Catholic Devotions in Mid-Nineteenth-Century America* (University of Notre Dame Press, 1986); Joseph P. Chinnici, *Devotion to the Holy Spirit in American Catholicism* (New York/Mahwah: Paulist Press, 1985); Jay P. Dolan, *Catholic Revivalism: The American Experience, 1830-1900* (University of Notre Dame Press, 1978); Joseph P. Chinnici, "Organization of the Spiritual Life: American Catholic Devotional Works, 1791-1886," *Theological Studies* 40 (June 1979), pp. 229-255.

[4]Chinnici, *op. cit.*, p. 34.

CHAPTER NINE

The United States Catholic School Phenomenon
Harold A. Buetow
Catholic University

Catholic schooling in the United States is a phenomenon of which all can be proud: the Roman Catholic Church, its leaders, the laity whose sacrifices made it possible, the clergy who worked for it, all who had the vision to make it different from any other place in the world, and especially those religious, lay teachers and administrators who worked and continue to work very hard and to sacrifice for it. The enterprise has a larger number of undeclared heroes and saints than any other comparably-sized group. It seems from many points of view to be a miracle of U.S. Catholic society. Bishop William McManus, who had a career-long involvement with Catholic schools, put it well:

> Nowhere else in the world has a local church, having decided that state-supported public education without religious education was an injustice to its young members and to its own institutional future, established schools of its own, financed by voluntary contributions and enriched with a full program of religious formation and education.[1]

Catholic schools constitute not a system but a pattern: one in which all parts have elements in common, but in which each part, and often each school, differs from all others. This pattern has made many contributions to our country.[2] For one thing, U.S. Catholic schooling has many "firsts." The first school of any kind was Roman Catholic in many areas: Louisiana, Kansas, the District of Columbia, North Dakota, Ohio, Kentucky, lower California and Baltimore. The first textbook within the confines of the present U.S. was the *Doctrina Breve* of Juan Zumarraga, brought from Mexico. The first dictionaries and formulations of Indian languages were compiled by missionaries. The first printing press in Michigan was that which the Reverend Gabriel Richard, S.S., brought to his school at Spring Hill.

The first structured schools established in the U.S. were founded by the Sisters of Charity under St. Elizabeth Bayley Seton and by the Sisters of Loretto in Nazareth, Kentucky, about a quarter of a century before others. West of the Mississippi, the first literary magazine was Catholic (*The Catholic Cabinet*, 1843-45), as was the first chartered university (St. Louis, 1832). The first high school diploma awarded in the state of Colorado was given by St. Mary's Academy, Denver. The Ursuline Sisters, in addition to being the first women to

---

[1] Bishop William McManus, "Building Support for Catholic Schools and Teachers," *Origins*, Vol. 18, No. 1 (May 19, 1988), p. 13.
[2] Much of the material in this section is condensed from Buetow, *Of Singular Benefit: The Story of U.S. Catholic Education* (New York: Macmillan, 1970), and its brief update, *A History of United States Catholic Schooling* (Washington, DC: National Catholic Educational Association, 1985).

take care of a military hospital within the confines of the present U.S., were the first to give the U.S. a woman who contributed a work of literary and historical merit (Madeleine Hachard), to give the country a woman druggist (Sister Frances Xavier Hebert), to establish an orphanage, and to shelter and work for the protection of girls.

There have been many other frequently-overlooked contributions of Catholic schooling to our country. The recruitments of religious-order teachers took place at a time when the U.S. was a cultural desert. John Quincy Adams called the Catholic educator, Reverend Simon Gabriel Bruté "the most learned man of his day in America." Others also had degrees from respected European universities. When possible, the schools accommodated non-Catholics at Nazareth Academy in Kentucky; for example, from 1815 to 1881 fully two-thirds of the female students were Protestant. The same Sisters of Charity of Nazareth for several years gave free service to schools in the mining sections of Ohio, maintained schools in poor urban and rural areas while refusing lucrative offers elsewhere, provided free service to orphans in the Louisville area from 1831 to 1923, and performed innumerable other works for the needy.

The teaching religious often sacrificed to the point of heroism. When the first Ursulines who came to New Orleans in 1727 landed at the mouth of the Mississippi after three months on the turbulent Atlantic Ocean, they still had to make a long and tedious trip through mosquito- and snake-infested bayous and swamps to the town, which then contained more than its share of a rough population. The first community of American origin, the Visitation Nuns, lived in a combination convent and school whose walls were not plastered from 1799 to 1811, at which time a sister lathed and plastered most of them herself. The first Sisters of Charity at Emmitsburg, Maryland, became sick from the lack of heat and food. For the Sisters of Charity of Nazareth, Kentucky, the first accommodations were a log house with one room below and one above, with a nearby hut serving as a kitchen.

As Father Frederic Baraga (1797-1868) was dying, he forced upon a visiting priest all the money he had ($20) for the visitor's school. When three Sisters of Loretto and two Sisters of Charity were travelling with others to Santa Fe in 1867, some of the party contracted cholera and all were frequently attacked by Indians; so disturbing was the experience that one Lorettine, Sister Mary Alphonsa Thompson, aged eighteen, literally died of fright. On the other end of the age scale, Philippine Duchesne was 72 years of age when she went to work among the Potawatomi. And Katherine Drexel, by the time of her death in 1955, had given a fortune to the Catholic education of Indians and Blacks, and set in motion the contributions of others to Catholic schooling.

In addition, most of the sisters faced a paucity of vocations, often took on such work for support as laundering, frequently made long journeys and allowed their dedication to carry them into the middle of border warfare and riots. Long before such was the practice elsewhere, they set up free schools for the poor beside their boarding schools, from which they derived necessary financial support. In addition to eradicating religious illiteracy, they contributed to the country as well as to their Church a cultural enrichment and a fullness of life. From all groups of Catholic teachers (religious, clergy and lay) came outstanding leaders of whom any educational system would be proud. Most of these were unsung. They brought their work to what the Bible calls the *anawim*: the downtrodden, outcast, powerless, poor members of society. Research indicates that schools have a much greater effect upon this group than upon those from better-educated parents.

It was because of the laity's ideals of sacrifice that the religious came when they did, and it was their willingness to undergo double taxation that financially supported their schools for so long. Lay responsibilities in Catholic schooling, sometimes considered new today, are really age-old. For example, from the time of the establishment of New York City's St. Peter's Free School in 1800 until 1831 the teachers were exclusively lay, and in six of the first seven schools founded between 1800 and 1860 in Savannah, Georgia, the teachers were all lay.

Many non-Catholics have throughout history paid tribute to the contributions of Roman Catholic schools. Non-Catholics were happy to pay tuition for their children to attend the early Catholic school at Goshenhoppen, Pennsylvania. The entire citizenry of Detroit elected to Congress Father Gabriel Richard who set up their city's school system and laid the early foundations of the University of Michigan. Visitation Academy in Georgetown was for many years recognized as the best secondary school opportunity for the daughters of governmental representatives of all denominations; Protestants went out of their way to congratulate Jesuit Leonard Neale for his schooling efforts on their behalf. A mid-nineteenth-century visitor from England, generally recognized as perceptive, wrote that the schooling of higher-echelon Protestants seemed to be entrusted to Catholic priests and nuns. In 1877, Henry Kiddle, superintendent of schools for New York City, felt that the teachers in parochial schools were better prepared than and superior to teachers in government schools.

Unfortunately, Catholic schooling has been categorized as "private," in contrast with "public" schooling. This differentiation has pejorative connotations. The "private" is at times equated with the "personal," which in most contexts connotes that everyone must live and die alone. "Private" signifies a separation from common purposes, meaningful participation in the common weal, and interest in helping society for the better. There is no such thing as a "private" school. By its nature, every school takes its students from the public and returns them, for good or for ill, to the public. Every school uses texts and other materials from publishers who are public, forms its curricula in accord with its vision of public needs, abides by at least minimum public standards set by the state, accepts teachers who were trained in publicly-approved institutions according to certain criteria. The only ways in which Catholic schools differ from their "public" counterparts are in their goals, their methods of funding and their administration by church authorities. Catholic school goals are consonant with the best interests of the nation: Daniel Webster said that "whatever makes men good Christians makes them good citizens." Catholic school funding is mostly from freewill donations.

It is therefore more accurate and more appropriate to designate Catholic schools as denominational, church-affiliated, or non-government schools, and government-funded ones as "government" schools, terminology I shall use in my discussion here. The United States is unique in the Western world in its explicit omission of formal religion from its schools; if this terminology suggests a parallel to the Soviet Union and other totalitarian regimes, let that be a matter for further thought.

RUMINATIONS FROM HISTORY

European Prologue

United States Catholic schools had their prologue in Europe. The years around and after Columbus first came to America in 1492 were a time of expanding trade, culminating in a commercial revolution and the discovery of new worlds. The ultimate motivation for the founding of America, however, went way beyond that. There was, for example, the devotional life of the people. The popular piety of the early emigres obliterated the sharp distinctions which some moderns make between the sacred and the secular. The Church was present at not only the great life events of birth, marriage and death, but also in the organizations of crafts and professions, the offices of government, and international relations. Theology and science were interpenetrated, and in the popular thought of the time "the sky hung low": the connections between the sacred and the secular were close. On that ethos the Church had a dynamic life in the present world, and not just in a world to come.

The Colonial Period: Transplantation

The Catholic settlements in New Spain and New France preceded the Protestant settlements of New England. In their missions to Mexico, Central America, South America and the borderlands of what became the United States (Florida, Louisiana, New Mexico, Texas, Arizona, and California), the missionaries had one chief aim: to spread the Catholic faith. But since the provisions of the royal patronage under which the Church operated also regarded missionaries as agents of the state, the goals of church and state were fused and furthered by the system of schooling implemented in New Spain. Although the overall system involved measures of force and compulsion, it at least rivalled the mother country in being progressive and Christian.

Half a century before Jamestown was founded by the English, the University of Mexico was conferring degrees (on Europeans at any rate) in law and theology. The Indian schools introduced Native Americans to Christianity within the Spanish way of life. Frequently the missionaries' secular counterparts exploited the Native Americans, a situation which the missionaries deplored.

The large mission schools, sometimes managing more than two thousand Indians, frequently contained a weaving room, blacksmith shop, tannery, wine press and warehouses. The missionaries introduced irrigation ditches, vegetable gardens, grain fields, and on the ranges thousands of horses, cattle, sheep and goats. When possible and advantageous to the Indians, the missionaries taught them to read and write, but for a people moving from primitive living into a different civilization the missionaries considered technical training as the most appropriate schooling.

French missionaries focused their efforts on areas now known as Maine, New York and Louisiana, and also on the Great Lakes and the Illinois country. The missionaries there found the Indians difficult to Christianize and educate. Indian aversion to anything abstract or spiritual together with their nomadic way of life made any stable school influence difficult. The French fur traders and their families found it practical to follow the Indian nomadic way, so that schooling for the French settlers was practically as impossible as it was for the Indians.

Not all Indians can be grouped together, however. Gabriel Marest, S.J., testified, for example, that "[t]he Illinois are much less barbarous than other savages."[1] Marest at the same time expressed the opinion that a change had been wrought in the Illinois due in part to the influence of the Christian religion. Herbert Priestley has observed that "amid white and red men alike the Church sought to raise the level of civilization by educational ministrations."[2] Into the wilderness the missionaries followed their nomad flocks and it is from the pens of the missionaries in shaky canoes or in dark forests of smoky wigwams that we gain a knowledge of their endeavors in the wilderness which for the most part was New France. The *Relations of the Jesuits* alone filled forty-one volumes, and they are but a small part of the entire literary output.[3]

In terms of lasting results, the French efforts at schooling, education and civilization in the North American continent can perhaps be termed a failure. This was despite the fact that hundreds of priests (Jesuits, Franciscans, Sulpicians, Carmelites, Capuchins and secular priests) spent a great part of their lives and often their blood on behalf of Christian formation and education.

It was the Thirteen Colonies along the Atlantic coastline, however, that set the pattern for the future development of what became the United States. The branches of Christianity with headquarters in Geneva, Edinburgh and Canterbury provided a deeper stamp than Rome on what became the public motto: *Novus Ordo Seclorum* (A New Order of Things).

By the beginning of the eighteenth century, the colonial settlements on the eastern seaboard had become a prosperous extension of British society, in which the prevailing outlook on life and the world was unmistakably influenced by a Puritan ethos. Simultaneous with all of this was a wide, sweeping intellectual revolution: the rationalistic and faith-excluding Enlightenment. Even before 1700, the Age of Reason had begun to create theological problems, but it also provided a philosophical base for the unfolding work of the Founding Fathers.

Catholics in the thirteen original colonies were an insignificant and powerless minority. In 1790 they numbered no more than 35,000 in a population of over four million. They shared the contemporary attitudes toward education: that it is the responsibility of the parents and that formal schooling should be church-controlled. They wanted the education of their children to be Catholic, and sacrificed toward that end. Families who could afford it sent their children abroad, to such colleges as St. Omer's in Flanders and to the convent schools of Europe. To provide preparation, the Jesuits offered such schools as those at Newtown Manor and Bohemia, about which we know little. In November, 1791, Georgetown College was founded by John Carroll (1735-1815) and staffed

[1]*Jesuit Relations and Allied Documents* (Cleveland: Burrows Brothers, 1896-1901), Vol. 12, ch. 66, p. 231.
[2]Herbert Ingram Priestley, *The Coming of the White Man, 1492-1848* (New York: The Macmillan Co., 1950), p. 246.
[3]William Bennet Munroe, *Crusaders of New France* (New Haven: Yale University Press, 1920), pp. 131-132.

by other priests, all of whom had been Jesuits until the Jesuits were suppressed by the papacy in 1773.

Of all the wonderful features of the Constitution, that great document written in 1787, the one that pertains most to Catholic education is the part of the First Amendment having to do with religion: "Congress shall make no law respecting an establishment of religion, or prohibiting the free exercise hereof." The interpretation of those words as applied to schools has constituted about 95 percent of church-state issues. Senator Robert Packwood said: "Every member of the Constitutional Convention came from a state that prior to the adoption of the Constitution and after, levied taxes — collected those taxes, and gave the taxes to churches to run primary and secondary schools."[1] Interpretations by the Supreme Court and legal scholars have, however, differed, many interpreting "disestablishment" to mean "separation" of religion from government and from the people.

Early National Period: Formative Foundations

During the era beginning with Thomas Jefferson's inauguration (1800), several traditions developed in American religion: religious freedom, a relatively distinct separation of church and state, a growing acceptance of denominationalism, the growth of the "voluntary principle" in matters pertaining to church membership and support, and the advance of patriotic piety with its belief in the divinely-appointed mission of the new nation. Less worthy were the attacks on Catholicism, inspired by nativism and including among their targets Blacks and Jews as well. The Church in this period was straitened by poverty and insecurity, teacher shortage, and a scarce and scattered Catholic population.

One of the most serious complaints about the United States situation at this time voiced by the Church's Councils of Baltimore (1829-84) pertained to the laws by which some of the states denied the right of the Church to possess property. Because of these laws, lay trustees were designated to hold church property in their names. This resulted in the difficulty called trusteeism, in which some lay officers at times became defiant of the authority of the hierarchy. This sometimes hindered the progress of schools.

Preeminent among church leaders who perceived that the success of the Church in the new republic would depend on the establishment of Catholic schools was the first Roman Catholic Bishop, John Carroll, who set his Church on a course that enabled it to expand, to absorb new immigrants and to establish schools. This was the beginning of a pattern for this country's bishops to take an interest in schools, a pattern which would come to be taken for granted.

When the westward movement carried Catholics along with others beyond the Alleghenies, the wilderness did not decrease their sacrificing efforts to provide schools. A number of Catholic elementary schools of the period were set up in log cabins, church basements, sacristies, choir lofts, rectory and convent rooms, and abandoned buildings. The goals, determination, leadership and perseverance

---

[1]United States Senate, *Committee on Finance,* Subcommittee Hearings on Tuition Tax Credits, 1978.

of the Catholics of the time set the pattern of Catholic schools on firm formative foundations.

The preparation of teachers, at least up to the time of the Revolution, had
been unheard of, and teacher standards, in Catholic as well as all other schools,
were low. Throughout this period and into the next, teacher-sexton and teacher-
organist combinations were not uncommon. The priest-teachers in the boys'
schools were often learned men, educated on the Continent, and of unrivalled
academic ability, but were few in number, and hampered by other duties. Consequently, they developed a system of student-teaching whereby the better students in the more advanced classes taught those in the lower grades. Scarcity of
teachers was a problem to all denominations. In that respect, Catholic schools
were more fortunate than most others in having groups of religious: dedicated
teachers living in community who gave themselves without consideration of
much financial remuneration. The teaching sisterhoods founded during this period were trained by educated priests during the sisters' beginning periods; thereafter they themselves trained their novices within their congregations.

One of the first communities dedicated to Catholic schooling to originate in
this country was the Visitations Nuns. Another was the community of the Sisters of Charity, which came into being through the zeal of Elizabeth Bayley Seton. When Seton died in 1821, in her forty-seventh year, the Sisters of Charity
numbered nearly fifty and were rapidly increasing. Many are of the opinion that
she laid the foundation for the Catholic school pattern as it eventually evolved in
the United States. Enrollments of students were small in comparison with the
population because an educational consciousness had not yet awakened, and
among the citizenry as a whole there was little interest in schooling.

Later National Period: Transition

During the decades before the Civil War, the popular Puritan hope for the
Kingdom of God on earth led to desires for reform. One of the areas of reform
was schooling. On the principle that the extension of knowledge would dissi-
pate human misery and provide a better day, Enlightenment ideals and the rationale of Harvard's Puritan founders converged. Idealists refused to be satisfied
with the fact that America's literacy rate was then probably unequalled anywhere
else in the world.

Clearly outstanding as the age's most effective educational crusader was Horace Mann (1796-1859). Despite his conviction of the need to eliminate sectarian religion from government schools, he was equally convinced that the schools
must instill the historic Protestant virtues, a conviction evidenced also in the
enormously popular works of instruction written by two New England ministers, Samuel G. Goodrich (1793-1860), known as Peter Parley, and the prolific
Jacob Abbott.

Another relevant phenomenon during this period of the Roman Catholic
Councils of Baltimore was immigration, a source of tremendous influence on the
country's churches as well as on this country's fabled diversity. After the early
immigrants from the French Revolution and the Napoleonic wars, the tempo
began to accelerate. Trouble in Ireland occasioned the first huge wave, a great
movement of Germans and Scandinavians dominated the next phase, and after
1890 the "great Atlantic migration" culminated in a vast exodus of Eastern Eu-

ropean Jews, Southern Italians, Poles and Balkan peoples. Before the gates were narrowed, over forty million immigrants had come to these shores.

The Catholic Church expanded immensely through immigration, embracing also the geographical phenomenon of the westward movement. Other expansion took place through conversions to Roman Catholicism. Conversions were not an unmixed blessing, however, with the country now experiencing the most violent religious discord in its history. Within the Roman Catholic Church, immigration led to active ethnic tensions, particularly between the French, Irish and Germans.

But conflicts and disagreements even more violent than those within Catholicism arose from without: the phenomena of American nativism and anti-Cathlicism. Emotional revivalism intensified such views. Anti-Catholicism offered to many a motive for Protestant solidarity. Political fears and economic pressures exacerbated the situation. All of these causes brought anti-Catholic agitation beyond the original Thirteen Colonies and carried anti-Catholic publications and horror literature about Roman Catholicism. And the agitation went beyond words. In Boston, after years of mounting tensions, on August 11, 1834, a well-organized group burned the Ursuline convent in Charlestown.

Between 1840 and 1842 in New York, the political rift widened further with the school crisis, answered forcefully by the blunt and perhaps pugnacious Catholic Bishop John Hughes, "Dagger John," who served from 1842 to 1864. As a result of his heated fight with New York City's Common Council, on April 9, 1842 New York State passed the Maclay Bill, which extended the common school system of the State to New York City. No school teaching any religious sectarian doctrine was to receive any money from the common school fund, and only government schools were to be provided for. The government-school, church-school dichotomy deepened.

In contrast to the forceful Hughes was the peace-loving Bishop of Philadelphia, Francis Patrick Kenrick. When the nativists in his city threatened violence, Kenrick issued an explanatory and conciliatory statement. But his quiet and dignified conduct did not prevent the violence in Philadelphia that led to wild and bloody rioting in May 1844. Two Roman Catholic churches and dozens of Irish homes were burned, militia fired point blank among advancing crowds, a cannon was turned against St. Philip Neri Church, and for three days mob rule prevailed in the city and its suburbs. Thirteen people were killed. Since that time, in the face of succeeding confrontations the advisability of the Hughes or Kenrick procedures have been argued.

Nativism synthesized into a movement of opposition to minorities on the ground of their being "un-American." It opposed Blacks, Catholics and Jews, asserted Anglo-Saxon superiority, and succeeded in restricting immigration. Some of the anti-Catholic bigotry was in high places and awesome: even from a president of the United States, Ulysses S. Grant, and in 1876 in the many proposals for a hostile amendment to the Federal Constitution by Senator James G. Blaine. Variants of the Blaine Amendment, which prohibited government money for religious enterprises, succeeded in appearing in many state constitutions.

Nevertheless Catholic schools continued to contribute. The fact that most of the Church's growth took place through immigration eliminated the possibility of the Church's becoming aristocratic or her schools becoming elitist, as had happened elsewhere and could have happened here. As this period wore on, it became increasingly obvious that all youth needed more schooling. The needs of an ever more industrial society for trained personnel increased. Catholic schools were, however, slower than their government counterparts to make necessary curricular changes. When the government schools took positions against religious instruction, though, and it became increasingly obvious that for the first time in history a government was attempting an educational pattern without formal religion, it became equally clear that the Church was going to have to step up its schooling efforts.

The Church's elementary schools therefore grew. On the secondary level, the original strain of academies now proliferated as Catholics and others attempted to satisfy the desires of the upper classes. The teaching communities of sisters and brothers increased (each community warranting a volume in itself). Nativist opposition to Catholic culture caused Catholic schooling, along with the rest of the Church, to change from a leaven mentality to one of siege.

The Church's hierarchy expressed themselves first at the Provincial Councils of Cincinnati, conducted for the most part by and for Germans, who from the beginning, for a variety of reasons, were in favor of Catholic schools. The entire United States hierarchy at the Councils of Baltimore then legislated encouragement and support. For the most part, they had a loyal clergy and laity behind them.

Compromise plans to help Catholic schooling as well as local communities were established in such cities as Savannah, Georgia; Hartford, Connecticut; Lowell, Massachusetts; and Poughkeepsie, New York. These plans provided for the major part of parochial school funding, especially teacher salaries and building maintenance, to be paid by community taxes. The institutions were called public-parochial schools. Some exist to this day, to the satisfaction and happiness of the local communities, parents, students, teachers and others involved.

Growth: Immigration at High Tide

The period from 1885 to 1917 was a critical one for organized religion; materialism and its cult of success, pragmatism, naturalism and hostile extensions of Darwinism permeated the country. The shift in the patterns of immigration which put the Protestant Establishment, already hurt by the Civil War, in a worsened position, led to a revival of the movement to restrict immigration, to a new kind of political machinery, and to new outbreaks of nativism.

Connected with the last phenomenon, just as the Supreme Court reflected the mood of the time in its 1896 decision providing "separate but equal" treatment for Blacks, so too the Court reflected the populace concerning Catholics. Most of the cases of church-state relationships pertained to schooling. The cases were tried in state and federal courts and did not evidence much consistency. In 1899, for example, in *Bradfield v. Roberts*,[1] the Supreme Court sustained a federal statute authorizing construction grants to a Roman Catholic hospital corporation (Providence Hospital in Washington, DC). The Court would not, however, grant the same latitude to church-affiliated schools.

---

[1]175 U.S. 291 (1899).

In schooling, Catholics followed the lead of the government sector and were beginning the formation of organizations to bring their educators together for discussions of problems and possible solutions. The Catholic Educational Association (later to add the adjective "National") was formed in 1904 from previously-existing smaller groups, and other Catholic educational associations formed about the same time.

Because child labor had finally come to an end and states were legislating compulsory schooling laws, the school population in both the government and non-government sectors zoomed. In Catholic elementary schools, this factor combined with the legislation of the Third Plenary Council of Baltimore of 1884 to bring about crowded classrooms and inadequate equipment. The decrees of this Council were the culmination of Catholic legislation that had begun as early as the beginnings of the Republic.

The Council decreed that, wherever possible, there was to be a parochial school near every church; priests who did not cooperate were to be removed; laity who did not cooperate were to be reprimanded by the bishop; and, unless other provisions for the religious education of their children were possible, Catholic parents were to send their children to Catholic schools. The Council also voted to increase the number of high schools and to raise standards. It was concerned also with the establishment of Catholic colleges, encouraging wealthy Catholics to give generously for this purpose. How much subsequent growth was due specifically to the Council will probably never be accurately determined.

On the secondary level of Catholic schooling, as of its government counterpart, there were striking developments. This period witnessed, for example, the founding of the first Central Catholic High School. But Catholics as well as the nation at large would have to wait until after World War I for meaningful interest in this level of schooling. The Catholic University of America was established in 1889, conceived as not only the apex of Catholic schooling in the United States, but also as the agent to unify and guide it, to raise its standards through a program of affiliation and to prepare its teachers.

There was among Catholics as among others the inception of professionalism among teachers; perhaps surprisingly, before 1900 when teachers in all schools were limited in their preparation and horizons, there was evidence that Catholic teachers were sometimes better prepared than their counterparts elsewhere. Religious communities attempted teacher preparation through practices like individual instruction, scholasticates, apprenticeships, lectures, summer schools and institutes. There was, however, evidence that they were less prepared for teaching older children or teaching the sciences.

Concerning students in this period, there were developments in both theory and practice. With regard to theory, government schools welcomed the introduction from abroad of the ideas of Johann Pestalozzi, Johann Herbart and Friedrich Froebel, a factor that would later contribute to the growth of progressive education. In the government schools, there was interest also in the area of the tests and measurements movement of Edward L. Thorndike, who held the principle that everything that exists, exists in quantity and can be measured. This Procrustean Bed of schools began its demise with the perception of individual differences by such government-school leaders as William T. Harris, Charles W. Eliot and John Dewey. Most of these developments, however, left Catholic educationists in an intellectual ferment. They could not accept the theorists completely: Pestalozzi because of his pantheism, progressive education because of what they considered undue permissiveness for the child and a forgetfulness of original sin, or Thorndike because of his empiricism.

Within, there was further ferment because of the Bouquillon controversy on the state's right to educate. In December 1891, the Reverend Thomas Bouquillon, professor of moral theology at Catholic University, published a pamphlet, *Education: To Whom Does It Belong?*, challenging the up-to-then church thinking that the state has only a substitutional right in education. Bouquillon's position clearly substantiated that of John Ireland, the influential Archbishop of St. Paul, Minnesota. Bouquillon wrote that education "belongs to the individual, physical or moral, to the family, to the state, to the Church, to none of these solely and exclusively, but to all four combined in harmonious working." [1]

Within a week, Rene I. Holaind, S.J., professor at the Jesuit Seminary at Woodstock College (Maryland), published *The Parent First* in response. The two pamphlets promoted intense and bitter public discussion. An official statement of papal representative Francesco Satolli settled nothing. Pope Leo XIII pleaded for an end to the controversy. Bouquillon's position was vindicated in Pope Pius XI's encyclical on education in 1929.

In the area of practice, Catholic school students comprised several immigrant minority groups. Immigrants were blamed for many of society's ills, even by government educators. Catholic educators tried to meet this prejudice by making their students not only Catholic, but also American. For Catholic immigrants, the parish was the unit that was familiar from their places of origin; an integral part of this, especially among the Germans, was the parish school. The parish school made the immigrant child's transition to the United States slower than the government schools and therefore, in the light of subsequent research, psychologically more sound.

In this time of the extremely slow process of eliminating the evils of child labor, a higher percentage of immigrants' children than among the total population were working; for them, extensive schooling was out of the question. Another minority group, Blacks, did not contain many Catholics, for complex reasons. Nevertheless, during this period religious communities were started both for and of Blacks. Also, the Second and Third Plenary Councils of Baltimore had urged attention to the religion and education of Blacks.

Because of Catholic rejection of such innovators as Pestalozzi and Herbart, improvements in Catholic textbooks that could have resulted from accepting the good in these theorists did not come, by and large. As a result, some Catholic texts wound up academically inferior to many in government-school use. Unfortunately, this same predisposition to reject change and improvement from outside also frequently resulted in poor quality in that area in which Catholic schools found a prime reason for their existence—catechetics, the imparting of religious truths. Rote memorization (not uncommon in all schools of the time in most subjects) of the Catechism of Baltimore III was too frequent. Before the end of this period, however, an awareness of the inadequacy of this procedure grew.

---

[1] For bibliographical and other details of the Bouquillon controversy, see Buetow, *Of Singular Benefit, op. cit.,* pp. 170-175.

At the end of this period, despite the many reasons for optimism, there was no more unanimity among Catholics *vis-à-vis* the desirability of maintaining their school system than before; Irish-Americans wanting a way out of the ghetto often tried the government school as their passport, many upwardly mobile Catholic immigrants became government-school teachers, many good Catholics served on government-school boards, and even some priests disagreed as to the desirability of Catholic schools. Among the last, the most famous was the Reverend Edward McGlynn of New York City. He took the position, still with us, of preferring to provide church resources for the cryingly needful area of social welfare rather than for schools.

New Maturation: Post-World War I to Post-World War II

Running through the currents of the excitements of war, contractions of spirit in the post-world-war periods, Red scares, and economic depressions and regressions as well as booms, was a steady acceleration of growth (economic at least), population movement and governmental expansion which gradually brought the country to a state of advanced technocratic crisis. Many came to doubt that the Redeemer Nation was capable of redeeming anyone or anything. Somehow the United States had become the victim of individualism, exploitation and world policemanship.

As for religion in schooling, the Supreme Court continued the ambivalent trends of the late nineteenth century. Its decisions during this period centered around two areas. The first was government aid to non-government schools. The Court decided that non-government schools have the right to exist and that the state can legally supply non-sectarian textbooks and transportation to their students.

There were memorable dicta. In *Meyer v. Nebraska* in 1923, for example, Justice James C. McReynolds wrote for the majority:

> The fundamental theory of liberty upon which all governments in this Union repose excludes any general power of the state to standardize its children by forcing them to accept instruction from public teachers only. The child is not the mere creature of the state; those who nourish him and direct his destiny have the right, coupled with the high duty, to recognize and prepare him for additional obligations.[1]

Pierce v. Society of Sisters in 1925,[2] also known as the *Oregon School Case,* has been called the Magna Carta of parochial schools, because it defended their right to exist. The briefs and oral discussion in this case contain just about every possible argument in favor of and in opposition to non-government schools.

The second area of decision was religion in government schools. State courts continued to contradict one another, and the federal courts continued to show their confusion. The upshot was to prevent the formal presentation of or-

---

[1]*Meyer v. Nebraska,* 262 U.S. 390 (1923).
[2]*Pierce v. Society of Sisters,* 268 U.S. 510, 45 S.Ct. 571, 69 L.Ed. 1070 (1925).

ganized religion in government schools. The greatest church-state cooperation in schooling came with the Servicemen's Readjustment Act of 1944. Commonly called the "GI Bill of Rights," this legislation enabled the government to pay tuition and other schooling expenses of servicemen returning from World War II and later from the Korean conflict in any school of their choice, even schools of theology.

In 1948 in *McCollum*,[1] the Supreme Court outlawed released-time programs for religious instruction on government-school premises. In the 1952 *Zorach*[2] case, it allowed released-time programs if the students desirous of religious instruction would leave the government-school grounds to go to religious centers for religious instruction or denominational exercises. However there was a minimum of administrative cooperation from government schools.

The Church's continuing to take seriously her role as an agent of schooling led to several expressions: In 1918, its Code of Canon Law left no doubt about the Church's right to educate, and legislated responsibilities accordingly. In 1919, when the National Catholic Welfare Conference (later called United States Catholic Conference) was formed as an arm of the bishops, it included a Department of Education. In contradistinction to the National Catholic Educational Association, which functions as an organization related to the profession of education, USCC's Department of Education serves in an advisory capacity to the hierarchy. Several factors led to the rise to a position of importance of another organization, the Confraternity of Christian Doctrine, founded in this country in 1902.

Catholic school goals during this time opposed the government school search for a pragmatistic kind of social efficiency. Catholic schools' declaration of the ultimate goal of education was the same as ever: the formation of the whole person, on a supernatural as well as on a natural plane. As their proximate goal, they sought the formation of persons adaptable to the contingencies of Christian living in this country's democracy. The U.S. hierarchy touched upon this in the 1919 Pastoral Letter and again in their 1950 Pastoral which was entitled, "The Child: Citizen of Two Worlds."[3] It was a recurring theme at the NCEA meeting in the 1920's. After 1938, the Commission on American Citizenship, formed that year, engaged in the matter and defined a social program.

On the elementary level, because of its concern over the dignity and the spiritual nature of the person, the Catholic school pattern only gradually and reluctantly accepted the testing and measurement movement. It opposed at first the "activity program" and the utilitarian bases of curricular decisions in the government school, but then gradually adapted what was acceptable from the new theorists in the light of Catholic principles, urged on by Monsignor George Johnson of Catholic University.

On the secondary level, financial strain hindered the building of laboratories and the development of vocational training, thus adding to other reasons for the retention of college preparatory curricula. On this level, the introduction of so-

[1]*McCollum v. Board of Education,* 333 U.S. 306 (1952).
[2]*Zorach v. Clauson,* 343 U.S. 306 (1952).
[3]Raphael M. Huber, "The Child: Citizen of Two Worlds," *Our Bishops Speak* (Milwaukee, MI: Bruce, 1952), pp. 161-169.

cial emphases to the curriculum was more gradual. Common to both levels, there was an attempt to make the catechism come to life. Assisting in this effort were the liturgical movement; psychologically-oriented catechesis; and catechism renewal through a return to the early Christian narrative-historical approach, Christocentrism, the Bible, the kerygmatic method, eye-catching illustrations and the use of audio-visual materials.

For teachers in general, the time after World War I ushered in a new era in preparation, salaries, admission standards and inspections. For Catholics, the 1920's added to previous programs of teacher training on the diocesan level. At the end of the 1950's the sister-formation program added new dimensions to the making of a sister-teacher. Throughout the period, the search for a higher level of professional training of teachers in Catholic schools was further motivated by statements of Popes Pius XI and Pius XII. The Catholic school teacher increase was not only qualitative but quantitative, the quantitative jump during this period being more than 100 percent. Lay teachers were being upgraded, in both number and position, coming into their own, especially after World War II.

With the growth of child psychology, the student, too, was becoming less the "forgotten person" of Catholic schools. While some government-school educators were opting for a consideration of the "whole child" and not just statistics, Catholic school educators were continuing their opposition to the current naturalism in interpreting the child. The Reverend Thomas Shields of Catholic University, himself a psychologist, adapted the best of the growing psychological movement to Catholic schools. Catholic concern for the dignity of the person resulted during the 1950's in the beginning of attention to exceptional children as well as continued attention to such minorities as Blacks.

Catholic attitudes to Blacks often followed their neighbors, but Catholics are proud of the many instances of Catholic acceptance of Blacks prior to the Brown Desegregation Decision of 1954.[1] Militating against these movements

---

[1]Among these were the schools in Baltimore in the early National Period; the first schools for Blacks near St. Louis by Madame Philippine Duchesne and the Religious of the Sacred Heart in 1818; the endeavors of Bishop John England in Charleston, South Carolina, in the mid-1820's; the founding of a religious order of Black nuns, the Oblate Sisters of St. Francis, in Baltimore in 1825, for poor Black children; the failed attempts of the Reverend Charles Nerinckx in 1824; the "Special Report of the Commissioner of Education, District of Columbia, 1868," praising the DC Catholic free schools for Blacks.

There was concern for the education of Blacks expressed by the Second Plenary Council of Baltimore in 1866 and the Third Plenary Council in 1884; the establishment of Black religious communities like the Oblate Sisters of Providence, the Sisters of the Holy Family, and the Handmaids of the Most Pure Heart of Mary; the work of the Josephites and other orders of priests among Blacks, starting after the Civil War; the Franciscan Sisters from Mill Hill, London, England, the only white sisterhood in 1881 devoting themselves to work among Blacks; the white Sisters of the Blessed Sacrament, founded in 1891 by Mother Katherine Drexel for school work among Blacks; the founding of the Catholic Student Mission Crusade in 1918 to interest Catholic students in Blacks; the founding of Xavier University of Louisiana in New Orleans in 1918 for the education of Blacks.

There was also the establishment in 1920 of St. Augustine's Seminary in Bay St. Louis, Mississippi, to train black candidates for the Society of the Divine

were the bigotry and prejudice of some Catholics, often deep-seated, and the paucity of Black Catholics. On the other hand, burned-out schools, churches, convents and rectories in the South testify to areas where Catholic leaders moved too fast for the local population.

Concerning the education of women, there were among Catholics as among others the remnants of a double standard. On the college level, Catholics moved more slowly than others in the direction of coeducation, on the moral grounds of supposed dangers in the mixing of the sexes. On the middle level, they voiced such objections as that each sex has different needs, that coeducation presents moral problems to the adolescent, and that the presence of the opposite sex distracts from study. Pope Pius XI in *The Christian Education of Youth* opposed coeducation, and a further instruction from Rome on the subject in 1957 resulted in high schools that were coinstitutional rather than coeducational—that is, they presented separate classroom instruction to each sex, but had them share some facilities such as cafeteria, chapel, and library. On the elementary level, U.S. Catholic schools never had any difficulty in having boys and girls together.

RUMINATIONS ABOUT THE PRESENT

The years from about the 1960's on mark interesting contrasts with the previous periods. The terms "Post Puritan" and "Post Protestant" are beginning to be applied to the United States. The age of the WASP and the age of the melting pot, if there ever was one, is coming to a close. Terms like "secular," "permissive," "the Death of God," and "the great moral revolution" describe the culture of our time. The country is experiencing a basic change in moral and religious attitudes. America's "civil religion" is being subjected to severe criticism. Declining growth rates and widespread budgetary problems reveal a loss of institutional vitality, to the churches as well as every other institution.

Word; the formation of the Catholic Interracial Council by John LaFarge, S.J., in 1934; clergy conferences around the same time for the welfare of Blacks; and the 1943 statement of the bishops of the country on the need for equality.

In New Orleans, Archbishop Joseph F. Rummel had by 1949 integrated the archdiocesan Holy Name societies, sodalities, and Councils of Catholic Men and Women, and his pastoral letter of March 1953 eliminated segregation in the Churches. In North Carolina, Bishop Vincent S. Waters integrated Catholic Churches, schools, and hospitals in June 1953. In the Archdiocese of Washington, DC, Archbishop (later Cardinal) Patrick A. O'Boyle ended segregation in the schools in the autumn of 1948. And so it went with many others: Archbishop Robert E. Lucey of San Antonio, Texas, Bishop Joseph Ritter of Indianapolis and St. Louis, and Cardinal Albert Meyer of Chicago, to cite a few.

For many reasons, youth show an estrangement from traditional forms of religious nourishment. Sydney E. Ahlstrom summarized these characteristics into three: metaphysical, moral and social

> 1) A growing commitment to a naturalism or "secularism" and corresponding doubts about the supernatural and the sacral;
> 2) A creeping (or galloping) awareness of vast contradictions in American life between profession and performance, the ideal and the actual;
> 3) Increasing doubt as to the capacity of present-day ecclesiastical, political, social and educational institutions to rectify the country's deep-seated woes.[1]

The spiritual result of all this is enormous. Many critics see time-honored United States church life as irrelevant to the country's actual condition and regard church-going America not as a moral leaven but as an obstacle to change. This brought widespread frustration even to church ministers.

In the Roman Catholic Church, the reverberations of the revolution begun with the election of Pope John XXIII in 1958 remain deeply felt. A wave of questioning of all traditional structures, such as the parish church, is taking place. Those Catholics committed to the sacral aim of "saving souls" have grave problems with a Catholic schooling which they see as producing an intellectual atmosphere in which the traditional faith does not seem to flourish sufficiently. Since the mid 1960's, Catholic school enrollments have been on a downward slide.

These cataclysmic changes bring about two important questions: the continued existence of Catholic schools and their identity. The questions are intertwined, and the question of Catholic schools' continued existence is intensifying. One example of a weakening resolve is a week-long symposium of 300 representatives of 22 Catholic educational organizations in May, 1988, in Dayton, Ohio, on "The Future of the Educational Mission of the Roman Catholic Church in the United States." A report on the meeting said: "With parochial school enrollment showing no sign of ending a 23-year decline, a growing number of Roman Catholic educators have begun to question the church's longstanding reliance on such schools as the bedrock of religious education."[2]

Some spoke in the schools' favor. Yet in a series of statements issued at the final session, the delegates called on the Church to "develop more effective uses of our changing resources" and to create new structures for "the delivery of education to all peoples."[3] Among proposed solutions to the spate of criticism of the Catholic schools and the difficulties they face have been suggestions to abandon Catholic schools and concentrate efforts solely on religious education; to opt for a complete restructuring of the existing system; to drop some levels, leaving the agonizing problem of which ones; and to merge schools instead of closing them, in order to prevent student loss, as far as possible.

Elsewhere, Bishop William McManus stated that "[t]he U.S. Catholic Church's enthusiastic commitment to Catholic schools has diminished almost to

---

[1] Sydney E. Ahlstrom, *A Religious History of the American People* (New Haven and London: Yale University Press, 1972), p. 1087.
[2] *The New York Times,* May 28, 1988, p. 1.
[3] *Ibid.*

the point of only being tolerant toward them."[1]   Observing the Church's failure to build new schools, he continued forthrightly that this "has done a grave injustice to the Church and has caused a scandalous injustice in the lives of several million young Catholics who have been deprived of Catholic schools."[2]

If Catholic schools no longer have a Catholic identity, they don't deserve to exist at such sacrifice, simply to duplicate what is being done elsewhere. One can no longer take for granted that schools called St. John's or St. Mary's are Catholic. If they do have a Catholic identity, there is no comparably effective way to form youth after the mind and heart of Christ, and the effort deserves the same measure of sacrifice that our forebears gave it. The measure of identity is detectable in six areas: atmosphere, goals, curriculum, students, teachers, and the secondary agents of family, church and state.[3]

Atmosphere

Every school must deal with atmosphere, conditions or climate, parts of which come from outside the school, others from inside. The atmosphere is integral to education and gives the school its flavor, and thus is important. The external atmosphere comprises the economic, political, cultural and social structures in which the school finds itself.

Over 57 percent of all Catholic-school pupils in the U.S. are in the middle eastern states and Great Lakes region. Ten states account for almost 70 percent of Catholic school enrollment. The first five (New York, Pennsylvania, Illinois, California and Ohio) comprise almost half (49.9 percent) of the enrollment. In many ways, this reflects national population statistics. There are exceptions: notably Louisiana as the nineteenth most populated state and Wisconsin as the sixteenth, both with high Catholic-school enrollments. Louisiana, Wisconsin, New Jersey and Massachusetts seem to indicate the influence of early Catholic cultures and history.

At present, about 48 percent of Catholic elementary schools are in urban areas, about 25 percent in suburban areas, and about 27 percent in rural areas. Secondary schools have shown the same general trends. In 1981, about 89 percent of all Catholic elementary schools had less than 500 pupils. Secondary schools were more evenly distributed over various enrollment ranges. Today, an increasing percentage of elementary schools have fewer than 500 pupils, while an increasing percentage of secondary schools exceed 500 pupils. As to ownership, most elementary schools are single-parish schools (about 85 percent); others are inter-parish, diocesan or private. Secondary schools are divided differently: single-parish (14.6 percent), inter-parish (11.4 percent), diocesan (35.5 percent), and private (38.5 percent). Parish elementary schools are supported mainly by parish subsidies (46 percent) and tuition (43 percent); the remainder

[1]McManus, *op. cit.*, p. 13.
[2]*Ibid.*, p. 15.
[3]Some of the materials in this section are from Buetow, *The Catholic School: Its Roots, Identity and Future* (New York: Crossroad, 1988).

comes from fund-raising efforts, volunteer work, contributed services from religious communities, and voluntary contributions.[1] More important to the Catholic school atmosphere than these statistics is its spiritual climate. This means especially the school's formation of Christian community. The hierarchy, other administrators and teachers must do all in their power to form the school community. One way to help make this possible is by applying the church's many encyclicals about social justice to school personnel. Students, too, must be acceptable as active participants in the Christian community that is the Catholic school, and should be able to find there a climate which complements that of the good Catholic home.

Goals

Goals are especially precious to the Catholic school. What had been for Greek education the *morphosis* of human personhood became for New Testament times and thereafter the more profound *metamorphosis;* for early Christians their religion's invitation to God-likeness was precious, and they held equally valuable *metanoia* or change of heart. For Catholics, of course, the practical application of immutable goals to the ever-changing present is an ongoing process.

All who are interested in Catholic schools should have input into their goals: society at large, the State, the Church community, parents and (particularly) the school community of faculty, students and staff. In this shared responsibility and participatory decision-making to formulate meaningful, specific goals, the process as well as the result can have many beneficial results. Not least among them is the establishment of a sense of community and the provision of insights that will be lived and will unite. The commonly-enunciated goals of "educated person," "liberation," and "salvation" have for Catholic schools specific meanings which are in many ways unique.

Curriculum

Goals are reflected in and implemented by the curriculum. The two major qualities that differentiate the Catholic-school curriculum from others are the importance it openly accords to religion and its unique presentation of values. The Catholic school's inclusion of the Roman Catholic religion is unabashedly and without question or doubt a contribution not only to its students, but also to the community and the nation. The question of how best to present religion in the curriculum, however, is not simple. Some schools are of the opinion that religion should permeate the entire curriculum. Others view their parish schools as part of the entire faith community, into which religious curricula should be integrated. Still others prefer to view the integrity of each subject, including religion, on its own merits, with its own academic criteria.

---

[1]These and other statistics in this section are from Frank H. Bredeweg and Bruno V. Manno, eds. *United States Catholic Elementary and Secondary Schools 1983-1984: A Statistical Report on Schools, Enrollment, and Staffing* (Washington, DC: National Catholic Educational Association, 1984).

The values taught in the Catholic school are especially important (again to the community and nation) in our time of crisis for their absence. Values originate with God by way of such revelation as the New Testament, with our neighbor broadly considered, and with ourselves. Catholic theories differ from others with regard to the imparting and acquiring of values, as well as in the specific values they prize and cherish. But, as with religion, the method of including values in the curriculum can be complicated.

Students

The end, purpose and center of the Catholic-school enterprise is the student. Since the time of Jesus, who showed a reverence and a solicitude for the human person never shown before or since, Catholics see the person, and hence the student, as having a dignity greater than all the rest of God's vast creation. In a good Catholic-school setting, students experience their dignity as persons before they know its definition. Catholic schools consider the person as the image and glory of God.

Catholic schools admit, embrace and work with those the Bible calls the *anawim,* the voiceless, powerless and unacceptable in society: "whatever you did for one of the least brothers of mine, you did for me" (Mat. 26:40). This embrace includes the underprivileged of all faiths and of none; women, with whom Jesus allowed his radical conduct to become public knowledge; and non-Catholic students, before whom the Church allows her teaching to speak for itself.

Catholic-school success with the *anawim* in inner-city schools is beyond dispute.[1] James S. Coleman and Andrew Greeley provide statistical evidence to show, for example, that Catholic high schools are more economically effective than are government high schools, and that students of Catholic high schools reach superior academic achievement.[2] The data show that among the motives for sending children to Catholic schools are the desire for a disciplined environment and the wish for children to secure moral and religious values.

Catholic schools have been enrolling an increasing number of non-Catholic students.[3] Much of this is the Church's contributions to Blacks. Also, a small "new immigration," mostly to cities, has comprised such Catholic minorities as Puerto Ricans and Mexicans. Varying degrees of success have been determined in part by the fact that Christian doctrine turns off some ethnic groups and is culturally acceptable to others. For example, the Black, Indian and Oriental races have not historically embraced the Catholic religion, while the Spanish have.

What raises people to their highest dignity is grace, the call to share in God's own nature. That grace is of the supernatural order does not make it

---

[1] There are, for example, studies by James S. Coleman, Thomas Hoffer, and Sally Kilgore; also those of Andrew Greeley. See Andrew Greeley, "Catholic High Schools: An Effective Inner-City Ministry," *National Catholic Reporter,* August 31, 1984, pp. 11-12.

[2] Cincy Currence, "A 'Catholic Schools Effect' Is Reaffirmed by Its Champions, Coleman and Greeley," *Education Week,* Vol. IV, No. 11 (November 14, 1984), pp. 1 and 11.

[3] *The New York Times,* September 6, 1984, p. B3.

something added to the top of nature like cream on milk, but the sacred and the natural permeating each other, intertwined organically like spring rain in the earth. The life of grace is therefore an aspect of the education which Catholic schools provide their students.

Because the individual does not live alone, but coexists with others, there are inevitable individual-community tensions. Isaiah's "Suffering Servant" passage and its New Testament referents remind the Catholic that how to live this phenomenon is exemplified in Jesus: an individual who takes upon himself the sins of the whole world, one who is allied yet alone. Catholic-school students are taught to realize their individuality and separateness from all around them, but at the same time realize their relationship to the universe, to nature and to other people.

An area in which we have a right to look for great things in Catholic schools is discipline. The word is from *discipulus,* which has the same root as the word for a follower of Jesus. More important are the philosophical and theological factors behind discipline, such as the concept of redemption. This means that Catholic schools should look upon their students with high aspirations. In the age-old controversy of the use of fear or love, Machiavelli and his followers opt for fear. Catholic-school teachers inevitably try to choose love, and attempt to help their students understand why.

Catholic schools see psychological insight into the stages of human growth and development (infancy, childhood, pre-adolescence, adolescence and adulthood) as important, because religious growth takes place commensurate with the readiness of each period. Many major psychological theories of individual growth and development admit a connection between Christianity and the personal formation that is education.

Teachers

Catholic schools emphasize the front-line importance of the teacher as one who forms human beings. This can be conceived of as a priestly role as mediator between the learner and the world of reality, or as a transmitter of the best of humankind's heritage, or as a role-model, or as a combination of all these and more. Catholics circumvent the debate over whether teaching is a profession and see in teaching a noble vocation, calling for detachment from self, a commitment that avoids sermonizing, generosity, concern for truth and justice, breadth and depth of vision, habitual spirit of service, fraternal solidarity and total moral integrity. The standards are high and the demands difficult.

Teachers guide youth toward eternal realities, with no one able to tell where the teacher's influence ends. Catholic teachers personify the integration of culture, faith and life. Christ-like, they represent their individual incarnational model. They effectuate a union of the Catholic school with the local church. Historically, they are in the tradition of the New Testament: Jesus the teacher, the apostles' ministry, and St. Paul's inheritance of the Jew's tremendous respect for teaching. They share in the noble tradition of the early Church and in the history of Christianity in their love of learning, desire for God, and preservation of culture and civilization. In the modern period, Vatican Council II and the recent popes convey an awareness of the importance of teachers.

Good Catholic teachers are ethically sensitive. This concerns particularly their obligations to students, to parents, to the community and to colleagues. With their students, Catholic teachers strive not only for a meeting of minds, but for a warm personal relationship. This entails respect, sensitivity, sympathy, concern, some degree of self-revelation, reciprocal dialogue, trust and openness. Good Catholic teachers welcome and encourage opportunities for contact with parents, supplement the education begun in the students' homes, meaningfully cooperate with parents and keep parents informed. They realize their importance to the community, especially the local community of faith. To accomplish all this, they are supportive of colleagues: working together as a team, being active in professional organizations, participating in retreats and being selflessly enthusiastic about continuing education.

To form such high-calibre Catholic-school teachers requires special care. Proper formation is a happy blend of professional training, progress in faith and personal growth. Professional training takes for granted proficient background in such areas as language, art, literature, mathematics and science, and ability in thinking, reasoning and understanding. The formation should be in a wide range of cultural, psychological and pedagogical areas in accordance with the discoveries of modern times.

Superadded for the Catholic teacher is the faith dimension. The Catholic teacher must be alert for opportunities to witness to faith. Prayer, sharing, service, follow-up kindnesses and other exercises inculcate habits of reflection and deepening faith. The personal growth expected of Catholic teachers begins with psychological and spiritual maturity, recognizing the need for a philosophy of life and of education. Conduct is also important, giving students an example of Christian behavior.

Preeminent among Catholic-school teachers is the teacher of religion, the subject area that is the *raison d'etre* of Catholic-schools' existence and the heartpiece of their identity. The qualities that describe all Catholic-school teachers should apply in an outstanding way to religion teachers. For adequacy, religion teachers should have appropriate graduate degrees in the human sciences, but especially in religious pedagogy.

The "master teacher" is the principal. Principals are to be instructional leaders, managers of time and resources, communicators, observers and evaluators of staff, creators of the school's climate and leaders in goal-setting and attainment, school-community relations, discipline and teacher support.

Unfortunately, the short supply of teachers for both the government and non-government sectors has in some places led to the acceptance of substandard qualifications. There has been the relatively new Catholic-school phenomenon of strikes. And Catholic-school teachers have sometimes absorbed, at times from secular training, the very positions and attitudes which historically inspired sacrifices for establishing and maintaining Catholic schools: empiricism, for example, and relativism, form over substance and process over content, a predilection for "methods" courses, solipsism, naturalism, materialism and positivism. At times they have even unwittingly reflected some of these positions in their teaching.

Lay teachers have come to hold almost the same majority that religious sisters, brothers and priests held in the 1960's. Overall, this has not resulted in any less Catholicity, despite the misgivings of some parents. In a 1984 study of the

National Catholic Educational Association, in most areas lay teachers were not found to be dramatically different from religious-community teachers, and all were more religiously committed than the average Catholic.[1]

Family and Church

The primary agents, co-principals or partners of education are God and the self-activity of the student. The secondary agents are the family, the Church and the state. The nuclear family (married parents and their progeny) comes first not only chronologically, but also in the order of priority. This God-ordained institution, this "domestic church," this basic unit of society, this first school forms the earliest, deepest and most persistent influence on a person's subsequent behavior, value judgments and life decisions. Unfortunately, however, modern times have brought problems. The retreat from the home caused by two working parents and broken marriages has applied to Catholics as well as to others. Also lessening parental involvement in education and schooling are such other current family trends as decreasing parental self-confidence regarding child-rearing, suburban family problems like increasing violence within the family, and an increased variety of family structures.

The family's role and responsibilities have to do with begetting life, not only physical, but also spiritual. Except for cases of neglect, abuse, rejection of children, or any combination of these, parental rights can neither be usurped nor surrendered. The basic element in parents' educational duty is to love, which engenders self-esteem and proper self-love on the part of their children, from which can arise fulfillment of the basic Christian law of love of God and neighbor. The family is to form a loving community of persons, serve life, participate in the development of society and share in the mission of the Church.

Because people follow witnesses more readily than teachers and because children need beacon personalities, Christian parenthood is a serious obligation. Parents should be given training in parenting, in home-school cooperation and, while preserving child autonomy, in ways to bring their children up with religion in a secularist society. The Christian family is at the heart of the Church's mission to exemplify God's love for His children. Because of complications like changing male and female expectations, it is difficult to assign precise roles to fathers and mothers; the area requires more research.

The Church, too, has rights and duties in schooling and education. The Church has rights because people have a spiritual nature as well as a physical one, because of social justice, and because of the need for the complete betterment of human life. Also, education is essentially a religious enterprise, dealing with the basic nature of reality, and a moral enterprise, dealing with forming the "good person," the "good life" and the "good society." The Church's serious duties to schooling are reflected in Church legislation.

In the particular Catholic school, the local Church, parish, religious community, or whoever, is the sponsoring organization in more ways than financial. The local Church is the reason the school came into existence, why the school is rooted in Catholic Christianity and why it remains a Catholic school. The local

[1]*NCEA Notes, Secondary Department*, Vol. 17, No. 1 (September 1984), pp. 3-5.

Church continuously gives the Catholic school the richness of the Christian tradition, exerts its ongoing influence without interfering with its autonomy, is the speculative model of the Christian community and the practical model of the living faith community, interfaces with the school in a way in which the strengths of each minister to the other's weaknesses, and is a wise and compassionate mediator between the school and the Church at large.

The Catholic school, with the complements of the Church, and with no desire for power, wants to educate children toward the most elevated concrete ideal possible: Jesus Christ and his evangelical message.

The State

The State, comprising both society and government plus sovereignty, has true rights in schooling and education. But the State should not be what current circumstances have made it: schooling and education's sole, dominant, or most powerful partner. The confused, chaotic and mutually contradictory decisions of the U.S. Supreme Court contravene the Judeo-Christian historical and philosophical perspective, deny substantive Church participation beyond the right of Church-school existence, make possible government monopoly over schools, and prevent meaningful parental choice.

The Catholic Church favors true choice, because it avoids any suggestion that the child is the mere creature of the State, avoids any debasing ideology which can turn schools into instruments of political power, is a right due to parents in distributive justice, and provides to all human beings the fundamental right to their own culture. True choice fosters satisfaction, involvement and enrichment; it is inherently instructive. Through its market influences it can help teachers and administrators; substitute parental love for State custodial care; communicate to children the State's endorsement of their parents: and provide decision-making ability, already possessed by the rich, to the poor.

But to achieve the real possibility of true choice, the financial difficulties of non-government schools have become so overpowering as to require requests for further assistance from the State. Aside from currently existing public-parochial schools, the two most widely-proclaimed methods of providing such assistance for true choice in schooling are vouchers and tuition-tax credits. Vouchers in this sense are certificates given to parents to pay for tuition or other costs at any eligible government or non-government school, religious or secular, within or outside the student's school district. Tuition-tax credit is a procedure whereby income-tax-paying parents receive a credit from their income tax for an agreed-upon amount for each of their children's tuition, no matter what school their children attend, and non-income-tax-paying poor parents receive an enabling fee for the same purpose.

On the federal level, the legislative branch seems more in touch with the grass roots of the country than does the judiciary. But countering the good will that often exists in legislatures has been hostile prejudice from pressure groups like the government-school "Establishment." This prejudice has not, however, been from the total population, where polls show that the people more and more favor Catholic schooling, though not understanding completely what Catholics schools are about, perhaps indicating a need for better Catholic-school public relations. In the judicial branch, whose philosophy of legal Realism is a merging of Positivism and Utilitarianism, the Supreme Court's mystifying inconsistency continues. Some scholars interpret current tendencies to be in the direction of an "accommodation principle" to religion.[1]

As in the adage that "he who pays the piper calls the tune," questions remain about government aid to non-government schools. How much government interference would be tolerable? Some of the areas in which non-government schools in general, and Catholic schools in particular, want to retain control are the determination of their own philosophy, the design of their curriculum, the choice of teachers and teaching materials, and the admission and deportment of students.

Among other arguments given against financial help from the government are that it would undermine government-school support, offer false hope to poor people who are incompetent to avoid entrepreneurial school charlatans, cause loss of Catholic-school identity, possibly decrease Catholic-school volunteerism, unconstitutionally advance religion, and discriminate along racial, ethnic or ideological lines. Among the arguments for government financial help to non-government schools are the American principle of citizen sovereignty, beneficial cooperation and competition among schools, the streamlining of bureaucracy, and the enabling of Catholic and other non-government schools to contribute to a more just society.

At the present time, three values underlie the First Amendment's Establishment Clause: neutrality, religious accommodation and separation. Neutrality means that the government must treat all religions in a similar manner. Accommodation recognizes the inevitability of some contacts between government and religion, as well as the propriety of some of these contacts. Separation seeks to prohibit government from favoring religion over irreligion or vice versa, thus ensuring the integrity of both church and state.

---

[1]*Lynch v. Donnelly*, 52 *Law Week* 4317 (March 6, 1984). This was a controversial 5-4 decision, in which the Supreme Court rendered the surprising decision that the use of tax money for a Christmas nativity scene was permissible. This decision refused to use strict scrutiny standards in assessing the "religious effect" of the crèche. In an important 1983 accommodation decision as applied to schooling, *Mueller v. Allen,* the Court declared constitutional the plan which permitted parents of Minnesota schoolchildren to deduct from their taxes expenses incurred in providing "tuition, textbooks and transportation" for their children. The Court came to see that the "wall" of separation between church and state is a useful metaphor, but is not an accurate description of the reality. The Constitution, the Court saw,

> does not require complete separation of church and state; it affirmatively mandates accommodation, not merely tolerance, of all religions, and forbids hostility toward any. Anything less would require the "callous indifference"...that was never intended by the Establishment Clause.

Mueller V. Allen, 103 S.Ct. 3062 (1983). See also Neal Devins, "The Supreme Court and Private Schools: An Update," *This World* 8 (Spring-Summer 1984), pp. 13-26.

The Court also stressed the positive role that non-government schools play:

> Parochial schools...have provided an educational alternative for millions of young Americans;...afford wholesome competition with our public schools;...relieve substantially the tax burden.... The State has, moreover, a legitimate interest in facilitating education of the highest quality for all children within its boundaries, whatever school their parents choose for them.

Mueller v. Allen, op. cit.

To determine whether a particular statute is constitutional, the Court has developed a three-pronged test: "First, the statute must have a secular legislative purpose; second, its principal or primary effect must be one that neither advances nor inhibits religion; finally, the statute must not foster an excessive government entanglement with religion."[1] If any of these elements is not satisfied, the Court will find the statute unconstitutional. The secular effect and entanglement prongs are especially difficult. Perhaps as part of its new tendency toward the accommodation of religion, the Court has come to note that "the wall of separation that must be maintained between church and state 'is a blurred, indistinct, and variable barrier depending on all the circumstances of a particular relationship'."[2] The tripartite test in particular cases, therefore, seems to resemble more a merely helpful signpost than a set formula.

What to do about government usurpations of individual, family and Church rights involves, at an initial minimum, instruction in the rights of the family and the Church, encouragement of those two partners, and familiarization with the realities of life in our Republic. The last is reflected in a court dictum that says: "The law helps those who help themselves, generally aids the vigilant, but rarely the sleeping, and never the acquiescent."[3] Catholic school proponents have many unused constitutional rights open to them.

Current Problems

Catholic schools are in no way to be considered as the sole answer to the furtherance of Catholic ideals: There are too many other considerations in the picture, like culture, sociology, and history. In Holland, West Germany and France, Catholic schools have for over two generations been relieved of many anxieties by being financially supported by the State,[4] and Catholicism in those countries is confused, lethargic or barely recognizable.

Yet Catholic schools are an important part of the answer. In the current talk about other ways of fulfilling the educational mission of the Roman Catholic Church, no one has come up with a better means than the Catholic school for forming youth. That statement, however, presupposes a school that is aware of its proper identity as Catholic and is trying in a living way to meet ever-changing needs. Such Catholic schools, if they maintain their identity, deserve a measure of effort comparable to the effort of the past.

It may seem to some people, perplexed by the seriousness of current problems, that it would be best to relegate the religious aspect of education to the home and church rather than to the school, and have everybody get behind the

---

[1]*Lemon v. Kurtzman,* 403 U.S. 602 (1971), at 612-613.

[2]*Wolman et al. v. Walter et al.,* 433 U.S. 229 (1977), citing *Lemon v. Kurtzman* at 614.

[3]*Hannan v. Dusch,* Supreme Court of Appeals of Virginia, 154 Va. 356, 379, S.E. 824, 831 (1930).

[4]For the treatment of church-affiliated schools in England, Scotland, Australia, West Germany, France, Belgium, Holland, and the United States, see Sr. Raymond McLaughlin, *The Liberty of Choice: Freedom and Justice in Education* (Collegeville, MN: Liturgical Press, 1979).

government schools and improve them. It is the considered opinion of this writer that that will not work for many reasons. That kind of dichotomy between religion and the rest of life does not harmonize with the nature of the person, of society or of religion. The compartmentalization of life is not possible from any academically respectable anthropological, sociological, psychological or other viewpoint. The child comes away from that kind of situation thinking that religion is a *solely* private and personal affair, with no social consequences or significance.

Further, omitting religion from the school gives the child the impression that religion is unimportant, all the important items being covered by the school curriculum. That kind of education is superficial and gives short shrift to providing insights into the meaning of life. In the long run that procedure would be harmful to the country at large. And it lacks the challenge and friendly competition (as well as the cooperation and interaction) that any large enterprise like the government-school Establishment and the church-affiliated-school pattern need for their betterment.

CONCLUSION

In addition to financial benefits to the citizenry, the equal and open existence of Catholic schools offers advantages to the State, individuals, society and human activity. The schools offer an educational alternative for youth; provide wholesome competition with government schools; facilitate high-quality education; can be a source of commitment, direction and vigor to the community of humankind; offer to human activity a proper and beneficial mean between otherworldly faith and immersion in earthly endeavors, and between the faith which many profess and the practice of their daily lives; and foster and elevate all that is true, good and beautiful in the human community. For individuals, they offer meaning to life, teachings that elevate the dignity of human nature, proclamations of the rights of humankind, and a presentation of truths of the moral order.

Because history, philosophy, psychology, politics, sociology and other disciplines have consistently shown Catholic schools to be of singular benefit to our nation, and current circumstances are making it more difficult for them to continue, C.S. Lewis' statement on another matter could have been written of this predicament:

> Such is the tragi-comedy of our situation —we continue to clamor for those very qualities we are rendering impossible.... We laugh at honour and are shocked to find traitors in our midst. We castrate and bid the geldings be fruitful.[1]

---

[1] C.S. Lewis, *The Abolition of Man* (New York: Macmillan Co., 1955), p. 35.

CHAPTER TEN

Changing and Remaining the Same:
A Look at Higher Education*

Philip Gleason
University of Notre Dame

The expression "identity crisis" has pretty well passed out of fashion. We hear it much less often than we did a few years ago. Yet the concern Catholic educators feel about maintaining the distinctive religious character of their schools suggests that the problem it designates is still very much with us. And one can confidently predict that it will remain, for what psychologist Erik Erikson had in mind when he coined the expression is a perennial paradox: how to change without becoming completely different; how to remain the same without stultifying oneself by losing touch with changing reality.[1]

Erikson was of course primarily concerned with identity as a personal problem. But he was also deeply interested in history, and paid careful attention to it in analyzing issues related to identity. That should not really be surprising (although it probably seems so) for the interaction of continuity and change is what history is all about. And to bring continuity and change into balance is to negotiate an identity crisis. That being the case, it seems reasonable to inquire whether the past history of Catholic higher education in this country may not afford useful perspectives on the problem of continuity and change as it presents itself to us today.

In seeking to show that history can enrich our understanding of the problem, I will be speaking of continuity in terms of *tradition,* and change in terms of *adaptation.* The first part of the discussion points out that tradition and adaptation are so closely intertwined as to be almost inseparable. The second and third parts identify two periods in which the pace of change was intense enough to justify speaking of them as crises. The conclusion offers some brief comments on Americanization as an overall perspective on the subject.

THE INTERLINKAGE OF TRADITION AND ADAPTATION

For most of us, "traditional" usually means what we remember of former times. That doesn't really carry us back very far; hence it is not surprising that some of our "traditions" are of quite recent vintage. Most people, for example, are taken aback when told that only three Catholic colleges in the country offered an academic major in religion in 1937, and they are even more astonished to

---

[1]For the concept of identity and its vogue, see my article, "Identifying Identity: A Semantic History," *Journal of American History* 69 (March 1983), pp. 910-931.

*Permission has been granted to reprint this article which was given as a lecture in the Georgetown Bicentennial Series, October 27, 1987, and subsequently published in *Current Issues in Higher Education,* Summer, 1989.

learn that teaching theology to undergraduates was not seriously proposed until two years later.[1]

In fact, tradition is being modified almost continuously, and adaptations quickly merge with older ways and soon become an indistinguishable part of the tradition they modified. Once stated the point is obvious. It will be worthwhile, however, to give a few examples to indicate how pervasively the novelty of American circumstances required adaptations that soon became part of the customary pattern. The experience of the teaching orders that played so crucial a role in the history of Catholic higher education in this country illustrates how flexible "tradition" could be in this regard.

Consider the case of the preeminent teaching order, the Jesuits. In Europe, where their schools were supported by endowments, they charged no tuition. In this country, schools had to be self-supporting, and the Jesuits found it impossible to continue the European tradition of free education. Although the Americans had trouble convincing their superiors in Rome, they were at length (in 1833) given permission to charge tuition in their schools, and thereafter took such an arrangement for granted.[2]

The absence of fixed endowments, and the fact that they existed in a religiously pluralistic society in which Catholics formed at first a tiny minority, likewise dictated that Jesuits and all other teaching communities of men and women accept non-Catholic students. Until the middle of the nineteenth century it was not at all unusual for Protestants to constitute a third to a half of the student body in Catholic colleges and academies, a fact that doubtless seems surprising to those who assume the early colleges were founded simply to "protect the faith" of Catholic youngsters.[3]

Because of the popular demand for education, religious communities found schools and colleges the ideal means for establishing a toe-hold, an institutional base from which they could derive support, recruit new members and expand their operations. Thus education played a crucial role in the development of religious communities in this country, even if that was not the work for which they were primarily founded. The Vincentians, for example, were drawn into collegiate education almost immediately on arriving in Missouri in 1818, and found it impossible to withdraw even though many in the community regarded it as a departure from their real mission.[4]

---

[1]Philip Gleason, *Keeping the Faith: American Catholicism Past and Present* (Notre Dame, IN: University of Notre Dame Press, 1987), pp. 143-147.

[2]Gilbert J. Garraghan, *The Jesuits of the Middle United States,* (New York: American Press, 1938), Vol. I, pp. 303-308.

[3]One of the first colleges to follow a "Catholics only" policy was Holy Cross. Its doing so was used as an argument against it by those who opposed its being granted a charter by the Massachusetts Legislature in 1949. See Walter J. Meagher and William J. Gratton, *The Spires of Fenwick: A History of the College of the Holy Cross 1843-1965* (New York: Vantage Press, 1966), pp. 50ff.

[4]See Frederick J. Easterly, *The Life of the Rt. Rev. Joseph Rosati, C.M.* (Washington: Catholic University of America Press), p. 141. According to a forthcoming history prepared by the editorial staff of the Vincentian Studies Institute, the feeling that colleges interfered with the Vincentians' principal works

The Christian Brothers furnish a particularly interesting example of the interaction of tradition and adaptation and the complications that could result. In Europe, the Brothers did not teach Latin because mastery of that language was a mark of upper-class status, and their founder, John Baptist de la Salle, intended them to teach the poor. In the United States, however, they taught all comers (of the male sex); and since secondary schools or colleges couldn't be taken seriously if they didn't teach Latin, the Brothers taught that too. They did, that is, until 1900 when headquarters in France *required* them to stop doing so. The French superiors, who looked at matters from the European perspective, regarded what was really a matter of educational democraticization as an indication that the American Brothers had betrayed their community's commitment to the lowly.[1]

In terms of organizational structure the great adaptation was the long, slow and painfully achieved transformation of the Catholic college understood as a *Gymnasium*, that is, a school combining both secondary and (what we call) collegiate studies, into two separate institutions, namely, an American-style high school and an American-style college. It is a complicated story. Here I will simply assert the following: 1) Catholic colleges started out as *Gymnasia*; 2) they began making adjustments almost at once; but 3) the changeover was not completed until the first quarter of the twentieth century.

More or less the same is true of curricular content. Catholic educators began with an ideal of the prescribed classical curriculum and tried to realize it in practice. They had to bow to realities from the first, however, for in the nineteenth century only a small minority of their students (probably under ten percent) finished the classical course and received the A.B. degree. The Jesuits, whose commitment to the classics seemed an essential element of their heritage, were particularly troubled by the curricular compromises they had to make. They held their noses while offering the "commercial course" in the nineteenth century, only giving in to "electivism," and the departmental system that accompanied it, around the first World War. Writing in the 1960's, Robert I. Gannon, S.J., formerly president of Fordham, still remembered the new approach being spoken of as "the depart from the mental system."[2]

THE CRISIS OF INSTITUTIONAL MODERNIZATION

The changes that Father Gannon referred to were part of the first of two crises of adaptation. It took place between 1900 and 1925, primarily in the areas

(seminary education and giving missions) persisted well into the twentieth century.

[1]The best introduction to this curious episode, and its considerable literature, is Ronald Eugene Isetti, "Americanization, Conflict and Convergence in Catholic Higher Education in Late Nineteenth-Century California," in Carol Guarneri and David Alvarex, eds., *Religion and Society in the American West: Historical Essays* (Lanham, MD: University Press of America, 1987), pp. 333-352.

[2]Robert I. Gannon, *Up to the Present: The Story of Fordham* (Garden City, NY: Doubleday, 1967), p. 106. Still the best overview of this process is Miguel A. Bernad, "The Faculty of Arts in the Jesuit Colleges in the Eastern Part of the United States: Theory and Practice (1782-1923)" (Ph.D. dissertation, Yale University, 1951).

of organizational structure and curriculum. Those who opposed the changes regarded what was going on as *secularization,* and in a sense it was. But toward
the end of the period, the Catholic "identity" of the colleges and universities was
given a more elaborate articulation through the adoption of Neo-scholasticism as
the official philosophy of Catholic education.

Space does not permit anything like a full discussion of these changes, or of
the larger realignment in American education of which they were a part. Let me
simply list some of the most important.

1. Socially, the most obvious change was the vast enlargement of the
clientele, including women. There were only three or four Catholic schools for
women offering college-level work in 1900. By 1930, forty-five women's colleges were accredited by the NCEA, while twenty-nine more were still too new
to have gained accreditation. The first steps toward co-education took place in
this era, and between 1899 and 1926 the total number of collegiate, professional
and graduate students in Catholic institutions increased seven-fold (from 6,500 to
46,000).[1]

2. Professional education likewise expanded tremendously in this era. The
term "professional" should be understood here as including not only law,
medicine and dentistry, but also vocationally-oriented programs in engineering,
pharmacy, journalism, music and education. The last-named, education, was especially important since it was intimately linked to the rapid multiplication of
women's colleges, and also to the beginnings of graduate education in Catholic
institutions. Except at the Catholic University of America, graduate study in
Catholic schools was confined mainly to masters-degree work until after World
War II.

3. With respect to undergraduate studies, the great change was the definitive
separation of secondary from collegiate instruction, that is, the rejection, at long
last, of the *Gymnasium*-derived structure. Since prep-level students still outnumbered "true collegians" by about two-to-one on the eve of World War I, this
was a wrenching adjustment for Catholic colleges, and a number of them did not
survive it.

"Standardization" was the term most often applied to these changes at the
time.[2] It involved the differentiation of collegiate and secondary studies on the
basis of college-admission standards expressed in high school "units," a
quantitative measure of study-time that came into use between 1900 and 1910.
The analogous measuring-stick on the college level, introduced just a little later,
was the "semester hour" or "credit." A "standard college" was thus defined as an

[1]For overall statistics, see "Report on the Attendance at Catholic Colleges and
Universities in the United States," *Catholic Educational Association Bulletin* 12
(August 1916), pp. 5-19; "Report of the Commission on Standardization," *ibid.,*
23 (November 1926), pp. 87-123; for women's colleges, see Mary J. Oates,
Higher Education for Catholic Women: An Historical Anthology (New York: Gar-
land, 1987); for coeducation, William P. Leahy, "Jesuits, Catholics and Higher
Education in Twentieth-Century America" (Ph.D. dissertation, Stanford University,
1986), ch. 3.
[2]This is discussed briefly in my essay, "American Catholic Higher Education: A
Historical Perspective," in Robert Hassenger, ed., *The Shape of Catholic Higher
Education* (Chicago: University of Chicago Press, 1967), esp. pp. 36-39, 44-46.

institution that accepted students who had completed sixteen high-school "units" and gave them a degree after they had been exposed to 120 semester hours of college work. Other "standards" dealt with such matters as the academic preparation needed by college teachers, the minimum number of departments a college should have, library holdings, laboratory equipment and value of endowment.

Standardization of this kind was made necessary when the old classical curriculum was displaced by the rise of new fields of study. As new subjects proliferated and became more specialized, and as specialization was extended to students through the elective principle, it became harder to specify what a college education should include. In the absence of any consensus as to content, the standardizing bodies (more familiar to us as accrediting agencies) in effect said it didn't matter *what* subjects one studied so long as one studied them long enough in institutions that met agreed-upon "standards" in respect to procedures, personnel and facilities.

The standardizing movement gave secondary and collegiate education its modern framework, the shape we take so much for granted that we assume it was always there. The reformers who championed standardization in Catholic institutions performed an invaluable service. That they encountered great resistance is understandable since traditionalists regarded it as sheer surrender to materialistic secularism and a betrayal of the Catholic liberal arts heritage that integrated true humanism and the true faith.

The critics were not, of course, wholly wrong. In the 1930's they were joined by Abraham Flexner, Robert Hitchins and Mortimer Adler in their flaying of the superficiality and crass vocationalism that electivism and quantitative standardization permitted. Their most telling criticisms centered on the breakdown of curricular coherence which, for Catholics, also implied a failure to integrate faith and learning as adequately as the classical curriculum had done. Widespread uneasiness over this problem was one of the factors that led Catholic educators to take up the teaching of neo-scholasticism philosophy so fervently in the 1920's.[1]

It is true that the "Scholastic Revival" had already been under way for more than a half-century, and I do not mean to imply that Thomism was not studied until after World War I. But it was only in the 1920's that neo-scholasticism became a real school philosophy, a system of thought that was taught to undergraduates on a mass basis as the "official" philosophy of the Catholic Church. Although they are obviously not the whole story, three features of the higher educational scene played a role in this development: 1) the tremendous expansion and growth already sketched; 2) the institutional modernization that introduced specialized departments of philosophy where more professionalized teachers held forth in required courses extending over twelve credit hours or more; and 3) the aforementioned uneasiness over the loss of curricular unity and the need to find a new way of integrating faith and knowledge.

---

[1]For a revealing contemporary statement, see James A. Burns, "Position and Prospects of the Catholic College," *National Catholic Educational Association* 24 (November 1927), pp. 128-140. See also Gleason, "Neo-scholasticism as Preconciliar Ideology," *U.S. Catholic Historian* 7 (Fall 1988), p. 408.

Neo-scholasticism, and the broader intellectual and cultural revival of which it was the central element, thus articulated a Catholic worldview within which institutionally modernized Catholic colleges and universities prospered from the 1920's through the 1950's. In other words, *tradition was reinforced on the ideological level, even while adaptation was avidly pursued on the organizational level.*

This kind of situation obviously entailed tensions, which became more intense after World War II, as overall enrollments surged and graduate work expanded dramatically. The controversy over Catholic intellectual life set off by Monsignor John Tracy Ellis' famous blast in *Thought* (Autumn, 1955) testified to the seriousness of the strains.[1] Knowing what happened next, we are tempted to think that everyone should have been prepared for fundamental readjustments on the ideological level. The fact is, however, that when they came in the 1960's, those changes took everyone by surprise, and we have not yet figured quite how to accommodate them. This brings me to the second crisis of change.

THE CRISIS OF IDEOLOGICAL MODERNIZATION

The crisis of ideological modernization is part of the present moment. Its beginnings date back more than a quarter of a century, and are quite remote from the experience of the younger faculty in Catholic colleges, not to mention the students, to whom Vatican II is hardly less "historical" than Trent. To such persons, it might seem extravagant to characterize as a "crisis" what they are apt to regard as long overdue reforms, attended, in their coming, by pleasantly exhilarating episodes of righteous militance. The "Catholic identity" issue, which emerged in the middle 1960's, did (and still does) represent a real crisis. It is a crisis because it required Catholic institutions to decide whether they wish to remain Catholic, and if they do, to devise new ways to operationalize that decision.

What are some of the changes whose combined effects add up to crisis? Most obvious are the structural, curricular and disciplinary changes (such as the shift to lay boards of trustees, the reduction or elimination of course requirements in religion and philosophy, and the relaxation of *in loco parentis*) which eroded the "traditional" religious identity and atmosphere of Catholic institutions. But these changes flow from deeper shifts in the realm of ideas and values. They are really byproducts of the more fundamental crisis of ideological modernization.

The nature of that crisis can be put in a nutshell by saying that a working consensus no longer exists among Catholic academics and administrators about what it means, in intellectual terms, to be a Catholic and about how Catholic faith should influence the work one does as a scholar and teacher.

I do not mean that they have all given up on these matters. The point, rather, is that disagreement, uncertainty and confusion abound. Some, of course, *have* given up. It would be idle to deny that the faculties of Catholic institutions include a considerable proportion who are indifferent to the preservation of

---

[1] John Tracy Ellis, "American Catholics and the Intellectual Life," *Thought* 30 (Autumn 1955), pp. 551-588. See also Gleason, *Keeping the Faith*, pp. 71-78.

their school's religious character, and a smaller percentage who are discreetly unsympathetic to that goal. Many others, however, are still actively committed to the ideal of relating faith and learning, both in their personal teaching and by means of curricular programs. The trouble is that conservatives, moderates, progressives and radicals disagree deeply about how these things are to be done. What is worse, they often suspect each other of bad faith. The resulting climate of confusion and mistrust nourishes the kind of superficial cynicism to which it sometimes seems academics are naturally predisposed, and which itself becomes a factor in the situation because it encourages people to say "a plague on all your houses" and join the ranks of those who have given up on the whole project.

It is in my view, which I cannot develop in detail here, that the collapse of neo-scholasticism played a key role in these developments. Ideas, intellect, truth: these are the very crux of higher education. And whatever one may think of its intrinsic validity, neo-scholastic philosophy and theology functioned for two generations before the Council as the agreed-upon Catholic system for reconciling the claims of faith and reason, establishing the rational grounding for religious claims, and articulating the implications of faith in the areas of personal morality (e.g., natural law teaching on birth control), social ethics (e.g., subsidiarity and the common good), even international relations (e.g., just war teaching).[1] Neo-scholasticism, in other words, constituted the *intellectual foundation* which the Catholic identity of Catholic institutions of higher education rested on in the half-century before the Second Vatican Council.

Neo-scholasticism no longer functions that way, and nothing has taken its place. The only thing that even looks like a candidate is peace-and-justice education.[2] That approach is closely linked to newly emerging trends in theology, but whether it will furnish an adequate base for a distinctive Catholic presence in American higher education remains to be seen. We are thus, as I see it, still in the midst of the crisis of ideological modernization. Rather than speculate on how it will develop in the future, I will conclude with a few very general comments about the way tradition and adaptation have interacted over the long haul.

I want to propose that *Americanization* constitutes the most useful perspective on the subject. Since adjustment to the local environment meant adapting to American circumstances, that might seem a tautology. To give it more concrete content, let us consider three very American principles that have shaped the adaptations made by the colleges.

1. *Democratization* changed the relationship of the schools to the clientele, as illustrated by the examples of the Jesuits' charging tuition and the Christian Brothers' teaching Latin. Democratization was also at work in the extension of higher education to women. The elective principle was interpreted as a democratization of studies, and in recent years faculty participation in governance has been linked with democratic ideal.

---

[1] The same general argument is sketched in my *Keeping the Faith,* pp. 172-176.
[2] For evidence of a conscious effort to develop this rationale, see David M. Johnson, ed., *Justice and Peace Education: Models for College and University Faculty* (Maryknoll, NY: Orbis Books, 1986), esp. pp. v-vi.

2. *Freedom* is another cornerstone value. One of its less obvious implications is voluntaryism: the principle that people are free to launch their own endeavors and carry them forward by their own efforts. That is, to a considerable extent, the key to the whole activity of Catholic higher education in this country, including the "proliferation" of Catholic colleges and universities, which critics have so often lamented, without, apparently, perceiving how proliferation is connected with freedom and voluntaryism. A more recent, and more positively evaluated, example of freedom's influence is the new concern for academic freedom that has established itself in Catholic institutions in the past two decades.

3. *Secularity, or religious neutrality,* is the last of the American principles that have affected Catholic higher education. In its practical working out, secularity/neutrality tended to become *secularization,* understood here as that separation of religion from social and political life which has expanded outward from the constitutional separation of church and state to include many other areas of life which were earlier thought of as falling within the purview of the churches. As the state expanded into these areas, the churches withdrew or at least attenuated their involvement. In higher education this development occurred in the pace-setting institutions between 1880 and 1910. Catholics, although quite hostile to the secularizing tendency through the 1950's, have become much more sympathetic in the past quarter century. This shift is part of the rethinking of church/world relationships since the Second Vatican Council. In higher education, the changeover to lay boards of trustees parallels the juridical "secularization" that took place when clergymen were displaced from the boards of leading Protestant institutions around the turn of the century.

Assuming that this makes clear what I meant in calling Americanization the most useful perspective on the kind of adaptations Catholic colleges and universities have made, it remains only to say what I think about it. Let me conclude with two observations.

The *first* is that these factors, forces, tendencies, principles (whatever one wishes to call them) will continue to act upon our colleges and universities and will, therefore, have to be dealt with.

The *second* is that while I regard them, and Americanization *in globo,* as good things, I do not regard democratization, freedom and secularity/neutrality as the kind of good things of which it is impossible to have too much, and which are to be favored everywhere and under all circumstances. Rather they should be seen as part of our heritage: an important part, since we are *American* Catholic educators. But all parts of that heritage, and contemporary needs as well, must be balanced against each other as we endeavor to do justice to both continuity and change in negotiating the still-continuing crisis of identity.

CHAPTER ELEVEN

American Catholic Sexual Ethics, 1789-1989
Leslie Griffin
University of Notre Dame

In his 1785 description of American Catholicism, John Carroll reported that:

> The abuses that have grown among Catholics are chiefly those, which result with unavoidable intercourse with non-Catholics, and the examples thence derived: namely more free intercourse between young people of opposite sexes than is compatible with chastity in mind and body; too great fondness for dances and similar amusements; and an incredible eagerness, especially in girls, for reading love stories which are brought over in great quantities from Europe.[1]

Carroll's text illustrates a number of concerns of American Catholic sexual ethics from 1789 until the twentieth century. As Catholics worked out their relationship to the new United States, they struggled to live and to interpret a Catholic sexual ethic amid the mores of the general non-Catholic public. Throughout these centuries, a constant worry of Catholic clergy and hierarchy was that Catholics would be corrupted by their association with those outside the faith. "Keeping company" with non-Catholics, e.g., in their dances, festivities and amusements, or in dating or marriage, might undermine appropriate moral standards for Catholic youth and adults.

The history of American Catholic sexual ethics is of course part of a larger story, in which Catholics have struggled to be at the same time loyal Americans and loyal Catholics. In the field of Catholic sexual ethics, a division between American and Catholic interpretations of sexuality erupts after the Second Vatican Council; up to that point, the story is one of basic continuity in teaching an ethic whose content remains fairly constant from 1789 to 1965.

In the later eighteenth century, and in the early years of the nineteenth century, the official Catholic sexual ethic clearly identified heterosexual marriage as the sole appropriate locus for sexual activity, and heterosexual marriage between Catholics as the norm. American Catholic sexual ethics arose from European interpretations of sexuality. In the eighteenth and nineteenth centuries, European moral theology consisted primarily of moral manuals. These manuals were rooted in the writings of Hermann Busenbaum and Alphonsus Liguori, and served primarily to guide confessors in the sacrament of penance. As such, their purpose was to explore the level of sinfulness of certain actions.[2]

---

[1] *Documents of American Catholic History,* John Tracy Ellis, ed. (Wilmington: Michael Glazier, 1987), Vol. I, p. 149.
[2] See Hermann Busenbaum, *Medulla Theologiae moralis* (Munster, 1650); Alfonso Maria de Liguori, *Theologia moralis,* 3 vols. (Bassani: Suis Typis Remondini Edidit, 1822).

A perceived strength of these manuals was precisely their lack of originality. New manuals were necessary over time which could include the pressing questions arising in later ages. Yet a similarity in format, style and content persists among these manuals. Continuity rather than innovation is the hallmark of Catholic sexual ethics.

Francis P. Kenrick, Archbishop of Baltimore, wrote the first American manual of moral theology, *Theologia Moralis,* in 1841, in imitation of the Liguori approach. Kenrick wrote his volumes because the seminary students were in need of texts responsive to the American context. In France, Jean Gury's *Compendium Theologiae Moralis* (1850) also reproduced Liguori's basic organization and style of argumentation, and became an important source for American moral theology. It was updated in 1865, and was revised again by Antonio Ballerini. The Gury manual was the standard for the *Compendium Theologiae Moralis* of Aloysius Sabetti, an American Jesuit who taught moral theology at Woodstock. Sabetti's volumes (later edited by Timothy Barrett) became one of the standard manuals used in seminaries throughout the United States. Both Kenrick and Sabetti employed American and English legal sources, including non-Catholic sources. Both tomes were used during the nineteenth century.[1]

John Noonan argues that Gury (in 1869) is the first moral theologian to mention love as a rational purpose for marital coitus. Peter Gardella, however, in *Innocent Ecstasy: How Christianity Gave America an Ethic of Sexual Pleasure,* states that Noonan is only "formally correct"; Kenrick anticipates Gury by 26 years. Kenrick opens his section on marriage with a discussion of love. Gardella attributes this to the American context of Kenrick's writings; given the constant migration life in the United States, Gardella believes that personal love is especially important in the American context. Gardella asserts: "Until the 1920's, no Catholic moralist equaled Kenrick in relating sex to a larger pattern of marital behavior centered on love."[2]

Gury, Sabetti-Barrett, and Kenrick are in agreement on certain fundamentals in sexual ethics. Sexual ethics is treated in certain key locations in the manuals: under the sixth and ninth commandments, under the sacrament of matrimony,

---

[1]For the history of the use of manuals in American Catholic moral theology, see the fine article by John P. Boyle, "The American Experience in Moral Theology," in Catholic Theological Society of America, *Proceedings of the Forty-First Annual Convention* 41 (1986), pp. 23-46; Paul McKeever, "75 Years of Moral Theology in America," *American Ecclesiastical Review* 152 (1965), pp. 17-32; David F. Kelly, *The Emergence of Roman Catholic Medical Ethics in North America: An Historical-Methodological-Bibliographical Study* (New York: The Edwin Mellen Press, 1979). See also Joanne Petro Gury, S.J., *Compendium Theologiae Moralis* (Lyons: J.B. Pelagaud, 1859); *Theologiae moralis [volumina] concinnatae a Francisco Patricio Kenrick,* 3 vols. (Philadelphiae apud Eugenium Cummiskey, 1841-1843; 2nd ed. Mechlin: Dessain, 1860-1861); Aloysius Sabetti, S.J., *Compendium Theologiae Moralis* (Ratisbon: Fr. Pustet, 1897; rev. ed., 1906, 1924). References to sexual ethics in the manuals can be found in sections on the sixth and ninth commandments and on the sacrament of matrimony.
[2](New York: Oxford, 1985), p. 23. See John T. Noonan, Jr., *Contraception: A History of Its Treatment by the Catholic Theologians and Canonists* (New York: New American Library, 1967), pp. 583-584.

and (less frequently) under the cardinal virtue of temperance. The sixth and ninth commandments prohibit sins of impurity (in deeds and in thoughts, respectively). As manuals for confessors, the texts identify sexual sins in terms of their gravity. A pivotal argument is that there is no *parvitas materiae*, no small or slight matter, in the sixth and ninth commandments; all sexual sins contain grave matter. Patrick Boyle explains the concept of parvity of matter:

> The manualists classified sin according to the seriousness of the matter. Mortal sins *ex toto genere suo* are sins whose matter is so evil that there is no possible situation in which gravity of the evil can be lessened. The matter is intrinsically evil. Mortal sins *ex genero suo* are sins whose matter can be either serious or light depending upon the circumstances which specify the act. In this category sins within the same species may be moral or venial depending upon the seriousness of the matter....It has been a long established teaching in pre-Vatican II moral theology that the matter in every sexual sin falls into the *ex toto genere suo* category. For centuries moral theologians and the papal magisterium of the Church held that there can be no parvity of matter in sins against the sixth and ninth commandments.[1]

A definition of venereal pleasure often opens the discussion of these commandments. Next, sins of impurity are divided into consummated and non-consummated acts. All sins of impurity are mortal if they are direct and voluntary. They may be venial if indirect or involuntary. (This means that sexual pleasure in marriage and indirect pleasure outside marriage are not necessarily mortal sins.) The consummated sins of impurity are fornication, adultery, incest, rape, abduction and sacrilege. Consummated sins which are in addition against nature are masturbation, sodomy and bestiality. Intentional non-consummated sins of impurity are also mortally sinful. These include a catalogue of touches, looks, reading and conversation, all dangerous, because all could lead to venereal pleasure. The teaching on parvity of matter guarantees that if venereal pleasure, however slight, is willed in these actions they are mortally sinful. Carroll's criticism of dances, love stories and association of young men and women is comprehensible in such a context.

In the sections on marriage, there is a lengthy treatment of the rite of marriage, including, e.g., what counts as an engagement, how to announce the banns, what an impediment is, what a valid marriage is, what the priest's responsibilities are. An additional feature of this section is frequently a discussion of the marital debt, including some analysis of when it is reasonable for spouses to refuse sexual relations (danger of venereal disease, risk to life, unreasonable frequency of demands). Here are also listed the prohibitions of any interference with the proper end of the marital act, namely, of contraception or of "onanism."

In the United States in the nineteenth century, both priests and moral theologians warned that occasions of sins of impurity and dangers to the sacrament of matrimony were posed by the non-Catholic presence. For example, in clerical discussions of the nineteenth century (as evident, e.g., in the *American Ecclesiastical Review*) proper preparation for and participation in marriage are a constant

---

[1]Patrick J. Boyle, S.J., *Parvitas Materiae in Sexto* in *Contemporary Catholic Thought* (Lanham, MD: University Press of America, 1987) pp. 2-3.

concern. The cases of conscience presented and analyzed by priests often focus on the special problem of mixed marriages. These cases of conscience become a familiar forum for discussions of sexual (i.e., marital) activity. In such cases, for example, priests try to resolve whether a baptized person whose first marriage was to a non-baptized person can marry a Catholic, or whether a Catholic and a non-Catholic Christian can wed, or whether Catholics can be bridesmaids in Protestant weddings. Throughout, there are severe warnings against the dangers of mixed marriages as threats to the faith.[1]

These cases of conscience provide an interesting perspective on the moral theology and pastoral guidance of the age. First, it is clearly priests who are to resolve these cases. Sexual and marital cases are presented in Latin, with an explanation that this is the usual procedure and that the cases have international appeal. Moreover, the editors of an early issue of the *American Ecclesiastical Review* explain that they try to limit subscriptions to priests and students of theology.[2] In sexual ethics, there is also concern that certain suggestive materials should not be accessible to lay readers. Second, the style of moral reflection is casuistical, a casuistry which cites the manualists in support of its conclusions. Moreover, it is a casuistry which relies on theological opinions for questions which are open to dispute.[3] Finally, attention is paid to acts and to the sinfulness of certain acts.

Parallel approaches to sexual sin are found in Catholic revival movements of the nineteenth century. According to Jay Dolan, its preachers taught a "rigorous moralism," with drunkenness and *impurity* identified as the two major sins. Preachers (like moralists) had to approach the topic of sexuality with caution: "Whatever the people do not know in reference to this vice...they need not and should not learn from the missionary." The preacher could "express, in two or three sentences, his abhorrence of it, and then dismiss it in disgust, as being too abominable to be treated before a Christian audience."[4] Dolan notes that the dance hall received the harshest criticism; also prohibited were "bad reading," "excursions and picnics, shows and the theatre" and the "company of people of different sexes."[5]

---

[1]Volume I of the *American Ecclesiastical Review* appears in 1889; see also *The Casuist: A Collection of Cases in Moral and Pastoral Theology*, 5 vols. (New York: Joseph F. Wagner, 1906; rev ed. 1924).
[2]"Conferences," *American Ecclesiastical Review* 9 (1983), p. 367.
[3]Probable opinions are clearly important to these authors. See the *New Catholic Encyclopedia* (New York: McGraw-Hill, 1967), articles on "Probabilism" and "Probabiliorism," in vol. 11, pp. 814-815, and on "Equiprobabilism," in vol. 5, pp. 502-503. See also John Mahoney, *The Making of Moral Theology: A Study of the Roman Catholic Tradition* (Oxford: Clarendon Press, 1987), ch. 4.
[4]From Joseph Wissel, *The Redemptorist on the American Missions* (New York: John Ross and Son, 1875), pp. 83-84, cited by Jay P. Dolan, *Catholic Revivalism: The American Experience 1830-1900* (Notre Dame: University of Notre Dame Press, 1978), p. 110. See also Jay P. Dolan, *The American Catholic Experience: A History from Colonial Times to the Present* (Garden City, NY: Doubleday & Co., 1985), p. 227.
[5]*Ibid.*, p. 111.

At the same time, in the eighteenth and nineteenth centuries, the synodal and conciliar legislation of the American Church, in addition to the national pastorals of the American Bishops, demonstrate the resolution of the U.S. hierarchy to defend the indissolubility of marriage and to prevent the dangers of mixed marriages. The longest decree of the first National Synod in 1791 is on the sacrament of matrimony. In addition to a discussion of the banns, and of the marriage rite, there is strong opposition to mixed marriages. "Mixed marriages were to be discouraged as much as possible. The Fathers of the Synod realized how difficult it would be to avoid marriages with non-Catholics, especially in those places where few Catholics resided, but the pastors were urged to exercise every holy influence to prevent these unions."[1] The synodal statement makes some provisions if these marriages should occur: e.g., the children should be raised Catholic, the priests should not be so antagonistic to the marriage that the parties turn to a Protestant minister, the standard wedding blessing cannot be announced.

Councils and pastorals of 1840, 1866 and 1884 condemn such marriages, and there are ringing condemnations of divorce in the 1866 Second Plenary Council. These conclusions are summarized in the Baltimore Catechism (1889) which states that

> The Church does forbid the marriage of Catholics with persons who have a different religion or no religion at all because such marriages generally lead to indifference, loss of faith, and to the neglect of the religious education of the children.[2]

Dolan adds:

> Catholic fiction stressed the peril, especially to children, of such mixed marriages; spiritual guidebooks somberly discussed this 'grave question,' and only in exceptional cases could such a marriage be allowed. Though the numbers did increase during the twentieth century, religiously mixed marriages were not common during the nineteenth century.[3]

A more homely illustration of the opposition of mixed marriages is found in an 1880 issue of a Catholic magazine, *The Ave Maria.* The editors offer a series of letters from the 1854 *Catholic Telegraph,* citing them as "An example of Moral Heroism" rare for this age. A (Presbyterian) fiancé writes to his (Catholic) beloved, asking her to worship with him in a Protestant church, since "in our happy country all religions are alike." (He also adds that the Protestant service will be better for business than the Catholic.) She refuses, saying that she has yielded her heart but not her soul to him, and that she cannot "surrender

---

[1]Peter Guilday, *A History of the Councils of Baltimore, 1791-1884* (New York: Arno Press, 1969), p. 67. See also his *The National Pastorals of the American Hierarchy (1792-1919)* (Washington, DC: National Catholic Welfare Council, 1923).

[2]Third Plenary Council of Baltimore, *Baltimore Catechism, No. 3* (New York: Benziger Brothers, 1885), p. 228.

[3]Dolan, *American Catholic Experience,* p. 228.

God to win a husband."[1] He writes back a more formal letter, requiring that they be married by a minister only; she refuses, and ends the engagement. Such is Catholic heroism in a religiously pluralistic society.

One explanation for the style and substance of Catholic sexual ethics for much of the nineteenth century is that it is the era of the immigrant Church. Dolan estimates that in 1830, there were 318,000 Catholics in the U.S. By 1850, that number had risen to one and one half million; by 1860 to 3,103,000 and by 1890 to close to nine million.[2] Overwhelming numbers of Catholics taxed Catholic clergy, with a severe priest shortage as the outcome. This scarcity resulted in the entrance of foreign priests into the U.S.; moreover, American priests were sent abroad to study, and returned to staff the seminaries. European modes of thought were thus perpetuated in the United States. John Tracy Ellis characterizes the first foreign priests as French and Irish, inheritors of a rigorist, Jansenist tradition, especially in sexual ethics. As the nineteenth century progresses, the Church was "Europeanized." By the mid-nineteenth century, Ellis notes

> so strongly had the textbooks of Roman Jesuits established themselves in American seminaries, that even the works of Francis Patrick Kenrick, then Bishop of Philadelphia, were making a relatively slow progress in spite of the recommendation they had received from the bishops of the Fifth Provincial Council of Baltimore in May, 1843.[3]

Jay Dolan's conclusion is that the Republican movement of the 1790's (American Catholicism's first "romance with modernity") was drowned by the waves of immigrants.[4] Adding to the difficulty of American Catholic relationships is the growth of anti-Catholicism in the United States in response to immigration. Such anti-Catholicism made it easier for Catholics to view "keeping company" with Protestants as corruptive, and to turn with more loyalty to Roman teaching.

By the end of the nineteenth century, however, some significant changes occur. The American Church appears poised to provide intellectual leadership, and another "Catholic romance with modernity" occurs in the 1890's.[5] Robert Cross traces the roots of liberal Catholicism to this era.[6] In moral theology, Thomas Bouquillon, the Belgian-born priest who is the first professor of moral

---

[1]N.A., "A Beautiful Example of Moral Heroism," *The Ave Maria* 16 (1880), pp. 191-192.

[2]Dolan, *Catholic Revivalism*, p. 25.

[3]John Tracy Ellis, "The Formation of the American Priest: An Historical Perspective," in *The Catholic Priest in the United States* (Collegeville: St. John's University Press, 1971), p. 32; see also pp. 19-22. Kenrick writes to his brother that seminaries are not taking his books lest "they appear to hurt the majesty of the city [Rome] by introducing the work of a stranger" (p. 32).

[4]Jay Dolan, "A Catholic Romance with Modernity," *The Wilson Quarterly* 5 (1981), pp. 120-133.

[5]*Ibid.*

[6]Robert D. Cross, *The Emergence of Liberal Catholicism in America* (Cambridge: Harvard University Press, 1958).

theology at Catholic University, questions the traditional role of moral theology in identifying sins, and brings social scientific analysis to his moral theology.[1] Yet the developments do not extend to changes in the field of sexual ethics. The papal condemnations of Americanism and Modernism occur in 1899 and 1907, and the work of many American theologians and clerics is viewed with suspicion. Gerald Fogarty reports,

> With the condemnation of Americanism a new spirit was breathed into the American Church, a spirit of Roman authority and discipline, of loss of American independence and episcopal collegiality. With it also came the stifling of intellectual life in the new nation.[2]

Both Fogarty and Ellis agree that American theology would not be renewed until the 1940's.

In sexual ethics, Peter Gardella argues that by the turn of the twentieth century, American theologians are even more conservative than their European counterparts. By this point, Adolphe Tanquerey, at St. Mary's Seminary in Baltimore, authors what Gardella calls the "second moral theology that drew on American materials and experiences." But this moral theology is "prudery triumphant," according to Gardella, because sexual questions are treated in separately bound volumes, and in the appendix, and not in the central parts of the text as in the past. Moreover, Tanquerey's conclusions are even stricter than those of Liguori.[3] Tanquerey fails to include a section on the sixth and ninth commandments, and even within the section on marriage, Tanquerey omits the usual treatment of the marital debt.

The first moral manual written in English, Thomas Slater's *A Manual of Moral Theology for English-Speaking Countries,* appears in 1908. Yet, the sections which treat sins of impurity remain in Latin. Slater rejects those who argue that moral theology should be a discipline of ideals; it is for confessors, and for discerning sin.[4]

In 1911 the sterilization of criminals and of the mentally defective becomes a pressing question for Catholic moralists, as laws supporting such practices are promulgated in a number of states (the first, in Indiana, in March 1907). There is room for discussion of the issue because theologians find ambiguity in the papal texts. An essential question is: Does the prohibition against direct sterilization apply only to the innocent? John Ryan describes a "discussion which

[1]On Bouquillon, see Cross, *Liberal Catholicism,* pp. 96-98, 142-144; Boyle, "American Catholic," pp. 32-33.
[2]Gerald P. Fogarty, S.J., *The Vatican and the American Hierarchy from 1870 to 1965* (Wilmington: Michael Glazier, 1985), p. 190. On Americanism and Modernism, see also Dolan, *American Catholic Experience,* ch.11; Ellis, "The Formation," pp. 57-74.
[3]Gardella, *Innocent Ecstasy,* p. 37. Gardella attributes this to anti-Catholicism, as well, and argues that Protestant discomfort with discussions of sexuality restricted American Catholic discussions. See A. Tanquerey, *Synopsis Theologiae Moralis et Pastoralis,* 3 vols. (Rome: Desclee, 1908).
[4]Thomas Slater, S.J., *A Manual of Moral Theology for English-Speaking Countries,* 2 vols. (New York: Benziger Brothers, 1912).

involved a dozen writers, twenty-four articles, one hundred and sixty-six pages and more than 62,000 words in the *American Ecclesiastical Review,* vols. 42-27 in the years 1910-1912."[1] Ryan views sterilization as a question of human welfare, and opposes it. It is not intrinsically wrong, but Ryan finds the arguments which support it unpersuasive. His approach to the subject is informative; he clearly identifies this as a subject open to discussion and disagreement. Moreover, he uses an analysis of proportionate good, which takes into account the numbers of persons who have been and will be affected by the problem.

John Ryan is also the earliest American moral theologian[2] to address the new subject of "birth control" in an *American Ecclesiastical Review* article in 1916.[3] On this subject, he says there is "no possibility of a difference of opinion." Again the American influence: Ryan worries that non-Catholics will persuade Catholics that birth control is not sinful, and that many Catholics already use it because they are unaware of its sinfulness. Ryan concedes that "chaste abstention" can be used to limit family size.[4] The 1919 National Pastoral addresses the subject of contraception, arguing that "the selfishness which leads to race suicide with or without the pretext of bettering the species is, in God's sight, 'a detestable thing'."[5] The letter opposes a double standard in sexual ethics, arguing that both men and women must maintain *purity* before marriage. There is also a strong argument against divorce, identifying it as "our national scandal."[6]

William Halsey's *The Survival of Innocence: Catholicism in an Era of Disillusionment, 1920-1940* identifies the era after the First World War as a time of Catholic innocence, an innocence which included a belief that there are clear-cut standards of morality. While Protestant Americans are disillusioned after the war, Catholicism begins to establish itself in American life, in part because of its stable interpretation of life.

> The problem with American innocence and the Catholic involvement with it, however, was the tendency to absolutize answers and narrow premises. In cultural forms it tended to repress the possibility of doubt, preventing moments of healthy unease.[7]

In Catholic sexual ethics, certainties abound. A new moral manual appears in 1929, *Moral Theology* by John McHugh and Charles Callan. McHugh and Callan are critical of manuals which refer too much to theologians' opinions, and prefer to give principles and rules rather than opinions. They argue that moral theology and moral manuals are not just about sin. Instead, they proposed an

---

[1]John A. Ryan, *Moral Aspects of Sterilization* (Washington, DC: National Catholic Welfare Conference, 1930), p. 3.

[2]According to Noonan, *op. cot.,* p. 502.

[3]John A. Ryan, "Family Limitation," *American Ecclesiastical Review* 54 (1916), pp. 684-696.

[4]Ryan also discussed the circumstances under which a wife could refuse intercourse with her husband.

[5]Guilday, *National Pastorals,* p. 313.

[6]*Ibid.,* p. 315.

[7](Notre Dame, IN: University of Notre Dame Press, 1980), p. 7.

ideal understanding, a positive view, of the moral life, in the spirit of Thomas Aquinas. That is, they want to help readers "escape from moral disease and death," but also "to live the life of grace and virtue."[1]

Yet there are only minor changes in sexual ethics, and portions of the text remain in Latin. First, sexual questions are treated under the virtue of temperance, in the section on sins of impurity. The listing of sins remains unchanged, although contraception has moved into the same section with other sexual sins, after pollution. Gardella calls attention to the text which argues that "sex pleasure has been ordained by God as an inducement to perform an act which is both disgusting in itself and burdensome in its consequences." He comments, "Catholic theology fell from the liberality of Kenrick, with his Liguorian tolerance for nature and his personal concern for love, to the repugnance of McHugh in less than a hundred years."[2] Gardella finds this approach more restrictive than that favored by European theologians of the same era, and blames it on the strong Protestant environment surrounding American Catholic sexual ethics.

In the 1940's American theology reawakens; several new sources shed light on sexual ethics in the United States. In 1940, *Theological Studies* commences publication, and includes an annual (sometimes semiannual) feature entitled "Notes on Moral Theology." Throughout the 1940's and 1950's, Jesuits John Lynch, Gerald Kelly, John Ford, John Connery and Joseph Farraher review Catholic moral theological literature, both European and American. In 1946 the Catholic Theological Society of American is founded and its *Proceedings* are published annually. The journals are a record of the multitude of issues that confront moral theologians in the twentieth century. Rhythm and other means of birth control take center stage; other prominent topics include sterility tests, sterilization, courtship and marriage (and proper limits/conditions to them), artificial insemination, the problem of divorce, *amplexus reservatus* (vaginal penetration without orgasm) and *copula dimidiata* (partial vaginal penetration), homosexuality, psychiatry and the Kinsey reports.

In *Theological Studies,* the authors review the opinions of moral theologians on these questions, in which discussion and disagreement can take place among moralists on a number of issues. An article in the first volume of *Theological Studies* discusses sex morality and chastity, reviews the manualist tradition on the subject, and urges avoidance of direct venereal pleasure.[3] Chastity and sex morality, and the delineation of mortal and venial sins in this area, remain a concern of the Jesuit authors in the years following 1940.[4]

---

[1] John A. McHugh, O.P., and Charles J. Callan, O.P., *Moral Theology: A Complete Course,* 2 vols. (New York: Joseph Wagner, 1929; rev. ed., 1958), Vol. 1, p. iv.
[2] Gardella, *op. cit.,* p. 38. McHugh and Callan, pp. 484-565, 596-624. By 1958, McHugh and Callan have revised the text to read: "Now, sex pleasure has been ordained by God as an inducement to perform an act which has for its purpose the propagation and education of children" (p. 518).
[3] Gerald Kelly, S.J., "A Fundamental Notion on the Problem of Sex Morality," *Theological Studies* 1 (1940), pp. 117-129.
[4] See. e.g., John C. Ford, S.J., "Notes on Moral Theology, 1942," *Theological Studies* 3 (1942), pp. 593-598.

Gerald Kelly's 1941 text, *Modern Youth and Chastity*, illustrates the era's sexual ethic. It is a textbook for college students; it thus places the manualist tradition in a broader context, although the basic content has not changed. Sexual expression is appropriate only in the context of marriage. Unmarried Catholics must be wary of any actions which could lead to venereal pleasure. Kelly distinguishes between direct (always unchaste) and indirect (sinful or not according to circumstances) venereal actions. Catholic youth are warned to distance themselves from serious relationships in which there is no possibility of marriage (and from non-Catholics). Young people should act with restraint around members of the opposite sex, and should avoid proximate occasions of sin.

Kelly also includes a traditional formulation of the sixth and ninth commandments. According to the sixth commandment, the following division of sins is employed:

Mortal Sin: a) All directly venereal actions.
b) All other actions performed for the purpose of stimulating or promoting venereal pleasure.
c) All actions involving the proximate danger of performing a directly venereal action or of consenting to venereal pleasure.

Venial Sin: Indirectly venereal actions performed without a relatively sufficient reason.

No Sin: Indirectly venereal actions performed with a relatively sufficient reason.

For the ninth commandment, the following categories apply:

Mortal Sin: a) The *willful approval* of unchaste actions.
b) The willful entertaining of any thoughts *for the purpose of* stimulating or promoting venereal passion.
c) The willful harboring of thoughts which involve the *proximate danger of* performing an unchaste action, or consenting to venereal pleasure.

Venial Sin: Thinking about sexually-stimulating things without a sufficient reason.

No Sin: Thinking about sexually-stimulating things with a sufficient reason.[1]

Modern Youth and Chastity also includes a more positive context for sexuality. Kelly describes friendship, general sexual attraction, personal sexual attraction and physical sexual attraction. He explains what makes a good marriage partner, and connects marriage to sexual attraction and friendship.

Certain gender expectations also figure in Kelly's analysis. Men are attracted to grace, emotional susceptibility, beauty, tenderness; women to strength,

---

[1]Gerald Kelly, S.J., *Modern Youth and Chastity* (St. Louis: The Queen's Work, 1941), pp. 82, 84.

courage, energy and calm deliberation.[1] When he is looking for a wife, a man should ask "Can she cook, and make the house a home? Has she that womanly quality that instinctively puts things in order?"[2] He praises the *Notre Dame Bulletin* story of a man who left a broom on the floor of his room. Five women stepped over it; one picked it up. Kelly concludes: "The wise man proposed [to the sixth]—and there is much to be said for his wisdom."[3]

Given the long history of American Catholic opposition to "keeping company," the *Theological Studies* discussion of this issue in the 1940's and 1950's is of interest. In 1948 Gerald Kelly (writing in agreement with Francis Connell) states: "it is a mortal sin to keep company with a non-Catholic with a view to marriage unless one has good reason to believe that one has or will have before the marriage a justifying cause for entering the union."[4] "Justifying cause" here means reason to believe that the partner will convert, or that a dispensation is possible. By the 1950's, moral theologians are still assessing certain social events. European texts (including Liguori) had limited visits between unmarried persons of the opposite sex and remained critical, for example, of dances. The concern, of course, is that such events may be occasions of sin. While Francis Connell defends such strict standards, John Connery, John Ford and Gerald Kelly disagree. Connery argues that American conditions are different and justify a less strict standard; in the United States, dancing is certainly not an occasion of sin. On this issue, then, the American environment causes moral theologians to distinguish themselves from a European standard.[5] However, "going steady" remains suspicious; while Connell opposes it, Ford and Kelly would prefer to assess it on an individual basis. On the other hand, certain "social" events remain reprehensible; in 1963 Joseph Farraher warns against attendance at non-Catholic weddings; even Catholic parents should not attend a child's wedding outside the Church.[6]

In *Theological Studies* and the *CTSA Proceedings* in the 1940's and 1950's, there are hints of the changes that will occur after the Second Vatican Council. By 1942, the personalism of Herbert Doms is well-known in the U.S., but Francis Connell's rejection of Doms provides occasion for him to reiterate the traditional ranking of the ends of marriage: procreative, primary; unitive, secondary.[7] In 1953 Gerald Gilleman's *The Primacy of Charity in Moral Theology* is assessed, as is Bernard Haring's *The Law of Christ* in 1957-1958. Both

---

[1]*Ibid.,* p. 14.

[2]*Ibid.,* p. 35.

[3]*Ibid.*

[4]"Notes on Moral Theology, 1947," *Theological Studies* 9 (1948), p. 120.

[5]See John C. Ford, S.J., and Gerald Kelly, S.J., *Contemporary Moral Theology, Volume One, Questions in Fundamental Moral Theology* (Westminster, MD: The Newman Press, 1958), ch. 9, for a summary of this discussion. See also John R. Connery, "Notes on Moral Theology," *Theological Studies* 16 (1955), p. 584; Francis J. Connell, C.SS.R., "Juvenile Courtships," *American Ecclesiastical Review* 132 ((1955), pp. 181-190.

[6]"Notes on Moral Theology," *Theological Studies* 24 (1963), pp. 58-59.

[7]Francis J. Connell, C.SS.R., "The Catholic Doctrine of the Ends of Marriage," The Catholic Theological Society of America, *Proceedings of the Foundation Meeting* 1 (1946), pp. 34-45.

Gilleman and Haring wished to expand the purview of moral theology through emphasis on charity and on a Christ-centered life. The leading American moral theologians are cautious about such enterprises, preferring to leave these issues to ascetic and pastoral theology.[1]

Another perspective on the moral theology of the 1950's can be found in a summary of the moral seminar at the Catholic Theological Society of America in 1950. The participants studied seminal tests and artificial insemination. Their overview provides some indication of the act-centered, probabilistic, casu-istic approach to moral theology dominant in this era. For sterility tests, the conclusions run as follows:

> Objectionable methods—masturbation, interrupted intercourse, condomistic intercourse, use of a vaginal sheath or of a contraceptive pessary. Licit to a greater or lesser degree—puncture of testicle, rectal massage, post-coital aspi-ration of vagina, use of a tassette, perforated condom, cloth condom, use of semen accidentally deposited outside of the vagina, as well as of that adhering to penis after intercourse, use of the emission produced during an involuntary pollution, also of the semen found in the male urethra after normal coitus, and lastly the use of a cervical spoon.[2]

A similar listing follows for judging methods of artificial (i.e., assisted) insemi-nation.

The predominant and representative moral text of the 1950's is John Ford and Gerald Kelly's *Contemporary Moral Theology*, volume one (1958) on fun-damental moral questions; volume two (1963) on marriage questions. These volumes incorporate much of the material from Ford and Kelly's "Notes," yet also add original material. They stake out a middle ground approach to morality: They are responsive to contemporary criticisms of past manuals, but they warn against the excesses of new approaches to moral theology. Noteworthy is their tremendous reliance on magisterial teaching; the theologian must not only accept magisterial teaching but also incorporate it into his writing. In addition, they argue that good moral theology requires good casuistry. They retain as well a concern for identifying levels of sinfulness; they include in volume one a

---

[1] Gerald Kelly, "Notes on Moral Theology," *Theological Studies* 14 (1953), pp. 31-38; John R. Connery, "Notes on Moral Theology," *Theological Studies* 18 (1957), p. 562.

[2] The Catholic Theological Society of America, "Summary of the Moral Seminar," *Proceedings of the Fifth Annual Meeting* 5 (1950), p. 157. It is no wonder that James Hennesey, S.J., *American Catholics: A History of the Roman Catholic Community in the United States* (New York: Oxford, 1981), notes of this era: "A Pervasive moralism characterized American Catholics of the 1950's....Moral the-ology, curiously immune to the influence of Christian history and dogma and heavily influenced by the legalistic approach of canonists and the abstractions of scholastic philosophers, dominated the scene. On the popular level, long lines at Saturday afternoon and evening confessions gave impressive witness to the phenomenon. Legalism, too, loomed large, reflected in and assisted by the will-ingness of churchmen (Pius XII in the van) to legislate the tiniest minutiae of church observance. Moralism was confused with religiousness, ethics with theol-ogy" (p. 288).

discussion of occasions of sin which rehearses the Connell-Connery discussion about company-keeping and dancing. In sexual matters, they are critical of Marc Oraison's psychiatric evaluation of sexual actions because it identifies acts such as masturbation, homosexuality, fornication, adultery and conjugal onanism as only materially mortal sins, instead of as formally mortal. However, more attention is paid to psychiatric developments and their implications for human action than in the past.[1]

In volume two, the input of contemporary theology is evident. The first half of the book is devoted to the ends of marriage. Here Ford and Kelly acknowledge the importance of personalist insights into the unity of the couple in marriage, but their aim "is to vindicate, theologically and canonically, for the so-called personalist (secondary) ends of marriage the essential place they deserve, while at the same time *defending their essential subordination to the primary ends.*"[2] Such an approach enables them to view marriage in a positive light (emphasize, e.g., marriage as vocation) while retaining traditional prohibitions. Mixed marriages are still "*per se hindrances to the realization of the vocational ideal of marriage,*"[3] although Ford and Kelly do not wish to exclude them in all cases, since they may serve to propagate the faith.

Part two of *Contemporary Moral Theology: Marriage Questions* treats practical questions of marital sexuality: orgasm, *amplexus reservatus* and *copula dimidiata*, oral-genital acts, incomplete sexual acts, contraception and periodic continence, and sterilizing drugs. Ford and Kelly employ traditional analyses of the marital act, and reinforce their prohibitions by including papal pronouncements on sexuality.

The constant subject of the 1940's and 1950's, whether in journals or magazines, or in works like *Catholic Moral Theology*, is birth control. In *Theological Studies*, in 1942, the issue is whether or not a wife may cooperate with *coitus interruptus* on the part of her husband. The survey of recent literature suggests that she can do so only with grave reason (such as abandonment) but she must actively resist condomistic intercourse.[4] By 1944, Planned Parenthood is identified as "one of the most powerful attacks on the chastity of the nation" and Catholic doctor John Rock (later a major player in the debate over the pill) is criticized for the use of masturbation in research.[5] By the 1950's, the licitness of rhythm is the cynosure, as moral theologians distinguish between moral and immoral uses of rhythm. "How long can one practice rhythm?" as well as "Can one practice rhythm without sufficient reason?" are pressing questions. In 1957 Connery and Kelly discuss how many children is "enough," and whether

---

[1]There are some sections in which they cite other moral theologians and the traditional manuals at length, and some in which they do not.
[2]Ford and Kelly, *Contemporary,* p. v., my emphasis.
[3]*Ibid.,* p. 161.
[4]John C. Ford, "Notes on Moral Theology, 1942" *Theological Studies* 3 (1942), pp. 596-598. There is long rooting in the manual traditions on the marital debt to allow this limited cooperation.
[5]John C. Ford, "Notes on Moral Theology, 1944" *Theological Studies* 5 (1944), p. 506.

Catholics are obliged to bear a certain number of children.[1] *Amplexus reservatus* is at times advocated as a permissible method for couples, but is later prohibited. The focus, then, is on what circumstances justify Catholic couples in limiting family size by the rhythm method.

Throughout these years, there is constant, vigorous opposition to artificial methods of birth control. By 1960, John Lynch calls contraception "tiresome," "theologically, a dead issue."[2] Theologians discuss whether a Catholic president should sign laws permitting contraceptives.[3] In the early 1960's, moral theologians criticize Catholic doctor John Rock's espousal of the birth control pill for Catholics; Rock publishes these views in a 1963 book, *The Time Has Come.* In chapter thirteen of *Contemporary Moral Theology*, "Can the Catholic Teaching Change?", Ford and Kelly assess the status of church teaching on contraception. After a lengthy review of theological opinions on the subject, they conclude:

> 1) The Church is so completely committed to the doctrine that contraception is intrinsically and gravely immoral that no substantial change in this teaching is possible. It is *irrevocable*.
> 2) It is not easy at present to assign a technical dogmatic note to the doctrine. But it is safe to say that it is "*at least* definable doctrine," and it is very likely already taught infallibly *ex iugi magisterio*.
> 3) Since the doctrine is at least definable, it must be included in some way within the object of infallibility. At the minimum, therefore, it is a part of the secondary object of infallibility and may be proposed as a truth which is absolutely *tenenda*. And there are good, though not yet convincing, reasons for holding that this doctrine is a part of the *depositum fidei* and can thus be infallibly taught as *credenda*.[4]

They join the criticism of Dr. John Rock, asserting in a (footnote) comment that "Dr. Rock's opinions in this matter have no standing whatever with Catholic theologians and directly contravene the authoritative teaching of the Catholic Church, which is binding on all Catholics."[5]

By 1964, however, there are dramatic developments in the birth control controversy. John Lynch warns of "a threat of moral schism within our own ranks,"[6] because people are questioning what Lynch views as the unquestionable teaching on contraception. Two articles, from *European* theologians W. van der

[1]See, e.g., *Theological Studies* 11 (1950), pp. 71-77; 14 (1953), pp. 54-57; 18 (1957), pp. 593-595; see also Orville Griese, *The "Rhythm" in Marriage and Christian Morality* (Westminster, MD: Newman Press, 1944) and "Objective Morality of the Rhythm Practice," *American Ecclesiastical Review* 120 (1949), pp. 475-479.
[2]"Notes on Moral Theology," *Theological Studies* 21 (1960), p. 227.
[3]John Connery, "May A Catholic President Sign...?" *America* 102 (December 12, 1959), pp. 353-354.
[4]Ford and Kelly, *Contemporary*, Vol. 2, p. 277.
[5]*Ibid.*, p. 377.
[6]"Notes on Moral Theology," *Theological Studies* 25 (1964), p. 232.

Marck and Louis Janssens,[1] justify the use of the pill by Catholics. Lynch describes this as the first time in church history that Catholic moral theologians have opposed the common teaching of the Church.

By 1964, the Second Vatican Council begins to influence American theology. In that year, an issue of *The Commonweal* devoted to the subject of birth control appears, with Daniel Callahan's essay "Authority and the Theologian."[2] The title is significant; from this point on, sexual ethical questions are inextricably linked to ecclesiological questions about church authority. Callahan concedes that "there was a remarkable harmony among the ideals of the magisterium, the theologians and the married laity"[3] until the mid-1950's. However, social factors, including overpopulation and the changing role of women, have changed this consensus, while new theological insights (including those from the Council) have made the old manuals "appear dangerously inadequate, if not altogether misleading."[4] In the midst of a "theological revolution," the "Center Party" (Callahan's description of Ford and Kelly) had "remained firmly imbedded in the atmosphere of the past," fearful of change, "years behind the revolution," like "government civil servants" trying to put the best light on official teaching.[5] Callahan urges theologians to maintain their integrity by taking stances contrary to the magisterium on birth control, if necessary.

1965 witnesses some telling changes in two journals, *Studies* and the *CTSA Proceedings*, which have recorded developments in the American theological community since the 1940's. For example, in the *CTSA Proceedings* of 1965, Charles E. Curran brings a new analysis to the subject of masturbation, rejecting the traditional approach which examined the act "statically," apart from the person. Curran reviews masturbation in light of fundamental option theory and empirical evidence (especially from psychology), and asserts that masturbation does not always involve grave matter. Because of fundamental option theory (which views individual choices in relationship to one's whole orientation toward God) Curran argues that the traditional teaching on parvity of matter must be rethought. Curran concludes:

> In the past, we moralists spent most of our time interpreting the documents of the magisterium for the Christian people. Today the Vatican Council and theologians are beginning to recognize the importance of the experience of Christian people. Theologians must also interpret the experience of Chris-

---

[1]This lends support to Fogarty's (*The Vatican*, p. 193) assertion that "the stifling atmosphere following the condemnation of Modernism had perhaps more effect in the United States than in Europe. In Europe critical scholarship went underground; in the United States it was nipped in the bud."

[2]80, no. 11 (June 5, 1964), pp. 319-323. Other authors in this volume include Richard McCormick, Bernard Haring, George Casey, Thomas Burch, E. Schillebeeckx and Louis Dupre.

[3]*Ibid.*, p. 320.

[4]*Ibid.*

[5]*Ibid.*, p. 321.

tian people for the magisterium. Previous teachings must be examined in the light of the circumstances of the times in which they were formed.[1]

In the same year, Richard McCormick publishes his "Notes on Moral Theology" in *Theological Studies*. In 1965, McCormick states that if Paul VI fails "to speak soon and authoritatively" about contraception, Catholics may be justified in applying "principles of probabilism" to the questions. From 1965 to 1968, McCormick weighs the teaching on contraception in connection to this question of doubt. McCormick's "Notes" exemplify the ecumenical openness and the critical engagement of magisterial thought which characterize American Catholic moral theology after the Council.[2]

While Curran and McCormick lead a new generation of American Catholic moral theologians, other U.S. Catholics participate in the papal birth control commission. In addition to the presence of American Bishops and American Jesuit moral theologian John Ford, the lay scholar John Noonan, and Patrick and Patricia Crowley, leaders of the Christian Family Movement, are included as expert consultants. Even the Vatican recognizes the importance of the experience of married persons, as lived and studied by the Crowleys, as a source of ethical insight. Within the committee, John Noonan's historical analysis of contraception provides powerful scholarly impetus for a change in official church teaching, while John Ford is an ardent advocate of the *status quo,* and defender of papal authority.[3]

In his 1968 presidential address to the Catholic Theological Society of America, Walter Burghardt, S.J., chides the members for their failure to develop an American theology

> whose neuralgic problems arise from our soil and our people; a theology with a distinctive style and rhetoric; a theology where not only is the Catholic past a critique in the American present, but the American present challenges and enriches the Catholic past; where the Catholic theologian is heard because he is talking to living people, about themselves, in their own tongue.[4]

One month later, on July 29, 1968, Pope Paul VI issues his statement on birth control, *Humanae Vitae.* While neither an American Catholic theology nor an American Catholic sexual ethic yet exists, the new papal encyclical provokes

[1]"Masturbation and Objectively Grave Matter," reprinted in *A New Look at Christian Morality* (Notre Dame: Fides Publishers, 1968), p. 215. Curran employs Richard McCormick's analyses; see Richard A. McCormick, S.J., "The Priest and Teen-Age Sexuality," *Homiletic and Pastoral Review* 65 (1964-1965), pp. 379-387; "Adolescent Masturbation: A Pastoral Problem," *Homiletic and Pastoral Review* 60 (1959-1960), pp. 527-540.
[2]Richard A. McCormick, S.J., *Notes on Moral Theology 1965-1980* (Lanham, MD: University Press of America, 1981), p. 51; see also pp. 38-51, 109-116, 164-168. Notes from later years are found in *Notes on Moral Theology 1981-1984* (Lanham, MD: University Press of America, 1984).
[3]For history of the commission, including a list of the other American members, see Robert Blair Kaiser, *The Politics of Sex and Religion: A Case History in the Development of Doctrine, 1962-1984* (Kansas City, MO: Leaven Press, 1985).
[4]*Proceedings of the Twenty-Third Annual Convention* 23 (1968), p. 22.

an American response. At a press conference in Washington, DC, on July 30, Charles Curran presents a statement with 87 (later 600) signatures of theologians which justifies dissent for Catholics from the birth control teaching. In September of 1968, the Board of Trustees of Catholic University authorizes an investigation into Curran and other professors who had signed the statement. Curran was not new to such controversy; already in 1967, the Trustees had blocked Curran's promotion to tenure and associate professor. Curran was reinstated in 1967 after a strike by students and faculty; in 1968, the Board of Inquiry cleared Curran and his fellow professors.[1]

In post-*Humanae Vitae* sexual ethics, then, Catholics are divided over their relationship to magisterial teaching. For while many theologians signed the Washington statement, other theologians, joined by numerous bishops, defend Paul VI. Meanwhile, studies show that in 1965, 77% of American Catholic women under 45 used some form of birth control, with only 14% employing rhythm. Although in 1955, "only 30 percent of Catholic women younger than 30 had been using contraception," by 1970 "two-thirds of U.S. Catholic women, and three-fourths of Catholic women younger than 30, were using birth control methods disapproved by the church."[2] Many theologians critical of official teaching cite this lay practice as evidence of the magisterium's error. *Humanae Vitae* is a watershed in American Catholic history, as it ushers in an era in which individual conscience and experience grow in importance as sources of norms for sexual ethics, and in which Catholics openly debate the merits of magisterial teaching.

One way to understand sexual ethical developments after 1968 is to realize that most of the actions outlawed as sins of impurity in the manuals are open to question in the American theological community. Even a glance at McCormick's "Notes on Moral Theology" over the past twenty years demonstrates that divorce and remarriage, premarital sexual relations, reproductive technology, homosexuality, and the roles of men and women in marriage and the family, are controverted questions. Jesuit John McNeill's 1976 book, *The Church and the Homosexual,* alerts Catholics to reconsider traditional prohibitions on all homosexual activity. McNeill is silenced after the book's publication, and is dismissed from the Jesuits in 1988 when he breaks his silence to criticize a 1986 Vatican letter on homosexuality.[3] Philip Keane employs a person-centered approach to criticize act-centered assessments of sexual conduct.[4] Throughout the 1970's, Catholic hospital policies, especially those which regulate sterilization,

---

[1]See Kaiser, *op. cit.,* pp. 208ff; see also William H. Shannon, *The Lively Debate: Response to Humanae Vitae* (New York: Sheed & Ward, 1970), and Charles E. Curran, Robert E. Hunt, and the "Subject Professors" with John F. Hunt and Terrence R. Connelly, *Dissent In and For the Church: Theologians and Humanae Vitae* (New York: Sheed & Ward, 1969).

[2]Kaiser, *op. cit,* p. 218; see also Andrew M. Greeley, *The American Catholic: A Social Portrait* (New York: Basic Books, 1977).

[3](Kansas City, KS: Sheed, Andrews and McMeel, 1976); see also *Taking a Chance on God: Liberating Theology for Gays, Lesbians, and Their Lovers, Families and Friends* (Boston: Beacon Press, 1988).

[4]Philip S. Keane, *Sexual Morality: A Catholic Perspective* (New York: Paulist Press, 1977).

are challenged by a number of Catholic theologians.[1] In the 1970's and 1980's, many ethicists move to a limited acceptance of reproductive technologies by married couples.

Meanwhile, the entire history of Christian thought on sexual ethics is called into question by the rise of feminist scholarship. Feminist scholars demand that sexual norms promote the well-being of women as well as men. Traditional assumptions about women's sexuality and sexual desire, about women's roles in marriage, family and reproduction, are challenged. Many feminist theologians reject self-sacrifice as a norm for Christian women in the family, and propose instead a standard of "mutuality" in relationship. Finally, feminist thought argues that the experience of women (so long ignored in the Christian tradition) is a resource and a starting point essential to ethical reflection on sexuality. Margaret Farley identifies the "moral revolution" that emerges from "new patterns of relationship" between women and men. This revolution changes the assessment of sexual conduct; for Farley, human actions must be measured by the standard of a "just love," which respects the concrete reality of the person, and not by abstract assessments of human acts. In a work such as *Between the Sexes,* Lisa Sowle Cahill presupposes the equality of women and men, and then moves to identify norms which promote such equality. Cahill relies on a revised natural law approach, which is reluctant to provide *absolute* norms for human sexual conduct.[2] Moreover, by 1985, it is Cahill who takes over the review of sexual ethical literature in *Theological Studies.*

Curran's publications and career after 1968 exemplify many of the developments in contemporary Catholic sexual ethics. Curran employs a revised natural law approach, which rejects a physicalist interpretation of human sexuality. Fundamental option theory leads him to reject "no parvity of matter." His anthropology accepts the reality of sinfulness in human life. His ethical stance is historically conscious and inductive, and questions the existence of absolute prohibitions of identifiable acts. Over the past twenty years, he has challenged absolute prohibitions of premarital sex, divorce, sterilization, and artificial insemination, as well as contraception and masturbation, while insisting that sexual conduct must still be guided by moral standards of responsibility and relationality. His theory of compromise permits a limited acceptance of homosexual relations. Amidst his lengthy corpus of theological and ethical arguments, in his 1988 book, *Tensions in Moral Theology,* Curran argues that "the primary questions or problem in developing a sexual ethic today is not the ethical question itself but the ecclesiological question of dissent and authoritative church teaching."[3] The 1986 Vatican ruling that finds him "not suitable nor eligible to

[1] Richard McCormick, "Sterilization and Theological Method," *Theological Studies* 37 (1976), pp. 471-477; John P. Boyle, *The Sterilization Controversy* (New York: Paulist Press, 1977).
[2] Margaret A. Farley, "New Patterns of Relationship: Beginnings of a Moral Revolution," in *Woman: New Dimensions,* Walter J. Burghardt, S.J., ed. (New York: Paulist Press, 1975), and *Personal Commitments: Beginning, Keeping, Changing* (San Francisco: Harper & Row, 1986); Lisa Sowle Cahill, *Between the Sexes: Foundations for a Christian Ethics of Sexuality* (Philadelphia: Fortress Press and New York: Paulist Press, 1985)
[3] (Notre Dame: University of Notre Dame Press, 1988), p.77.

teach Catholic theology" cites his writings on contraception, masturbation, abortion, euthanasia, premarital sex, homosexuality, sterilization and artificial insemination.[1]

The challenge to traditional moral norms after 1968 is also evident in the 1977 book, *Human Sexuality*. In 1972, the Catholic Theological Society of America appointed a committee to study sexual ethics; William Carroll, Agnes Cunningham, Anthony Kosnik, Ronald Modras and James Schulte are appointed members. In the tradition of Kenrick, Sabetti, Slater, Ford and Kelly, *Human Sexuality: New Directions in American Catholic Thought* seeks to relate the Christian tradition of sexual ethics to the North American context.

The text bears witness to many of the crucial differences in post-conciliar American Catholic theology; even the ecclesial status of the composers (two laymen and one woman religious, in addition to two priests) reflect a change. New interpretations of theological and ethical methodology are present as well. The authors employ Scripture, the Christian tradition and empirical sciences as sources for Christian ethics, and examine them in light of biblical scholarship and historical consciousness. The traditional moral manuals are given brief treatment. Kosnik *et al.* reject a strict act-centered analysis of sexuality as well as the teaching on parvity of matter. Instead, they take their "universal principle" or "fundamental criterion"[2] from Vatican II: it is the "nature of the person and his acts." They replace the traditional ends of marriage, "procreative" and "unitive," with "creative" and "integrative" goals; sexuality should foster "creative growth toward integration."[3] The commission members next identify particular values that contribute to creative growth toward integration. These are that sexual expression be self-liberating, other-enriching, honest, faithful, socially responsible, life-serving and joyous. Only at a third level (after the fundamental principle and these values) does the question of concrete rules or norms for specific actions (e.g., masturbation, premarital sex) emerge. However, the authors prefer to employ the term "guidelines" for this level. The fourth level of analysis is the individual person's decision, which must not be viewed merely as conformity to pre-existing rules.

It is under the rubric "guidelines," then, that Kosnik *et al.* treat the specific actions, the sins of impurity, so important to the manualist tradition. They review homosexual relations, masturbation, premarital sex, bestiality, sterilization, artificial insemination, adultery and other actions. While they are critical of some of these activities, they insist that these actions cannot be assessed independently of persons.

[1]*Ibid.*, p. 7. For Curran's sexual ethics, see also *A New Look at Christian Morality* (Notre Dame: Fides, 1968); "How My Mind Has Changed, 1960-1975," in *Horizons* 2 (1975), pp. 187-205; *Catholic Moral Theology in Dialogue* (Notre Dame: University of Notre Dame Press, 1976); *Themes in Fundamental Moral Theology* (Notre Dame: University of Notre Dame Press, 1977); *Issues in Sexual and Medical Ethics* (Notre Dame: University of Notre Dame Press, 1978); *Transition and Tradition in Moral Theology* (Notre Dame: University of Notre Dame Press, 1982).
[2](Garden City, NY: Doubleday, 1979), p. 116. See also Dennis Doherty, ed., *Dimensions of Human Sexuality* (Garden City, NY: Doubleday, 1979).
[3]*Ibid.*, p. 106.

It would be a mistake, however, to interpret the CTSA report as a definitive statement of American Catholic sexual ethics. For the "epiphenomenon"[1] over the book—loud praise *and* loud protest—illustrates the pluralism of opinion in the American Catholic moral theological community. On the ecclesial front, Anthony Kosnik is disciplined for his participation in the project.[2]

Yet American Catholic voices also laud and protest a work which reiterates the traditional prohibitions of the sixth and ninth commandments, the 1975 Declaration on Sexual Ethics, *Persona Humana,* issued by the Congregation for the Doctrine of he Faith. That document reaffirms prohibitions on masturbation, homosexuality and premarital sex, as intrinsically evil actions, and reasserts the traditional teaching on parvity of matter.[3] Some members of the American theological community continue to criticize "revisionist" sexual ethics and to defend official magisterial teaching. For example, a 1985 book by Donald Lawler, Joseph Boyle and William E. May defends official magisterial teaching on sexuality, not only against the secular influences of American society (whose permissiveness trivializes sex), but against "the work of these Catholic writers [which] suffers from the same essential shortcomings as that of their secular counterparts."[4]   Their solution is to explain the positive, personalistic interpretations of sexuality in the Catholic tradition that render the traditional prohibitions of certain types of conduct meaningful.

Many challenges, then, are posed to traditional Catholic sexual ethics after *Humanae Vitae,* even as it retains defenders in Rome and in the United States. Many ethicists abandon an act-centered analysis for a focus on persons in relationship. Many reject a physicalist, "order of nature" approach to sexuality, and lean toward "order of reason" approaches in which persons transcend biology. Absolute norms are questioned, and proportionalist modes of assessment become popular. The field of moral theology expands to include women as well as men, laity as well as priests. Experience is recognized as an important source of ethical reflection. Andre Guindon argues that over the past twenty years, much American Catholic ethics has undergone a

> substantial paradigmatic shift. The new model recognizes that human sexuality is more than a corporeal reality and, consequently, that human sexual acts cannot be reduced to 'genital acts.' This change of perspective has been but-

[1]Daniel Maguire, "Human Sexuality: The Book and the Epiphenomenon," The Catholic Theological Society of America, *Proceedings of the Thirty-Third Annual Convention* 33 (1978), pp. 54-76.
[2]See Curran, *Tensions,* p. 76.
[3]Sacred Congregation for the Doctrine of the Faith, *Declaration on Sexual Ethics* (Washington, DC: United States Catholic Conference, 1977); see also Boyle, *Parvitas,* pp. 84-85.
[4]Rev. Donald Lawler, O.F.M.Cap., Joseph Boyle, Jr., and William E. May, *Catholic Sexual Ethics: A Summary, Explanation, and Defense* (Huntington, IN: Our Sunday Visitor, 1985), p. 12. For an explanation of the moral/theological perspective which undergirds their argument, see Germain Grisez, *The Way of the Lord Jesus, Volume One, Christian Moral Principles* (Chicago: Franciscan Herald Press, 1983).

tressed by a prevailing awareness of the inadequacy of a deontological, con-
fession- and act-centered approach to ethics in a Christian context.[1]

Moreover, the new model is historically conscious, employs a wide range of
sources, views sexuality in a broad context, and respects theological as well as
scriptural developments. While Guindon is appreciative of these changes, however, he warns that contemporary Catholic moralists are still

> embedded, like everyone else, in a culture which construes 'sex' as genital
> acts. This embeddedness is so compelling that, though they assert their crit-
> ical distance, most Catholic moralists seem to buy the inventory of sexual
> activities wholesale from the old textbooks which they denigrate in their the-
> oretical considerations.[2]

The manuals may still exert strong influence on American Catholic sexual
ethics, even as ethicists struggle to develop new frameworks, such as Guindon's
"sexual lifestyles" or Margaret Farley's "just love," capable of encompassing the
changes in traditional ethical analysis.[3]

As we have seen, according to Jay Dolan, American Catholics have twice
before confronted modernity. In the late 1790's the influx of immigrants and a
foreign clergy stopped the development of a republican Church. In the 1890's
the condemnations of Americanism and Modernism uprooted a burgeoning
American Catholic theological community. In the 1990's the American Church
again confronts modernity, and in sexual ethics its romance appears to be with
the experience of Christians as a central source of ethical reflection on sexuality.

In sexual ethics, however, modernity confronts American Catholics with
many challenges. In their book *Intimate Matters: A History of Sexuality in
America,* John D'Emilio and Estelle B. Freedman argue that

> over the last three and a half centuries, the meaning and place of sexuality in
> American life have changed: from the family-centered, reproductive sexual
> system in the colonial era; to a romantic, intimate, yet conflicted sexuality in
> nineteenth-century marriage; to a commercialized sexuality in the modern pe-

---

[1] Andre Guindon, "Sexual Acts or Sexual Lifestyles: A Methodological Problem in
Sexual Ethics," *Eglise et Theologie* 18 (1987), p. 315. Guindon's essay studies
the writings of Charles Curran, Philip Keane, Lisa Sowle Cahill and Anthony
Kosnik (in the CTSA report).
[2] *Ibid.*
[3] Guindon urges an approach which examines sexual lifestyles—conjugal, familial,
gay and celibate—and which espouses a "sexual language which is integrated,
relational, generous, and responsible" (p. 329). See also *The Sexual Creators: An
Ethical Proposal for Concerned Christians* (Lanham, MD: University Press of
America, 1986). Another ethicist who avoids the act-centered approach is Margaret Farley. She proposes norms of justice for sexuality. "Most generally, the
norms are respect for persons through respect for autonomy and relationality; respect for relationality through requirements of mutuality, equality, commitment,
and fruitfulness." See "An Ethic for Same-Sex Relations," in *A Challenge to
Love: Gay and Lesbian Catholics in the Church,* edited by Robert Nugent (New
York: Crossroad, 1983), p. 105.

riod, when sexual relations are expected to provide personal identity and individual happiness, apart from reproduction.[1]

It is not yet clear if the lived experience of American Catholics conforms to these stages. As Anne Patrick notes,

> our historical narrative has focused on professional, clerical moral theology...a full account of the American experience in moral theology should...[do] justice to the efforts and contributions of lay women and men, or religious sisters and brothers, and of ordinary parish priests.[2]

So too, the full story of American Catholic sexual ethics, of the experience of Catholics through two centuries of this country's history, awaits retrieval.

It is clear, however, that Catholic moral theological reflection on sexual ethics does not correspond to these stages. Personalism makes a late entry into American Catholic sexual ethics in the 1950's, and most moral theologians remain critical of a sexual ethic which is too individualistic in focus. As American Catholics begin to highlight the lived experience of women and men as a valid source of moral norms, the American milieu and its interpretation of sexuality, will have a profound impact on their discussions. They will need to take account of the demands of the "stage three" lifestyle of their compatriots. For example, in a climate in which sexual relations furnish great possibilities for personal meaning, they also carry the prospect of meaninglessness, and persons may need to learn to "discipline sexuality precisely in order to prevent it from contributing to a general personal apathy."[3] As in the days when they struggled with the influence of mixed marriage, divorce, dances and other socials, in the next century the struggle will be for American Catholics to discern the proper relationship between the values embodied in the Christian tradition on sexual ethics and the daily experience of individual Catholics in the United States.

---

[1](New York: Harper & Row, 1988), pp. xi-xii.
[2]Anne E. Patrick, "A Response (II) to John Boyle," The Catholic Theological Society of America, *Proceedings of the Forty-First Annual Convention* 41 (1986), p. 50.
[3]Margaret A. Farley, "Sexual Ethics," in the *Encyclopedia of Bioethics,* 4 vols. (New York: The Free Press, 1978), p. 1587.

CHAPTER TWELVE

The History of American Catholic Medical Ethics

David F. Kelly
Duquesne University

The last few decades, from 1960 to the present, have given rise to a significant increase in the importance of medical ethics in the United States. So clear has this growth been that many contemporary scholars forget that health care ethics existed as an important field of study within Roman Catholic moral theology for all of this century in the United States and for centuries before this one in Europe. Indeed, prior to the last thirty years or so, medical ethics was almost a Catholic field of study.[1] This essay will trace the development of American Catholic medical ethics, beginning with some introductory discussion of its origins in European moral theology and pastoral medicine.[2]

EUROPEAN CATHOLIC ROOTS

Medicine and religion have long been related to one another, both within and without the Christian Church. Many societies have combined the work of health provider and spiritual leader. The "holy person" would offer not only religious counsel but healing treatment as well. This changed after the fifth century B.C. in Greece, when Hippocrates began the process of what we might call "scientific medicine," where medicine can become a *techne,* that is, an art with its own method of investigation, diagnosis and prescription.[3] For the next

---

[1]Contributions from other sources were rare. Joseph Fletcher wrote on the first Protestant works in the field in 1954 (a work strongly criticized and even condemned by Catholic moralists of that time), and commented that Protestant and Jewish literature was almost entirely lacking; see *Morals and Medicine* (Princeton University Press, 1954; reprinted Boston: Beacon Press, 1960), pp. xix, 16-17. Some brief discussion is found in a few works by Protestant ethicists, but there is little or no systematic development. Philosophers who did not rely on any faith tradition made few applications of their ethics to medical issues. Professional associations of physicians did talk about medical ethics, but, as will be noted later, they did little real ethical study of medical practice or policy.

[2]The material presented in this essay can be found in greater detail in Kelly, *The Emergence of Roman Catholic Medical Ethics in North America: An Historical, Methodological, Bibliographical Study* (New York: Edwin Mellen Press, 1979), and in Kelly, "Roman Catholic Medical Ethics and the Ethos of Modern Medicine," *Ephemerides Theologicae Lovanienses,* 59 (1983), pp. 46-67.

[3]This has been called a process of secularization, but I agree with other modern scholars that this is not accurate. Hippocrates did not deny the sacred character of medicine or of nature; he affirmed it. What he did deny was the religious concept then in vogue of the arbitrary, often whimsical causing of illness by the local gods. To some extent, this "secularized" health care; no longer would illnesses be cured by praying to the god who had given them. But it is not a secularization in the real meaning of that term; religion and medicine were not seen as enemies or

millennium or so, until the fifth and sixth centuries A.D., physicians were not usually priests or monks, though Christian physicians clearly related their vocation as physicians to their faith as Christians. They were called to heal as Jesus had healed.[1]

This changed along with the collapse of Roman structures in the early Middle Ages. From the seventh through the twelfth centuries, Christian monks took over the practice of medicine, seeing it as a part of their religious duties rather than as their primary vocation. There was little attempt to advance medical knowledge.[2]

Thomas Aquinas and other major theologians of the High Middle Ages introduced into Western Christianity a theological matrix which again made medical advances possible. For Aquinas the study of nature, of creation as God had created it, was a way of giving glory to God. Medical practice could thus again become an art, a *techne*, rather than just an obligation, an *officium*. This theological change, similar in some ways to the one proposed earlier by Hippocrates, served as a basis for the advancement of "scientific" medicine within a theocentric Christian environment.[3]

The real secularization of medicine occurred in the eighteenth century with the Enlightenment. Now physical and spiritual healing were separated and religion was privatized. Scientific progress was extolled as the future of humankind; religion was often seen as the enemy of real science, useful only to the degree that it might promote right action by the people and thus contribute something visibly and measurably useful to the community.[4]

The development of medical ethics as a distinguishable area within Catholic moral theology is related rather clearly to the variations in the relationship of Christianity and medicine we have been tracing. The more medicine ventured out on its own, as a discipline in its own right, the more theologians and pastors attended to it and tried to establish a dialogue with physicians at the interface of medicine and religion.

There is little or nothing about medical ethics in the New Testament, though there are, of course, passages concerned with human sexuality, an area which will be treated in many works of pastoral medicine and medical ethics.[5]

---

even as totally unrelated. For discussion of this, see Robert M. Veatch, "Codes of Medical Ethics in Medical Education," in *The Teaching of Medical Ethics,* Veatch, *et al.,* eds. (Hastings-on-Hudson, NY: Hastings Center, 1973), p 143; Ludwig Edelstein, *The Hippocratic Oath, Text, Translation, and Interpretation* (Baltimore: Johns Hopkins Press, 1943); and P. Lain Entralgo, *Doctor and Patient* (New York: McGraw-Hill, 1969), pp. 42-44.

[1]See Heinrich Pompey, *Die Bedeutung der Medizin fur die kirchliche Seelsorge im Selbstverstandnis der sogenannten Pastoralmedizin* (Fribourg, Germany: Herder, 1968), p. 17; Entralgo, *op. cit.,* pp. 53-57.

[2]Pompey, *op. cit.,* pp. 17-20; Entralgo, *op. cit.,* pp. 60-70.

[3]Pompey, *op. cit.,* pp. 23-30; Entralgo, *op. cit.,* pp. 87-94.

[4]See Albert Niedermeyer, *Allgemeine Pastoralmedizin* (Vienna: Herder, 1955), Vol. I, pp. 15-16. The ideal pastor of this period was often seen as one who would bring proper hygiene to his parishioners.

[5]Paul mentions *pharmakeia* in his list of vices in Gal. 5:20, but the exact meaning is unknown, though it might mean abortion. See Daniel Callahan, *Abortion: Law,*

The writers of the patristic period do introduce a number of directly "medical ethical" issues, such as abortion and contraception, but there is no real attempt at any systematization.[1] In the *Libri Penitentiales* of the seventh and following centuries, small booklets written to help confessors assign proper penances, some issues of medical ethics are grouped together, but no real development is yet apparent, nor is there any recognition of physicians or of moral problems proper to medicine.[2]

It is in conjunction with the development of medicine in the High Middle Ages under the influence of scholastic theology that the first attempts are made to speak more formally to the ethical issues of health care. The *Summae* for confessors now replaces the *Libri*. The newer books are longer and better organized. Some of them, and some of the moral treatises written by the major theologians, are organized according to the Commandments or the Virtues, and include sections on the Sacraments and on specific vocations or states in life. Moral questions relating to health care are grouped primarily under the fifth and sixth commandments or under the corresponding Virtues of Justice and Chastity, under the Sacrament of Matrimony, and now for the first time in a special section concerned with the moral obligations of physicians, who are included along with clerics, judges and some others as worthy of special attention.[3] In a real way this is the beginning of Medical Ethics in Catholic Moral Theology. As medicine begins now to develop as a discipline in its own right, with its own schools and practicing professionals, theologians attempt to initiate a dialogue with medicine.

The moral manuals written in response to the call of the Council of Trent for a disciplined and consistent education of clergy continue the organizational rubrics of the *Summae*. Scores of these were produced from the sixteenth through the first half of the twentieth centuries and all include discussion of health care questions.[4]

Choice, and Morality (New York: Macmillan, 1970, reprinted Macmillan Paperbacks, 1972), p. 410.

[1]Callahan, *op. cit.*, p. 410; John T. Noonan, Jr., *Contraception: A History of Its Treatment by the Catholic Theologians and Canonists* (Cambridge: Harvard University Press, 1965, reprinted New York: New American Library Mentor, 1967), pp. 78-175.

[2]For a collection of these, see John Thomas McNeill and Helene M. Gamer, eds. and trans., *Medieval Handbooks of Penance* (New York: Columbia University Press, 1938). Medicine is mentioned in the *Penitential of Bartholomew Iscanus,* but only in passing (McNeill and Gamer, p. 350).

[3]The literature here is too great to be listed in a brief essay. For a description of some *summae,* see Pierre Michaud-Quantin, *Sommes de casuistigues et manuels de confession au moyen âge (XII-XVI siecles), Analecta Mediaevalia Namurcensia,* No. 13 (Louvain, Belgium: Nauwelaerts, 1962).

[4]For an overview, see L. Vereecke, "Moral Theology, History of (700 to Vatican Council I)," *New Catholic Encyclopedia,* Vol. 9, 1967; for further detail on how these books treated health care questions, see Kelly, *The Emergence of Medical Ethics, op. cit.*, pp. 28-42.

Pastoral Medicine

With the eighteenth century and the Enlightenment, a new rubric came into common use to describe what was now becoming a separately recognized field of study with a growing body of literature separate from the general works in moral theology. "Pastoral Medicine" investigated the relationship of religion and medicine. In a time when the two were taking separate, even antagonistic paths, pastoral medicine tried to maintain a dialogue. Pastors and theologians wrote to physicians about the spiritual and ethical implications of medicine; doctors taught pastors how to provide first aid and hygiene to their parishioners.[1] The topics included in these disparate works were varied indeed, anything which had to do with soul and body could be part of the literature. Works in pastoral medicine included such issues as diet and hygiene, first aid for pastors, basic anatomy and psychology, mysticism and science, revelations and visions, miraculous healings, asceticism, emotional disorders and moral culpability, and a complete range of sexual ethical issues, including those we might call "medical" as well as such topics as celibacy and methods of sexual intercourse.

It is possible to trace a development within these topics, however, a development which influenced the growth of Medical Ethics in the United States in the twentieth century. Whereas the earlier works in pastoral medicine emphasized teaching rudimentary medicine to pastors (the Enlightenment notion that priests and religious were useless unless they knew and practiced science for the people), as the literature grew during the nineteenth and early twentieth centuries, it became more and more interested in what we would now call "health care ethics." Moral questions came to the fore. The principle of selection for topics in pastoral medicine was by the beginning of this century primarily the actual professional practice of health care personnel. It was this practice and the procedures it included which needed ethical guidance. The first work in pastoral medicine available in English for American readers was Carl Cappellmann's *Pastoral Medicine,* translated in 1878 from the Latin original. This work was the most clear to that date in emphasizing the moral topics which had been only one, often minor, subdivision of pastoral medicine. Cappellmann includes these other areas in his work and recognizes that they are part of pastoral medicine. But he explicitly wants to reduce the emphasis on these other areas in order to offer moral guidance to physicians in their professional practice.[2]

This trend within pastoral medicine to emphasize ethical discussion is at least partly the result of Enlightenment influence. Ethics is, after all, the "useful, practical" side of religion, precisely the side which the Enlightenment supported. It is not surprising, then, that American theologians, who grew up in a "practical" Enlightenment-born nation, should make some of their greatest contributions to Catholic theology in the area of ethics.

---

[1]For more detail, see Kelly, *The Emergence, op. cit.,* pp. 55-80; also Kelly, "Roman Catholic Medical Ethics and the Ethos of Modern Medicine," *op. cit.,* pp. 50-54.

[2]C. Cappellmann, *Pastoral Medicine* (1877), trans. by William Dassel (1978) (New York: F. Putset, 1882). See especially his introduction, pp. 1-3.

THE EARLY PERIOD (1900-1940)

For reasons which will become apparent, Catholic Medical Ethics in the United States can be divided into three somewhat distinct periods. The early period preceded the Second World War and the papacy of Pius XII. It was a time when American Catholics were able to deal with medical issues more or less on their own terms, and the approach they took showed this relative isolation. After the War, and with the papacy of Pius XII, some questions arose which required a defense of the Catholic position. This brought some change in emphasis into the discipline from 1940 up to the Second Vatican Council in the 1960's. The third period has followed the Council and is a time of rapid and even radical change, when Catholics are no longer alone in the field, and when health care ethics has become an ecumenical and rapidly growing field.

Name and Definition

Beginning just before the turn of the century, Catholic moral theologians, especially in the United States, developed a specific subdivision of moral theology which would later be known as "medical ethics." I have identified thirteen books written before 1940 by American Catholic scholars which are in some way works in medical ethics.[1] Several of these saw multiple editions and revisions over the years. As the discipline developed from its roots in general moral theology and European pastoral medicine, it tended to continue the trend already apparent within pastoral medicine itself. That is, American writers emphasized in a more and more consistent fashion the moral issues of medical practice which had been but one of the areas of interest in pastoral medicine.

Some works were clearer at this than others. The first American book in the field, written in 1897 by the Belgian-born Jesuit theologian Charles Coppens, was directed explicitly to medical students at the John A. Creighton Medical College in Omaha. The title, *Moral Principles and Medical Practice,* shows the emphasis on the immediately practical concerns which will characterize the definition of the discipline in the United States.[2] Coppens' reason for including some topics and excluding others is clearly their practical importance for physicians in their professional practice. For example, when he introduces some questions of sexual ethics in a chapter on venereal excesses, he does not do as pastoral medicine had done, simply because such topics were part of the wide range of issues concerned with body and soul, medicine and religion, but because the physician might be called upon to give advice to patients in this regard. Coppens' book, which was reprinted in a fourth edition in 1905 and which formed the basis of a "new, revised edition" co-authored by Henry Spalding in

---

[1] For a complete chronological list of the major works in medical ethics, see Kelly, *The Emergence, op. cit.,* pp. 7-12, 455-459.
[2] *Moral Principles and Medical Practice: The Basis of Medical Jurisprudence* (New York: Benziger Brothers, 1897), p. 222.

1921, was clearly influential in moving the American discipline in this more practical direction.[1]

Coppens' work is also interesting from the perspective of the rubric which was to designate the discipline. As his subtitle, *The Basis of Medical Jurisprudence,* shows, Coppens calls it "medical jurisprudence." In medical schools of the period and in professional associations of physicians such as the American Medical Association, two rubrics were available which might have been used: "medical ethics" and "medical jurisprudence." The first of these would ultimately be accepted, but not without considerable resistance. The reasons for this, if studied in any detail, would take us too far from our main topic, but some brief summary is helpful. The "medical ethics" of the professional medical associations was not in any real sense the moral (ethical) investigation of medicine or health care; it did not really intend to apply moral principles to medical practice. Rather it dealt largely with questions of medical etiquette, of how doctors should treat each other, of how to resist governmental regulation and national health insurance, of how to ensure that the profession would be protected against outsiders or alternative practitioners, even of what kind of horse and buggy to ride.[2] The approach was largely self-serving. That is, the principle goal of "medical ethics" was to defend the prestige of the medical profession. Not that this was all bad. Patients and doctors are not enemies and in many ways what benefits the profession of medicine is also helpful to the health of the nation. But clearly this is not automatically true. The codes of "medical ethics" together with the literature explaining and defending them were not moral theology or ethics in any real sense.[3] Moral theologians recognized this, and were reluctant to adopt the term as the rubric for their discipline. Some explicitly rejected it.[4]

---

[1] The second and third editions, both printed in 1897, were really reprints of the first. The fourth was slightly changed. The 1921 edition included some additional essays by the co-author. The book was quoted by other moralists and was translated for Europeans into French, German and Spanish. A German reviewer, an expert in pastoral medicine, gave it a "high rating in the literature of pastoral medicine" (Niedermeyer, *Allgemeine Pastoralmedizin,* Vol. I, p. 65, translation mine).

[2] For a particularly scathing attack on the "medical ethics" of the late nineteenth and early twentieth centuries, see Donald Enloe Konold, *A History of American Medical Ethics, 1847-1912* (Madison: State Historical Society of Wisconsin for the Department of History, University of Wisconsin, 1962). The horse-and-buggy example is taken from Daniel Webster Cathell's *Book on the Physician Himself and Things that Concern His Reputation and Success,* 10th ed. (Philadelphia: F.A. Davis, 1898). This book, which saw at least 10 editions, is generally classified as a work in "medical ethics." It is sexist, racist and self-serving.

[3] A similar situation can be found in works of "nursing ethics," often called "professional adjustments" or "professional trends." These were largely discussions of etiquette and tended to emphasize propriety in language and dress. Charles McFadden, whose *Medical Ethics for Nurses* appeared in 1946, explicitly says he is *not* writing a book in "nursing ethics."

[4] Austin O'Malley and James J. Walsh, *Essays in Pastoral Medicine* (New York: Longmans, Green and Co., 1906), p. v; Henry S. Spalding, *Talks to Nurses: The Ethics of Nursing* (New York: Benziger Brothers, 1920), pp. 14-15. One moralist

"Medical Jurisprudence" offered an alternative, one which Coppens adopted. He argued that since jurisprudence deals with law and since medical jurisprudence deals with medicine and (civil) law, including the area of forensic medicine, it is proper to extend the field to include the moral principles which underlie the law.[1] Coppens' suggestion was never widely adopted; the rubric never became popular for the emerging discipline. But it is an example of the hesitation moralists of the period had in using the seemingly more obvious "medical ethics."

After Coppens' book, a series of works were written by Catholic scholars. Some of these followed his lead in emphasizing moral questions; others remained closer to the kinds of issues typical of works in pastoral medicine. The first American work to use the rubric "pastoral medicine" is a good example of the older approach. Alexander E. Sanford, a Catholic physician, wrote *Pastoral Medicine: A Handbook for the Catholic Clergy* in 1904. His book was intended to tell clergy what they needed to know about medicine, not to investigate the moral issues of medical practice.

There were other similar books, but as the early decades of the century passed, the American discipline came to emphasize primarily the moral dimensions of medical practice. Its goal was to inform health care professionals concerning their moral responsibilities as doctors and nurses. Thus the topics chosen for inclusion were those procedures which nurses and physicians encountered in their professional practice. Since these tended to be mostly physical interventions to cure physical ailments, Catholic medical ethics naturally began to analyze this kind of procedure connected with health care. It came to be "physicalist" and "individualist." It was interested in a moral analysis of the medical procedures actually done by health care professionals.

One example of this emphasis was the trend in some of the literature to underline the problem of abortion as of primary importance. Coppens' book stresses abortion, analyzing it in more detail than the other issues he treats. In 1904 Andrew Klarmann went even further when he argues that abortion ought to be the only issue central to pastoral medicine. His *The Crux of Pastoral Medicine: The Perils of Embryonic Man* was revised in four editions to become a 300-page analysis of abortion and fetal care.[2] Patrick Finney's *Moral Problems in Hospital Practice: A Practical Handbook,* published in 1922 shows a similar emphasis, as most of the 200-page book is devoted to questions of obstetrics and gynecology.[3] Catholic medical ethics never restricted itself to this one topic, of course, but abortion and similar issues would continue to be of central importance.

of this period does use the term. In 1921 Michael Bourke wrote a 24-page pamphlet called *Some Medical Ethical Problems Solved* (Milwaukee: Bruce, 1921).
[1]See especially pp. 17-19.
[2](New York: F. Putstet, 1904, 1905, 1907, 1912, 1915).
[3](St. Louis, MO: B. Herder).

Associations and Journals

The founding of two major Catholic Associations with their respective journals was of considerable significance to the growth of Catholic medical ethics. The Catholic Hospital Association of the United States and Canada was begun in 1915

> for the promotion and realization of progressively higher ideals in the religious, moral, medical, nursing, educational, social and all other phases of hospital and nursing endeavor and other consistent purposes especially relating to the Catholic hospitals and schools of nursing in the United States and Canada.[1]

The separate Catholic Hospital Association of Canada would begin its formal existence in 1954 and the United States organization would later change its name to the Catholic Health Association. Its journal, *Hospital Progress,* now *Health Progress*, began publication in 1920. The Association was affiliated in 1933 with the American Catholic hierarchy through the National Catholic Welfare Conference and has continued to be connected to the formal structure of the hierarchy over the decades.

When the CHA was founded in 1915, there were 541 Catholic hospitals in the United States.[2] The number grew rapidly through the 1950's (by 1963 there were 857), and the influence of the CHA in establishing moral policy within the hospital system increased. The Association published a brief code of ethics in 1921 which dealt with operations connected with pregnancy and reproduction.[3] This "Surgical Code for Catholic Hospitals" lasted until 1948, when it was replaced by the "Ethical and Religious Directives for Catholic Hospitals." The "Surgical Code" includes two sets of operations which

> are unethical and may not therefore be performed: One. Operations involving destruction of foetal life....Two. All operations involving the sterilization or mutilation of men or women, except where such follows as the indirect and undesired result of necessary interference for the removal of diseased structures.[4]

---

[1]R. Shanahan, "Catholic Hospital Association," *New Catholic Encyclopedia,* Vol. 3, (1967), p. 268. The citation is from the official statement of purpose. See also Edward F. Garesché, "The Catholic Association of the United States and Canada," *Month,* 145 (1925), pp. 341-351.

[2]J. Flanagan, "Hospitals, Modern," *New Catholic Encyclopedia,* Vol. 7, (1967), p. 167.

[3]See an article entitled "Catholic Nurses in Council," *Month,* 162 (1933), p. 296; see also an editorial comment in *Month,* 162 (1933), p. 492. For the Code itself, see *Graduate Nurses: Symposium of Ethical Inspiration,* Leo Gregory Fink, ed. (New York: Paulist Press, 1938), pp. 293-295.

[4]This is quoted from the "Surgical Code," in Fink, *op. cit.*

Through this and subsequent codes, as well as through its journal *Hospital Progress,* the CHA was and is of considerable influence in setting the actual practice in Catholic hospitals on issues of this type.

The National Federation of Catholic Physicians' Guilds was formed in 1932 "to promote spiritual aims and ideals as they apply to members of the medical profession."[1] Individual guilds had existed for some time on the local level in this country and guilds were common in England and on the Continent.[2] In 1932 eleven local guilds joined to form the Federation. By 1964 there were 104 local guilds with 7,000 members.[3] The Federation began publication of *Linacre Quarterly* in 1932, and has consistently emphasized medical moral issues. As one author pointed out in 1938, such guilds are important so that Catholic physicians "may keep themselves sensitively and fundamentally in touch with sound Catholic principles in questions involving important medico-ethical problems as they arise."[4]

Methodology

The area of methodology is complex and problematic. It inevitably involves issues of debate and controversy, since it concerns method and judgments reached in accordance with the method, which are now so much in dispute within Catholic Health Care Ethics. It is impossible even to attempt a description of the method used in the first forty years of the discipline without implying some sort of critical judgment, since the very terms used in the description are those of today's Catholic theologians, many of whom find the method of previous generations seriously deficient. In addition, the matter itself is complex, involved as it must be with difficult normative and metaethical issues. This essay will not attempt a complete analysis, but will give a limited overview of the basic methodological approaches of the discipline.

Catholic Health Care Ethics in the United States, in dialogue with European Pastoral Medicine, developed a methodology which was intended to enable it to arrive at universally applicable solutions to medical ethical questions. The method was based on a cause-and-effect analysis which ethicists found quite appropriate when applied to the kinds of topics emphasized in the discipline: physical interventions (operations and medications) for physical ailments. Indeed, it is quite likely that in some real way the very compatibility of this ethical method to the supposed "scientific" method of cause-and-effect analysis (diagnosis and prescription) of modern medicine made it even more attractive to Catholic moralists called upon to offer specific answers to the moral questions physicians posed.

[1] W.J. Egan, "National Federation of Catholic Physicians' Guilds," *New Catholic Encyclopedia,* Vol. 10, 1967, p. 236.
[2] Charles Plater, "Why a Catholic Medical Guild?" *The Catholic Mind,* 29 (1931), p. 311.
[3] Egan, *op. cit.,* p. 236.
[4] James F. McDonald, "Why Catholic Physicians' Guilds?" *Catholic Mind,* 36 (1938), p. 59.

Contemporary critics of this method have called it "physicalism." Physicalism is an emphasis in moral analysis on the physical and biological properties, motions and goals of the action under consideration. The ethical judgment which results, whether the action is right or wrong, is applied whenever the physical act is the same. In the Catholic medical ethics of this period, this emphasis was dominant to the relative neglect of other aspects of human behavior, such as social, psychological, relational and spiritual aspects.

Catholic moralists did not intend, of course, to eliminate these other realities when doing ethics. Indeed, it was their stated purpose to investigate the practice of medicine precisely from the spiritual and moral perspective, to enhance medical practice by introducing human dimensions of morality into what was often seen as a purely scientific endeavor. Often in the works of the period this theme is important. And medical moralists of the time include such important theological principles as God's role in ruling human life and the meaning of human suffering in the context of Jesus' redemptive love. Nonetheless the actual analysis of medical procedures quite clearly subordinates these important themes from Christian anthropology to a precise method which in fact reaches its final conclusions on the basis of a physicalist analysis of acts.

Though no attempt can be made here at detail, some mention is necessary of the principle of double effect. As the discipline continued its development, this principle was refined so that by 1940 or so it had become the central framework for the application of physicalist criteria to medical procedures.[1] The principle enabled moralists to make clear distinctions, on the basis of the action itself, between direct and indirect abortions, sterilizations, mutilations, euthanasia and even, for a few authors, between direct lies and indirect falsehoods called mental reservations.[2] A similar insistence on the biological goal of sexual intercourse resulted in the condemnation of all methods of contraception which were said to interfere in the act or in the biological process. This physicalist method was refined by American scholars during the first half of the century.

Examples are many. We have already noted that Charles Coppens' 1897 work limited detailed exploration to the issue of abortion. Though his analysis lacks the precision of later writers, and though he is somewhat confused especially in his treatment of ectopic pregnancy (he refuses to give a clear answer when it is known that the "growth" is a fetus),[3] he does use the principle of double effect and physicalist criteria to deal with the issue. No "direct" abortion is permitted for any reason. Contraception is forbidden and if a woman should die as a result of childbearing...

---

[1]There has been and still is considerable controversy as to whether or not this principle was the central framework in medical ethics or just one principle among many others. For one recent discussion, see Bernard Hoose, *Proportionalism: The American Debate and Its European Roots* (Washington, DC: Georgetown University Press, 1987), pp. 101-103. For a detailed argument on this point, see Kelly, *The Emergence, op. cit.,* pp. 259-264, which shows that it was a general framework device, and not just one of many principles applied to medical ethics.

[2]For a complete analysis, see Kelly, *The Emergence, op. cit.,* pp. 244-279.

[3]First ed., p. 79.

well, such temporal dangers and sufferings as attend child-bearing are the lot of womankind, just as the dangers and hardships of the battlefield, the mine, the factory...are the lot of men....women, as a rule...patiently submit to God's sentence pronounced in Paradise, 'I will multiply thy sorrows and thy conceptions.'[1]

Andrew Klarmann's book, *The Crux of Pastoral Medicine: The Perils of Embryonic Man*, is quite similar to Coppens'. He allows indirect abortion in the case of cancer of the uterus but, like Coppens, is unwilling to accept this in the case of ectopic pregnancy. He is less flexible than his predecessor, however, in that he condemns any attempt at aborting an ectopic fetus as a direct abortion, suggesting that in such a case "a Christian mother must...make herself a willing martyr to her conjugal vows."[2]

Other works of the first two decades of the century are similar. The most clearly physicalist analysis of this period is found in Patrick Finney's 1922 manual, *Moral Problems in Hospital Practice: A Practical Handbook*.[3] He lists the four conditions of the principle of double effect and like his predecessors considers any operation to save the life of the mother with an ectopic pregnancy to be a direct abortion and thus always forbidden.[4] He applied physicalist criteria to sterilization and to other kinds of mutilation.

It was T. Lincoln Bouscaren who "solved" the problem of ectopic pregnancy in a thesis he wrote in 1933.[5] His solution made physicalism a more precise instrument for use in Catholic medical ethics and is an excellent example of how this method works. Bouscaren, an American-born Jesuit educated in Rome, argued that if the fetus were removed from the fallopian tube the abortion would indeed be direct and hence forbidden. But if the tube were removed with the fetus inside it the abortion could be considered indirect and hence permitted, since the act could be considered the removal of a pathological organ similar to the removal of the cancerous womb of a pregnant woman, which had already been accepted as an indirect abortion. Bouscaren is quite clear that the decisive difference is the physical causal chain of events which the procedure entails.[6]

Catholic hospital chaplains were relieved to see Bouscaren's thesis accepted by at least some Catholic moralists. It meant that women need no longer be told they had to die even though a relatively simple operation could save them. Bouscaren's "solution" solidified the hold that physicalism had on Catholic moral method. The case of ectopic pregnancy had been likely to become an area where even Catholics would object to the results. Bouscaren and those who agreed with him (not all did, but enough did to enable the opinion to become a permitted, or "probable" opinion) had removed the rather startling conclusion from Catholic medical ethics that women and fetuses had to die when the woman might be saved. And they did it using the same kind of approach which had created the problem in the first place, but now with a new twist. The issue contin-

[1]*Ibid.*, pp. 123-124.
[2]*Ibid.*, p. 101.
[3](St. Louis, MO: B. Herder).
[4]*Ibid.*, p. 135.
[5]*Ethics of Ectopic Operations* (Chicago: Loyola University Press, 1933).
[6]*Ibid.*, pp. 160-162.

ues to be a problem today when salpingostomy (cutting the embryo out of the tube) is a possible procedure which can in some cases preserve the fallopian tube. This procedure is forbidden by Bouscaren's physicalist criteria. But at least women no longer need die from ectopic pregnancy. The issue which would finally lead to serious attack on physicalism and to the conclusion that it is simply not tenable, would be the birth control controversy in the 1960's and 1970's.

By 1940, physicalist criteria had been established as central to medical ethical analysis. No one name had been accepted for the discipline, as "medical ethics" and "medical jurisprudence" both had disadvantages. The definition of the discipline had been set as determined by the criterion of selection of topics: the daily professional practice of medical personnel. This criterion resulted in an emphasis on physical interventions like surgery and medication, topics which were "solved" by the physicalist criteria emphasized at the time.

THE MIDDLE PERIOD (1940-1960)

It is during the next two decades that Catholic Medical Ethics established itself, especially in the United States, as a self-conscious field of study with its own sense of definition and method. Whereas the early period had no truly comprehensive works in medical ethics (some of the pastoral medicine volumes include a vast array of topics, but are not really works in medical ethics; some of the books we have noted do have such analysis but tend to limit the scope of topics), the 1940's and 1950's will produce a significant number of more or less complete manuals in medical ethics.

Name and Definition

The first, and arguably the most important of the manuals, was that of Charles McFadden, an Augustinian priest who taught at Villanova University. His *Medical Ethics* was the most widely used manual of the time and saw six editions between 1946 and 1967.[1] The first edition, entitled *Medical Ethics for Nurses*, shows the importance given to nurses by Catholic moralists. Unlike the approach used in "nursing ethics" and "professional adjustments" within the nursing profession, where the emphasis was almost totally on etiquette and on following doctors' orders,[2] Catholic medical moralists tended more to believe that nurses, like physicians, should be able to understand the intricacies of medical morality. McFadden is explicit: "It is the experience of the author that the mat-

---

[1]*Medical Ethics for Nurses* (Philadelphia: F.A. Davis, 1946); *Medical Ethics* (2nd ed. 1949, 3rd ed. 1953, 4th ed. 1956, 5th ed. 1961, 6th ed. 1967).

[2]Martin Benjamin, in a recent review, cites the following statement by nurse Sarah Dock from the *American Journal of Nursing* in 1917: "The first and most helpful criticism I ever received from a doctor was when he told me that I was supposed to be simply an intelligent machine for the purpose of carrying out his orders" (*Hastings Center Report*, April-May 1988, p. 38). Benjamin correctly notes that the nurse's role in ethical decision-making has not been widely recognized. The exception, however, was Catholic Medical Ethics, where the nurse was *supposed* to know the right thing to do even if the doctor didn't.

ter is neither too abstract nor too comprehensive for the nurse to master."[1] This aspect of Catholic Medical Ethics is an interesting contrast within what must generally be considered, at least for the perspective of today's feminist critique, a sexist discipline. Many of the topics analyzed and many of the procedures condemned by moralists of the time concerned women in a more direct way than men. Women were the ones who were called upon directly to suffer and die (we have seen a couple of quotes already to that intent). Men were the ones who made the decisions (almost no authors were women and those who were usually co-authored works with male theologians); moral judgments were determined by the hierarchy, who were, and still are, all male. Nonetheless, in this secondary yet still important way Catholic Health Care Ethics did involve women nurses in the process of learning, if not of creating and developing, health care ethics.

McFadden's use of the phrase "medical ethics" as title of his manual was influential in leading the discipline to accept the rubric as its name. From this point on "medical ethics" will be an accepted designation, and during the 1940's and 1950's it will be the one most widely used.[2] But McFadden takes care to disassociate his meaning of the term from that of the medical and nursing professions. He will deal with ethics; they are interested in etiquette.[3] Other authors of the period will make the same distinction.

McFadden's book includes the entire range of issues that came to constitute the material definition of Roman Catholic medical ethics of the time. The emphasis is practical. Most emphasized are questions of direct physical medical intervention (abortion, mutilation, sterilization, euthanasia, artificial insemination). Sexual issues are included only insofar as they are needed to deal with medical procedures such as artificial insemination and contraception. McFadden's purpose, as seen both in his formally stated goal and in the topics he treats, is to analyze and answer the ethical questions which arise within the actual professional practice of health care personnel.

The most important American Catholic medical ethicist of the period was the Jesuit moralist Gerald Kelly. Educated in Rome, Kelly taught for 26 years at St. Mary's College in Kansas. From 1947 to 1953 he wrote "Notes on Moral Theology" for *Theological Studies,* and he was generally considered the foremost medical moralist of his time. His articles were consistently cited by Catholic authorities and by other authors.

In the late 1940's it became clear that the "Surgical Code for Catholic Hospitals," promulgated by the Catholic Hospital Association in 1921, was no longer adequate. The CHA appointed a committee, with Kelly as its chairman, to revise the code. The result was the "Ethical and Religious Directives for Catholic Hospitals."[4] First formulated in 1949, revised in 1954 and again in

---

[1]*Medical Ethics for Nurses, op. cit.,* p. xi (included in later editions as "Preface to First Edition").
[2]Though not by all authors. Protestant scholar Joseph Fletcher, for example, rejects it completely (*Morals and Medicine, op. cit.,* p. 5).
[3]3rd ed., p. 3.
[4]The Directives are widely available, as small pamphlets published by the CHA, in *Hospital Progress* and *Linacre Quarterly,* and as appendices in many of the medical

1971, the Directives were not at first intended to be binding on individual dioceses unless the Bishop so directed, but were rather to serve as guidelines for
dioceses which did not have their own codes.[1] They quickly became the accepted
code, however, which was seen as binding in Catholic hospitals in the United
States.

The 1949 Directives include a longer "ethical" section which is said to bind
all patients regardless of religion and a shorter "religious" section on the spiritual
care of Catholic patients. The "ethical" directives are largely limited to forbidding those procedures which physicalist criteria had come to judge as always
immoral: direct abortion, euthanasia, artificial insemination, masturbation for
sterility testing, direct sterilization, and contraception by any means except periodic continence (rhythm). Skin grafts and blood transfusions are permitted and
other organ transplants are said to be under debate; incidental appendectomy,
lobotomy and narcotherapy are allowed with proper safeguards. The "religious"
directives speak of preparation for the sacraments and burial of amputated limbs
and fetuses; no mention is made of the religious care of non-Catholic patients.

The 1955 Directives are mostly identical, adding a few specifications. One
important clarification is added to the "religious" section, however, when the
Directives explicitly permit a Catholic hospital to call non-Catholic clergy to
minister to their patients. There had been some dispute about this and a number
of Catholic moralists, including McFadden in his first edition, had forbidden this
as encouraging false religion. McFadden changed his opinion in later editions.[2]
Doubtless non-Catholic patients had usually had access to their ministers —
there was no reason why patients themselves or their families could not make
the call — and the spiritual care of non-Catholic patients was seldom if ever actually hindered in Catholic hospitals. But the attitude of seeing this as cooperation in false religion was odious and its passing welcome.

Gerald Kelly wrote a number of articles concerning the issues addressed in
the Directives. First published from 1949 to 1954 as five booklets, *Medico-
Moral Problems* was revised and published as a one-volume book in 1958.[3]
These articles constitute a comprehensive treatise on medical ethics. Kelly here
continues the direction we have seen as Catholic Medical Ethics emphasizes the
procedures which make up the actual professional practice of nurses and physicians. Among these procedures, Kelly, like the Directives, stresses issues related
to reproduction. Though Kelly was never able to transcend either the definitional
or the physicalist methodological limitations of his discipline, he was able to
speak directly and without mystifying jargon. He admitted it when he did not
know the answer to a case. On a few questions, such as ectopic pregnancies and
the use of artificial hydration and nutrition, Kelly accepted the less restrictive
position more quickly than some of his colleagues. He died in 1964, just as the

ethics manuals. The most recent 1971 version is published by the United States
Catholic Conference, Department of Health Affairs.
[1]Catholic Hospital Association, "Ethical and Religious Directives," *Linacre Quarterly,* 15, Nos. 3-4 (July-Oct., 1948), p. 1.
[2]For his restrictive judgment, see *Medical Ethics for Nurses,* 1946, *op. cit.,* p.
333. By 1949, in the second edition, McFadden had changed his mind (pp. 407-
408).
[3](St. Louis, MO: The Catholic Hospital Association, 1949-1954, 1958).

Pill controversy was beginning. Gerald Kelly was the most influential, and arguably the best, of the Catholic moralists of the 1940's and 1950's.

The 1950's saw the publication of a number of new manuals in Catholic Medical Ethics. Among the more important were those of John Kenny, Edwin Healy, Thomas O'Donnell and Patrick O'Brien.[1] Kenny and Healy use the rubric "medical ethics" in their titles; by now this is an accepted designation. All show the same emphasis on physical interventions for physical illnesses which has become typical. Catholic Medical Ethics has now become a self-conscious field of study. Its goal is to analyze and make ethical judgments concerning those procedures which physicians and nurses do in their professional practice. In this analysis it is still, in 1960, virtually alone.

Methodology

The middle period of American Catholic Medical Ethics (1940-1960) continues the pervasive use of the same physicalist criteria we have already noted. The major manuals of these two decades found the principle of the double effect, with its cause and effect precision, especially apt at supporting ethical judgments on the procedures stressed in modern medicine. But in addition to this there was an often subtle yet clear and considerable increase in the role that Church authority, particularly the authority of Pope Pius XII, played in medical ethical analysis. The manuals now came to rely more and more heavily on Church decisions. This reliance often overshadowed other forms of reasoning and argumentation. Thus, in addition to physicalism, American Catholic Medical Ethics came in an increased way under the influence of what I have called "ecclesiastical positivism."[2]

Ecclesiastical positivism in medical ethics (or in moral theology, generally) is not, of course, a creation of the 1940's and 1950's. With the papacy of Pius XII (1939-1958), however, more stress is given to papal authority in medical ethics than had previously been the case. Whereas in the earlier period the emphasis was on working out the fundamental physicalist methodology and in developing the specifications needed to apply it to difficult cases, now there is a shift toward a defense of these principles and conclusions. Whereas earlier literature is directed mainly to Roman Catholic readers, and presumes their agreement, now Catholic moralists are more aware of the diversity of their audience. Both Catholics and non-Catholics may need convincing. Thus Catholics are urged to respect the inerrant authority of the Church, which is said to guarantee the decisions reached, even though these may be disputed by non-Catholic physicians. Non-Catholics, too, are asked to respect the decisions of the Catholic Magisterium, which is said to be the only authority capable of cor-

---

[1] John P. Kenny, *Principles of Medical Ethics* (Westminster, MD: The Newman Press, 1952, 2nd ed., 1962); Edwin F. Healy, *Medical Ethics* (Chicago: Loyola University Press, 1956); Thomas J. O'Donnell, *Morals in Medicine* (Westminster, MD: The Newman Press, 1956, 2nd ed., 1959); Patrick A. Finney and Patrick O'Brien, *Moral Problems in Hospital Practice: A Practical Handbook* (St. Louis, MO: B. Herder, 1956). This was a revision of Finney's 1922 book.

[2] For a detailed analysis, see Kelly, *The Emergence, op. cit.,* pp. 311-320.

rectly interpreting the natural law. Since the natural law binds all people, the interpretations of the Catholic Magisterium are said as well to bind everyone. The obvious question of how the natural law, which is supposed to be available to "unaided human reason," can be known in fact only by the Catholic hierarchy, was seldom raised at the time, and has never received a satisfactory answer.[1]

One of the causes for this shift toward ecclesiastical positivism was the increasing integration of Catholics into the mainstream of American life. In 1900 there were an estimated 12 million Catholics in the United States.[2] By 1940 the number had probably risen to 30 million, though the official *Catholic Directory* for the year put it at 23 million. The year 1921 marked the first of a number of restrictive immigration laws, which led to a relative stabilization of the American Catholic population. John Tracy Ellis notes that second and third generation Catholics refused to stay in Catholic ghettos and spread out into the American culture.[3] As they did, Catholic hospitals became an important part of the American health care system, offering medical services to non-Catholics, who in turn became more active in the Catholic institutions. The Second World War also increased the interaction of Catholics and others in medicine. American Catholic scholars were beginning to move out into wider intellectual circles. Thus what had needed (or had seemed to need) little defense in a literature directed mainly to Catholics now came to demand a more explicit apologetic.

The degree of interest in medical ethics shown by the new pope also contributed to the emphasis on church authority. There had until now been relatively few papal interventions in the area.[4] But during the 1940's and 1950's Pope Pius XII and his curial agents issued large numbers of statements of various kinds on medical ethics. Writing in 1955, Gerald Kelly estimated that there were to that moment about sixty different pronouncements by the pope. These were listed in a number of the manuals and gathered in anthologies. Thus, although Catholic Medical Ethics still proclaimed that its teachings were based on natural law and not on magisterial decree, in practice it was often the decisions of the pope which caused American Catholic moralists to change their ideas and how they expressed them. Though rejected in theory, ecclesiastical positivism — the notion that right and wrong is posited by the Church rather than discovered by human reason in the Natural Law — came to be of central operative importance in the Catholic Medical Ethics of the 1940's and 1950's.

[1]No attempt at analysis is possible here. For one early query, see Norman St. John-Stevas, *Life, Death and the Law* (Cleveland: World Publishing, 1961), pp. 29-31. See also Gregory Baum, "The Right to Dissent," *Commonweal*, August 23, 1968; *The Magisterium and Morality, Readings in Moral Theology*, No. 3. Charles E. Curran and Richard A. McCormick, eds. (New York: Paulist Press, 1982); John Boyle, "The Natural Law and the Magisterium," in *ibid.*, pp. 430-460.
[2]John Tracy Ellis, *American Catholicism*, (Chicago: University of Chicago Press, 1969), pp. 124-125.
[3]*Ibid.*, pp. 167-168.
[4]Writing in 1919, Austin O'Malley notes how few there are, and how many questions remain undecided (*The Ethics of Medical Homicide and Mutilation* [New York: Devin-Adair, 1922], preface).

This combination of physicalism and ecclesiastical positivism is apparent in McFadden's *Medical Ethics*. He clearly insists that his is a work in ethics, based on the Natural Law and not on specifically Catholic or Christian sources of revelation. Indeed, in his third edition he says he has eliminated the constant use of the word "Catholic," since he wants to be clear that the judgments of the Natural Law bind everyone, not just Catholics.[1] Yet his manual stresses the pronouncements of the magisterium and often cites them as part of his analysis. In one instance he explicitly changes his mind from an earlier edition, based not on reasoning but on a statement of Pius XII.[2] Physicalist criteria play the central role in McFadden's method. Indeed, he goes into more detail on physicalist specifications than many of his contemporaries, and some of his applications are simply absurd.[3] Yet McFadden's manual, which we have noted as the most influential textbook of the period, is generally typical of the physicalist and positivist method used by Catholic moralists of the time.

Gerald Kelly demonstrates the growing importance during these decades of magisterial decisions. In one of the articles included in his *Medico-Moral Problems*, Kelly asks why it is that non-Catholics are bound to follow the "Ethical" section of the "Ethical and Religious Directives." In the first version of this article (1949) he insists mainly on the scientific expertise of Catholic moralists. Because they are the only ones studying medical ethics with any seriousness, it is normal that they alone have gathered the skill needed to interpret the natural law. The directives bind, however, not because of church authority, but because they are proper interpretations of Natural Law made by expert scientists.[4] By 1958, when papal pronouncements have proliferated, Kelly must change his argument. In the 1958 version of the same article, Kelly argues that magisterial teaching, guaranteed by divine help, "is a practical necessity for most men."[5] Kelly has here shifted his emphasis away from Natural Law — though he still insists, of course, that the magisterium does not *make* moral law; it interprets

---

[1]Healy, *op. cit.,* 3rd ed., p. xiii.

[2]3rd ed., p. 72; 4th ed., p. 71.

[3]One example is his discussion of the number and size of holes required in a perforated condom if this method is to be used to gather semen for sterility testing. Unlike some other Catholic moralists of the time, he concludes that since it is unlikely that the quantity of semen which gets through the holes will be sufficient for conception, the entire procedure is immoral (4th ed., pp. 95-97). Since the whole idea is that the married couple have been unable to conceive, such detail shows how physicalism reduces itself to patent absurdity. Another example of the same kind is found in his analysis of truth telling. He says that as long as the physical words might possibly designate the truth, the doctor can say them even though the patient has little realistic chance of knowing what they really mean and even though the doctor obviously intends that the patient be deceived, though for supposedly benevolent motives. Thus, a physician can tell a feverish patient that his temperature is normal, and "mentally reserve" that it is normal only for someone racked with a disease that causes high fever (3rd ed., pp. 371-373). If the patient thinks the doctor means it is normal for normal (not-sick) people, that is the patient's misinterpretation.

[4]Part I, 1949, pp. 5-9.

[5]*Medico-Moral Problems,* 1958 ed., p. 29.

the Natural Law — toward the authority of the Catholic Magisterium. He finds this role of authority particularly necessary in the matter of artificial contraception.[1] The physicalist use of the double effect principle is also of central importance in Kelly's analysis, though he does avoid some of the more startling conclusions to which this method can lead.[2] The manuals of Kenny, Healy, O'Donnell, and Finney and O'Brien differ in some emphases, but are essentially similar.[3]

A number of important issues were analyzed and conclusions reached during these decades. In some cases American Catholic Medical Ethics made substantial contributions to what must be seen as humane and theologically valid judgments. Possibly the most significant of these is the development and application of the traditional concepts of "ordinary" and "extraordinary" means of preserving and prolonging life. Pope Pius XII revived this centuries-old distinction, insisting that it was not morally obligatory to make use of unreasonably burdensome or humanly useless treatment to prolong life.[4] Only "ordinary," i.e., humanly reasonable procedures, were obligatory. Gerald Kelly argued that this meant that medically-induced (artificial) nutrition need not be used in all cases.[5] Other American moralists also insisted on the humane application of the distinction. In this way Catholic Medical Ethics developed a tradition which remains of value today in supporting a national consensus opposed to the technological vitalism of some approaches to modern medicine.

Another topic of importance to be resolved during this period was that of organ transplantation. Though some moralists were at first opposed (McFadden for one), an agreement gradually emerged that this procedure was not the "direct" mutilation forbidden by a physicalist interpretation of the principle of totality, but was rather a gift of self to other supported by the Christian principle of love of neighbor in the context of God's creative love for and alliance with His people.[6] This was one of the very few analyses in Catholic Medical Ethics during this period to break with the physicalist method. In this case, too, the fact that

[1] 1958 ed., pp. 153-155.
[2] He does not insist on waiting until the Fallopian tube is about to burst in a woman with an ectopic pregnancy (1958 ed., pp. 213-217); he does not reject altogether the use of perforated condoms in sterility testing (pp. 218-227); he does not use the physicalist analysis of lies and mental reservations.
[3] See Kelly, *The Emergence, op. cit.,* pp. 371-395.
[4] "Prolongation of Life: Allocution to an International Congress of Anesthesiologists," *The Pope Speaks,* 4 (1957-1958), pp. 393-398.
[5] *Medico-Moral Problems,* 1958 edition, p. 130; "The Duty of Using Artificial Means of Preserving Life," *Theological Studies,* 11 (1950), pp. 218-220; "The Duty to Preserve Life," *Theological Studies,* 12 (1951), pp. 550-556, esp. p. 555.
[6] The position was advanced, against the opinion then generally held that organ transplantation was a direct mutilation forbidden by the principle of totality, by Bert Cunningham in his doctoral dissertation, "The Morality of Organ Transplantations," *Catholic University of America Studies in Sacred Theology,* 86 (Washington, DC: Catholic University of America Press, 1944). For further detail see Kelly, "Individual and Corporatism in a Personalist Ethic: An Analysis of Organ Transplants," in *Personalist Morals: Essays in Honor of Professor Louis Janssens,* J.A. Selling, ed. (Leuven: University Press, 1988), pp. 150-157.

Catholic tradition had come to support the procedure was important, perhaps even essential, for the acceptance of organ transplants in the United States.

In 1960 Catholic Medical Ethics in the United States stood virtually alone in the field. It had developed and was applying and defending a precise, presumably adequate, and universally applicable methodology. But the 1960's would bring two new factors, tremors which would shake the discipline. Within the Church there would be Vatican II and all that went with it. And as philosophers and non-Catholic theologians discovered medical ethics, there would be competition and extra-Catholic dialogue. The name, the definition, and the method were to undergo criticism from within and without.

THE LATER PERIOD (1960 TO THE PRESENT)

Perhaps the most obvious characteristic of Roman Catholic Medical Ethics from the mid-1960's to the present is that it is no longer the only source or even the single most important source of medical ethical scholarship. Indeed, except for certain methodological discussions where Catholic scholars and members of the hierarchy continue to discuss specifically Catholic approaches, it is no longer possible to locate Catholic Medical Ethics as truly distinct. The field is now essentially ecumenical, and Catholics join theologians from other traditions and philosophers who represent no particular religious matrix. There has been an unprecedented growth in medical ethics in the last three decades. The literature is enormous. Whereas *Hospital Progress* and *Linacre Quarterly* had been virtually alone as medical ethics journals, such periodicals now abound, led by the prominent *Hastings Center Report,* which began publication in 1971. Medical ethics think-tanks have grown up all over the country; hospitals have ethics committees and there are associations of such committees as well as consultants to help them get started; the federal government and state governments have commissions and task forces; law courts hear cases; hospitals and medical schools hire ethicists; medical journals publish articles on ethics. Catholic Medical Ethics plays an important role in this, but it no longer plays the only role; it does not even play the leading role.[1]

Name and Definition

We have noted that American Catholic Medical Ethics stressed those explicitly medical procedures such as surgery and other interventions which had come to typify the medical profession's actual practice. In contrast to this individual professional approach, today's field has extended its topical array to include the entire sphere of individual and structural, microethical and macroethical issues connected directly or indirectly to medicine and biology. Political, social, psychological, national and international concerns now constitute an important part of medical ethics. This is due partly to the ecumenical growth in the field and partly to the changing emphasis since Vatican II within Catholic moral theology from individual to structural issues. Most of today's scholars applaud this ex-

---

[1] The number of Catholic hospitals has declined since 1960.

pansion.[1] Earlier American manuals were too strictly limited to individual acts and procedures. Since the 1960's there has been a trend to return to some degree to the wider definition found in European Pastoral Medicine,[2] though American authors have never expanded the field to include the entire range of topics in that earlier body of literature.

The name given to the discipline has reflected this definitional change in emphasis. Though "medical ethics" remains one of the accepted rubrics, it has been joined by "bioethics," "biomedical ethics" and "health care ethics." Each suggests the centrality of "life" and "health" rather than of professional medicine. The first two reflect as well the growing importance of biology, especially of genetic research, and of its potentially radical social effects. The third, "health care ethics," most clearly emphasizes the structural aspects of health care, which stretch well beyond the medical profession. This rubric also has the essential advantage of including nurses and other health care professionals and para-professionals as central to the project. The term "medicine" is sometimes restricted to the practice of licensed physicians; "medical ethics" used to mean physicians' codes of etiquette and advancement. For these reasons, "health care ethics" is probably the single best rubric, and has been used as the title of the recent volume by Benedict Ashley and Kevin O'Rourke, the most complete Catholic manual of the last twenty years.[3] The more traditional "medical ethics" will continue in general usage, however, and if properly understood, actually has the advantage of including nurses and others in the practice of medicine.

Methodology

The physicalist and positivist frameworks of the 1940's and 1950's are now beset with radical challenges from both within and without the Catholic community. It is true that some continue to support them with little change.[4] And some have developed refined methodological precisions which eliminate certain of the more obvious mistakes they lead to.[5] But what can rightly be called the

---

[1]For one suggested list of topics, see Richard A. McCormick, "Issue Areas for a Medical Ethics Program," in Veatch, *op. cit.,* pp. 103-121.

[2]And in a few Canadian works as well. For example, compare Jules Paquin, *Morale et médecine* (Montreal: Comité des hôpitaux du Québec, 1955) to any of the 1950's manuals in the United States. For detail see Kelly, *The Emergence, op. cit.,* pp. 193-199. Similar tendencies can be found in other French Canadian authors, possibly resulting from their acquaintance with French works in Pastoral Medicine.

[3]Benedict M. Ashley and Kevin D. O'Rourke, *Health Care Ethics: A Theological Analysis,* 2nd ed. (St. Louis, MO: The Catholic Health Association of the United States, 1982).

[4]The best source for this approach is *Ethics and Medics,* a newsletter published by the Pope John Center in Braintree, Massachusetts.

[5]Germain Grisez best exemplifies this attempt. His work on act-analysis, distinguishing divisible from indivisible acts, has resulted in a better approach to the principle of double effect than that of previous moralists (*Abortion: The Myths, the Realities and the Arguments* [New York: Corpus Books, 1970], pp. 329-346; *The Way of the Lord Jesus, Vol. I: Christian Moral Principles* [Chicago: Francis-

center — Richard McCormick calls it "the extreme middle"[1] — in contemporary Catholic health care ethics has rejected both frameworks.

Emphasis on the physical analysis of individual acts and human faculties has been replaced by an emphasis on the human person considered as individual and as a social being. It is the human person adequately considered who is the basis for ethical analysis.[2] Thus physicalism has been criticized by personalism. The principle of double effect, once of central importance, has been challenged by a less precise but far more adequate methodological approach which many call proportionalism. Acts are no longer decisive in themselves. Contexts and consequences are of primary operative importance. Themes of central symbolic significance in Christian anthropology, such as the meaning of God's sovereignty over creation and the meaning of human suffering, are freed to engage us in the vital task of discerning, in Catholic theological context, the meaning of human life.[3]

Similarly, the "extreme middle" of contemporary American Catholic Medical Ethics has rejected the almost automatic deference given to official Church documents by Catholic moralists of the 1940's and 1950's. This rejection is not a denial of the Catholic tradition; nor is it a rejection of the role of the bishops and the pope. Rather it is a return to the tradition of Natural Law, according to which God has visibly sacramentalized in the very ongoing act of creation the divine will for human behavior. The Natural Law, as Thomas Aquinas put it, is the participation of the rational creature in the Eternal Law of the very divine plan.[4] Moral truth is not extrinsic. It is not imposed on persons from without, either by a testy God or by God's chosen representatives. Rather it is the discovered way to human thriving. And in the process of this discovery all humans have a share. Contemporary Catholic health care ethics is thus returning to the best of its own tradition.

THE FUTURE

This essay will conclude by asking one question about the future. Will American Catholic Health Care Ethics survive? At one level, of course, the answer is easy. Catholicism will survive in the United States; so will its medical ethics. But on another level the question can be asked in a different way: will "the extreme middle" survive the post-Vatican II period? Will the center hold?

can Herald Press, 1983], pp. 298-299). He has continued a reliance on physicalism, however, coupled with an ecclesiastical positivism which goes beyond even that of most of the older tradition (for one discussion see Bernard Hoose, *Proportionalism*, pp. 111-112).

[1] *Health and Medicine in the Catholic Tradition* (New York: Crossroad, 1987), p. 3.

[2] The phrase comes from the official Vatican II commentary on the document on the Church. Louis Janssens has developed its ethical implications (see his "Artificial Insemination" Ethical Considerations," *Louvain Studies*, 8 [1980], pp. 3-29; see McCormick, *Health and Medicine in the Catholic Tradition*, pp. 15-20).

[3] Theological principles like these are really hermeneutic themes essential to any theological health care ethics. For detail, see Kelly, *The Emergence, op. cit.*, pp. 436-437; Kelly, "Roman Catholic Medical Ethics and the Ethos of Modern Medicine," *op. cit.*, pp. 58, 65-67.

[4] *Summa Theologiae*, Ia, IIae, 91,2, *in corp.*

The answer to that question is, unfortunately, not apparent. The kind of writing and teaching now being done by so many Catholic moralists will probably continue to be done. But what is not self-evident is that it will continue to be done as Catholic writing and teaching. There are signs of a restriction now, of a return from dialogue to condemnation, of a rejection of the Catholic theological center.[1] Oppression of this kind closes down the very theological work which defines the best of Catholic health care ethics.

Prior to the last twenty-five years or so, Roman Catholic medical moralists were virtually alone in attempting a rigorous study of the ethical analysis of medicine. Despite serious shortcomings in that analysis, Catholic theologians and Catholic pastors accomplished something of true significance. Catholic Medical Ethics played an important role in the creation of the contemporary multifaceted discipline which health care ethics has become. In a number of areas Catholic Medical Ethics laid a base for analyses and conclusions which are now becoming standard medical ethics procedure in the United States and elsewhere. Today Catholic theologians are active along with their non-Catholic colleagues in further developing and refining important health care policy in this nation. But the future contribution of Catholic theology will be seriously hampered if the center fails to survive. Catholics are no longer alone as medical ethicists. A return to the restrictive methodologies of the past would serve only to isolate Catholic theology from the discipline. Scholars would refer to Catholic Medical Ethics as an intriguing but largely irrelevant anomaly, and the contribution of Catholic theology to medical ethics would atrophy. If, however, Catholic Health Care Ethics remains faithful to the message of Jesus Christ and to the best of the Catholic theological heritage, it can continue to be an essential component in American health care as it continues to serve the revelation of God.

---

[1] A number of examples can be cited. Vatican reaction to the theological scholarship of Charles Curran, to the women religious who signed the statement on abortion in the *New York Times,* to Archbishop Hunthausen, and to sterilization policy in some Catholic hospitals has led to a sense of fear among American Catholic Bishops and Theologians.

CHAPTER THIRTEEN

Lay Participation in the Catholic Church in America, 1789-1989

Robert F. Leavitt, S.S.
St. Mary's Seminary and University, Baltimore

The story of the laity in the Catholic Church from the American Revolution to the present is a highly episodic tale. It is characteristically told as a string of small chapters within the dominant hierarchical narrative, chapters with headings like "trusteeism," "immigrant Church," "labor movement," "Americanism," "Catholic Action" and "Lay Ministry." Each chapter contributes its own small part to the historical flow of Catholicism in our country, but the chapters themselves are rarely, if ever, extracted and read together as a theological history in themselves. In a limited fashion, this is the task of this essay.[1]

Our story pivots retrospectively around those special moments of lay awareness and activity since the founding of our country.[2] The theological meaning of those moments, of course, cannot be evaluated by measuring them against the standard of Vatican Council II or, as often happens, against some ideal ecclesial construct. They must be measured against a "sliding" scale of ecclesiological consciousness and cultural appraisal which history alone provides. Their significance lies in the lessons they teach about a church gradually appreciating its own nature and, in the process, reevaluating the cultural milieu of which it is a part. The "pilgrim" Church was a reality before it became a conciliar theme. And, "reading the signs of the times" was always a part of the Church's exegesis of culture, even if we no longer fully share some assessments that have previously been made.

The key motif of our narrative and theological essay is the "participation" of the laity in the life and mission of the Church. The definition, focus and organizational forms that this participation has taken these last two hundred years have varied considerably. Lay participation in the Church has been influenced by American cultural forces as well as Vatican initiatives, waxing and waning under the irregular pressure of social and ecclesial dynamics.

---

[1] On the history of Catholics in the US, see Sydney E. Ahlstrom, *A Religious History of the American People* (New Haven: Yale University Press, 1972); James Hennesey, S.J., *American Catholics: A History of the Roman Catholic Community in the US* (New York: Oxford University Press, 1981); John Tracy Ellis, *American Catholicism* (Garden City, NY: Doubleday, 1985); *Encyclopedia of the American Religious Experience: Studies of Traditions and Movements*, Charles H. Lippy and Peter W. Williams, eds. (New York: Charles Scribners), Vol. I; *Documents of American Catholic History*, John Tracy Ellis, ed. (Wilmington: Michael Glazier, 1987), Vols. 1-3.

[2] See Andrew M. Greeley, *The American Catholic: A Social Portrait* (New York: Basic Books, 1977), ch. 1. Greeley prefers what he calls "the mosaic with permeable boundaries" model to the melting pot or the mosaic images of Catholic assimilation.

For historical as well as theological reasons, we cannot judge earlier ideas of lay involvement against contemporary models. Any deficiency in a model of lay participation must somehow lie within the historical and religious horizon of the period itself, and not be anachronistically determined from a later standpoint. For that reason, we are not as interested in the "theories" of lay participation that have been proposed in the past as in the often spontaneous structural adaptations which lay and clergy have invented in response to a particular set of needs and circumstances.

After making some brief observations about the European historical background on the topic of lay participation, and then reviewing the colonial period in America, we will track the story of lay involvement in the Church from 1789 to the present, concluding with the recent Synod on the Laity as the international harbinger, perhaps, of a new period of national lay participation in the Church.

A EUROPEAN AND COLONIAL PROLOGUE

The Reformation in the sixteenth century and the Enlightenment in the seventeenth and eighteenth centuries, as much as theology and canon law, have profoundly influenced the Church's thinking about the role of the laity in the modern period. Luther's theology undercut the ecclesiological grounds for the strong distinction of clergy and laity. In denying the sacramentality of orders, the weight of his theological axe fell sharply on the clerical branch. Onto this wound, though, he grafted a "high" theology of the Christian (lay) vocation founded in baptism.[1] The Reformation thus established a theological tension between clergy and laity which aggravated an already unsteady opposition. It would subsequently mean that, in Rome, any "lay movement" not explicitly subordinating itself to the hierarchy was viewed as possibly subverting it.

The Calvinist and Zwinglian reform movements followed in Luther's footsteps and radicalized further his critique of the hierarchical principle. The Reformation promoted the lay principle, already bolstered by renaissance humanism, at the expense of the clerical one. Memories of Montanism, the Cathari and Waldenses, not to mention Marsilius of Padua's *Defensor Pacis*, filled the theological armory of the Counter Reformation response. The Catholic Church asserted an even stronger theology of the hierarchy as part of its own apologetic and practice.

The Enlightenment is, of course, the threshold of modernity itself. From Montaigne and Voltaire to Locke, Hume and Kant, their epoch laid the social, political and moral foundations of the modern period.[2] Kant's aphorism summing up Enlightenment, *sapere aude* (dare to know) was couched as a maxim of free inquiry, yet the animus of the Enlightenment was directed to a large extent against religion, especially Catholicism. Voltaire openly proclaimed *ecraser*

---

[1]On Luther's theology, see Paul Althaus, *The Theology of Martin Luther* (Philadelphia: Fortress Press, 1966), chs. 22 and 23.
[2]See Peter Gay, *The Enlightenment: An Interpretation* (New York: W.W. Norton & Company, 1977). For a summary of the effects of the Enlightenment on secularity and religion, see Peter L. Berger, *The Sacred Canopy: Elements of a Sociological Theory of Religion* (Garden City, NY: Doubleday, 1969).

l'infame (erase the infamy) against the Church. For the *philosophes*, this was a Church exalting hierarchy against democracy and dogma against independent thought, a medieval religious institution in alliance with a medieval political one.

Like the Reformation, the Enlightenment was yoked to a growing national consciousness and changing political realities. The Church was increasingly regarded as an intruder in national culture as well as a purveyor of obscurantist doctrine. The Enlightenment "mentality" scorned metaphysics and mystery in favor of science and sociology. In the main, its proponents were laymen, Protestants or lapsed Catholics. The word for the laity in French, *laic*, and the word for secularist, *laiciste*, have the same root because the Enlightenment virtually identified them.

> "The dominant feature of this period is the apostacy of the educated laity, and their determination to promote by every means in their power the complete secularization of society."[1]

The French Revolution enacted laws to disenfranchise the Church and undermine its clerical dimension, e.g., in the Civil Constitution of the Clergy. Throughout the nineteenth century, French laicism continued to promote liberal political and social arrangements which were seen in Rome as detrimental to its moral and religious interests.

So, the European religious and ideological drama, from the Reformation through the Enlightenment, is an essential prologue and context to understand the Catholic Church's approach to the issue of the laity in the United States. Our own political evolution, nourished by Enlightenment principles and conducted by Protestant colonialists, would leave the Vatican wary and suspicious of the new American experiment.

In February 1604, King James I ordered all priests to leave England in less than a month. The first permanent English settlement in America was in Jamestown three years later. Sir George Calvert, who became a Catholic himself about 1624, helped to establish a broad spirit of religious toleration for Catholics in Virginia and Maryland.

In June 1632, King Charles I designated the land north of Virginia as a colony, named *Terra Mariae* or "Maryland" after Queen Henrietta Marie. Catholicism was officially established in this new colony in 1634 when three Jesuits arrived on the *Ark* and the *Dove*. The first indications of an active

---

[1]Stephen Neill and Hans-Ruedi Weber, *The Laymen in Christian History* (London: SCM, 1963), p. 311. Also see *Theology in Transition: A Bibliographical Evaluation 1954-1964*, Elmer O'Brien, S.J., ed. (New York: Herder & Herder, 1965), p. 18: "The dictionary of Larousse defines *'laic'* as 'one who does not belong to the Church,' and with this handicap to live down one can understand that French theologians have been foremost in magnifying the position of the laity in the Church."

Catholic laity date from the end of this decade when Captain Cornwaleys, Fulk Brent, and Thomas Greene were defending religious liberty in Maryland.[1]

Because English Catholics in the new colony sent their children to the continent for schooling, Maryland Catholicism nurtured a very well-educated laity. Though small in numbers, they were often quite wealthy and influential during the early 18th century.

During the same period, anti-Catholicism was transferred to the northern colonies and cultivated by Fox's *Book of Martyrs* and the *New England Primer*. In 1688, Boston executed a Catholic, Ann Glover, as a witch. The settlement of English, German and Irish tradespeople in the 1750's increased the Catholic lay population in Pennsylvania, Delaware and Maryland. It also abetted continuing anti-Catholic prejudice expressed, for example, in the use of "transubstantiation oaths" to bar Catholics from holding public office. In 1776, American Catholics constituted about one percent of the total colonial population, concentrated in Maryland, Pennsylvania and the Maritimes.

The Church in colonial America amounted to scattered congregations in these areas, served mostly by Jesuits. Laity sought to establish themselves economically and to resist religious intolerance. "With no effective episcopal government for 150 years, colonial Catholicism everywhere developed independent ways which in the post-colonial era would be accommodated to more traditional Church polity with difficulty."[2]

ESTABLISHMENT AND IMMIGRATION: 1789-1860

After the Revolution, the task of organizing the Catholic Church in the new nation began. In the colonial period, American Catholics were under the jurisdiction of the vicar apostolic of the London District. John Carroll (1735-1815) led an effort to work out practical and spiritual arrangements for the clergy between the years 1782 and 1784, but the issue of appointing a bishop dragged on and was complicated by varied political concerns. Finally, with the bull *Ex Hac Apostolicae*, Carroll was appointed Bishop of Baltimore (November 6, 1789). He was consecrated in England by the Benedictine Bishop Charles Walmesley in Lulworth Castle in August 1790.[3]

His missionary experience gave Carroll a very practical ecclesial sense about how best to establish the Catholic Church in the new nation. He strongly endorsed education for clergy and laity, establishing strong precedents in Georgetown Academy (1790) and St. Mary's Seminary (1791) for the future of Catholic higher education in America. He favored the election of bishops by the clergy and less episcopal control of property, causes that would not find acceptance in Rome and would cause him considerable trouble at home.

Gradually, the structure of the Catholic Church in the United States came to resemble the European arrangement. But, the revolution had changed the

---

[1]James Hennesey, "Catholicism in the English Colonies," in *Encyclopedia of the American Religious Experience, op. cit.,* Vol. I, p. 354.

[2]Debra Campbell, "Catholicism from Independence to World War I" in *Encyclopedia of the American Religious Experience, op. cit.,* Vol. I, p. 369.

[3]See Hennesey, *American Catholics, op. cit.,* pp. 69-88.

Church's legal status into something that neither canon law nor theology nor European ecclesiastical culture understood or appreciated.

The issue of "trusteeism" (the lay administration of local Catholic parishes) inaugurated a long period of ecclesiastical tension, beginning with Carroll and lay Catholics in New York and Philadelphia. The requirements of canon law confronted the colonial customs of "congregational" Catholicism, nationalism and lay rights. These three forces together made the issue of trusteeism emblematic of the emerging Catholic laity in America.[1]

Between 1790 and 1820, the Catholic lay population grew from 35,000 to 195,000. But the phenomenon of mass immigration afterwards boosted Catholic numbers by 1860 to 3,103,000. This made the Catholic Church the largest religious body in America by 1865.[2] Concurrent with the westward expansion, immigration diversified and increased the Catholic population in waves. First Irish, and then German, Catholics established themselves in various regions, mostly in the east and midwest, deeply rooting an ethnic Catholicism in the country. This fostered tensions with movements which periodically reasserted themselves in groups such as the American Protectionist Association (APA), in the anti-immigration laws of the 1920's, and criticism of the presidential bids of Al Smith and John Kennedy.

In the mid-nineteenth century, prominent converts to Catholicism sharply contrasted with the immigrant image of the expanding Church and recalled the elite Catholic laity of the colonial and revolutionary eras like the Calverts and the Carrolls. An episcopal pastor in New York, James Roosevelt Bayley, a relative of Elizabeth Seton, converted in 1840. Others included James McMaster (a newspaper editor), Levi Silliman Ives (Episcopal bishop of North Carolina), William Henry Anderson (professor at Columbia), and Eliza Allen Starr (poet and essayist).[3] But the two converts who best exemplified the effort of lay Catholics to reconcile their new-found religious faith with American culture were Isaac Hecker and Orestes Brownson. The foundation of the Paulists by Hecker in 1858, like Elizabeth Seton's establishment of the Sisters of Charity over fifty years earlier, represented an outlet for lay dedication and evangelization which church structures did not readily provide.

A history of lay activity in the Church would be overly literal not to view the establishment and flourishing of religious orders in America as part of the nineteenth century metamorphosis of lay Catholicism. Catholic education in the United States, from the Ursulines in Louisiana in the early eighteenth century through the establishment of Notre Dame by the Congregation of the Holy Cross in 1842, became a distinctive feature of the Church in this country. Laity benefitted from the educational mission of these groups, and the orders, in turn, fertilized their own growth from the educational ovum. Between 1789 and 1859, 51 women's religious communities, 16 of which were native American congre-

---

[1] Jay Dolan, *op. cit,* pp. 158-194, treats the issue of trusteeism in the broad context of the development of parochial organization in nineteenth-century Catholicism.

[2] See Ahlstrom, *op. cit.,* p. 527.

[3] Campbell, *op. cit.,* p. 364.

The Catholic Church had its American historic roots in states prominent for slavery, e.g., Louisiana, Virginia and Maryland. But neither the hierarchy nor the laity in the nineteenth century saw the institution of slavery as a violation of human rights. Immigrants, not emancipated slaves, occupied the Church's attention after the Civil War, even though it is reckoned that over 100,000 Blacks from Louisiana were Catholics. The Oblate Sisters of Providence (1829) and the Josephites (1874) ministered to Blacks in a thoroughly segregated Catholic Church. Meanwhile, some black Catholics distinguished themselves as ecclesiastics, such as the Healy brothers: James became Bishop of Portland, Maine (1875) and Patrick, President of Georgetown (1873-82).[1]

The First Plenary Council of Baltimore, held in October 1829, dealt with the institutional issues of the Catholic Church in America in the first half of the nineteenth century.[2] It secured episcopal authority, clerical incardination, church property, sacramental uniformity for immigrant ethnic differences, and the primacy of schools and a catechism. Religious women served immigrant parishes on the frontier where priests were not plentiful and the religious orders began to marshall a vast army of servants for educational and charitable purposes.

LABOR AND AMERICANISM: 1870 TO 1920

The new immigrants in the last part of the nineteenth century came from southern and eastern Europe. They would eventually swell the Catholic population to 16 million by 1910. They took the place of the Irish immigrants of the 1830's who were now acceding to civil service jobs in the police and fire departments. The first Irish mayor of Boston was elected in 1884. The rise of industrialization in the urban east at this time found a ready supply of workers in both old and new Catholic immigrants. Organized labor soon became the burning social issue with Catholic laity increasingly taking positions of leadership in the movement. At this time, labor unions required an oath of secrecy and were connected with socialist principles. *Qui Pluribus* in 1846 committed the Church against socialism, so it was understandable why a number of bishops actively opposed the unions. The violent episode of the Molly Maguires in 1877 among Pennsylvania coal miners confirmed lay and episcopal reservations about the union movement. The Knights of Labor, under the leadership of Terence Powderly, eventually won recognition by the bishops in 1886 and, with Gibbons' intercession at Rome, the Vatican's approval. Lay participation in the labor movement through women such as Mary Harris ("Mother") Jones and Mary Kenney O'Sullivan strengthened the Church's presence in the cities among working people.[3]

Labor movements were not the only expression of Catholic lay activity in the late nineteenth century. This period witnessed the rise of fraternal lay organizations whose purposes overlapped social and spiritual concerns. Irish and German immigrants had already created their own societies (the Ancient Order of

---

[1]*Ibid.*, p. 366.
[2]See *Pastoral Letters of the US Catholic Bishops*, Hugh J. Nolan, ed. (Washington, DC: USCC, 1984), pp. 35-49.
[3]Campbell, *op. cit.*, p. 368.

Hibernians and the German Catholic Central Verein), and in 1882 the Knights of Columbus, founded as an insurance association to assist widows and orphans, came into existence. Catholic laity also became involved in parish organizations such as the Rosary Altar Society, the Sodality of our Lady, the Holy name Society and Scapular Confraternities. They provided devotional supports for lay men and women. On the occasion of the American centennial (1889), a lay congress met in Baltimore organized by Catholic lay leaders Brownson, Onahan, Spaunhorst and Foy. "Lay representatives at Baltimore discussed a wide array of topics from education and charities to journalism, labor organizations, and lay activities."[1] In 1893, the congress met in Chicago and heard Rose Hawthorne Lathrop as well as other speakers who criticized the failure to reach out to Blacks and Indians, opposed the arms race, and generally promoted lay participation in the Church.[2] In the late nineteenth century reading circles and summer schools flourished among Catholic lay women, but disappeared by the end of the First World War.

> Because it witnessed the emergence of a new, articulate, and confident breed of lay leaders with a vision for the future, the period between 1885 and 1893 has been called the 'lay renaissance.' By the middle of the 1890's, however, the lay renaissance had foundered, in part, because other issues had deflected the attention of the hierarchy.[3]

By the end of the century, the American hierarchy was predominantly Irish, but the more recent waves of German immigrants, carrying a formidable linguistic barrier with them, presented a serious pastoral difficulty. Peter Paul Cahensly, a wealthy member of the German Parliament, travelled to America in 1874 and, concluding that German defections from Catholicism in America were happening at an alarming rate, petitioned Rome to establish national parishes and even national bishops for the German immigrants. This precipitated what gradually became known as the controversy over Americanism.[4] Two schools of thought on this issue were reflected in the hierarchy. Led by Gibbons and Ireland, the liberals took a positive view of adaptation, regarding the American experiment as a milieu conducive to the development of Catholicism. The conservatives (those spokesmen chiefly were Corrigan, McQuaid and the midwestern German bishops) did not wish to sacrifice distinctive marks of Catholic identity in a predominantly Protestant country. In a letter of 1895, Leo XIII praised the American hierarchy, but held that equality of all religions before the law was not, perhaps, the best arrangement. This probably would have been the end of it except that the French translation (1897) of Elliott's biography of Isaac Hecker, in which his approach to pastoral adaptation in America was described, met with fierce opposition from French conservatives. They reported the issue to Rome and Leo XIII, without consulting the American hierarchy, ultimately stated his

[1]*Ibid.*, p. 369.
[2]*Ibid.*
[3]*Ibid.*
[4]See Gerald P. Fogarty, *The Vatican and the American Hierarchy from 1870 to 1965* (Wilmington: Michael Glazier, 1985), ch. VI, for a thorough treatment of the Americanism controversy.

opinion in *Testem Benevolentiae* (1899). The errors condemned in the letter included assertions that one can modify doctrines to win converts and that individual judgment has rights against ecclesiastical authority. Liberals denied what they called the "phantom heresy" while conservatives felt vindicated. The scars of the controversy, however, continued long into the twentieth century when clergy and lay leaders struggled over how Catholicism should relate, no longer to the American political system, but now to its evolving cultural ethos.

In 1908, the Catholic Church in the United States ceased being a mission church and became a national hierarchy in its own right. Catholic participation in World War I, as in the Civil War fifty years earlier, helped to establish the patriotic credentials of the immigrants despite their foreign religious loyalty.

The Catholic Encyclopedia, published in 1910, summarized the ecclesial status of the laity in succinct canonical categories:

> The juridical condition of the laity in the Christian society is therefore determined by two considerations: their separation from the clergy, which excludes them from the performance of acts reserved to the latter; and second, their subjection to the spiritual authority of the clergy, which imposes certain obligations on them, while at the same time it confers on them certain rights.[1]

Noting that lay servers at Mass wear the cassock to "safeguard the principle of excluding the laity"[2] from liturgical rites, the article devotes no consideration at all to the theology or practice of the Catholic laity, in the Church and society, such as we have briefly reviewed.

Despite their subservient, nearly invisible place in the canonical field of vision, the Catholic laity in America had achieved a remarkable pastoral record. They had become a church with multiple ethnic groups, developed significant religious and lay institutions, organized themselves to protect their economic interests, and endured nativist prejudice while demonstrating their patriotism in two wars. One of them had signed the Declaration of Independence and the other had become chief justice of the Supreme Court. Lacking a theology or spirituality tailored for their new role in the United States, the American laity had elaborated, without realizing it, an *ad hoc* and distinctive American and ecclesial *modus vivendi*.

CATHOLIC ACTION AND SOCIAL ACTION: 1920-1945

The next period of lay activity in the Church will witness an increase in new organizations of lay involvement as well as a pronounced emphasis on social justice. Once again, these steps will be overshadowed by a recrudescent nativism.

The new immigrants who arrived in America at the beginning of the twentieth century once again ignited nativist hostility, now abetted by the rising

---

[1]*The Catholic Encyclopedia* (New York: Encyclopedia Press, 1910), Vol. VIII, p. 749.

[2]*Ibid.,* p. 750.

tide of Fundamentalism and made yet more menacing by the Ku Klux Klan. In 1928 the Democratic Party nominated the Irish Catholic governor of New York, Al Smith, for president. This provoked outright charges of the incompatibility of Catholicism with American Constitutional principles. Public fears were spread and reinforced by political cartoons showing Smith assembling his new Cabinet composed of the Pope and bishops. Not until 1960, and John Kennedy's successful bid for the presidency, would the nativist calumny be driven back decisively.

In the time between the wars, hierarchy and laity joined forces in building an impressive Catholic educational system. It even became common for the construction of schools to precede the building of churches once new parishes were established. Educational ventures expanded from the primary to the secondary level as Catholics recognized the benefits of schooling for social and economic advancement. But the underlying reason for the extraordinary phenomenon of Catholic schools was the protection of a religious culture.

The American democratic experiment made possible the progress of religion without legal or moral interference. The First Amendment guaranteed the disjunction of religion from politics, but just as important, it allowed the religious groups to compose their own responses to the ethos of the surrounding culture. The Catholic response was to preserve a religious heritage through its own social and educational apparatus, but at the same time to participate increasingly in the economic and political life of the nation. It allowed Catholics to exist as a group "in two worlds," at once, much as the counter-cultural covey might cautiously carry out transactions with the surrounding culture. In theological terms, it was a Catholic version, ethnic and a bit gothic, of the neo-orthodox critique.

Helping to secure this world apart were a new array of Catholic lay organizations. The Catholic Daughters of America were founded in 1903, the National Christ Child Society (for needy children) began in 1916, and the National Council of Catholic Women in 1920. At the theological extremes, Opus Dei was established in 1928 and the Catholic Worker Movement in 1933. These organizations, and many more like them, afforded Catholic laity numerous apostolic outlets not provided by the standard parish enterprises, the Rosary Altar Society, the Holy Name Society and the Scapulars.

The Catholic lay journal, *Commonweal,* began publication in 1924 to provide intelligent commentary on issues of public policy and faith, much like its Jesuit counterpart, *America* (1909). Along with the general Catholic migration to the middle-class went a new intellectual ferment among laity and clergy, sparked by the awareness of European thought and the involvement in American social issues.[1]

Naturally, the Depression hit the Catholic immigrant population very hard. Roosevelt would win Catholic lay support arguing that his social reconstruction programs answered the call of *Rerum Novarum* and *Quadragesimo Anno,* while Father John A. Ryan helped to fashion public policies in the spirit of the great social encyclicals. At the same time, some Catholic laity would be listening to the zealotry of Father Coughlin on the far right, and other intrepid ones devouring the leftist Christian anarchism of Peter Maurin, philosopher for the *Catholic*

---

[1]Ahlstrom, *op. cit.,* pp. 1007ff.

Worker. The pluralism of Catholic social thought in America, voiced by clergy and laity alike, would become an increasingly prominent feature of Catholic intellectual life after the next war.

In Europe, new voices on the laity's behalf began to be heard. Around 1900, the German movement called "Reform Catholicism" petitioned the Vatican to recognize the maturity of the Catholic laity in that country. Pius XI responded to this request in 1925 when he condemned the arch-conservative French lay movement *Action Francaise* and approved what he called "Catholic Action." Though defined defensively as the cooperation of the laity in the work of the hierarchy, it added official impetus to the yearning for greater lay involvement in the Church. Combined with the liturgical movement (originating in 1909 in Belgium) which promoted greater lay participation in the Mass, the European seeds were now planted for a new American vision of lay participation in the Church.

LAY ASSIMILATION
AND THE CONCILIAR APOGEE: 1945-1965

In Europe the 1940's were a significant period theologically and magisterially. The decade began with Pius XII's *Mystici Corporis Christi* (1941) which was an ecclesiological breakthrough, substituting the Pauline theme of the "Body of Christ" for the medieval canonical image of the "perfect society." The effect of the Pauline metaphor was to construct the hierarchical principle on top of a more basic biblical concept of the Church. Identifying the lay role in the Church passively and legally, such as the canonical view had established, would not succeed with a more organic theological category such as the "Body of Christ."[1]

Three years later, the Vatican issued *Divino Afflante Spiritu,* the "Magna Carta" of modern biblical studies. This opened the door for applying the historical methods in biblical exegesis, and more broadly paved the way for a more critical historical consciousness in the Church as a whole. One expression of this was the development of patristic studies in France which seemed to shift the categories of theological discussion from medieval scholasticism back to the Fathers. Called *nouvelle theologie* by its detractors, the patristic revival, in its own way, contributed theological paradigms not captured by scholastic categories. The work of De Lubac on grace and Teilhard de Chardin on evolution came under ecclesiastical fire, but it was clear that a new theological awakening was taking place in Europe. At the end of the decade, Pius XII issued *Humani Generis* condemning aspects of this new theological speculation.[2]

Finally, the appearance in 1947 of *Mediator Dei,* the great encyclical on the liturgy, made possible a new and much more active participation of the laity in the Mass. This was reinforced in 1956 with the revision of the services for Holy Week. Two years later, the "Dialogue Mass" dramatically symbolized what par-

---

[1]*Ibid.,* pp. 1012-1015.
[2]See O'Brien, *op. cit., passim.* The great modern theological work on the laity is Yves Congar, *Lay People in the Church: A Study for a Theology of the Laity,* trans. by Donald Attwater (Westminster: Newman Press, 1957).

ticipation meant in worship. All these developments in Europe set the stage for the further evolution of lay consciousness in America.

Lay Catholicism in the 1950's continued in the channels dug by earlier generations: involvement in parish organizations and national lay apostolates, support for parochial schools, the preservation of Catholic culture.[1] However, the earlier immigrant phenomenon was finished and its place taken by the post-war baby boom and suburban Catholic migration. The laity became increasingly more educated, but John Tracy Ellis and Thomas O'Dea criticized the Catholic community for impeding, with its ghetto mentality, the development of a genuine class of Catholic intellectuals in America. Some were *bona fide* intellectuals (John Courtney Murray, Thomas Merton, Daniel Callahan, William F. Buckley, Jr.), but in the 1950's when Catholics succeeded to secular prominence it was largely in television and the movies. Bing Crosby and Fulton J. Sheen brought a distinctive celebrity style to post-war Catholicism, a sign of genuine arrival in modern America: fame and recognition. Catholics were now so well accepted as Americans that Cardinal Spellman could lock horns with no less than Eleanor Roosevelt over federal aid to parochial schools and still not provoke a serious nativist reaction.

Will Herberg's *Protestant, Catholic, Jew* (1956) observed that by the 1950's Catholicism was just another way to be American. The "triple melting pot" absorbed the seasoning of each religious tradition while it flavored them in turn with its own distinctive American taste. Two decades later, Robert Bellah would be describing America's "civil religion" and in the 1980's Martin Marty began to speak of the "public church."[2] The issue of the assimilation of Catholics into the mainstream of American life would gradually yield to the larger issue of the secularization of American life, the drying up of the old Protestant ethos, and its replacement by Fundamentalism. Once digested and assimilated, what piquancy would Catholicism provide for American culture?

American Catholic journals, like *Cross Currents,* published articles by major European intellectuals (Jacques Maritain, Romano Guardini, Jean Danielou) giving interested laity a much broader theological and religious sensibility. The 1950's drew to a close with the publication of *We Hold These Truths* by John Courtney Murray, S.J., a highly original theological essay demonstrating the compatibility of Catholicism with American constitutional democracy. The Church, in America at least, had assimilated the Enlightenment.

John Kennedy's election as president in 1960 became the symbol of how far Irish Catholicism had come, but his exchanges with the Houston Ministerial Conference and Norman Vincent Peale, while astute as politics, did not show much Catholic commitment or intellectual depth. One could not tell from Kennedy's answers exactly what his Catholicism meant to him. Twenty years later Geraldine Ferraro, also one of immigrant stock, dodged the abortion issue

---

[1]For a survey of the kind of organizations and activities that were typical of laity in the 1950's, see Leo R. Ward, *Catholic Life, U.S.A.: Contemporary Lay Movements* (St. Louis: B. Herder, 1959).
[2]See Robert Bellah, *The Broken Covenant: American Civil Religion in Time of Trial* (New York: Seabury Press, 1975); Martin Marty, *The Public Church: Mainline — Evangelical — Catholic* (New York: Crossroads Books, 1981).

by distinguishing her private disagreement as a Catholic from her public allegiance to *Roe v. Wade*. Thus, a new generation of Catholic laity, who held more political influence than ever before, seemed poorly equipped to argue the value and compatibility of Catholic social ethics with American democratic pluralism.

The apogee of Church teaching on the laity, no doubt, was Vatican Council II (1963-1965). *The Dogmatic Constitution on the Church*[1] was the first doctrinal conciliar text in the history of the Church to treat the laity explicitly. It began

> Everything that has been said of the People of God is addressed equally to laity, religious, and clergy.[2]

Instead of defining the laity restrictively and canonically, the council went on:

> The term 'laity' is here understood to mean all the faithful except those in Holy Orders and those who belong to a religious state approved by the Church. That is, the faithful who by Baptism are incorporated into Christ, are placed in the People of God, and in their own way share the priestly, prophetic, and kingly office of Christ, and to the best of their ability carry on the mission of the whole Christian people in the Church and in the world.[3]

The Old Testament image of the People of God now assumes a certain priority over the Pauline image of the Body, and with this change in metaphors goes a new emphasis on the laity's active participation in the whole life of the Church. The laity's mission is identified with the mission of the white Church.

Another document which advanced the cause of the laity was *The Constitution on the Sacred Liturgy*.[4] It affirmed that

> In the restoration and promotion of the sacred liturgy the full and active participation by all the people is the aim to be considered before all else, for it is the primary and indispensable source from which the faithful are to derive the true Christian spirit.[5]

The liturgical renewal was the most immediate and visible effect of Vatican Council II and helped to establish the new theological currency of the term "lay participation." The dramatic change of Latin to the vernacular now made possible a heightened sense of clergy and laity in one activity. The prominent liturgical roles that laity began to play in the Mass, alongside the priest, had the consequence of popularly identifying lay participation in the Church with expanding liturgical roles. The development of lay ministry in the post-Vatican II era would owe much of its impetus to this phenomenon.

[1]*(Lumen Gentium,* 1964), ch. IV.
[2]*Ibid.,* p. 30.
[3]*Ibid.,* p. 31.
[4]*(Sacrosanctum concilium,* 1963).
[5]*Ibid.,* p. 14.

Finally, Vatican Council II issued its statement on the laity, the *Decree on the Apostolate of Lay People.*[1] It began by clearly defining the vocation of lay people and specifying their participation in the mission of the Church. Harkening back to the "Mystical Body" image, the Council says:

> in the organism of a living body no member plays a purely passive part, sharing in the life of the body it shares at the same time in its activity.[2]

The aim of the decree is to overcome lay inertia, and affirm the need for the participation of the laity in the mission of the Church. While there is one Christian holiness, namely participation in Christ,

> lay spirituality will take its particular character from the circumstances of one's state in life (married and family life, celibacy, widowhood), from one's state of health and from one's professional and social activity.[3]

But, lay participation in the Church's mission is inevitably specified in different fields of activity or apostolates. The Council reaffirms the importance of individual and group apostolates, cooperation with the hierarchy, and special training for apostolic activity.

Of course, all the documents of Vatican Council II have implications for the laity, not just these three, but it is fair to say that these provided the doctrinal foundations, liturgical expression and apostolic thrust for a new consciousness of lay participation in the Church.

The *Declaration on Religious Liberty*[4] was surely the distinctive American contribution to Vatican Council II, a result of the experiment in democracy of which American Catholics had been a part for almost two hundred years. The Declaration affirmed that

> the principle of religious liberty contributes in no small way to the development of a situation in which men can without hindrance be invited to the Christian faith, embrace it of their own free will and give it practical expression in every sphere of their lives.[5]

In short, it allows for a new kind of evangelization and witness. The full meaning of lay participation in the Church for the future rests as much with this claim as with the normal liturgical and ecclesial organs of its expression.

[1](*Apostolicam Actuositatem*, 1965).
[2]*Ibid.*, p. 2.
[3]*Ibid.*, p. 4.
[4](*Dignitatis humanae*, 1965).
[5]*Ibid.*, p. 10.

LAY PARTICIPATION IN THE CHURCH
SINCE VATICAN COUNCIL II

The aftereffect of Vatican Council II on American Catholic laity was generally one of surprise mixed with pockets of exhilaration and dismay. The burst of
energy from Rome enlivened the American Church at all levels and began to
produce a series of organizational adaptations which changed both the surfaces
and symbols of Catholic life. Without any theological preparation for the new
overtures sounded by Vatican Council II, lay Catholics, like many of the clergy,
spontaneously fell back on their instincts to assess what had happened. For
some, the Council confirmed a "style" of openness and freedom which suited the
American temper very well. For others, though, it tampered with the distinctive
traits of Roman Catholicism which had made the Church robust in America.

These reflexive responses aligned themselves with a growing trend of new
lay "camps," *The National Catholic Reporter* and *The Wanderer* becoming house
organs for the respective parties. In 1965 Reverend Gommar A. DePauw
founded the Catholic Traditionalist Movement committed to preserving the Latin
liturgy, while Catholics United for the Faith (CUF) was formed in 1968. These
were not mainstream movements, however, as most Catholic laity welcomed the
changes and participated actively in establishing new patterns of Catholic lay involvement.

The civil rights movement of the 1960's enlisted the support of socially
conscious laity. Together with the anti-war (or peace) movement, it shaped a
new generation of Catholic laity who mobilized with clergy and ecumenical
groups to defend human rights and to protest an unpopular war.

Since the 1960's, the face of the American Catholic laity has visibly
changed colors. Blacks began to assert their rights and needs as Catholic laity.
New immigrants arrived from the southern hemisphere and the far east posing
new cultural challenges for the recognition and assimilation of ethnic groups.

In parishes laity became more active in liturgy and on parish councils. Religious women, who were formerly the backbone of the Catholic school system,
transferred their interest and energies to emerging parochial opportunities.

Women's consciousness of their role in the Church focused on opening up
all church ministries, including ordination, to women. This eventually caused
the Vatican in 1976 to provide a biblical and doctrinal explanation for the tradition of restricting priestly ordination to men. The debate, however, only
intensified in the aftermath.

Lay spirituality, a somewhat neglected theme despite the emphasis on it at
Vatican Council II, expressed itself soon after the Council in the charismatic
movement. Beginning at Duquesne University in 1966, this movement responded to a new quest for religious experience associated with the Holy Spirit,
healing, speaking in tongues and other "charismatic" gifts. Despite its merits as
a form of spiritual enthusiasm, the charismatic renewal nevertheless sat uneasily
in the Vatican II ecclesial landscape.

The Catholic bishops in America responded to the council's call for lay participation in the Church by formalizing structures at the national level. The
USCC established its standing Committee on the Laity which has actively promoted the exchange of information on a whole range of lay issues. In 1971 the

National Council of Catholic Laity was formed in Cincinnati. Independently, the Call to Action Conference (1976) in Detroit urgently tried to breathe new life into an active, but uncertain lay movement. The bishops responded with their pastoral letter, *Called and Gifted: The American Catholic Laity 1980.*

These organizational developments during the 1970's, and many more too numerous to mention, reflected both the vitality of the lay movement after the Council, but also, and somewhat paradoxically, its sense of disorientation and confusion. In 1976, the Vatican, for what seemed like tensions over policy, reorganized its lay consistory and established the Pontifical Council on the Laity. Two years later, a conference at Chicago's National Center for the Laity outlined the major tasks facing the lay movement: changing language about *belonging to* the Church to *being* the Church, relating work and faith, avoiding the clericalization of the laity, overcoming the immaturity of the laity, and shaping a creative spirituality of lay life.

In the 1980's lay theologians, a new breed of laity in American Catholicism, addressed these issues. Leonard Doohan envisioned a "lay-centered" Church in which laity would increasingly assume leadership roles within the Church. He offered "models" of lay theologies to order the rather diffuse religious and theological literature on the laity. Increasingly the themes of empowerment and leadership have come to prominence in discussions of the laity.[1]

More recently, the Pallotine Institute for Lay Leadership and Apostolate Research (PILLAR) has tried to locate the emerging lay problematic beyond the usual considerations of leadership. Instead, it has shifted the question to the philosophical and theological ways of dealing with modernity and faith. In *American & Catholic: The New Debate,* Joe Holland provides three contemporary, but cumbersome, Catholic versions of what H. Richard Niebuhr attempted in his famous "Christ and Culture" typology.[2]

This question of faith and culture returns us, by a long detour, to the underlying thread that has accompanied Catholicism through its whole history in

---

[1]Leonard Doohan, *The Lay-Centered Church: Theology and Spirituality* (Minneapolis: Winston Press, 1984); Doohan, *The Laity: A Bibliography* (Wilmington: Michael Glazier, 1987). On the theme of "leadership," see James D. Whitehead and Evelyn Eaton Whitehead, *The Emerging Laity: Returning Leadership to the Community of Faith* (Garden City, NY: Doubleday, 1986). Greeley, *op. cit.,* offers a sociological analysis of the laity after the council. Three themes characterize Greeley's "portrait" of the American Catholic laity: (1) They are underrepresented in prestige positions in culture and the media, (2) their ethnicity has allowed them to absorb and reject different aspects of the American ethos, and (3) they can no longer be assumed to agree with the official positions of the Catholic Church. In Greeley's view, this last trait marks them as "communal Catholics." In this phenomenon, American pluralism seems to have fashioned a kind of Catholic version of "denominationalism."

[2]*American and Catholic: The New Debate,* Joe Holland and Anne Barsanti, eds. (South Orange, NJ: Pillar Books, 1988). Also see James H. Moorhead, "Theological Interpretations and Critiques of American Society and Culture," in *Encyclopedia of the American Religious Experience,* Vol. 1, pp. 101-115, for a survey of the history of the faith-culture problematic in American Protestantism from the Puritans to the present.

America. In the past Catholics sought to shape their faith in response to the dominant Protestant ethos of the country; today they seek to articulate it in relation to another cultural "center of gravity" — either secularism, or liberal democracy, or technology. The appraisal one makes of long-term social and cultural trends such as these, and their compatibility with Catholic ideals, turns out to be the critical background position for any theology striving to come to grips with modernity.

In a seminal essay on the future of religion in the modern period, Daniel Bell has sketched out in broad strokes the complex ideological lines of force which have shaped the modern world.[1]

> From the seventeenth through the nineteenth century there occurred what I shall call 'The Great Profanation,' a change in moral temper, in the relation of the individual to the existential questions of culture, which undermined the cultural foundations of the Western religious answers that had given men a coherent view of the world.[2]

Direct experience replaced revelation, tradition, authority, even reason, as the "touchstone" of religious judgment. For Bell, the "profanation" he speaks about is different from secularization because it goes to the heart of the religious vision of the self. Modernity, in the religio-cultural sense, means

> the turning away from the authority of the past, the shrinking of the realm of the sacred, and the Faustian quest for total knowledge...[3]

Modernity substituted new political and aesthetic religions for traditional ones, but in Bell's view, these alternatives are now exhausted and the religious field is once again open for fresh candidates. His guess (in 1979) was that the contest would be among (1) moralizing religion (Fundamentalism), (2) redemptive religion (the reconciling power of Tradition), and (3) mystical religion (Eastern mysticism). On the margins of all three are the cults.

> When the institutional framework of religions begins to break up, the search for direct experience which people can feel to be 'religious' facilitates the rise of cults.[4]

The 1980's have verified his conjecture all too well.

Bells' sociological analysis ranges far and wide over the past three hundred years attempting to give perspective to the difficult, seemingly intractable problems facing culture's search for religious meaning. It proposes a deep exegesis of modernity that moves ahead of the standard liberal and conservative appraisal.

---

[1]Daniel Bell, "The Return of the Sacred? The Argument on the Future of Religion," in *The Winding Passage: Essays and Sociological Journeys 1960-1980* (New York: Basic Books, 1980), pp. 324-354.
[2]*Ibid*, p. 334.
[3]*Ibid*, p. 335.
[4]*Ibid*, pp. 349-352.

Read as a gloss on *Gaudium et Spes*, this kind of exegesis is a first, and necessary, chapter in defining the role of the laity for the future.

EPILOGUE: THE SYNOD ON THE LAITY (1987)

On January 30, 1989, Pope John Paul II published his Apostolic Exhortation on the Laity, *Christifideles Laici*.[1] It was based on the 1987 world Synod of Bishops, and the theme of "Vocation and Mission of the Laity in the Church and in the World 20 Years After the Second Vatican Council."

Christifideles Laici is a very long and exhaustive treatment of the subject of the laity based on the teaching of Vatican Council II, the New Code of Canon Law, and other post-conciliar developments in society and the Church which bear on the theme of the laity. It prefers the scriptural motifs of the "Workers in the Vineyard" and the "Vine," evoking a Johannine symbolism of the Church. The Matthean summons "You go into my vineyard too,"[2] is reiterated several times to underline the importance of lay participation.

Divided into five sections, the document covers the baptismal identity of the lay faithful, their ministries and offices in the Church, co-responsibility for the mission, states of life and the formation of the laity. Out of this very comprehensive survey, we can select a few themes which are particularly relevant to the situation of the laity in America.

First, the spiritual situation of the modern world receives considerable attention in the introduction. The phenomena of secularism, atheistic humanism and international conflict are singled out as the global context for lay involvement in our times. In treating the laity's co-responsibility for the Church's mission, the exhortation again reviews the need for re-evangelization in secularized societies which were formerly Christian. The mission of the laity, then, is sharply located at the cultural frontiers of modernity. This corresponds to some of the more recent developments in lay Catholicism in which an evaluation of the culture is a prerequisite for evangelization and mission.

Second, the cultural, social, economic and political tasks of the laity are strongly underlined in the document. Social justice, founded in the dignity of the human person, is stressed and specified in various areas (right to life, family, religious liberty, charity, public life, social and economic life).

Third, turning explicitly to lay participation in the life of the Church, the exhortation takes up the issue of lay ministry. The text clearly demarcates what is proper to the laity whose ministry is based on Baptism and what pertains to the ordained whose ministry is based on the Sacrament of Orders. It states:

---

[1]See *Origins,* Vol. 18, No. 35 (February 9, 1989), pp. 561-595. Many commentators have emphasized Pope John Paul II's philosophical mentality which is interwoven with the biblical imagery of his writings. His major philosophical work, *The Acting Person* (Holland: D. Reidel, 1979), treats the concepts of action, integration and participation which are central to his exhortation on the laity.

[2]Matthew 20: 3-4.

> The various ministries, offices, and roles that the lay faithful can legitimately fulfill in the liturgy, in the transmission of the faith and in the pastoral structure of the church ought to be exercised in conformity to their specific lay vocation, which is different from that of the sacred ministry.[1]

The Synod itself asked that *Ministeria Quaedam* (1972) be reconsidered and studied in light of present practice.

Fourth, the status of women in the Church was also treated in some depth at the Synod and in the exhortation. The text called upon the Church to recognize and use the gifts of men and women for its life and mission. Framed within the anthropological and theological foundations of masculinity and femininity, the exhortation asserted that

> without discrimination, women should be participants in the life of the church and also in consultation and the process of coming to decisions.[2]

Fifth, the document concludes on the important theme of the continuing formation of the laity. The final section deals with lay spirituality under the heading of "a total integrated formation for living an integrated life." Being members of the Church and citizens of society can lead to "parallel" lives which the exhortation wants to avoid at all cost. So, it regards continuing formation as a necessary means to assure that the spiritual and secular dimensions of the lay vocation are properly unified and integrated.

Christifideles Laici is an impressive statement of the status and mission of the laity in the modern world. Though aware of the obstacles presented by modernity, the exhortation offers an inspiring, coherent and progressive vision of the lay vocation at the end of the twentieth century.

As we have seen, the story of the American Catholic laity since 1789 is largely a narrative of representative episodes and ventures in response to different social and ecclesial issues. In the process, the Catholic laity in this country have developed an energy, style and vision which is distinctively American. The Catholic ghetto secured a Roman Catholic identity for them through the 1950's, but since then laity have been searching for a new sense of themselves. In some essentials ways, their destiny remains caught up in the unfolding of the American experiment at home and around the world. Richard John Neuhaus has called our times the "Catholic Moment," arguing

> that this is the historical moment at which Roman Catholicism has a singular opportunity and obligation to take the lead in reconstructing a moral philosophy for the American experiment in republican democracy.[3]

---

[1]*Ibid.*, p. 572.
[2]*Ibid.*, p. 586.
[3]Richard John Neuhaus, "The Catholic Moment," in *American and Catholic, op. cit.*, p. 17. For a complete statement of his position, see Richard John Neuhaus, *The Catholic Moment: The Paradox of the Church in the Post-Modern World* (San Francisco: Harper and Row, 1987).

Should this moment materialize, it will have happened because the Catholic laity fully grasps its ecclesial calling and is capable of engaging in it effectively. As we recall our past and prepare to shape Catholicism in America for the next century, this should be our highest priority.

CHAPTER FOURTEEN

The Contribution of the Laity and Religious in the Development of American Catholic Spirituality

Sonya A. Quitslund
George Washington University

If "Spirituality is faith made explicit in life"[1] is there such a thing as an American Catholic spirituality and if so, where do we find it? Any attempt to isolate such a phenomenon seems doomed from the start because of its multiple cultural, national and ethnic origins. Moreover, the history of spirituality recognizes two basic types which lead either to the obliteration of or the affirmation of self. While both can be found within the American experience, this paper proposes that the second reflects the American spirit more accurately and is where we might find a distinctive American contribution to Christian spirituality.

Even though "American Puritanism and republicanism created an environment for Catholics that demanded, in terms of style and content, a religious response that had no effective model,"[2] American Catholic devotional or spiritual life has generally reflected European trends. Only in the later nineteenth century and mid-twentieth century did a set of historical circumstances and a spiritual crisis affecting the universal church generate a response that might be called distinctively American. Issues of authority clashed with an American sense of independence and personal responsibility. Prophetic voices called attention to the presence of the Holy Spirit and challenged the Church to prepare for new options in the dawning of a new age.

The dominant issues, infallibility and *Humanae Vitae,* were eventually resolved in the consciences of those involved, but the underlying spiritual malaise that turned them into truly critical matters was not so easily settled. At the heart of the problem lay a crisis of faith acerbated by world events as well as an exaggerated emphasis on authority. Fingering human sinfulness in apocalyptic tones went counter to an essentially optimistic American spirit. This made religion irrelevant to some. Prophetic figures, however, emerged in each age highlighting the role of the Holy Spirit, affirming human potential and calling for confidence in the future.

The massive immigration of the late nineteenth century effectively overwhelmed and subdued this prophetic voice, a pattern repeated, although to a lesser degree, in the twentieth century with the influx of refugees. Attention to serious spiritual ills suffered neglect as efforts focused on to the multiple needs of the newcomers.

The situation of the universal Church, however, differed considerably. The nineteenth century began with the Pope in captivity (1810-1814) and the very

---

[1]Mary Jo Weaver, *New Catholic Women* (NY: Harper & Row, 1985), p. 180.
[2]Patrick Carey, ed., *American Catholic Religious Thought* (NY: Paulist Press, 1987), p. 4.

existence of the European Church threatened by the rising spirit of nationalism. It culminated with the seizure of the vast papal states and the stripping of all temporal power from the papacy except for the minuscule territory of the Vatican State. While the twentieth century has been torn by two world wars, the threat to the Church shifted to Eastern Europe, to African rejection of colonially-imposed Christianity and the communist takeover of China. These historical events, joined to the secular spirit of the modern and post-modern eras, deepened the faith crisis, especially in America when the Church appeared allied with the wrong side in matters affecting human rights: labor, authority, slavery, war, women.

In both centuries two groups were discernible: a majority, essentially faithful to the devotional tradition of the past, and a vocal minority, who insist all deserve more than they are getting. They call for a total community in which the spiritual spills over into the material, temporal, secular world, Christianizing it in the process. The historical survey to follow will show how some of these ideas slowly filter down. The spiritual insights of the 1880's and 1890's are negatively affected by subsequent church and world events, so that by the 1920's the spiritual enthusiasm of people like Hecker and Brownson faded from the scene. Will history repeat itself as church and world events in the late twentieth century seem ready to threaten the recent surge in religious earnestness?

Perhaps concerted efforts on the part of women, religious and lay, to develop a new Christian spirituality that takes its cue from the affirmation of human nature found in the book of *Genesis* rather than being rooted in Platonic dualism and gnostic anti-materiality (which provided a basis for the devaluation of women), will break the pattern. The spiritual revitalization that feminists want to bring to American Catholicism may ultimately be a unique and invaluable contribution to world-wide Catholic spirituality.

The list of canonized or beatified American saints is not long and not the primary source for our research. With the exception of Isaac Jogues and the other North American Jesuit martyrs of French origin, all have been canonized since 1975. They reflect the multi-national make-up of the American Church: Blessed Kateri Tekakwitha (1656-1680), the first Native American so honored; the Spanish Franciscan who labored in California, Blessed Junipero Serra; the French educator Philippine Duchesne (1769-1852) who wanted to work among the Indians; the Italian Frances X. Cabrini (1850-1917), the first American citizen canonized, who dedicated her life to the poor, sick and orphaned; and the German bishop who labored so diligently in Pennsylvania, John Neumann (c. 1812-1869).

Elizabeth Ann Seton (1779-1821) and Katherine Drexel (1858-1955), as native-born Americans, might serve as more likely sources for an "American spirituality." Their lives reveal a struggle with older, monastic forms, inherited from Europe, a yearning to express something distinctively American in their journey into God. The causes of other Americans have also been introduced, such as the Capuchin friar Solanus Casey of Detroit, and Cornelia Connelly, founder of the Sisters of the Holy Childhood.

With the exception of Kateri, all of these saints were religious women or men, even though Elizabeth Seton and Cornelia Connelly had been married and mothers before founding their communities. As such, their sanctity and spirituality is not readily translatable into lay life nor is it necessarily appropriate.

Even religious life today, especially that of many communities of women, has made considerable changes in terms of spiritual formation and the kind of spirituality expected of vowed members. For example, the IHM's originally described their charism as "self-abnegation and renouncement of self-will"; today it is "The Love of Jesus Christ [that] unites us in community and impels us to proclaim the good news of salvation."[1]

> There is a grave need today for a program of spirituality that shows the Lord present and working in the secular world and that inspires and strengthens lay people to live out their evangelical commitment....Spirituality must be prophetic in outlook and redemptive in its ability to bear unavoidable suffering on behalf of the Kingdom...a paschally oriented spirituality...[to] inspire us to continue confidently and joyfully no matter what we experience.[2]

The following overview attempts to trace the spiritual odyssey of American Catholicism with special emphasis on developments in the late nineteenth century and mid-twentieth century. It raises the question: has the institutional Church taken its responsibility to form Christian spirituality sufficiently seriously?[3] Perhaps this is to be *the* task of the Church for the third century.

HISTORICAL OVERVIEW

The historical method of American Catholic historians up to the present has hampered easy access to the American spiritual legacy because they gave more attention to the record of American Catholic material accomplishments than to the spiritual, and little recognition to women.[4] Others who attempt a spiritual

---

[1]Carol Quigley, ed., *Turning Points in Religious Life* (Wilmington: Glazier, 1987), p. 249.

[2]Frederick G. McLeod, "Issues and Trends in Spirituality 1987," in *Review for Religious,* Vol. 47, No. 2 (Mar.-April, 1988), pp. 252-253

[3]Cornelia Connelly insisted one of the key tasks of her order was to promote its own spiritual development and that of its neighbors. Caritas McCarthy, *Spirituality of Cornelia Connelly: In God, For God, With God* (Lewiston, NY: Edwin Mellen Press, 1986).

[4]Jay P. Dolan, *The American Catholic Experience* (Garden City: Image, 1985) is one of the first to attempt a more sociological approach. I acknowledge my indebtedness to him for many of the facts and some of the analysis in the survey that follows. According to James Kenneally, "Eve, Mary and the Historians: American Catholicism and Women" in *Horizons,* Vol. 3, No. 2 (Fall 1976), pp. 200-201, only one leading historian of the American Church treats women specifically, but does little more than list their names: Constantine McGuire, *Catholic Builders of the Nation,* 5 vols. (Boston: Continental Press, 1923). He also notes that *Notable American Women,* 3 vols. (Cambridge: Harvard University Press, 1971) lists 70 Catholics but few of these are mentioned in histories of American Catholicism. Only three were born Catholic and two of them apostatized. Generally one-third of feminists left the Church of their birth for liberal ones or abandoned religion. What really needs to be done is to make a serious examination of the effect of Catholic anti-feminism on Catholic women. The spirituality of those "driven" from the Church is also an important facet to American Catholic spiritu-

analysis rely on personal testimonies, the activities of bishops, the legislation of the Baltimore councils and synods, as well as the literature of the day.[1] The weakness of this is that most of it comes from clerical hands telling people how to pray and what to say. Does it really tell us how the laity experienced God? What follows makes no claim at being comprehensive due to the constraints of space, and represents a first attempt to focus more exclusively on religious and lay contributions as a form of compensatory history. This means the roles played by some truly great bishops must necessarily be overlooked or mentioned only in passing.

Columbus and many of the Spanish who followed him were religiously motivated. Some were truly pious. Cortés attended daily Mass but proved ruthless in his relations with the Indians. Others, sixteenth century missionaries such as Antonio de Montesinos, O.P. and Bartolomeo de Las Casas, O.P., ultimately persuaded the Crown and the people to recognize that Indians had human rights. In 1573 the Franciscans began to establish missions in Florida, and by 1655 they had 38. However, by 1708 all but St. Augustine had been destroyed by the English.

The Jesuit Eusebius Kino went to California in 1681, then to Mexico and Arizona. Even with 40 years of Jesuit presence, the native religion remained very much alive with only a thin veneer of Christianity.[2] The Franciscans, initially more successful, made 54,000 converts in 65 years but due to a high mortality rate and their treatment of the Indians, only 15,000 remained in the missions by 1836.[3]

With minimal success in terms of conversions, the French Jesuits proved the most inspirational in terms of influence on later American Catholics. The often gruesome tales of the martyrdom of North American Jesuits inspired generations of young Catholics to generous missionary dedication in China, Latin America and Africa. The French tried to adapt their program to the culture of the people but their methods were eventually challenged by religious authorities. Their expulsion from the Spanish and French colonies ended this more enlightened approach.[4] Today, as Native Americans attempt to recapture their ancient religious traditions, American spirituality stands to profit from the profound sense of how the spiritual world permeated all of reality.[5]

The English Jesuits ultimately became the first diocesan priests in the young colonies (with the society's suppression in 1773). They left a lasting imprint on the American Church by forming lay leaders in their schools and initiating many into Ignatian spirituality through retreats. Moreover, the first

---

ality. Cf. Weaver, *op. cit.*, pp. 1-15, a careful analysis of many recent Catholic historical works on American Catholicism.

[1] Joseph Chinnici, "Organization of the Spiritual Life: American Catholic Devotional Works, 1791-1866," *Theological Studies*, Vol. 40, No. 2 (June 1979), pp. 229-255. Also Weaver, *op. cit.*, p. 10 citing Gerda Lerner.

[2] John L. Kessell, *Mission of Sorrows: Jesuit Guevavi and the Pimas 1691-1767* (Tucson: University of Arizona Press, 1970).

[3] Sherburne F. Cook, *The Conflict Between the California Indian and White Civilization* (Berkeley: University of California Press, 1976).

[4] Dolan, *op. cit.*, p. 59.

[5] Cautions suggested by Sam D. Gill, *Mother Earth: An American Story* (Chicago: University of Chicago Press, 1987) will need to be taken into consideration.

American bishop came from their ranks. They favored a partner union of church and state that respected the rights of both, placing spiritual values above material ones.[1]

English speaking Catholicism began in Maryland with Father Andrew White, S.J., who celebrated the first Mass in Maryland on St. Clement's Island in 1634. Although the civil authorities denied the first Jesuits permission to live with the Indians for the purpose of converting them, Father White chose to disobey in the name of religion. He started a mission in 1639 and eleven months later baptized his first converts, but by 1641 the Governor authorized the settlers to shoot on sight any Indians on Kent Island, thus seriously undermining further missionary efforts. But White's legacy of civil disobedience in the name of a higher calling remains.

By 1646 no Jesuits were left in Maryland. The next Jesuits to arrive (1648) became gentlemen farmers, slaveholders and educators. The penal laws which outlawed Mass and proselytizing limited their ministry. In 1700 there were about 2500 Catholics in Maryland, mostly wealthy; by 1765, 20,000. In 1718 Catholics lost the right to vote. The Church survived penal laws, the 1773 suppression of the Jesuits, 150 years without a bishop, all without priestly defections. The people clung to the faith during a time when for most Catholics contact with priests was rare. By the 1760's the Jesuit plantations functioned as parish churches and devotional societies were organized for the women. Religious vocations began to appear. Mary Diggs became the first American nun. By 1776, 36 wealthy young women had taken vows (the cost of the trip to Europe and the dowry ruled out vocations for the poor).[2]

Between 1773 and 1800 Father Joseph Durkin, S.J., developed devotion to the Sacred Heart and established confraternities for the perpetual adoration of the Blessed Sacrament, whose members committed themselves to one-half hour of prayer at home on stated days. Devotion to the Sacred Heart helped to counter Jansenist influences which tended to minimize the humanity of Christ. In the nineteenth century, Father McElroy, S.J., founder of Boston College, was among the first priests to institute what came to be known as the parish mission.[3] Thus the early Jesuits gave a specific and lasting direction to American spirituality.

Two authors played a key role in the spiritual development of the people at this time: John Gother (†1704) and Richard Challoner (†1781). Gother fostered devotion to Jesus and His life, a personal, interior piety which stressed faith and favored congregational participation. Challoner's *Garden of the Soul* also emphasized interior, personal piety but urged Catholics to be engaged in the world in a way consistent with the Gospels and the ten commandments. Both urged devotion to the Mass as the chief act of prayer and worship.[4] Prayer remained

[1]R.E. Curran, *Maryland Jesuits* (Baltimore: Corporation of Roman Catholic Clergymen, Maryland Province of the Society of Jesus, 1976), p. 5. Detailed studies exist on the work of the Jesuits in every area of the United States.

[2]*Ibid.*, pp. 33, 59.

[3]Dolan, *op. cit.*, p. 86.

[4]John Gother, *Instructions for Particular States and Conditions of Life,* ed. Rev. M. Comerford (Dublin: H.M. Gill, 1888); *Instructions and Devotions for Hearing*

essentially personal, and life remained disciplined and sober. Increased numbers of Catholics led to a shift from home to parish by mid-eighteenth century which significantly altered religion's domestic character. It became more public and congregational, with greater stress on devotion to the Blessed Sacrament, the Sacred Heart and external ritual.[1]

Because the colonial situation encouraged a loose attitude toward church law, some clerical writers became preoccupied with a concern for uniformity and a Roman emphasis. Fearing American Catholics were not Roman enough, they stressed rubrics and externally identifiable practices when they spoke of "spiritual life." Out of this emerged a "strong awareness of the communal dimension of prayer, witness to the universal church" and a refusal to reduce Christian life to strictly internal convictions, which Chinnici calls a "mystique of salvation."[2]

AMERICAN INDEPENDENCE

Under the leadership of John Carroll (1736-1815), the American clergy drew up a constitution for the Catholic Church in 1783 granting them wide operational autonomy, necessitated by the political conditions of the day. Carroll's request for an American bishop in whose election Rome would have no role was dictated by spiritual concerns as well as political expediency. The appointment of Carroll as "Superior of the Mission" by Rome in 1784 reflected a unique understanding of American Catholicism: it was to be free and independent of all foreign influence or jurisdiction, or so the first clergy thought.[3]

Faced with a growing population and an aging clergy, the education and formation of native clergy became the priority, and in 1791 the future Georgetown University was founded. The program of studies, in part a reaction to the overly rationalistic climate of the eighteenth century, proposed to develop individuality and to train imagination and feelings. Carroll insisted on his vision and criticized the discipline imposed at first as unsuitable for "freedom-loving, high-spirited American boys."[4]

The arrival of the first community of nuns on American soil added yet another dimension to the growing Catholic community. In 1790 four Carmelites, three natives of Maryland, settled near Port Tobacco, Maryland, and by 1800 had 18 members. In 1799 the Visitandines started the first Catholic school for girls in the United States. The Ursulines had already begun teaching in New Orleans (French territory) in 1727. The first parochial school opened in Frederick in 1824 under the direction of the Sisters of Charity. Carroll's concern for the edu-

---

Mass (London: T. Meighan, 1740), pp. 4-5; Edwin H. Burton, *The Life and Times of Bishop Challoner, 1691-1781,* 2 vols. (New York: Longmans, Green, 1909).

[1]Dolan, *op. cit.,* pp. 94-95.

[2]Chinnici, *op. cit.,* pp. 230-235. *Pious Guide to Prayer and Devotion, Containing Various Practices of Piety Calculated to Answer the Various Demands of the Different Devout Members of the Roman Catholic Church* (Georgetown: James Doyle, 1792).

[3]Carey, *op. cit.,* p. 11 points out the Bull erecting Baltimore as a diocese stipulated the clerical right to elect an American bishop was restricted to the first election. Carroll tried to keep this from the public.

[4]Curran, *op. cit.,* p. 43.

cation of both boys and girls endured and ultimately became a distinctive feature of the American Church.

Had his vision and desire that imagination and feelings be developed been respected and followed, the subsequent story of American spirituality might have been quite different. Although the Jesuits were restored in the early 1800's, most who came over the next 30 years were from Europe and did not understand the United States or the peculiar Jesuit position as landowner. Moreover, Carroll became increasingly conservative and even authoritarian as archbishop.

His insistence that religious toleration was not a pragmatic concession to religious pluralism but a fundamental human right endorsed by the Declaration of Independence of 1776 stood very much in the tradition of the sixteenth-century Spanish missionaries' insistence on the basic human rights and dignity of the Indians. This vision faded in the following century as tensions created by the massive immigration mounted. Only with the dawn of Vatican II did these ideals once again regain the limelight in official ecclesiastical circles and find graphic expression in the lived spirituality of some American Catholics.[1]

Suitable priests proved a major concern because bishops and religious superiors did not always send their best. Sometimes they sent problems. It is not surprising that power struggles began to break out between the clergy and lay trustees. The laity wanted "to participate in the selection of their pastors, and to dismiss them if they abused their authority...."[2] The trustees defended a communal conciliar view of the Church over a more hierarchical one, a decisive advance toward a new definition and lay understanding of Church that received official recognition at Vatican II. In the ensuing battle, spiritual considerations fell as some priests and bishops preferred to see a congregation leave the Church rather than yield on the issue of authority. Interdicts and excommunications were not unusual. In 1850, 67 percent of the pastors stayed in the parish less than 6 years; by 1900, 63 percent stayed more than 6 years, a shift that strengthened the authority of the pastor.[3]

Frightened by the anarchy of the French Revolution (1789) and by the potential for turmoil now associated with democracy, the institutional Church directed its energies to shoring up its authority. The influx of immigrants and European priests to serve them helped in this regard. The French Sulpicians and the restored Jesuits (Europeans) brought a stern morality, baroque piety and strong prejudices against American institutions and ideas. Baroque piety went against much of what might be considered the freedom-loving, imaginative American spirit with its insistence on the importance of structures, hierarchical

---

[1]This is especially reflected in lay involvement in the Civil Rights and Peace and Pro-Life movements, in lay missionaries in Appalachia, South and Central America, in ritualized protests first in draft offices, then at nuclear sites and at abortion clinics. Mention should also be made of efforts on behalf of religious minorities, e.g., Soviet Jews.

[2]Carey, "The Laity's Understanding of the Trustee System: 1785-1855," *Catholic Historical Review* 64 (July 1978), pp. 365-366.

[3]Dolan and Jeffrey Burns, "Parish History Study" (unpublished, 1982), data available at Cushwa Center for the Study of American Catholicism, University of Notre Dame.

mediation, saints, external religious behavior, a pessimistic view of human nature and self-discipline.[1]

What the clergy thought of the laity has been documented. Father Stephen Badin writing to Carroll about the "pollution of sins and vicious habits among American Catholics," pointed to "pride, abuse or excess of liberty and an ungovernable spirit of independency [sic]" as the root of the problem. Father J.B. David called upon the reader of *True Piety* to "acknowledge the corruption of government and your impotency to all good without...grace..." He reminded his retreatants that Adam had received 900 years of rigorous penance for his one sin, and asked them to compare theirs to his: "His was only one sin, and yours are multiplied over the hairs of your head."[2]

While some early nineteenth-century literature had a more positive spiritual anthropology, it was soon superseded by a more negative tone. Growth in the spiritual life seemed to mean greater awareness of one's sinfulness and the necessity of penance, rather than deeper consciousness and enjoyment of the Spirit. The *Catholic Laity's Directory* of 1822 even contained an explicit rejection of a more interior approach to Christian life.[3]

On his deathbed Carroll identified as one of this greatest consolations:

> that I have always been attached to the practice of devotion to the Blessed Virgin Mary, that I have established it among the people under my care and placed my diocese under her protection.[4]

In the nineteenth century devotion to Mary multiplied. Even before the definition of the Immaculate Conception in 1854, the Seventh Provincial Council of Baltimore (1849) urged its devotion. The Second Plenary Council in 1866 promoted Marian piety as a defense against unfaith. The bishops placed the U.S. under the protection of the Immaculate Conception in 1846 and in 1914 began work on a shrine to honor Mary.

By 1815 two conflicting views of what should characterize the American Catholic Church challenged the right of the other to exist: the ideal of an indigenous church and that of a European transplant. The massive European immigration soon decided the issue in favor of the latter.[5]

THE IMMIGRANT CHURCH 1820-1920

A total of 10 groups representing 28 languages came during these years to enrich the American Church. Devotionalism which reigned supreme until the mid-nineteenth century became one of the means of controlling what otherwise risked appearing as a chaotic religious scene with the proliferation of national

---

[1]Chinnici, *op. cit.*, p. 237.
[2]Archives of Baltimore, June 9, 1802. J.B. David, *True Piety or the Day Well-Spent. Being a Catholic Manual of Chosen Prayers, Devout Practices, and Solid Instruction, Adopted by a Catholic Clergyman of Baltimore* (Warner and Hanna, 1809), p. 225.
[3]*The Catholic Laity's Directory*, 1822, p. 30.
[4]Annabelle Melville, talk cited in *Catholic Standard*, January 12, 1989, p. 3.
[5]Dolan, *op. cit.*, p. 124.

churches that often recruited their own clergy. Bishops tried to strengthen their authority. They put external conformity at the center of Catholic life — temporal and spiritual. Taking their cue from the crisis state of affairs in Europe, the clergy warned the laity in apocalyptic tones as jubilee years multiplied in 1846, 1854, 1858 and 1864, calling them to repent and to prepare for judgment.

The Irish probably had the greatest impact on the direction the young Church took. By 1900, 62 percent of the bishops were Irish.[1] This had serious consequences for the Church and only recently have they begun to be addressed. Spanish-speaking Catholics in the newly acquired Southwest territories lacked native clergy, so often they improvised, mixing folk traditions with Catholicism. Served by mostly French clergy who generally failed to appreciate or to understand their spirituality,[2] they are still struggling to overcome a second-class status.

Even more tragic is the actual loss of over 200,000 Eastern Rite Catholics. By 1916, 163 of their parishes had joined Orthodoxy rather than sacrifice aspects of their tradition which further impoverished the spiritual pool for American Catholic spirituality.[3] A narrowness of vision and outright prejudice were among some of the weaknesses that characterized this era. The concern for authority and uniformity may have stabilized the Church but it certainly impeded spiritual growth in the nineteenth century.

By the 1860's devotionalism dominated the religious scene. At least 60 percent of the societies founded between 1860 and 1900 were devotional; 73 percent of the 80 prayerbooks and 98 percent of the 130 guides to devotions published in the nineteenth century were printed after 1840.[4] A proliferation of Catholic papers and periodicals after 1850 also helped promote these devotions. Even parish missions increased threefold.

Until ethnic mixed marriages became more common among Catholics after 1880, Catholic communities tended to be religiously and ethnically exclusive. Moreover, prior to 1880, most parish societies were devotional in nature; after 1800 more diversified goals (social, recreational, charitable, educational) set the stage for a Catholic attempt at a social gospel movement. Parish life centered around Sunday Mass, Vespers, Benediction and devotions. The most popular included devotions to the Sacred Heart, the Blessed Sacrament, the Immaculate

[1]Richard A Schoonherr, "Ethnicity and Status Attainment: The Case of the Roman Catholic Clergy," (unpublished paper), cited by Dolan, *op. cit.,* pp. 143ff. In 1972, 37 percent of the clergy and 48 percent of the hierarchy were still Irish or of Irish ancestry.
[2]James H. Defouri, *Historical Sketch of the Catholic Church, U.S.A.* (San Francisco: McCormick Bros., 1887), pp. 67, 122; Robert E. Lucey, "The Catholic Church in Texas," in *The Catholic Church USA,* L.J. Putz, ed. (Chicago: Fides Publishers Assoc., 1956), p. 228.
[3]Paul R. Magocsi, "Ukrainians," *Harvard Encyclopedia of American Ethnic Groups,* pp. 999-1001, Keith P. Dyrud, "The Establishment of the Greek Catholic Rite in America as a Competitor to Orthodoxy" in *The Other Catholics,* Dyrud, M. Novak and R.J. Veccli, eds. (New York: Arno Press, 1978), pp. 191-192.
[4]Ann Taves, "Relocating the Sacred: Roman Catholic Devotions in Mid-Nineteenth Century America" (unpublished Ph.D. dissertation, University of Chicago, 1983), pp. 10-13.

Conception, the rosary, novenas and saints for special needs like Saints Joseph, Patrick, Jude and Anthony, as well as monthly devotions honoring Mary in May, the Sacred Heart in June, the Holy Souls in November. Indulgences further enhanced these devotions.

Religion took a legalistic and authoritarian turn. Sermons often tinged with an anti-world, anti-Protestant tone, identified the two chief sins as drunkenness and impurity. Sermons nurtured guilt and promoted confession. Laws and rules strengthened the struggle against sin. Devotions provided an emotional outlet, although some tended to reinforce a negative sense of self. Two qualities characterized the spirituality of the day: individualism which flowed from the conviction of one's personal responsibility for one's own salvation, and a stress on values identified as feminine: emotionalism, sentimentalism, docility.[1]

Several factors contributed to the enduring success of devotionalism, even though *The Imitation of Christ* and De Sales' *Introduction to the Devout Life* enjoyed popularity at the time, taking one a step beyond the ritual of devotions. Many Catholics were poor immigrants struggling to survive under what seemed to be hostile conditions. Devotions, because in the vernacular, offered a link to the world left behind. This generation resisted Americanization. Resentment of the "foreign" ways of a clergy and hierarchy dominated by the Irish often led to bitter fights to preserve a national identity. Because the immigrants felt threatened by the Protestant presence which surrounded them, they clung to their various national devotions and feast days tenaciously and celebrated them with deep emotion in their ethnic enclaves.

The development of the parochial school system, even though barely more than one-third of the parishes had schools during this period, nevertheless contributed in its own way to the devotional spirituality of the day. It created the potential out of which a more sophisticated or a deeper form of spirituality could emerge; for, in promoting literacy, it also fostered *Catholic* literacy. Numerous publications tried to capitalize on the fertile soil thus prepared. But this potential for a more in-depth exposure to the Christian tradition, and to the lives of the saints and their writings, was not sufficiently exploited in the nineteenth century to alter in any drastic way the basic form of American Catholic spirituality. The *Syllabus of Errors* with its blanket condemnation of anything new, the condemnation of Americanism and Modernism at the turn of the century, fostered paranoia, suspicion and distrust of any departure from the past.

Ninety-one of the 119 women's orders in nineteenth-century America were of European or Canadian (and therefore French) origin. Since they played a key role in the spiritual formation of the children, it is obvious that most youth, at least initially, were more apt to be influenced by European models than by American. Many sisters could not even speak English. The parish school functioned in many instances as a means to keep a foreign language and its culture alive. Ninety-five percent of the German parishes and 71 percent of the Polish

---

[1]Dolan, *op. cit.*, pp. 227-229, 231. Cf. Ann Douglas, *Feminization of American Culture* (New York: Knopf, 1977) for an excellent presentation of the Protestant picture.

had schools for this express purpose.[1] Only in the 1920's when certification became necessary did radical changes occur. Concerted efforts were then made for the exclusive use of English in the schools. After 1920, Catholic secondary schools and colleges that had followed the European, Jesuit model began to conform to the American pattern.

The nineteenth century as a whole did little to promote a distinctive American spirituality. The majority of lay and religious Catholics were immigrants, often preoccupied with survival and with preserving their ethnic heritage. National reaction to the massive, increasingly Catholic immigration occurred in two stages: the development of a public school system viewed in its promotion of Americanization as a not too subtle means of "protestantizing" the immigrant, and the enactment in the 1920's of immigration quotas which tended to curb the supposed "Catholic threat."

Americanism and Modernism discouraged intellectual curiosity and contributed to the development of a fortress mentality which impeded the emergence of a truly American Catholic spirituality. In effect, it "paved the way for the Romanization of the American Church."[2] The resulting image of a timeless, perfect church, characteristic of early twentieth-century ecclesiology, was quite at odds with the late eighteenth-century view that motivated Carroll as he drew up the young Church's constitution. He had believed the Church could and should be adapted to the American cultural context.

The picture, however, was not totally negative. By the end of the century the predominance of women in all Christian churches and the tacit social acceptance of religion as belonging to woman's sphere led to the efforts to put more "muscle" into religion, to attract men back into the pews: for example, Father Finn's books and the Holy Name Society. Moreover, prophetic voices began to be heard in the post-civil war era, notably Orestes Brownson (1803-1876) and his disciple, Isaac Hecker (1819-1888), founder of the Paulists. They tried to fashion a more consciously American style of Catholicism which stressed the role of the laity in bringing about harmony between church and state, and their obligation to follow the promptings of the Spirit. Brownson especially defended civil and religious freedom. In the 1860's and 1870's, he analyzed the interconnections between political theory, ecclesiology, the role of the Christian in society and its devotional expression. He found a bureaucratic system of government led to the overdirection of the faithful, made them weak, timid, subordinate to the clergy regarding issues of church property, political responsibility and attitude concerning the civil rights of their wives and parental rights of education — all of which fostered a mechanistic devotionalism.[3]

---

[1]Colman Barry, O.S.B., *The Catholic Church and German Americans* (Milwaukee: Bruce Pub., 1953), p. 272; Dolan and Burns, *op. cit.,* pp. 279, 293.

[2]Dolan, *op. cit.,* p. 319. See E. Wakin and J.F. Scheuer, *The De-Romanization of the American Catholic Church* (New York: New American Library, 1970), for the reversal of this process.

[3]Orestes Brownson, "Civil and Religious Freedom" in *Brownson's Quarterly Review* (July 1864), p. 327; "Rights of the Temporal," in *ibid.,* No. 22 (Oct. 1860), pp. 490-492; *Devotion to the Holy Spirit in American Catholicism,* Joseph Chinnici, O.F.M., ed. (New York: Paulist Press, 1985), p. 7.

Calling for a new spiritual discipline to train people in self-reliance, courage, individual initiative and intellectual development, he acknowledged that this need not eliminate spiritual devotions. However, such activities would flow from interior dispositions and an awareness of the mystery of Christ.[1] Brownson offered an ecclesiology at once more incarnational and open to the guidance of the Holy Spirit.

Hecker started with the religious wants, needs and experiences of the individual. He looked for new models of holiness because he believed the Spirit worked in a revelatory fashion within the individual and even within American culture. In 1875, offering a more positive view of human nature, Hecker called for a new spirituality which would recognize the action of the Holy Spirit on souls and through them energize and renew the earth. He criticized docility and passivity as well as the mechanical piety of the day for inculcating complete submission to the external authority and discipline of the Church, and little more. Some branded excessive reliance on devotions and emotions as spiritually unhealthy, and warned young women in particular of the danger of too many devotions.[2] Both Brownson and Hecker believed the Church, after 300 years of excessive preoccupation with issues of authority ought to reassert the importance of the Holy Spirit in the interior life of the individual, and in the future pay more attention to the internal dimension of Christian life.[3] Few, however, heeded this call for a more refined type of piety and preaching; most, from the pope on down continued to foster devotional Catholicism for both personal and social reasons, since it served as a means of affirming Catholic identity in a Protestant society.

Efforts to present the Holy Spirit as "an integrative force symbolizing social, political and ecclesiological renewal," and to use this approach to fashion a new theological spiritual synthesis ended with a series of Novena Sermons on the Holy Ghost by Father Thomas Hopkins in 1901. The spirituality that prevailed had no specific social content or application. While interest in the Holy Spirit surfaced in the 1930's and 1940's, it bore noticeable fruit only in the 1960's and 1970's. But as Chinnici notes, throughout the time from 1870 to 1980, the Holy Spirit served as a central symbol for the American Catholic experience, the community's spiritual identity and some of its most significant choices.[4]

Some bishops initially shared Brownson's and Hecker's view of the special lay vocation to work, speak and act, but generally gave little positive attention to woman's role beyond the home. With American exuberance they agreed American Catholicism should be the model and agent of reform for the European Church. But Leo XIII in his condemnation of Americanism, which singled out

---

[1]Brownson, "Rights of the Temporal," pp. 470, 496; "Recent Events in France," *Brownson's Quarterly Review* 18 (Dec. 1871), p. 499.
[2]Isaac Hecker, *The Church and the Age* (New York: Office of the Catholic World, 1887), p. 7; Archives of the Paulist Fathers, Mission Chronicles (Nov. 1863 mission in St. Louis, MO), Vol. II, p. 13; George Deshon, *Guide for Young Catholic Women*, p. 143.
[3]Carey, *op. cit.*, pp. 22, 23, 30.
[4]Chinnici, *op. cit.*, pp. 89ff.

the French translation of Hecker's life as being behind the rejection of the idea the Church ought to adapt its doctrine of the modern age, sounded the death knell to such ideas. He also warned against any idea that the Church in America could be different from the rest of the Church.

One wonders if any connection existed between the views expressed and positions taken by American bishops at the time of Vatican I and the rather severe tone of *Testem Benevolentiae*. The American hierarchy was divided over the matter of papal primacy and infallibility. Some believed it needed to be balanced with the rights and powers of the national episcopacy. Many argued for constitutional limits to the papacy and considered papal infallibility merely a theological opinion, not a well-grounded doctrine.[1] In the end, all submitted but interpreted the dogma in a moderate way, spelling out the limits and extent of papal power.

Very few American Catholics were immediately involved in the intellectual world touched by Americanism and Modernism, but they were very much involved in the pragmatic side of life. Even as the Romanization process was underway, something very American was also at work. Surrounded by phenomenal success stories, many believed that in the land of opportunity, no one need be poor, if only he or she worked hard. Charitable institutions and efforts multiplied, many motivated by the belief poverty could be wiped out.

The Saint Vincent de Paul Society arrived in the U.S. in 1845. Considered by 1880 the most important charitable agency in the Church, it offered the best expression of the nineteenth-century lay apostolate. Religious women operated 119 hospitals and 267 orphanages. Most of the immigrant groups had fraternal organizations that took care of the needs of their own people. One such group was The German *Central Verein* founded in 1855, noted for its strong lay leadership. Concentrated in the midwest, such groups are typically remembered for their publications and especially for their educational works.

The Catholic Total Abstinence Union of America, established in 1872, represented the most enduring reform sponsored by nineteenth-century Catholics; in the labor movement they also helped bring about better working conditions and better wages. With *Rerum Novarum* in 1891, the social agenda became a religious matter of human rights. Already in 1889, the laity had organized a national Catholic congress to discuss current concerns and again in 1893 at Chicago where men and women discussed the encyclical and social questions for three days. Black Catholics were even more active; they held five congresses in the 1880's and 1890's to protest segregation and discrimination in Catholic churches and schools. In the North, religious orders were assigned to black parishes, thus removing this issue from diocesan concerns for decades to come.

Unfortunately, the bishops were more concerned with internal problems like schools and Americanism than with the broader social issues of systemic proportions. The building momentum of the laity faltered and by 1910 was diffused within the Catholic community. Middle-class Catholics identified poverty,

---

[1] Seven of the 49 Americans at Vatican I spoke out, signed petitions or wrote against the doctrine. Only four clearly favored it. Twenty-two left before the vote; one voted against it (total vote was 533 for, 2 against). Carey, *op. cit.*, pp. 27, 29.

housing, political and educational reform as more immediate concerns than the human rights of workers or Blacks. Some priests, like Father William Kerby of CUA, as well as lay leaders who recognized the systemic nature of evil underlying poverty, urged a shift from the earlier "band-aid" charity or relief work to a head-on confrontation with the more basic issue of the causes of poverty and its consequences.

Finally a lay voice had emerged that no longer responded to social problems simply out of expediency and pragmatism, but out of serious reflection in the light of the gospel. Even though Cardinal Gibbons opposed lay congresses (and effectively ended them), the laity did not sit still. A creative tension now existed that was not nationalistic or destructive as it had been at times in the past. The American Federation of Catholic Societies was founded in 1901 and by 1913 included women. The goal of this lay group was to build a Christian America based on Catholic principles with special attention to intemperance, the violation of Sunday and divorce.[1]

The Bishops' Program of Social Reconstruction of 1919 was the culmination of 30 years of Catholic efforts for social reform, but priests and the laity, not the bishops, had provided the initial thrust for this reform (which unfortunately died in the 1920's). The American public's favorable reception of this plan for post-war reconstruction brought a measure of acceptance and recognition to Catholics, especially to the hierarchy, even though the document itself was by one individual, Father John Ryan.

The role played by the laity in the area of social justice and reform was prophetic of a certain discernible shift in spiritual leadership from the shoulders of the chief pastors to priests and people. This marked the rest of the twentieth century and started to define the contours of a distinctive American Catholic spirituality. A host of new priorities called forth by human tragedy, injustice and a sense of responsibility to present and future generations for the health of the planet slowly replaced an earlier spirituality content with stacking up indulgences for the future and blind to or unwilling to confront the dehumanizing conditions of society with any attempt at effective action. This spirituality originated from within; it was not dictated from outside.

If nineteenth-century Catholics chafed at an excessively Irish bit, twentieth-century Catholics suffered from spiritual reins too loosely and indecisively held.[2] At a time when the laity most wanted leadership, it was not there, forcing them to grow up and take responsibility for their own decisions. This proved a difficult, painful process for both hierarchy and laity, a process that is not yet finished.

In 1924 Thomas Turner organized his fellow black Catholics. Ten years later, Catholic Interracial Councils began to explore the issue of discrimination but not until 1947 did Cardinal Ritter order integration and threaten excommunication. Only in the 1950's did the hierarchy as a whole include racial justice as part of social justice.

[1]Dolan, *op. cit.,* pp. 341.
[2]For example, endless bickering over communion in the hand, clumsy implementation of liturgical reform, upholding patriotism (Vietnam War) and pro-war attitudes, altar girls, women's ordination.

As Blacks flocked to the cities, whites moved to the suburbs. Experienced initially as a financial crisis by the Church, much energy and perhaps up to half of the sermons each year were directed to raising funds for new churches and schools. The resulting segregation only added to the spiritual impoverishment of the people.

Ritual and a fascination for the miraculous continued to mark typical Catholic spirituality in the first half of the twentieth century. The ever popular novenas differed from one part of the country to another, but generally honored Mary (Perpetual Help, Miraculous Medal, Our Lady of Sorrows) and reinforced the sense of sin and guilt, the need for heavenly help. The messages of Lourdes and Fatima strengthened defenders of this spirituality who published 10,000 Marian titles between 1948 and 1957. The emphasis on Mary tended to reinforce the feminine nature of religion. Sodalities in honor of Mary took on new life, especially under Dorothy J. Willmann and Daniel Lord, S.J. Summer schools of Catholic Action sponsored by the sodalities offered more rigorous training for the laity and justice.[1] The Dominicans sponsored teams of Our Lady under lay leadership which presented a more challenging spiritual life to married couples.

Other developments fostered renewed interest in lay spirituality. The retreat movement, often based on an abbreviated form of the Ignatian Exercises, especially in high schools, stressed sin, judgment, heaven and hell. A more positive note appeared with the liturgical movement under the leadership of men like Virgil Michel and Martin Hellriegel. Viewed as a primary agent for Christian solidarity and social reconstruction, annual conferences began in 1940 which highlighted the link between liturgical prayer and social justice. Finally, even though of European origin and with an emphasis on the spiritual nature of Catholicism, the "new theology" found a receptive audience among the young intellectuals of the day.

Family-oriented groups like the Cana Conference and the Christian Family Movement, as well as student and worker groups, developed a social action focus grounded in a solid program of spiritual development. Gradually focus shifted from the parish to the broader community as the members understood the Church increasingly as Christ's Mystical Body. The flourishing Catholic school system contributed significantly to this intellectual/spiritual renaissance. Not only did 59 percent of the parishes have schools by 1959, but there were 116 colleges and universities for women and 59 for men.[2]

Vocations had mushroomed. New orders emerged to work with Blacks or in foreign lands. Paulists and Glenmary missionaries took America for their mission field. Maryknoll went abroad. Year by year the number of converts mounted as the Church continued to grow, even without an enormous influx of immigrants. In 1960 alone the Church boasted a record 146,212 converts.

But all was not well. In 1956 John Tracy Ellis criticized the lack of American Catholic intellectual life and called devotional Catholicism and its culture a liability. Sheed and Ward's publication of European lay thinkers like

---

[1] The earliest example appeared in the 1890's; soon up to 10,000 per year attended. Rural life summer schools were also popular into the 1940's and 1950's. *Ibid.*, pp. 258, 381.
[2] Dolan, *op. cit.*, pp. 397, 399.

Chesterton, Maritain and Claudel helped provide an intellectual stimulus. Lay publications like *Jubilee* and *Commonweal* tried to fill the void and eventually gained respect.

Dorothy Day (1897-1980) and the *Catholic Worker* with its goal of making the Catholic Church the "dominant social dynamic force" proved harbingers of a long overdue spiritual renewal. Day epitomized a "balance between active Christianity and searching prayerfulness," offering modern Catholic spirituality" a blend of ancient asceticism, a medieval expression of religious experience and a modern social and ecumenical consciousness."[1] Hospitality houses run by laity were intended to be witness to the truth that the spiritual is far more central to life than the material. They hoped to change people's hearts, to effect a radical reconstruction of society, and argued for a spiritual solution to society's ills. The meaning of "faith made explicit in life" finds its best expression in Dorothy Day's own words:

> Yes, we have lived with the poor, with the workers...the unemployed, the sick....We have all known the long loneliness and we have learned that the only solution is love that comes with community.[2]

Because Dorothy Day was radically for peace, the *Catholic Worker* became the hub of the emerging American Catholic peace movement. To many her pacifist stance during World War II was unpatriotic and so support for her work diminished.[3]

The Grail, the creation of a Dutch Jesuit in 1921 to train women for the lay apostolate for service to the poor and interracial justice, arrived in the U.S. in 1940. The leaders set about preparing women for a new Catholicism. The members led an intense spiritual-liturgical life, and they offered retreats and workshops to help initiate others into a more humanistic spirituality. When the women's movement began, the Grail became very active in it, in a distinctively ecumenical way. As early as 1978 a workshop focused on alternate images of God and forms of worship. By 1984 it went even further with a workshop on "Sophia and the Future of Feminist Spirituality." Although it dealt with the topic in the light of the Judeo-Christian traditions, it presented Sophia as a goddess-like figure.[4]

Two other transplants from Europe, the Young Christian Students and the Young Christian Workers, originally meant to be arms of Catholic Action and hence under the hierarchy, developed into independent lay movements in the U.S. Fathers Reynold Hillenbrand and Louis Putz used them to encourage lay responsibility and deliberately kept them as far removed from the hierarchy as possible.[5]

---

[1]Weaver, *op. cit.,* p. 188.
[2]Quoted in Doris Grumbach, "Father Church and the Motherhood of God," *Commonweal* 93 (December 11, 1970), pp. 268-269.
[3]Cf. Robert Ellsberg, *By Little and By Little: The Selected Writings of Dorothy Day* (New York: Alfred A. Knopf, 1988).
[4]Weaver, *op. cit.,* pp. 185ff. Also Alden V. Brown, *The Grail Movement in the U.S., 1940-1972* (Ph.D. dissertation, Union Theological Seminary, 1982).
[5]Dolan, *op. cit.,* p. 416.

These groups injected new blood into the American Church and set the stage not only for a Catholic Reformation but for a laity ready to take charge. By 1960, many were as well or better educated than the clergy and hierarchy. A Catholic ran for president, a new pope called for a council and wanted to open the windows to let in some fresh air.

Suddenly, in the midst of the euphoria and agony of Vatican II, American nuns and priests began to renounce commitments taken up to 20 or 30 years earlier, and in some cases, publicly to flaunt church teaching and laws. Two hundred forty-one seminaries closed between 1964 and 1986. As nuns left, tuitions climbed in parochial schools, enrollments declined and schools closed. Many laity and clergy were confused and upset by the rapidity of change and the way in which change (especially liturgical) was implemented. Some even left the Church because of these changes. From 1963 to 1974 church attendance dropped from 71 percent to 50 percent, monthly confessions from 37 percent to 17 percent.[1] In more recent years, many turned to other traditions, even to Hare Krishna or the Unification Church, or joined the ranks of the unchurched.

If John Tracy Ellis voiced concern in 1956 regarding Catholic intellectual life, the critical voices of the 1960's and 1970's were more apt to be directed to the emptiness of Catholic spiritual life, a life that had been theologically and theoretically rooted in the Mystical Body. In the wake of World War II and the resultant social upheaval, sincere people question the reality of God and the relevance of religion. The Death of God movement struck a resonant chord in the hearts of many, not in Nietzchean rebellion but from the very depths of their souls. "God" seemed an empty word and one may wonder if this was a result of the sterility of life in the churches. In this context the growing momentum created by the marriage of liturgy and justice finally exploded.

Suddenly people asked: where does the Church stand on women's rights, on the environment, on racial justice, on political accountability, on peace in a nuclear age? The official Church was slow to respond. Many like Greeley have singled out *Humanae Vitae* as the arch culprit responsible for the crisis of faith in the Church. Certainly, if polls have any validity, nothing touched so many Catholics so quickly and so intimately as this decision. Perhaps it, more than any other single event, forced Catholics to make a mature decision for which they knew they would be eternally accountable. Once again the issue of authority and how it should be exercised came to the forefront, as well as that of religious freedom and the primacy of the individual conscience (which Vatican II had said was immune from coercion in religious matters).[2] People began to question what constituted Catholic identity and who determined it. It seemed that many laity, not withstanding denunciations from the pulpit, decided they determined their Catholicity and their right to call themselves Catholic.

[1] Andrew M. Greeley, *The American Catholic* (New York: Basic Books, 1977), pp. 127, 132.
[2] Dolan, *op. cit.*, p. 436.

A FEMINIST SOLUTION

As with many other movements affecting the American Church in the 1960's, the women's movement also had European antecedents. The St. Joan's Alliance dated from the English suffrage movement and women like Gertrud Heinzelmann of Switzerland in 1962 raised their voices urging that the ordination of women to the priesthood be considered at Vatican II. As American women turned to the study of theology, they discovered that the apparent devaluation of women in the Church was a shockingly consistent pattern throughout Christian history. Some turned their efforts to a revision of this tradition. Others proposed alternate options: 1) leave the Church because sexism is intrinsic to its very origins, nature and message; 2) get into the power structure and redeem the institution by eliminating its sexist structures and language; or 3) develop a feminist spirituality to give the movement staying power and ultimately to transform the entire Catholic community.

The first solution obviously offers nothing to American Catholic spirituality. The second, however, offered some very positive suggestions, especially once people engaged in serious reflection about the nature of power and the nature of the priesthood. Theologians of the movement cautioned women about the need to define power and priesthood as experienced, and then to reflect on how to redefine and restructure power and priesthood so they will no longer be experienced as oppressive and dehumanizing but enabling, liberating and affirming. For most, role reversal was never a viable option, let alone desired. The Women's Ordination Conference, among other groups, has played an important role in pursuing this issue singlemindedly, speaking from its earliest moments in 1975 of a "future priesthood now" which intended to humanize the office for both women and men.

From this very narrow issue of priesthood, two important consequences resulted: the bonding of religious and lay women who found they had a common cause, and a reaching out from the very beginning to include men: not to use them to try to gain access to power but simply to affirm a union with them. There was a recognition that men also shared this experience of oppression in the Church, an oppression from arbitrary use (abuse) of power in a very juridically-oriented institution, from which even bishops were not immune, nor priests, nor nuns, nor lay women and men, and an oppression from sexual stereotypes imposed by Church and society. Most women seeking ordination in the 1970's and 1980's were quite clear they did not want to be ordained into the existing priesthood. Many of these women experienced their call to priesthood while already ministering in the community. They wanted the notion of priesthood to be expanded along the lines of Vatican II's concept of service, so that their particular gifts, their service or ministry could be recognized and formally authenticated: whether to youth, the aged, the imprisoned, the ill or dying, or in the more traditional liturgically centered parish community.

At the same time as these developments on the theoretical level, significant changes occurred on the practical level. Lay people began to pick up the slack left by decreasing numbers of nuns and priests, despite increasing numbers of Catholics. Feminists regarded the decline in traditional vocations as a clear sign from the Holy Spirit that their calls were authentic, despite the negative Roman reaction to the idea of women priests. Team ministry (priest plus nuns or lay people) or parishes staffed by the non-ordained became a reality. By 1988 seminars for priests on how to explain "priestless Sundays" were spreading in the west and the midwest. Parishes closed or consolidated for lack of clergy to staff them. These significant changes were totally unexpected but suggest the possible return to the early American Catholic experience of a more domestic or lay-oriented, lay-run Church.

Furthermore, leaders of the Women's Ordination Conference engaged in ongoing dialogue with the bishops, even suggesting the agenda, in an attempt to affirm their love for and loyalty to the Church, their willingness to serve the Church and to accept their shared responsibility for its direction. They were suggesting a more conciliar-oriented ecclesiology.

The Catholic women's movement, drawing its leadership from religious women, academic women and others concerned has thus tried to anticipate the immediate and future needs of the Church and to propose remedies or solutions that will further humanize the ministry of the Church to be able to accomplish this spiritual, redemptive mission.

The third solution, however, is apt to have the most far reaching effect on American Catholic spirituality. In defining "feminism" the key element is the affirmation of the full personhood of woman. In developing a feminist spirituality, it is clear that one is most fully human, most fully free only when one totally affirms the full personhood of the other. As such the feminists, in proposing a spirituality for women, are not just concerned about women. They are careful to affirm the being and needs of both women and men. The goal is human partnership, not the manipulation or the exclusion of others. In effect, feminist authors propose a new model of human maturity based on the conviction that human and religious development are inseparable.

Denise Carmody in her book *Seizing the Apple: A Feminist Spirituality of Personal Growth* singles out four areas she considers crucial for a fully adequate feminist spirituality: prayer, work, family life and politics. Joann Wolski Conn has edited a book that attempts to understand self-sacrificial motifs, dependence, socialization and its consequences for women's spirituality. She insists on the need to deal with one's low self-esteem and the detrimental effects of some aspects of Christian tradition that reinforce a negative view of self. As such it is directed more specifically to women, but if taken seriously would definitely have a positive impact on anyone touched by it. Like Carmody, Conn agrees spirituality must include every dimension of human life: It is not just about prayer but the actualization of self-transcendency by the Holy.[1]

[1]Denise Carmody, *Seizing the Apple: A Feminist Spirituality of Personal Growth* (New York: Crossroads, 1984). Joann Wolski Conn, *Spirituality: Resources for Christian Development* (New York: Paulist Press, 1986).

Rosemary Ruether has been one of the consistent prophetic voices within feminism associated with the women's spirituality movement. She summarizes its goal:

> to transcend itself in human-church in a redemptive community that encompasses all people and rights the human relationship with nature. The vision of redemption must be universal. None are redeemed if some are still damned.[1]

These authors reject the traditional view of complementarity so dear to church documents because it too easily leads to theories of woman's inferiority and subordination so detrimental to a healthy spirituality. Other authors continue to work from within the confines of complementarity, such as Ronda Chervin.[2]

CONCLUSIONS

The good-hearted, more docile Catholics still hold the majority. However, a new breed, small though it may be, stands heir to Father White's civil disobedience, to Father Carroll's temerity with Rome, to Dorothy Day's tenacity in the face of criticism and misunderstanding, and is making its mark on the Church today. Because of their visions, these spiritual pioneers are willing to take a stand and suffer the consequences, regardless of the pressure lawfully constituted authority may put on them. Those who run afoul of authority are more apt to be people profoundly involved in the community that surrounds them, than those caught up in theological semantics or flagrant violations of church law to suit personal convenience. They are people of conviction whose views are not readily changed: they are stubborn and exasperating persons to those who do not share their views.

They function as prophets in our midst and prophets have never been particularly esteemed or loved by their contemporaries because they make them/us feel uncomfortable. They are willing to suffer for an ideal because they value spiritual integrity more than material comfort or social acceptance. They challenge the shallowness of our convictions and lives. They propose changing the way we pray in a most radical way. Prayer becomes a challenge to become one with everyone, "that they may be one" because it is rooted in scripture, in Christ. We are to let the Spirit cry forth from within. In actively participating in the liturgical life of the Church, we are invited to let go of comfortable, familiar, automatic ways of prayer, to expose ourselves to Infinite Mystery, to the penetrating power of the divine Word, to stand poised on the edge of an infinite abyss. We are being forced to rethink our very Catholic identity. No longer do fish on Friday, Latin ritual, ember days, fasting, novenas, indulgences and processions pass

[1]Rosemary Ruether, "The Development of My Theology," *Religious Studies Review*, Vol. 15, No. 1, Jan. 1989, p. 4.
[2]Ronda Chervin, *Feminine, Free and Faithful* (San Francisco: Ignatius Press, 1986). *Woman's Tale: Journal of Inner Exploration* (New York: Seabury Press, 1980).

as adequate signs of our Catholicity. We are challenged to bear fruit, to take the Eucharistic grace received at the liturgy out into the world to transform it. As a sign of our willingness, our ability to share this love with others, with the oppressed, the suffering, the outcast, the sinner, the unloved, we are urged to turn to the person next to us with a "sign of peace."

A number of essentially lay-led groups have offered encouraging signs of spiritual renewal in our day: charismatic and cursillo movements, revitalized third orders, prayer groups, Bible study groups, parish Renew. Of these, prayer groups have perhaps served as the greatest catalytic force or seedbed for vocations, for social justice action and for Renew (about 80 percent involved in Renew have come from prayer groups). But now these groups consist mainly of women and are dwindling. Those in social justice groups seem to have left their original prayer affiliations behind. This is not to say they do not pray but rather reflects something of the limitations of the lay state: a limit of time and the necessity to make hard decisions about priorities.

Does the current tapering off in spiritual movements mean that we are facing a spiritual decline such as the American Church experienced at the end of the nineteenth century? Only peace and abortion continue to be issues that rally significant numbers across the country.

From the hierarchy on down, there has been a new awareness of and a new openness to the Spirit, even for some a readiness to let the Spirit lead. The spirituality we see in Americans today, in the Berrigans, Murrays, Mertons, Hunthausens, Currans, Foxes, Kanes, Mansours, the women of WOC, of the National Assembly of Religious Women, of the Leadership Conference of Women Religious, the National Coalition of American Nuns, the 24 religious women who signed the *New York Times* statement, to mention the more familiar, is that of dissenters and prophetic figures who with the courage of their convictions dared to speak a controversial word. Some, like the Berrigans, John Courtney Murray, or Thomas Merton have in a sense been vindicated. Many Americans now regret the war, what it demanded of and did to a whole generation of young women and men; we no longer need to apologize for believing separation of church and state is a good thing; the right of religious freedom and a real respect and appreciation for other religious traditions are widely accepted.

These prophetic witnesses were preceded by a host of others, too numerous to list, but for the record let us recall Lucy Burns (1874-1966): opposed by bishops she spent more time in jail than any other American suffragist; Leonora Barry (1849-1930): denounced by priests for her activity in the labor movement campaigning for child labor laws; Mary Harris or "Mother Jones" (1830-1930): organizer for the United Mine Workers, she planned her own (Catholic) funeral and once said, "I'm waiting for the fellows in the Church to come out and fight with me, and then I'll go in." She accused Catholicism of "abandoning the revolutionary thrust of the Gospel."[1] Martha Avery (1851-1929) launched the Catholic Truth Guild; Anna Dengel (1892-1980) struggled to get the Code of Canon Law changed so nuns could be medical doctors and started an association of lay women to get around it in 1926 (which eventually became the Medical

---

[1]Weaver, *op. cit.*, p. 24.

Missionary Sisters).[1] Anita Caspary and the IHM's, the Sisters for a Christian Community founded by Lilanna Kopp, the Association of Contemplative Sisters, even though forbidden by Rome to organize, went ahead and have yet to be recognized or approved by the Vatican congregation for Religious (CRIS).

To be free we must be willing to assume the risks of freedom. Whether right or wrong, all the above by their actions and their decision to stay in the Church have demonstrated their conviction that Christ came to set us free, that freedom is of the essence of Catholicism, and that this freedom is no vague abstraction but is made explicit in the very lives they live. As such it is an integral dimension of their faith and their spirituality.

The admission of past sin is one of the greatest signs of spiritual growth and development in the Catholic Church in recent years. The American Catholic Church through the leadership of its bishops has taken matters a step further. Since 1980 they have made it increasingly clear that social justice is an essential part of the church's mission. They have recognized the sin of racism in church and society, duly and repeatedly condemned it and have made some sincere attempts to atone for it. Some American bishops have publicly apologized for the failure of the Church in the past to protest injustices against Native Americans. They have recognized and condemned militarism but have not yet made significant steps beyond that. They are in the process of condemning sexism in society, recognizing its presence in members of the clergy and laity but are faltering in terms of condemning its presence in church structures and proposing the kind of creative remedies we need.

These failures of courage keep the institution from being on the cutting edge of its prophetic vocation and challenge its credibility in the eyes of the mature Catholic. It also offers a distinct challenge to that mature Catholic to bring the entire Body of Christ, the people of God, into a positive, creative confrontation with the perceived evil so that out of the encounter will come a stronger, purer, truer Christian community.

Not only do we have a tradition of loyal, positive, constructive, even creative dissent, but it constitutes a dominant element of what we might call an American Catholic spirituality. Ours is a prophetic and political spirituality rooted in a doctrine of the Holy Spirit and expressed in social justice commitments, for in moving beyond self we learn to trust our own experience and our faith becomes truly explicit in life. Let us earnestly pray that the American Church will not succumb to fear in the face of the often difficult demands of the Spirit for structural change, that we do not experience yet another spiritual decline into devotionalism, authoritarianism and the stifling of the Spirit.

---

[1] *Ibid.*, see especially chapter 1 "Who Can Find a Valiant Woman?" pp. 18-35.

CHAPTER FIFTEEN

American Catholics and Social Reform, 1789-1989

Mel Piehl
Valparaiso University

In 1893 Cardinal James Gibbons explained to the Parliament of Religions at the Columbian Exposition in Chicago what he understood to be the essential Catholic motive for social engagement: The "fatherhood of God and the brotherhood of Christ," he said, "has inspired the Catholic Church in the mission of love and benevolence. This is the secret of her all-pervading charity. This idea has been her impelling motive in her work of the social regeneration of mankind."[1]

The assertion of a spiritual purpose for social action has been a distinguishing characteristic of American Catholicism from the early days of the republic to the present. But in the course of American history, Catholics' actual relations to various forms of social action and social reform have been shaped not only by their own changing understandings of what Christian faith called them to do, but by their historical experience of American society and culture. High spiritual motives did lead many Catholics to intense moral and social commitments, but the actual content of their social thought and action was also deeply affected by their own social values and by their peculiar and complex relations with the larger American society, including movements of social reform.

In terms of social outlook, American Catholicism prior to the great immigrations of the 1830's was predominantly conservative and favorably inclined toward the more hierarchical and regulative strands of the new nation's republican social order. The primary reason was that Catholics had greatly benefitted by one of the enlightened social changes of the American Revolution, the national separation of church and state. But the tiny Catholic minority concentrated in Maryland and Pennsylvania also knew how fragile that achievement was in an overwhelmingly Protestant society. The institutionalization of religious liberty in the federal constitution, and its personal expression in the enlightened toleration of the early federal officials, forged a deep attachment to the national American republican experiment on the part of Catholics who were highly aware that such sentiments were not unanimously favored by their fellow citizens. In an address to George Washington in 1790, for instance, the Catholic clergy asserted that

> the prospect of national prosperity is peculiarly pleasing to us, on another account; because, whilst our country preserves her freedom and independence, we shall have a well founded title to claim from her justice, the equal rights of citizenship... [They are] rights rendered more dear to us by the remembrance of former hardships.

---

[1] Quoted in Charles Shanabruch, *Chicago's Catholics* (Notre Dame, IN: University of Notre Dame Press, 1981), p. 129.

They prayed for the preservation of those rights by the Washington government, and told the new president that they expected "the full extension of them from the justice of those States, which will still restrict them."[1]

An additional reason for Catholic elites to emphasize the conservative features of the new American republic came from the radical French Revolution. Catholics had even more reason than most conservative Americans to be horrified by the anti-religious dimensions of events in France, since it was their own Church that was being pilloried and plundered. The spread of pro-revolutionary "republican societies" in the United States, and the seeming affinity of some Jeffersonian Republicans for anti-clerical and levelling social ideas derived from France, made American Catholics eager to stem the dangerous virus. John Carroll wrote in 1794:

> We are threatened here with the dissemination of the French political errors....Our alliance with them, and the habits of intimacy formed during the war between many Americans and some French officers, who have since taken a leading part in their revolution, are active means of spreading the infatuation, and it requires all the firmness and integrity of our great President Washington and the persons acting under him, to withstand the torrent.[2]

While an essentially conservative version of Catholic Americanism formed the dominant strand of respectable Catholic social thought in the early nineteenth century, and remained the bedrock of most Catholic social pronouncements long afterward, other voices also appeared on the scene. By actively promoting the economic and social change associated with the dynamic capitalism of the young republic, while advocating amelioration of its more harmful effects, a few urban reformers ironically helped put Catholicism more in touch with the general direction of American society in the nineteenth century than did the more traditional Catholic elites. The most visible forerunner of what eventually became a small tribe of Irish American Catholic reformers was Matthew Carey, a Dublin-born political agitator and printer who advocated policies that would release the latent energy of the working classes and presumably spread to them the benefits of emerging capitalism. Carey initially championed unfettered economic individualism as the best way to open economic opportunity to the wage earner, but after the depression of 1819 turned increasingly toward a Hamiltonian belief in economic planning, protectionism and federal spending to develop an economic infrastructure that would, he believed, work to promote the interests of both manufacturer and laborer. At various times, Carey promoted nearly every "humanitarian reform" that emerged among civic minded urban elites of the early nineteenth century, including public education, prison reform and relief for the poor. In most of these efforts, Carey exhibited the common early nineteenth-century reformer's combination of paternalistic benevolence (derived from religious and humanitarian duty toward those less fortunate) and the peculiarly

---

[1]"The Address of the Roman Catholics to George Washington, Esq., President of the United States," in Thomas O'Brien Hanley, ed., *The John Carroll Papers* (Notre Dame, IN: University of Notre Dame Press, 1976), Vol. I, p. 410.
[2]Carroll to John Troy, July 12, 1794, *Carroll Papers,* Vol. II, p. 121.

American belief that the primary task of reform is to enable those not presently prospering under American capitalism to do so, either by expanding the benefits of the system or by better fitting the marginalized to enter it. But his extensive personal charitable involvements with the working classes and the poor also could lead him to arguments that religion should actively promote social justice. He strongly urged, for example, that the clergy preach sermons criticizing the low wages of working women in Philadelphia: "I do not mean actual charity sermons; of these there are enough...I mean sermons on the inhumanity of cutting down the wages of female labour...."[1]

As Catholics multiplied in American cities in the early nineteenth century, self-sacrificing priests like Father Alexander Mupiatti and the Cuban American Felix Varela, religious orders like the Sisters of Charity and the Sisters of Mercy, and committed lay persons like the saintly New York black Catholic Pierre Toussaint and the Society of St. Vincent de Paul, began what eventually became a massive Catholic charitable effort on behalf of orphans, the poor and the infirm in American cities. Unlike Carey, most of them did not extend their spiritually motivated practice of the works of mercy to advocacy of social reform. The emphasis of most nineteenth-century Catholic social thought was in fact quite the opposite: poverty and social suffering were consequences of sin, existing social arrangements were divinely ordained and not to be tampered with, and charity was a spiritual opportunity and duty pointing toward the supernatural world and not this one. Even though immigrant Catholics were at the bottom of American society, most soon came to share the democratic and capitalistic belief in the virtues of the American economic and social order, and saw no fundamental difficulties in reconciling the higher spiritual and moral principle of their faith with the emerging bourgeois values of their energetic and expansive society.

If Carey and the practitioners of Catholic charity represent the beginning of the Catholic encounter with the rapidly expanding social ethos of urban, bourgeois America, Catholics also had to come to terms with the quite different outlook of a region where social values were increasingly shaped by the institution of slavery. By the early nineteenth century the expansion of the peculiar institution and the rise of northern abolitionism forced some Catholics to consider the relationship of their ancient religion to human bondage. Although a few lay Catholics supported colonization of Blacks in Africa, almost no Catholic, clerical or lay, joined the abolitionist cause. What emerged as the prevalent Catholic response to abolitionism was only a slight variation on the dominant proslavery ideology: slaves should be treated humanely and given the benefits of religion, but slaveholding was compatible with Catholic faith, and in any case the Church as such could not interfere with a purely political question.

The most notable Catholic expositor of this position was the learned Bishop of Charleston, John England. England's attempt to operate a school for free Blacks had suggested to some that he might be sympathetic to anti-slavery. But after Pope Gregory XVI issued an apostolic letter against the slave trade in 1838, England hastened to clarify his views in a series of letters to Secretary of State

[1]Quoted in James Roohan, *American Catholics and the Social Question, 1865-1900* (New York: Arno Press, 1976), p. 54.

John Forsyth, and in the process elaborated the most sophisticated Catholic response to the anti-slavery movement of the antebellum years. In an elaborate
analysis drawing on both theology and church history, England argued that
Catholicism had always worked to promote Christ's essential teachings about
spiritual equality and human dignity, but that it had done so most effectively by
quietly spreading Christian moral principles to human hearts rather than by
overtly confronting even cruel social institutions and practices. After demonstrating to his satisfaction how the Church had worked to ameliorate the barbarous exploitative practices of early medieval Europe by slowly altering the
moral values of the ruling classes, England concluded that

> I have shown that the Saviour did not repeal the permission to hold slaves,
> but that he promulgated principles calculated to improve their condition, and
> perhaps, in the progress of time, to extinguish slavery.[1]

If Jesus himself had been a long-range rather than an immediate abolitionist, it
seemed that his Catholic followers certainly need not support an immediate end
to slavery on religious grounds, whatever their "personal wishes" concerning the
institution.

> There is no danger—no possibility, on our principles—that Catholic theol-
> ogy should ever be tinctured with the fanaticism of abolitionism. Catholics
> may and do differ in regard to slavery, and other points of human policy,
> when considered as ethical or political questions. But our theology is fixed,
> and is and must be the same now as it was in the first eight or nine centuries
> of Christianity.[2]

England put it more bluntly in a letter to the editors of his Catholic journal:

> I have been asked by many a question which I may as well answer at once,
> *viz.*: whether I am friendly to the existence or continuation of slavery? I am
> not—but also see the impossibility of now abolishing it here. Whether it
> can and ought to be abolished is a question for the legislature and not for
> me.[3]

Catholics who believed in the meliorist influence of religion on harsh social
practices like slavery pointed to personally kind masters, and to slaves who were
baptized in the faith because of their owners' Christian teaching and example.
England even claimed that black Catholic slaves "are everywhere distinguished as
a body for orderly habits and fidelity to their masters, so much so that in Maryland, where they are numerous, their value is 20 to 25 per cent above that of
others."[4] That the proof of black Catholic faithfulness should suggest a rise in
the price of human flesh pointed up the contradictions that plagued even the
most sincerely religious white Catholics in the South. In fact, Catholic mas-

---

[1] Ignatius Aloysius Reynold, ed., *The Works of the Right Reverend John England*,
5 vols. (Baltimore: John Murphy and Co., 1849), p. 127.
[2] *Ibid.*, p. 108.
[3] *United States Catholic Miscellany*, February 17, 1841.
[4] Reynold, *op. cit.*, Vol. III, p. 104.

ters, including priests, bishops, and men's and women's religious orders, differed little if at all in their treatment of Blacks from their Protestant and nonreligious neighbors. An illustration of how involvement with the system could undermine religious values is the painful story of Jesuit slaveholding in Maryland. Historian R. Emmett Curran has shown how admonitions from superiors to look on slaves as "brothers in Jesus Christ" were rendered ineffectual by the harsh realities of bondage. The tension between spiritual teaching and social practice reached a kind of moral climax when the Jesuits finally sold all their slaves to Louisiana in 1838, amidst heartrending scenes of family separation. The slaves, many of them Catholic, bore their fate with "heroic courage and Christian resignation," and begged for rosaries to aid them in their ordeal.[1]

While some Catholics felt the gap between Christian teaching and American social reality as an intellectual or moral dilemma, those "marginalized" Catholics who existed outside dominant institutions and ideologies had less difficulty reconciling the mandate of religious charity with their own social location and function. This is particularly true of the most distinctive group of American Catholics in the nineteenth century, the women who organized themselves into religious communities in order to bring the spiritual and ethical principles of the Gospel into the society. Though these women seldom adopted any systematic social critique or attempted to alter institutions in ways that might be labelled reform, their own active charitable mission and activities on behalf or the Gospel diverged in some ways from prevailing social norms, and thus constituted a kind of reformist challenge to the dominant American social values and institutions.[2]

Many of the notable early American religious women like Mother Elizabeth Seton of the Emmitsburg Sisters of Charity, Catherine Spalding of the Sisters of Charity (Nazareth), Angela Sansbury of the Dominican Sisters, and Elizabeth Lange of the Oblate Sisters of Providence—a Black order founded in Maryland—struggled to obtain sufficient religious autonomy and social freedom to be able to chart their own directions in providing forms of Christian service to orphans, the sick, the uneducated and the poor. While their own economic and social backgrounds differed considerably, all the female religious orders had to find adequate economic means to sustain their missions, since they lacked the permanent endowments of the European orders. This necessity further encouraged their active entry into the fields of teaching, nursing and social service where they could secure a minimal income in addition to funds received by donation.

These developments meant that American Catholic sisters became in some respects more entangled with the ordinary institutions and values of American society than their European counterparts. They wrote constitutions, incorporated according to state laws, bought and sold property, and owned slaves. Yet their

[1]R. Emmett Curran, S.J., "'Splendid Poverty': Jesuit Slaveholding in Maryland, 1805-1838" in Randall M. Miller and Jon L. Wakelyn, eds., *Catholics in the Old South* (Macon, GA: Mercer University Press, 1983), pp. 125-146.
[2]For the history of early American women religious, see Mary Ewens, *The Role of the Nun in the Nineteenth Century* (Salem, NH: Ayer Company, 1984) and Barbara Misner, *Highly Respectable and Accomplished Ladies* (New York: Garland, 1988). For sisters in the South, see Frances Jerome Woods, "Congregations of Religious Women in the Old South," in *Catholics in the Old South,* pp. 99-124.

relative social and economic autonomy also meant that Roman Catholic sisters represented a dramatically visible alternative to prevalent American values concerning women's spheres, social position and relations with men. Because they were communities of unmarried, childless women who justified their position and activities on the basis of higher spiritual ideals, Catholic women religious aroused especially harsh opposition from American defenders of male supremacy, the patriarchal family and the cult of female domesticity. Much of this opposition was part of the general nativist Protestant hostility to Catholicism, but the particular ferocity directed at the Catholic sisters—epitomized by *The Awful Disclosures of Maria Monk* and the burning of the Ursuline Convent in Boston in 1834—suggest that the Catholic belief in the religious superiority of the female virgin called to a life of Christian service was seen as a particular threat to nineteenth-century American cult of true womanhood.[1] Of course, with few possible exceptions, nineteenth-century Catholic sisters did not think of themselves as directly challenging prevalent American social norms, and in practice their own vision of "spiritual motherhood" tended in some ways to reinforce conventional ideas of women's roles among those they served. Yet in exemplifying a form of female moral and social autonomy deeply rooted in Catholic religious tradition, while at the same time attempting to exemplify the values of Christian charity and service, Catholic women religious represented a striking social alternative to American gender arrangements.

In the middle of the nineteenth century, however, the possibility that American society would look to Catholicism for social instruction was virtually nonexistent. With the transformation of American Catholicism by the great waves of immigration, the Church came to be seen as a near-foreign body in American society, isolated and vulnerable to the periodic assaults of vocal anti-Catholics that began in the 1830's and were periodically renewed well into the mid-twentieth century. Forced to fend off these attacks while ministering as best it could to the vast legions of new arrivals, the Church had little energy to devote to transforming the wider social order.

Furthermore, Catholics could hardly ignore the fact that "social reform" in America was initially lined with many of the same forces and values that displayed such hostility to their religion. It was often the most energetic and socially engaged sectors of American society (social reformers with their roots in evangelical Protestantism) who were also prominent in the anti-Catholic movements of the day. The numerous early nineteenth-century reform movements on behalf of sabbath observance, peace, prison reform, better treatment of the handicapped, and so on, were generally organized by Protestant clergy or pious lay people who not only failed to invite Catholics into their efforts, but promoted the identification of genuine Americanism with their faith.[2]

The greatest of the antebellum reform movements, abolitionism, included prominent anti-Catholic ministers like Lyman Beecher, Samuel Crothers and

[1]Joseph G. Mannard, "'Maternity...of the Spirit': Nuns and Domesticity in Antebellum America," *US Catholic Historian,* Vol. 5, (Summer/Fall 1986), pp. 305-324.
[2]Marty, *Righteous Empire: The Protestant Experience in America* (New York: Dial, 1970), pp. 89-99.

George Bourne, some of whom were even convinced that Catholicism was the hidden hand upholding the slave power.[1] Dorothea Dix, justly famed as a crusading Protestant reformer on behalf of the mentally ill, was also notably anti-Catholic and in her role as superintendent of nurses during the Civil War she fought vigorously to prevent Catholic sisters from serving as nurses in battle-field hospitals.[2] For many Protestant reformers, the Roman Catholic religion— no less than war or liquor or slavery—was one of the evils to be reformed out of American society.

This experience of being on the receiving end of "reform," of feeling the heat of righteous indignation directed at cherished beliefs and values, helped inoculate immigrant American Catholicism against standard American reform outlook, with its tendency toward abstract moralism and claims of disinterested benevolence. Like American Southerners, perhaps, American Catholics existed enough outside the mainstream Yankee Protestant experience to see the self-righteousness and intemperate zeal that often tainted even the loftiest reform efforts. The Church's American experience thus reinforced Catholicism's conservative theological tendency to expect the permanence of sin in the world even while striving to overcome it on a spiritual plane. Even those American Catholics who became aware of social evils seldom looked to make the Church itself a direct instrument of social change in the same way that some American Protestants did.

The sobering effect of Catholic theology on Yankee reformist zeal is well-illustrated by one of nineteenth-century Catholicism's most famous converts, Orestes Brownson. Brownson, whose earlier career had given him a thorough familiarity with the spirit of Yankee reform movements, came to believe that much of the impetus for social reform arose from essentially spiritual yearnings that could only be satisfied by salvation within the Church, not by moralizing activism. Brownson therefore no longer looked to social transformation as the primary means to improve the human condition, because the root of the problem lay elsewhere, in human sin and self-seeking. Accordingly, most of his post-conversion writing focused more on matters of theology and philosophy than on social analysis. When he did take up social questions, his ideas revealed an increasing emphasis on the necessary moral foundations of stable social institutions, on natural law, and on hierarchical order, the last eventually linked with a typical Catholic idealization of the Middle Ages.[3]

But the necessary cautions of theological orthodoxy did not mean that American Catholics always found a comfortable fit between their highest religious values and dominant social and economic interests. On the contrary, when thoughtful Catholics like Brownson or Archbishop John Hughes of New York did take care to reflect on American society and capitalist economic development from the vantage point of Christian moral teaching, they found it severely wanting. As early as 1844, Hughes had denounced "the spectacle of the starving la-

[1]Louis Filler, *The Crusade Against Slavery* (New York: Harper & Row, 1960), pp. 148-149.
[2]Ewens, *op. cit.,* pp. 225-229.
[3]Arthur M. Schlesinger, *Orestes A. Brownson: A Pilgrim's Progress* (Boston: Little, Brown, 1939).

borer maintaining a contest of competition with the bloated capitalist"; he sharply criticized the moral assumptions of orthodox laissez-faire economics.[1] And despite his increasingly conservative social assumptions, the Catholic Brownson effectively used Christian ideas to criticize the reduction of the human being to "economic man", a "producing, distributing, and consuming machine, placed in the same category with the steam-plough, patent reaper, spinning jenny, and the power loom." He also retained an astute sense of the way concentrated economic power in American society tended to enhance capitalist control of the ostensibly democratic polity and to increase the dependence of the wage earner. "Employers in vain pretend that the interests of capital and labor are the same," he wrote in 1872. "They are not so under a civilization based on Mammon, or under a civilization that seeks only the advancement of material interests, and invests capital only for the sake of material profit. In the struggle, the stronger party, under a material system, is always sure to succeed. And this is always the party of capital; for labor seeks employment to live; capital for profit and gain."[2]

This kind of spiritually-based social criticism, however, was an isolated phenomenon, and did not form the basis for any program of social reform. Catholic leaders continually called for a generalized "return to Christianity" as the solution to the evils of the age, but this was overwhelmingly presented in purely personal terms. Meanwhile Catholics were being drawn deeply into the existing institutions and values of American life. Operating as a minority in a social environment radically different from any the Church had previously known in its history, American Catholicism could not attempt to shape social institutions in any significant way, but mainly reacted to the diverse social movements that developed in the United States, and thereby came into contact with the Catholic faithful.

Two of the most significant social reforms that gained strength in the half century after the Civil War were the labor movement and the women's movement. The Church's rather differing relations with these two American developments further demonstrates how difficult it was for a still intellectually underdeveloped American Catholicism to chart a religiously proper course in relation to main currents of American reform.

In general, the official church response to American movements for women's rights and related reforms affecting the family varied from indifferent to hostile. Catholic leaders universally professed regard for "Christian womanhood," and proclaimed the Catholic Church as the true guardian of women's interests through the ages, as did Archbishop John Ireland in 1896:

---

[1] John Hughes, "A Lecture on the Importance of a Christian Basis for the Science of Political Economy and Its Application to the Affairs of Life," in Lawrence Kehoe, ed., *Complete Works of the Most Rev. John Hughes,* 2 vols. (New York: 1865), p. 521.

[2] Orestes A. Brownson, "Charity and Philanthropy," *Catholic World* 4 (1867), p. 445; Brownson, "The International Association," *Catholic World* 14 (1872), p. 696.

In prechristian civilization woman was a slave, without honor or rights, the mere toy of passion.....In the Christian civilization...the woman was the queen of the home, and as the Christian religion grew in power, so grew the dignity of womanhood influence and in the respect awarded to it.[1]

But official Catholic spokesmen also generally scorned women's reform movements and warned Catholics against them, especially when they seemed to raise issues about the relations of men and women within the family. Cardinal James Gibbons, for example, said,

I regard 'woman's rights' as the worst enemy of the female sex. They rob woman of all that is amiable and gentle, tender and attractive, they rob her of her innate grace of character, and give her nothing in return but masculine boldness and brazen effrontery.[2]

Rooted as it was in diverse currents of evangelical Protestantism, Enlightenment theories of human rights, and modern ideas about sexuality, the American women's movement had few points of contact with traditional Catholic thought or values concerning family life or women. For their part, many women's rights advocates felt little need to find common ground, and simply assumed or invited the hostility of the "reactionary" Catholic hierarchy. Perhaps the most dramatic and sustained instance of such mutual incomprehension and hostility involved the birth control movement. Led by Margaret Sanger, whose father was himself a disaffected Catholic, Sanger found in the official Catholic Church a suitably dramatic opponent to a cause that was, for her and her followers, the touchstone of women's emancipation. For the most part the official Church reciprocated with just the expected kind of opposition on which Sanger thrived. In 1921, for example, church officials under the direction of Monsignor Joseph Dineen used city police to shut down a Sanger meeting in New York's Town Hall on the grounds that there might be children in the audience.[3]

Yet despite the general suspicion regarding American women's movements by official church spokesmen, the actual response of American Catholics to efforts on behalf of women were somewhat more diverse. The Church, for example, did not initially approve the establishment of American women's colleges as vehicles for women's emancipation and entry into the worlds of politics and the professions. But Catholic women, led by the religious orders, successfully pushed for the establishment of Catholic women's colleges. For instance, the long battle of Sister Mary Euphrasia of the Sisters of Notre Dame de Namur to establish Trinity College in Washington eventually won the support of Cardinal Gibbons, who provided her with crucial support for the college against the stub-

---

[1]John Ireland, *The Church and Modern Society* (Chicago: D.H. McBride, 1896), p. 333.

[2]Quoted in Elizabeth Carr Worland, "American Catholic Women and the Church to 1920" (dissertation, St. Louis University, 1982), p. 135.

[3]Peter Fryer, *The Birth Controllers* (New York: Stein and Day, 1966), p. 211. On Sanger's crusade and its ideological relations to religion, see David M. Kennedy, *Birth Control in America* (New Haven: Yale University Press, 1970).

born opposition of European Catholic authorities.[1] Gibbons was partly motivated by embarrassment at the fact that Catholic women would attend secular
colleges, but his position—and that of many other Catholics who endorsed
women's education—indicates how the American Church was often altered by
American women's reform movements at the practical if not at the intellectual or
theological level.

On the most widely debated women's reform of the late-nineteenth and early
twentieth century, the movement for suffrage, the Church took no official doctrinal position, so that Catholic men and women, clergy and laity, freely assumed various positions. Prominent members of the hierarchy like Gibbons and
Archbishop John Williams of Boston vocally opposed suffrage. So did laymen
like Orestes Brownson and John Boyle O'Reilly. Also joining the prominent
opponents of reform were a number of notable female Catholic writers and intellectuals, including convert and evangelist Martha Moore Avery, essayist Agnes
Repplier, and novelist and social critic Katherine Conway.[2] The arguments of
Catholic opponents of suffrage resembled those of Protestant and secular critics,
but they also drew on distinctly Catholic views that movements for women's
rights were artificial substitutes for true religious elevation of the status of
women, which they asserted had been degraded since the Reformation.

But some Catholics supported suffrage, including bishops like Patrick
William Riordan of San Francisco, John Lancaster Spalding of Peoria, and
Austin Dowling of Des Moines. Priest-reformers like John A. Ryan and
Thomas Scully of Massachusetts backed women's rights, and influential
Catholic politicians like Thomas A. Walsh of Montana played important roles
in the eventual passage of the Nineteenth Amendment. Some Catholic women
also supported the cause, and their most visible leaders worked to counter the
widespread perception that Catholics were automatically opposed to women's
rights or to changing women's place in American society. Among the leaders in
this endeavor were middle-class reformers like Margaret O'Foley of Massachusetts and Lucy Burns (an associate of Alice Paul in the Congressional
Union and Woman's Party), and women's labor advocates like Mary Kenney
O'Sullivan and Leonora Barry. They argued that influential Catholic women in
the early Church and the Middle Ages, such as Catherine of Siena and Joan of
Arc, had never been passive guardians of virtue, but active participants and reformers of society; therefore, they argued, politics could be an appropriate vehi-
cle for Catholic women's efforts to better American society and bring it closer to
Christian norms.[3]

---

[1]Worland, *op. cit.*, pp. 81-92.
[2]James J. Kenneally, "Eve, Mary, and the Historians: American Catholicism and
Women," in Janet Wilson James, ed., *Women in American Religion* (Philadelphia:
University of Pennsylvania Press, 1980), pp. 191-206. On Conway's extraordinary Catholic outlook, which enabled her to be both an activist career woman and
novelist and an advocate of the Catholic ideal of motherhood, see Paula M. Kane,
"The Pulpit of the Hearthstone: Katherine Conway and Boston Catholic Women,
1900-1920," *US Catholic Historian*, Vol. 5 (Summer/Fall 1986), pp. 355-370.
[3]Worland, *op. cit.*, pp. 159-186.

While the suffrage reform prompted these articulate and socially alert elites to debate women's roles from their Catholic perspectives, the great majority of American Catholics were not so attuned to political or religious argument on such matters. Most of them were immigrants, or at most only a generation or two removed from the immigrant experience. Often shaped by devotional Catholicism and its pessimistic piety that saw human life as so corrupted by sin that it must suffer the manifold evils of this world rather than overcome them, they were commonly suspicious of any social changes that might even remotely threaten such a fundamental institution as the family, or alter the arrangement of gender roles within it. This was especially true when many of their religious leaders depicted such changes as contrary to Catholic teaching and divine law, or linked changes in women's status with religiously unacceptable proposals such as divorce and birth control. The Chicago archdiocesan weekly *New World*, for instance, suggested that God had sent the "Irish Marys, Italian Marias, and Polish Hildas" to America to save the country from feminist college graduates. Because "crude and dangerous moral and social heresies" were attacking home and family, it said that "we must arm our Catholic mothers, our Catholic sisters and our Catholic daughters with those virtues that make for the preservation of home and family."[1]

However, the sense that American society was beginning to open the door to a new kind of relation between the sexes was not without its effects on American Catholics, especially women. It prompted widespread discussions about family stability, the responsibility of family roles, and the dangers of radical individualism in America.

While the dominant reaction was defensive and hostile, some more favorable voices were heard. Mary O'Sullivan of Boston, for instance, asserted that "the time has gone by when a girl was born to no higher destiny than humiliating dependence on fathers or brothers, or a sordid, loveless marriage."[2] The talk of suffrage prompted Margaret Moore of Syracuse to write in the diocesan *Catholic Sun*,

> No true woman ever married a man for the sake of becoming his dependent....Rather, does not the wife earn her right to the home and income by labors greater than the husband's? Is it not as an equal companion that she expects and has a right to be treated?

But an anonymous female letter writer to the same paper probably spoke for a larger number of Catholics:

> Equality of the sexes is not the nature of things. The woman's place is in the home and the difference between men's and women's vocations is that one is active and the other passive. If a woman does her best to please her husband he will be happy and she successful in holding his love.[3]

---

[1]Quoted in Shanabruch, *op. cit.*, pp. 138-139.
[2]Quoted in Kenneally, *op. cit.*, p. 205.
[3]Quoted in David J. O'Brien, *Faith and Friendship: Catholicism in the Diocese of Syracuse, 1886-1986* (Syracuse, NY: Catholic Diocese of Syracuse, 1987), p. 164.

Catholicism's response to labor and economic reform movements also caused disagreement and conflict, but since these issues cut less close to the bone of religion itself, it was far easier for the Church to find acceptable points of congruence between American reform movements and the moral traditions and teachings of the Church, including the encyclicals of the popes beginning with Leo XIII. Indeed, for many Catholics in the late nineteenth and early twentieth century, the phrase "social reform" simply meant labor and economic reform, an indication of the success the movement eventually came to enjoy within important sectors of the Church. The fact that American Catholicism could plausibly claim to be a defender of the rights of workers eventually came to be a proud index of its relevance to modern American society, and an important reason for its ability, unlike much of European Catholicism, to retain the loyalty of the working masses.

The history of the Church's relations to issues of labor and economic reform, though marked by considerable local variation, went through three broad phases at the national level. The first period, roughly from the Civil War to the turn of the century, was marked by growing recognition of the depth of economic grievances, and by various kinds of practical accommodation between the Church and labor, even though most church leaders were suspicious of organized labor and unable to develop any real theological or moral justification for unions or state regulation of capitalism. The first landmarks in this phase were the Molly Maguire episode and the railroad strikes of 1876-77, in which the deceptive cruelty of the mine owners and railroad barons against their workers awakened some Catholic thinkers to the need for reforms, and moved may Catholic workers toward labor organization. This was followed by the rise of the Knights of Labor and the debate over secret societies, which culminated in Cardinal Gibbons' famous defense of the Knights as a legitimate organization not hostile to the Church.

At the same time, growing Catholic charitable efforts, such as those of the Society of St. Vincent de Paul and various religious orders, prompted a growing awareness among some Catholic leaders of the extent of American social problems. In the pages of journals like *The American Catholic Quarterly* and more popular papers like the *Boston Pilot,* thoughtful Catholics began to ponder how their faith could appropriately respond to social problems of labor and poverty. The difficulties of working out an accommodation were often evident in the 1880's and 1890's, as in the tangled affair of Edward McGlynn, a New York priest who was suspended in part for backing reformer Henry George.[1]

The second phase, lasting roughly from the turn of the century to 1919, was marked by a more coherent American Catholic stance on issues of labor and economic justice, by the development of more sophisticated theological and moral reflection on these issues, and by the organizational elaboration of Catholic social institutions under the direction of the hierarchy. Several different but broadly convergent forces worked toward these changes within the Catholic community. First, many Catholics found in the ideologically safe American la-

---

[1]Roohan, *op. cit.,* pp. 161-331; Aaron I. Abell, *American Catholicism and Social Action: A Search for Social Justice, 1865-1950* (Notre Dame, IN: University of Notre Dame Press, 1963), pp. 27-136.

bor movement a religiously acceptable way to protect their interests and work for fairer economic arrangements. By World War I, Catholics formed a majority of members and leaders of the American Federation of Labor, and influential "labor priests" like Peter C. Yorke and Peter Dietz forged important links between the Church and labor-oriented causes.[1] Second, the impulse of Catholic charity, which had earlier taken root in a wide range of institutional efforts to serve the poor but had generally steered away from general social concern, expanded into broad national reform efforts designed to alter what many increasingly saw as the environmental cause of poverty. Especially through the extensive efforts and writing of Father William Kerby of Catholic University, some Catholics were moved to see that their religiously motivated social service would not be undermined but deepened by expanding it to the reform of general social policies and institutions.

> The zealous Christian will endeavor to obtain the greatest possible advantage out of everything good and helpful in the modern temper....But he will, at the same time, seek to protect the precious inheritance of the teaching and law of Christ concerning the poor.[2]

Finally, the learned priest-reformer John A. Ryan forged an impressive intellectual synthesis of neo-scholastic Catholic philosophy and the broad streams of American progressive reform. Ryan's tireless efforts and the extraordinary circumstances of World War I combined to produce the Bishops' Program for Social Reconstruction of 1919, which advocated, among other things, a minimum wage, federal housing for workers, and labor participation in the management of industry. Although not universally applauded by Catholics, and shoved to the rear in the political and religious climate of the 1920's, the Bishops' Program became the fundamental charter for twentieth-century American Catholic reformers and marked, as historian Joseph McShane has said, a new and mature phase of the Church's involvement in American social life.[3]

Particularly interesting in this progressive era of Catholic social reform were the vigorous efforts of the minority of socially conscious Catholic women who worked along the frontiers where the issues of labor, social welfare, and women's rights intersected and overlapped. The Catholic social settlements of the era, though far less publicized than Protestant houses, were focal points for Catholic women's involvement in a wide range of social reforms, and often fostered connections between charitable service and wider social change. Some of these settlements were run by religious orders, like the Sisters of Our Lady of Christian Doctrine founded in 1908 by Marion F. Gurney (Mother Marianne of Jesus) on the Lower East Side of New York, the Sisters of Charity of Mount Saint

---

[1]Marc Karson, *American Labor Unions and Politics, 1900-1918* (Carbondale, IL: Southern Illinois University Press, 1956), p. 224, 528.

[2]Quoted in Patrick Bernard Lavey, "William J. Kerby, John A. Ryan, and the Awakening of the Twentieth-Century Catholic Social Conscience, 1899-1919" (Ph.D. dissertation, University of Illinois, 1986), p. 202.

[3]Joseph M. McShane, *Sufficiently Radical: Catholicism, Progressivism, and the Bishops' Program of 1919* (Washington, DC: Catholic University of America Press, 1986), p. 282.

Joseph-on-the-Ohio, the Servants of the Immaculate Heart of Mary, and the Helpers of the Holy Souls. But most were run by Catholic lay women; Annie Leary's settlement on Charlton Street in New York, Mary Workman's Brownson House in Los Angeles, Josephine Brownson's Weinemann Settlement in New York, and Grace O'Brien's numerous settlements were motivated by Catholic competition and fear of the inroads being made by Protestant settlements in immigrant Catholic neighborhoods.

In other cases, what began as middle-class Catholic women's efforts to serve immigrants or "working girls" turned into advocacy of broader social reforms once the structural character of the female labor problem was discovered. For example, Caroline Gleason of the Catholic Women's League of Portland, Oregon, working closely with the reform-minded priest Father Edwin O'Hara, became a prime mover of the Oregon minimum wage law.[1] The Women's Trade Union League, which was one of the few reform groups in the Progressive era to combine successfully middle-class women's concerns and labor issues, included substantial Catholic participation. By 1911, nine of its ten officers were Catholics. Among its early stalwarts was the prominent women's and labor advocate Mary Kenney O'Sullivan, a former dressmaker who battled widely on behalf of labor, women's rights and peace causes. O'Sullivan eventually broke with the WTUL and turned to the radical Industrial Workers of the World when the more cautious women's group failed to support the Lawrence textile strike of 1912.[2]

The era in which Catholic involvement with labor and economic causes had begun to intersect with women's rights and other American social reform movements receded after about 1920. While non-Catholic American social criticism in many areas tended to assume political and cultural directions that even socially conscious Catholics could not accept (for instance, by incorporating ideas of Marxist economics, uninhibited sexuality, birth control, and anti-religious pessimism and materialism of various kinds), the accumulated intellectual and institutional effects of the papal condemnations of Americanism and modernism cut the official Church off from many currents of American thought and society. The new kinds of clerical control imposed by church figures like Cardinal William O'Connell of Boston, and the increasingly rigid applications of canon law to a range of Catholic institutions and activities, made it difficult for official Catholicism to respond positively to the diverse social problems and forces in American culture. Accordingly, most Catholic social efforts had to be closely aligned not only with orthodox theology but with what was understood to be the unified social stance of the universal Church.[3]

---

[1] Abell, *op. cit.*, pp. 165-168. Thomas O. Wood, "The Catholic Attitude Toward the Social Settlement Movement, 1886-1914" (unpublished dissertation, University of Notre Dame, 1958), pp. 65-70.

[2] Worland, *op. cit.*, pp. 109-117. James A. Kenneally, "Catholic and Feminist: A Biographical Approach," *US Catholic Historian,* Vol. 3 (Spring 1984), pp. 239-250.

[3] William M. Halsey, *The Survival of American Innocence: Catholicism in an Era of Disillusionment* (Notre Dame, IN: University of Notre Dame Press, 1980).

Despite these inhibitions, however, American Catholicism in the period from World War I to Vatican II spawned a rich variety of Catholic social movements and causes. Most of them actually drew strength from formally religious understandings of "modern social evils" as well as from engagement with the particular conditions of American life. It was not only the historical importance of economic issues in those years, but the universal Church's greater perceived experience and knowledge in that sphere that made them the natural focus of socially conscious Catholic reform efforts. And unlike its minimal involvement with other areas of social reform, the Catholic involvement in labor and economic concerns displayed the institutional strengths of the Church and became an important force in shaping the modern American approach to industrial problems.

At the national level, both Franklin Roosevelt's New Deal and the rise of the Congress of Industrial Organizations in the 1930's benefitted from substantial Catholic involvement, especially early in the decade. Operating from their different perspectives, members of the hierarchy, socially conscious Catholic activists, Catholic union leaders, Catholic politicians, and the masses of Catholic voters concentrated in the urban North—all found reasons to support Roosevelt and the New Deal, especially in its early years. In the later 1930's, some members of the hierarchy became more critical of the "statist" elements of the New Deal, and the maverick Father Charles Coughlin, who enjoyed a great following among poorer Catholics in the cities, turned against Roosevelt and toward an increasingly vicious anti-Semitism that finally led the Church to silence him.

The more respectable Catholic involvement with labor and reform movements in the 1930's encompassed a variety of outlooks and activities, most of them well within the pragmatic liberal traditions of American progressivism. The official Social Action Department of the National Catholic Welfare Conference, led by John Ryan and Raymond McGowan, worked on behalf of a range of "progressive" economic causes, most of them closely aligned with the New Deal outlook.[1]

Father Francis Haas and others became influential labor mediators who tried to defend workers' rights and promote social justice. The National Catholic Rural Life Conference, founded in 1923, became an important advocate for social policies affecting the quality of life on the farms. The Association of Catholic Trade Unionists, founded in 1937, worked to create a specifically Catholic presence within the new Congress of Industrial Organizations (which had strong Catholic participation) but also to battle anti-religious elements—especially communism and gangsterism—within the unions.[2]

---

[1]David J. O'Brien, *American Catholics and Social Reform* (New York: Oxford University Press, 1968). George Q. Flynn, *American Catholics and the Roosevelt Presidency* (Lexington: University of Kentucky Press, 1968). Alan Brinkley, *Voices of Protest: Huey Long, Father Coughlin, and the New Deal* (New York: Alfred A. Knopf, 1982).

[2]Thomas A. Blantz, *A Priest in Public Service: Francis J. Haas and the New Deal* (Notre Dame, IN: University of Notre Dame Press, 1982). Neil Betten, *Catholic Activism and the Industrial Worker* (Gainesville, FL: University Press of Florida, 1976).

Most of these liberal American Catholic reformers and the movements with which they were associated considered themselves to be carrying out the broad Catholic mandate to establish social justice as presented in the modern papal encyclicals, and also to be operating in the distinctive American tradition of Catholic social reform going back to Cardinal Gibbons and the Bishops' Program of Social Reconstruction. While thoroughly orthodox in religious motive and practice they also tended to operate as pragmatic reformers in the American tradition—or to see the American liberal tradition itself as an expression of "Catholic" principles of justice—and seldom felt it necessary to offer elaborate theological or spiritual underpinnings for their work.

A somewhat different type of Catholic social movement that appeared in the 1930's and 1940's was self-consciously religious and even "integralist," less connected to the traditions of American liberalism, and often strongly influenced by European Catholic social, intellectual, or spiritual currents—especially those associated with the "Catholic revival." It was often the numerically small movements of this sort which also strongly emphasized the distinctive role of the laity in bringing Christian values to society at large. Among socially conscious movements that fit this description were the Grail, Catherine de Hueck's Friendship House, the various "Specialized Catholic Action" groups like the Young Christian Students and the Young Christian Workers, the Christian Family movement, and the group formed around the magazine *Integrity*. The Catholic Worker movement, founded by Dorothy Day and Peter Maurin in 1933, also fits this category, although Day also brought to her movement the distinctive social outlook and traditions of native American radicalism.[1]

Many of these "integralist" or "personalist" reformers found their greatest theological inspiration in the American branch of the liturgical movement led by the Benedictine Virgil Michel which, with its emphasis on the doctrine of the Mystical Body of Christ, had closely linked the liturgical renewal to the idea of a Christian reform of society. Because they took a religious point of departure somewhat more distant from ordinary American culture and values, these movements tended to see a greater gap between prevalent American social values and those ideally upheld by the Church and the Gospel, to be more "marginal" in terms of their relations to the general society, and to develop a more "countercultural" approach to reform by emphasizing the necessity for difficult religious and personal transformation among their adherents as the first step toward a deeper Christian reform of American society.

The two decades of general American affluence that followed World War II marked an end to the era in which Catholic social reform could be almost exclu-

---

[1]Alden Brown, "The Grail Movement in the United States, 1940-1972: The Evolution of an American Catholic Laywomen's Community" (Ph.D. dissertation, Union Theological Seminary, 1982). Elizabeth L. Sharum, "A Strange Fire Burning: A History of the Friendship House Movement" (Ph.D. dissertation, Texas Tech University, 1977). Dennis Robb, "Specialized Catholic Action in the United States, 1936-1949" (Ph.D. dissertation, University of Minnesota, 1972). Jeffrey M. Burns, *American Catholics and the Family Crisis* (New York: Garland, 1988). Mel Piehl, *Breaking Bread: The Catholic Worker and the Origin of Catholic Radicalism in America* (Philadelphia: Temple University Press, 1982).

sively identified with labor and economic issues. These concerns certainly did not disappear in the 1950's and 1960's, and notable advocates of labor and economic justice like Monsignor George Higgins of the NCWC Social Action Department effectively carried on the Ryan tradition of liberal Catholic reform, with its links to the labor movement and the liberal wing of the Democratic Party. In some cases this social reform tradition could spawn effective engagement with new causes—most notably when official Catholic support and the backing of Catholic politicians like Robert Kennedy could combine with grass roots efforts to support groups like Cesar Chavez's United Farm Workers.[1]

But the emergence of new issues to center stage in the 1950's and the 1960's, particularly race, war and women's rights, created quite different reform dynamics within the Church and American society at large.[2] When these changes intersected with the dramatic religious transformations in Catholicism at large brought on by Vatican II, the result was a new dimension of American Catholic social engagement, and troubled debates about the direction and meaning of such activities. Many of the traditional liberal-labor Catholic reforms no longer seemed adequate to the new challenges of the time, as American liberalism itself came under increasing challenge. Some of the older lay-oriented personalist-integralist movements, especially those partially rooted in the European Catholic social traditions like the Grail and the Christian Family Movement, also underwent severe self-questioning and internal transformation in the 1960's. However, the Catholic Worker movement, perhaps because Dorothy Day had incorporated into its life something of the semi-anarchistic traditions of American social radicalism along with its orthodox Catholicism, actually underwent a revival in the 1960's and remained a small but influential presence in the American Catholic social tradition in the 1970's and 1980's.

The issue that most fundamentally altered the landscape of Catholic social reform, and of American liberal reform generally, was race. Catholics had always been involved with the race question in this country, but their engagement was rather marginal until the civil rights era of the 1950's and 1960's. So long as most Blacks lived in the rural South and most white Catholics in the urban North, the primary Catholic concern with racial justice arose among the small black Catholic community and the very few white Catholics who sought to evangelize or engage in religious service among Blacks. With few exceptions, white Catholics accepted prevalent American racial patterns and seldom considered how vast the distance was between their cherished religious beliefs and the racial oppressions of their society. Black Catholics occasionally raised eloquent voices to appeal to their co-religionists, notably in the five Black Catholic Lay Congresses organized by Daniel Rudd in the 1880's and 1890's, but they were far

---

[1]Gerald M. Costello, *Without Fear or Favor: George Higgins on the Record* (Mystic, CT: Twenty-Third Publications, 1984).

[2]The history of concern for peace is sometimes placed under the heading of social reform, but it has not been included in this survey because it is more tied to American Catholics' relations to issues of national defense and war than to domestic social concerns. For a history of the Catholic peace movement, see Patricia McNeal, *The American Catholic Peace Movement* (New York: Arno Press, 1978).

from the view of most Catholics.[1] Among the few white Catholics who deplored racial suppression, though with varying degrees of sensitivity to the depth of the problem, were Father John Slattery, an influential Josephite who worked to evangelize Blacks; Mother Katherine Drexel of the Blessed Sacrament Sisters whose concern for evangelization and social service to Blacks and Indians carried over to lobbying on their behalf; Father John LaFarge who helped establish the Catholic Inter-racial Council in 1934; Catherine de Hueck of the Friendship House movement which worked in black neighborhoods and advocated integration in Catholic institutions; and the Catholic Worker movement.

But it was the migration of Blacks to northern cities, the rise of the civil rights movement, and the increasing national attention to segregation and racial inequality that began to stir broader Catholic concern in the 1950's. Some early Catholic attention was focused on bishops like Joseph Rummel of New Orleans and Joseph Ritter of St. Louis who mandated integration in Church-run schools and other institutions. By the late 1950's a growing number of socially conscious Catholics applauded and even joined the movement against legal segregation and discrimination in the South. In 1960 the Catholic Inter-racial Council was transformed into the National Catholic Conference for Interracial Justice, and in cooperation with Protestant groups played an important role in encouraging Catholic civil rights activity in the early 1960's. The presence of Catholic priests, and especially nuns, in the 1965 march from Selma to Montgomery, Alabama, was widely noted, and some believe it brought a new sense of urgency to those unaccustomed to seeing traditional religious figures engaged in such unconventional forms of social action.

But this hopeful, progressive and morally clear-cut phase of Catholic civil rights involvement did not last long. Even while the more obvious indicators of official segregation in the American Catholic Church and American society were slowly being eliminated, it became evident that the American racial crisis cut far deeper, and that it was intimately entangled with both white and racial attitudes and ways of life, and with issues of poverty, housing, education and jobs. And especially in the urban North, the conflict over race-related issues soon revealed how much white American Catholicism was, in a phrase of the 1960's, not a part of the solution but part of the problem. While a socially conscious minority of priests, sisters and lay people such as Father James Groppi of Milwaukee became increasingly radical and confrontational in their assault on what some now define as "institutionalized racism" in both Church and society, substantial numbers of ordinary white Catholics resisted changing deeply ingrained attitudes or ways of life where race was concerned. Polls and survey research generally showed that white Catholic racial attitudes differed little from those of non-Catholics, whether they lived near Blacks in the cities or among the increasing majority of Americans who had left the cities for the nearly all-white suburbs,

---

[1]Congress of Colored Catholics of the United States, *Three Catholic Afro-American Congresses* (Cincinnati: American Catholic Tribune, 1893; Arno Press reprint, 1978).

partly to escape urban and racial problems.[1]   While many white Catholics sympathized with the efforts of federal and voluntary agencies to take forceful steps to open opportunity to Blacks, others overtly or silently participated in the "white backlash" against further political efforts toward racial equality.

The conflicts within American Catholicism over racial questions, which melded into the more general American social crises of the late 1960's, were a major factor in disrupting what had been one of the primary presumptions of almost all earlier Catholic social reform efforts: that the divinely ordained Church itself already embodied a morally superior form of social understanding, and that the task of Catholics was to bring these moral truths to society at large.   By 1968, when the Black Catholic Clergy Caucus could declare that "the Catholic Church in the United States is primarily a white racist institution," even Catholics who disagreed no longer expected the official Church to have in its portfolio clear, coherent answers to America's deep social problems.[2]

Once the question of the proper relation of the Catholic faith and ethics to various social values and institutions became controverted, the deep political conflicts within and about American society became translated into moral and even theological conflicts within the Church itself.   In the first hopeful glow after Vatican II, liberal American Catholics imagined that a popularly reformed Church, now understood as the "people of God" rather than a hierarchical and clericalized "perfect society," would be a newly potent instrument for reforming American society in accord with generally agreed-upon Catholic principles.   But with the eruption in the 1960's of deep conflicts within American Church not only over race and war, but over issues regarding the treatment of women, clergy participation in politics, and authority within the Church itself, social concerns assumed a much greater prominence in the total life of American Catholicism than they ever had before.   From the official bishops' conference to Catholic seminaries and universities to the ordinary parish, larger numbers of American Catholics were drawn to consider the moral implications of their religious beliefs, and to ask questions about how those values related to a socially troubled nation and world.

A variety of answers developed.   At the popular official intellectual levels, there were many who looked with varying degrees of skepticism or disfavor on the new varieties of social reform, especially to the extent that they turned into criticisms of the institutional Church itself.   Even among those Catholics who attempted to link their faith to what they saw as urgent social issues, several major strands of religiously informed social thought and action emerged intact from the cauldron of the 1960's, and continued with varying degrees of influence into the 1970's and 1980's.   In many cases these perspectives overlapped or coincided on particular issues, but they tended to develop their own agendas of social reform, and their own characteristic strategies and emphases concerning the relation between the Catholic Church and American social reform, or more broadly, between faith and social action.

---

[1]Richard A. Lamanna and Jay J. Coakley, "The Catholic Church and the Negro," in Philip Gleason, ed., *Contemporary Catholicism in the United States* (Notre Dame, IN: University of Notre Dame Press, 1969), pp. 147-193.
[2]Quoted in Lamanna and Coakley, *op. cit.,* p. 169.

Most spectacular and distressing to many Catholics and others was the new "Catholic Left" that emerged in the 1960's. Spawned primarily by opposition to the war in Vietnam, but also by other domestic and foreign policy issues, this relatively small but intensely committed movement made national headlines by speaking out against the war, which it came to see as the most visible symptom of a deeper moral and social evil embedded in American institutions and life, including the Catholic Church. Identified especially with the Berrigan brothers, the Catholic Left moved from conventional forms of protest to more militant acts of civil disobedience in the late 1960's and early 1970's, including raids on draft boards and the destruction of draft records.

Plagued by both internal dissensions and the fierce prosecution of the Federal Bureau of Investigation, the Catholic Left faded as a coherent movement. While the Catholic Left was never directly influential within most of the "institutional Church" it disdained, and although it served as a negative reference group for many American Catholics, it did leave a legacy of highly politicized religious social criticism that sees a deep discontinuity between genuine Catholicism and most of the institutions and values of American society. In the 1980's this legacy found affinities with some versions of the diverse "liberation theology" movements coming out of Latin America affecting the North American Catholic Church.[1]

A second stream of social thought and action within the American Church is closely identified with the changing perspectives of American religious orders, especially women religious. Along with their lay supporters (some of them former priests and nuns) they increasingly linked their own religious mission to reforms of Church and society in ways that American Catholics and even the universal Church found difficult to ignore, if only as a potentially dangerous threat. Evolving out of the long history of social service as practiced by both male and female religious in the United States, but especially influenced by the internal "renewal" process mandated by Vatican II, many of the religious orders began to define their fundamental religious mission in relation to the social and structural reform of American society. Initially led by influential reformers such as Marie Augusta Neal and Mary Luke Tobin, but soon followed by a host of increasingly sophisticated social activists and critics, the sisters began to make public social concerns a crucial focus of their activities. A major sign of the transition came in 1970-1971 when the Conference of Major Superiors of Women acted on their own to change their name to the Leadership Conference of Women Religious and began to encounter serious conflicts with Vatican authorities, partly over their growing affinity with the general American women's movement. In December 1971 American sisters formed Network, a Washington-based lobby for social justice, while coalitions like the National Coalition of American Nuns and the National Black Sisters Conference emphasized social concerns within various orders and communities.[2]

---

[1]Charles Meconis, *With Clumsy Grace: The American Catholic Left, 1961-1975* (New York: Seabury Press, 1979).
[2]Mary J. Weaver, *New Catholic Women* (San Francisco: Harper & Row, 1885). Mary Ewens, "Political Activity of American Sisters Before 1970," and Nancy

By the end of the 1970's activist American sisters were increasingly involved in a range of domestic and international social concerns, from women's equality in Church and society to nuclear war and third world hunger. Developing out of the long history of North American Catholic involvement in Latin America, issues concerning Central and South America assumed even greater importance through the 1980's. Besides this publicly visible activism, many women religious practiced social justice concern within local parishes and communities. A 1982 survey of the Sisters of St. Joseph in New York state, for example, found them living in inner city housing in order to experience and work on behalf of poor residents' concerns, running shelters for abused women, serving illegal aliens, and advocating the cause of Native Americans on the Mohawk reservation.[1] By 1980, sisters in even smaller dioceses like that of Davenport, Iowa, were to be found holding workshops on race and poverty, supporting the cause of migrant workers, and encouraging the teaching of social justice in Catholic schools.[2] The ways in which many of these activities integrated acts of direct social service with social advocacy demonstrated how religiously-inspired charity and public social service among American Catholic reformers had often come to go hand-in-hand.

Another somewhat overlapping strand of Catholic social reform was more closely tied to urban parishes and neighborhoods, where clerical and lay activists worked to link the Catholic Church with broader community issues and concerns. Rooted in earlier efforts like the "Back of the Yards" Council promoted by Monsignor Bernard Sheil and Saul Alinsky in Chicago in the 1930's and 1940's, these efforts to link the life of the local Catholic Church with public social reform aroused both strong loyalties and fierce opposition as they spread from northern "ethnic" neighborhoods to Hispanic barrios. Principal figures in the movement to mobilize both lay and hierarchical support for social justice at the local level included longtime Chicago activists Ed Marciniak and Monsignor John Egan, Monsignor Geno Baroni, Father Henry Browne of New York, and Archbishop Patricio Flores of San Antonio. Less nationally visible but perhaps more significant in the long run was the deliberate and religiously grounded process by which some urban parishes in the 1970's and 1980's gradually shifted their priorities to make social awareness and action a significant part of their mission. At the heavily black Church of the Gesu and Most Blessed Sacrament in Philadelphia in the 1970's, for example, the Church worked to control internal expenses and put as many resources as possible into a parish-bound Community Relations Committee and a neighborhood group called START (Southwest Area Teams Alleviating Racial Tension).[3]

In some dioceses and parishes, the long-established St. Vincent de Paul societies began to work for better nutrition for the poor and elderly while running

Sylvester, "Post-Vatican II Sisters and Political Ministry," in Madonna Kolbenschlag, ed., *Between God and Caesar* (New York: Paulist Press, 1985), pp. 41-73.
[1]Cecelia Holbrook, "Agents of Change: The Sisters of St. Joseph in New York State," *U.S. Catholic Historian,* Vol. 2 (Winter 1982), pp. 29-35.
[2]Madeline Marie Schmidt, *Seasons of Growth: A History of the Diocese of Davenport, 1881-1981* (Davenport, IA: Diocese of Davenport, 1981), p. 284.
[3]Joseph J. Casino, "From Sanctuary to Involvement: A History of the Catholic Parish in the Northeast," in Dolan, *op. cit,* Vol. I, p. 96.

community pantries. Such efforts might not be typical of parish life, but they represented one sign of the new importance of social action in the American Church.

The most nationally visible strand of Catholic social reform was the official one centered in the National Conference of Catholic Bishops and its administrative arm, the United States Catholic Conference. Continuing the long North American tradition of official Catholic social statements and action going back to the Ryan era and before, the bishops made social concerns of far greater importance within the American Church, and brought Catholic social perspectives before the wider American public in unprecedented ways. Throughout the 1970's and 1980's, a stream of hearings, studies, drafts and official pronouncements on practically every major social question, from the Equal Rights Amendment to hunger to prime-time television poured out of the bishops' committees and agencies, with varying degrees of public attention and implementation. In their advocacy of social reform, the bishops and their politically and intellectually sophisticated operatives like Father J. Bryan Hehir tried to walk a line between the increasingly vigorous social justice constituencies within the Church and their own sense of what was religiously justified and practically acceptable, both within the American context and the international theological and ecclesiastical environment in which they functioned. Most of their statements went unnoticed outside narrow ecclesiastical circles, but others became touchstones of wider debate in the ideologically charged environment of contemporary American politics. Depending on their own political and religious perspectives, Catholics and other Americans applauded or criticized the bishops' most important statements, while working to interpret them in the most favorable light.

Major landmarks of recent official social teaching include the bicentennial hearings and subsequent statements in 1976, the statement on nuclear war, *The Challenge of Peace,* issued in 1983, and the 1986 statement on the economy, *Economic Justice for All.*[1] Widely publicized and analyzed in both the secular and religious media and the academy, these statements commanded attention even from those Catholics and non-Catholics who disagreed with them. But some of the limitations of the bishops' social perspectives were displayed when they issued the draft statement on women in 1988. In contrast to the widespread respect that greeted the earlier pastoral letters, the statement on women had little impact outside the Church, and faced considerable criticism even within. This response pointed to the great difficulty official Catholicism has had in dealing with modern American social changes related to women and sexuality. In its relations to questions concerning women, it seems, American Catholicism in the late twentieth century may be in the same early stage of response that it was with labor questions in the late nineteenth century.

In its increasingly complex encounter with American social reform of the last two centuries, Roman Catholicism has tried to test social movements by the standard of religion. As they became more at home in American culture, some American Catholics began to examine more critically which social values embedded in the teaching or practice of the Church were really essential corollaries

---

[1]National Conference of Catholic Bishops, *The Challenge of Peace: God's Promise and Our Response* (Washington, DC: United States Catholic Conference, 1983)

of Catholic faith and which were nonreligious adaptations to a particular social environment, whether in the European past or the American present. Even if the answers were not always clear, or if a few Catholics began simply to equate religion with social reform—long a tendency in American Protestantism—the conviction that authentic religion must yield not only personal but social transformation has come to be an important feature of modern American Catholicism. From American Catholic efforts to improve society, however flawed, the Church has gained a deeper insight into the relation of faith to the world, and American society has added a valuable religious dimension to its own impulse to reform.

NOTES ON CONTRIBUTORS

Harold A. Buetow (Rev.) is Professor of Education at The Catholic University of America. He earned his Ph.D. from The Catholic University of America and his J.D. from the Columbus School of Law at The Catholic University of America. Father Buetow is the author of *The Catholic School: Its Roots, Identity, and Future* and the Catholic Book Award Winner for *Of Singular Benefit: The Story of US Catholic Education.*

Patrick W. Carey is Associate Professor of Historical Theology at Marquette University. He earned his Ph.D. from Fordham University. Dr. Carey is the author of *An Immigrant Bishop: John England's Adaptation of Irish Catholicism to American Republicanism* (1982); *People, Priests and Prelates: Ecclesiastical Democracy and the Tensions of Trusteeism* (1981); *American Catholic Religious Thought* (1987), and has contributed to a number of periodicals.

Cyprian Davis, O.S.B., is Professor of Church History in the St. Meinrad School of Theology. He earned his Ph.D. in Historical Sciences from the University of Louvain. Father Davis is the author of numerous articles dealing with monastic history and spirituality and the history of black Catholics and black Spirituality. He is the author of a text for high school students on Church history and is currently completing a book on the history of black Catholics in the United States.

John Tracy Ellis (Monsignor) is Professorial Lecturer in Church History at The Catholic University of America. He earned his Ph.D. at The Catholic University. He is the author of numerous books including *Cardinal Consalvi and Anglo-Papal Relations; The Life of James Cardinal Gibbons, Archbishop of Baltimore, 1834-1921; John Lancaster Spalding, First Bishop of Peoria.*

Virgina Geiger, S.S.N.D., is Professor of History and Philosophy at the College of Notre Dame of Maryland. She has earned her Ph.D. at The Catholic University of America. She is the author of *Daniel Carroll, A Framer of the Constitution: Daniel Carroll; One Man and His Descendants;* editor of *Maryland Our Maryland;* and editor of *The Living Constitution, 1787, 1987, 2187.*

Philip Gleason is Professor of History at the University of Notre Dame. He received his Ph.D. from the University of Notre Dame. Professor Gleason is the author of *Keeping the Faith: American Catholicism Past and Present,* and is a contributor to numerous periodicals. He is presently at work on a general history of Catholic higher education in the United States.

Leslie Griffin is Assistant Professor of Theology at the University of Notre Dame. She earned her Ph.D. in Religious Studies from Yale University. Dr. Griffin has authored several articles on Christian and political ethics in *Theological Studies, The Journal of Religious Ethics* and *New Theology Review.*

John A. Gurrieri (Rev.) is currently a Fellow at the Institute for Ecumenical and Cultural Research at St. John's University in Collegeville, Minnesota, where he is pursuing research on the History of Sacramental Theology and Liturgical praxis. He is a candidate for a Ph.D. at the Institut Superieur de Liturgie, Institut Catholique de Paris. Father Gurrieri is the former Executive Director on the Bishops' Committee on the Liturgy of the National Conference of Catholic Bishops. He is the author of several articles in *Worship, The Living Light, Liturgy, The New Catholic Encyclopedia* and *Pastoral Music.*

David F. Kelly is Professor of Theology at Duquesne University. He studied at the Catholic University of Louvain in Belgium and earned his Ph.D. in Theology at the University of Saint Michael's College in Toronto. Professor Kelly is the author of *The Emergence of Roman Catholic Medical Ethics in North America* and *A Theological Basis for Health Care and Health Care Ethics.* He has contributed numerous articles on moral theology and medical ethics.

Robert F. Leavitt, S.S., is President-Rector of St. Mary's Seminary and University in Baltimore, Maryland, where he also earned his Ph.D. Father Leavitt teaches Systematic Theology and specializes in the field of Fundamental Theology. His recent article, "Catholic Vision of Pluralism," will appear in the forthcoming book, *Contemporary Issues of Medical Ethics.*

Dolores Liptak, R.S.M., is Director of the Catholic Archival and Historical Services. She received her Ph.D. at the University of Connecticut and her Archival Certification at the University of Dayton, the National Archives and Diocesan Archives. She is the author of *Immigrants and Their Church* and *European Immigrants and the Catholic Church in Connecticut, 1870-1920.*

Mel Piehl is Associate Professor of History and Humanities in Christ College, the honors-humanities college of Valparaiso University. A Danforth and Woodrow Wilson Fellow, he earned his Ph.D. from Stanford University. Dr. Piehl is the author of *Breaking Bread: The Catholic Worker and the Origin of Catholic Radicalism in America.* He has written numerous articles on the Catholic Worker Movement and American Catholicism.

Sonya Quitslund is Assistant Professor of Religion at George Washington University and has earned her Ph.D. from The Catholic University of America. Her book, *Beauduin A Prophet Vindicated,* received a book of the year award in 1973. She has written over 30 articles in such journals as *Nouvelle Revue Theologique, Journal of Ecumenical Studies, Bible Today, Liturgy,* and *Carmelite Studies* on biblical, feminist and ecumenical topics.

Joel Rippinger, O.S.B., is an instructor in Theology and History at Marmion Academy and Marmion Abbey, Aurora, Illinois. He received his M.A. in History from the University of Notre Dame, his S.T.L. in Monastic Studies from the University of Saint Anselm, Rome. He has served as a member of the editorial board of the *American Benedictine Review.* He has authored articles on

Benedictine history and spirituality and has presently completed a volume on the *History of the American Benedictines.*

Margaret Susan Thompson is Associate Professor of History and Director of American Studies at Syracuse University. She earned her Ph.D. at the University of Wisconsin-Madison. She has authored many articles for periodicals and her forthcoming book, *The Yoke of Grace: American Nuns and Social Change, 1808-1917,* will be published by Oxford University Press.

Stephen J. Vicchio is Chairman and Associate Professor of Philosophy at the College of Notre Dame of Maryland. He earned his M.A. from Yale University and his Ph.D. from St. Andrew's in Scotland. He is the author of *A Careful Disorder, Voice from the Whirlwind,* the introduction to *On Vital Reserves* (two essays of William James) and the introduction to the new edition of Jacques Maritain's *Introduction to Philosophy.* He has contributed to numerous scholarly publications.